ORACLE8
Black Book

ORACLE8
Black Book

Michael R. Ault

 CORIOLIS GROUP BOOKS

an International Thomson Publishing company I(T)P®

Albany, NY • Belmont, CA • Bonn • Boston • Cincinnati • Detroit • Johannesburg • London
Madrid • Melbourne • Mexico City • New York • Paris • Singapore • Tokyo • Toronto • Washington

Oracle8 Black Book

Limits of Liability and Disclaimer of Warranty

Trademarks

The Coriolis Group, Inc.
An International Thomson Publishing Company
14455 N. Hayden Road, Suite 220
Scottsdale, Arizona 85260

602.483.0192
FAX 602.483.0193
http://www.coriolis.com

Library of Congress Cataloging-In-Publication Data
Ault, Michael R.
    Oracle8 black book / by Michael R. Ault.
       p.   cm.
    Includes index.
    ISBN 1-57610-187-8
    1. Relational databases. 2. Oracle (Computer file) I. Title.
  QA76.9.D3A939   1997
  005.75'75–dc21   97-37926
                                             CIP

Printed in the United States of America
10 9 8 7 6 5 4 3 2

Publisher
Keith Weiskamp

Project Editor
Ann Waggoner Aken

Production Coordinator
Michael Peel

Cover Design
Anthony Stock

Layout Design
April Nielsen

CD-ROM Development
Robert Clarfield

*As with my previous missives, this book is dedicated to my loving family.
My wife Susan and daughters Marie and Michelle again have had to put up with me
working late hours and many weekends when I should have been paying attention to them.*

Acknowledgments

This book would not have been possible without the help and assistance of many people. Chief among the midwives of the birthing process for this book were Don Burleson, who dragged me kicking and screaming into the Coriolis fold; Ann Waggoner Aken, my dedicated and long-suffering editor; the dedicated copy editor Susie Holly, who had to put up with my sometimes caustic wit; and last, but not least, Michael Peel, production coordinator for the book.

It would be difficult to mention all of the folks who also assisted with page layout, printing, and the other myriad tasks associated with this type of undertaking, but I hope all of you know that I appreciate your efforts.

Contents

Practical Guide To User-Defined Types 157

Chapter 5   Oracle8 Data Storage Features   183

Chapter 9   The Oracle8 Data Dictionary   367

Introduction

In my previous books, I attempted to teach prospective DBAs and Unix administrators how to progress from a junior level to a more senior level by use of general discussion and example. This book is a departure from that motif and is designed to be a hands-on reference for the developer and DBA alike. In the following chapters, we will discuss Oracle8 object-related jobs and tasks, and give real, concrete examples of how they should be accomplished—we won't discuss theory. This book will not discuss Oracle processes, except when germane to a problem or solution. The book will not breakdown the sga, pga, uga, or any memory area unless again, it bears directly on whatever problem we are solving. This book will also not discuss general database internals tuning unless it is in light of a particular solution. For information on those types of topics, I refer the reader to my other books. This book is more of a reference book, a "book of tools" for the working developer/DBA to use.

Each chapter in this book is divided into two sections: technical information and then Practical Guides to performing specific tasks. The Practical Guide sections are all based on techniques hand-tested on several versions of Oracle. When necessary, the differences are pointed out. Any humor is solely the responsibility of the author. The book is divided into 13 chapters and an appendix. Read carefully; there will not be a test so you have to depend on your own memory.

- Chapter 1—Provides an overview of relational and object-oriented terminology and technology. The Practical Guide provides concrete examples of how to apply these to database design. Actual conversion examples are given.

- Chapter 2—Provides an overview of database structured design methodology. The Practical Guide demonstrates real-world application of the structured design concepts and provides a template for use in object-oriented diagramming.

- Chapter 3—Discusses Oracle8 and how triggers are used to provide encapsulation and data hiding. Example triggers are shown, and the dreaded mutating table is slain.

- Chapter 4—Discusses Oracle object/relational structures and insights into the use of the user-defined types. Comparisons to Java are utilized to demonstrate Oracle8's object-oriented capabilities.

- Chapter 5—Demonstrates Oracle8 data storage features. Partitioned tables, nested tables, **VARRAY**s, index-only tables, and **LOB** storage examples are given.

- Chapter 6—Examines the new **LOB** features of Oracle8. Techniques for reading, inserting, and using **LOB** datatypes in the database are demonstrated including the **DBMS_LOB** package.

- Chapter 7—Examines the PL/SQL enhancements specifically dealing with collection data types such as **VARRAY** and nested tables. The Practical Guide demonstrates the use of collection methods and data types.

- Chapter 8—Deals with the new parallel and distributed options of Oracle8. Techniques for use of parallel insert, update, and delete are discussed and demonstrated. Advanced queuing is also discussed.

- Chapter 9—Demonstrates how the Oracle8 data dictionary has been altered for the new features of Oracle8. The book's companion appendix provides complete definitions of the major sets of data dictionary items such as the dollar ($), GV_$, and DBA_ views and tables. The Practical Guide shows how these tables and views are used to find information about Oracle8 objects.

- Chapter 10—Provides information on application tuning with practical demonstrations of the use of Oracle provided tuning tools and scripts. All scripts discussed in Chapter 10 are provided on the com-panion CD-ROM, which also includes the Precise/SQL SQL-tuning tool from Precise Software Solutions.

- Chapter 11—Provides information on tuning Oracle internals. The Practical Guide provides scripts, techniques, and guidelines for Oracle internal tunings. All scripts shown are provided on the companion CD-ROM along with the Q Diagnostic program from Savant Corporation.

- Chapter 12—Covers the Oracle-supplied tuning and utility scripts, and demonstrates their use.

- Chapter 13—Covers Oracle and Java topics. The Practical Guide shows examples of the use of Java with Oracle, including queries against the Oracle database using JDBC and JSQL, and the retrieval and display of objects (such as images) from the database. The companion CD-ROM contains the JDK1.1.4, JDBC, and JSQL development tool sets for use with Oracle8.

- Appendix—Provides a reference for DBA_ and V$ views and ($) dollar tables.

Chapter 1

Oracle And The Object Paradigm

For years, Oracle has been one of, if not the, major contender in the relational database arena. Now with Oracle8, Oracle Corporation enters full force into the object-relational database world. With this new object orientation for Oracle comes a new bag of jargon that developers and database administrators (DBAs) have to get a grip on.

Notes…

1

Object-Oriented Terms

What follows is a generic list of object-oriented terminology with definitions. These, as well as Oracle-specific object-oriented terms, will be used throughout the book.

- *Encapsulation*—The feature of an object-oriented program that means it is completely standalone. It is not dependent on another object, nor is another object dependent upon it for its function. Because an encapsulated object is passed attributes and returns attributes with no other external communication required (i.e., no global or public variables, no external calls to other objects or methods), it is said to implement *data hiding* or *binding*.

- *Polymorphism*—The feature that allows a single method to be used by multiple classes or objects. An example would be overloading an Oracle PL/SQL function to handle multiple datatypes. An overloaded function (or procedure) in PL/SQL simply has several functions or procedures of the same name and argument structure, except that one of the passed arguments is a different datatype. The users have no idea that multiple functions or procedures exist; they simply call the function or procedure and get the results back.

- *Inheritance*—Allows subclasses to inherit behaviors from their superclass. Usually, a superclass is a general class of generic functions with subclasses that exhibit more and more specialized behavior. Oracle8 will not support inheritance until release 8.1, at the earliest.

- *Persistence*—Allows for object data to be available across executions.

- *Passive database*—One that does not store the implementations of the methods defined for a class. The database must provide implementation of methods in its application code.

- *Active database*—One that stores implementations of the methods for its classes. The methods are stored and retrieved with the objects. An active database, by its very nature, is robust and flexible.

Oracle-Specific Object Terms

Oracle8 has specific definitions for the Oracle object-oriented extensions. These involve how Oracle uses object technology. This section presents some of these Oracle-specific definitions to complete this discussion of object-oriented jargon.

- *Object type*—Datatypes that define Oracle objects. An Oracle object is one instance of an Oracle object type. Oracle objects can be *persistent*, such as tables or views, or *transient*, such as a memory construct in PL/SQL. The **CREATE TYPE** command is used to create an Oracle object type. Persistent object types have object identifiers (OIDs), while non-persistent object types do not. These are sometimes referred to as *complex objects*. Object types were called *abstract data types* in early release documentation.

- *Object table*—A table of Oracle object types. If a pre-Oracle8 table is ported to Oracle8, it doesn't automatically become an object table. To get a relational table to behave as if it were an object table, it must be made part of an object view. Only objects represented by true object tables have OIDs. Object tables were referred to as *extent tables* or *typed tables* in early Oracle8 documents.

- *Object identifier (OID)*—Consists of a 128-byte hexadecimal value, guaranteed to be globally unique. Only objects stored in an object table have OIDs. By itself, an OID cannot be used to locate an object instance; only a **REF** (discussed later), which contains location data, can be used for this purpose. This OID is used to enforce object identity.

- *Object*—A single instance of an object datatype, which may or may not have an associated OID. If the object is from an object table, it will have an OID; if it is from Oracle call interface variables or PL/SQL variables, it will not.

- *Nested object*—An object whose object type is used to specify a single column in an object table.

- *Nested table*—The **CREATE TYPE** command can be used to create a type that is actually a table; this table type can then be used to create a table of that type, which can be used as a column in a second object table. This results in a nested table. Don't worry if this is confusing now. In the next few chapters, you will see examples that should reduce the fog factor.

- *Datatype*—The three types of datatypes in Oracle8 are: *built-in*, the standard **NUMBER**, **DATE**, **VARCHAR2**, **LONG**, **LONG RAW**, **BLOB**, etc.; *library*, types built by a third party and supplied to the user (generally, a specialized form of the user-defined datatype); and *user-defined*, specialized types built by users or VARs. User-defined types (UDTs) with methods provide enforcement of classes. UDTs are made of the atomic datatypes or attributes and methods.

- *Method*—A stored procedure written in PL/SQL that performs operations on types. This enforces object behaviors.

- *Large object (LOB)*—New in Oracle8 is extended coverage for large objects. The types of LOB: character LOB (CLOB); binary LOB (BLOB); national character LOB (NCLOB); and a LOB stored externally to the database, a BFILE that is generally to be used for long binary files, such as digitized movies or audio tracks.

- *External procedures*—Another new Oracle8 feature, the ability to call procedures that don't reside in the database from PL/SQL. By procedures, I mean a 3GL program. The current version (8.0.2) supports only C, but more languages will be available by the time of the general release of Oracle8. External procedures are also referred to as *3GL callouts*. One problem with them is that for each process that makes a

3GL callout, a new callout process is created, and because they don't yet work with MTS, this will effectively double the number of operating-system processes required in an environment that uses callouts.

- *Constructor*—An Oracle kernel-generated method to instantiate an Oracle object-type instance. It is differentiated from a user-created method in that it is system-created and automatically applied when a call is made to an object type or when an object type is needed and does not have an implicit or explicit **SELF** parameter (to use a bit of "objectspeak").

- *Forward type definition*—The ability to define an object type and then use that type in a second, third, or any number of subsequent type definitions. I prefer to call this a type-in-type. In this special case, both types refer to each other in their definitions. This involves the use of an incomplete type. For you C programmers, this is identical to forward declaration.

- *Object view*—Allows normal relational tables to be referenced like objects in an object relational database. The object-view process supplies synthesized OIDs for relational rows.

- *Encapsulation*—The process where attributes and behaviors are stored together. Oracle's new type specifications allow storage of attributes and methods together in the database.

- *Persistence*—Oracle allows both persistent and nonpersistent data structures. Persistent structures are in the form of tables, object tables, clusters, etc., and nonpersistent structures are in PL/SQL types.

A quick review of these terms and their definitions could lead you to conclude that they are varnish-overs of existing technology. Maybe this is the case, maybe not. That doesn't change the fact that the new kid on the block is object oriented, and we all have to follow the leader.

Indeed, in many cases object-oriented design and implementation will be difficult until a base of objects and development techniques is established. This is what is known as the bleeding edge, and we are it. Besides Oracle, several other database systems are, or claim to be, object databases. The next section takes a quick look at these other offerings.

Other Object Databases

This is by no means a complete list of every company that has brought out an "object" database. These are, however, the ones that have established a following:

- *Objectivity/DB 2.0*—From Objectivity Inc. Provides persistence on a class basis. Accesses persistent objects via handles. Uses DDL similar to C++ (also supported by third-party design tools). Provides several DBA/Development tools and data browsers. Uses passive database technology.

- *ONTOS DB 2.2*—From ONTOS Inc. Provides persistence on a class basis. Accesses persistent objects via a pointer. Uses C++ headers or a provided DB design tool to generate schemas. Provides DBA configuration and design tools. Uses passive database technology.

- *VERSANT Release 2*—From Versant Object Technology Corp. Provides persistence on an object basis. Uses C++ headers or utilities provided for DDL/schema design and build. Provides DBA configuration and data tools. Uses passive database technology.

- *ObjectStore 2.0*—From Object Design Inc. Provides persistence on an object basis. Accesses objects via pointers. Uses C++ headers or utilities provided for DDL/schema design and build. Provides DBA configuration and data tools. Uses passive database technology.

- *GemStone Version 3.2*—From Servio Corp. Provides persistence on the basis of class. Accesses classes via nonpersistent pointers. GemStone offers either standard implementation for structures using C, C++, or SmallTalk and visual programming in Servio's own GeODE interface. Provides DBA configuration and data tools in addition to the GeODE interface. Uses active database technology.

All of these database systems provide for the standard database features, such as recoverability, lock management, consistency, constraints, indexing, etc.

Oracle8 provides persistence on an object basis. Database schema are created using standard SQL with object extensions. Access to persistent objects is via reference (object to object) or handles (names). Oracle Corp. provides many configuration, design, and object-broker utilities. Oracle8 uses active database technology. It stores objects via a proprietary storage structure that uses named data areas called *tablespaces*. Objects are stored in internal formats inside the storage structures. Detailed metadata is provided for all levels of the data structure.

Goals Of Object-Oriented Programming

The goal of object-oriented programming is simple: provide jobs for all of those C++, Visual Basic, and Visual C++ programmers out there. Seriously, object-oriented programming has some definite predefined goals:

- *Code reusability*—Ultimately, the top goal for object-oriented programming is to develop a full set of off-the-shelf reusable components that can be used universally to develop software, just as a set of boards is used to assemble a modern computer.

- *Separate form and function*—Through data hiding, encapsulation, and polymorphism, you no longer have to worry about the "hows," but only the "whats" (once someone writes fully reusable "hows," that is).

- *Make programming more engineering and less art*—By providing a standard set of reusable components, software engineers can concentrate on building applications instead of building tools to build applications.

Characteristics Of An Object-Oriented System

Essentially, object-oriented systems are those where code units (objects) have been pushed down into the same area as the data that they act upon. In other words, data units and code units are indistinguishable. This produces objects that can be readily reused and behave in an object-oriented manner.

Users should see a consistent look and feel as they move through the object-oriented application. This consistent look and feel is brought about by reusing screen and interface objects throughout the application.

From the maintenance programmer's viewpoint, an object-oriented system consists of a series of objects that the maintenance programmer can alter at will, with assurance that the object will still function within the application framework, as long as the programmer doesn't change the "messages" that the object understands. In addition, modifications to objects will be transferred throughout the structure of the application—that is, modifications to type primitives will promulgate to wherever they are used in the system.

The drawback of the object-oriented system is much larger executables. This is a result of the pairing of data and behaviors, and the required code to ensure inheritance, polymorphism, and encapsulation. The use of shared class libraries also increases the size of executables. Another reason for the larger executables is the use of generalized coding practices instead of pinpoint solution coding, which is used in non-object-oriented applications.

This increase in size of object-oriented program applications also results in slower applications. Any losses in speed, however, will (hopefully) be regained in better, more robust, more easily maintained applications.

Benefits Of The Object-Oriented Approach

The object-oriented approach to application development has several benefits:

- *Reusable code*—If the application is done right, it will produce multiple objects, such as screen handlers, printer objects, and I/O objects, that will be reusable in other projects and in multiple sections of the application.

- *Ease of maintenance*—The object approach allows individual objects to be upgraded, refined, and replaced without touching any of the rest of the code base. This should speed maintenance and, as long as the maintenance programmer follows the object interface rules, allow maintenance to be done at the single-object level.

- *Standardization of application interfaces*—If all applications use the same interface objects, then all of your applications will have the same look and feel to your users. This reduces operator errors and the learning curve in introducing new applications.

Oracle8 And The Object-Oriented Paradigm

What does all of this mean in relation (no pun intended) to Oracle8? How does Oracle8 measure up to the standards for object-oriented applications? This section will answer these questions before moving into the Practical Guide section of the chapter.

To be object oriented, a database system would have to exhibit at least some of the characteristics of an object-oriented system. Does Oracle8 meet this criterion? Let's start by seeing how Oracle8 enforces the principles of object-oriented programming.

- *Principle one*—Actions in object-oriented programming are initiated by transmission of a message to an agent (i.e., an object) responsible for the action.

Oracle's implementation—The use of methods in types allows messages to be sent to objects built of these types. The action (method) is then carried out on the data stored in the type.

- *Principle two*—Messages in object-oriented programming encode the request for action and are accompanied by any arguments (information) needed by the agent to carry out the action.

  Oracle's implementation—Messages in the form of method calls are sent to objects built of Oracle types. Arguments may be passed with these method calls. Based on the contents of the message, Oracle types implement methods on the data contained in the types.

- *Principle three*—If an object accepts a message, it accepts the responsibility to carry out the action. The action is carried out via a method.

  Oracle's implementation—If a method doesn't exist in a specific type, an error is returned.

- *Principle four*—All objects can be considered instances of specific classes. A class is a grouping of similar objects. Objects exhibit both state (values) and behavior (methods).

  Oracle's implementation—Types can be used to build objects or can be used in other types that can then be used in objects. Types have attributes that when used to build objects, exhibit state (values). Each type can incorporate methods to enforce behavior for that type.

- *Principle five*—All objects of a specific class use the same method in response to similar messages. Classes may exhibit relations to subclasses and superclasses.

  Oracle's implementation—If a type that contains a method is used in an object, the method will be used no matter what object the type is used to build. If a type contains a subtype, the subtype's methods are available to the supertype when dealing with the subtype.

- *Principle six*—All subclasses inherit attributes and, perhaps, methods from its superclass(es).

  Oracle's implementation—Oracle will not use inheritance until the 8.2 release. All methods are local to the type they inhabit and aren't inherited up or down the type-subtype chain for an object.

- *Principle seven*—The class hierarchy (subclass-class-superclass tree) is walked up from whatever class is initially referenced until the appropriate method is found to deal with a message. If no method is found, an error is issued. This is known as *method binding*.

  Oracle's implementation—Oracle type methods are local to the type they inhabit until later releases of Oracle. Unless the method is in the specific type being addressed, an error is returned. There is no walking of the class hierarchy.

- *Principle eight*—The issuer of a message doesn't need to know *how* the message action is carried out, just that if the message is accepted by an object, the action *will* be carried out. This is called *information hiding*.

  Oracle's implementation—Oracle type methods are fully compliant with this principle. The issuer of a call to a method doesn't have to concern itself with how it is carried out by the Oracle type method. If a method exists (i.e., the message is accepted), then the action will be carried out.

- *Principle nine*—A subclass can exhibit different behaviors from its superclass—that is, a subclass can override the behaviors by applying exceptions. Often, the method used will have the same name. Therefore, multiple subclasses will have the same method, but will arrive at the action required by different routes. This is polymorphism.

  Oracle's implementation—Pseudo-polymorphism can be built into Oracle by using overloading in type methods, stored functions, procedures, or with trigger logic. I call this *pseudo-polymorphism*, because it cannot be directly implemented at the type-subtype level until later releases of Oracle8.

How does Oracle measure up? Other than lacking inheritance and having only pseudo-polymorphism, pretty good. While not 100 percent in compliance with object orientation, Oracle is much closer than many people think. Once full inheritance is established, along with polymorphism, it will be fully compliant. Oracle is promising this for late 1998 or early 1999.

Practical Guide To

Task Completion

- Migrating To Oracle8
- Developing A Type Hierarchy
- Defining Type Methods (Behaviors)
- Converting Relational Structures To Objects
- Loading Data Using SQLLOADER
- Moving Data From Load Tables Into Database Object Structures

Migrating To Oracle8

The long-awaited moment approaches. The long-heralded release of Oracle8 into production is happening, so now what do we DBAs and application developers do? We migrate. Of course, we should take the proper steps to ensure that we migrate properly (see Figure 1.1).

How do we accomplish this migration? Planning. Planning is the only way to minimize points of possible failure in your migration path from Oracle7 to Oracle8. In this guide, I will provide a logical framework for planning your migration and, hopefully, shine a light on the pitfalls that you should avoid along the way (see Figure 1.2).

Preparing To Migrate

Your preparation should involve reviewing the installation and operation manuals, performing controlled tests of new features, and, then, finally bringing Oracle8 into full use.

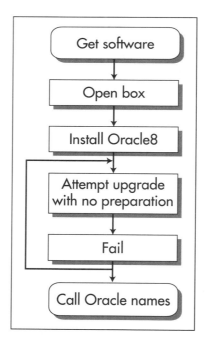

Figure 1.1

The usual migration path.

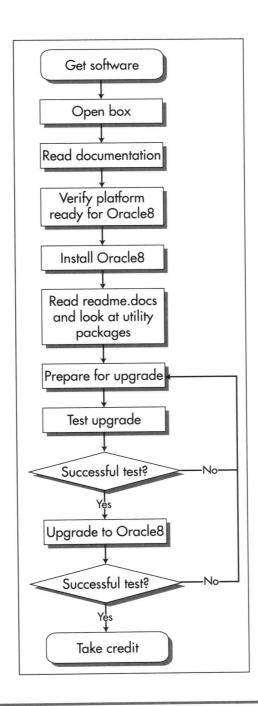

Figure 1.2

The proper migration path.

Invariably, Oracle users will ask the "experts" hundreds of questions about installation and migration to Oracle8 that should have been answered by reading the documentation and testing new features before implementation. You have to take the time to study the new-features sections of the manuals, read the readme.doc, and review utility scripts for "hidden" changes.

A couple of weeks after I mentioned the compatible parameter in one of my "Dear SYSOP" columns for the now defunct *OREVIEW* magazine, Oracle came out with a spate of bugs that related to that parameter. Were the two related? Probably. This just demonstrates that people thought they had immigrated to a new version of Oracle, when, in fact, because of the setting of the parameter, they hadn't even tested the new features that depended on a new redo log format. Reading the documentation before they migrated would have prevented this.

Oracle8 will take up to 50 percent more space for initial load than Oracle7. Do you have enough free space? You may want to run both Oracle8 and your Oracle7 system in parallel. Do you have enough memory or CPU? At least as of version 8.0.2 (beta2), no one could provide a good method for estimating the sizes of nested tables and tables with **VARRAY**s. I would plan on at least another 25 to 50 percent space hit if you plan to use these features a great deal. For that matter, the new OID takes 16 bytes all by itself, so for large applications, here is another hit on space.

For those operating systems that fall prey to disk-space fragmentation, defragment. Oracle requires contiguous space.

Don't begin your migration without a clear plan of how to get from your Oracle7 instance to your Oracle8 instance. Decide on your path, preferably one that doesn't lead over a cliff. Review the possible methods to migrate your system, choose the best for your situation, and then plan, plan, plan.

Finally, how do you know if your migration is successful? How will you know that the system is functioning correctly after the migration is complete? You should:

- Have a test plan.

- Evaluate your existing system prior to migration to check its performance characteristics.

- Have a standard set of test cases to run against the old database and the new.

Testing The Migration Process

If at all possible, test your migration path—even if it is on a small database that you create specifically for the test (in fact, this is the best way). Repeat the test until you know exactly what you are doing. I know, the bosses will be yelling if you are a bit late with the production migration, but hurrying to meet a schedule is probably the best path to disaster. When you rush, you forget important steps, overlook potential problems, and just plain do stupid things.

Testing The Migrated Test Instance

If you are lucky enough to have the space available to do a nonproduction test migration, be sure to test that what you ended up with is at least as good as what you started with. Find the causes of any anomalous behavior and fix them before you spend all weekend migrating your production database—only to have it malfunction, when the boss is looking, of course.

Protecting Your Retreat Path

Protect your retreat path by ensuring that you have a complete backup of your Oracle7 instance.

One beta tester, who shall remain nameless, decided to install the Oracle8 beta2 on his NT server without backing up the 5GB Oracle7 test database he had just spent a week preparing. The beta install crashed the NT Oracle7 instances so completely that they couldn't be restored without a backup.

Be sure that you parse out enough time to allow multiple reinstalls and migrations as needed. If you plan out the time needed to the nearest second, chances are you won't make your schedule. Better to finish early than to have everyone breathing down your neck because you didn't meet your schedule.

Again, cut a full backup or a full export of your source database. I cannot stress this enough. At worst, having a full backup wastes some disk or tape space for a while; at best, it will save your hide from falling over the cliff.

Prepare the source database as completely as possible:

- *Remove unneeded tables*—Drop all those temporary tables, test tables, and no-longer-used tables.

- *Remove unneeded views*—Review the contents of the Oracle view **dba_views** and get rid of outdated or unused views.

- *Drop defunct users*—If the database has been in operation for a while, it may have several defunct users. Why carry dead weight with you?

- *Do space management*—Consolidate multiple datafiles, or, conversely, split up datafiles that are too big to perform properly.

- *Tune your source database*—Make sure your database is running at tip-top performance.

Migrating The Source Database

Following the pretested methodology, migrate the source database to its new Oracle8 home. Immediately after the migration successfully completes, shut down and perform a complete cold backup. This gives you a starting point, should something go awry with subsequent testing. An export will do nearly as well, but don't use a hot backup at this point, because it will not afford full recoverability at this stage of migration. The backup should contain all datafiles, control files, redo logs, parameter files, and SQL scripts used to build any of the database objects.

The Three T's: Tune, Tweak, And Test The New Database

Using the knowledge you gained from your thorough review of the documents, readme files, and utility scripts, tune and tweak the new Oracle8 instance to optimum performance. Once the database is tuned, test it using your predeveloped test cases.

What Next?

Once the database is migrated to the Oracle8 instance structure, you need to consider which new features you want to implement (after all, if you didn't want the new features, why did you migrate?) and how you are going to implement them.

Let me make a statement that I'm sure will have some of you shuddering: If you are completely happy with your application, don't force-fit it into Oracle8's new features. Change for the sake of change is unwise. If you have a good, viable reason to implement these new features, by all means do so. Oracle8 will function very well with an Oracle7 application resting inside of it. Don't feel that you must convert your applications immediately to the new features. Take some time and get familiar with the ride of the new database and watch for its quirks before you start a pell-mell conversion.

A Detailed Look At The MIG80

No, this isn't a new Russian fighter plane. MIG80 is the migration utility that Oracle has provided to get your Oracle7 database into an Oracle8 database. Essentially, you have two main paths and a rocky third to migrate from Oracle7 to Oracle8. These are:

- For small instances (not more that a gigabyte or two), export the Oracle7 database, build the Oracle8 database, and import.

- For large instances (many gigabytes), use the MIG80 facility.

- For those who like pain, unload all Oracle7 tables into flat files, build the Oracle8 database using DDL scripts, and use the SQLLOADER to reload data.

The MIG80 path, of course, involves the use of the MIG80 utility. Oracle8 has made changes to virtually all database structures:

- Datafile file headers

- Data dictionary

- Controlfile structure

- Rollback segment structure

The MIG80 utility, properly used, makes sure that the existing Oracle7 structures are altered to the new Oracle8 structures. This is a one-way path, and, once started, the only way to go back to the Oracle7 instance you knew and loved is to recover from the backup or the export you dutifully made prior to starting, right?

Let's take a more detailed look at the actual procedure to use the MIG80 utility.

 You must start at the 7.1.6, 7.2.3, or 7.3.3 (or higher) release level of Oracle. A version 6 database must be migrated to at least 7.1.6 before it can be converted to Oracle8.

1. Back up the source Oracle7 database or perform a complete export.

2. Drop any users or roles named "migrate."

3. Resolve all pending transactions in a distributed environment.

4. Bring all tablespaces online or make sure they are offline normal or temporary, not immediate. Resolve any save undo situations in tablespaces (see migration manual).

5. Shut down normal (not immediate or abort).

6. Install the Oracle8 software. Do not do a complete install, as this will attempt to build an Oracle8 instance and may damage your existing instance beyond recovery. Do a partial, software-only install.

7. Install the MIG80 utility into the Oracle7 **ORACLE_HOME** by using oracleinst on Unix or its equivalent on your operating system.

8. Unset the **TWO_TASK** environmental variable on Unix or **ORA_DFLT_HOLSTER** on VMS.

9. Set the following init.ora parameter: **ORA_NLS33=$ORACLE_HOME/migrate** (or its equivalent location on your system).

10. Run the MIG80 utility on the Oracle7 database according to the directions for your system. This creates an Oracle8 data dictionary and a binary convert file. You will need 1.5 times the amount of space that your current dictionary occupies as free space in your system tablespace area for the new dictionary. If you aren't sure you have the space, run MIG80 in **CHECK_ONLY** mode first. You aren't past the point of no return yet. This step obliterates the Oracle7 catalog views, but you can recover them by doing the following if you need to abandon the migration at this point:

   A. Start up the Oracle7 database in normal mode.

   B. Drop the user "migrate."

   C. Rerun catalog.sql.

   D. If using server manager, rerun catsvrmg.sql.

   E. If using parallel server, rerun catparr.sql.

   F. If using Symmetric Replication, run catrep.sql.

 This will be a 7.3 database if you abandon it at this point.

11. Remove any obsolete initialization parameters from the database's init<SID>.ora file.

12. Set compatible to 8.0.0.0 or not at all.

13. Change the locations specified by the **CONTROL_FILES** parameter to a new location.

14. Remove the old control files; they will re-create.

15. From SVRMGR, issue the commands: **CONNECT INTERNAL** and **STARTUP NOMOUNT**.

16. From SVRMGR, the DBA issues the **ALTER DATABASE CONVERT** command on the Oracle8 side. This command creates a new controlfile, converts all online file headers to Oracle8 format, and mounts the Oracle8 instance. This is the point of no return.

17. The DBA issues the **ALTER DATABASE OPEN RESETLOGS** command on the Oracle8 side, which automatically converts all objects and users defined in the new dictionary to Oracle8 specifications. It also converts all rollback segments to Oracle8 format.

18. Finish converting the catalog to a full Oracle8 catalog by running cat8000.sql, usually located in the $ORACLE_HOME/rdbms/admin subdirectory on Unix. Then run catalog.sql, located in the same place. Finally, run catproc.sql to rebuild the PL/SQL and utility packages. If needed, also run any other "cat".sql scripts to install any purchased options as required.

19. Shut down and back up your new Oracle8-ready database.

Pitfalls To Avoid

What are the pitfalls? I wish I knew. Honestly, it would be impossible to tell you all the possible points of failure. Essentially, most will be resource related, such as not enough space. Here's a quick list of possible points of failure:

- *Not enough space in the **SYSTEM** tablespace when using MIG80 to migrate.* MIG80 will complain and abort if it doesn't have the space to create the new dictionary tables. You will need at least 1.5 times the space your current dictionary occupies as free space in the **SYSTEM** tablespace to use MIG80. Run MIG80 in **CHECK_ONLY** mode to verify that space is available (among other nice items to know).

- *Incorrect block sizes.* If you are using the export/import method, both databases must have matching block sizes, and block size must be at least 2,048 bytes. Oracle8 will not accept a smaller block size than 2,048 bytes.

- *Attempting to migrate from a 16-bit to a 32-bit machine using MIG80.* Come on, get serious. The only methods that work are methods two and three (export/import or SQLLOADER). I opt for export/import in this situation.

- *Going from one character set to another.* For MIG80, this isn't a problem, but for the other methods, it could be. Be sure to check your NLS parameters.

- *Performing migration steps out of order.* Obviously, don't do this.

- *Not fulfilling the prerequisites for migration* (as explained in the previous sections).

- *Allowing other users to access the database during migration.*

- *Working with a database that's not at least version 7.1.6.* I'm not kidding, it checks for this and errors out if it isn't.

- *Not setting permissions properly, if re-creating control files in a different location.*

- *All tablespaces not online or in an offline normal or temporary status when the Oracle7 instance is shut down.* Be sure there is no outstanding undo in any of the tablespaces.

- *An initialization file smaller than 2K in size.* (This has always been a limit; it just wasn't checked before. Anything over 2K was ignored and not read.) Move all comments to the end if they are important, and delete unneeded lines.

Developing A Type Hierarchy

One of the first steps in beginning an object-oriented development project is to develop a type hierarchy, which will determine inheritance characteristics for a set of classes, subclasses, and superclasses. Some may question whether or not this step is important for Oracle8, because Oracle8 doesn't yet support inheritance. I suggest that an ounce of prevention is worth a pound of cure. If you design your types in Oracle so they will easily map into the predefined type structure, then you will be miles ahead when Oracle does support inheritance.

Any object-oriented class structure has four general classes of types (from Timothy Budd, *An Introduction to Object-Oriented Programming*, Addison-Wesley Publishing, 1991):

- *Data manager, data, or state*—Classes that maintain data or state information.

- *Data sink or data source*—Classes that generate data (a source) or accept data for processing (a sink).

- *View or observer*—Classes that allow data objects to be viewed, displayed, or printed. They generate user-viewed instances of other objects.

- *Facilitator or helper*—Classes that maintain no state information themselves, but facilitate complex processing. A synonym for this type would be a *catalyst type*.

How do these classes relate to Oracle8 development? Oracle8 provides the data manager class that maintains data and state of objects. Using Oracle development tools, you can construct classes that perform the functions of view or observer classes. Using PL/SQL, C++, Visual Basic, or other tools, you can build the facilitator and helper classes. Data sources usually pre-exist, although they can be built using any of the tools already mentioned. Data sinks are constructed in the same fashion as data sources.

Types generally move from the abstract to the concrete. For example, a superclass for all objects that move people and goods could be called *vehicle. Vehicle* has the property of moving people or goods by physical means (if you want to include matter transports "a la Star Trek," then you would call the class *transporters*). Physical means are defined as being by road, track, sea, or air. This is a pretty loose class; notice a distressing lack of attributes.

You can now add subtypes to the class (or type) hierarchy—automobile, truck, train, and airplane. You can further enhance your type structure by adding attributes to each of the subtypes now defined, as shown in Figure 1.3.

You'll notice that the hierarchy shown in Figure 1.3 has one supertype, several types, and subtypes, with attributes demonstrated. The best way to determine status in a type hierarchy is to apply the "*has a, is a*" test. This test is simply a semantic one. If you can say that something *is a* something else, then it is a subtype of that something else. For example, a wife *is a* female, a husband *is a* male. A woman *is a* female, a man *is a* male. Therefore, wife and woman are two subtypes of female, and man and husband are subtypes of male.

As long as you can *is a* your way up a hierarchy, then you haven't reached the ultimate supertype. For example, husband *is a* man *is a* male *is a* human *is a* primate *is an* animal *is a* living creature. The generalized *living creature* is the ultimate supertype for husband (or for that matter, wife).

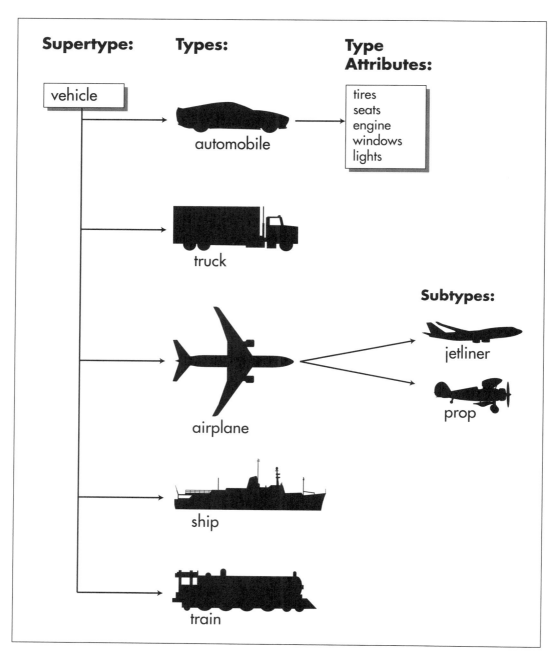

Figure 1.3

Example of a type hierarchy.

Determining attributes can sometimes be more difficult. For example, a husband *has a* wife, a wife *has a* husband; so, are wife and husband attributes or types? I'll let you decide. A general test is that if an object *has a* something, then that something is probably an attribute, not a subtype.

This doesn't mean that attributes can't be types. A company *has an* employee, but an employee *has a* job. If an object has a *has a* associated with it, then it is most likely a separate object that may have a reference back to the first object. This is how we resolve the husband/wife tangle from the previous example, by saying a wife is married to a husband.

An example from Figure 1.3 would be with the automobile type and its attribute list. An automobile *has a* tire (actually, more than one), but a tire *has a* size, *has an* inflation limit, *has a* tread type, *has a* manufacturer. It is the same with virtually every other part of an automobile as well.

You should identify the least granular type levels and start there in your application. For example, if you are building an automobile-rental tracking application, you don't need to walk the type hierarchy back up to the vehicle level or allow for trains, planes, ships, or trucks, so you start at the automobile and track down the chain. Start at the top level that applies to your application and work on the type dependency chain from there.

Defining Type Methods (Behaviors)

Type methods in Oracle8 define type behaviors. Oracle8 automatically builds constructor, modifier, and destructor methods when a type is created. When selected, special behaviors—such as computing total price, determining status from value (or state if you prefer), or defining order of return—all can be built into an Oracle8 type.

Once a type hierarchy is established and you have a list of types, dependent types, and attributes, you need to draw up a list of type behaviors. These behaviors can be brought about by external action requests via messages, or by internal actions required by change of state. Methods are probably most useful for change-of-state actions. For example, a method could be defined to automatically update a purchase-order object's total attribute upon addition, update, or deletion of a line item. A method could be defined to notify via a message (called an *alert*) a second object that, upon completion of the purchase-order object, initiates an action to order more of whatever is on the purchase order.

You must decide which types will have which behaviors, then translate these behaviors into methods. A method should never attempt to update, add, or delete another type's attribute state. It may send a message that causes the message type to initiate an action, but cannot do the action itself. A sure sign that a type may have to be broken into multiple subtypes is when you find yourself giving it too many behaviors. Behaviors should be atomic in nature. If a behavior affects multiple attributes in a type, then it should be externalized into a helper class object (such as a PL/SQL function, procedure, or trigger).

Here are some fatal design flaws when defining methods:

- *Types with too many methods*—Dependent types are hidden within the type's structure and should be placed into their own type.

- *Types with no methods*—The type probably isn't a type and may be deleted or absorbed into another type.

- *Types with methods that will never be used*—This is often the result of a non-communicating development team. Not everyone understands the type's true function in the type structure or hierarchy.

- *Types with disconnected methods*—This usually happens to the first or last types defined. It is a result of thinking, "We know we need this behavior, but not just where." If you have methods assigned to a type that don't directly affect the type or its attributes, it doesn't belong there.

- *Multiple types with the same method*—This usually happens to types that are actually subtypes to a common supertype. In Oracle8, multiple types with the same method should be moved to an external procedure until true inheritance becomes available. Once Oracle8 offers true inheritance, create a supertype and place a common method there.

Converting Relational Structures To Objects

The Oracle7 structure to be converted consists of 8 tables, 8 primary keys, and 11 foreign keys, with supporting indexes for the primary and foreign keys. Figure 1.4 shows the entity relational diagram for this structure. The actual table definitions are shown in Listing 1.1. This structure shows that the **clients** entity and, thus, **CLIENTS** table, and the **clients_info_number** entity and, thus, **CLIENTS _INFO_NUMBERS** table, are the two main entities. All of the other entities are dependent upon these two controlling entities. This will evolve under Oracle8 into two objects, **CLIENTS** and **CLIENTS_INFO_NUMBERS**, which will absorb the other entities into a hierarchical object structure, as shown in Figure 1.5.

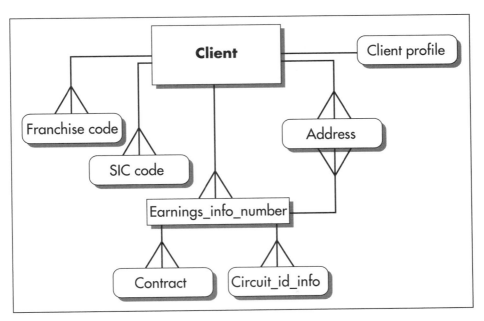

Figure 1.4*

Sample entity relational diagram for relational structure.

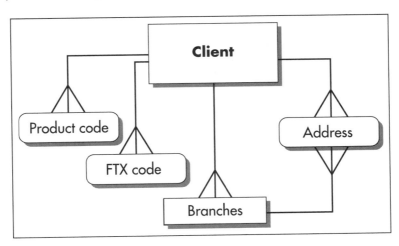

Figure 1.5*

Object-oriented ERD for conversion example.

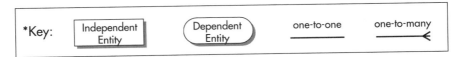

Listing 1.1 Oracle7 creation script for application fragment.

```
CREATE TABLE CLIENTS (
  clients_id              INTEGER   NOT NULL,
  customer_name           VARCHAR2(35) NOT NULL,
  active_flag             VARCHAR2(1),
  fax                     VARCHAR2(20),
  lookup_no               VARCHAR2(9) NOT NULL,
  phone                   VARCHAR2(20),
  corporate_name          VARCHAR2(30),
  lookup_parent           VARCHAR2(9),
  lookup_str_adrs         VARCHAR2(25),
  lookup_city             VARCHAR2(20),
  lookup_state            VARCHAR2(2),
  lookup_zip              VARCHAR2(5),
  lookup_zip_ext          VARCHAR2(4),
  lookup_type             CHAR(2),
  lookup_parent_flag      CHAR(1),
  creation_ts             DATE,
  creation_sy_user        INTEGER,
  spp_rating              CHAR(2),
  rating_date             DATE,
  competitor_loss         INTEGER,
  note                    VARCHAR2(250),
  last_contact_ts         DATE,
  delete_status           CHAR(1),
  name_soundex            CHAR(4),
  sales_volume            VARCHAR2(15),
  sales_volume_code       CHAR(1),
  total_employees         VARCHAR2(9),
  line_of_bus             VARCHAR2(19),
  pct_growth_sales        VARCHAR2(4),
  territory_covered       CHAR(1),
  ceo_first_name          VARCHAR2(13),
  ceo_last_name           VARCHAR2(15),
  ceo_middle_initial      VARCHAR2(1),
  ceo_suffix              VARCHAR2(3),
  ceo_prefix              VARCHAR2(10),
  ceo_title               VARCHAR2(30),
  mrc                     VARCHAR2(4),
  sub_indctr              CHAR(1),
  CONSTRAINT PK_clients
    PRIMARY KEY (clients_id)
        USING INDEX
        TABLESPACE APPL_INDEX
)
TABLESPACE APPL_DATA
;
```

```
CREATE TABLE CLIENTPROFILES (
  clientprofiles_id           INTEGER NOT NULL,
  clients_id                  INTEGER NOT NULL ,
  revnum                      INTEGER,
  created_by                  INTEGER,
  creation_ts                 DATE,
  delta_sy_user               INTEGER,
  delta_ts                    DATE,
  industry                    INTEGER,
  business_descrip            VARCHAR2(160),
  primary_contact             INTEGER,
  num_locations               SMALLINT,
  equipment                   INTEGER,
  equipment_brand             VARCHAR2(32),
  year_equip_installed        INTEGER,
  voice_network               INTEGER,
  business_strategy           VARCHAR2(160),
  bell_perception             INTEGER,
  lan_info                    VARCHAR2(160),
  long_dist_carrier           INTEGER,
  revenue                     NUMBER(9,2),
  internet_flag               CHAR(1),
  isp                         VARCHAR2(32),
  home_page                   VARCHAR2(50),
  cust_market_info            VARCHAR2(160),
  co_type                     INTEGER,
  msa_flag                    CHAR(1),
  msa_term                    SMALLINT,
  csa_flag                    CHAR(1),
  maint_provider              VARCHAR2(32),
  telecom_budget              NUMBER(9,2),
  fiscal_end                  DATE,
  equip_vendor                VARCHAR2(32),
  long_dist_bill              NUMBER(10,2),
  contact_frequency           INTEGER,
  video_flag                  CHAR(1),
  CONSTRAINT PK_clientprofiles
   PRIMARY KEY (clientprofiles_id)
      USING INDEX
      TABLESPACE APPL_INDEX,
   CONSTRAINT FK_clientprofiles_1
   FOREIGN KEY (clients_id)
      REFERENCES CLIENTS
)
TABLESPACE APPL_DATA
;
```

```
CREATE INDEX FK_clientprofiles_1 ON CLIENTPROFILES
(
    clients_id
)
TABLESPACE APPL_INDEX
;

CREATE TABLE CLIENTS_INFO_NUMBERS (
clients_info_nmbrs_id           INTEGER NOT NULL ,
userid                          INTEGER,
clients_id                      INTEGER,
listing_name                    VARCHAR2(100),
clients_number                  CHAR(13),
service_class                   VARCHAR2(5),
installed_lines                 NUMBER(4),
restrict_code_1                 VARCHAR2(14),
restrict_code_2                 VARCHAR2(14),
restrict_code_3                 VARCHAR2(14),
restrict_code_4                 VARCHAR2(14),
restrict_code_5                 VARCHAR2(14),
billing_name                    VARCHAR2(40),
phone                           VARCHAR2(10),
disconnect_reason               CHAR(2),
disconnect_date                 DATE,
btn                             CHAR(13),
old_clients_number              CHAR(13),
service_address                 VARCHAR2(100),
con_ctrl_number                 CHAR(15),
term_agreement                  CHAR(13),
shared_tenant_svcs              VARCHAR2(10),
installation_date               DATE,
 CONSTRAINT PK_clients_info_nmbrs
  PRIMARY KEY (clients_info_nmbrs_id)
    USING INDEX
    TABLESPACE APPL_INDEX,
 CONSTRAINT FK_clients_info_nmbrs_1
  FOREIGN KEY (userid)
    REFERENCES USERS,
 CONSTRAINT FK_clients_info_nmbrs_2
  FOREIGN KEY (clients_id)
    REFERENCES CLIENTS
)
TABLESPACE APPL_DATA
;
```

```
CREATE INDEX FK_clients_info_nmbrs_2 ON CLIENTS_INFO_NMBRS
(
    clients_id
)
 TABLESPACE APPL_INDEX
 ;
CREATE INDEX FK_clients_info_nmbrs_1 ON CLIENTS_INFO_NMBRS
(
    userid
)
TABLESPACE APPL_INDEX
 ;

CREATE TABLE ADDRESSES (
addresses_id                   INTEGER NOT NULL ,
addrtype                       INTEGER NOT NULL ,
clients_info_nmbrs_id          INTEGER,
clients_id                     INTEGER,
address1                       VARCHAR2(80),
address2                       VARCHAR2(80),
address3                       VARCHAR2(80),
address4                       VARCHAR2(80),
address5                       VARCHAR2(80),
address6                       VARCHAR2(80),
address7                       VARCHAR2(80),
address8                       VARCHAR2(80),
address9                       VARCHAR2(80),
address10                      VARCHAR2(80),
address11                      VARCHAR2(80),
address12                      VARCHAR2(80),
address13                      VARCHAR2(80),
address14                      VARCHAR2(80),
address15                      VARCHAR2(80),
  CONSTRAINT PK_addresses
   PRIMARY KEY (addresses_id)
     USING INDEX
     TABLESPACE APPL_INDEX
  CONSTRAINT FK_addresses_1
   FOREIGN KEY (userid)
     REFERENCES USERS,
  CONSTRAINT FK_addresses_2
   FOREIGN KEY (clients_id)
     REFERENCES CLIENTS(clients_id),
  CONSTRAINT FK_addresses_3
   FOREIGN KEY (clients_info_nmbrs_id)
     REFERENCES CLIENTS_INFO_NMBRS
  )
 TABLESPACE APPL_DATA
  ;
```

```
CREATE INDEX FK_addresses_3 ON ADDRESSES
(
    clients_info_nmbrs_id
)
TABLESPACE APPL_INDEX
;
CREATE INDEX FK_addresses_2 ON ADDRESSES
(
    clients_id
)
TABLESPACE APPL_INDEX
;
CREATE INDEX Fk_addresses_1 ON ADDRESSES
(
    userid
)
TABLESPACE APPL_INDEX
;

CREATE TABLE CIRCUIT_ID_INFO (
    circuit_id_info_id          INTEGER NOT NULL,
    clients_info_nmbrs_id       INTEGER,
    connect_type                CHAR(1),
    connected_number            VARCHAR2(36) NOT NULL,
    CONSTRAINT PK_circuit_id_info
    PRIMARY KEY (circuit_id_info_id)
      USING INDEX
     TABLESPACE APPL_INDEX,
 CONSTRAINT FK_circuit_id_info_1
  FOREIGN KEY (clients_info_nmbrs_id)
   REFERENCES CLIENTS_INFO_NMBRS
)
TABLESPACE APPL_DATA
;

CREATE TABLE SUB_CODES (
   sub_codes_id                 INTEGER NOT NULL,
   sub_code                     VARCHAR2(8) NOT NULL,
   clients_id                   INTEGER NOT NULL,
 CONSTRAINT PK_sub_codes
  PRIMARY KEY (clients_id,sub_codes_id)
    USING INDEX
    TABLESPACE APPL_INDEX,
 CONSTRAINT FK_sub_codes
  FOREIGN KEY (clients_id)
     REFERENCES CLIENTS
)
TABLESPACE APPL_DATA
;
```

```
CREATE INDEX FK_sub_codes_1 ON SUB_CODES
(
    clients_id
)
TABLESPACE APPL_INDEX
;

CREATE TABLE FTX_CODES (
    ftx_codes_id                INTEGER NOT NULL,
    ftx_code                    CHAR(8) NOT NULL,
    clients_id                  INTEGER,
    ftx_code_desc               VARCHAR2(32),
    primary_ftx_code_ind        CHAR(1),
  CONSTRAINT PK_ftx_codes
  PRIMARY KEY (clients_id,ftx_codes_id)
     USING INDEX
     TABLESPACE APPL_INDEX,
 CONSTRAINT FK_ftx_codes
  FOREIGN KEY (clients_id)
     REFERENCES CLIENTS
)
TABLESPACE APPL_DATA
;

CREATE INDEX FK_ftx_codes_1 ON FTX_CODES
(
 clients_id
)
TABLESPACE APPL_INDEX
;

CREATE TABLE CONTRACTS (
    contracts_id                INTEGER NOT NULL,
    clients_info_nmbrs_id       INTEGER,
    contract_no                 CHAR(15),
 CONSTRAINT PK_contracts
  PRIMARY KEY (clients_info_nmbrs_id,contacts_id)
   USING INDEX
   TABLESPACE APPL_INDEX,
 CONSTRAINT FK_contracts_1
  FOREIGN KEY (clients_info_nmbrs_id)
     REFERENCES CLIENTS_INFO_NMBRS
 )
TABLESPACE APPL_DATA
 ;
```

```
CREATE INDEX Fk_contracts_1 ON CONTRACTS
(
 clients_info_nmbrs_id
)
TABLESPACE APPL_INDEX
;
```

Many of the table structures in Listing 1.1 violate third normal form. Unfortunately, certain design restrictions (i.e., much of this was from a third-party application and, therefore, verboten to touch) forced this design.

To convert this relational structure into an object-relational structure, you have to know the dependencies. In this case, you are working against the following business rules:

1. **CLIENTS** and **CLIENTS_INFO_NUMBERS** can have independent existence, but, usually, for every one client, there may be many or no **CLIENTS_INFO_NUMBERS** records.

2. A **CLIENTS_INFO_NUMBER** can be created without a parent **CLIENTS**.

3. **ftx_code** and/or **sub_code** entities are dependent (i.e., they can't exist without the parent) on **CLIENTS**.

4. A **CONTRACT** and/or **CIRCUIT_ID_INFO** are dependent on **CLIENTS_INFO_NUMBER**.

5. In some cases, the records in **ADDRESS** are dependent on **CLIENTS** and, sometimes, on **CLIENTS_INFO_NUMBER**.

6. There can be no more that six **FRANCHISE** codes and no more than three **FTX_CODES** per client.

7. Up to three **ADDRESSES** can tie to a **CLIENTS_INFO_NUMBERS**, but only one can tie to the client.

8. A single **CLIENTS_INFO_NUMBERS** can be tied to multiple contracts.

9. A single **CLIENTS_INFO_NUMBERS** can be tied to multiple circuit/phone numbers.

10. A **RESTRICT_CODE** indicator (up to five) is used on a per-**CLIENTS_INFO_NUMBERS** basis to restrict access to that number's information (this promulgates back up to any client information as well).

11. A **CLIENT** may have one client profile.

Under Oracle8, relationships are shown by using **REF** statements. **REF** relationships are one-to-one. Because you can't make **CLIENTS_INFO_NUMBERS** dependent on **CLIENT** (see Rule 1 in the next section), you need the two main object structures **CLIENTS** and **CLIENTS_INFO_NUMBERS**. These will relate by a **REF** from **CLIENTS_INFO_NUMBERS** to **CLIENTS**. All of the other dependent entities will roll up into one: a type, a nested table, or **VARRAY** internal object.

For dependent entities whose behavior is limited to a fixed number of occurrences per parent record, Oracle suggests the use of **VARRAY**s, which are stored in line with the parent records in *RAW* format. Tests show, however, that this wastes space; a nested table may be more efficient. For multiple relations where the ultimate number is unknown or is extremely high, or the size of the resulting RAW would be too long (like anytime in early releases), I suggest using a nested table. For related one-to-one data, such as the **restrict_code** data and the **CLIENTPROFILES DATA**, I suggest using a type specification.

Some Rules For Using Types

1. A **VARRAY** or **NESTED TABLE** cannot contain a **VARRAY** or **NESTED TABLE** as an attribute.

2. When using nested tables, you must specify a store table in which to store their records.

3. Store tables inherit the physical attributes of their parent table.

4. You cannot specify default values for **VARRAY**s.

5. You cannot use constraints (even **NOT NULL**) in type definitions (they must be specified using an **ALTER TABLE** command).

6. You cannot index a table column specified as a **VARRAY**.

7. You cannot partition a table using **VARRAY**s or nested tables.

8. **VARRAY**s cannot be directly compared in SQL.

9. Incomplete types (forward typing) are allowed, but an incomplete type cannot be used in a **CREATE TABLE** command until it is complete.

10. The scalar parts of a type can be indexed directly in the parent table object.

11. **VARRAY** and **NESTED TABLE** subattributes cannot be indexed directly on a parent table object.

12. **NESTED TABLE STORE TABLE** attributes can be indexed.

Let's look at how this maps into the **CREATE TYPE**, **VARRAY**, and **NESTED TABLES** of Oracle8. Listing 1.2 shows the code to implement the structure as re-mapped to Oracle8.

Listing 1.2 Oracle8 code to implement application fragment.

```
REM There can be multiple contracts so lets
REM make it a nested table
REM
CREATE TYPE circuit_t AS OBJECT (
   connect_type    CHAR(1),
   connected_number    VARCHAR2(36)
) ;

CREATE OR REPLACE TYPE circuit_list AS TABLE OF circuit_t;
REM
REM There can be multiple contracts, lets make it a
REM nested table.
REM
CREATE OR REPLACE TYPE contract_t AS OBJECT (
    contract_number   CHAR(15)
);
CREATE OR REPLACE TYPE contract_list AS TABLE OF contract_t;
REM
REM There was a fixed number of franchise codes allowed and it was small
REM so use a VARRAY.
REM
CREATE OR REPLACE TYPE sub_t AS OBJECT (
   sub_code     VARCHAR2(8)
);
REM
REM sub_v is aVARRAY of 10 elements
REM
CREATE OR REPLACE TYPE sub_v AS VARRAY(10) OF sub_t;
REM
REM There is a fixed number of SIC codes and it is small
REM so use a VARRAY.
REM
CREATE OR REPLACE TYPE ftx_t AS OBJECT (
   ftx_code                CHAR(8) ,
   ftx_code_desc     VARCHAR2(32),
      primary_ftx_code_ind   CHAR(1)
);
REM
REM ftx_v is a VARRAY of 6 elements.
REM
CREATE OR REPLACE TYPE ftx_v AS VARRAY(6) OF ftx_t;
REM
```

```
REM The LOOKUP information is a one-to-one type
REM data set so use a type definition directly into the object.
REM
CREATE OR REPLACE TYPE lookup_t AS OBJECT (
     lookup_no                VARCHAR2(9) ,
     lookup_parent            VARCHAR2(9),
     lookup_str_adrs          VARCHAR2(25),
     lookup_city              VARCHAR2(20),
     lookup_state             VARCHAR2(2),
     lookup_zip               VARCHAR2(5),
     lookup_zip_ext           VARCHAR2(4),
     lookup_type              CHAR(2),
     lookup_parent_flag       CHAR(1)
);
REM
REM The address information is fairly long, so even though
REM it is a fixed number of values, lets put it in a nested table.
REM This data is from a legacy system, addresses can have from
REM 5 to 15 lines of data.
REM
CREATE OR REPLACE TYPE address_t AS OBJECT (
  addrtype                   INTEGER ,
  address1                   VARCHAR2(80),
  address2                   VARCHAR2(80),
  address3                   VARCHAR2(80),
  address4                   VARCHAR2(80),
  address5                   VARCHAR2(80),
  address6                   VARCHAR2(80),
  address7                   VARCHAR2(80),
  address8                   VARCHAR2(80),
  address9                   VARCHAR2(80),
  address10                  VARCHAR2(80),
  address11                  VARCHAR2(80),
  address12                  VARCHAR2(80),
  address13                  VARCHAR2(80),
  address14                  VARCHAR2(80),
  address15                  VARCHAR2(80)
);
REM
REM address_list is a nested table definition.
REM
CREATE OR REPLACE TYPE address_list AS TABLE OF address_t;
REM
REM The restrict_code data is a one-to-one type relation
REM so lets use a type definition directly into the object.
REM
```

```
CREATE OR REPLACE TYPE restrict_code_t AS OBJECT (
        restrict_code_1                VARCHAR2(14),
        restrict_code_2                VARCHAR2(14),
        restrict_code_3                VARCHAR2(14),
        restrict_code_4                VARCHAR2(14),
        restrict_code_5                VARCHAR2(14)
);
REM
REM The CEO data is a one-to-one relationship so just use
REM a type definition directly into the object.
REM
CREATE OR REPLACE TYPE ceo_t AS OBJECT (
    ceo_first_name                     VARCHAR2(13),
    ceo_last_name                      VARCHAR2(15),
    ceo_middle_initial                 VARCHAR2(1),
    ceo_suffix                         VARCHAR2(3),
    ceo_prefix                         VARCHAR2(10),
    ceo_title                          VARCHAR2(30)
);
REM
REM The client table is the master in this set. Now that
REM the dependent types, VARRAYs, Nested Tables, and
REM REF table have been created, go ahead and create it.
REM
CREATE OR REPLACE TYPE client_t AS OBJECT (
clients_id                         INTEGER ,
addresses                          address_list,
customer_name                      VARCHAR2(35) ,
active_flag                        VARCHAR2(1),
fax                                VARCHAR2(20),
lookups                            lookup_t ,
phone                              VARCHAR2(20),
corporate_name                     VARCHAR2(30),
creation_ts                        DATE,
creation_sy_user                   NUMBER(38),
spp_rating                         CHAR(2),
rating_date                        DATE,
competitor_loss                    INTEGER,
last_contact_ts                    DATE,
delete_status                      CHAR(1),
name_soundex                       CHAR(4),
sales_volume                       VARCHAR2(15),
sales_volume_code                  CHAR(1),
total_employees                    VARCHAR2(9),
line_of_bus                        VARCHAR2(19),
pct_growth_sales                   VARCHAR2(4),
territory_covered                  CHAR(1),
mrc                                VARCHAR2(4),
```

```
ceo                            ceo_t,
sub_indctr              CHAR(1),
ftx_codes               ftx_v,
sub_codes               sub_v,
MEMBER PROCEDURE do_soundex(id IN integer, nor_val IN varchar2)
);
REM
REM Now create the object clients which contains
REM nested tables, types, and normal attributes
REM
CREATE TABLE CLIENTSV8 OF client_t
OIDINDEX oid_clientsV8 (TABLESPACE APPL_INDEX)
NESTED TABLE ADDRESSES STORE AS ADDRESSESV8
        PCTFREE 10
        PCTUSED 80
        INITRANS 5
        MAXTRANS 255
        TABLESPACE APPL_DATA
        STORAGE (
                INITIAL 20m
                NEXT 10m
                MINEXTENTS 1
                MAXEXTENTS 10
                PCTINCREASE 0
        )
;
ALTER TABLE CLIENTSV8 ADD
        CONSTRAINT PK_clientsv8
                PRIMARY KEY (clients_id)
        USING INDEX
                PCTFREE 20
                INITRANS 5
                MAXTRANS 255
                TABLESPACE APPL_INDEX
                STORAGE (
                        INITIAL 10m
                        NEXT 10m
                        MINEXTENTS 1
                        MAXEXTENTS 121
                        PCTINCREASE 0
                        FREELISTS 5
                )
;
ALTER TABLE CLIENTSV8 MODIFY
    customer_name NOT NULL;
CREATE OR REPLACE TYPE BODY client_t IS
MEMBER PROCEDURE do_soundex(id IN integer, nor_val IN varchar2) IS
sx_val integer;
```

```
BEGIN
    sx_val:=soundex(nor_val);
    UPDATE CLIENTSV8 SET name_soundex=sx_val WHERE clients_id=id;
END;
END;
/
REM
REM The clients_info_data is an independent one-to-many
REM from CLIENTSV8. We will REF client_t and CLIENTSV8
REM
CREATE OR REPLACE TYPE clients_info_t AS OBJECT (
  clients_info_nmbrs_id        INTEGER,
  clients_id_r                 REF client_t,
  listed_name                  VARCHAR2(100),
   earning_number              CHAR(13),
   service_class               VARCHAR2(5),
  restrict_code                restrict_code_t,
  no_of_lines                  NUMBER(4),
  disconnect_date              DATE,
  disconnect_reason            CHAR(2),
  billing_name                 VARCHAR2(40),
   phone                       VARCHAR2(10),
   btn                         CHAR(13),
   old_clients_number          CHAR(13),
   service_address             VARCHAR2(100),
  con_ctrl_number              CHAR(15),
  term_agreement               CHAR(13),
  shared_tenant_svcs           VARCHAR2(10),
  installation_date            DATE,
  contracts                    contract_list,
  circuits                     circuit_list,
MEMBER PROCEDURE get_client_id_ref
(client_id IN integer, earning_id IN integer)
);
REM
REM clients_info_numbers is a table definition
REM
CREATE TABLE   CLIENTS_INFO_NUMBERSV8 OF clients_info_t
    (clients_id_r WITH ROWID
      SCOPE IS tele_dba.clientsv8)
      OIDINDEX oid_clients_info_nmbrsV8 (TABLESPACE APPL_INDEX)
      NESTED TABLE CONTRACTS STORE AS CONTRACTSV8
      NESTED TABLE CIRCUITS STORE AS CIRCUITSV8
      PCTFREE 10
       PCTUSED 80
       INITRANS 5
       MAXTRANS 255
       TABLESPACE APPL_DATA
```

```
        STORAGE (
                INITIAL 20m
                NEXT 10m
                MINEXTENTS 1
                MAXEXTENTS 10
                PCTINCREASE 0
        )
;
ALTER TABLE CLIENTS_INFO_NUMBERSV8 ADD
        CONSTRAINT PK_clients_info_numbersV8
                PRIMARY KEY (clients_info_nmbrs_id)
        USING INDEX
                PCTFREE 20
                INITRANS 5
                MAXTRANS 255
                TABLESPACE APPL_INDEX
                STORAGE (
                        INITIAL 10m
                        NEXT 10m
                        MINEXTENTS 1
                        MAXEXTENTS 121
                        PCTINCREASE 0
                        FREELISTS 5
                )
;
CREATE TYPE BODY clients_info_t AS
MEMBER PROCEDURE get_client_id_ref
(client_id IN integer, earning_id IN integer)
IS
BEGIN
        UPDATE CLIENTS_INFO_NUMBERSV8 z
    SET Z.clients_id_r =
    (SELECT REF(x) FROM CLIENTSV8 x
        WHERE X.clients_id=client_id)
    WHERE Z.clients_info_nmbrs_id=earning_id;
END;
END;
/
```

One thing to notice in this code is the use of the following coding conventions:

- All **TYPES** end in "_t".

- All **VARRAY**s end in "_v" (I use "_vw" for views).

- All **NESTED TABLES** end in "_list".

- When used in a DDL statement, native datatypes are capitalized, while user-defined types are lowercase.

- The entities are singular, while the tables or objects that they become are plural or are a plural or neutral form.

- All **REF** columns end in "_r".

- All primary keys have the prefix "PK_" followed by the table name.

- All foreign keys have the prefix "FK_" followed by the table name and arbitrary integer.

- All lookup keys have the prefix "LU_" followed by the table name and arbitrary integer.

- All unique value keys have the prefix "UK_" followed by the table name and an arbitrary integer.

- All OID indexes have the prefix "OID_" followed by the table name.

Also notice that each section is remarked (in the new code) to tell what is going on and why. This is a good practice and should be emulated. (I don't say this is the best way or the only way; you should develop a methodology that makes sense to your environment.)

The Oracle7 DDL must have the primary tables created first and then the related tables (or all tables, then the constraints). The Oracle8 code must have all types, **VARRAY**s, and **NESTED TABLES**, as well as related tables, before the primary tables are defined. If methods used in the type bodies are dependent on specific tables existing, then those tables must be created before the type bodies. This indicates that the Oracle8 system will require more analysis on the front end to build properly. If this analysis is not done properly, the rebuilding is more complex than with an Oracle7 database structure.

Notice that the number of indexes drops from 19 to 4. This is because as tables are made into nested tables, Oracle8 adds another column (**SETID$**) that is in the structure of their store tables. This **SETID$** value is added to the applicable indexes to establish the proper relations. This is done "under the covers," and DBAs need not concern themselves with it. The store tables inherit the physical attributes of their master table. The store tables can be modified just as regular tables can; thus, if required, you can add performance-enhancing indexes, as well as alter storage parameters.

Again, the order is critical. Notice that the type bodies come after the table created with the types (for **client_t** and **clients_info_t**). This is because the methods included in the bodies depend on the **CLIENTS** and **CLIENTS_INFO_NUMBERS** tables being valid. Also, see that the **CLIENTS** table is created prior to the **CLIENTS_INFO_NUMBERS** table. This is required because the column **CLIENTS_ID_R** references the **CLIENTS** table.

*A **REF** can refer to only one entry in a referenced object; therefore, references always go from the dependent table to the controlling table, from the many side of the relation to the one side.*

In the table definition for the **CLIENTS_INFO_NUMBERS** table, examine the first couple of lines that follow the **CREATE** line. These commands

```
clients_id_r WITH ROWID
SCOPE IS tele_dba.clientsv8
```

"finish" the **REF** command that was started in the type declaration. Because a type is generic in nature, you cannot limit the scope of a **REF** value inside a type declaration. Instead, you must restrict the value at point of use—in this case, the table creation. These commands allow the **ROWID** pseudo-column to be stored with the OID from the **REF**ed object table. This storing of the **ROWID** and OID speeds any **UNREF** activities. The **SCOPE** command restricts all **REF**s from this column to the specified table. This also reduces the space requirements for the **REF** column value and speeds access.

The **OIDINDEX** clause in both **CREATE TABLE** commands creates an index on the object identifier that can then be used to speed **REF** type queries against the tables. In this situation, the **CLIENTS_INFO_NUMBERSV8** object table will be **REF**ing the **CLIENTSV8** object table, so placing the **CLIENTSV8** OIDs into an index is a performance-enhancing idea. The **OIDINDEX** on **CLIENTS_INFO_NUMBERSV8** is just good form.

Summary

What can we summarize from the conversion example? Here are a few conversion guidelines:

- Attribute sets that are one-to-one with the main object should be placed in a **TYPE** definition and used directly.

- Attribute sets that have a low, fixed number of occurrences should be placed into **VARRAY**s (this may not be true if constraints or direct comparisons are required).

- Attribute sets with many occurrences, or that require constraints and value-to-value comparison, should be placed in nested tables.

- If a type is to be used in a **REF**-able object, the object must be created using the **AS OBJECT** clause.

- **REF** clauses in a **TYPE** declaration must be finished via an **ALTER TABLE** command on the final object table if scoping or **ROWID** storage is required.

- Use of **WITH ROWID** and **OIDINDEX** clauses should be encouraged to speed access and, in some cases, reduce storage requirements.

- Analysis of dependencies is critical to success.

Oracle8 will require a great deal more front-end analysis to prevent recoding. It is a new view of the world, and you will have to change your perception of how the database works in order to use the provided features fully.

 ## Loading Data Using SQLLOADER

Once a database has been built, you have many options for loading data. One option is to use SQLLOADER, an Oracle utility.

SQLLOADER reads flat files from the operating system, including EBCDIC format files, and loads them into Oracle database structures. SQLLOADER is controlled by the data loaded into a control file about the flat file structure and by commands either specified on the command line or placed in a parameter file.

The data can be either fixed-length records that are positionally delimited or via files where a special character known as a *delimiter* is used to separate variable-length fields within a variable-length record. Usually, a comma is used (by default) as a record separator in variable-length records, but you can specify different delimiters.

Let's examine a typical scenario for both a fixed-length record file and a variable-length delimited file.

SQLLOADER With Fixed-Length Records

Some data files have fixed-length records with fixed-format fields. You can load them by using the **POSITION** keyword with a position specifier.

The following example illustrates how to load a fixed-length format file.

Example data file:

```
5       Internal IS Services   Building 5             1
10      Programming Services   Building 10            3
12      Computer Operations    Building 5             2
15      Accounting Services    Headquarters           1
20      Human Resources        Headquarters           2
9       Non-Human Resources    Laboratory Building 5  1
```

In this case, the department number takes up 1:2, the department name 7:28, the building 29:50, and the floor 51:52.

Example table (which you load the data into):

```
CREATE TABLE DEPARTMENTS (
    Depno       NUMBER(3)      NOT NULL,
    Depname     VARCHAR2(30)   NOT NULL,
    Building    VARCHAR2(30)
    Floor       NUMBER(2)    );
```

Example control file:

```
LOAD DATA
INFILE *
INTO TABLE DEPARTMENTS
(DEPNO      POSITION(1:2)    INTEGER EXTERNAL,
DEPNAME     POSITION(7:28)   CHAR,
BUILDING    POSITION(29:50)  CHAR,
FLOOR       POSITION(50:51)  INTEGER EXTERNAL)
BEGINDATA
5       Internal IS Services Building 5             1
10      Programming Services Building 10            3
12      Computer Operations  Building 5             2
15      Accounting Services  Headquarters           1
20      Human Resources      Headquarters           2
9       Non-Human Resources  Laboratory Building 5 1
```

Because the number of records is small, you can edit the data file to include the control information. If the number of records was prohibitive, or, if you wanted to load files again and again, you could have placed the control information into a second file, and the **INFILE** clause would contain a fullpath description of the data-file location. The **ENDDATA** clause would be removed.

Actually, you don't have to specify the ending position for the integer values, but it is good form to do so. If you don't specify a loading mode, SQLLOADER will assume **INSERT** by default. The four loading modes are:

- **INSERT**—Inserts into empty tables
- **REPLACE**—Deletes all data in the table and loads the new data
- **APPEND**—Adds data to the end of the file
- **TRUNCATE**—Truncates the existing data and loads the new data

Nonfixed-Length Delimited Data

When the records in the data file to be loaded are delimited variable-length records, this is known as loading *stream-format* records. Generally, stream-format records have little or no blank padding, and the fields back right up onto each other, with only a field delimiter between them.

Notice in this next example, you are appending data to the file. If you wanted to load data into an empty table, you could leave off the **APPEND** statement in the control file, and SQLLOADER would do a load into an empty table (defaulting to **INSERT**). If you specified **REPLACE**, the existing data would be dropped and the new data loaded. If you specified **TRUNCATE**, the table would be truncated and the new data added. A truncation cannot be rolled back.

Example data file:

```
5,Internal IS Services,"Building 5",1
10,Programming Services, "Building 10",3
12,Computer Operations,"Building 5",2
15,Accounting Services,"Headquarters",1
20,Human Resources,"Headquarters",2
9,Non-Human Resources,"Laboratory Building 5",1
```

Example table:

```
CREATE TABLE DEPARTMENTS (
    Depno     number(3)      Not Null,
    Depname   varchar2(30)   Not Null,
    Building  varchar2(30)
    Floor     number(2)   );
```

Example control file (since the number of records is small, you can edit the data file to include the control information):

```
LOAD DATA
INFILE *
INTO TABLE DEPARTMENTS
APPEND
FIELDS TERMINATED BY ',' OPTIONALLY ENCLOSED BY ' " '
(DEPNO,DEPNAME,BUILDING,FLOOR)
BEGINDATA
5,Internal IS Services,"Building 5",1
10,Programming Services, "Building 10",3
12,Computer Operations,"Building 5",2
15,Accounting Services,"Headquarters",1
20,Human Resources,"Headquarters",2
9,Non-Human Resources,"Laboratory Building 5",1
```

Moving Data From Load Tables Into Database Object Structures

Usually, your data in the flat operating-system files is not nicely formatted for loading into Oracle tables. The data to be loaded are likely from legacy systems and will not be in any form even remotely resembling third normal form. Generally, the data from legacy systems contains multiple rows of identical information, duplicate values, and will probably have to be loaded into multiple Oracle tables. For example, an input flat file, as seen in Listing 1.3, has the following structure:

Listing 1.3 The structure for an example input flat file.

BRANCH_NMBR	CHAR(13)
INT_CODE	CHAR(3)
LISTED_NM	VARCHAR2(100)
SHORT_SRVC_ADRS	VARCHAR2(100)
DETAIL_HOUSE_NMBR	VARCHAR2(8)
DETAIL_SFX	VARCHAR2(4)
DETAIL_DRCTNL_PRFX	CHAR(2)
DETAIL_STR_NM	VARCHAR2(44)
DETAIL_DRCTNL_SFX	CHAR(2)
DETAIL_THRGHFR	VARCHAR2(6)
DETAIL_SUPPL_ADRS_UN_TYP	CHAR(4)
DETAIL_SUPPL_ADRS_UN_DATA	VARCHAR2(10)
DETAIL_SUPPL_ADRS_ELEV_TYP	CHAR(4)
DETAIL_SUPPL_ADRS_ELEV_DATA	VARCHAR2(10)
DETAIL_SUPPL_ADRS_STRUC_TYP	CHAR(4)
DETAIL_SUPPL_ADRS_STRUC_DATA	VARCHAR2(10)
DETAIL_POSTAL_COMM	VARCHAR2(32)
DETAIL_ST	CHAR(2)

DETAIL_ZIP	CHAR(5)
BILLING_NM	VARCHAR2(20)
BILLING_ZIP	CHAR(5)
BILLING_CTY	VARCHAR2(10)
BILLING_ST	CHAR(2)
BILLING_ADRS	VARCHAR2(60)
PHN_NMBER	CHAR(10)
COS	VARCHAR2(5)
TRBL_CUST_DSGNT	VARCHAR2(70)
BILLING_PHN_NMBR	CHAR(10)
NMBER_OF_PROD	NUMBER(3)
SWITCH_RSN	CHAR(2)
REVENUE	NUMBER(9,2)
PRCDNC_CD	NUMBER(2)
MTCH_GRD	VARCHAR2(7)
CONF_CD	CHAR(2)
HO_NMBR	CHAR(9)
BSNSS_NM	VARCHAR2(30)
SCNDRY_NM	VARCHAR2(30)
STR_ADRS	VARCHAR2(25)
CTY_NM	VARCHAR2(20)
STATE	CHAR(2)
PHYS_ZIP_CD	CHAR(5)
ZIP_4	CHAR(4)
CONTACT_ADRS	VARCHAR2(25)
CONTACT_CTY	VARCHAR2(20)
CONTACT_ST	CHAR(2)
CONTACT_ZIP_CD	CHAR(5)
CONTACT_ZIP_4	CHAR(4)
PHN_NMBR	CHAR(10)
OWNER_FRST_NM	VARCHAR2(13)
OWNER_MI	CHAR(1)
OWNER_LST_NM	VARCHAR2(15)
OWNER_SFX	CHAR(3)
OWNER_PRFX	VARCHAR2(10)
OWNER_TITLE	VARCHAR2(30)
MNGMNT_RESPY_CD	CHAR(4)
SALES_VOL	VARCHAR2(15)
SALES_VOL_CD	CHAR(1)
EMPL_TOTAL	VARCHAR2(9)
STAT_IND	CHAR(1)
SUBSDY_IND	CHAR(1)
ULT_HO	CHAR(9)
HDQRT_HO	CHAR(9)
PRNT_HO	CHAR(9)
PRNT_CTY	VARCHAR2(20)
PRNT_ST	CHAR(2)
HRCHY_CD	CHAR(2)
DIAS_CD	CHAR(9)

```
SML_BSNSS_IND          CHAR(1)
CTTG_FILE_IND          CHAR(1)
PBLC_PRVT_IND          CHAR(1)
LN_OF_BSNSS            VARCHAR2(19)
PRMY_FTX_CD_1          CHAR(8)
FTX_CD_2              VARCHAR2(8)
FTX_CD_3              VARCHAR2(8)
PRMY_FTX_CD_1_DESC     VARCHAR2(32)
FTX_CD_2_DESC         VARCHAR2(32)
FTX_CD_3_DESC         VARCHAR2(32)
ULT_NM               VARCHAR2(30)
PRNT_NM              VARCHAR2(30)
PCT_GRWTH_SALES        VARCHAR2(4)
LGL_STAT_IND          CHAR(1)
TRTRY_CVRD            CHAR(1)
FRNS_IND             CHAR(1)
PROD_CD_1            VARCHAR2(8)
PROD_CD_2            VARCHAR2(8)
PROD_CD_3            VARCHAR2(8)
PROD_CD_4            VARCHAR2(8)
PROD_CD_5            VARCHAR2(8)
PROD_CD_6            VARCHAR2(8)
```

Even without knowing a thing about the business this is for, an experienced developer can see that at least five to six different tables are loaded into this one file, if the tables are in third normal form. How can you load this type of flat file into Oracle? Actually, you have four options:

1. Create a 3GL program using embedded SQL to read the file and load into the appropriate tables.

2. With SQLLOADER, make multiple passes through the data file, using loader logic control statements to parse the data properly.

3. Load the file into a *flat* structure database table and use stored procedures to parse the data into the appropriate tables.

4. Create a 3GL program and a set of PL/SQL conversion routines where the 3GL program calls the PL/SQL routines to load the data.

Option 1 will involve days of testing, loading, and reloading, unless the person doing the 3GL is experienced with Oracle embedded SQL. Option 2 can be quite involved, although if you get it to work, it can be very fast. Option 3 is probably the best if you have the space in the database structure. It allows you to load the data using SQLLOADER, which can be extremely fast, and process the data using Oracle stored functions and procedures, which are normally very efficient. Option 4, a hybrid of 1 and 3, allows for when you don't have the space in the database to have two copies of the data (the flat version and the regular version).

Let's examine Option 3 for the previous example file. We will load the data into the following tables, as shown in Listing 1.4:

Listing 1.4 Example table structures for load example.

```
TABLE CLIENTS (
        clients_id              INTEGER NOT NULL,
        customer_name           VARCHAR2(35) NOT NULL,
        active_flag             VARCHAR2(1) NULL,
        fax                     VARCHAR2(20) NULL,
        ho_no                   VARCHAR2(9) NOT NULL,
        phone                   VARCHAR2(20) NULL,
        corporate_name          VARCHAR2(30) NULL,
        ho_parent               VARCHAR2(9) NULL,
        ho_str_adrs             VARCHAR2(25) NULL,
        ho_city                 VARCHAR2(20) NULL,
        ho_state                VARCHAR2(2) NULL,
        ho_zip                  VARCHAR2(5) NULL,
        ho_zip_ext              VARCHAR2(4) NULL,
        ho_type                 CHAR(2) NULL,
        ho_parent_flag          CHAR(1) NULL,
        creation_ts             DATE NULL,
        creation_sy_user        NUMBER(38) NULL,
        competitor_loss         INTEGER NULL,
        name_soundex            CHAR(4) NULL,
        module_code             VARCHAR2(4) NULL,
        sales_volume            VARCHAR2(15) NULL,
        sales_volume_code       CHAR(1) NULL,
        total_employees         VARCHAR2(9) NULL,
        subsidiary_indctr       CHAR(1) NULL,
        small_bus_indctr        CHAR(1) NULL,
        cottage_file_indctr     CHAR(1) NULL,
        pub_pri_indctr          CHAR(1) NULL,
        line_of_bus             VARCHAR2(19) NULL,
        pct_growth_sales        VARCHAR2(4) NULL,
        legal_status_indctr     CHAR(1) NULL,
        territory_covered       CHAR(1) NULL,
        owner_first_name        VARCHAR2(13) NULL,
        owner_last_name         VARCHAR2(15) NULL,
        owner_middle_initial    VARCHAR2(1) NULL,
        owner_suffix            VARCHAR2(3) NULL,
        owner_prefix            VARCHAR2(10) NULL,
        owner_title             VARCHAR2(30) NULL,
        franchise_indctr        CHAR(1) NULL)
```

```
TABLE BRANCHES (
        branch_id               INTEGER NOT NULL,
        userid                  INTEGER NULL,
        clients_id              INTEGER NULL,
        listed_name             VARCHAR2(100) NULL,
        branch_number           CHAR(13) NULL,
        service_class           VARCHAR2(5) NULL,
        no_of_prods             NUMBER(4) NULL,
        switch_reason           CHAR(2) NULL,
        billing_name            VARCHAR2(40) NULL,
        phone                   VARCHAR2(10) NULL,
        switch_date             DATE NULL,
        btn                     CHAR(13) NULL,
        man_fid                 VARCHAR2(5) NULL,
        old_branch_number       CHAR(13) NULL,
        service_address         VARCHAR2(100) NULL,
        int_code                CHAR(3) NULL,
        installation_date       DATE NULL)

TABLE ADDRESSES (
        addresses_id            INTEGER NOT NULL,
        addrtype                INTEGER NOT NULL,
        branch_id               INTEGER NULL,
        address1                VARCHAR2(80) NULL,
        clients_id              INTEGER NULL,
        address2                VARCHAR2(80) NULL,
        address3                VARCHAR2(80) NULL,
        address4                VARCHAR2(80) NULL,
        address5                VARCHAR2(80) NULL,
        address6                VARCHAR2(80) NULL,
        address7                VARCHAR2(80) NULL,
        address8                VARCHAR2(80) NULL,
        address9                VARCHAR2(80) NULL,
        address10               VARCHAR2(80) NULL,
        address11               VARCHAR2(80) NULL,
        address12               VARCHAR2(80) NULL,
        address13               ARCHAR2(80) NULL,
        address14               VARCHAR2(80) NULL,
        address15               VARCHAR2(80) NULL)

TABLE PRODUCT_CODES (
        product_codes_id        INTEGER NOT NULL,
        product_code            VARCHAR2(8) NOT NULL,
        clients_id              INTEGER NOT NULL)
```

```
TABLE FTX_CODES (
        ftx_codes_id            INTEGER NOT NULL,
        ftx_code                CHAR(8) NOT NULL,
        clients_id              INTEGER NULL,
        ftx_code_desc           VARCHAR2(32) NULL,
        primary_ftx_code_ind    CHAR(1) NULL)
```

The initial data load is done using SQLLOADER into a flat table whose structure exactly matches the input file structure. The records are nondelimited fixed length, so the control file looks like Listing 1.5:

Listing 1.5 Example SQLLOADER control file for loading flat table.

```
--SQLLOADER control file for LOAD_TEST
LOAD DATA
INFILE '/export/home/FLAT_FILES/BRANCH.LIST'
INSERT INTO TABLE APPL_DBO.LOAD_TEST
(
BRANCH_NMBR                     POSITION(1:13)         CHAR(13).
INT_CODE                       POSITION(14:16)        CHAR(3),
LISTED_NM                      POSITION(17:116)       CHAR(100),
SHORT_SRVC_ADRS                POSITION(117:216)      CHAR(100),
DETAIL_HOUSE_NMBR              POSITION(217:224)      CHAR(8),
DETAIL_SFX                     POSITION(225:228)      CHAR(4),
DETAIL_DRCTNL_PRFX             POSITION(229:230)      CHAR(2),
DETAIL_STR_NM                  POSITION(231:274)      CHAR(44),
DETAIL_DRCTNL_SFX              POSITION(275:276)      CHAR(2),
DETAIL_THRGHFR                 POSITION(277:282)      CHAR(6),
DETAIL_SUPPL_ADRS_UN_TYP       POSITION(283:286)      CHAR(4),
DETAIL_SUPPL_ADRS_UN_DATA      POSITION(287:296)      CHAR(10),
DETAIL_SUPPL_ADRS_ELEV_TYP     POSITION(297:300)      CHAR(4),
DETAIL_SUPPL_ADRS_ELEV_DATA    POSITION(301:310)      CHAR(10),
DETAIL_SUPPL_ADRS_STRUC_TYP    POSITION(311:314)      CHAR(4),
DETAIL_SUPPL_ADRS_STRUC_DATA   POSITION(315:324)      CHAR(10),
DETAIL_POSTAL_COMM             POSITION(325:356)      CHAR(32),
DETAIL_ST                      POSITION(357:358)      CHAR(2),
DETAIL_ZIP                     POSITION(359:363)      CHAR(5),
BILLING_NM                     POSITION(364:383)      CHAR(20),
BILLING_ZIP                    POSITION(384:388)      CHAR(5),
BILLING_CTY                    POSITION(389:398)      CHAR(10),
BILLING_ST                     POSITION(399:400)      CHAR(2),
BILLING_ADRS                   POSITION(401:460)      CHAR(60),
PHN_NMBER                      POSITION(461:470)      CHAR(10),
COS                            POSITION(471:475)      CHAR(5),
TRBL_CUST_DSGNT                POSITION(476:489)      CHAR(14),
BILLING_PHN_NMBR               POSITION(490:499)      CHAR(10),
NMBER_OF_LN                    POSITION(500:502)      DECIMAL EXTERNAL(3),
SWITCH_RSN                     POSITION(503:504)      CHAR(2),
```

```
REVENUE                POSITION(505:513)    DECIMAL EXTERNAL(9),
PRCDNC_CD              POSITION(514:515)    DECIMAL EXTERNAL(2),
MTCH_GRD               POSITION(516:522)    CHAR(7),
CONF_CD                POSITION(523:524)    CHAR(2),
HO_NMBR               POSITION(525:533)    CHAR(9),
BSNSS_NM              POSITION(534:563)    CHAR(30),
SCNDRY_NM            POSITION(564:593)    CHAR(30),
STR_ADRS             POSITION(594:618)    CHAR(25),
CTY_NM               POSITION(619:638)    CHAR(20),
STATE                 POSITION(639:640)    CHAR(2),
PHYS_ZIP_CD          POSITION(641:645)    CHAR(5),
ZIP_4                 POSITION(646:649)    CHAR(4),
CONTACT_ADRS         POSITION(650:674)    CHAR(25),
CONTACT_CTY          POSITION(675:694)    CHAR(20),
CONTACT_ST           POSITION(695:696)    CHAR(2),
CONTACT_ZIP_CD       POSITION(697:701)    CHAR(5),
CONTACT_ZIP_4        POSITION(702:705)    CHAR(4),
PHN_NMBR             POSITION(706:715)    CHAR(10),
OWNER_FRST_NM        POSITION(716:728)    CHAR(13),
OWNER_MI             POSITION(729:729)    CHAR(1),
OWNER_LST_NM         POSITION(730:744)    CHAR(15),
OWNER_SFX            POSITION(745:747)    CHAR(3),
OWNER_PRFX           POSITION(748:757)    CHAR(10),
OWNER_TITLE          POSITION(758:787)    CHAR(30),
MNGMNT_RESPY_CD      POSITION(788:791)    CHAR(4),
SALES_VOL            POSITION(792:806)    CHAR(15),
SALES_VOL_CD         POSITION(807:807)    CHAR(1),
EMPL_TOTAL           POSITION(808:816)    CHAR(9),
STAT_IND             POSITION(817:817)    CHAR(1),
SUBSDY_IND           POSITION(818:818)    CHAR(1),
ULT_HO               POSITION(819:827)    CHAR(9),
HDQRT_HO             POSITION(828:836)    CHAR(9),
PRNT_HO              POSITION(837:845)    CHAR(9),
PRNT_CTY             POSITION(846:865)    CHAR(20),
PRNT_ST              POSITION(866:867)    CHAR(2),
HRCHY_CD             POSITION(868:869)    CHAR(2),
DIAS_CD              POSITION(870:878)    CHAR(9),
SML_BSNSS_IND        POSITION(879:879)    CHAR(1),
CTTG_FILE_IND        POSITION(880:880)    CHAR(1),
PBLC_PRVT_IND        POSITION(881:881)    CHAR(1),
LN_OF_BSNSS          POSITION(882:900)    CHAR(19),
PRMY_FTX_CD_1        POSITION(901:908)    CHAR(8),
FTX_CD_2             POSITION(909:916)    CHAR(8),
FTX_CD_3             POSITION(917:924)    CHAR(8),
PRMY_FTX_CD_1_DESC   POSITION(925:956)    CHAR(32),
FTX_CD_2_DESC        POSITION(957:988)    CHAR(32),
FTX_CD_3_DESC        POSITION(989:1020)   CHAR(32),
ULT_NM               POSITION(1021:1050)  CHAR(30),
```

```
PRNT_NM                         POSITION(1051:1080)    CHAR(30),
PCT_GRWTH_SALES                 POSITION(1081:1084)    CHAR(4),
LGL_STAT_IND                    POSITION(1085:1085)    CHAR(1),
TRTRY_CVRD                      POSITION(1086:1086)    CHAR(1),
FRNS_IND                        POSITION(1087:1087)    CHAR(1),
PROD_CD_1                       POSITION(1088:1095)    CHAR(8),
PROD_CD_2                       POSITION(1096:1103)    CHAR(8),
PROD_CD_3                       POSITION(1104:1111)    CHAR(8),
PROD_CD_4                       POSITION(1112:1119)    CHAR(8),
PROD_CD_5                       POSITION(1120:1127)    CHAR(8),
PROD_CD_6                       POSITION(1128:1135)    CHAR(8)
)
```

Because this flat file contains the initial 10,000 records on a multimillion record load, you will want to use an external control file—hence, the full **INFILE** specification. Also, because you will be doing multiple loads, you should standardize the commands used to invoke SQLLOADER by use of a parameter file:

```
userid=APPL_dbo/APPL_dbo
control=load_test.ctl
skip=1
load=10000
direct=true
rows=2000
```

So, to load the data from the branch.list file into the **LOAD_TEST** table, the command is:

```
SQLLDR PARFILE=LOAD_TEST.SH
```

Once the data is loaded into the **LOAD_TEST** table, you must use PL/SQL procedures to parse it into the Oracle database tables (described earlier). First, load the **CLIENT** cluster of tables, as shown in Listing 1.6, because the **BRANCH** table is dependent upon the **CLIENT** table.

Listing 1.6 Example PL/SQL procedure for data conversion.

```
CREATE OR REPLACE PROCEDURE load_clients(rows IN NUMBER) AS
--
--
CURSOR proc_row(row NUMBER, maxr NUMBER) IS
   SELECT idrow FROM BATCH_CONTROL
   WHERE numrow BETWEEN row AND maxr;
--
--
CURSOR get_client_data(rowcount number, maxrows number) IS
```

```
SELECT
    NVL(rtrim(bsnss_nm),'Not Available') bsnss_nm,
    NVL(rtrim(scndry_nm),'Not Available') scndry_nm,
    NVL(rtrim(ho_nmbr),'9999') ho_nmbr,
    phn_nmbr,prnt_ho,str_adrs,cty_nm,load_test.state,phys_zip_cd,
    zip_4,stat_ind,sales_vol,sales_vol_cd,empl_total,sml_bsnss_ind,
    cttg_file_ind,pblc_prvt_ind,ln_of_bsnss,pct_grwth_sales,
    lgl_stat_ind,trtry_cvrd,ceo_frst_nm,ceo_lst_nm,ceo_mi,
    ceo_sfx,ceo_prfx,owner_title,mngmnt_respy_cd,frns_ind,
    prod_cd_1,prod_cd_2,prod_cd_3,prod_cd_4,prod_cd_5,
    prod_cd_6,prmy_ftx_cd_1,prmy_ftx_cd_1_desc,ftx_cd_2,
    ftx_cd_2_desc,ftx_cd_3,ftx_cd_3_desc,detail_house_nmbr,
    detail_sfx,detail_drctnl_prfx,detail_str_nm,detail_drctnl_sfx,
    detail_thrghfr,detail_suppl_adrs_un_typ,
    detail_suppl_adrs_un_data,detail_suppl_adrs_elev_typ,
    detail_suppl_adrs_elev_data,detail_suppl_adrs_struc_typ,
    detail_suppl_adrs_struc_data,detail_postal_comm,
    detail_st,detail_zip,mlng_adrs,mlng_cty,
    mlng_st,mlng_zip_cd,mlng_zip_4,user,sysdate
FROM
    LOAD_TEST,BATCH_CONTROL2,
WHERE
    BATCH_CONTROL2.numrow BETWEEN rowcount AND maxrows
    AND LOAD_TEST.rowid=BATCH_CONTROL2.idrow;
--
--
  CURSOR get_ei_data (hn NUMBER) IS
  SELECT
  LOAD_TEST.listed_nm,load_test.ernng_nmbr,
  LOAD_TEST.cls_of_srvc,load_test.nmber_of_ln,
  LOAD_TEST.switch_rsn,load_test.billing_nm,
  LOAD_TEST.billing_adrs,load_test.billing_cty,
  LOAD_TEST.billing_st,load_test.billing_zip,
  SUBSTR(load_test.branch_nmbr,1,10),
  LOAD_TEST.man_fid,load_test.short_srvc_adrs,
  LOAD_TEST.int_code
  FROM LOAD_TEST
  WHERE LOAD_TEST.ho_nmbr=hn;
--
--
  userid              NUMBER;
  this_day            DATE;
  cursor_name         INTEGER;
  ret                 INTEGER;
  maxrows             NUMBER;
  sql_com             VARCHAR2(500);
  maxcount            NUMBER;
  rowcount            INTEGER:=1;
--
```

```
-- Clients, ftx codes, product codes, addresses
--
sec_name                LOAD_TEST.scndry_nm%TYPE;
ho                      LOAD_TEST.ho_nmbr%TYPE;
phone1                  LOAD_TEST.phn_nmbr%TYPE;
bus_name                LOAD_TEST.bsnss_nm%TYPE;
par_ho                  LOAD_TEST.prnt_ho%TYPE;
street                  LOAD_TEST.str_adrs%TYPE;
city                    LOAD_TEST.cty_nm%TYPE;
state                   LOAD_TEST.state%TYPE;
phys_zip_cd             LOAD_TEST.phys_zip_cd%TYPE;
zip_4                   LOAD_TEST.zip_4%TYPE;
stat_ind                LOAD_TEST.stat_ind%TYPE;
sales_vol               LOAD_TEST.sales_vol%TYPE;
sales_vol_cd            LOAD_TEST.sales_vol_cd%TYPE;
empl_total              LOAD_TEST.empl_total%TYPE;
sml_bsnss_ind           LOAD_TEST.sml_bsnss_ind%TYPE;
cttg_file_ind           LOAD_TEST.cttg_file_ind%TYPE;
pblc_prot_ind           LOAD_TEST.pblc_prvt_ind%TYPE;
ln_of_bsnss             LOAD_TEST.ln_of_bsnss%TYPE;
pct_grwth_sales         LOAD_TEST.pct_grwth_sales%TYPE;
lgl_stat_ind            LOAD_TEST.lgl_stat_ind%TYPE;
trtry_cvrd              LOAD_TEST.trtry_cvrd%TYPE;
owner_first_nm          LOAD_TEST.owner_frst_nm%TYPE;
owner_lst_nm            LOAD_TEST.owner_lst_nm%TYPE;
owner_mi                LOAD_TEST.owner_mi%TYPE;
owner_sfx               LOAD_TEST.owner_sfx%TYPE;
owner_prfx              LOAD_TEST.owner_prfx%TYPE;
owner_title             LOAD_TEST.owner_title%TYPE;
mngmnt_respy_cd         LOAD_TEST.mngmnt_respy_cd%TYPE;
frns_ind                LOAD_TEST.frns_ind%TYPE;
prod_cd_1               LOAD_TEST.prod_cd_1%TYPE;
prod_cd_2               LOAD_TEST.prod_cd_2%TYPE;
prod_cd_3               LOAD_TEST.prod_cd_3%TYPE;
prod_cd_4               LOAD_TEST.prod_cd_4%TYPE;
prod_cd_5               LOAD_TEST.prod_cd_5%TYPE;
prod_cd_6               LOAD_TEST.prod_cd_6%TYPE;
prmy_ftx_cd_1           LOAD_TEST.prmy_ftx_cd_1%TYPE;
prmy_ftx_cd_1_desc      LOAD_TEST.prmy_ftx_cd_1_desc%TYPE;
ftx_cd_2                LOAD_TEST.ftx_cd_2%TYPE;
ftx_cd_2_desc           LOAD_TEST.ftx_cd_2_desc%TYPE;
ftx_cd_3                LOAD_TEST.ftx_cd_3%TYPE;
ftx_cd_3_desc           LOAD_TEST.ftx_cd_3_desc%TYPE;
detail_house_nmbr       LOAD_TEST.detail_house_nmbr%TYPE;
detail_sfx              LOAD_TEST.detail_sfx%TYPE;
detail_drctnl_prfx      LOAD_TEST.detail_drctnl_prfx%TYPE;
detail_str_nm           LOAD_TEST.detail_str_nm%TYPE;
detail_drctnl_sfx       LOAD_TEST.detail_drctnl_sfx%TYPE;
```

```
detail_thrghfr                      LOAD_TEST.detail_thrghfr%TYPE;
detail_suppl_adrs_un_typ            LOAD_TEST.detail_suppl_adrs_un_typ%TYPE;
detail_suppl_adrs_un_data           LOAD_TEST.detail_suppl_adrs_un_data%TYPE;
detail_suppl_adrs_elev_typ          LOAD_TEST.detail_suppl_adrs_elev_typ%TYPE;
detail_suppl_adrs_elev_data         LOAD_TEST.detail_suppl_adrs_elev_data%TYPE;
detail_suppl_adrs_struc_typ         LOAD_TEST.detail_suppl_adrs_struc_typ%TYPE;
detail_suppl_adrs_struc_data        LOAD_TEST.detail_suppl_adrs_struc_data%TYPE;
detail_postal_comm                  LOAD_TEST.detail_postal_comm%TYPE;
detail_st                           LOAD_TEST.detail_st%TYPE;
detail_zip                          LOAD_TEST.detail_zip%TYPE;
mlng_adrs                           LOAD_TEST.mlng_adrs%TYPE;
mlng_cty                            LOAD_TEST.mlng_cty%TYPE;
mlng_st                             LOAD_TEST.mlng_st%TYPE;
mlng_zip_cd                         LOAD_TEST.mlng_zip_cd%TYPE;
mlng_zip_4                          LOAD_TEST.mlng_zip_4%TYPE;
--
-- Branch Number, addresses
--
list_name                           branch_nmbrs.listed_name%TYPE;
earn_nmbr                           branch_nmbrs.earning_number%TYPE;
cos                                 branch_nmbrs.service_class%TYPE;
nol                                 branch_nmbrs.no_of_lines%TYPE;
dr                                  branch_nmbrs.disconnect_reason%TYPE;
btn                                 branch_nmbrs.btn%TYPE;
bn                                  branch_nmbrs.billing_name%TYPE;
mf                                  branch_nmbrs.man_fid%TYPE;
srvc_adrs                           branch_nmbrs.service_address%TYPE;
int_code                            branch_nmbrs.int_code%TYPE;
billing_adrs                        LOAD_TEST.billing_adrs%TYPE;
billing_cty                         LOAD_TEST.billing_cty%TYPE;
billing_st                          LOAD_TEST.billing_st%TYPE;
billing_zip                         LOAD_TEST.billing_zip%TYPE;
subsdy_ind                          LOAD_TEST.subsdy_ind%TYPE;
--
--
--
BEGIN
 BEGIN
  /*
   First clear out the batch_control of old entries
  */
  sql_com:='TRUNCATE TABLE batch_control';
  cursor_name:=DBMS_SQL.OPEN_CURSOR;
  DBMS_SQL.PARSE(cursor_name,sql_com,dbms_sql.v7);
  ret:=DBMS_SQL.EXECUTE(cursor_name);
  DBMS_SQL.CLOSE_CURSOR(cursor_name);
  COMMIT;
 END;
```

```
BEGIN
 --
 --
 sql_com:='INSERT INTO batch_control (control_var)
 SELECT UNIQUE(ho_nmbr) FROM LOAD_TEST';
 cursor_name:=DBMS_SQL.OPEN_CURSOR;
 DBMS_SQL.PARSE(cursor_name,sql_com,dbms_sql.v7);
 ret:=DBMS_SQL.EXECUTE(cursor_name);
 DBMS_SQL.CLOSE_CURSOR(cursor_name);
 COMMIT;
END;
BEGIN
 --
 --
 sql_com:='UPDATE batch_control a SET idrow = (SELECT
    MIN(rowid) FROM LOAD_TEST WHERE
    control_var=LOAD_TEST.ho_nmbr)';
 cursor_name:=DBMS_SQL.OPEN_CURSOR;
 DBMS_SQL.PARSE(cursor_name,sql_com,dbms_sql.v7);
 ret:=DBMS_SQL.EXECUTE(cursor_name);
 DBMS_SQL.CLOSE_CURSOR(cursor_name);
 COMMIT;
END;
--
-- For each run, reset the batch_control_seq by dropping and
-- rebuilding it.
--
BEGIN
 sql_com:='UPDATE batch_control
    SET numrow=batch_control_seq.nextval
    WHERE control_var IS NOT null';
 cursor_name:=DBMS_SQL.OPEN_CURSOR;
 DBMS_SQL.PARSE(cursor_name,sql_com,dbms_sql.v7);
 ret:=DBMS_SQL.EXECUTE(cursor_name);
 DBMS_SQL.CLOSE_CURSOR(cursor_name);
 COMMIT;
END;
BEGIN
 SELECT MAX(numrow) INTO maxcount FROM batch_control;
 IF maxcount>0 THEN
 maxrows:=rowcount+rows;
 DBMS_OUTPUT.PUT_LINE('Rowcount:'||TO_CHAR(rowcount)||
  'Maxrows:'||TO_CHAR(maxrows));
 dbms_output.put_line('Opening cursor get_client_data');
 OPEN get_client_data(rowcount,maxrows);
 dbms_output.put_line('Fetching cursor get_client_data');
```

```
    FETCH get_client_data INTO
        bus_name,sec_name,ho,phone1,par_ho,street,city,
        state,phys_zip_cd,zip_4,stat_ind,sales_vol,sales_vol_cd,
        empl_total,sml_bsnss_ind,cttg_file_ind,pblc_prot_ind,
        ln_of_bsnss,pct_grwth_sales,lgl_stat_ind,trtry_cvrd,
        owner_first_nm,owner_lst_nm,owner_mi,owner_sfx,owner_prfx,
        owner_title,mngmnt_respy_cd,frns_ind,prod_cd_1,
        prod_cd_2,prod_cd_3,prod_cd_4,
        prod_cd_5,prod_cd_6,prmy_ftx_cd_1,prmy_ftx_cd_1_desc,
        ftx_cd_2,ftx_cd_2_desc,ftx_cd_3,ftx_cd_3_desc,
        detail_house_nmbr,detail_sfx,detail_drctnl_prfx,
        detail_str_nm,detail_drctnl_sfx,detail_thrghfr,
        detail_suppl_adrs_un_typ,detail_suppl_adrs_un_data,
        detail_suppl_adrs_elev_typ,detail_suppl_adrs_elev_data,
        detail_suppl_adrs_struc_typ,detail_suppl_adrs_struc_data,
        detail_postal_comm,detail_st,detail_zip,
        mlng_adrs,mlng_cty,mlng_st,mlng_zip_cd,
        mlng_zip_4,user,this_day;
dbms_output.put_line(bus_name||' '||sec_name||' '||ho);
LOOP
  LOOP
    dbms_output.put_line(bus_name||' '||sec_name||' '||ho);
    EXIT WHEN get_client_data%NOTFOUND;
    INSERT INTO CLIENTS (
          clients_id,customer_name,delta_ts,delta_sy_user,
          ho_no,phone,corporate_name,ho_parent,ho_str_adrs,
          ho_city,ho_state,ho_zip,ho_zip_ext,creation_ts,creation_sy_user,
          name_soundex,active_flag,sales_volume,sales_volume_code,
          total_employees,subsidiary_indctr,
          small_bus_indctr,cottage_file_indctr, pub_pri_indctr,
          line_of_bus,pct_growth_sales,legal_status_indctr,
          territory_covered,owner_first_name,owner_last_name,
          owner_middle_initial,owner_suffix,owner_prefix,
          owner_title,mrc,franchise_indctr
            )
        VALUES (
          clients_id_seq.NEXTVAL,bus_name,this_day,
          userid,ho,phone1,sec_name,par_ho,street,
          city,state,phys_zip_cd,zip_4,this_day,
          userid,soundex(bus_name),stat_ind,sales_vol,
          sales_vol_cd,empl_total,subsdy_ind,sml_bsnss_ind,
          cttg_file_ind,pblc_prot_ind,ln_of_bsnss,
          pct_grwth_sales,lgl_stat_ind,trtry_cvrd,
          owner_first_nm,owner_lst_nm,owner_mi,
          owner_sfx,owner_prfx,owner_title,
          mngmnt_respy_cd,frns_ind);
```

```
      IF frns_ind IS NOT NULL THEN
        IF prod_cd_1 IS NOT NULL THEN
          INSERT INTO product_codes VALUES(
          product_codes_id_seq.NEXTVAL,
          prod_cd_1,
          clients_id_seq.CURRVAL);
        END IF;
        IF prod_cd_2 IS NOT NULL THEN
          INSERT INTO product_codes VALUES(
          product_codes_id_seq.NEXTVAL,
          prod_cd_2,
          clients_id_seq.CURRVAL);
        END IF;
        IF prod_cd_3 IS NOT NULL THEN
          INSERT INTO product_codes VALUES(
          product_codes_id_seq.NEXTVAL,
          prod_cd_3,
          clients_id_seq.CURRVAL);
        END IF;
        IF prod_cd_4 IS NOT NULL THEN
          INSERT INTO product_codes VALUES(
          product_codes_id_seq.NEXTVAL,
          prod_cd_4,
          clients_id_seq.CURRVAL);
        END IF;
        IF prod_cd_5 IS NOT NULL THEN
          INSERT INTO product_codes VALUES(
          product_codes_id_seq.NEXTVAL,
          prod_cd_5,
          clients_id_seq.CURRVAL);
        END IF;
        IF prod_cd_6 IS NOT NULL THEN
          INSERT INTO product_codes VALUES(
          product_codes_id_seq.NEXTVAL,
          prod_cd_6,
          clients_id_seq.CURRVAL);
        END IF;
    END IF;
      IF prmy_ftx_cd_1 IS NOT NULL THEN
        INSERT INTO ftx_codes VALUES(
        ftx_codes_id_seq.NEXTVAL,
        prmy_ftx_cd_1,
        clients_id_seq.CURRVAL,
        prmy_ftx_cd_1_desc,
        'Y');
```

```
END IF;
IF ftx_cd_2 IS NOT NULL THEN
   INSERT INTO ftx_codes VALUES (
   ftx_codes_id_seq.NEXTVAL,
   ftx_cd_2,
   clients_id_seq.CURRVAL,
   ftx_cd_2_desc,
   'N');
END IF;
IF ftx_cd_3 IS NOT NULL THEN
   INSERT INTO ftx_codes VALUES (
   ftx_codes_id_seq.NEXTVAL,
   ftx_cd_3,
   clients_id_seq.CURRVAL,
   ftx_cd_3_desc,
   'N');
END IF;
IF detail_house_nmbr IS NOT NULL THEN
  INSERT INTO addresses (
  addresses_id,addrtype,clients_id,
  address1,address2,address3,address4,
  address5,address6,address7,address8,
  address9,address10,address11,address12,
  address13,address14,address15
 )
 values (
  addresses_id_seq.NEXTVAL,
  1,
  clients_id_seq.CURRVAL,detail_house_nmbr,
  detail_sfx,detail_drctnl_prfx,detail_str_nm,
  detail_drctnl_sfx,detail_thrghfr,detail_suppl_adrs_un_typ,
  detail_suppl_adrs_un_data,detail_suppl_adrs_elev_typ,
  detail_suppl_adrs_elev_data,detail_suppl_adrs_struc_typ,
  detail_suppl_adrs_struc_data,detail_postal_comm,
  detail_st,detail_zip
    );
 END IF;
IF mlng_adrs IS NOT NULL THEN
  INSERT INTO addresses (
  addresses_id,addrtype,clients_id,
  address1,address2,address3,
  address4,address5
   )
  VALUES (
  addresses_id_seq.NEXTVAL,
  2,
  clients_id_seq.CURRVAL, mlng_adrs,
  mlng_cty,mlng_st,mlng_zip_cd,mlng_zip_4
    );
```

```
   END IF;
--
--
OPEN get_ei_data(ho);
FETCH get_ei_data INTO
  list_name,branch_nmbr,cos,
  nol,dr,bn,billing_adrs,
  billing_cty,billing_st,billing_zip,
  btn,mf,srvc_adrs,int_code;
LOOP
  EXIT WHEN get_ei_data%NOTFOUND;
INSERT INTO branch_nmbrs (
  branch_nmbrs_id,clients_id,listed_name,
  branch_number,service_class,no_of_lines,
  switch_reason,billing_name,btn,man_fid,
  service_address,int_code)
VALUES (
  branch_nmbrs_id_seq.NEXTVAL,
  clients_id_seq.CURRVAL,
  list_name,branch_nmbr,cos,
  nol,dr,bn,btn,mf,srvc_adrs,
  int_code);
 IF bn IS NOT NULL THEN
   INSERT INTO addresses (
   addresses_id,addrtype,branch_nmbrs_id,
   address1, address2,address3,address4,address5
   )
   VALUES (
   addresses_id_seq.NEXTVAL,
   3,
   branch_nmbrs_id_seq.CURRVAL,
   bn,billing_zip,billing_cty,billing_st,billing_adrs
   );
END IF;
FETCH get_ei_data into
  list_name, earn_nmbr,cos,nol,dr, bn,
  billing_adrs,billing_cty,billing_st,billing_zip,
  btn,mf,srvc_adrs,int_code;
END LOOP;
  CLOSE get_ei_data;
rowcount:=rowcount+1;
FETCH get_client_data INTO
     bus_name,sec_name,ho,
     phone1,par_ho,street,
     city,state,phys_zip_cd,zip_4,
     stat_ind,sales_vol,sales_vol_cd,
     empl_total,sml_bsnss_ind,cttg_file_ind,
```

```
            pblc_prot_ind,ln_of_bsnss,pct_grwth_sales,
            lgl_stat_ind,trtry_cvrd,owner_first_nm,owner_lst_nm,
            owner_mi,owner_sfx,owner_prfx,
            owner_title,mngmnt_respy_cd,frns_ind,
            prod_cd_1,prod_cd_2,prod_cd_3,prod_cd_4,
            prod_cd_5,prod_cd_6,prmy_ftx_cd_1,
            prmy_ftx_cd_1_desc,ftx_cd_2,ftx_cd_2_desc,
            ftx_cd_3,ftx_cd_3_desc,detail_house_nmbr,
            detail_sfx,detail_drctnl_prfx,detail_str_nm,
            detail_drctnl_sfx,detail_thrghfr,
            detail_suppl_adrs_un_typ,detail_suppl_adrs_un_data,
            detail_suppl_adrs_elev_typ,detail_suppl_adrs_elev_data,
            detail_suppl_adrs_struc_typ,detail_suppl_adrs_struc_data,
            detail_postal_comm,detail_st,detail_zip,
            mlng_adrs,mlng_cty,mlng_st,mlng_zip_cd,
            mlng_zip_4,userid,this_day;
      END LOOP;
       maxrows:=rowcount+rows-1;
       rowcount:=rowcount-1;
       CLOSE get_client_data;
       COMMIT;
      OPEN get_client_data(rowcount,maxrows);
END LOOP;
END IF;
END;
END;
```

The previous procedure uses a batch update method using a temporary table to
hold the **ROWID**s and a row number. A method that performs better than the one
shown for populating the temporary table is to select the distinct values into a table,
use a **MIN()** function to retrieve the **ROWID** where it first matches the distinct value,
and then create a second temporary table adding a **ROWNUM** column. Once you
have the temporary table populated, you batch through it in update sizes that are
just shy of filling your rollback segment extent size.

The next procedure populates the branch table using a similar technique:

```
CREATE OR REPLACE procedure load_branch(rows IN NUMBER) AS
--
--
  CURSOR proc_row(row NUMBER, maxr NUMBER) IS
     SELECT idrow FROM batch_control
     WHERE numrow BETWEEN row and maxr;
--
--
```

```
   CURSOR get_branch_data (
    start_row number, end_row number) IS
    SELECT
     listed_nm,branch_nmbr,cos,nmber_of_ln,
     switch_rsn,billing_nm,billing_adrs,billing_cty,
     billing_st,billing_zip,SUBSTR(branch_nmbr,1,10),
     man_fid,cris_srvc_adrs,cent
    FROM LOAD_TEST A, BATCH_CONTROL B
     WHERE B.numrow BETWEEN start_row AND end_row
     AND A.rowid=B.idrow;
 --
 --
   sql_com                    VARCHAR2(500);
   maxcount                   NUMBER;
   rowcount                   INTEGER:=1;
   cursor_name                INTEGER;
   ret                        INTEGER;
   maxrows                    NUMBER;
   userid                     NUMBER;
   this_day                   DATE;
 --
 -- Branch Number, addresses
 --
 list_name                   branch_nmbrs.listed_name%TYPE;
 branch_nmbr                 branch_nmbrs.branch_number%TYPE;
 cos                         branch_nmbrs.Service_class%TYPE;
 nop                         branch_nmbrs.no_of_prods%TYPE;
 sr                          branch_nmbrs.switch_reason%TYPE;
 btn                         branch_nmbrs.btn%TYPE;
 bn                          branch_nmbrs.billing_name%TYPE;
 mf                          branch_nmbrs.man_fid%TYPE;
 srvc_adrs                   branch_nmbrs.service_address%TYPE;
 int_code                    branch_nmbrs.int_code%TYPE;
 billing_adrs                LOAD_TEST.billing_adrs%TYPE;
 billing_cty                 LOAD_TEST.billing_cty%TYPE;
 billing_st                  LOAD_TEST.billing_st%TYPE;
 billing_zip                 LOAD_TEST.billing_zip%TYPE;
 --
 --
BEGIN
 BEGIN
  /*
   First clear out the batch_control of old entries
  */
  sql_com:='TRUNCATE TABLE batch_control';
  cursor_name:=DBMS_SQL.OPEN_CURSOR;
  DBMS_SQL.PARSE(cursor_name,sql_com, dbms_sql.v7);
```

```
 ret:=DBMS_SQL.EXECUTE(cursor_name);
 DBMS_SQL.CLOSE_CURSOR(cursor_name);
 COMMIT;
END;
BEGIN
 --
 -- Now populate batch_control with values
 --
 sql_com:='INSERT INTO batch_control(numrow,idrow)
 SELECT rownum,rowid FROM LOAD_TEST';
 cursor_name:=DBMS_SQL.OPEN_CURSOR;
 DBMS_SQL.PARSE(cursor_name,sql_com,dbms_sql.v7);
 ret:=DBMS_SQL.EXECUTE(cursor_name);
 DBMS_SQL.CLOSE_CURSOR(cursor_name);
 COMMIT;
END;
--
-- Now chunk through the insert process
--
BEGIN
 SELECT MAX(numrow) INTO maxcount FROM batch_control;
 IF maxcount>0 THEN
  maxrows:=rowcount+rows;
  DBMS_OUTPUT.PUT_LINE('Rowcount:'||TO_CHAR(rowcount)||
  'Maxrows:'||TO_CHAR(maxrows));
  DBMS_OUTPUT.PUT_LINE('Opening cursor get_branch_data');
  OPEN get_branch_data(rowcount,maxrows);
  DBMS_OUTPUT.PUT_LINE('Fetching cursor get_branch_data');
  FETCH get_branch_data INTO
    list_name,branch_nmbr,cos,nop,sr,bn,
    billing_adrs,billing_cty,billing_st,billing_zip,btn,
    mf,srvc_adrs,int_code;
  LOOP
     LOOP
       EXIT WHEN get_branch_data%NOTFOUND;
       IF branch_nmbr IS NOT NULL THEN
        INSERT INTO branch_nmbrs (
        branch_nmbrs_id,listed_name,
        branch_number,service_class,
        no_of_prods,switch_reason,
        billing_name,btn,man_fid, service_address,
        int_code)
     VALUES (
        branch_nmbrs_id_seq.NEXTVAL,
        list_name,branch_nmbr,cos,nop,
        dr,bn,btn,mf,srvc_adrs,int_code);
```

```
  IF bn IS NOT NULL THEN
    INSERT INTO addresses (
     addresses_id, addrtype,branch_nmbrs_id,
     address1,address2,address3,address4,address5
     )
    VALUES (
     addresses_id_seq.nextval,
     3,
     branch_nmbrs_id_seq.CURRVAL,
     bn,billing_zip,billing_cty, billing_st,billing_adrs
     );
    END IF;
 END IF;
 FETCH get_branch_data INTO
  list_name,branch_nmbr,cos,
  nop,sr,bn,billing_adrs,billing_cty,
  billing_st,billing_zip,btn,mf,
  srvc_adrs,int_code;
 rowcount:=rowcount+1;
END LOOP;
 CLOSE get_branch_data;
COMMIT;
maxrows:=rowcount+rows-1;
rowcount:=rowcount-1;
OPEN get_branch_data(rowcount,maxrows);
 END LOOP;
END IF;
END;
END;
```

Foundations For Object-Oriented Development

Before you can fully use the object-oriented extensions for Oracle supplied in Oracle8, you must understand object-oriented analysis and design as it applies to database systems, especially Oracle. This chapter is an overview of object-oriented systems analysis, functional decomposition, and object-oriented entity relation diagramming (OOERD).

Notes...

Chapter 2

Object-Oriented Systems Analysis

In previous paradigms, we performed analysis based more on computer limitations than on what made sense for the objects being modeled. The relational model is very powerful if you are dealing with numbers and text, but it falls down when complex objects, such as video, audio, or real-world objects, are forced upon it. Once it is fully realized, the object-oriented approach, with its concentration on objects and their behaviors, will be a powerful tool in the hands of programmers.

To realize the full potential of object orientation, we must apply new analysis techniques to the problems we wish to solve using the new paradigm. Unfortunately, no fully realized CASE tools exist for object-oriented analysis. Some come close, but none provide for the full functionality needed. This is also true of the modeling techniques that have been developed. Some are too simplistic, giving only a broad overview, while others provide perhaps too detailed a look at object messaging, generating diagrams that look like bowls of spaghetti with a few odd-shaped meatballs thrown in.

I'm afraid we must work with the tools provided until something better comes along. Let's examine some of these techniques.

Object-Oriented Modeling Frameworks

One of the first modeling techniques for object-oriented modeling is known as CRC/RDD, which stands for class, responsibility, and collaboration cards/responsibility-driven design. It is perhaps one of the easier techniques to use and involves neither complex software or hardware, nor an extremely long learning curve.

CRC/RDD depends on written requirements being present and uses textual analysis to determine key objects. For each object, which represents a class, a diagram is prepared, usually on a 3x5 card. The card contains the class name, superclasses, and members. The cards are then used to generate more specific subsets of subsystems, contracts (messages), and collaboration graphs.

This is a good technique for getting at what objects, methods, and collaborations are required, but it is just a starting point to more advanced methods. For more information on the use of CRC/RDD methods, look at *An Introduction to Object Oriented Programming* (by Timothy Budd, Addison-Wesley, 1991) or *Object-Oriented Methods, 2nd Edition* (by Ian Graham, Addison-Wesley, 1996). The method is broken down into these 10 steps:

1. Using the nouns in the specification statement, identify the application objects. Organize them into classification structures.

2. Find responsibilities by searching out the verbs in the specifications. These correspond to methods in other analysis techniques.

3. Assign responsibilities (methods) to the classes.

4. Examine the class structures and refine the responsibilities assignments.

5. Find collaborations (i.e., objects that act together via messaging).

6. Discard or absorb classes with no responsibilities.

7. Refine class structures.

8. Group responsibilities into contracts (methods).

9. Use collaborations to define subsystems.

10. Flesh out the design.

As you can see, the dynamics of the method can be applied, even if the cards and other paraphernalia aren't. Responsibilities are grouped according to whether they are for knowing or doing. Collaborations can exist between objects or with the server to help a class fulfill a responsibility.

A second method has been put forth in a paper by Choad/Yourdon (1990, 1991, 1991a), presenting a simplified notation for OOERD. This method is gaining popularity. Indeed, the notation I put forth later in the chapter to handle Oracle peculiarities is based loosely on this method. The method put forth by Choad/Yourdon breaks down into five stages:

- *Subjects*—The application is broken down into subjects, which are equivalent to levels or layers in standard data flow diagrams. If they contain more than five objects, then more analysis is probably required.

- *Objects*—The objects are identified in detail from within the subjects through standard data analysis identification of business entities.

- *Structures*—Classification and composition structures are identified. This is determined by and determines inheritance. These structures have been likened to specialization/generalization trees.

- *Attributes*—Attributes are detailed, and relationships are identified and assigned cardinality. This is done by applying the techniques of extended relational analysis (ERA).

- *Services*—This equates to operations or methods. Each object is provided with methods for creation and deletion of instances, getting and putting values and other special behaviors as required.

Choad furthers the Object-Oriented Analysis (OOA) section in his 1991a extension by adding three more components:

- Human interaction component (HIC)

- Task management component (TMC)

- Data management component (DMC)

Together, these three components form the problem domain component of the design. This method introduces APO (a part of), AKO (a kind of), and other notations that are useful for determining hierarchy and inheritance.

Essentially, the basic part of the diagram consists of a round-cornered box that is subdivided into three sections: name space, attribute space, and method space. Each object has one box. If the object has instances, it is surrounded by an outer round-cornered box that is usually gray. Lines with double arrows denote message traffic. Relations are shown using classic Yourdon bar-circle-crow's feet notation. Hierarchies are shown using either rounded forks for the AKO relation or triangular forks for the APO relation.

Based firmly as they are in the object-oriented paradigm, both of the techniques mentioned so far—CRC/RDD and OOERD—are good for modeling strictly object-related applications, such as vending machines, process flows, or automated teller machines. When modeling specialized systems, however, such as Oracle8 and its implementation of object-oriented ideas and constructs, both fall short.

Object-Oriented Entity Relational Modeling

Oracle8 has numerous structures that just don't map into standard or object-extended entity relational diagrams. Partitioned tables, index-only tables, object views—none of these is represented in standard notations. The concepts of nested tables, **VARRAY**s, and included types are also difficult to show in standard diagrams. To this problem I would like to propose the following set of extensions, loosely based on Choad/Yourdon diagram techniques. Figure 2.1 shows how these map out graphically and show the example conversion ERD from Chapter 1 in the new notation.

The new notation consists of:

- *Objects*—Standard Yourdon notation of a rounded box with a gray or solid-color outer box if the object has instances

- *Types*—Treated as a single object with a single round-cornered box

- *Nested tables*—Double round-edged box with outer box shown as a dashed line

- *VARRAY*—Box with three rounded corners and a square upper-left corner with a small box to show the **VARRAY** limit

- *Public method*—Square-edged box placed on edge of master type

- *Private method*—Dashed-edge box placed inside master type

- *Relational table*—Round-edged box with divider surrounded by square-edged box (most will be created from a type specification)

- *Index-only table*—Round-cornered box with outer dashed square-edged box; inner box has divider

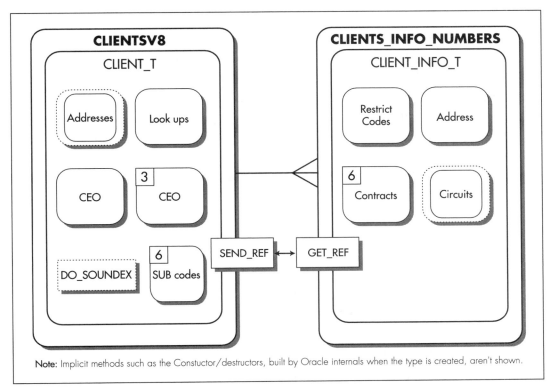

Figure 2.1

Example OOERD using Oracle object-oriented symbol extensions.

- *Partitioned table*—Inner multiple (3) overlapping round-edged boxes with dividers surrounded by outer square-edged box

- *Object view*—Inner round-edged box with divider surrounded by square outer box, surrounded by dashed round-edged box (showing that it is a relational table with an object view wrapper allowing it to participate in REFs)

- *Messages*—A standard double-arrow line

- *REFs*—Standard crow's feet notation

Other relations between relational tables are shown with standard notation.

No doubt, this method of showing Oracle databases that use object-oriented constructs has deficiencies, but I haven't seen a better way yet. I have included a VISIO stencil file on the CD-ROM enclosed with this book that provides these symbols for your use. Figure 2.2 shows all of the symbols defined here.

Using these symbols, the designer is now equipped to model Oracle8 databases (at least until something better comes along). The attributes for each object can either be entered into the space inside each of the diagram boxes or provided as a separate blown-up version. If this method were to be automated, I would place scrolling boxes in each of the sections where attributes, methods, or classes are shown. Included on the CD-ROM is the Rational Rose UML-based modeling tool. It uses a modified CRC structure for modeling Oracle8 structures.

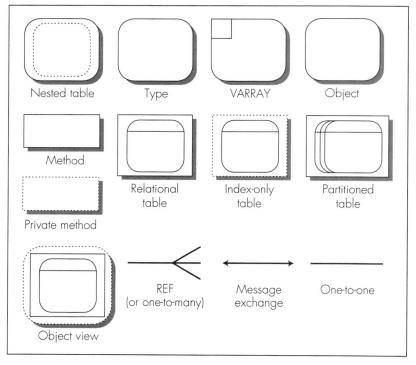

Figure 2.2

Symbols for modeling Oracle object-oriented extensions.

Project Methods

Projects need to be carefully planned. In the Navy, we followed the axiom, "Plan your work, work your plan." This applies to software development as well as fixing a pump as big as the car you drove in high school. Many excellent methodologies are available, and all of them boil down to five steps:

- Listening to the users

- Defining rules

- Developing prototypes

- Refining

- Implementing

If you don't do the first step properly (listening to users), then none of the rest will succeed. You must listen to users and define the rules of the business based on what you hear. This listening must be done at the proper level, or you will define improper rules. In the laboratories where I used to work in the nuclear industry, you would be hard pressed to find anyone above the lowest level of management who could name the equipment or state the methods or procedures being used on a project.

Naturally, if you interviewed people at this level about what was required for a laboratory information system, you would get a fully different answer than if you interviewed the laboratory technicians and first-level management. This is why I usually discount most surveys that begin, "In a survey of upper management..." So, the first rule is: Always interview at the proper level for each part of the system.

This is not to say that upper management shouldn't be interviewed; they know what reports and outputs are required, but any specifications on input, usage, and general system response requirements should be gathered at the lowest level possible. This is where the layered approach is used at its best. The layered approach divides system functionality into layers, with each layer corresponding to a level of interaction.

- At the lowest level (systemwise) is the base system administration layer. This layer consists of maintenance programs and screens, such as those used to input look-up values, calculation factors, etc. At this level, interview the system and application managers. Sometimes, this level is divided into two sublevels: system and application administration.

- The next level is the object information collection layer (input/output), which corresponds to the general user level. At this level are the major interaction screens where data may be input or displayed and where ad-hoc queries and reports are generated.

- The top level (in a basic application) is the upper management report layer. This level may involve screens that allow upper management to select canned reports for generation and, increasingly, screens to allow ad-hoc scenario generation ("what-if queries"). Generally, the data that reaches the upper level has been summarized, condensed, and purified (not how many pounds of peaches did Register X sell, but how many peaches did Store or Division X sell).

Each of these main levels may be divided into multiple sublevels (for example, a level for each division that inputs data into the system, or a level for intermediate managers). Figure 2.3 shows an example of project levels, who to interview, and what should be expected. Don't be surprised if input from each level sounds as though it comes from a different application.

Level	Who To Interview	For Specification Of
Level 3 Upper Management Roll-up data, summaries	CEO, VP, Senior managers	High-level Report requirements, scenario types
Level 2 General User Tuning data, Back-up requests, Look-up maintenance	Data Entry, Mid-Managers, Users	Data Input and display screens, user-level reports
Level 1 System/Application Manager	DBA, SA, Operators	System monitoring and maintenance screens and routines, back-up and recovery routines

Figure 2.3

Example project levels.

Each level will provide a level of abstraction for the business rules, which will define the system. Once a set of business rules for each level is generated, use it to model the objects, methods, and messages required at each level.

Once you understand the levels for a project, you must reconcile the OOERDs for each level into a coherent OOERD for the application. This will involve determining how data should be rolled up to each successive layer of the application. For example, the maintenance level will consist mostly of graph-type data entry and view screens for the input of the basic system reference objects and menus for the performance of maintenance functions, such as backup, restoration, and monitoring. You may also create menus for data loading at this level.

The user level of the application will consist of "stylish" data-entry forms that use pull-down menus and List Of Values (LOV) screens based on the look-up values provided at the first level, as well as adding the data that is the purpose for the system.

The highest level of the application will provide graphs, charts, and summary reports for use in trend and *information* analysis. Notice that I didn't say *data* analysis. At the top levels, management shouldn't be interested in data; they should be interested in information, which is summarized data. Summarized data provides trend analysis at a glance. This also requires the ability to display graphs and charts. In addition, the upper level will desire the ability to play what-if games with the information.

Essentially, as you move up the levels chart, the data moves from look-up (basic, core data) to input data (operational, detail data), to information (summarized, rolled-up data). You move from the concrete through multiple levels of abstraction to the highest level of abstraction.

Interview Techniques

Interview techniques are critical to the success of projects. You must be able to listen to the users at the various levels of a project. Most methods suggest that two people conduct each interview—one to ask questions and lead discussion and the other to record what is said. Some methods suggest the use of recordings (with permission, of course). You must find a style that works for you. Even if you arrive on a site and are immediately handed a code specification, be sure to find out how it was generated and, if necessary, ask to conduct spot interviews if you don't have confidence in the results.

Interviews should be conducted at the user's work area if possible; if that is not possible or advisable, choose a neutral location. Interviews should be nonconfrontational. You want the users to feel that they own the system, not that it is being thrust upon them.

Ask general questions at first and move toward the specifics, using answers as your guideline. If there are existing systems in place, gauge the users' feelings about those systems. Find out what they like and, most important, what they don't like about the existing systems. Find out what they expect the new system to provide. Nothing is gained by replacing an unusable system with a faster unusable system.

Joint Application Design (JAD) sessions may be a faster method of gathering requirements, but be sure to keep them small—no more than five to ten users at a time—or they will dissolve into chaos.

To derive a complete view of the system, you must review any pre-generated system specifications and requirements, interview users at all levels, and review existing systems for strengths and weaknesses.

Analyzing Interview Results

Once you have a complete set of interview, specification, and system reviews, you need to analyze the results for redundancy and remove the redundancies. Then you need to put the requirements in order of priority and take them back to the people you interviewed at each level to review the results. Gather any additional requirements and re-analyze. Repeat as required until the people at each level approve the requirements.

Once a final set of requirements is in hand, a textual analysis, sometimes called the Abbot method, is used to develop a list of types, objects, and methods:

1. Identify types (from the nouns in the specification).

2. Classify identified types into classification structures. For Oracle, this is a specification of objects, types, nested tables, varrays, index-only tables, and partitioned tables.

   - Objects are the top level of type. Use the *is a* test to determine this (for example, the major item we deal with is a car). Determine top-level objects in Oracle by determining how deep types are nested.

At least for now, an object cannot be used as a subtype within an object if it contains complex subtypes, such as nested tables or varrays. If a single one-to-many relation is involved, it may be safely absorbed; if it is a middle participant in a string of one-to-many relations, then it cannot. In the case of a string of one-to-many relations, you should use REF columns to relate objects. All REF objects should be resolved by methods in both the parent and child object.

- Nested tables are for a type of *has a,* relations which are known as *has some* relations where the number of related objects is unknown or large (for example, to use an extension of the example in Chapter 1, each car has some screws).

- Varrys are *has some* relations, which are fixed in number (for example, each car has four tires).

- Index-only tables are for *is a* types with a limited, small number of *has a* relations (such as look-up tables; for example, each car light is a light bulb that has a manufacturer on the approved list).

- Partitioned tables are for *is a* types with a large number of instances (for example, this system monitors a telephone connection or a circuit connection for each small business in a five-state region).

- A general type is for collections of related attributes used in a supertype, such as an address type, a spouse type, a child type, any collection of attributes that pertain to an *is a* that is a *has a* for another type and could resolve to a one-to-one relationship.

3. Find methods (use the verbs in the specification).

4. Assign methods to objects.

5. Determine which methods require data from other objects and define passing methods in those objects and define any required message passing. An example would be REF columns between objects.

6. Determine which attributes may require internal methods (total price, age, number of children) and assign those methods to their objects.

7. Use methods that require data from other objects to determine subsystem boundaries and collaborations.

8. Discard types or objects that have no methods or collaborations, or absorb them into other objects.

9. Attributes are resolved by the *has a* or *has some* test. Some attributes, however, may actually be objects or types if they also have attributes. This indicates either a super-subtype relation or an independent object REF relationship. An example would be a car *has an* engine, an engine *has some* parts. Clearly, because many engine parts are *has some* relations (*has some* screws, *has some* bolts, *has some* spark plugs), an engine is not only an attribute of a car, but also an object in its own right and should probably be separate. (Depending on the level of abstraction, if all you care about is engine size and fuel type, then a simple subtype will do.)

Once you have a listing of types, objects, and tables, diagram the system and use diagrammatic analysis to further determine hidden relations. By laying out the diagram so that no REF or relationship lines cross, you will be setting up the subsystem levels in your applications. Where objects cannot be clearly laid out with no crossing REF or relation lines, look for objects that may have been improperly resolved.

With OOERD in hand, you can create your first prototype to show users. For each level of user, attempt to prototype the most complex/most used process first and then move to the least complex/least used.

Practical Guide To

Object-Oriented Development

- Techniques For Interviewing (Requirements Capture)
- Developing An OOERD From A List Of Objects/Types And Rules

Techniques For Interviewing (Requirements Capture)

First, prepare some basic, open-ended questions about the general business and its use, such as:

- What does the business do?

- What (products, services, etc.) does the company provide?

- Who are the company's suppliers?

- What are the company's long-term goals?

- What are the company's short-term goals?

- Who are the company's customers?

Once you establish a base of knowledge about the business and its goals, you can focus more on the application. This also serves to familiarize you with the users and their interaction style. Next, ask some open-ended questions about the application to be built:

- How do you see the proposed application helping the business?

- How does the application help you (sell, provide) your (product, service)?

- Where does the application fit into the supply chain for the company?

- Will the application interface with any suppliers' or customers' systems?

- How do you envision the application supporting the company's long-term goals?

- How do you envision the application supporting the company's short-term goals?

These questions will help focus the discussion onto the application and where the users envision the application fitting into the scheme of things with the company. Use the responses from this series of questions to derive more detailed questions to "drill down" to a final set of requirements questions, such as:

- You have said that you sell X. What elements of this transaction need to be captured by the system?

- What different types of Xs do you sell/manufacture/purchase?

- Do you need to track information about your suppliers, such as names of contacts, addresses, approval status?

- You have said that you build Y for sale to company Z, using components from companies I and J. Do any of these companies provide online catalogs or interfaces you want to use?

- When I asked you where this application fits into the company's long-term goals, you stated it would be the foundation application. Could you expand on this? What other applications do you foresee it interfacing with?

- When you finish a month/quarter/year, what reports do you currently use/generate?

Once the final questions are answered, you begin sifting the answers for redundancies. Don't try to do this as answers are recorded, or you may remove some critical seeming redundancy that actually describes nearly similar transactions.

You need to choose your prototype carefully. Choose a prototype that models either the most complex operation at a specific level or models the most frequently used major transaction for that level. Move from the most complex/most used to the least complex/least used modules. This ensures that the majority of system functionality is completed, should money or time run out.

The iterations of prototyping/coding/prototyping need to be time-boxed. This means you should set a definite cutoff on iterations, elapsed time, or both for the prototyping phase. By setting definite limits that everyone is aware of, you will help focus the effort on what is important and limit scope creep.

When prototyping reports, try to solve them graphically if possible. A graph showing average sales or total per day or other time-based data is usually easier to understand than a column of numbers. Also be prepared to have a report of the values that the graph is based upon, however.

All projects must overcome two syndromes, which I call the NIH and pot-roast syndromes. NIH stands for not invented here and usually applies to any new technologies you will try to use. The pot-roast syndrome is best described by a short story:

A man noticed his wife cutting the edge off of a pot roast before placing it in the roasting pan. He asked her why she did this, to which the wife responded that her mother had taught her to do so. Her curiosity piqued, the wife called her mother and asked the reason, to which the mother responded that her mother had taught her to do so. Luckily, the grandmother was still alive, so they called her. Her answer was, "Goodness! You are still doing that? I did it because it was the only way the roast would fit in my pan."

The moral: Look for the reasons that reports and procedures are done the way they are. If the answer is, "It has always been done this way," see if there is a better way or if the report or process can be eliminated.

When I worked at a NASA project, a weekly status report for all financial aspects of the project was printed. This usually tied up the high-speed printer for hours and killed several trees per week. When asked why the report was generated, the users said they needed the last five pages of summary and just assumed the entire report had to be generated to get them. It turned out the five pages of summary could be reduced to one graph. Don't be afraid to ask why until you find out, especially with legacy reports and processes.

Example Interview

In this practical guide, we will demonstrate a typical interview with responses. The application is to be developed for Susan's Spaghetti Emporium, a restaurant that wants to automate. From a general walk-through of the business, we have determined the following levels for the application:

- System/Database management
- Restaurant floor
- Kitchen
- Purchasing
- Management reports and summaries

Because this is a small operation, the owner will handle both the system/database management, and management reports and summaries levels. The wait staff, bus staff, and hostesses will handle the restaurant-floor level, and the chef will handle the kitchen and purchasing levels.

Here is the transcript of the interview with the restaurant-floor personnel (introductions, general chat, and other extraneous material have been removed):

What do you do in your jobs?

Hostess: Greet customers, take reservations, seat customers, handle queuing of customers when the restaurant is backed up, handle telephone calls to the restaurant, schedule wait staff and bus staff.

Wait staff: Take drink and food orders, bring food to the tables when it is ready, keep drinks full, and help clear tables as required.

Bus staff: Clear tables when the customers are done, gather linen that has been soiled, replace linen and silverware with clean linen and silverware as needed, help bring out large orders.

What are some of the frustrations of your jobs?

Hostess: I really hate it when I forget frequent customers' names. It isn't bad when I can see them, but with reservations over the phone, I have trouble recognizing voices and names. We have been having problems with tracking when tables are cleared and ready for new customers. It is so embarrassing when a customer points out an open table I didn't know about. It is hard to remember how many people can be seated at a specific table or if the table can be moved for large groups. Right now, we use a manual scheduling method. It really becomes a hassle tracking vacations, time off, sick days, and scheduling.

Wait staff: I hate it when I put an order in and it comes back wrong. I don't have the best handwriting, so I guess it is mostly my fault. When it is really busy, it is hard to know when a food order is ready, so sometimes the orders get cold before I realize they are ready. I really get frustrated trying to remember everyone's drinks for refills. It is frustrating to see people waiting when there are empty tables in my section. It is frustrating to try and keep track of when I have to work. I hate last-minute changes.

Bus staff: It frustrates me trying to figure out when customers have left, like how do I know if they have left or just gone to the bathroom? Anyway, it is also hard to keep track of linen; it falls on me to make sure we have enough on hand. It can be frustrating when we run low on silverware as well. It is really frustrating to have everyone yelling for tables when I know I just cleared several. I had to cancel some time with my kids because of a schedule change; I really hate that.

What do you envision the new application doing for you?

Hostess: I would like it to track how many times a customer has called for reservations and how many times they have been in the restaurant, if possible. That way, it could flag me when I put reservations in that this is a frequent customer. It would be great if it would give me an indication of cleared tables, so I could tell at a glance when I can seat people. If it could help with scheduling, it would be worth a lot to me.

Wait staff: It would be great if I could enter orders in and have them sent to the kitchen. If there was some sort of automatic notification when an order was ready, it would be great. If it would keep drinks straight for me, it would be wonderful. Automatic notification to the hostess when tables are clear would be a big help.

Bus staff: I'm not sure what would help me. I need to know when a table is ready for clearing, keep track of linen used against available stocks, and keep track of the amount of silverware on hand. Sounds like it would mean a lot of work for me to enter the information, and I don't need any more work.

We can now generate a list of rules with some of the data we have gathered:

- The restaurant takes reservations.

- If the restaurant is full, customers are placed on a wait list on a first-come, first-served basis, except for those with reservations.

- Tables must be tracked as to status: cleared, occupied, ready to be cleared, or reserved.

- Orders must be tracked as to placement, ready status, and whether they are complete, canceled, or returned.

- If an order is returned, the reason should be captured.

- Frequent customers should be flagged as such when placing reservations.

- Customers should be tracked for frequency of reservations and visits.

- Tables should be tracked for capacity and location.

- Orders should automatically be sent to the kitchen and bar, and their status sent back to the wait staff.

- Table status should be automatically sent to the hostess station when it changes.

- Customers place orders that are taken by wait staff and filled by the kitchen.

- Tables are used by customers and cleared by bus staff.

- Orders have the following status: placed, filled, canceled, returned.

- Order quantities should be tracked by the wait staff.

So, what have we learned so far? Let's do a preliminary analysis and see what we come up with for the restaurant-floor level of the application. We have the following potential objects/types:

- Customers

- Reservations

- Orders

- Drinks

- Tables

- Linens

- Silverware

- Schedules

The following subtypes/attribute candidates have been identified:

- Customers
  - Frequent customers
  - Queued customers
  - Seated customers
  - Finished customers
  - Customer name
  - Customer drink
  - #Reservations
  - #Visits
- Reservations
  - Customer names
  - Time (assumed)

- Orders
  - Drink
  - Food
  - Placed orders
  - Ready orders
  - Canceled orders
  - Returned orders
- Drinks
  - Customer name/position?

- Tables
  - Cleared tables
  - Occupied tables
  - Table capacity
  - Tables ready for clearing
- Linens
  - Linens on hand
  - Soiled linens
- Silverware
  - Silverware on hand
  - Silverware used
  - Silverware missing
- Schedules
  - Wait staff schedule
  - Bus staff schedule
  - Vacation days
  - Days off

Armed with this information, we can now go back and ask more specific questions to refine our model.

How are tables currently tracked?

Each table has a number that corresponds to its location in the restaurant; however, this sometimes gets confusing when tables are moved for large groups.

How are linens currently tracked?

Tracked? When the hamper fills, we call and they come get it and give us a new one. We don't actually own the linens; we use a service.

How is silverware tracked?

We all sit down in the morning and make up the sets and wrap each with a napkin. Periodically during the day, we unload the dishwasher and wrap the clean silverware in napkins. Any extra pieces are put in the extras box, and we go through that once a week to make up however many sets we can. Then we order new sets as required for lost, damaged, or stolen sets.

What customer information is tracked?

We keep all comment cards in a shoe box. Once in a while, we sit down and send out flyers to the customers who have given us addresses. Other than that, all we have are the reservation books.

You said you manually prepare schedules. How exactly is this done?

I ask who wants to work when, and then try to schedule accordingly. Some always want to work nights, some days, and some just don't care. I try to keep the hours even and not overwork anyone, you know, try to keep it fair. If we know we are going to have a busy night, I may have to assign a waitperson to do busing. We have to watch hours for the part-time help; if they get over their hour limit, we can't work them any more for the week.

You said one of the things you do is keep track of queued customers. What exactly are they?

On busy nights, we sometimes have a waiting list. It is sometimes hard to keep the list straight, especially when folks get frustrated and leave. We have no way of knowing who is still here and who has left. It is also hard to notify the right customers when we have a table for them.

You've talked about silverware and linens. What about plates, bowls, glasses?

Oh, all of those have to be tracked as well. We try to keep track of breakage each night, so we can order replacements.

I've noticed you sell liquor, beer, and wine. Anything special in those areas?

Keeping track of the wine list is tough. It is really bad when someone orders a special wine, and we have to tell them we are out. All of the waitpersons have to have a liquor server license to serve any alcohol, so if one is under age, I need to assign a second waitperson to help in their area. We also have to track if someone tries a fake ID on us. Our beer list is also a tough spot. If we could have what is in stock readily available to the wait staff, it would help a lot. Alcoholic drink orders and food orders are kept separately. We have a roving bar waitperson who gets the alcohol orders when the wait staff are busy.

You've said there may be more than one person working a table and you have this roving bar waitperson. How are tips kept straight?

All tips are placed in a central jar, and at the end of the night, it is portioned out according to the volume each person handled. We do tip share for the helpers and roving wait staff. The chef gets 25 percent right off the top.

Based on these answers, what additional rules can we infer?

- Wait staff is scheduled to work according to full- or part-time status and hours worked.

- Wait staff needs liquor licenses to serve liquor; otherwise, they need assistance in their area.

- Linens, flatware, and glassware (including plates and such) should be tracked.

- Schedules should be generated for wait staff and bus staff, taking into account vacations, sick time, and hours worked.

- Silverware is ordered when numbers drop below a certain order threshold.

- Linen service is contacted when the number on hand drops below a certain order threshold.

- Beer, wine, and liquor orders are placed when levels drop below certain order thresholds.

- Inventories of specialty beers and vintage wines should be automatically tracked and orders placed when quantities drop below certain order thresholds.

- Order quantities should be tracked by the wait staff.

- Liquor inventory is kept by the barkeeper, as is the inventory of draft beer and jug wine.

We now have enough information to do further analysis. Let's see how this shakes out into what we have so far:

- Customers

  Customer name

  Customer status

  Frequent customer

  Customer address

  Customer comments

  Customer drink preference

  #Reservations

  #Visits

  Favorite table (assumed)

- Wait list

  Customer name

  Time placed on list

  Number in party

- Reservations

  Customer name

  Date

  Time (assumed)

  Number in party

  Occasion (assumed)

  Table

- Orders

  Table number

  Employee placing order

  Status

    Placed

    Ready

    Canceled

    Completed

    Returned (assumed)

    Reason

  Type

    Drink

        Name

        Price

    Food

        Item number

        Short name

        Price

- Tables

  Table number

  Table status

    Cleared

    Occupied

    Ready to clear

    Reserved

  Table capacity

  Location

- Linens

  Linens on hand

    Type

        Tablecloths

        Napkins

        Kitchen towels

  Soiled linens

    Type

        Tablecloths

        Napkins

        Kitchen towels

  Order threshold

    Type

        Tablecloths

        Napkins

        Kitchen towels

- Silverware
  - Silverware on hand
    - Type
      - Knife
      - Fork
      - Spoon
    - Number
  - Silverware missing
    - Type
      - Knife
      - Fork
      - Spoon
    - Number
  - Order threshold
    - Type
      - Knife
      - Fork
      - Spoon
    - Number

- Dishes
  - Breakage
    - Date
    - Type
      - Glasses
      - Plates
      - Cups
      - Saucers
    - Number
- Schedules
  - Job
  - Week
  - Wait staff schedule
    - Name
    - License status
    - Date
    - Time start
    - Time finish
  - Bus staff schedule
    - Name
    - Date
    - Time start
    - Time finish

- Employees
  - Name
  - Birth date
  - License number
  - Usual assignment
  - Vacation days
  - Days off
  - Employment status
    - Full-time
    - Part-time
  - Work status
    - Vacation
    - Sick
  - Hours this week
  - Preferred shift
- Wine List
  - Vintage
  - Type
  - Winery
  - Quantity on hand
  - Order threshold

- Beer list
  - Name
  - Brewer
  - Quantity on hand
  - Order threshold
- Liquor (assumed)
  - Type
  - Distiller
  - Quantity on hand
  - Order threshold
- Menu (assumed)
  - Item number
  - Item description
  - Short name
  - Item cost

Our list is getting fairly complete. The items marked as assumed were added by the analyst, based on required support structures he felt were needed. Based on the inferred rules and the above list of objects/types, we can proceed to the layout of an initial OOERD for the restaurant-floor level of our application.

Developing An OOERD From A List Of Objects/Types And Rules

We have been given the following list of rules and possible objects/types:

- The restaurant takes reservations.

- If the restaurant is full, customers are placed on a wait list on a first-come, first-served basis, except for those with reservations.

- Tables must be tracked as to status: cleared, occupied, ready to be cleared, or reserved.

- Wait staff is scheduled to work according to full- or part-time status and hours worked.

- Wait staff needs a liquor license if they serve liquor; otherwise, they need assistance in their area.

- Orders must be tracked as to placement, ready status, and whether they are complete, canceled, or returned.

- If an order is returned, the reason should be captured.

- Frequent customers should be flagged as such when placing reservations.

- Customers should be tracked for frequency of reservations and visits.

- Tables should be tracked for capacity and location.

- Linens, flatware, and glassware (including plates and such) should be tracked.

- Orders should automatically be sent to the kitchen and bar, and the status sent back to the wait staff.

- Table status should be automatically sent to the hostess station when it changes.

- Schedules should be generated for wait staff and bus staff, taking into account vacations, sick time, and hours worked.

- Silverware is ordered when numbers drop below a certain order threshold.

- The linen service is contacted when the number on hand drops below a certain order threshold.

- Beer, wine, and liquor orders are placed when levels drop below certain order thresholds.

- Inventories of specialty beers and vintage wines should be automatically tracked and orders placed when quantities drop below certain order thresholds.

- Customers place orders that are taken by the wait staff and filled by the kitchen.

- Tables are used by customers and cleared by the bus staff.

- Orders have the following status: placed, filled, canceled, returned.

- Order quantities should be tracked by the wait staff.

- Liquor inventory is kept by the barkeeper, as is the inventory of draft beer and jug wine.

- Based on further analysis, we can now refine our model and derive the following revised object-attribute list:

- Customers

  Customer name

  Customer status

  Frequent customer

  Customer address

  Customer comments

  Customer drink preference

  #Reservations

  #Visits

  Favorite table (assumed)

- Wait List

  Customer name

  Time placed on list

  Number in party

- Reservations

  Customer name

  Date

  Time (assumed)

  Number in party

  Occasion (assumed)

  Table

- Orders
  - Table number
  - Employee placing order
  - Status
    - Placed
    - Ready
    - Canceled
    - completed
    - Returned (assumed)
    - Reason
  - Type
    - Drink
    - Name
    - Price
  - Food
    - Item Number
    - Short name
    - Price

- Tables
  - Table number
  - Table status
    - Cleared
    - Occupied
    - Ready to clear
    - Reserved
  - Table capacity
  - Location
- Linens
  - Linens on hand
    - Type
      - Tablecloths
      - Napkins
      - Kitchen towels
  - Soiled linens
    - Type
      - Tablecloths
      - Napkins
      - Kitchen towels
  - Order threshold
    - Type
      - Tablecloths
      - Napkins
      - Kitchen towels

- Silverware

  Silverware on hand

    Type

      Knife

      Fork

      Spoon

    Number

  Silverware missing

    Type

      Knife

      Fork

      Spoon

    Number

  Order threshold

    Type

      Knife

      Fork

      Spoon

    Number

- Dishes

  Breakage

    Date

    Type

      Glasses

      Plates

      Cups

      Saucers

    Number

- Schedules

  Job

  Week

  Wait staff schedule

    Name

    License status

    Date

    Time start

    Time finish

  Bus staff schedule

    Name

    Date

    Time start

    Time finish

- Employees
  Name
  Birth date
  License number
  Usual assignment
  Vacation days
  Days off
  Employment status
    Full-time
    Part-time
  Work Status
    Vacation
    Sick
  Hours this week
  Preferred shift
- Wine list
  Vintage
  Type
  Winery
  Quantity on hand
  Order threshold

- Beer list
  Name
  Brewer
  Quantity on hand
  Order threshold
- Liquor (assumed)
  Type
  Distiller
  Quantity on hand
  Order threshold
- Menu (assumed)
  Item number
  Item description
  Short name
  Item cost

This level can be subdivided into four areas: hostess, wait staff, bus staff, and bar with the objects/types breaking out into the following subdivisions:

Hostess

- Customers

  Customer name

  Customer status

  Frequent customer

  Customer address

  Customer comments

  Customer drink preference

  #Reservations

  #Visits

  Favorite table (assumed)

- Wait list

  Customer name

  Time placed on list

  Number in party

- Reservations

  Customer name

  Date

  Time (assumed)

  Number in party

  Occasion (assumed)

  Table

- Schedules

  Job

  Week

  Wait staff schedule

    Name

    License status

    Date

    Time start

    Time finish

  Bus staff schedule

    Name

    Date

    Time start

    Time finish

- Employees
  Name
  Birth date
  License number
  Usual assignment
  Vacation days
  Days off
  Employment status
    Full-time
    Part-time
  Work status
    Vacation
    Sick
  Hours this week
  Preferred shift
- Tables
  Table number
  Table status
  Cleared
    Occupied
    Ready to clear
    Reserved
  Table capacity
  Location

Wait Staff

- Orders
  Table number
  Employee placing order
  Status
    Placed
    Ready
    Canceled
    Completed
    Returned (assumed)
    Reason
  Type
    Drink
      Name
      Price
    Food
      Item number
      Short name
      Price

- Tables

  Table number

  Table status

  - Cleared

  - Occupied

  - Ready to clear

  - Reserved

  Table capacity

  Location

- Menu (assumed)

  Item number

  Item description

  Short name

  Item cost

- Wine list

  Vintage

  Type

  Winery

  Quantity on hand

  Order threshold

- Beer list

  Name

  Brewer

  Quantity on hand

  Order threshold

- Liquor (assumed)

  Type

  Distiller

  Quantity on hand

  Order threshold

Bus Staff

- Tables

  Table number

  Table status

  - Cleared

  - Occupied

  - Ready to clear

  - Reserved

  Table capacity

  Location

- Linens
    - Linens on hand
        - Type
            - Tablecloths
            - Napkins
            - Kitchen towels
    - Soiled linens
        - Type
            - Tablecloths
            - Napkins
            - Kitchen towels
    - Order threshold
        - Type
            - Tablecloths
            - Napkins
            - Kitchen towels

- Silverware
    - Silverware on hand
        - Type
            - Knife
            - Fork
            - Spoon
        - Number
    - Silverware missing
        - Type
            - Knife
            - Fork
            - Spoon
        - Number
    - Order threshold
        - Type
            - Knife
            - Fork
            - Spoon
        - Number

- Dishes

  Breakage

  - Date

  - Type

      - Glasses

      - Plates

      - Cups

      - Saucers

    - Number

Bar

- Wine list

  Vintage

  Type

  Winery

  Quantity on hand

  Order threshold

- Beer list

  Name

  Brewer

  Quantity on hand

  Order threshold

- Liquor (assumed)

  Type

  Distiller

  Quantity on hand

  Order threshold

We can list the responsibilities that will help us determine needed methods:

- Hostess is responsible for maintaining customer, reservation, and wait lists.

- Hostess prepares work schedules based on staff availability and status.

- Hostess is responsible for seating customers when tables become available.

- Hostess should notify wait staff when customer is seated in their area.

- Wait staff is responsible for waiting on customers.

- Wait staff uses menu and beer, wine, and liquor lists to serve customers.

- Wait staff takes orders, sends orders to the kitchen or bar, collects money and tips.

- Wait staff may help bus staff clear tables.

- Wait staff should notify bus staff when customer is finished.

- Bus staff is responsible for clearing tables when customers are finished.

- Bus staff tracks linen, silverware, and dishes for usage.

- Bus staff is responsible for notifying the hostess when a table is ready for the next customer.

- Bar staff is responsible for filling drink orders.

- Bar staff is responsible for tracking beer, liquor, and wine usage and inventory.

Figure 2.4 shows the OOERD generated from the previous rules and objects/types list. Figure 2.5 shows an enlargement of an object with attributes, types, and special tables shown.

Summary

In this case study we looked at a small restaurant and defined the objects, attributes, and responsibilities for the restaurant based on interview results with the staff. This demonstrates that traditional methods of requirements gathering can be used for object-oriented design. Further definition of methods will be accomplished as the application is developed.

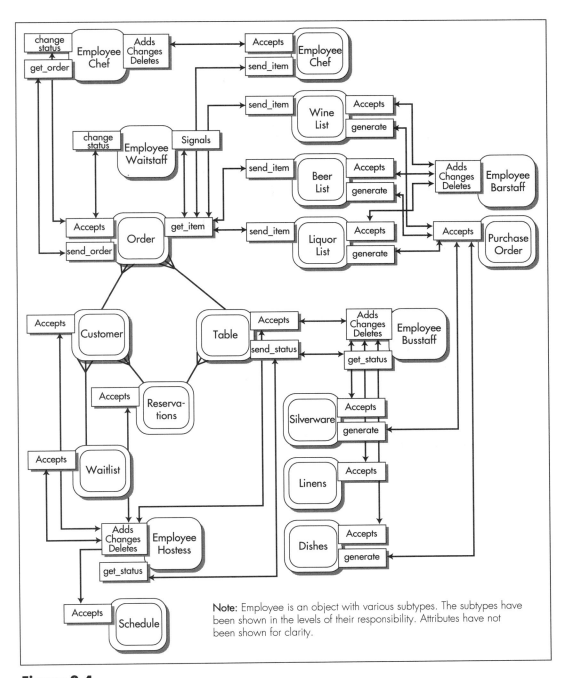

Note: Employee is an object with various subtypes. The subtypes have been shown in the levels of their responsibility. Attributes have not been shown for clarity.

Figure 2.4

Example OOERD from rules and objects/types list.

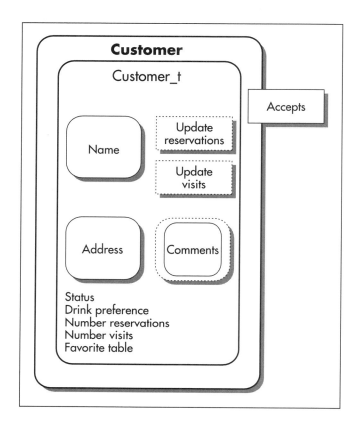

Figure 2.5

Example object specification.

Simulating Object Orientation With Oracle Triggers

*Triggers have been available, first in forms and then in the database, since version 6 of Oracle. In Oracle 7.3, they became compiled objects (rather than being parsed at runtime). In Oracle8, an additional trigger to allow the update of complex views (an **INSTEAD OF** trigger) was added to the 12 basic types of triggers available in Oracle7. By using these triggers, you can create a semblance of object orientation—that is, the passing of messages (events) to trigger-specific events (trigger actions) that act internally on an object (Oracle entity/table). This is a basic form of encapsulation.*

Notes...

Chapter 3

Oracle Triggers And Simulated Encapsulation And Data Hiding

Oracle triggers are stored PL/SQL code that acts on table attributes or other tables when a specific event occurs involving their parent table. The possible Oracle7 database-level triggers are:

- **BEFORE ROW**
- **AFTER ROW**
- **BEFORE ACTION**
- **AFTER ACTION**
- **FOR EACH ROW** (combined only with **BEFORE/AFTER** commands for four basic types)

Each of these triggers must be combined with one or all of the following:

- **INSERT**
- **UPDATE**
- **DELETE**

The four **BEFORE/AFTER** triggers are combined with the **INSERT/UPDATE/DE-LETE** triggers to form 12 types of available triggers. Prior to Oracle 7.3, the trigger code was stored as PL/SQL code and only parsed at runtime. With 7.3, the code is parsed into Oracle Pcode and stored identically to other stored objects, such as packages, procedures, or functions.

Oracle8 introduced a new trigger specifically for views. This new trigger, called **INSTEAD OF**, also combines with the **BEFORE/AFTER** and other triggers to specify that the actions be taken on the specified tables *instead of* the view. With later versions of Oracle (early versions forbid it), you can have multiple triggers of the same type on the same table; however, their firing order is not guaranteed.

When designing triggers, follow these guidelines:

- Do not use them to duplicate actions that can be better handled by Oracle internals, such as referential integrity.

- Limit the size of triggers to fewer than 60 lines or so. If the length gets much more than this, consider moving the functionality into functions or procedures.

- Be careful you don't define a recursive trigger, which causes itself to fire. An example of a recursive trigger would be an **AFTER INSERT** trigger on a table that performs an **INSERT** itself to that table or an **AFTER UPDATE** trigger that performs an **UPDATE** itself.

A common error that occurs with triggers is the mutating table. A mutating table is one that is currently being modified by an **UPDATE**, **DELETE**, or **INSERT** statement, or a table that might need to be updated by the effects of a declarative **DELETE CASCADE** referential integrity constraint. A mutating table is mutating only to the session that issued the statement in progress. The problem is that a trigger cannot query or modify a mutating table that contains the triggering statement. **BEFORE ROW** or **AFTER ROW** triggers fired by a single **UPDATE** do not cause this to occur.

If you need to update a mutating table, you have several methods to choose from:

- *Temporary table*—Create a temporary table to hold the values to be manipulated.

- *PL/SQL table*—Select the values into a PL/SQL table before taking the action that causes the table to mutate, then modify the PL/SQL table values.

- *Package variable*—Select the needed value into a package variable or variables.

For example, two **AFTER ROW** triggers can be used in place of one that causes a mutating table error: one to update a temporary table and a second that then updates the main table with the values from the temporary table.

The user of a trigger is not the executor. The executor becomes the owner of the trigger while the trigger fires; therefore, selection from **USER_USER** inside of a trigger always results in the owner of the trigger being returned. If the identity of the executor of a trigger is required for auditing purposes, it must be passed to the trigger.

You must have **CREATE TRIGGER** or **CREATE ANY TRIGGER** privilege to create triggers in your schema or in others schemas, respectively.

Because triggers are now stored objects, the creator of a trigger must have explicit grants on any objects used by the triggers, similar to the requirements for packages, views, or functions.

The dependencies for a trigger can be viewed by looking at the **ALL_DEPENDENCIES** view (from the owner) or via the **DBA_DEPENDENCIES** view for DBA users wishing to see the dependencies of any trigger.

Triggers And Object-Oriented Behavior

By acting based on events and being stored with a specific table, triggers emulate certain characteristics of object-oriented behavior. The concept of encapsulation allows that data and behavior should be encapsulated into a single entity to practice data hiding. This is accomplished on a primitive level by standard triggers. A simple form of messaging (i.e., taking specific actions on a table, sending a message that you are inserting, updating, or deleting from a triggers table) causes a trigger to fire and take actions based on how it was triggered (actually not a single trigger, but a set of triggers; if a single trigger is set to fire on multiple actions, then it comes closer to this behavior).

Not until the addition of conditional predicates in Oracle8 could you specify multiple actions based on action in a trigger. The conditional predicates are:

- **INSERTING**—Returns the value of **TRUE** if the trigger fires for an **INSERT** statement.

- **DELETING**—Returns the value of **TRUE** if the trigger fires for a **DE-LETE** statement.

- **UPDATING**—Returns the value of **TRUE** if the trigger fires for an **UPDATE** statement.

- **UPDATING** (column_name)—Returns a value of **TRUE** for an **UP-DATE** to the specified column.

Conditional predicates allow a single trigger to fire for multiple conditions and, based on the firing condition, take multiple actions. Use of the **IF-THEN-ELSE-END IF** construction and conditional predicates brings triggers closer to true object-oriented behavior.

You cannot set triggers for object columns or their attributes, varrays, nested tables, or LOB columns. PL/SQL functions or methods cannot be invoked in the trigger restriction. A trigger restriction is the SQL-based restriction specified in a trigger's **WHEN** clause.

Let's move on to the Practical Guide for this chapter, so I can actually demonstrate these techniques.

Practical Guide To

Creating And Using Triggers

- Creating A Basic Trigger
- Using Conditional Predicates
- Creating A **CASCADE UPDATE** Trigger
- Creating An **EITHER-OR** Trigger
- Calling Procedures From Triggers
- Using **FUNCTIONS** In Triggers
- Using The **INSTEAD OF** Trigger

Creating A Basic Trigger

To create a trigger, the user must have either the **CREATE TRIGGER** or **CREATE ANY TRIGGER** grant and have direct grants on any objects used by the trigger. You can use a basic trigger for verification, conversion, or auditing activities—among thousands of possible uses, both imaginable and unimaginable. The **CREATE TRIGGER** command is used to create all types of triggers and has the form:

```
CREATE OR REPLACE TRIGGER [schema.]trigger_name
    {BEFORE | AFTER | INSTEAD OF}
    {DELETE
    |INSERT
    |UPDATE      [of column [,column] ... ] } ] ...
ON [schema.] { table | view }
[ [ REFERENCING { old [as] old
                                |NEW [AS] new } ... ]
FOR EACH {ROW | STATEMENT} [WHEN {condition} ] ] ] pl/sql block
```

Where:

OR REPLACE - Replaces an existing trigger.
schema - Name of schema; if other than current schema, must have CREATE ANY TRIGGER grant.
table - Name of the table the trigger is to be applied to.
view - For INSTEAD OF triggers only, the name of the view the trigger applies to.
BEFORE - Indicates that the trigger executes before Oracle executes the triggering statement.
AFTER - Indicates the statement then the triggers are executed.
INSTEAD OF - For views only, Oracle executes the statement instead of the triggering statement.
DELETE - Fires on a DELETE statement.
INSERT - Fires on an INSERT statement.
UPDATE OF - Fires on UPDATE statement.
ON - Names the object; can be a table, object table, view, or Object view.
(Can be on index only tables, but cannot create triggers on SYS owned tables.)
REFERENCING - Specified correlation names between NEW and OLD and whatever is specified in their place.
FOR EACH ROW - Designates the trigger is a row trigger. Trigger is fired once for each row that is affected by the triggering statement.
(Except for INSTEAD OF triggers, a trigger is a statement trigger by default.)
WHEN - Specifies a specific condition under which the trigger is fired; the condition must be met or the trigger doesn't execute. By definition, INSTEAD OF triggers cannot have WHEN conditions.
PL/SQL block - The block of PL/SQL that is the purpose of the trigger to exist in the first place.
(Cannot contain COMMIT, ROLLBACK, SAVEPOINT, or SET CONSTRAINT commands.)

First, let's show a simple trigger to update a sum column on insertion into a table. The tables involved in the transaction are **purchase_orders** and **price_adjust**. **purchase_orders** has the columns **state_code**, **po_num**, **line_no**, **price**, and **adjusted_price**. The table **price_adjust** has the columns **state_code** and **adjust_rate**. As its name implies, **purchase_orders** contains information about various lines and prices for a company's purchase orders, and the **price_adjust** table contains the tax-adjustment figures for each state (of course, now that virtually every county and city has different rates, this is rather a simplistic view; but, hey, this is a simple trigger).

Essentially, we want the trigger to insert a value into the **adjusted_price** column for each line entered into the table, adjusted by the tax rate based on its state code. This makes the trigger an **INSERT** trigger.

```
CREATE OR REPLACE TRIGGER purchase_order_adjust
BEFORE INSERT ON purchase_orders
FOR EACH ROW
WHEN (new.price>0)
DECLARE
    adj_price NUMBER;
    RATE number;
BEGIN
  SELECT adjust_rate
  INTO rate
  FROM price_adjust
  WHERE state_code = :new.state_code;
  adj_price:=:new.price*rate;
  :new.adjusted_price:=adj_price;
END;
```

After we apply this trigger to the **purchase_orders** table, let's test it to see that it actually works. First, we must insert a value for the adjustment rate into the **price_adjust** table:

```
SQL> INSERT into price_adjust values ('GA',1.065)

1 row created.
```

Now that we have our reference table populated, let's try an **INSERT** into the **purchase_orders** table:

```
SQL> INSERT into purchase_orders
  2  (lineno,price,po_num,state_code)
  3  values
  4  (1,1000,1,'GA');

1 row created.
```

Did our trigger fire as we expected it to? Let's do a **select** and see:

```
SQL> select * from purchase_orders;

LINENO    PRICE    ADJUSTED_PRICE  PO_NUM    ST
--------  -------- --------------- --------  --
1         1000     1065                 1    GA
```

Yes, it worked. Now, what happens if we get a change for our purchase order, making Line Number 1 $2000?

```
SQL> UPDATE purchase_orders set price=2000 where po_num=1
  2   and lineno=1;

1 row updated.

SQL> select * from purchase_orders;

LINENO    PRICE    ADJUSTED_PRICE  PO_NUM    ST
--------  -------- --------------- --------  --
1         2000     1065                 1    GA
```

Rats! Now what? We have two options: Create an **ON UPDATE** trigger to handle this or modify our existing trigger to handle either an **INSERT** or **UPDATE**. Let's modify the existing trigger:

```
CREATE OR REPLACE TRIGGER purchase_order_adjust
BEFORE INSERT OR UPDATE ON purchase_orders
FOR EACH ROW
WHEN (new.price>0)
DECLARE
     adj_price NUMBER;
     RATE number;
BEGIN
   SELECT adjust_rate
   INTO rate
   FROM price_adjust
  WHERE state_code = :new.state_code;
  adj_price:=:new.price*rate;
   :new.adjusted_price:=adj_price;
END;
```

Look at the second line in the code. We added **OR UPDATE** and then recompiled the trigger. Here is the result:

```
SQL> UPDATE purchase_orders set price=2000 where po_num=1
  2    and lineno=1;

1 row updated.

SQL> select * from purchase_orders;

LINENO    PRICE    ADJUSTED_PRICE  PO_NUM    ST
--------  -------- --------------- --------  --
1         2000     2130            1         GA
```

We now have the desired behavior. For both **INSERT**s and **UPDATE**s, the adjusted price column is set to the price times the rate from the **price_adjust** table, based on the state. See how all of this is hidden from the user? Even at the base SQL level, the user has no indication that any of the trigger activity is occurring. This is a simple form of data hiding. Because the trigger is stored as only associated with a single table, it is also a simple form of encapsulation (except they aren't stored together as one entity).

Using Conditional Predicates

Conditional predicates allow a single trigger to decide what action to take based on the triggering action. For example, different actions could be taken if a table were inserted into, updated, or deleted from. The actions could be as simple as inserting a row into an auditing table for each table action or updating multiple tables with the results of a changed calculation.

For our example, we have a **purchase_orders** table with line number, price, adjusted price, purchase-order number, and state code; a **price_adjust** table with state code and adjustment rate; and a **billings** table with a total price, purchase-order number, and purchaser name.

The trigger we want to build updates the **total-price** column of the **billings** table each time a change is made to a **purchase-order-number** line item in the **purchase_orders** table. I know this wastes resources and calculated values shouldn't be stored in a database, but this is just an example.

Here is the trigger we want to create:

```
CREATE OR REPLACE TRIGGER maintain_total
BEFORE INSERT OR DELETE OR UPDATE
  ON purchase_orders FOR EACH ROW
```

```
DECLARE
new_total NUMBER;
chg_date DATE;
  BEGIN
    SELECT SUM(adjusted_price), sysdate
    INTO new_total,chg_date
    FROM purchase_orders
    WHERE po_num=:new.po_num;
     IF INSERTING THEN
       UPDATE billings
       SET po_amount=new_total,
           change_date=chg_date,
           change_type='INSERT'
       WHERE po_num=:new.po_num;
     ELSIF DELETING THEN
       UPDATE billings
       SET po_amount=new_total,
           change_date=chg_date,
           change_type='DELETE'
       WHERE po_num=:new.po_num;
     ELSIF UPDATING THEN
       UPDATE billings
       SET po_amount=new_total,
           change_date=chg_date,
           change_type='UPDATE'
       WHERE po_num=:new.po_num;
    END IF;
  END;
```

The code compiles fine. Let's run it:

```
SQL> UPDATE purchase_orders set price=3000 where po_num=1;
UPDATE purchase_orders set price=3000 where po_num=1
            *
ERROR at line 1:
ORA-04091: table TELE_DBA.PURCHASE_ORDERS is mutating, trigger/function may not see
it
ORA-06512: at "TELE_DBA.MAINTAIN_TOTAL", line 5
ORA-04088: error during execution of trigger 'TELE_DBA.MAINTAIN_TOTAL'
```

What happened? Remember the discussion about mutating table errors at the beginning of the chapter? This is a classic way of getting them. Essentially, we have a value that we are updating, so it is in a state of flux (our first trigger from the previous guide is firing at the same time this one fires, leaving a value in a transient state; hence, the mutation).

How can we fix this? We must change the trigger to an **AFTER** type trigger. This means eliminating all **OLD** and **NEW** references and using logic closer to that of a stored procedure using cursors. In pre-7.3 days, we would have done this anyway, because procedures were compiled and triggers were not. Here is the new trigger code:

```
CREATE OR REPLACE TRIGGER maintain_total
AFTER INSERT OR DELETE OR UPDATE
  ON purchase_orders
DECLARE
 adj_price NUMBER;
 RATE       number;
 new_total NUMBER;
 chg_date  DATE;
 po        NUMBER;
CURSOR get_po IS
   SELECT UNIQUE po_num
   FROM billings;
CURSOR get_total(po number) IS
   SELECT SUM(adjusted_price), sysdate
   FROM purchase_orders
   WHERE po_num=po;
  BEGIN
  OPEN get_po;
  FETCH get_po into po;
  LOOP
    EXIT WHEN get_po%NOTFOUND;
     OPEN get_total(po);
     FETCH get_total INTO new_total,chg_date;
    IF INSERTING THEN
     UPDATE billings
     SET po_amount=new_total,
         change_date=chg_date,
         change_type='INSERT'
     WHERE po_num=po and
           po_amount<>new_total;
    ELSIF DELETING THEN
     UPDATE billings
     SET po_amount=new_total,
         change_date=chg_date,
         change_type='DELETE'
     WHERE po_num=po and
           po_amount<>new_total;
```

```
  ELSIF UPDATING THEN
    UPDATE billings
    SET po_amount=new_total,
        change_date=chg_date,
        change_type='UPDATE'
    WHERE po_num=po and
          po_amount<>new_total;
  END IF;
CLOSE get_total;
FETCH get_po INTO po;
END LOOP;
END;
```

So, what happens now when we fire off an **UPDATE** into the table?

```
SQL> select * from billings;

PO_NUM    PO_AMOUNT  PURCHASER                              CHANGE_DA CHANGE_TYP
--------  ---------  -------------------------------------  --------- ----------
1         3195       Georges Shootery                       24-JUL-97 Initial

SQL> UPDATE purchase_orders set price=2000 where po_num=1;

1 row updated.

SQL> select * from billings;

PO_NUM    PO_AMOUNT  PURCHASER                              CHANGE_DA CHANGE_TYP
--------  ---------  -------------------------------------  --------- ----------
1         2130       Georges Shootery                       24-JUL-97 UPDATE
```

Our trigger works (and, yes, I did check it out on all three actions: **INSERT**, **UP-DATE**, and **DELETE**). What did we change?

- We made the trigger an **AFTER** action trigger instead of **BEFORE** action. This changed the timing to eliminate the conflict with the other trigger.

- Because we made the trigger an **AFTER** action trigger, the capability of using the **NEW** and **OLD** qualifiers disappeared, so now we have to use cursor logic instead.

- Using cursors, we have to loop through the entire set of purchase orders— not very efficient, but it works.

- We assumed that a change would affect a total amount. If a change doesn't alter the total, then no processing is done for the purchase order.

- We were able to combine two guides in one example: the use of conditional predicate logic and avoiding a mutating table error.

Creating A **CASCADE UPDATE** Trigger

Oracle provides a means to perform a cascading delete when a master table value is deleted, but what about when a record is updated (yes, I know this shouldn't be done, but, darn it, sometimes it has to be). Let's examine a method to perform a **CASCADE UPDATE**.

You might need a **CASCADE UPDATE** if you have a dependent table that could be dependent on one or more tables. For example, you may have two types of customer: one who has bought from you and for whom you have marketing information; and another who is new to you and may buy from you or go with another vendor. If you have dependent tables (such as an interaction log that tracks phone calls to and from customers), you would want to switch the dependencies from your new customer table to your established customer table.

Enforcing A *CASCADE UPDATE*

How would you enforce a **CASCADE UPDATE**? One method is to use data dictionary tables and views to backtrack foreign-key relations and then apply **UPDATE**s along this path. This may be a lengthy process, however, and can be a performance problem.

A simpler method is to implement a table-based **CASCADE UPDATE**. The table contains the information a procedure needs to update all tables that are dependent upon a main or master table. Therefore, the table has to contain the master table name, the dependent table(s), and, in case you can't duplicate the exact column name across all of the dependent tables, the column to update. The table DDL code shown here meets these requirements. If required, you could add a fourth column indicating an update order, and the cursor in the **update_tables** procedure detailed later could be altered to do an ordered retrieve of the information.

```
CREATE TABLE update_tables
(
   main_table   VARCHAR2(30) NOT NULL,
   table_name   VARCHAR2(30) NOT NULL,
   column_name  VARCHAR2(30) NOT NULL,
CONSTRAINT pk_update_tables
PRIMARY KEY (main_table,table_name,column_name)
USING INDEX
```

```
TABLESPACE tool_indexes)
STORAGE (INITIAL 100K NEXT 100K PCTINCREASE 0)
TABLESPACE tools
/
```

Column definitions are as follows:

- **main_table** holds the name of the table that the update cascades from.

- **table_name** holds the name(s) of the tables to cascade the update into.

- **column_name** is the name of the column in the target table(s) to update.

The table by itself would be of little use. Because the data in the table is dynamic (i.e., multiple tables and columns that will need to be addressed), you must enable your trigger to dynamically reassign these values. The easiest way to do this is to create a set of procedures that use the DBMS_SQL Oracle-provided package to dynamically reassign your update variables. The code segment in the next section shows the commented code for just such a procedures set. The set consists of two procedures, **update_tables** and **update_column**.

The *CASCADE UPDATE* Procedures

Use of the DBMS_SQL package to dynamically build the **TABLE UPDATE** command on the fly allows the same set of procedures to be used for any set of master-dependent tables that have entries in the source table.

The **update_tables** procedure accepts the master table name, the old value for the column to be updated, and the new value for the column. The procedure uses a standard cursor **FETCH** to retrieve the dependent table names and dependent table column names from the source table, shown previously. If desired, you could alter the table to accept an ordering value for each master-dependent set to allow the **CASCADE UPDATE** to be done in a specific order. Using this information and the new and old values for the column from the trigger call, the **update_column** procedure dynamically rebuilds the **TABLE UPDATE** command to update the appropriate tables.

```
-- First create package body
-- Decided to use package so that all procedures will
-- be in one place and very controllable
-- M. Ault 1/14/97 Rev 1.0
--
```

```
CREATE OR REPLACE PACKAGE cascade_update AS
--
-- First package is update_column.
-- This package actually does the work
-- using DBMS_SQL to dynamically rebuild the
-- UPDATEs at runtime for each table.
--
PROCEDURE update_column(
   old_value          IN VARCHAR2,
   new_value          IN VARCHAR2,
   table_name         IN VARCHAR2,
   update_column   IN VARCHAR2
);
--
-- Next procedure is update_tables.
-- It is the loop control procedure for
-- the trigger and calls update_column.
--
PROCEDURE update_tables(
   source_table   IN VARCHAR2,
   old_value          IN VARCHAR2,
   new_value          IN VARCHAR2
);
--
-- End of PACKAGE HEADER
--
END cascade_update;
/
--
-- Now build package body.
-- That actually holds the
-- procedures and code.
--
CREATE OR REPLACE PACKAGE BODY cascade_update AS

PROCEDURE update_column(
   old_value          IN VARCHAR2,
   new_value          IN VARCHAR2,
   table_name         IN VARCHAR2,
   update_column   IN VARCHAR2)
AS
--
-- define state variables for dbms_sql procedures
--
   cur                                INTEGER;
   rows_processed   INTEGER;
--
```

```
-- start processing
-- (dbms_output calls are for debugging
-- commented out during normal runtime)
--
BEGIN
--   DBMS_OUTPUT.PUT_LINE('Table name: '||table_name||' Column: '||update_column);
  --
  -- initialize the dynamic cursor location for
  -- the dbms_sql process
  --
  cur:=DBMS_SQL.OPEN_CURSOR;
  --
  -- populate the initialized location with the statement to be
  -- processed
  --
--DBMS_OUTPUT.PUT_LINE(
--'UPDATE '||table_name||' set
'||update_column||'='||chr(39)||new_value||chr(39)||chr(10)||
--' WHERE '||update_column||'='||chr(39)||old_value||chr(39)||' AND 1=1');
--
dbms_sql.parse(cur,
'UPDATE '||table_name||' set
'||update_column||'='||chr(39)||new_value||chr(39)||chr(10)||
' WHERE '||update_column||'='||chr(39)||old_value||chr(39)||' AND
1=1',dbms_sql.v7);
--
-- execute the dynamically parsed statement
--
rows_processed:=DBMS_SQL.EXECUTE(cur);
--
-- close dynamic cursor to prepare for next table
--
DBMS_SQL.CLOSE_CURSOR(cur);
--
-- END PROCEDURE
--
END update_column;

PROCEDURE update_tables(
source_table   IN VARCHAR2,
old_value IN VARCHAR2,
new_value IN VARCHAR2) as
--
-- Create the cursor to read records
-- from bbs_siteid_tables.
-- Use * to prohibit missing a column
--
```

```
CURSOR get_table_name IS
  SELECT
  *
 FROM
    update_tables
WHERE
main_table=source_table;
--
-- Define ROWTYPE variable to hold record from
-- tables. Use rowtype to allow for
-- future changes.
--
 update_rec update_tables%ROWTYPE;
--
-- start processing
--
BEGIN
--
-- open and fetch values with cursor
--
 OPEN get_table_name;
 FETCH get_table_name INTO update_rec;
--
-- now that cursor status is open and values in
-- variables can begin loop
--
LOOP
--
-- using the notfound status we had to pre-populate
-- record
--
    EXIT WHEN get_table_name%NOTFOUND;
--
-- Initiate call to the update_column procedure
--
    update_column(old_value, new_value, update_rec.table_name,
update_rec.column_name);
--
-- Now get next record from table
--
    FETCH get_table_name INTO update_rec;
--
-- processing returns to loop statement
--
 END LOOP;
--
-- close cursor and exit
--
```

```
 CLOSE get_table_name;
 --
 -- end of procedure
 --
 END update_tables;
 --
 -- end of package body
 --
 END cascade_update;
 /
```

The Final Piece, The Trigger

Once the source table and procedures are built, you need to design a trigger to implement against your master tables that automatically fires on update to the target master column. The following code shows an example of this trigger. Notice that the trigger passes the master table name to the **update_tables** procedure as well as the old and new values for the column being updated. This allows the **update_tables** procedure to select only the names and columns for the tables that are dependent upon the master table for which the trigger is implemented. This allows multiple master tables to use a single source table.

The calling trigger has to be in the form:

```
 CREATE OR REPLACE TRIGGER cascade_update_<tabname>
  AFTER UPDATE OF <column> ON <tabname>
  REFERENCING NEW AS upd OLD AS prev
  FOR EACH ROW
     BEGIN
        cascade_update.update_tables('<tabname>',:prev.<column>,:upd.<column>);
     END;
```

The values for **<tabname>** and **<column>** must be placed in these positions before compiling the trigger.

 Notice how the table name is passed to the procedure; this is the way it must be done.

Using the procedures and trigger described in this guide, a developer can enforce a cascade update against any set of master-dependent tables without the performance hit of searching the data dictionary for the relationship definitions.

Creating An **EITHER-OR** Trigger

In some applications, multiple master tables require common look-up or dependent tables. This defeats commonly used referential integrity clauses, such as foreign-key references, and maintenance of the required REF links might be difficult (we will examine this in Chapter 4's Practical Guide). The solution is what I call an **EOR** (short for **EITHER-OR**) trigger.

An **EOR** trigger verifies that an inserted value corresponds to the primary key value in either one (or more) table or another table, corresponding to the number of master tables you might have. For example, you may have a central address table where a part of the primary key is a value linking back to one of several master tables (such as employee, customer, and supplier tables all sharing a common address table). Figure 3.1 shows the ERD for this situation.

A quick look at Figure 3.1 shows the relationship we are talking about. It looks simple, but try to do the relationships using standard Oracle8 referential integrity. See Listing 3.1 for an example of what happens when this is attempted. The tables are reduced to their essential structures (i.e., a primary key only).

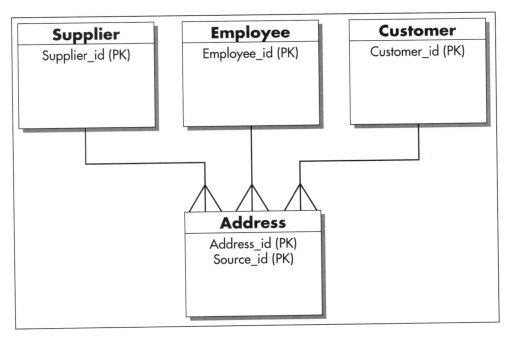

Figure 3.1

ERD for **EOR** trigger example.

Listing 3.1 Example of what happens when trying multiple foreign keys on a single column.

```
SQL> create table addresses (address_id number not null,
  2 source_id number not null, constraint pk_addresses
  3 primary key (address_id,source_id););

Table created.

SQL> create table customers(customer_id number not null,
  2 constraint pk_customers primary key (customer_id));

Table created.

sql> create table suppliers(supplier_id number not null,
  2 constraint pk_suppliers primary key (supplier_id))

Table created.

SQL> create table employees(employee_id number not null,
  2 constraint pk_employees primary key (employee_id));

Table created.

SQL> alter table addresses add constraint fk_addresses_1
  2 foreign key(source_id) references suppliers(supplier_id);

Table altered.

SQL> alter table addresses add constraint fk_addresses_2
  2 foreign key (source_id) references employees(employee_id);

Table altered.


SQL> alter table addresses add constraint fk_addresses_3
  2 foreign key (source_id) references customers(customer_id);

Table altered.

SQL> INSERT into employees values (1);

1 row created.

SQL> INSERT into customers values(2);

1 row created.
```

```
SQL> INSERT into suppliers values (3);

1 row created.

SQL> INSERT into addresses values (1,1);
INSERT into addresses values (1,1)
            *
ERROR at line 1:
ORA-02291: integrity constraint (SYSTEM.FK_ADDRESSES_3) violated -
parent key not found


SQL> INSERT into addresses values (1,2);
INSERT into addresses values (1,2)
            *
ERROR at line 1:
ORA-02291: integrity constraint (SYSTEM.FK_ADDRESSES_2) violated -
parent key not found


SQL> INSERT into addresses values (1,3);
INSERT into addresses values (1,3)
            *
ERROR at line 1:
ORA-02291: integrity constraint (SYSTEM.FK_ADDRESSES_3) violated -
parent key not found
```

You can see the need for the **EOR** trigger in the situation shown in Listing 3.1. What exactly does this trigger do? For each inserted or updated value, it performs an **IF/THEN** loop to test that the value being inserted exists in one of the master tables as a key. This leads to a key requirement on the master tables. The requirement limits the value for each of the master table's keys to specific ranges. For example, **customers.customer_id** would be limited to the range 1 to 10,000,000, while **supplier.supplier_id** is restricted to 10,000,001 to 20,000,000, and EMPLOYEES.EMPLOYEE_ID is restricted to greater than 20,000,001. These key restrictions are accomplished by pulling the values from an Oracle sequence that has had its range restricted by use of the **MINVALUE** and **MAXVALUE** clauses.

The trigger we want to build will be a **BEFORE ROW** trigger. The triggering events will be **INSERT** and **UPDATE**. The code for this trigger is shown in Listing 3.2.

Listing 3.2   Example EOR trigger code.
```
CREATE OR REPLACE TRIGGER eor_addresses
BEFORE INSERT OR UPDATE ON addresses FOR EACH ROW
```

```
DECLARE numrows INTEGER;
  CURSOR get_cus_count(s_id NUMBER) IS
    SELECT COUNT(*) FROM customers WHERE customer_id=s_id;
  CURSOR get_sup_count(s_id NUMBER) IS
    SELECT COUNT(*) FROM suppliers WHERE supplier_id=s_id;
  CURSOR get_emp_count(s_id NUMBER) IS
   SELECT COUNT(*) FROM employees WHERE employee_id=s_id;
   value_not_present EXCEPTION;
   id NUMBER;
BEGIN
  IF :new.source_id>20000000 THEN
    id:=:new.source_id;
    OPEN get_emp_count(id);
    FETCH get_emp_count INTO numrows;
    CLOSE get_emp_count;
    IF numrows<1 THEN
       RAISE value_not_present;
    END IF;
  ELSIF :new.source_id>10000000 THEN
    id:=:new.source_id;
    OPEN get_sup_count(id);
    FETCH get_sup_count INTO numrows;
    CLOSE get_sup_count;
    IF numrows<1 THEN
       RAISE value_not_present;
    END IF;
  ELSE
    id:=:new.source_id;
    OPEN get_cus_count(id);
    FETCH get_cus_count INTO numrows;
    CLOSE get_cus_count;
    IF numrows<1 THEN
       RAISE value_not_present;
    END IF;
END IF;
EXCEPTION
  WHEN value_not_present THEN
  RAISE_APPLICATION_ERROR(-20100, 'value not present in parent tables');
END;
/
```

Listing 3.3   Test of EOR trigger code.

```
SQL> TRUNCATE TABLE customers;
Table truncated

SQL> TRUNCATE TABLE employees;
Table truncated
```

```
SQL> INSERT into employees values (20000002);

1 row created.

SQL>
SQL> INSERT into customers values (10000001);

1 row created.

SQL>  INSERT into addresses values (1,1000);
 INSERT into addresses values (1,1000)
*
ERROR at line 1:
ORA-20100: value not present in parent tables
ORA-06512: at line 30
ORA-04088: error during execution of trigger 'SYSTEM.EOR_ADDRESSES'


SQL> INSERT into addresses values (1,20000002);

1 row created.

SQL> INSERT into addresses values (2,10000001);

1 row created.

SQL> INSERT into addresses values (1,20000003);
INSERT into addresses values (1,20000003)
            *
ERROR at line 1:
ORA-20100: value not present in parent tables
ORA-06512: at line 30
ORA-04088: error during execution of trigger 'SYSTEM.EOR_ADDRESSES'
```

Listing 3.3 shows a test of this trigger logic. Notice how we have truncated the test tables and redone the inserts to be in line with the key restrictions set up in the trigger. Also, notice the use of the user-generated (**value_not_present**) exception and the use of the custom error code (**raise_application_error**). You can then trap for the application error in your application using the **PRAGMA EXCEPTION_INIT** declaration:

```
PRAGMA EXCEPTION_INIT(bad_value , -20100);
```

Using this technique, you can trap for and report errors back to your users.

Calling Procedures From Triggers

Many times, application logic may be too complex for a simple trigger, or you may need to reuse the logic in other triggers or application segments. In this case, the use of a procedure or function is required. I suggest placing all procedures and functions for an application level into a single package. This provides for a common repository of standard application methods (not to be confused with type methods, which we will see later). This promotes the reuse of code—one of the basic tenets of the object-oriented paradigm.

In Creating A Basic Trigger, we created a trigger that updated a total column in a second table when a value or set of values in a table changed. This type of logic is better placed in a procedure, because it may also be needed by other application components. Listing 3.4 shows the original code for this trigger.

Listing 3.4   Code to build a trigger without using a procedure.

```
CREATE OR REPLACE TRIGGER maintain_total
AFTER INSERT OR DELETE OR UPDATE
 ON purchase_orders
DECLARE
 adj_price NUMBER;
 RATE       number;
 new_total NUMBER;
 chg_date  DATE;
 po         NUMBER;
CURSOR get_po IS
   SELECT UNIQUE po_num
   FROM billings;
CURSOR get_total(po number) IS
   SELECT SUM(adjusted_price), sysdate
   FROM purchase_orders
   WHERE po_num=po;
 BEGIN
 OPEN get_po;
 FETCH get_po into po;
 LOOP
   EXIT WHEN get_po%NOTFOUND;
    OPEN get_total(po);
    FETCH get_total INTO new_total,chg_date;
   IF INSERTING THEN
    UPDATE billings
    SET po_amount=new_total,
        change_date=chg_date,
        change_type='INSERT'
    WHERE po_num=po and
          po_amount<>new_total;
```

```
    ELSIF DELETING THEN
     UPDATE billings
     SET po_amount=new_total,
         change_date=chg_date,
         change_type='DELETE'
     WHERE po_num=po and
           po_amount<>new_total;
    ELSIF UPDATING THEN
     UPDATE billings
     SET po_amount=new_total,
         change_date=chg_date,
         change_type='UPDATE'
     WHERE po_num=po and
           po_amount<>new_total;
   END IF;
 CLOSE get_total;
 FETCH get_po INTO po;
 END LOOP;
 END;
```

Notice that the code in Listing 3.4 has some areas for building the **MAINTAIN_TOTAL** trigger that can be made into standardized procedure modules. At the beginning, we have the cursor **get_total**, which can be made easily into a standard application package that can be reused elsewhere. For example:

```
CREATE OR REPLACE PROCEDURE get_po_total(
  po IN NUMBER, po_total OUT NUMBER, todays_date OUT DATE) AS
  CURSOR get_total(po NUMBER) IS
    SELECT SUM(adjusted_price), sysdate
    FROM purchase_orders
    WHERE po_num=po;
BEGIN
  OPEN get_total(po);
  FETCH get_total INTO po_total,todays_date;
  CLOSE get_total;
END;
```

Now we need to place this procedure into a package that is specific to the application we are developing—in this case, a purchase-order information tracking system, or PITS. The header and package body for the PITS package will be:

```
CREATE OR REPLACE PACKAGE pits AS
PROCEDURE get_po_total(
  po IN NUMBER, po_total OUT NUMBER, todays_date OUT DATE);
END pits;
/
```

```
CREATE OR REPLACE PACKAGE BODY pits AS
PROCEDURE get_po_total(
  po IN NUMBER, po_total OUT NUMBER, todays_date OUT DATE) AS
  CURSOR get_total(po NUMBER) IS
    SELECT SUM(adjusted_price), sysdate
    FROM purchase_orders
    WHERE po_num=po;
BEGIN
  OPEN get_total(po);
  FETCH get_total INTO po_total,todays_date;
  CLOSE get_total;
END;
END pits;
/
```

Now, look at the trigger code in Listing 3.5. Notice how we have replaced several lines of code with a single procedure call.

Listing 3.5   Updated trigger code with procedure call added.

```
CREATE OR REPLACE TRIGGER maintain_total
AFTER INSERT OR DELETE OR UPDATE
  ON purchase_orders
DECLARE
 adj_price NUMBER;
 RATE      number;
 new_total NUMBER;
 chg_date  DATE;
 po        NUMBER;
CURSOR get_po IS
   SELECT UNIQUE po_num
   FROM billings;
BEGIN
   OPEN get_po;
   FETCH get_po into po;
   LOOP
     EXIT WHEN get_po%NOTFOUND;
   pits.get_po_total(po,new_total,chg_date);
   IF INSERTING THEN
     UPDATE billings
     SET po_amount=new_total,
         change_date=chg_date,
         change_type='INSERT'
     WHERE po_num=po and
           po_amount<>new_total;
```

```
  ELSIF DELETING THEN
   UPDATE billings
   SET po_amount=new_total,
       change_date=chg_date,
       change_type='DELETE'
   WHERE po_num=po and
         po_amount<>new_total;
  ELSIF UPDATING THEN
   UPDATE billings
   SET po_amount=new_total,
       change_date=chg_date,
       change_type='UPDATE'
   WHERE po_num=po and
         po_amount<>new_total;
 END IF;
FETCH get_po INTO po;
END LOOP;
END;
```

This replacement has changed the code a little, but the next one should have a much larger effect. We are going to move the update code into a separate procedure. The procedure code (placed in the PITS package) looks like this:

```
PROCEDURE update_billings (
   po IN NUMBER,
   new_total IN NUMBER,
   chg_date IN DATE,
   chg_type IN VARCHAR2) AS
BEGIN
  UPDATE billings
    SET  po_amount=new_total,
            change_date=chg_date,
            change_type=chg_type
   WHERE po_num=po and
              po_amount<>new_total;
END;
```

Our total package now looks like Listing 3.6.

Listing 3.6   Final version of PITS package.
```
CREATE OR REPLACE PACKAGE pits AS
 PROCEDURE get_po_total(
    po IN NUMBER,
    po_total OUT NUMBER,
    todays_date OUT DATE);
```

```
PROCEDURE update_billings (
   po IN NUMBER,
   new_total IN NUMBER,
   chg_date IN DATE,
   chg_type IN VARCHAR2);
END pits;
/
CREATE OR REPLACE PACKAGE BODY pits AS
 PROCEDURE get_po_total(
     po IN NUMBER,
     po_total OUT NUMBER,
    todays_date OUT DATE) IS
  CURSOR get_total(po NUMBER) IS
    SELECT SUM(adjusted_price), sysdate
    FROM purchase_orders
    WHERE po_num=po;
 BEGIN
  OPEN get_total(po);
  FETCH get_total INTO po_total,todays_date;
  CLOSE get_total;
 END;
--
PROCEDURE update_billings (
   po IN NUMBER,
   new_total IN NUMBER,
   chg_date IN DATE,
   chg_type IN VARCHAR2) AS
BEGIN
  UPDATE billings
    SET  po_amount=new_total,
            change_date=chg_date,
            change_type=chg_type
   WHERE po_num=po and
              po_amount<>new_total;
END;
END pits;
/
```

The final trigger code has been shortened considerably and made more readable, as shown in Listing 3.7. Note that all of the **UPDATE** commands, which took several lines of code, have been replaced by two lines: one to set the **chg_type** variable and one with the actual procedure call.

Listing 3.7   Final trigger code with procedure calls.

```
CREATE OR REPLACE TRIGGER maintain_total
AFTER INSERT OR DELETE OR UPDATE
  ON purchase_orders
```

```
DECLARE
 adj_price NUMBER;
 RATE      number;
 new_total NUMBER;
 chg_date  DATE;
 po        NUMBER;
 chg_type  VARCHAR2(10);
CURSOR get_po IS
   SELECT UNIQUE po_num
   FROM billings;
BEGIN
   OPEN get_po;
   FETCH get_po into po;
   LOOP
     EXIT WHEN get_po%NOTFOUND;
     pits.get_po_total(po,new_total,chg_date);
     IF INSERTING THEN
       chg_type:='INSERT';
       pits.update_billings(po,new_total,chg_date,chg_type);
      ELSIF DELETING THEN
       chg_type:='DELETE';
       pits.update_billings(po,new_total,chg_date,chg_type);
      ELSIF UPDATING THEN
       chg_type:='UPDATE';
       pits.update_billings(po,new_total,chg_date,chg_type);
      END IF;
   FETCH get_po INTO po;
   END LOOP;
   END;
```

What have we gained from the changes to the trigger? For one, we have made sure the code was reusable. Next, by moving the trigger code into reusable procedures, we are practicing information hiding. By having the code in external procedures, we can change the base code in the procedure without having to modify the trigger code. This will also be the first step toward moving the code into internal type methods, and the procedure will either act as a message-passing medium or can be completely eliminated. This implements one of the rules of object-oriented programming: No object should directly affect the data in another object.

Using **FUNCTION**s In Triggers

Functions always return a value, while procedures (as we saw in the previous Practical Guide) may or may not. Functions are useful for hiding complex computations or conversions. For example, a technical calculation, such as a radionuclide decay determination, should be done the same way each time to assure that this is to implement the calculation into a function. Other calculations, not quite so esoteric, should also be pushed out of triggers and into functions. An example of a simple function that can be pushed out would be a square-footage calculation for a real-estate program (because not many of us are nuclear chemists). Let's model this function into a trigger.

You have two tables, **HOUSES** and **ROOMS** (in later sections, you will make these into one object using object types and nested tables, but let's keep this simple for now). Houses have one or more rooms, and rooms have length and width dimensions. For this example, don't worry about other attributes other than the **HOUSE_ID** and **ROOM_ID** key values. These tables relate as shown in Figure 3.2.

The function will accept length and width, multiply them together, and return square feet:

```
LENGTH x WIDTH = SQUARE FEET
```

The **FUNCTION** code is shown in Listing 3.8. A function always returns a value. To use a function outside of its package, you must assert its purity. This is done by placing the **FUNCTION** in a **PACKAGE** called **realestate** and asserting its purity in the **PACKAGE** header, as shown in Listing 3.8.

Listing 3.8 FUNCTION PACKAGE code.

```
CREATE OR REPLACE PACKAGE realestate AS
FUNCTION square_feet(
    length IN NUMBER,
    WIDTH IN NUMBER)
RETURN NUMBER;
PRAGMA RESTRICT_REFERENCES(square_feet,WNDS);
END realestate;
/
CREATE OR REPLACE PACKAGE BODY realestate AS
 FUNCTION square_feet(
    length IN NUMBER,
    WIDTH IN NUMBER)
 RETURN NUMBER AS
 square_feet NUMBER;
 BEGIN
  square_feet:=length*width;
  RETURN square_feet;
 END;
END realestate;
/
```

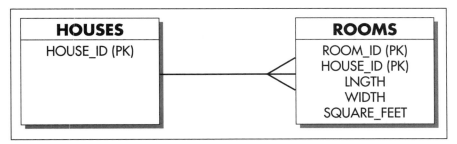

Figure 3.2

*ERD for **FUNCTION** example.*

Now that you have created the function, you can create the trigger code to populate the **square_fee**t column when a row is added to the **ROOMS** table. This is a **BEFORE INSERT OR UPDATE ROW** trigger. You can use the conditional predicates to restrict trigger firing only when width or length are inserted or updated. As more Oracle8 features are used, the functions will move into internal type methods, but will probably still be invoked via a trigger. Listing 3.9 shows the trigger code.

Listing 3.9   Code for trigger using function call.

```
CREATE OR REPLACE TRIGGER insert_sq_ft
BEFORE INSERT OR UPDATE ON rooms FOR EACH ROW
DECLARE
sq_ft NUMBER;
width NUMBER;
lngth NUMBER;
BEGIN
IF INSERTING THEN
  IF (:new.width<>0 AND :new.lngth<>0) THEN
    width:=:new.width;
    lngth:=:new.lngth;
    sq_ft:=realestate.square_feet(width,lngth);
    :new.square_feet:=sq_ft;
  END IF;
ELSIF UPDATING('WIDTH') OR UPDATING('LNGTH') THEN
  width:=:new.width;
  lngth:=:new.lngth;
  sq_ft:=realestate.square_feet(width,lngth);
  :new.square_feet:=sq_ft;
END IF;
END;
/
```

Notice that the code in Listing 3.9 does no explicit inserts or updates; it merely allows the statement to act on the row providing a new value for the **square_feet** column. The code also uses a special feature of the **UPDATING** conditional predicate, in which you can specify what columns have to be updated for the trigger to fire. See the difference between the **INSERTING** and **UPDATING** conditional statements in Listing 3.9. In the **INSERTING** statement section, you have to implicitly check if the values for width or length are being set.

We can convert this function into an internal method. This technique will be shown in a later section.

Using The **INSTEAD OF** Trigger

Earlier versions of Oracle did not allow updates to complex views. You could update simple views (based on a single table with no complex operations) as long as all **NOT NULL** columns were represented in the view and **UPDATE** statement. In late Oracle7 releases, simple join views could be updated as long as these conditions were true for both tables in the view. Now, with the **INSTEAD OF** trigger, even complex views based on multiple tables can be updated, inserted, and deleted.

The **INSTEAD OF** trigger can be specified only for views. Attempting to create one on a table will result in an "ORA-25002: cannot create **INSTEAD OF** triggers on tables" error.

Let's use the classic (if such a concept applies to tables) tables **EMP**, **DEPT**, and **PROJECT** to define a complex view and demonstrate an **INSTEAD OF** trigger. (This example is from "Oracle8 Server Application Developer's Guide," Release 8.0, June 1997, Part# A54645-01.) The view we will update is shown in Listing 3.10.

Listing 3.10   Complex view for INSTEAD OF demonstration.

```
CREATE VIEW manager_info AS
    SELECT e.name, e.empno, d.dept_type, d.depno, p.level.
                    p.projno
    FROM emp e, dept d, project p
    WHERE e.empno = d.mgr_no
    AND d.deptno = p.resp_dept;
```

As you can see by examining the view in Listing 3.10, it is based on three tables, a situation that prohibits any form of **INSERT** operation on the view (actually through the view to the underlying tables). Therefore, you can create an **INSTEAD OF** trigger that will take the place of any attempted **INSERT** action. Listing 3.11 shows the code for creating the **INSTEAD OF** trigger.

Listing 3.11 Example trigger using INSTEAD OF to INSERT INTO a complex view.

```
CREATE TRIGGER manager_info_insert
INSTEAD OF INSERT ON manager_info
REFERENCING NEW as N
---- new manager information
FOR EACH ROW
---- This is actually the default, not needed
BEGIN
    IF NOT EXISTS SELECT * FROM emp
            WHERE emp.empno = :n.empno
    THEN
            INSERT INTO emp
                        VALUES(:n.empno, :n.name);
    ELSE
            UPDATE emp SET emp.name = :n.name;
    END IF;
IF NOT EXISTS SELECT * FROM emp
            WHERE emp.empno = :n.empno
    THEN
            INSERT INTO emp
                        VALUES(:n.empno, :n.name);
    ELSE
            UPDATE emp SET emp.name = :n.name;
    END IF;
IF NOT EXISTS SELECT * FROM emp
            WHERE emp.empno = :n.empno
    THEN
            INSERT INTO emp
                        VALUES(:n.empno, :n.name);
    ELSE
            UPDATE emp SET emp.name = :n.name;
    END IF;
END;
```

One especially useful feature of the **INSTEAD OF** trigger is that it is the only means to update an object view (a special view used to provide object characteristics to a relational table). In fact, to modify an object instantiated by an object view into the user side object cache and flush it back into the persistent store, an **INSTEAD OF** trigger is the only method available via the Oracle call interface (OCI).

In conclusion, the **INSTEAD OF** trigger provides functionality that was missing from previous Oracle releases. The **INSTEAD OF** trigger brings more power and versatility to the view concept, allowing more extensive use of views in coding situations where only tables were allowed before.

The Oracle8 Object/ Relational Architecture

This chapter provides an overview of the Oracle8 object/ relational architecture. It addresses the concept of user-defined types (UDTs) and how they are used in relation to the object/relational model. The chapter also compares and contrasts Oracle types with the types defined in Java, and discusses pairing object behavior with data and the use of methods.

Notes…

Chapter 4

User-Defined Types (Composite Objects)

Until Oracle8 was introduced, Oracle allowed only complex datatypes (abstract datatypes or user-defined types) in PL/SQL—and even that was possible only since version 7.3. This restriction kept Oracle relegated to the "purely" relational data structures of tables, indexes, etc.

Oracle8 altered the entire method of constructing tables. This isn't to say that you can't build standard relational tables anymore. The format for the **CREATE TABLE** command allows for a purely relational construct with no advanced typing, but it also allows for the complete object-table specification, as well as specification of index-only tables, partitioned tables, and complex structures using attributes, types, nested tables, **VARRAY**s, and **REF**s.

A user-defined type (UDT) is a combination of more than one atomic datatype (such as **NUMBER**, **CHAR**, **VARCHAR2**) into complex data structures that can be used for building more complex objects. In addition, UDTs allow pairing of data with behavior through the use of PL/SQL internally stored methods.

Using UDTs

Why would you use a UDT? A classic example would be the use of an address complex type. Normally, you would either need a separate table for addresses or build into your table multiple fields to handle a single address. Addresses are then manipulated field by field. For example, a typical address table might consist of:

```
CREATE TABLE ADDRESSES (
    ADDRESS_ID number not null,
    employee_id number not null,
    STREET_ADDRESS varchar2(80),
    PO_BOX VARCHAR2(20),
    Suite VARCHAR2(20),
    city VARCHAR2(30),
    State_code char(2),
    zip_code  char(5),
    zip_ext char(4),
    CONSTRAINT pk_addresses PRIMARY KEY (address_id,employee_id)
    USING INDEX
    STORAGE (initial 100k NEXT 100k PCTINCREASE 0)
    TABLESPACE appl_indexes
);
```

Of course, using a separate table would require a foreign key and its additional index requirements, as well as additional storage and maintenance requirements. Insert logic would require not only an **INSERT** into the **employees** table, but also a separate **INSERT** into the **addresses** table. **SELECT**s from the tables would require join logic and **DELETE**s, even with **CASCADE DELETE** triggers still requiring additional transactional overhead.

How would you use a UDT to implement an address structure? The code is simple:

```
CREATE TYPE address_t AS OBJECT (
    STREET_ADDRESS varchar2(80),
    PO_BOX VARCHAR2(20),
    Suite VARCHAR2(20),
    city VARCHAR2(30),
    State_code char(2),
    zip_code  char(5),
    zip_ext char(4));
```

Next:

```
CREATE TABLE employees (
    employee_id NUMBER NOT NULL,
    FIRST_NAME  VARCHAR2(30),
    LAST_NAME VARCHAR2(20),
    Middle_initial CHAR(1),
    address  address_t);
```

Of course, if you add a name type

```
CREATE TYPE name_t  AS OBJECT(
    first_name VARCHAR2(20),
    last_name VARCHAR2(20),
    middle_initial CHAR(1));
```

the table becomes

```
CREATE TABLE employees (
    employee_id NUMBER NOT NULL,
    employee_name name_t,
    address address_t);
```

We will look at these processes in more detail in the Practical Guide later in this chapter. The previous example is not an object table. In early releases of Oracle8, the default for any type created was an object type, but now you must explicitly declare the table to be based entirely on an object type in order for it to be an object table. An example later in this section shows this syntax.

A Comparison With Java

Because Java comes closer than any other language to being the "ideal" object-oriented language, let's compare how it implements types with how Oracle implements them. Java types are usually implemented like C++ strucs, except that a single object file serves as the interface definition and implementation for a type (or *class*, in Java terminology). Attributes of a Java object and internal methods are accessed via dot notation, the same as in Oracle8 (as you shall see in the Practical Guide).

Java does all referencing for you; it does not allow manipulation of pointers. Oracle8 uses references that you can manipulate. A major difference between Java and Oracle8 is that no objects in Java are persistent, while types and objects created by them can be persistent in Oracle. If types are used in the context of PL/SQL, they don't have to be persistent. Oracle8 (and to a limited extent, Oracle7.3) is more flexible than Java as far as typing.

Java allows forward referencing, as does Oracle8. This eliminates the header requirements of such languages as C and C++. Java allows the definition of variables anywhere in the program body; Oracle8 (in PL/SQL) doesn't.

Both Java and Oracle8, in PL/SQL, allow method (procedure/function) overloading. This means that multiple methods, procedures, or functions can be declared with the same name but different argument types. This allows the same method to be called for various datatypes. Then, the Java or Oracle8 engine chooses the proper method, procedure, or function to use, based on the datatype of the argument.

The next section looks at a simple type definition (class in Java) in both Oracle8 and Java.

Example Type/Class Definition In Java And Oracle8

We will demonstrate using a simple **Room** type/class definition. In Java, this definition looks like Listing 4.1.

Listing 4.1   Example class definition in Java.

```
public class Room {
      public double l, w;      //The length and width of the room
      public double h;         //The height of the room

//Methods that return the square feet and cubic feet of the room
  public double square_feet() { return l * w; }
  public volume() { return l * w * h; }
}
```

The class definition in Listing 4.1 stores a room's height, width, and length and contains methods for calculating the square footage and cubic footage of the room. Listing 4.2 shows the same definition in Oracle8.

Listing 4.2   Example object type definition in Oracle8.

```
CREATE TYPE room_T AS OBJECT (
   lngth NUMBER,
   width NUMBER,
   height NUMBER,
MEMBER FUNCTION square_foot RETURN NUMBER,
pragma RESTRICT_REFERENCES(square_foot, WNDS, WNPS),
MEMBER FUNCTION volume RETURN NUMBER,
pragma RESTRICT_REFERENCES(VOLUME, wnds, wnps));
CREATE TYPE BODY room_T AS
MEMBER FUNCTION square_foot RETURN NUMBER IS
BEGIN
    RETURN lngth * width;
END;
MEMBER FUNCTION volume RETURN NUMBER IS
BEGIN
   RETURN lngth * width * height;
END;
END;
```

Unlike Java, Oracle8 requires you to declare the actual methods in a separate code section. This is the major difference between Listings 4.1 and 4.2.

Use Of Classes/Types In Java And Oracle8

Now that you have seen a basic example of how types and classes look in Java and Oracle8, let's examine how they are used. Listing 4.3 shows how Java would use the class created in Listing 4.1.

Listing 4.3   Example using class and method in Java.

```
Room LivingRoom = new Room();
double area;
LivingRoom.w = 10;
LivingRoom.l = 20;
area = LivingRoom.square_foot();
```

Notice how once you create an instance of **Room**, you can then call methods (**area**) that are part of the class by simply using the instance name you created and the method name using dot notation (**LivingRoom.area**).

Listing 4.4 shows the same process in Oracle8, SQL, and PL/SQL.

Listing 4.4   Example using types and method access in Oracle8, SQL, and PL/SQL.

```
In PL/SQL (persistent), first create an object table from type room:

CREATE TABLE rooms (room varchar2(20), room_dimensions room_T);
INSERT INTO rooms VALUES ('LivingRoom',room_dimensions(10,20,16));

DECLARE
    area NUMBER;
    volume NUMBER;
    roomtemp room_t;
  BEGIN
   SELECT room_dimensions INTO roomtemp
   FROM rooms r WHERE room='LivingRoom';
   area:=roomtemp.square_foot();
   volume:=roomtemp.volume();
   dbms_output.put_line('Square feet='||TO_CHAR(area));
   dbms_output.put_line('Volume='||TO_CHAR(volume));
   END;
```

```
In PL/SQL (nonpersistent):

DECLARE
   LivingRoom room_T:=ROOM_T(0,0,0);
   area number;
BEGIN
   LivingRoom.lngth := 10;
   LivingRoom.width := 20;
   area := LivingRoom.square_foot();
END;
```

As you can see, for nonpersistent values (Java and PL/SQL), you can have virtually identical code. For persistent objects (PL/SQL), you need to create the storage area and then use data access methods to perform operations. Oracle8 and Java methods can be accessed in virtually identical ways.

Object-Related Extensions To PL/SQL

The new shift toward objects has resulted in numerous extensions to PL/SQL. You must be aware of the object-related extensions to PL/SQL if you are to take full advantage of the new paradigm.

All new features of Oracle8 PL/SQL are documented in Appendix A of the *PL/SQL User's Guide And Reference*, Release 8.0, June 1997, PART# A54654-01. We will summarize them here.

External Procedures

Oracle8 supports the use of *external procedures*. External procedures are C (initially, with COBOL and other languages to follow) routines stored in a dynamic link library (DLL) or shared library that can be called via a defined library link from PL/SQL. The new **CREATE LIBRARY** command establishes the link to the external library. The general format for the command is:

```
CREATE LIBRARY lib_name IS|AS 'full_path_name';
```

Simply creating the library link is not enough, however, to use the procedures stored in the DLL. You must also register the procedures to the Oracle data dictionary. This is accomplished with the **EXTERNAL LIBRARY** call in a PL/SQL block. The **EXTERNAL LIBRARY** clause looks like

```
EXTERNAL LIBRARY library_name
   [NAME external_procedure_name]
   [LANGUAGE language_name]
   [CALLING STANDARD {C | PASCAL}]
   [WITH CONTEXT]
   [PARAMETERS (external_paramter[, external_parameter]...)];
```

where **external_parameter** stands for

```
{ CONTEXT
| {parameter_name | RETURN} [property] [BY_REF] [external_datatype]}
```

and **property** stands for

```
{INDICATOR | LENGTH | MAXLEN | CHARSETID | CHARSETFORM}
```

The **EXTERNAL LIBRARY** call acts as an interface between the external library routine and Oracle. Its arguments pass needed values to the external procedure and return results from the external procedure. Listing 4.5 shows an example.

Listing 4.5 Example function using an external procedure call.

```
CREATE FUNCTION decay_correct (
-- correct for the radioactive decay of an isotope
   ai      NUMBER, -- activity initial
   t       number, -- elapsed time (same units as t2)
   t2      number, -- halflife
RETURN NUMBER AS EXTERNAL
  LIBRARY c_utils
  NAME "decay_correct" -- Double quotes preserve lowercase
  LANGUAGE C;

Example use:

DECLARE
   activity number;
   elapsed_time number;
   half_life number;
   final_activity number;
BEGIN
...
   final_activity:=decay_correct(activity, elapsed_time, half_life);
...
END;
```

What actually happens when the call is made? First, the library alias is resolved. Then, via an external procedure call over a separate listener process, the external procedure is invoked in a new "extproc" process, and the values it needs are passed to it. Once the procedure completes, the extproc process returns the values it has processed. The extproc process remains active as long as the process that invoked it remains active; it dies only when the calling process dies or is killed.

The DBA for a system using the external processes must explicitly start a listener process for use by the external process mechanism.

Object Type Support

PL/SQL supports user-defined object types. You cannot create a UDT in PL/SQL; you can use only a predefined UDT. PL/SQL is used to construct any UDT methods. Object types map directly into classes defined in such languages as C++. Oracle types can be persistent (used to create an object or other table) or nonpersistent (used to create a PL/SQL table). In either case, the methods defined are available for use, as seen earlier in Listing 4.4.

If a type is defined as an object, then it can be used in PL/SQL declarations via a **REF** specification. For example, if you specify a type of car as an object type and create a table using the object type specified, then you can use a **REF** to specify that a PL/SQL variable is a **REF** to the object **car**, as seen in Listing 4.6.

Listing 4.6 Example of a type used in a PL/SQL declaration via a REF.

```
CREATE OR REPLACE TYPE car_t AS OBJECT (
    make varchar2(32),
    model varchar2(32),
    year number(4,0),
    option_package char(3),
    blue_book number,
    black_book number);

CREATE TABLE in_stock_cars OF car_t;

CREATE FUNCTION get_car (car_ref REF IN_STOCK_CAR) AS
 car_val car;
 CURSOR get_car (car_val  REF in_stock_car) AS
  SELECT DEREF(car_val) FROM dual;
```

```
BEGIN
 ...
 OPEN get_car(car_ref);
 FETCH get_car INTO car_val;
 CLOSE get_car;
 ...
END;
 (assuming that the passed REF value is valid and not dangling)
```

These code fragments create an object type and a table of objects from that type. Then, assuming some object instances were inserted into the object, you can use a PL/SQL procedure to manipulate them, using a **DEREF** to get the values from a passed **REF** value.

A **REF** value is closely related to the object identifier (OID) for an object instance. An OID is a unique identifier (supposedly global, but how this is guaranteed is not clear) that uniquely identifies the object being **REF**ed.

Also, notice the rebirth of the **dual** table. A **dual** table is a single-column single-value table that was used by triggers and procedures in late version 6 and version 7, but then fell out of use. Now with OIDs, it is being used again. Be sure to watch out for duplicate values getting into **dual**, as this will break your code.

Another new feature of PL/SQL is the **VALUE** clause, which allows the value of an object to be selected. For example, the code

```
DECLARE
    my_car car;
BEGIN
    SELECT VALUE(c)  INTO my_car FROM in_stock_cars c
    WHERE c.model='CORVETTE' and c.year=1969;
END;
```

would select the value for **in_stock_cars** that corresponds to a 1969 Corvette (hopefully there is only one or you will get an exception). When dealing with **REF** values and objects, take care that no **REF** is left without a proper tie to an object (say the master record got deleted and no one thought to send a message to the child records to delete themselves). This is called a dangling **REF**. The **IS |IS NOT DANGLING** clause checks for dangling **REF**s. For example, suppose you have a **cars_sold** table with the reference column **in_stock** that refers to **in_stock_cars**. The following code would eliminate any dangling **REF**s:

```
BEGIN
  UPDATE cars_sold SET stock_number = NULL WHERE in_stock IS DANGLING;
END;
```

PL/SQL And Collections

Collections are special types, such as nested tables or **VARRAY**s. These are specified using types and then can be used in PL/SQL. This allows multiple instances of an object to be associated automatically with a single instance of another master object. A classic use for this type of structure is a phone or email address list (which we all seem to accumulate). Listing 4.7 demonstrates this construct.

Listing 4.7 Examples of VARRAY and nested table builds.

```
rem For a VARRAY:

CREATE OR REPLACE TYPE email_t  AS OBJECT(
    email_address     VARCHAR2(64)
);
rem
rem email_v is a VARRAY of 10 elements
rem
CREATE OR REPLACE TYPE email_v AS VARRAY(10) OF email_t;

rem Or, if we really expect a lot of email addresses, a nested table:

CREATE OR REPLACE TYPE email_t  AS OBJECT(
    email_address     VARCHAR2(64)
);
rem
rem email_list is a nested table of email_t addresses
rem
CREATE OR REPLACE TYPE email_list AS TABLE OF email_t;
```

Until Oracle fixes the storage of **VARRAY**s, the best advice is to use only nested tables. Storage of **VARRAY**s can take up to 25 times the amount of storage required for a similar nested table.

An added benefit to using nested tables is that, after the storage table is created, you can specify indexes and constraints against the nested table, allowing another layer of business rule implementation. You cannot specify constraints or indexes against **VARRAY**s.

Inheritance And Polymorphism

Oracle will not support inheritance until version 8.1, at a minimum. You can simulate polymorphism through procedure, method, and function overloading.

Overloading is the process by which multiple procedures are contained in a single package with the same name and number of variables. Whatever variables are to be polymorphed, however, must be different datatypes in each of the procedures, functions, or methods.

This is an important statement: The procedure, function, or method must have its members contained in a single package or type body; you cannot produce polymorphic sets of procedures or functions through multiple independent procedure and function build scripts.

The Practical Guide includes examples of procedure, function, and method overloading.

Pairing Data With Behavior

Another cornerstone of the object-oriented paradigm is the pairing of data with behavior. To a limited extent, the use of triggers in previous versions of Oracle was a primitive attempt at this type of construct. Now, with Oracle8 and methods, Oracle comes much closer to providing true object-oriented pairing of data and behavior.

A method is a PL/SQL construct defined at the type level that can operate locally on the type itself (*intra-type*) or globally against other tables or objects (*inter-type*). For a true object-oriented implementation, you should use only intra-type methods in an application. All inter-type operations should be performed via a combination of method-to-procedure-to-method or method-to-method communications (message passing).

By sticking with inter-type methods only, you are using encapsulation and data-hiding, thus ensuring that the object is reusable and standalone. On the other hand, if you allow inter-type methods, then your objects will have inter-object dependencies, and you have defeated the purpose of the object-oriented paradigm.

The conversion example shown in the Chapter 1 Practical Guide has a method defined that reads a **REF** value from the parent table into a **REF** table. This reading of a **REF** from one table to another is an example of inter-type methods and should be avoided.

A better way of accomplishing the same end is to have a method in the dependent table that sends a request (message) for a **REF** to a method in the master table. This way, the behaviors are encapsulated in their own objects, and the dependent table is protected from changes in the master table structure. For example, what if the selection criteria changed in the master table? Not only would changes be required for the master, but you would also have to change the dependent table. On the other hand, if the method for returning the **REF** is internal to the master table, then the changes are isolated to the master table only. The Practical Guide presents an example of this **REF** request/**REF** passing method setup.

Practical Guide To

User-Defined Types

Creating A Basic Type

To create Oracle8 types, use the **CREATE TYPE** command. In earlier releases (previous to 8.0.2), the command's default behavior was to create an object type. Now, this must be explicitly stated. A basic type can be likened to a single relational table row and used to build rows in a table or act as a single set of values in a column. Definition of a type, whether it is an object or basic type, results in the creation of its required constructor methods, as well.

The following code segment creates a **CEO** type for use in a company table as a column set of values:

```
rem
rem The CEO data is a one-to-one relationship so just use
rem a type definition directly into the object.
rem
CREATE OR REPLACE TYPE ceo_t AS OBJECT(
    ceo_first_name          VARCHAR2(13),
    ceo_last_name           VARCHAR2(15),
    ceo_middle_initial      VARCHAR2(1),
    ceo_suffix              VARCHAR2(3),
    ceo_prefix              VARCHAR2(10),
    ceo_title               VARCHAR2(30)
);
```

Notice that this looks suspiciously like a table definition, except that you cannot declare constraints, tablespace definitions, or storage clauses. The type has no physical implementation except for a listing in the data dictionary tables. To create a table using the type, the table must reference the type as a normal datatype:

```
CREATE TABLE company (
    company_id          INTEGER NOT NULL,
    company_name      varchar2(32) NOT NULL,
    address                         address_t,
    ceo                             ceo_t,
    CONSTRAINT pk_company PRIMARY KEY (company_id)
    USING INDEX TABLESPACE appl_index
    STORAGE (INITIAL 1m NEXT 1m PCTINCREASE 0, FREELISTS 5)
    PCTFREE 20)
STORAGE (INITIAL 10m NEXT 10m PCTINCREASE 0)
PCTFREE 20 PCTUSED 70
TABLESPACE appl_data;
```

Notice how this code fragment makes two references to types: the **CEO** type (**ceo_t**) and the **ADDRESS** type (**address_t**). Later, you will discover that a company may have multiple addresses, and you will change this from a single- to a multivalued type.

Creating A Forward Type

In certain situations, you may have a type that references a second type that also references the original type. This recursive relationship is shown by such constructs as a manager object and an employee object, where the employee object makes a reference to the department object, which makes a reference back to the employee type:

```
CREATE OR REPLACE TYPE name_t AS OBJECT (
    first_name        VARCHAR2(32),
    last_name         VARCHAR2(32),
    middle_initial  VARCHAR2(3));

CREATE OR REPLACE TYPE dept_t AS OBJECT (
    number        INTEGER,
    manager REF employee,
    description VARCHAR2(60));

CREATE OR REPLACE TYPE employee_t AS OBJECT (
    name                    REF name_t,
    department        REF dept_t);
```

The code, as shown, will not work because of the circular references (notice that **dept_t** references **employee_t** through the **manager** attribute and that the **employee_t** type references the **dept_t** type through the **department** attribute). How can you make this work?

The forward type is incompletely specified. In this case, you can choose either **dept_t** or **employee_t** to make a forward type:

```
CREATE OR REPLACE TYPE dept_t;   ➡ Notice that this type is incomplete

CREATE OR REPLACE TYPE name_t AS OBJECT (
    first_name        VARCHAR2(32),
    last_name         VARCHAR2(32),
    middle_initial    VARCHAR2(3));
```

```
CREATE OR REPLACE TYPE employee_t AS OBJECT (
   name                    REF name_t,
   department              REF dept_t);

CREATE OR REPLACE TYPE dept_t AS OBJECT (     → Here we complete the type
   number         INTEGER,
   manager REF employee,
   description VARCHAR2(60));
```

This code works. Just remember that forward or incomplete types must be completed before building any tables or objects that use them.

Creating An Object Type

You specify an object type using the **AS OBJECT** clause of the **CREATE TYPE** command. The only way to create an object table is via an object type. An object table has an OID for each row that can be used in **REF**, **UNREF**, and **VALUE** commands, as in Listing 4.8.

Listing 4.8   Creating an object table with an object type.

```
CREATE OR REPLACE TYPE client_t as object  AS OBJECT(
   clients_id                    INTEGER,
   addresses                 address_list,
   customer_name             VARCHAR2(35),
   active_flag                VARCHAR2(1),
   fax                       VARCHAR2(20),
   lookups                       lookup_t,
   phone                     VARCHAR2(20),
   corporate_name            VARCHAR2(30),
   creation_ts                       DATE,
   creation_sy_user          NUMBER(38),
   spp_rating                    CHAR(2),
   rating_date                       DATE,
   competitor_loss               INTEGER,
   last_contact_ts                   DATE,
   delete_status                 CHAR(1),
   name_soundex                  CHAR(4),
   sales_volume              VARCHAR2(15),
   sales_volume_code             CHAR(1),
   total_employees            VARCHAR2(9),
   line_of_bus               VARCHAR2(19),
   pct_growth_sales           VARCHAR2(4),
   territory_covered             CHAR(1),
```

```
    mrc                                              VARCHAR2(4),
    ceo                                                   ceo_t,
    sub_indctr                                          CHAR(1),
    ftx_codes                                             ftx_v,
    sub_codes                                             sub_v,
MEMBER PROCEDURE do_soundex(id IN integer, nor_val IN varchar2)
);
```

This code creates a complex object that would take at least three or more relational tables to duplicate. The type specifications that end in **_V** are **VARRAY** specifications, and the attributes that have **_LIST** as a part of their name are nested tables. This specification also references a method called **DO_SOUNDEX**. A later section of this Practical Guide shows how to create a method.

To create a table from this type, you first need to complete the type specification by creating a type body for the specified method and specify a store table for the referenced nested table type, as in Listing 4.9.

Listing 4.9 Completing the type specification and specifying a store table.

```
rem Now create the object clients which contain
rem nested tables, types, and normal attributes.
rem
CREATE TABLE clientsV8 OF client_t
OIDINDEX oid_clientsV8 (TABLESPACE APPL_INDEX)
NESTED TABLE addresses STORE AS addressesv8  <---- Here is the store table
specification
        PCTFREE 10
        PCTUSED 80
        INITRANS 5
        MAXTRANS 255
        TABLESPACE APPL_DATA
        STORAGE (
                INITIAL 20m
                NEXT 10m
                MINEXTENTS 1
                MAXEXTENTS 10
                PCTINCREASE 0
        )
;
ALTER TABLE clientsV8 ADD    <---- Here we add a primary key to the table
specification
        CONSTRAINT PK_clientsv8
                PRIMARY KEY (clients_id)
```

```
            USING INDEX
                    PCTFREE 20
                    INITRANS 5
                    MAXTRANS 255
                    TABLESPACE APPL_INDEX
                    STORAGE (
                            INITIAL 10m
                            NEXT 10m
                            MINEXTENTS 1
                            MAXEXTENTS 121
                            PCTINCREASE 0
                            FREELISTS 5
                    )
    ;
ALTER TABLE clientsV8 MODIFY <------ Here we add a not null constraint to the table
      customer_name NOT NULL;
CREATE OR REPLACE TYPE BODY client_t IS <---- Here is the specification for the
method DO_SOUNDEX
MEMBER PROCEDURE do_soundex(id IN integer, nor_val IN varchar2) IS
sx_val integer;
begin
      sx_val:=soundex(nor_val);
      update clientsv8 set name_soundex=sx_val where clients_id=id;
end;
END;
/
```

 ## Creating A Nested Table Type

Oracle8 allows you to specify a special type known as a nested table, or table-within-table, type. You should use this type when the number of dependent instances of the type is large or unknown. A prime example is the **dependent** attribute of an employee object. Example code to implement a nested table type is shown in Listing 4.10.

Listing 4.10   Implementing a nested table type.

```
CREATE OR REPLACE TYPE dependent_t(
    relation            VARCHAR2(15),
    name                name_t,
    age                 NUMBER
);
rem
rem dependent_list is a nested table definition
rem
CREATE OR REPLACE TYPE dependent_list AS TABLE OF dependent_t;
```

```
CREATE OR REPLACE TYPE employee_info_t as object (
 employee_id        INTEGER,
 name                     name_t,
 dependents         dependent_list,
);
rem
rem employee_info is a table definition
rem
CREATE TABLE  employee_info OF employee_info_t
     OIDINDEX oid_emloyee_info (TABLESPACE APPL_INDEX)
      NESTED TABLE dependents STORE AS dependentsV8
      PCTFREE 10
       PCTUSED 80
       INITRANS 5
       MAXTRANS 255
       TABLESPACE APPL_DATA
       STORAGE (
               INITIAL 20m
               NEXT 10m
               MINEXTENTS 1
               MAXEXTENTS 10
               PCTINCREASE 0
       );
```

Notice how the store table for the nested table type is specified. The store table will take on the default storage attributes of the master table's tablespace. Hopefully, in future releases (after 8.0.3), you will be able to specify the storage of nested tables as a separate definition. You can alter the store table's storage characteristics with an **ALTER TABLE** command.

Inserts into a nested table automatically create an identifier in a pseudo-column called **SETID$** that refers to the master table.

Creating A **VARRAY** Type

Another special type is the **VARRAY**, or varying array, type. You should use it when the number of instances to be stored is small. This type is stored inline with the other table data. In early releases (up to 8.0.3), the **VARRAY** could take up to 25 times the amount of storage as a nested table for the same values. Unless you are using a newer release where this has been corrected, I suggest using the nested table instead of a **VARRAY**. Let's examine how they are created, anyway:

```
rem There is a fixed number of FTX codes and it is small
rem so use a VARRAY
rem
CREATE OR REPLACE TYPE ftx_t (
    ftx_code                                        CHAR(8) ,
    ftx_code_desc                                VARCHAR2(32),
        primary_ftx_code_ind                         CHAR(1)
);
rem
rem ftx_v is a VARRAY of 6 elements
rem
CREATE OR REPLACE TYPE ftx_v AS VARRAY(6) OF ftx_t;
```

Notice that the number of instances of the **VARRAY** is set at **6** in this example. This requires 676 bytes of **RAW** inline storage. You have no control over storage and can neither index nor constrain **VARRAY** values.

Populating Types

As stated in other sections, the creation of a type automatically creates a method (constructor) to populate the type. To call the method, use the original type name. The constructor is never called implicitly but must be called explicitly. You can use the constructor anywhere you use a function call. Here is an example **INSERT** into the **employee_info** table:

```
SQL> insert into employee_info
  2  values(1,name_t('Michael','Ault','R'),    <-- Note use of the name_t
                                                  constructor method
  3  dependent_list(    <-- Note use of dependent_list constructor method to build
                           insert array
  4  dependent_t('Wife',name_t('Susan','Ault','K'),'39'), <---- Note use of
                                                          dependent_t method
  5  dependent_t('Daughter',name_t('Marie','Ault','C'),23),
  6  dependent_t('Daughter',name_t('Michelle','Ault','E'),19))
  7* );

1 row created
```

Notice that the format for using the constructor methods walks down the type tree. In this case, the type tree for the dependent type looks like this:

```
dependents      <---- Attribute in table
                   dependent_list    <---- Nested Table Type
                                          dependent_t      <---- Base Type
```

Dependents is the attribute, so it isn't used in the type tree. Therefore, you start at the **dependent_list** type as the outermost method and end at **dependent_t**, the basic type constructor method. Because the type is for a nested table, you specify the **dependent_t** method multiple times for each **INSERT** into the nested table. Notice that you also use a constructor method, **name_t**, inside the innermost type constructor to perform the **INSERT** into the dependent's name attribute, which is itself a type.

Population of a **VARRAY** type is identical to population of a nested table type, except that you can insert only up to the maximum specified count of the **VARRAY**. **VARRAY**s must be full to the last entry entered; they cannot be sparse.

Using Other Built-In Methods For Collections

In addition to the constructor type, Oracle provides collection methods for use with **VARRAY**s and nested tables. You cannot use these methods outside of PL/SQL. You can use them only in procedural statements, not in DML. They are:

- **EXISTS**—Used with nested tables to determine if a specific element in a collection exists.

- **COUNT**—Returns the number of elements that a collection contains, not including **NULL** values. For **VARRAY**s, **COUNT** is equal to **LAST**. For nested tables, **COUNT** and **LAST** may be different because of deleted values in interstitial data sites in the nested table.

- **LIMIT**—Used for **VARRAY**s to determine the maximum number of values allowed. If **LIMIT** is used on a nested table, it will return a **NULL**.

- **FIRST** and **LAST**—Return the smallest and largest index numbers for the collection referenced. Naturally, they return **NULL** if the collection is empty. For **VARRAY**s, **FIRST** always returns 1; for nested tables, it returns the value of the first filled spot for that entry. **LAST** returns the last filled instance of a **VARRAY** and a nested table. For a **VARRAY**, **COUNT** will always equal **LAST**. For a nested table, **LAST** should always be greater than **COUNT**.

- **PRIOR** and **NEXT**—Return the prior or next value based on the input value for the collection index. **PRIOR** and **NEXT** ignore deleted instances in a collection.

- **EXTEND**—Appends instances to a collection. **EXTEND** has three forms: **EXTEND**, which adds one **NULL** instance; **EXTEND(n)**, which adds *n* **NULL** instances; and **EXTEND(n,m)**, which appends *n* copies of instance *m* to the collection. For **NOT NULL** specified collections forms, 1 and 2 cannot be used.

- **TRIM**—Removes instances from a collection. When used with no arguments, it removes the last instance. **TRIM(n)** removes *n* instances from the collection.

- **DELETE**—Removes specified items from a nested table or all of a **VARRAY**. When specified with no arguments, it removes all instances of a collection. For nested tables only, **DELETE(n)** removes the *n*th instance and **DELETE(n,m)** deletes the *n*th through *m*th instances of the nested table that relate to the specified master record.

Remember when using these methods that a **VARRAY** is a dense type. Its values start at 1 and go to the last filled value as far as the index is concerned, with no breaks and no **NULL** values allowed. A nested table is allowed to have deleted values (i.e., it can be "sparse"). Therefore, if you attempt to use a method that is inappropriate, such as **DELETE** with an argument against a **VARRAY**, you will receive an error.

Collection methods can raise the following exceptions:

- **COLLECTION_IS_NULL**—The collection referenced is atomically **NULL**.

- **NO_DATA_FOUND**—Subscript points to a **NULL** instance of the collection.

- **SUBSCRIPT_BEYOND_COUNT**—Specified subscript is beyond the number of instances in the collection.

- **SUBSCRIPT_OUTSIDE_LIMIT**—Specified subscript is outside the legal range (usually received from **VARRAY** references).

- **VALUE_ERROR**—Subscript is **NULL** or is not an integer.

You can use these collection methods in a variety of ways. In the case of a nested table where some of the values are **NULL**, selection using a standard cursor could result in an exception. Use the **FIRST** and **NEXT** collection methods to transverse these **NULL** values:

```
j := dependents.FIRST;
WHILE j IS NOT NULL LOOP
   process dependents(j)
   j := dependents.NEXT(j);
END LOOP
```

What does this code fragment do? First, it uses the **FIRST** collection method to get the index integer of the first valid record for the **dependents** nested table. Remember, a nested table is a sparse construct, so the first valid value may not be 1.

Next, it begins loop processing of values, assuming it didn't get a **NULL** value on the call to **FIRST**. Once the first value is processed, the counter is reset to the appropriate **NEXT** value. Once **NEXT** evaluates to **NULL**, the loop is exited.

Another example is a **VARRAY** where you want to process only the number of values that are in each **VARRAY** instance set. To do this, you can use **FIRST** and **LAST** or 1 and **COUNT**:

```
FOR j IN addresses.FIRST..addresses.LAST LOOP

-- or

FOR j in 1..addresses.COUNT LOOP
```

The next example shows how to determine if you can add a specific number of instances to a **VARRAY** using the **LIMIT** collection method:

```
IF (addresses.COUNT + 5) < addresses.LIMIT THEN
  -- add 5 more addresses
```

Again, let me stress, as shown in these code fragments, that collection methods can be used only in procedural statements, not in DML.

Creating A **REF** Request And **REF** Passing Method Set

In the body of this chapter, we discussed that you should create two methods to implement an object-oriented type set properly, where a dependent table object uses a **REF** to refer to a master table object. The first method, which for convenience I call the **get_ref** method, resides in the dependent table object-type specification; and the second, which I call **give_ref,** resides in the master table object type specification.

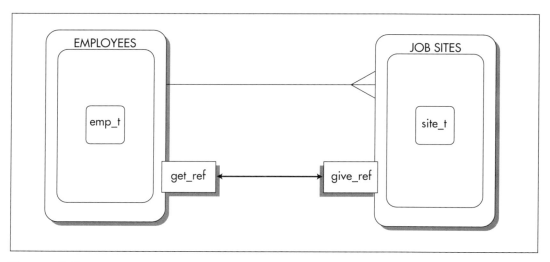

Figure 4.1

OOERD for example objects.

As its name implies, the whole purpose of the first method is to request the value of a specific **REF** from the master table. The whole purpose of the second method is to receive the request for the **REF**, get the requested **REF** from the master table object, and return the **REF** to the calling method. For this example, we have two object tables, **employees** and **job_sites**, which are related, as shown in Figure 4.1.

As you can see from looking at the OOERD in Figure 4.1, there are two object tables, their main types, and a single method in each. The code to implement this structure is shown in Listing 4.11.

Listing 4.11   Example implementation of a get_ref/give_ref method set.

```
CREATE OR REPLACE TYPE address_t  AS OBJECT(
   street      VARCHAR2(30),
   city        VARCHAR2(30),
   state       CHAR(2),
   zip         CHAR(5))
/
CREATE OR REPLACE TYPE emp_t AS OBJECT (
  employee_id                  INTEGER ,
  name                          name_t,
  birthdate                     DATE,
  hiredate                      DATE,
  address                       address_t,
  dependents                   dependent_list,
```

```
MEMBER FUNCTION give_ref(id IN integer)
RETURN REF emp_t,
PRAGMA RESTRICT_REFERENCES (give_ref,WNPS)
)
/


rem
rem Now create the object employees which contains
rem nested tables, types, and normal attributes
rem
CREATE TABLE employees OF emp_t
OIDINDEX oid_employees (TABLESPACE raw_INDEX)
NESTED TABLE dependents STORE AS dependentsv8a
        PCTFREE 10 PCTUSED 80
        INITRANS 5 MAXTRANS 255
        TABLESPACE raw_data
        STORAGE (
                INITIAL 20m NEXT 10m
                MINEXTENTS 1 MAXEXTENTS 10
                PCTINCREASE 0
        )
/

ALTER TABLE employees ADD
        CONSTRAINT PK_employees
                PRIMARY KEY (employee_id)
        USING INDEX
                PCTFREE 20
                INITRANS 5
                MAXTRANS 255
                TABLESPACE raw_index
                STORAGE (
                        INITIAL 10m NEXT 10m
                        MINEXTENTS 1 MAXEXTENTS 121
                        PCTINCREASE 0 FREELISTS 5
                )
/

ALTER TABLE employees MODIFY
    name NOT NULL
/

CREATE OR REPLACE TYPE BODY emp_t IS
MEMBER FUNCTION give_ref(id IN integer)
  RETURN REF emp_t  IS
  ref_val REF emp_t;
```

```
BEGIN
  SELECT REF(e) INTO ref_val
  FROM employees e
  WHERE e.employee_id=id;
  RETURN ref_val;
END;
END;
/

CREATE or replace TYPE company_t  AS OBJECT(
   company_name              VARCHAR2(32),
   company_business      VARCHAR2(32),
   company_contact          name_t,
   contact_home              VARCHAR2(20))
/

rem
rem The job_sites object is an independent one-to-many
rem from employees. We will REF emp_t and EMPLOYEES.
rem

CREATE OR REPLACE TYPE site_t as object  AS OBJECT(
  site_id                        INTEGER,
  company                      company_t,
  address                       address_t,
  employee_id_r            REF emp_t,
MEMBER FUNCTION get_ref
   (emp_id IN integer)
   RETURN REF emp_t)
/

rem
rem job_sites is an object table definition
rem

CREATE TABLE job_sites OF site_t
     (employee_id_r WITH ROWID
      SCOPE IS employees)
      OIDINDEX oid_job_sites (TABLESPACE raw_index)
       PCTFREE 10 PCTUSED 80
       INITRANS 5 MAXTRANS 255
       TABLESPACE raw_data
       STORAGE ( INITIAL 20m NEXT 10m
                         MINEXTENTS 1 MAXEXTENTS 10
                         PCTINCREASE 0
                       )
/
```

```
ALTER TABLE job_sites ADD
     CONSTRAINT PK_job_sites
          PRIMARY KEY (site_id)
     USING INDEX
          PCTFREE 20
          INITRANS 5 MAXTRANS 255
          TABLESPACE raw_index
          STORAGE (INITIAL 10m NEXT 10m
                             MINEXTENTS 1 MAXEXTENTS 121
                             PCTINCREASE 0 FREELISTS 5
                             )
/

CREATE TYPE BODY site_t AS
MEMBER FUNCTION get_ref (emp_id IN integer)
RETURN INTEGER IS
status INTEGER:=0;
BEGIN
     SELF.employee_id_r := emp_t.give_ref(emp_id);
     RETURN status;
EXCEPTION
WHEN others THEN
     status := 1;
     RETURN status;
END;
END;
/
```

The actual methods **get_ref** and **give_ref** are quite small and non-complex. To use the
methods, you call them as you would normal functions during **INSERT** or **UPDATE**
operations involving the **REF**ed row in the **employees** table object or the actual stored
REF value in the **job_sites** table object.

Overloading Procedures

Overloading an Oracle procedure is a primitive form of polymorphism, which simply allows you to call the same procedure name and get back different results based
on the input values (messages) sent to the procedure. In Oracle, you usually use this
technique to allow a single name to be used for a procedure set that accepts multiple
datatypes as input (such as **CHAR**, **VARCHAR2**, **NUMBER**, and **DATE**) and gives
the "same" result. A good example of this is the **DBMS_OUTPUT.PUT_LINE** set of
procedures. Listing 4.12 shows the **DBMS_OUTPUT** package header that contains
these procedure specifications.

Listing 4.12 Example of procedure overloading.

```
procedure put_line(a varchar2);
procedure put_line(a number);
procedure put_line(a date);
--  Put a piece of information in the buffer followed by an end-of-line
--    marker. When retrieved by get_line(s), the number and date items
--    will be formatted with to_char using the default formats. If you
--    want another format then format it explicitly and use the
--    put_line(<varchar2>) call. Note that this routine is overloaded on
--    the type of its argument. The proper version will be used depending
--    on argument type. get_line(s) return "lines" as delimited by
--    "newlines". So every call to put_line or new_line will generate a
--    line that will be returned by get_line(s).
--  Input parameters:
--    a
--          Item to buffer
```

Without doing anything different to your code, and as long as a single data item of that type is specified, **DBMS_OUTPUT.PUT_LINE** can process **VARCHAR2**, **NUMBER**, and **DATE** data items. If you use multiple data items, they must be explicitly converted to one of the datatypes—**VARCHAR2**, in this case.

Overloading can be done only within the boundaries of a package or type definition.

Overloading Functions

Like their more talented cousins procedures, functions can be overloaded. An overloaded function takes in one or more arguments (messages) and returns a single value. An overloaded function can take in one or more arguments where the main argument is of differing datatypes and return different datatype single values, depending on the type of the argument passed to the function. An example is found in the **DBMS_LOCK** package, shown in Listing 4.13.

Listing 4.13 Example of function overloading from DBMS_LOCK.

```
function  request(id in integer,
                  lockmode in integer default x_mode,
                  timeout in integer default maxwait,
                  release_on_commit in boolean default FALSE)
   return integer;
function  request(lockhandle in varchar2,
                  lockmode in integer default x_mode,
                  timeout in integer default maxwait,
                  release_on_commit in boolean default FALSE)
```

```
   return integer;
-- Request a lock with the given mode. Note that this routine is
-- overloaded based on the type of its first argument.  The
-- appropriate routine is used based on how it is called.
-- If a deadlock is detected, then an arbitrary session is
            chosen to receive deadlock status.
```

As Listing 4.13 shows, overloading functions and procedures is virtually identical.

Overloading Methods

Method overloading can be used to provide a common name for a method that actually consists of several methods that perform differently, depending on the values passed as messages to the method. An example is a method that updates a table attribute based on the value it is passed. If it were passed a date value, it would do the conversion to character; same with a number. Or perhaps it would insert into a **TYPE** attribute a code based on input value.

The technique for overloading a method procedure or function, as shown in Listing 4.14, is identical to overloading a standard procedure or function.

Listing 4.14   Example overloading of a type method.
```
SQL> create type test3 AS OBJECT(type_passed varchar2(8),
  2    member procedure input_type(in_char char),
  3    member procedure input_type(in_varchar varchar2),
  4    member procedure input_type(in_date date),
  5    member procedure input_type(in_number number))
  6  /

Type created.
```

This method overloading allows incorporation of polymorphism into object types.

Creating A **MAP** Or **ORDER** Method

A **MAP** or **ORDER** method provides for comparison of types. It is easy, relatively speaking, for Oracle to compare scalar values, such as **CHAR**, **VARCHAR2**, **NUMBER**, or **DATE**. But, how can it compare instances of a type that has multiple datatypes? The answer is to create a **MAP** or **ORDER** method but not both. There can be only one **MAP** or one **ORDER** method per type. You can specify only a **MAP** or an **ORDER** method but not both.

The **MAP–MEMBER** Function

The **MAP** type of the **MEMBER** function maps, at the time of use, all the values in the type to the specified function. For large comparisons, it is the most efficient **MEMBER** function of the two types **MAP** and **ORDER**. Listing 4.15 shows a **MAP** method declaration.

Listing 4.15   Example MAP method declaration.

```
CREATE OR REPLACE TYPE site_t AS OBJECT (
  site_id                        INTEGER,
  company                        company_t,
  address                        address_t,
  employee_id_r             REF emp_t,
MEMBER FUNCTION get_ref
   (emp_id IN integer)
   RETURN REF emp_t,
MAP MEMBER FUNCTION give_site_id
RETURN INTEGER)
/

CREATE TYPE BODY site_t AS
 MEMBER FUNCTION get_ref (emp_id IN integer)
 RETURN INTEGER IS
 status INTEGER:=0;
 BEGIN
    SELF.employee_id_r := emp_t.give_ref(emp_id);
    RETURN status;
 EXCEPTION
 WHEN others THEN
    status := 1;
    RETURN status;
 END;
 MAP MEMBER FUNCTION give_site_id
 RETURN INTEGER IS
 BEGIN
     RETURN site_id;
 END;
END;
```

The listing will return a **site_id** value whenever comparison values are required from the **site_t** type. This allows **GROUP BY**, **ORDER BY**, and other sort-dependent calls against the type to function properly.

The **ORDER–MEMBER** Function

The **ORDER** type of the **MEMBER** function allows for ordering of entries that don't have as easy a solution as simply returning a **site_id** that is stored in the table. An

ORDER function must return an integer value and is used only once per call. A **MAP** function is used recursively. An **ORDER** is most useful when you are comparing a small number of instances against a single value. A **MAP** is most useful when you are sorting large numbers of instances. Listing 4.16 is an example of an **ORDER** function.

Listing 4.16   Example of an ORDER function.

```
CREATE OR REPLACE TYPE site_t AS OBJECT (
   site_id                          INTEGER,
   company                          company_t,
   address                          address_t,
   employee_id_r                    REF emp_t,
MEMBER FUNCTION get_ref
   (emp_id IN integer)
   RETURN REF emp_t,
ORDER MEMBER FUNCTION give_order( site INTEGER)
RETURN INTEGER)
/

CREATE TYPE BODY site_t AS
 MEMBER FUNCTION get_ref (emp_id IN integer)
 RETURN INTEGER IS
 status INTEGER:=0;
 BEGIN
    SELF.employee_id_r := emp_t.give_ref(emp_id);
    RETURN status;
 EXCEPTION
 WHEN others THEN
    status := 1;
    RETURN status;
 END;
 ORDER MEMBER FUNCTION give_order( site INTEGER)
 RETURN INTEGER IS
 BEGIN
IF site<SELF.site
   THEN
       RETURN 1;
ELSIF site>SELF.site
   THEN
       RETURN -1;
Else
       RETURN 0;
 END;
END;
```

Listing 4.16 creates an **ORDER** function called **give_order** that returns -1, 1, or 0, depending on the comparison of the input value to the value of the instance attribute. Again, an **ORDER** function is used on a one-time basis (it can compare the input value to only the current instance value), while a **MAP** method maps all instance values into scalars when it is called.

Using Types In PL/SQL

You can use types as you use other scalar datatypes in PL/SQL. When a variable is first declared as a type, it is atomically **NULL** and can't be used until it is initialized; otherwise, it will return **NULL** values for all calls to the variable or its sub-attributes. For example, if you have a type **room**, which has the attributes **LNGTH** and **WIDTH**, and a single method **SQUARE_FOOT**, and you want to use it in a procedure, the code for the type specification would resemble Listing 4.17.

Listing 4.17   Example type specification with method.
```
CREATE TYPE room  AS OBJECT(
lngth NUMBER,
width NUMBER,
MEMBER FUNCTION SQUARE_FOOT
RETURN NUMBER);

CREATE TYPE BODY room AS
  MEMBER FUNCTION SQUARE_FOOT
  RETURN NUMBER IS
  area NUMBER;
  BEGIN
   AREA:=SELF.lngth*SELF.width;
    RETURN area
  END;
END;
```

To use the type in a function or procedure, you need to implicitly or explicitly set its values. Listing 4.18 shows an example of what happens when you use an uninitialized composite versus a properly initialized one.

Listing 4.18   Example of type use and method call from PL/SQL.
```
rem First, here is the uninitialized version.
rem
CREATE OR REPLACE PROCEDURE area (
lngth IN NUMBER, width IN NUMBER, area OUT NUMBER) AS
example_room room;
BEGIN
example_room.lngth:=lngth;
example_room.width:=width;
```

```
  area:=example_room.square_foot;
END;
/
SQL> set serveroutput on

SQL> DECLARE
  2    lngth NUMBER:=20;
  3    width NUMBER:=16;
  4    cal_area NUMBER:=0;
  5    BEGIN
  6    area(lngth,width,cal_area);
  7    dbms_output.put_line(cal_area);
  8*   END;
SQL> /
DECLARE
*
ERROR at line 1:
ORA-06530: Reference to uninitialized composite
ORA-06512: at "SYSTEM.AREA", line 4
ORA-06512: at line 6

rem Here is the initialized version
create or replace procedure area (
lngth in number, width in number, area out number) as
example_room room:=room(null,null);  <-- Notice the value of example_ROOM is
initialized here
BEGIN
example_room.lngth:=lngth;
example_room.width:=width;
area:=example_room.square_foot;
END;
/
SQL> SET SERVEROUTPUT ON

SQL> DECLARE
  2    lngth NUMBER:=20;
  3    width NUMBER:=16;
  4    cal_area NUMBER:=0;
  5    BEGIN
  6    area(lngth,width,cal_area);
  7    dbms_output.put_line(cal_area);
  8*   END;
SQL> /
320

PL/SQL procedure successfully completed.
```

Using REF, DEREF, And VALUE

REF and **DEREF** are Oracle-supplied routines that allow a developer to explicitly reference an object instance. The call to **REF** returns the OID of the object instance. An OID is a 128-byte base-64 number, which isn't very useful except as a handle to the object instance. To get the value or values stored in the instance that is referred to by a **REF**, you use the **DEREF** routine. **DEREF** returns the values in the object instance referenced by a specific **REF** value.

REFs establish relationships between two object tables, much as a primary-key/foreign-key relationship in relational tables. Relational tables have difficulty, however, if you need more than one table in a primary-key/foreign-key relationship related to a single table. An example is an address table that stores addresses from several entities. The use of **REF**s eliminates this problem, because an unscoped **REF** can refer to any accessible object table.

A **SCOPE** clause in a definition forces a set of **REF**s for a given column to be confined to a single object table. There can be only one **REF** clause for a given **REF** column. **REF** scope can be set at either the column or table level.

REF values can be stored with or without a **ROWID**. Storing a **REF** with a **ROWID** speeds dereferencing operations, but takes more space. If **WITH ROWID** is not specified with the **REF** clause, the default is to not store **ROWID**s with the **REF** values. **SCOPE** clauses prevent dangling references, as they will not allow **REF** values unless the corresponding entries in the **SCOPE** table are present.

You can add **REF** columns to nested tables with the **ALTER TABLE** command.

The **VALUE** routine returns the value of a **REF** call, much like the **DEREF** routine. Listing 4.19 shows the creation of an object type, a specification of an object table to hold the type instance, and a second table that references the object table. Also shown are some example operations with **REF** and **DEFREF**.

Listing 4.19   Example use of REF and DEREF.

```
SQL> CREATE TYPE dept_t AS OBJECT
  2  (dname VARCHAR2(100),
  3   address VARCHAR2(200));

Type created.

SQL> CREATE TABLE dept OF dept_t;

Table created.
```

```
SQL> CREATE TABLE emp (
  2  ename VARCHAR2(100),
  3  enumber NUMBER,
  4  edept REF dept_t SCOPE IS dept);

Table created.

SQL> INSERT INTO dept VALUES (dept_t('Home','5055 Forest Run'));

1 row created.

SQL> INSERT INTO dept VALUES (dept_t('Work','1800 Century Blvd'))

1 row created.

SQL> SELECT * FROM dept;

DNAME                                    ADDRESS
------------------------------------     ---------------------------------------------
Home                                     5055 Forest Run
Work                                     1800 Century  Blvd


SQL> SELECT REF(d) FROM dept d;

D
---------------------------------------------------------
0000280209A656BEEF11B811D1AD5B0060972CFBA8A656BEEE
11B811D1AD5B0060972CFBA8008000C10000

0000280209A656BEF011B811D1AD5B0060972CFBA8A656BEEE
11B811D1AD5B0060972CFBA8008000C10001



SQL> INSERT INTO emp SELECT 'Mike Ault',1, REF(d) FROM dept d
  2* WHERE d.dname='Home'
SQL> /

1 row created.

SQL> SELECT * FROM emp;

ENAME                                                ENUMBER
--------------------------------------------------   --------------------------------
Mike Ault                                                                          1
```

```
EDEPT
-------------------------------------------------------------------
0000220208A656BEEF11B811D1AD5B0060972C
FBA8A656BEEE11B811D1AD5B0060972CFBA8


SQL> SELECT ename,enumber,DEREF(edept) FROM emp;

ENAME                                                ENUMBER
------------------------------------------------- --------------------------------
DEREF(EDEPT)(DNAME, ADDRESS)                                       1
-------------------------------------------------------------------
Mike Ault
DEPT_T('Home', '5055 Forest Run')


SQL> spool off
```

Listing 4.20 demonstrates the **VALUE** routine. **VALUE** can assign the value from one instance of an object table to another. For normal selection, the standard **SELECT** works better, as shown in Listing 4.20.

Listing 4.20   Example of a VALUE routine.

```
SQL> select value(d) from dept d where d.dname like 'Home'

D(DNAME, ADDRESS)
----------------------------------------------------------
DEPT_T('Home', '5055 Forest Run')

SQL> SELECT * FROM dept d WHERE d.dname LIKE 'Home%';

DNAME                   ADDRESS
--------------------    --------------------
Home                    5055 Forest Run
```

Using The **DANGLING** Clause

The **DANGLING** clause tests for a dangling **REF**. In some situations, if the application is not coded properly, a **REF**ed value could be deleted without removing the **REF** value in a dependent table. If this deletion of a master object instance occurs without removal of the dependent **REF** value, the **REF** value left in the dependent table is said to be *dangling* and can result in problems for retrieves, updates, and deletes. An example of the use of this clause would be to set all dangling **REF** values to **NULL** via an **UPDATE** statement such as:

```
UPDATE emp SET edept=NULL WHERE edept IS DANGLING;
```

Unless you are absolutely sure that you have no dangling **REF** values, you should use the **DANGLING** clause to ensure that the records you retrieve are complete. The clause can be used with both **IS** and **IS NOT**:

```
SELECT ename, enumber, DEFRE(edept) FROM emp WHERE edept IS NOT DANGLING;
```

Always be sure that a **REF** value is not **NULL** before attempting to **REF** or **DEREF** it; otherwise, your session may be terminated (indeed, after several experiments along this line in version 8.0.2, Oracle caused my NT 4 box to reboot). The only way to do this is to use the **DANGLING** clause.

 ## Updating And Deleting Type-Based Objects

Type-based objects, just like relational objects, have to be updated and deleted. Updates will use more complex statements for type-based objects than are used for relational objects. **DELETE** statements are fairly straightforward for type-based objects, so we will cover them last.

You must update a type using a form of its constructor. For example, to update a value in a simple nested type, you simply use dot notation to specify which value to change, as shown in Listing 4.21.

Listing 4.21 **Example update of a simple nested type.**

```
SQL> r
  1  INSERT INTO employees
  2  VALUES (
  3  1,
  4  name_t('Mike','Ault','R'),
  5  '9-jun-56',
  6  '2-Feb-96',
  7  address_t('5035 tree summit','Alpharetta','Ga','30245'),
  8  dependent_list(
  9  dependent_t('Wife',name_t('Susan','Ault','K'),39),
 10  dependent_t('Daughter',name_t('Cynthia','Ault','M'),23),
 11  dependent_t('Daughter',name_t('Michelle','Ault','E'),19))
 12* )

1 row created.

SQL> COMMIT;

Commit complete.
```

```
SQL> UPDATE employees e SET e.name.first_name='Michael' WHERE
  2* e.name.first_name='Mike'

1 row updated.

SQL> COMMIT;

Commit complete.
```

The update of a nested table requires the new keyword **THE**. I usually do a mental translation to **THE SET**. The purpose of this new keyword is to allow you to perform DML on the internal values of a nested table as referenced from the master table. For example, let's change my daughter's name from Michelle to Clyde in the **employees** table. The **employees** table uses a nested table called **dependents** to store dependent data. Listing 4.22 shows the required DML to perform this update.

Listing 4.22   Example UPDATE statement using THE.
```
UPDATE THE
(SELECT dependents FROM employees e WHERE e.employee_id = 1) DEP
SET dep.first_name='Clyde' WHERE dep.firstname='Michelle';
```

A **DELETE** command, shown in Listing 4.23, is similar. Let's assume my first daughter meets a rich young DBA and moves out. She is no longer my dependent, so I have to remove her from the **dependents** list. This final example shows how this is done using the **THE** operator.

Listing 4.23   Example DELETE statement using THE.
```
DELETE THE
(SELECT DEPENDENTS FROM employees e WHERE employee_id=1) dep
WHERE dep.first_name='Cynthia';
```

Oracle8 Data Storage Features

*Oracle8 offers developers and DBAs several new storage options. Among these are partitioned tables and indexes, index-only tables, nested tables, and **VARRAY**s, as well as new LOB datatype storage options.*

Notes…

Chapter

5

Table Storage Options

This chapter starts with a discussion of the various new storage options for tables under Oracle8. We will also review the standard relational option extensions, such as index-only and partitioned tables.

Relational Tables

Standard relational tables are still available in Oracle8. These tables contain only simple attributes and are created by specifying the **CREATE** command, just as in previous releases of Oracle.

Oracle8 also allows complex relational tables. These tables may contain **VARRAY**s, nested tables, type columns, and even **REF** columns to object tables. Only pure relational tables can be partitioned. Relational tables do not have object identifiers (OIDs).

Relational tables can be used as object tables if they are made into an object view with a pseudo-OID.

Object Tables

Object tables are based on a type defined with the **AS OBJECT** clause. They can contain scalar attributes, type columns, nested tables, **VARRAY**s, and **REF** columns to other object tables. Object tables have OIDs and can be used in **REF** calls from procedures, functions, methods, and other tables.

Object tables cannot be used in partitioned tables; however, partitioned indexes can be generated for object tables.

Partitioned Tables

Oracle8 offers new functionality with the introduction of partitioned tables. In previous Oracle releases, the only way to get similar functionality was to partition your tables manually into segments located on different disks or to specify several identically structured tables and use a partitioned view. Neither of these alternatives to true partitioned tables was satisfactory for any but the most elementary of implementations.

Partitioned tables are partitioned by value range in Oracle8. Through some PL/SQL magic with triggers or a combination of triggers and other stored procedures or functions, however, a partitioning column can be populated based on any data conversions that can be distilled down to integer or numeric values.

A table may not be partitioned based on **ROWID** or **LONG** columns, or by keywords (such as salesmen names). The Practical Guide in this chapter shows a method to get around the keyword limitation.

Partitions give you added granularity in how tables and indexes are used, backed up, and recovered. Partitions allow for greater data access, because in a nonpartitioned environment, in order to do data maintenance, an entire table or index has to be taken out of service. With partitions, only the effected table segments are taken out of service, leaving the rest to be accessed by users.

You can use up to 16 columns to determine partitioning behavior. Each segment of a partitioned table can be given its own storage parameters, including being placed into a read-only tablespace. Partitioned tables cannot contain **VARRAY**s, nested tables, or types. Partitions can be added, dropped, or split.

Index-Only Tables

Index-only tables are another new feature of Oracle8. They allow for b-tree storage of data for an entire table. This results in faster retrieval of data. You should use these tables when the number of columns is small and the tables don't frequently experience updates or deletes. Index-only tables must have a primary key specified, as they are sorted on the primary key value into the b-tree.

Use index-only tables for lookup tables that in the past required both a regular table and an index. This can result in a major storage savings. An index-only table has no **ROWID**s and cannot be an object-type table, nested table, or use **VARRAY**s.

If an index-only table has extremely large rows, you must specify a **PCTTHRESHOLD** value; otherwise, any rows that exceed the **PCTTHRESHOLD** percentage of space in the index block will be rejected, unless you also specify the **OVERFLOW** clause. Do not use **PCTTHRESHOLD** without specifying an **OVERFLOW** area, or data loss could result.

PCTTHRESHOLD allows you to specify the column where the break in a row to move to the **OVERFLOW** area should occur. Only the last primary key column or a nonprimary key column can be specified for the break column in the **INCLUDING** clause.

Nested Tables

Oracle8 nested tables have no independent existence from their master tables. When a nested table's master table is dropped, the store table associated with the nested-table entry is also dropped. A nested table is created when a type created with the **AS TABLE** clause is referenced in a table column specification. If a type defined with the **AS TABLE** clause is used for a column definition, you must specify a **NESTED TABLE/STORE AS** clause for the column's store table, or an error will result.

A nested table's store tables take the storage characteristics of the tablespace in which they are created. You can change the storage characteristics (other than the **INITIAL** and **MINEXTENTS** specifications) of a nested table's store table with an **ALTER TABLE** command. You can add indexes and constraints to a nested table's store table using the **ALTER TABLE** and **CREATE INDEX** commands.

No DML can be issued against a store table. All **INSERT**, **UPDATE**, and **DELETE** operations have to be done through the master table and the constructor methods.

Clustered Tables

Oracle8 supports clustered tables. A clustered table shares one or more cluster attributes with a group of other tables. The cluster attributes are all stored in the same physical block. This shared storage allows for rapid retrieval using joins based on the cluster attributes (called the *cluster key*). Clustering can reduce storage requirements, because duplicate storage of cluster key values is not required.

You can use clustering on a single table to force storage of all key values into a single block. This single-table clustering can improve access speeds for retrievals based on cluster key values.

Clusters can be indexed or hashed. Hashed clusters do not use a clustered index but, instead, depend on either a default hashing algorithm supplied by Oracle or a user-supplied algorithm. If the number of data values to be stored in a cluster is known, then a hashed cluster can be faster than an indexed cluster, because no index lookups are required. However, a hash function requires an input of the number of expected values. If the number of values to be stored in the cluster is unknown, use an indexed cluster.

If the total size used to store the values for a cluster key exceeds the size of a data block (**db_block_size**), then chaining and performance degradation will occur. This means that if you cluster several tables, be sure that the number of cluster entries for each cluster key's unique value doesn't exceed database block size. If you plan on using clusters, I suggest using the largest database block size applicable on your system, unless you have some overriding reason not to do so.

Index Storage Options

Oracle8 offers several new index storage options. This section addresses partitioned indexes, reverse key indexes, and bitmap indexes (actually a late version 7 addition), along with the normal b-tree structure indexes.

Partitioned Indexes

Oracle8 offers partitioned indexes to go along with partitioned tables. These indexes can be locked to the tables and partitioned identically (referred to as *local*) or partitioned independently (referred to as *global*). Local partitioning makes more sense unless you have a specific performance reason to use global partitioning on your partitioned indexes.

You can use partitioned indexes against nonpartitioned tables. A standard index can use a maximum of 32 columns, but only 16 can be used in a local partitioned index because of the limit of 16 columns in a partition specification for a table.

Oracle automatically manages local partitioned indexes. Global indexes are the responsibility of the DBA.

A partitioned index can be prefixed or nonprefixed. A prefixed index uses the left portion of the index key for its partitioning logic. A nonprefixed index doesn't use the left-most section of the index for its partitioning logic and thus will not perform as well. Global nonprefixed indexes are not allowed.

An operation that renders one part of a local partitioned index invalid doesn't affect other partitions in the index. An operation that affects a partition of a global index may result in all partitions becoming invalid for use.

Bitmapped Indexes

Bitmapped indexes were introduced in Oracle7.3. They are created as bitmaps of the values in the index rather than as b-trees of the values. This conversion to a bitmap results in a several-fold decrease in storage requirements and a several-fold increase in speed of access times. Bitmapped indexes are suggested for use on low cardinality data, which has a low selectivity (few unique values). Tests have shown that a cardinality as low as 1:100 (key-value-to-stored-value ratio) can significantly benefit from bitmapped indexing over conventional indexes.

Unique And Non-Unique Indexes

Oracle8 also supports the standard unique and non-unique indexes. Such indexes use the b-tree storage model. Generally speaking, uniqueness is an internal table issue and should be addressed at that level. Oracle doesn't recommend using unique indexes if they can be defined at the table level via constraints. If all values in a non-unique index are unique, Oracle8 can use that index to enforce a primary key constraint.

Clustered Indexes

Oracle8 supports clustered indexes, which support table clusters. Table clusters are groups of tables that have one or more columns stored in the same data block or blocks, based on the cluster key specification. A cluster index must be created for non-hashed clusters. You cannot specify a clustered index for a hashed cluster.

Reverse Key Indexes

Oracle8 introduces the reverse key index. In a reverse key index, the bytes of the index block are stored in reverse order, excluding the **ROWID**. You cannot specify a **NOSORT** on a reverse key index. A bitmapped index cannot be reverse keyed.

Reverse key indexes are useful in situations where a sequential key value is used and the insert rate is high. In a standard index, a sequential key (such as a sequence-generated or date-based key) can result in disk hotspots at the leaf nodes. Reversing the index value causes more spread of values and thus reduces disk hotspots and contention. Reverse key indexes can also help reduce index sliding, which is caused by range **DELETE**s and **INSERT**s on indexes.

Reverse key indexes can be built based only on b-tree-style indexes.

Tablespace Options

Later versions of Oracle7 and Oracle8 increased the flexibility and complexity of managing Oracle tablespaces. Gone are the days when a DBA could simply specify a datafile size (or sizes) and a default storage clause and be done with tablespaces. The new options allow auto extension, creating true temporary tablespaces, and making a tablespace nonlogging (no redo generation). All of these are features that users of Oracle asked for, but I wonder if, in some cases, we will regret getting what we think we wanted.

Auto extension of tablespaces sounds good on the surface. In fact, other databases have long had the equivalent through server-managed files. Unless you are careful about how you set the **AUTOEXTEND** features, you could end up with a space-bound database rather quickly. With auto extension, you can set the minimum extent size, a maximum size, or you can set the maximum to unlimited, which I don't recommend.

Temporary tablespaces, as their name implies, allow only temporary segments to be created inside them. This is a good feature to prevent developers from creating "temporary" tables in the temporary tablespace that somehow never get deleted. You can change a tablespace from temporary to permanent and back the other way. Of course, a tablespace that contains permanent objects cannot be made temporary until all permanent objects are removed.

Nonlogging tablespaces are a good idea, except when you forget to reset them and then have to recover. Setting the **NOLOGGING** flag stops the majority of redo operations, except those that change dictionary settings or deal with new extent validation. **NOLOGGING** is overridden by any object-level logging set points.

Control Files

Control files are going to take a lot of people by surprise in Oracle8. In previous versions, control files were fairly static in size and usually the smallest database files.

This is no longer the case. Control files are used for a larger range of logging operations in Oracle8, mostly involving the expanded backup and recovery options available. This means storage for control files will increase by a factor of 10 to 20 times over previous versions. Thus, that little 1MB control file from your Oracle7 database will grow to 10MB, 20MB, or more in Oracle8. If you don't plan for this added space requirement, you could be in for a shock on some systems where space is tight.

LOB Storage

Oracle8 greatly extends the large object storage capability by adding **LOB**-based datatypes, such as **CLOB**, **NCLOB**, **BLOB**, and **BFILE**. These take the place of **LONG RAW**, although it is still available. Of these new datatypes, the most exciting is **BFILE**, coupled with the **DIRECTORY** specification, which allows automatic referencing of external **RAW** files from within Oracle8. Oracle8 also allows storage of **LOB** data in separate tablespaces from the rest of a table's data attributes, making space management easier for databases that use **LOB**s.

LOB Storage Clause

The **LOB** storage clause defines to Oracle8 how the **LOB** data item in a table is stored. The clause has the format shown in Figure 5.1.

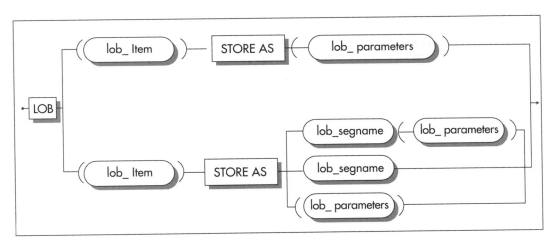

Figure 5.1

*Format of the **LOB** storage clause.*

The clause shown in Figure 5.1 defines a **LOB** data item's storage profile. This clause has a sub-clause, shown in Figure 5.2, that actually defines the key parameters.

The **LOB lob_parameters** clause allows you to specify the tablespace where you should store **LOB**s and the associated storage or as an alternative to specify inline storage. Inline storage is limited to 4K or less in total length. The **CHUNK** clause allows you to specify the number of database blocks to allocate per **LOB CHUNK** stored. **PCTVERSION** specifies how full the **LOB** storage area becomes before older

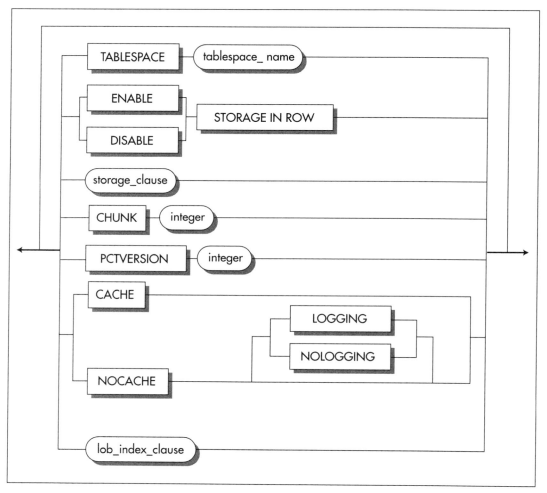

Figure 5.2

*Format of the **LOB lob_parameters** clause.*

versions of **LOB**s are overwritten. The **lob_index_clause** specifies the name of the **LOB** index and can be used if only one **LOB** item is specified. Figure 5.3 shows the **lob_index_clause**.

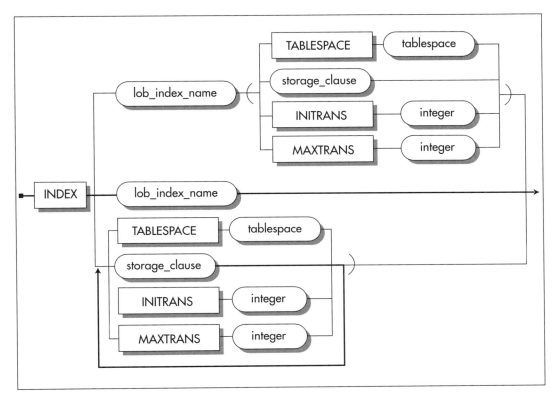

Figure 5.3

*Format of the **LOB lob_index_clause** section.*

Practical Guide To

Oracle Storage Structures

- Creating Relational Tables
- Creating Object Tables
- Creating Partitioned Tables
- Splitting A Partition
- Adding, Modifying, Renaming, Moving, Dropping, And Truncating Partitions
- Using The **EXCHANGE PARTITION** Clause
- Maintaining A Partitioned Table's Indexes
- Creating An Index-Only Table
- Creating Nested Tables
- Creating Clustered Tables
- Creating Partitioned Indexes
- Creating Bitmapped Indexes
- Creating Unique and Non-Unique Indexes
- Creating Reverse Key Indexes
- Using The Tablespace **AUTOEXTEND** Option
- Using Temporary And Permanent Tablespace
- Creating A Table With **LOB** Attributes
- Using **BFILE LOB** Datatypes

Creating Relational Tables

You create Oracle8 relational tables with the **CREATE TABLE** command. You can create a simple table without the use of types:

```
CREATE TABLE employees
(empid                   number,
emp_first_name      varchar2(30),
emp_last_name       varchar2(30),
emp_middle_initial   char(1),
emp_ssn                  char(11))
TABLESPACE appl_data
STORAGE (INITIAL 1m NEXT 1m PCTINCREASE 0 MINEXTENT 1 MAXEXTENT 30)
PCTFREE 20 PCTUSED 80
FREELISTS 10;
```

You can add constraints to a relational table in Oracle8:

```
CREATE TABLE employees
(empid                      number NOT NULL,
CONSTRAINT pk_employees PRIMARY KEY(empid)
USING INDEX TABLESPACE appl_index
STORAGE (INITIAL 1m NEXT 1m PCTINCREASE 0)
PCTFREE 20,
emp_first_name      varchar2(30),
emp_last_name       varchar2(30),
emp_middle_initial   char(1),
emp_ssn                  char(11))
TABLESPACE appl_data
STORAGE (INITIAL 1m NEXT 1m PCTINCREASE 0 MINEXTENT 1 MAXEXTENT 30)
PCTFREE 20 PCTUSED 80
FREELISTS 10;
```

A relational table can also use types in Oracle8:

```
CREATE TYPE emp_name (
first_name varchar2(30),
last_name varchar2(30),
middle_initial char(1));

CREATE TABLE employees
(empid                      number NOT NULL,
CONSTRAINT pk_employees PRIMARY KEY(empid)
USING INDEX TABLESPACE appl_index
STORAGE (INITIAL 1m NEXT 1m PCTINCREASE 0)
PCTFREE 20,
```

```
name                    emp_name,
emp_ssn                 char(11))
TABLESPACE appl_data
STORAGE (INITIAL 1m NEXT 1m PCTINCREASE 0 MINEXTENT 1 MAXEXTENT 30)
PCTFREE 20 PCTUSED 80
FREELISTS 10;
```

A relational table can be made from a nonobject type:

```
CREATE TYPE emp_name (
first_name varchar2(30),
last_name varchar2(30),
middle_initial char(1));

CREATE TYPE employee (
empid number,
name emp_name,
emp_ssn char(11));

CREATE TABLE employees OF employee
TABLESPACE appl_data
STORAGE (INITIAL 1m NEXT 1m PCTINCREASE 0 MINEXTENT 1 MAXEXTENT 30)
PCTFREE 20 PCTUSED 80
FREELISTS 10;
ALTER TABLE employees MODIFY employee.empid NOT NULL;
ALTER TABLE employees ADD CONSTRAINT pk_employees PRIMARY KEY (employee.empid)
USING INDEX TABLESPACE appl_index
STORAGE (INITIAL 1m NEXT 1m PCTINCREASE 0)
PCTFREE 20;
```

As long as the types used in the **CREATE TABLE** command are not object types, a relational table is the result. A relational table can even include **REF** calls to object tables, nested tables, and **VARRAY**s. A relational table cannot be used as the direct receiver of a **REF** call. A relational table—as long as it includes no types, **VARRAY**s, **REF**s, or nested tables—can be used as a partitioned or index-only table.

Creating Object Tables

Oracle8 object tables are created with the **CREATE TABLE** command using an object type as the target for the table creation. You create the object type with the **CREATE TYPE . . . AS OBJECT** command. Object tables differ from relational tables in that they have an integral OID that is guaranteed to be globally unique. The OID is a 128-byte base-64 number (petabyte-range capable).

```
CREATE TYPE emp_name (
first_name varchar2(30),
last_name varchar2(30),
middle_initial char(1));

CREATE TYPE employee AS OBJECT (
empid number,
name emp_name,
emp_ssn char(11));

CREATE TABLE employees OF employee
TABLESPACE appl_data
STORAGE (INITIAL 1m NEXT 1m PCTINCREASE 0 MINEXTENT 1 MAXEXTENT 30)
PCTFREE 20 PCTUSED 80
FREELISTS 10;
```

Creating Partitioned Tables

As the name implies, a partitioned table is split among one or more disk areas. This splitting is done by the database itself. Except during the initial creation, the DBA or developer has no need to be concerned with the mechanical aspects of the partitioning. Partitioning is controlled by a specified range of values for one or more of the columns in a table. With triggers, a DBA or developer can use application-specific logic to do partitioning using a derived column.

The **CREATE TABLE** command is used to create partitioned tables. Any attempt to create a partitioned table based on a type or containing a type will generate an "ORA-14114: partitioned table cannot have column with object, **REF**, nested table, array datatype" error, as shown in Listing 5.1.

Listing 5.1   Example creation of a partitioned table.

```
First, try using attribute assignment to a type:

SQL> CREATE TABLE part_test (part part_t)
  2   storage (INITIAL 1m NEXT 1m pctincrease 0)
  3   PARTITION BY RANGE (part_bin)
  4   (PARTITION before_100 VALUES LESS THAN (100),
  5   PARTITION before_200 VALUES LESS THAN (200),
  6*  PARTITION new_bins VALUES LESS THAN (MAXVALUE))
SQL> /
CREATE TABLE part_test (part part_t)
                          *
ERROR at line 1:
ORA-14114: partitioned table cannot have column with object, REF, nested table,
array datatype
```

NEXT, try direct type usage:

```
SQL> CREATE TABLE part_test OF part_t
  2  storage (INITIAL 1m NEXT 1m pctincrease 0)
  3  PARTITION BY RANGE (part_bin)
  4  (PARTITION before_100 VALUES LESS THAN (100),
  5  PARTITION before_200 VALUES LESS THAN (200),
  6* PARTITION new_bins VALUES LESS THAN (MAXVALUE))
SQL> /
CREATE TABLE part_test OF part_t
*
ERROR at line 1:
ORA-14114: partitioned table cannot have column with object, REF, nested table,
array datatype
```

Finally, do it correctly with no types to be seen:

```
SQL> CREATE TABLE part_test(part_bin NUMBER, part_name VARCHAR2(30),
  2  part_desc VARCHAR2(240), part_NUMBER VARCHAR2(15))
  3  STORAGE (INITIAL 1m NEXT 1m pctincrease 0)
  4  PARTITION BY RANGE (part_bin)
  5  (PARTITION before_100 VALUES LESS THAN (100),
  6  PARTITION before_200 VALUES LESS THAN (200),
  7* PARTITION new_bins VALUES LESS THAN (MAXVALUE))
SQL> /

Table created.

SQL> spool off
```

What if you want to partition by a particular type of object—for example, a type of tool (hammer, wrench, screwdriver, socket, etc.)? How can you accomplish this using partition logic as it currently exists? Use a trigger, as shown in Listing 5.2.

Listing 5.2 Demonstration of trigger to partition by a character value.

```
Creation of test table:
SQL> CREATE TABLE tool_test(tool_bin NUMBER, tool_name VARCHAR2(30),
  2  tool_desc VARCHAR2(240), tool_NUMBER number)
  3  STORAGE (INITIAL 1m NEXT 1m pctincrease 0)
  4  PARTITION BY RANGE (tool_NUMBER)
  5  (PARTITION before_2 VALUES LESS THAN (2),
  6  PARTITION before_3VALUES LESS THAN (3),
  7  PARTITION before_4 VALUES LESS THAN (4),
  7* PARTITION new_tools VALUES LESS THAN (MAXVALUE))
SQL /
```

Creation of the trigger:

```
SQL> create or replace trigger partition_tools
  2   before insert or update of tool_name on tool_test
  3   for each row
  4   declare
  5   tn varchar2(30);
  6   begin
  7   tn := upper(:new.tool_name);
  8   if tn like ('%HAMMER%')
  9   then
 10      :new.tool_number := 1;
 11   elsif tn like ('%SCREW DRIVER%')
 12   then
 13      :new.tool_number := 2;
 14   elsif tn like ('%WRENCH%')
 15   then
 16      :new.tool_number := 3;
 17   else
 18      :new.tool_number := 4;
 19   end if;
 20*  end;
SQL> /

Trigger created.
```

Insertion of test values spread among partitions:

```
SQL> insert into tool_test (tool_bin,tool_name,tool_desc)
  2   values (123,'jack hammer','air driven hammer');

1 row created.

SQL> insert into tool_test (tool_bin,tool_name,tool_desc)
  2* values (231,'roofing hammer','hammer used for roofing')

1 row created.

SQL> insert into tool_test (tool_bin,tool_name,tool_desc)
  2* values (432,'electric screw driver','electric driven screw driver)

1 row created.

SQL> insert into tool_test (tool_bin,tool_name,tool_desc)
  2* values (334,'phillips screw driver','cross head screw driver')

1 row created.
```

```
SQL> insert into tool_test (tool_bin,tool_name,tool_desc)
  2* values (334,'regular screw driver','flat head screw driver')

1 row created.

SQL> insert into tool_test (tool_bin,tool_name,tool_desc)
  2* values (545,'hex screw driver','hex head screw driver')

1 row created.

SQL> insert into tool_test (tool_bin,tool_name,tool_desc)
  2* values (667,'hex wrench','hex head wrench')

1 row created.

SQL> insert into tool_test (tool_bin,tool_name,tool_desc)
  2* values (776,'kucklescribe','writing implement (German)')
SQL> /

1 row created.

SQL> insert into tool_test (tool_bin,tool_name,tool_desc)
  2* values (786,'monkey wrench','plumbing wrench')
SQL> /

1 row created.

Test if values were distributed as planned:

SQL> select count(*) from tool_test partition (before_2)

  COUNT(*)
 --------
        2

SQL> select count(*) from tool_test partition (before_3)

  COUNT(*)
 --------
        4

SQL> select count(*) from tool_test partition (before_4);

  COUNT(*)
 --------
        2
```

```
SQL> select count(*) from tool_test partition (new_tools)

 COUNT(*)
--------
        1
```

Use this technique for as complex a hierarchical relationship as you can code-reduce into a set of integers.

Splitting A Partition

If a comparison of number of values per partition for a specific partitioned table shows that the partitions are not evenly distributed, then it is advisable to split the overloaded partition into two or more smaller partitions. The command to determine the number of entries in a specific partition is:

```
SELECT COUNT(*) FROM table_name PARTITION (partition_name);
```

To determine the distribution within the partition, a **SELECT** similar to this should be used:

```
SELECT COUNT(*),part_value FROM table_name PARTITION (partition_name) GROUP BY
part_value;
```

Once you have determined the value upon which to split the partition, use the **ALTER TABLE...SPLIT PARTITION** command:

```
ALTER TABLE tool_test SPLIT PARTITION new_tools AT (4)
INTO (PARTITION before_4, PARTITION new_tools);
```

Adding, Modifying, Renaming, Moving, Dropping, And Truncating Partitions

You can create individual table partitions in virtually the same way you create a full table. Use the **ALTER TABLE** command with the appropriate **PARTITION** clause to achieve the desired action. Table 5.1 shows the **PARTITION** clauses and their actions.

Table 5.1   The ALTER TABLE command PARTITION clauses.

Clause	Action
ADD PARTITION	Adds a partition to the specified partitioned table
MODIFY PARTITION	Modifies the specified partition's physical attributes
RENAME PARTITION	Renames the specified partition
MOVE PARTITION	Moves the specified partition to a new location
DROP PARTITION	Drops the specified partition
TRUNCATE PARTITION	Truncates the data in the specified partition

Here are example uses of the **PARTITION** clauses:

```
ALTER TABLE tool_test DROP PARTITION before_2;
ALTER TABLE tool_test TRUNCATE PARTITION before_2;
ALTER TABLE tool_test MOVE PARTITION new_tools TABLESPACE appl_data2;
ALTER TABLE tool_test MODIFY PARTITION new_tools STORAGE(MAXEXTENTS 10);
```

 ## Using The **EXCHANGE PARTITION** Clause

Under certain circumstances, such as archival storage of a partition's data, you may have to move a partition's data into a standard table. Or, if a new region is brought into a company, a new partition may have to be brought into an existing table. In both of these scenarios, existing table data is either moved *out* of the table partition in bulk or moved *in* to a table's partition in bulk. Bulk moves of partition data are accomplished via the **ALTER TABLE...EXCHANGE PARTITION** command.

If you have a table called **sales** and you want to move the first-quarter sales (partition **sales_qtr1**) into a normal table (**qtr1_97_sales**) for archival purposes, you would use this command:

```
ALTER TABLE sales EXCHANGE PARTITION sales_qtr1 WITH TABLE qtr1_97_sales;
```

If the target table exists, its data is put into a replacement partition, and the partition's data is moved into the table. If the table doesn't exist, you get an error. If you want to exchange a partition for an empty table, use the example in Listing 5.3 as a guide.

Listing 5.3 Example use of EXCHANGE PARTITION command.

First, show what happens when the table doesn't exist:

```
SQL> alter table tool_test exchange partition before_3 with table tool3;
alter table tool_test exchange partition before_3 with table tool3
                                                                  *
ERROR at line 1:
ORA-00942: table or view does not exist
```

Create blank table with same structure:

```
SQL> create table tool3 as select * from tool_test where 2=3;

Table created.
```

Show table is empty:

```
SQL> select count(*) from tool3;

  COUNT(*)
--------
       0
```

Show partition has values:

```
SQL> select count(*) from tool_test partition (before_3)

  COUNT(*)
--------
       4
```

```
SQL> alter table tool_test exchange partition before_3 with table tool3;

Table altered.
```

Show that values have been exchanged:

```
SQL> select count(*) from tool3;

  COUNT(*)
--------
       4
```

```
SQL> select count(*) from tool_test partition (before_3);

  COUNT(*)
--------
       0
```

Note: This is a DDL, not a DML, action and cannot be rolled back once it is done.

You can also make the **EXCHANGE** clause include indexes by adding **INCLUDING INDEXES** to the clause. The sub-clauses available with the **EXCHANGE** clause are:

- **INCLUDING INDEXES**
- **EXCLUDING INDEXES**
- **WITH VALIDATION**
- **WITHOUT VALIDATION**

Maintaining A Partitioned Table's Indexes

Indexes on a partitioned table can become unusable because of partition splits, drops, truncation, or exchanges. Two clauses allow disabling of a local set of indexes and rebuilding them for a partition. These clauses are shown here:

```
ALTER TABLE table_name MODIFY PARTITION part_name UNUSABLE LOCAL INDEXES;
ALTER TABLE table_name MODIFY PARTITION part_name REBUILD UNUSABLE LOCAL INDEXES;
```

Use the **ALTER INDEX** command to rebuild and maintain global indexes.

Creating An Index-Only Table

An index-only table has a b-tree type structure identical to that of Oracle standard indexes. It contains no **ROWID**s and must have a primary key. An index-only table primary key is used to build the b-tree structure.

```
CREATE TABLE part_lookup
(part_number number not null,
part_name VARCHAR2(30),
CONSTRAINT pk_part_lookup PRIMARY_KEY(part_number))
ORGANIZATION INDEX
STORAGE (INITIAL 1M NEXT 1m PCTINCREASE 0)
PCTFREE 40
TABLESPACE appl_index;
```

Index-only tables should be used where there are few columns and the values are frequently selected but not updated or deleted. The example code creates a part lookup index-only table. The **ORGANIZATION INDEX** clause tells Oracle to make this an index-only table.

You can make an index-only table into a regular table by exporting and dropping the index-only table, creating a blank normal table with the same name and structure, and importing with the **IGNORE=Y** flag into the blank table.

You cannot modify index-only tables. Any attempt to add columns or modify existing columns results in an "ORA-25182: Feature not available yet" error.

Index-only tables cannot have indexes built against them. Because types cannot be specified with constraints, index-only tables cannot be built based on types.

Creating Nested Tables

A nested table is built from a special form of user-defined type (UDT).

```
CREATE OR REPLACE TYPE address_t(
        addrtype              INTEGER      ,
        address1              VARCHAR2(80)  ,
        address2              VARCHAR2(80)  ,
        address3              VARCHAR2(80)  ,
        address4              VARCHAR2(80)  ,
        address5              VARCHAR2(80)  ,
        address6              VARCHAR2(80)  ,
        address7              VARCHAR2(80)  ,
        address8              VARCHAR2(80)  ,
        address9              VARCHAR2(80)  ,
        address10             VARCHAR2(80)  ,
        address11             VARCHAR2(80)  ,
        address12             VARCHAR2(80)  ,
        address13             VARCHAR2(80)  ,
        address14             VARCHAR2(80)  ,
        address15             VARCHAR2(80)  );

rem
rem address_list is a nested table definition
rem

CREATE OR REPLACE TYPE address_list AS TABLE OF address_t;
```

Notice that the basic type is created first and then used to create the special table type. The **TABLE TYPE CREATE** command does not create the physical table; it only allows the type to be used for building a nested table. You can use an object type to create a nested table type. Design-wise, this is useless, because nested tables are automatically related by the **SETID$** column in their defined store tables.

To use a nested table, you must make a store table definition at the time the master table is created.

```
CREATE TABLE clients OF client_t
NESTED TABLE clients_data STORE AS clients_store
NESTED TABLE addresses STORE AS addresses_store
        PCTFREE 10
        PCTUSED 80
        INITRANS 5
        MAXTRANS 255
        TABLESPACE SCOPUS_DATA
        STORAGE (
                INITIAL 20m
                NEXT 10m
                MINEXTENTS 1
                MAXEXTENTS 10
                PCTINCREASE 0
        )
;
```

This shows that to instantiate a nested table, you must define a store table. (Note the store table specifications for **clients_data** and **addresses**. **addresses** is an implementation of the previously defined **address_list** nested table type.) Nested table store tables assume the default storage characteristics of the tablespace where they are stored. The default tablespace for a nested table store table should be small. Use the **ALTER TABLE** command against a store table to set the values you desire. For example, to modify the characteristics of the store table created for the **addresses** nested table, the command would be:

```
ALTER TABLE addresses_store
STORAGE (NEXT 10M PCTINCREASE 0)
PCTFREE 20 PCTUSED 80
FREELISTS 10;
```

Indexes and constraints can also be built against a store table once it is defined.

Creating Clustered Tables

Creating a clustered table in Oracle8 is identical to creating a clustered table in previous versions of Oracle. Clustered tables can be either index or hash clustered. Index clustered tables store together the rows having the same cluster key value. Hash clustered tables store together the rows that have the same calculated hash value.

```
CREATE CLUSTER purchase_order
   (po_number NUMBER(10) )
SIZE 512
STORAGE ( INITIAL 100K NEXT 50K PCTINCREASE 0);

CREATE TABLE po_items
 (po_number NUMBER(10) NOT NULL,
  line_number NUMBER(3) NOT NULL,
  item_number NUMBER(5),
  item_price NUMBER(9,2),
CONSTRAINT pk_po_items PRIMARY KEY (po_number, line_number))
CLUSTER purchase_order (po_number);

CREATE TABLE po_details
(po_number NUMBER(10) PRIMARY KEY,
purchaser_id NUMBER NOT NULL,
credit_rating CHAR(3))
CLUSTER purchase_order (po_number);

CREATE INDEX clidx_purhcase_order ON CLUSTER purchase_order;
```

If you know you are going to have only 5,000 purchase orders as a maximum before archiving the cluster data and truncating the cluster tables, you could use a **HASH** cluster and gain some speed:

```
CREATE CLUSTER purchase_order
(po_number NUMBER(10))
SIZE 512 HASHKEYS 5000
   STORAGE (INITIAL 100k NEXT 100k PCTINCREASE 0);
```

The tables in a hash cluster are created in the same way as in an index cluster. No cluster index is built for a hash cluster. Hash clusters should be used only where the maximum number of entries in the hash cluster is known ahead of time. If desired, you can specify your own **HASH** function by using the **HASH IS (. . .)** clause with the **CREATE CLUSTER** command. The **HASH IS** value must be a SQL statement. The internal hash algorithm returns values from 0 to hashkeys-1. The entered value of hashkeys is rounded up to the nearest prime number. If **HASH IS** is used, then Oracle divides the column value by the calculated value and uses the remainder for the hash value. The **SIZE** value should be a divisor of **db_block_size**.

The clustered table's storage is taken from the storage defined for the cluster itself. Determine the size for the largest table, and set storage values accordingly or set the **MAXEXTENTS** to unlimited.

Clustering of single tables can provide dramatic improvements in query speed on the cluster key value because of the localized storage of key values.

Creating Partitioned Indexes

Oracle8 offers partitioned indexes, as well as partitioned tables. Partitioned indexes can be either local (lock-stepped to the table partitions) or global (DBA- or developer-defined). Local indexes can also be either prefixed or nonprefixed.

Local Prefixed Partitioned Indexes

Local prefixed partitioned indexes use the leftmost portion of the partition key for the table they are defined on.

Notice in Listing 5.4 that the index locations are specified. If this is not done, the indexes will be co-located with the data segments. By using the **LOCAL** option and prefixing the index, you can assure that the indexes will be partitioned identically to the tables and that maintenance on one section of the index won't affect other segments.

Listing 5.4 Example use of local partitioned indexes.

```
CREATE TABLE clients
(client_id NUMBER NOT NULL,
client_name VARCHAR2(20) NOT NULL,
street_address  VARCHAR2(30),
suite_or_po   VARCHAR2(10),
city VARCHAR2930),
state CHAR(2),
zip CHAR(5))
PARTITION BY RANGE (client_id)
(PARTITION client_1 VALUES LESS THAN (10000)
STORAGE( INITIAL 1M NEXT 1M PCTINCREASE 0)
TABLESPACE client_data1,
PARTITION client_2 VALUES LESS THAN (20000)
STORAGE( INITIAL 1M NEXT 1M PCTINCREASE 0)
TABLESPACE client_data2,
PARTITION client_3 VALUES LESS THAN (30000)
STORAGE( INITIAL 1M NEXT 1M PCTINCREASE 0)
TABLESPACE client_data3,
PARTITION client_4 VALUES LESS THAN (MAXVALUE)
STORAGE( INITIAL 1M NEXT 1M PCTINCREASE 0)
TABLESPACE client_data4
  );
```

```
CREATE INDEX pi_clients
ON clients (client_id)
LOCAL
(PARTITION pi_client_1
STORAGE( INITIAL 100k NEXT 100k PCTINCREASE 0)
TABLESPACE client_idx1,
PARTITION PI_client_2
STORAGE( INITIAL 100k NEXT 100k PCTINCREASE 0)
TABLESPACE client_idx2,
PARTITION pi_client_3
STORAGE( INITIAL 100k NEXT 100k PCTINCREASE 0)
TABLESPACE client_idx3,
PARTITION pi_client_4
STORAGE( INITIAL 100k NEXT 100k PCTINCREASE 0)
TABLESPACE client_idx4
 );
```

Global Partitioned Indexes

If you want maximum spread of the data values (for large tables) but want the indexes to be more specific, you should use global indexes. For example, an orders table may be spread by order date into 12 months, but you may want the indexes on the partitioned table to be based on quarters, as shown in Listing 5.5.

Listing 5.5   Example use of global partitioned indexes.

```
CREATE TABLE orders (
order_date      DATE not null ,
ORDER_NUMBER number NOT NULL,
ORDER_TOTAL number(9,2),
SALESPERSON_ID number)
partition by range (ORDER_DATE)
(partition ORDERS_1 values less than ('31-jan-97'),
partition orders_2 values less than ('28-feb-97).
...
partition orders_12 values less than ('31-jan-97'));

create INDEX pi_orders
ON orders(order_date)
GLOBAL
PARTITION BY RANGE(ORDER_DATE)
(PARTITION pi_orders1 VALUES LESS THAN ('30-MAR-97'),
PARTITION pi_orders2 VALUES LESS THAN ('30-JUN-97'),
PARTITION pi_orders3 VALUES LESS THAN ('31-SEP-97'),
PARTITION pi_orders4 VALUES LESS THAN (MAXVALUE));

(For clarity, I just show the bare bones of the command. You should specify storage
and tablespace information. Notice how the last index partition specifies MAXVALUE
for its range. This is a good practice for GLOBAL indexes or errors may result.)
```

Global indexes are prefixed by definition. Nonprefixed global indexes have no benefit, so they should not be allowed.

A nonprefixed local index is good to use for non-unique values and where quick selection is required for column values. However, scanning a nonprefixed index is more expensive.

Global or local indexes can become invalid due to the following operations:

- **ALTER TABLE MOVE PARTITION**
- **ALTER TABLE TRUNCATE PARTITION**
- **ALTER TABLE SPLIT PARTITION**
- **ALTER INDEX SPLIT PARTITION**
- **IMPORT PARTITION** (with bypass index maintenance)
- **SQLLOADER** conventional path (with bypass index maintenance)
- Direct path **SQLLOADER**

If one partition of an index is marked **IU** (unusable), you can still use the other partitions. The partition of the index marked **IU** can be rebuilt without rebuilding the other index partitions. For example, the command

```
ALTER INDEX pi_clients1 REBUILD PARTITION;
```

would rebuild the **pi_clients1** partition of the **pi_clients** partitioned index.

Creating Bitmapped Indexes

Use a bitmapped index for low cardinality data where the use of a normal b-tree index doesn't make sense. A bitmapped index on low cardinality data can improve query speed many times over a b-tree or no index on the same column. Example columns that would be good candidates for a bitmapped index are **gender**, **hair_color**, **eye_color**, **zip_code**, etc.

```
CREATE BITMAP INDEX bm_clients_1
ON clients(zip_code)
STORAGE(INITIAL 1M NEXT 1M PCTINCREASE 0)
TABLESPACE appl_index;
```

Bitmapped indexes can also be partitioned. They take considerably less space (up to 100 times) than an equivalent regular b-tree index. A bitmapped index equates the **ROWID** to a bit identifier for the value of the key column. That's all that is stored in the index. Bitmapped indexes are appropriate for complex ad hoc queries that contain lengthy **WHERE** clauses involving low cardinality columns. Oracle8 allows multiple-column bitmapped indexes.

Under Oracle8, bitmapped indexes should be used on foreign key indexes associated with star schemas in data warehouse applications. Don't use bitmaps in high-update applications. Because of their compressed format, a single block could contain many values, and the minimal locking for a bitmapped index is at the block level.

For obvious reasons, bitmapped indexes cannot be declared unique. Large block sizes help bitmapped-index efficiency. All columns that are **NOT NULL** should be declared as such if they are used in a bitmapped index. Fixed-length datatypes make better bitmapped indexes than variable-length datatypes (i.e., use **CHAR** if possible). Bitmapped indexes are not used with the rule-based optimizer, nor can they be used to enforce referential integrity.

For bitmapped-index creation, three initialization parameters have an impact:

- **COMPATIBLE**—Must be explicitly set to 7.3.2 or higher.

- **CREATE_BITMAP_AREA_SIZE**—Defaults to 8MB. Low cardinality requires less space, and high cardinality may require more.

- **BITMAP_MERGE_AREA_SIZE**—Defaults to 1MB. A larger value will improve performance for large bitmapped-index creations.

 ## Creating Unique And Non-Unique Indexes

Unique and non-unique indexes are nothing new in Oracle. They are created using the **CREATE UNIQUE INDEX** and **CREATE INDEX** commands:

```
CREATE INDEX lu_clients ON clients(client_name)
STORAGE (INITIAL 1M NEXT 1M PCTINCREASE 0)
TABLESPACE appl_index;

CREATE UNIQUE INDEX pk_clients ON clients(clients_id)
STORAGE (INITIAL 1M NEXT 1M PCTINCREASE 0)
PCTFREE 20
TABLESPACE appl_index;
```

PCTUSED cannot be specified when you use the **CREATE INDEX** command. The initialization parameters that most affect index creation are those that deal with the sort area. An index can contain a maximum of 32 columns.

Creating Reverse Key Indexes

Oracle8 reverse key indexes provide for situations where the information being indexed is extremely linear, resulting in skewing of the b-tree and generation of hot-spots in the storage structure. Examples would be a large insert based on a sequence primary key value or where a date is used for a key value.

The inversion of the index bytes (with the exception of the **ROWID**s) results in a more random distribution in these linear insert situations:

```
CREATE UNIQUE INDEX pk_clients ON clients(client_id)
REVERSE
STORAGE (INITIAL 1M NEXT 1M PCTINCREASE 0)
TALESPACE appl_index;
```

Reverse indexes can be used only on b-tree type indexes. They can be used wherever b-tree indexes are used.

Using The Tablespace **AUTOEXTEND** Option

In most other database systems, file handling is passed off to the operating system. This passing of the responsibility for file management makes other database systems easier to manage, up to a point. In Oracle, the DBA has always had ultimate control over datafiles. Datafile size, placement, and other file-management concerns are under the sole purview of the DBA. In past releases (prior to 7.2), this meant DBAs had to monitor tablespace usage closely, because any required addition to a tablespace was manually accomplished through the addition of multiple physical datafiles to the tablespace. The **AUTOEXTEND** option has removed this requirement:

```
CREATE TABLESPACE appl_data
DATAFILE '/oracle01/ORTEST1/data/appl_data01.dbf' SIZE 200M AUTOEXTEND ON
NEXT 10M MAXSIZE 300M
DEFAULT STORAGE (INITIAL 1M NEXT 1M PCTINCREASE 1 MINEXTENTS 1 MAXEXTENTS 20)
ONLINE;
```

This code creates the tablespace **appl_data** with a single datafile **appl_data01.dbf** that has an initial size of 200MB. The datafile can automatically extend in 10MB segments to a maximum size of 300MB.

Also, notice the setting for **PCTINCREASE**. A setting of 0 will result in no automatic coalescence of free space. Setting **PCTINCREASE** to 1 ensures that the tablespace will be automatically coalesced as required, without incurring excessive penalties if someone creates a table without specifying a storage clause.

Problems could occur if you use the **AUTOEXTEND** feature for tablespaces and specify **MAXSIZE UNLIMITED**. This tells the system that you don't care how much the tablespace datafile extends, so it could possibly eat an entire disk or array if, for example, you had a runaway query generating sorts.

Using Temporary And Permanent Tablespace

In Oracle versions prior to 8, all tablespaces were permanent. A permanent tablespace contains persistent objects (i.e., tables, indexes, and clusters). A temporary tablespace can contain only temporary segments (sort, index, and table-build segments).

The following code creates a temporary tablespace called **temp**. It can be used only for temporary type segments. Any attempt to use **temp** for a permanent segment will result in an error.

```
CREATE TABLESPACE temp
DATAFILE '/oracle03/ORTEST1/data/temp01.dbf' SIZE 200M
DEFAULT STORAGE (INITIAL 3M NEXT 3M PCTINCREASE 0)
TEMPORARY
ONLINE;
```

To create a permanent tablespace called **users**, you would use this code:

```
CREATE TABLESPACE users
DATAFILE '/oracle04/ORTEST1/users01.dbf' SIZE 10M
DEFAULT STORAGE (INITIAL 100K NEXT 100K PCTINCREASE 1)
PERMANENT
ONLINE;
```

You actually don't have to specify the **PERMANENT** keyword, as this is the default for tablespace creation. A permanent tablespace can contain permanent objects, such as tables, indexes, or clusters, as well as temporary segments. You can change a permanent tablespace to a temporary one, as long as it contains no permanent objects. You can change a temporary tablespace to a permanent one at any time. This code demonstrates the conversion of a tablespace from temporary to permanent and from permanent to temporary:

```
ALTER TABLESPACE temp PERMANENT;

ALTER TABLESPACE users TEMPORARY;
```

Creating A Table With **LOB** Attributes

Large objects (**LOB**s) have special problems that must be addressed when they are to be stored and used in an Oracle database. In releases previous to Oracle8, you had two choices for storage of binary large objects (**BLOB**s):

- Store them internal to the database as a **LONG RAW**, which could be up to 2GB in length.

- Store a pointer to the **BLOB** location, and use the Oracle Call Interface (OCI) or 3GL with embedded SQL and PL/SQL to access the objects. A **LONG RAW** cannot be randomly accessed—it is an all-or-nothing proposition.

In Oracle8, the concept of **LOB** has been amplified with several new datatypes: **BLOB**, **CLOB**, **NCLOB**, and **BFILE**. With the exception of **BFILE**, these new **LOB** datatypes can be stored either inline with the rest of the table data (if they are less than 4K-1 bytes in size) or in a separate **LOB** storage tablespace area. The **LOB** datatypes (other than **BFILE**) support random access of data within the **LOB** and data conversions via the **DBMS_LOB** package against their contents.

You can use the **LOB** storage area with various **CHUNK** sizes, with a **CHUNK** being a multiple of the database block size up to a maximum **CHUNK*DB_BLOCK_SIZE** of 32K. This allows for optimal storage of **LOB** type data. For example, if you are storing video that is blocked at 4K and you have a database block size of 2K, you can specify the **LOB** storage **CHUNK** at 2K to give 4K chunks of **LOB** storage to the specified video. A **LOB** datatype cannot exceed 4GB in size. If you are creating a database whose primary purpose is to store **LOB** objects (such as a video or picture library), set **DB_BLOCK_SIZE** to a divisor of or equal to the expected **LOB** blocking size to allow for optimal storage.

A **BFILE** is a pointer to an external **LOB** file. It is also limited to a maximum of 4GB or to the operating system's file size limit, whichever is smaller. A **BFILE** is a read-only file and is not maintained by Oracle. It can be randomly accessed, but any sequential access must be programmed by the developer, as it is not supported by Oracle.

The following code defines the storage for the **LOB** data attribute **picture_lob**. It assumes a blocking size of 8K and a **db_block_size** of 2K, setting the CHUNK size to 4K, so that the picture **BLOB**s are stored at their blocking size. In addition, the **LOB**s are indexed for rapid retrieval:

```
CREATE TYPE name_t (
first_name    VARCHAR2(30),
last_name     VARCHAR2(30),
middle_initial    CHAR(3));
CREATE TYPE picture_data_t (
pic_title    VARCHAR2(30),
pic_desc VARCHAR2(80),
pic_date   DATE,
pic_owner   name_t);
CREATE TABLE   pictures (
picture_data     picture_data_type,
picture_lob        BLOB)
LOB  (picture_lob) STORE AS
                          (TABLESPACE pic_lob_ts
                            STORAGE  (INITIAL 10k NEXT 10k)
                            CHUNK 4
                             NOCACHE LOGGING
                             INDEX (TABLESPACE pic_lob_index_ts
                                      STORAGE (INITIAL 256 NEXT 256)));
```

Using **BFILE LOB** Datatypes

The **BFILE** datatype allows access to the externally stored **LOB**. The **BFILE** is actually a two-part type consisting of a directory alias defined using the **CREATE DIRECTORY** command, and the name of the **LOB** file located in the directory. The Oracle-provided **DBMS_LOB** package provides access to **LOB**s and the capability to manipulate them. **DBMS_LOB** is required if you use PL/SQL against the **BFILE** datatype. The only other way to access **BFILE**s is from the Oracle call interface. The procedure **BFILENAME** populates the **BFILE** datatype. Listing 5.6 shows an example of the use of the **LOB** datatypes **BFILE** and **BLOB**, and several of the Oracle supplied **LOB** handling routines.

Listing 5.6   Example use of LOB datatypes.

```
SQL> CREATE DIRECTORY gif_directory AS 'E:\Oracle3\Ortest1\bfiles';
(Note: In 8.0.2 this failed to populate the DIR$ table OS_DIR column. A direct
insert worked, however.)
```

```
SQL> CREATE TYPE bfile_t (
 2:   bfile_id        NUMBER,
 3:   bfile_desc    VARCHAR2(30),
 4:   BFILE_LOC       BFILE);
SQL> CREATE TABLE graphics_table OF bfile_t
 2: STORAGE (INITIAL 10M NEXT 10M PCTINCREASE 0);
SQL> INSERT INTO graphics_table VALUES (
 2: bfile_t(1, 'April book of days woodcut', bfilename(gif_directory,'APRIL.GIF')));
...
SQL> INSERT INTO GRAPHICS_TABLE VALUES (
 2: bfile_t(12,'March book of days woodcut',bfilename(gif_directory, 'MARCH.GIF')));

SQL> SET SERVEROUTPUT ON

SQL> DECLARE
 2:   id          NUMBER;
 3:   image1      BLOB;
 4:   locator     BFILE;
 5:   bfile_len   NUMBER;
 6:   bf_desc     VARCHAR2(30);
 7:   bf_name     VARCHAR2(30);
 8:   bf_dir      VARCHAR2(30);
 9:  CURSOR get_id IS
10:     SELECT bfile_id,bfile_desc FROM graphics_table;
11: BEGIN
12:    open get_id;
13: LOOP
14:    FETCH get_id INTO id, bf_desc;
15: EXIT WHEN get_id%notfound;
16:    SELECT bfile_loc INTO locator FROM graphics_table WHERE bfile_id=id;
17:    dbms_lob.filegetname(locator,bf_dir,bf_name);
18:    dbms_lob.fileopen(locator,dbms_lob.file_readonly);
19:    bfile_len:=dbms_lob.getlength(locator);
20:    dbms_output.put_line(bf_desc||' Length: '||to_char(bfile_len)||
21:    ' Name: '||bf_name||' Dir: '||bf_dir);
22:    dbms_lob.fileclose(locator);
23: END LOOP;
24: END;
25: /

April book of days woodcut Length: 140725 Name: APRIL.GIF Dir: GIF_DIRECTORY
May book of days woodcut Length: 146689 Name: MAY.GIF Dir: GIF_DIRECTORY
June book of days woodcut Length: 147605 Name: JUNE.GIF Dir: GIF_DIRECTORY
July book of days woodcut Length: 155666 Name: JULY.GIF Dir: GIF_DIRECTORY
August book of days woodcut Length: 153032 Name: AUGUST.GIF Dir: GIF_DIRECTORY
September book of days woodcut Length: 150092 Name: SEPTEMBE.GIF Dir: GIF_DIRECTORY
October book of days woodcut Length: 150243 Name: OCTOBER.GIF Dir: GIF_DIRECTORY
```

```
November book of days woodcut Length: 136762 Name: NOVEMBER.GIF Dir: GIF_DIRECTORY
December book of days woodcut Length: 134564 Name: DECEMBER.GIF Dir: GIF_DIRECTORY
January book of days woodcut Length: 158974 Name: JANUARY.GIF Dir: GIF_DIRECTORY
February book of days woodcut Length: 150416 Name: FEBRUARY.GIF Dir: GIF_DIRECTORY
March book of days woodcut Length: 81408 Name: MARCH.GIF Dir: GIF_DIRECTORY

PL/SQL procedure successfully completed
```

The procedure I wanted to test, **DBMS_LOB.LOADFROMFILE**, won't be available until version 8.0.3, but it allows you to copy **BFILE LOB** values from the external directory location into an internal **LOB** value. This will make loading **LOB**s into the database much easier than using 3GL or OCI calls. In the Chapter 6 Practical Guide, I demonstrate the use of **DBMS_LOB.LOADFROMFILE**.

Other **DBMS_LOB** package routines are:

- **COMPARE**—Compares two **LOB** values.

- **INSTR**—Determines the position of the specified string in the **LOB**.

- **SUBSTR**—Returns part of the **LOB** starting at the specified substring.

- **APPEND**—Adds one internal **LOB** to the end of another internal **LOB**.

- **COPY**—Copies an internal **LOB** into another internal **LOB**.

- **ERASE**—Erases an internal **LOB**.

- **FILECLOSE**—Closes an external **BFILE**.

- **FILECLOSEALL**—Closes all external **BFILE**s.

- **FILEEXISTS**—Verifies that a specified **BFILE** exists.

- **FILEGETNAME**—Gets the file name and directory alias for a specified locator value.

- **FILEISOPEN**—Verifies a **BFILE** is open.

- **FILEOPEN**—Opens a **BFILE** for reading.

- **GETLENGTH**—Gets the length of a **BFILE**.

- **LOADFROMFILE**—Loads an external **BFILE** into an internal **LOB**.

- **READ**—Reads a **LOB** into a buffer.

- **TRIM**—Trims an internal **LOB**.

- **WRITE**—Writes a buffer into an internal **LOB**.

Listing 5.7 shows an example procedure for copying external **BFILE**s into an internal table. This code reads the basic information from **graphics_table**; gets the **BFILE** locator; and, using the **DBMS_LOB** package, opens, gets the length, and copies the external **BFILE** into an internal **BLOB**. The internal **BLOB** is then loaded into the **internal_graphics** table, and the **DBMS_LOB** package is used to close the **BFILE**.

Listing 5.7   Example procedure for copying external BFILEs into internal BLOBs.

```
CREATE TABLE  internal_graphics (
graphic_id                NUMBER,
graphic_description  VARCHAR2(30),
graphic_lob               BLOB)
LOB  (graphic_lob) STORE AS
                               (TABLESPACE grph_lob_ts
                                 STORAGE   (INITIAL 10k NEXT 10k)
                                 CHUNK 4
                                  NOCACHE LOGGING
                                  INDEX (TABLESPACE grph_lob_index_ts
                                               STORAGE (INITIAL 256 NEXT 256)));


CREATE OR REPLACE PROCEDURE load_graphics AS
  id                NUMBER;
  image1        BLOB;
  locator        BFILE;
  bfile_len     NUMBER;
  bf_desc      VARCHAR2(30);
  bf_name      VARCHAR2(30);
  bf_dir           VARCHAR2(30);
CURSOR get_id IS
    SELECT bfile_id,bfile_desc FROM graphics_table;
BEGIN
  open get_id;
LOOP
  FETCH get_id INTO id, bf_desc;
  EXIT WHEN get_id%notfound;
  SELECT bfile_loc INTO locator FROM graphics_table WHERE bfile_id=id;
  dbms_lob.filegetname(locator,bf_dir,bf_name);
  dbms_lob.fileopen(locator,dbms_lob.file_readonly);
  bfile_len:=dbms_lob.getlength(locator);
  insert into temp_blob values(empty_blob());
  select temp_blob into image1 from temp_blob;
```

```
   dbms_log.loadfromfile(image1, locator, bfile_len);
   insert into internal_graphics values (id,bf_desc,image1);
   dbms_output.put_line(bf_desc||' Length: '||to_char(bfile_len)||
   ' Name: '||bf_name||' Dir: '||bf_dir);
   dbms_lob.fileclose(locator);
delete temp_blob;
END LOOP;
END load_graphics;
/
```

Oracle has supplied some great new tools for use by Oracle developers. The new datatypes and the expanded **LOB** datatype coverage will make creating object-oriented systems and systems that need to handle complex video, picture, or sound clip type data much easier.

Chapter 6

Using The New Multimedia Datatypes

Oracle8 offers several new datatypes that make building and maintaining multimedia databases much easier than with previous releases. This chapter looks at the use of these new datatypes, their limits, and their structure.

Notes…

Chapter

6

Internal **LOB** Multimedia Datatypes

Oracle has two basic **LOB** datatypes:

- *Internal datatypes* are **BLOB** (binary large object), **CLOB** (character [single-byte] large object), and **NCLOB** (national character [multibyte] large object).

- *External datatypes* are actually pointer constructs to external file locations—a locator, or **BFILE**.

Internal **LOB** datatypes can be stored either inline (up to a maximum of 4,000 bytes) or in an external **LOB** storage area (up to 4GB or the maximum datafile size on your platform) that is specified by a **LOB** storage declaration.

Differences Between **LOB** And **LONG RAW**

The following list explains **LOB** operations that can't be done with **LONG RAW**:

- **LOB**s can be attributes of user-defined datatypes (objects).

- The **LOB** locator is stored in the table column, either with or without the actual **LOB** value. **BLOB**, **NCLOB**, and **CLOB** values can be stored in separate tablespaces, and **BFILE** data is stored in an external file on the server.

- When you access a **LOB** column, the locator is returned.

- A **LOB** can be up to 4GB. **BFILE** maximum size is operating-system dependent but cannot exceed 4GB.

- **LOB**s permit efficient, random, piecewise access to and manipulation of data.

- You can define one or more **LOB** datatype columns in a table.

- With the exception of **NCLOB**, you can define one or more **LOB** attributes in an object.

- You can declare **LOB** bind variables.

- You can select **LOB** columns and **LOB** attributes.

- You can insert a new row or update an existing row that contains one or more **LOB** columns and/or an object with one or more **LOB** attributes. (You can set the internal **LOB** value to **NULL**, leave it empty, or replace the entire **LOB** with data. You can set the **BFILE** to **NULL** or to point to a different file.)

- You can update a **LOB** row/column intersection or **LOB** attribute with another **LOB** row/column intersection or **LOB** attribute.

- You can delete a row containing a **LOB** column or **LOB** attribute and thereby delete the **LOB** value. Note that for **BFILE**s, the actual operating-system file is not deleted.

BLOB Datatypes

BLOBs store raw data. While they are similar to **LONG RAW**, they have a greater capacity (4GB versus 2GB) and greater flexibility. You can have multiple **BLOB**s per table or type. **BLOB**s participate in transactions and can be parsed, appended, deleted, or added via PL/SQL and SQL, whereas **LONG RAW** is limited to one per table, can't be used in types, and can't participate in standard transactions. Before they can be used, **BLOB**s must be initialized using the **EMPTY_BLOB()** function in either an **INSERT** or **UPDATE** command.

CLOB Datatypes

CLOBs store single-byte character data. They can be defined in types and tables and are limited to 4GB in length. **CLOB**s participate fully in transactions and can be accessed piecewise. Before they can be used, **CLOB**s must be initialized using the **EMPTY_CLOB**() function in either an **INSERT** or **UPDATE** command.

NCLOB Datatypes

NCLOBs store multibyte character data. Each value stored in an **NCLOB** must have the same number of bytes per character. Varying-byte characters are not supported through **NCLOB**s. **NCLOB**s are a maximum of 4GB or the size of the maximum file size on your system. The number of characters an **NCLOB** can store depends on the bytes per character for the character set used. **NCLOB**s can't be used in type definitions, but they can be used in table definitions. You can access **NCLOB**s via the PL/SQL interface.

External LOB Datatypes

External datatypes can be of any format: text, graphic, GIF, TIFF, MPEG, MPEG2, JPEG, etc. When read into the database, they have to be moved into a compatible format (**BLOB**, **CLOB**, or **NCLOB**).

The **BFILE** datatype acts as a pointer or locator for the actual external datafiles. It is a two-part locator—the first part is the file name, and the second part is the internal alias for the full path directory where the files reside. The directory alias is defined with the **CREATE DIRECTORY** command:

```
CREATE OR REPLACE DIRECTORY gif_dir AS '/usr/graphics/gif';
```

Once a directory alias is established, you are granted access through an object grant on the directory alias via the **GRANT** command:

```
GRANT READ ON DIRECTORY gif_dir TO system;
```

BFILEs can be up to 4GB in length or up to your system's maximum file size, whichever is smaller. **BFILE**s are piecewise read only. To perform any manipulations of **BFILE** data, the **BFILE** locator must open the **BFILE** physical file, and the **DBMS_LOB** package must read the contents into an internal **LOB**. The Server Image Cartridge (addressed later in this chapter), if installed, provides a way to write **LOB**s back out to physical files.

You should call the **BFILENAME**() function as part of a SQL **INSERT** to initialize a **BFILE** column or attribute for a particular row. This associates it with a physical file in the server's file system.

The **DIRECTORY** object, represented by the **directory_alias** parameter to the **BFILENAME()** function, must already be defined using SQL DDL before this function is called in a SQL DML statement or a PL/SQL program. **BFILENAME()**, however, does not validate privileges on this **DIRECTORY** object, nor does it check if the physical directory that the **DIRECTORY** object represents actually exists. These checks are performed only during file access using the **BFILE** locator initialized by the **BFILENAME()** function.

You can use **BFILENAME()** as part of a SQL **INSERT** and **UPDATE** statement to initialize a **BFILE** column. You can also use it to initialize a **BFILE** locator variable in a PL/SQL program, and then use that locator for file operations. If the corresponding directory alias and/or file name does not exist, however, then PL/SQL **DBMS_LOB** routines that use this variable will generate errors.

The **DBMS_LOB** Package

Oracle8 provides the **DBMS_LOB** package, which is used to access and manipulate **LOB** values in both internal and external storage locations.

Routines That Can Modify **BLOB**, **CLOB**, And **NCLOB** Values

The **DBMS_LOB** package contains the following procedures, which are used to modify **LOB** datatypes:

- **APPEND()**—Appends the contents of the source **LOB** to the destination **LOB**.

- **COPY()**—Copies all or part of the source **LOB** to the destination **LOB**.

- **ERASE()**—Erases all or part of a **LOB**.

- **LOADFROMFILE()**—Loads **BFILE** data into an internal **LOB** (8.0.3 and higher).

- **TRIM()**—Trims the **LOB** value to the specified shorter length.

- **WRITE()**—Writes data to the **LOB** from a specified offset.

Routines That Read Or Examine **LOB** Values

In addition to routines used to modify **LOB** values, routines that provide data about **LOB**s are also provided by the **DBMS_LOB** package. These include:

- **GETLENGTH()**—Gets the length of the **LOB** value.

- **INSTR()**—Returns the matching position of the *n*th occurrence of the pattern in the **LOB**.

- **READ()**—Reads data from the **LOB** starting at the specified offset.

- **SUBSTR()**—Returns part of the **LOB** value starting at the specified offset.

Read-Only Routines Specific To **BFILE**s

BFILEs are special **LOB** datatypes because they are externally stored to the rest of the database datafiles. **BFILE**s require special routines. They include:

- **FILECLOSE()**—Closes the file.

- **FILECLOSEALL()**—Closes all previously opened files.

- **FILEEXISTS()**—Checks if the file exists on the server.

- **FILEGETNAME()**—Gets the directory alias and file name.

- **FILEISOPEN()**—Checks if the file was opened using the input **BFILE** locators.

- **FILEOPEN()**—Opens a file.

Datatypes

Parameters for the **DBMS_LOB** routines use the following datatypes:

- **BLOB**—For a source or destination binary **LOB**.

- **RAW**—For a source or destination **RAW** buffer (used with **BLOB**).

- **CLOB**—For a source or destination character **LOB** (including **NCLOB**).

- **VARCHAR2**—For a source or destination character buffer (used with **CLOB** and **NCLOB**).

- **INTEGER**—To specify the size of a buffer or **LOB**, the offset into a **LOB**, or the amount to access.

Defining **LOB** Storage

If you have not defined **LOB** storage and **LOB** attribute size exceeds 4,000 characters, the attributes that overflow will automatically be placed in the table owners default tablespace. If **LOB** storage is allowed to go to a default storage location, you will not get optimal use of resources. This will cause contention for disk resources, which will reduce your system performance.

LOB storage is defined by the **CREATE** or **ALTER TABLE** commands. The **LOB** storage clause, shown in Figure 6.1, defines the **LOB** storage profile.

The **LOB** storage clause uses a **LOB** parameters section to specify the **LOB** tablespace, storage in row, **CHUNK** and **PCTVERSION** settings, as well as **CACHE** status and, if **NOCACHE** is specified, whether the **LOB** storage should be **LOGGING** or **NOLOGGING** as well as the specification for the **LOB** index. The **LOB** parameters section of the **LOB** storage clause is shown in Figure 6.2.

The **LOB** index is specified through the **LOB** index clause. You can name or let the system name the index and then specify the normal index storage variables. Figure 6.3 shows the **LOB** index clause.

Whether the datatype is **BLOB**, **CLOB**, or **NCLOB**, the storage clause format is identical. **LOB** storage specifications can be applied to **BFILE** datatypes, but doing so doesn't make sense. If you do not specify the **segname** parameter, the Oracle system will give the segment some wonderful name, such as SYS_LOB0000001562C0035$. I suggest you name the segments.

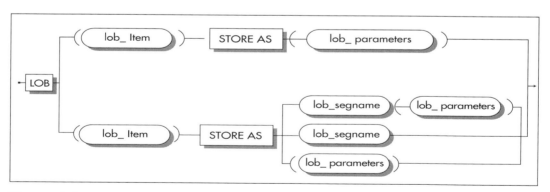

Figure 6.1

LOB storage clause.

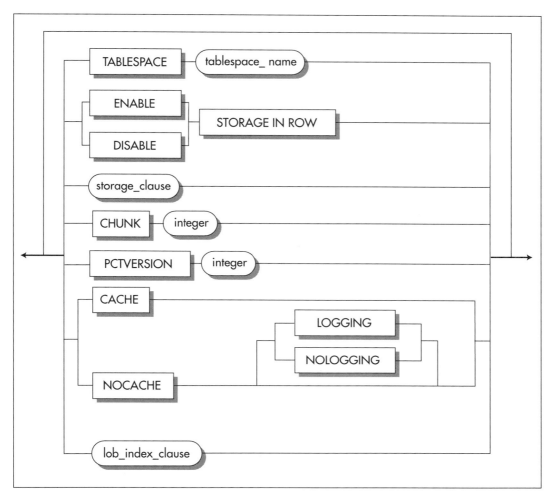

Figure 6.2

LOB parameters section of the *LOB* storage clause.

The Server Image Cartridge And **LOB**s

The Oracle8 Server Image Cartridge (once it is functional) will provide the means to intimately manipulate **LOB** values, including conversion between image formats, cropping, and other image functions. The cartridge consists of two **TYPE** specifications—ORDIMGB and ORDIMGF—and their associated methods.

ORDIMGB is used for **BLOB** work, and ORDIMGF is used for **BFILE** work. Each image file, if it is in one of the supported formats, contains information about itself.

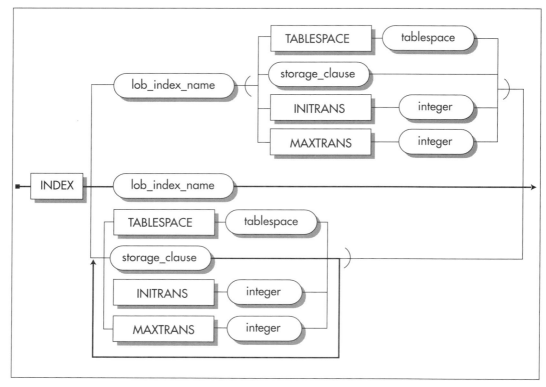

Figure 6.3

LOB index clause.

This information concerns size, compression, and other image-pertinent data.

Each of the object **TYPE** specifications contains the attributes specified in Table 6.1.

The **TYPE** definitions also contain the **METHOD** definitions, as shown in Table 6.2.

The **COPYCONTENT** (dest **IN OUT BLOB**) method copies an image without changing it. The **SETPROPERTIES** method reads the internal properties of the image and loads them into the **TYPE** attributes. The **PROCESS** (command **IN VARCHAR2**) method allows processing of the image via command entry when the method is called. Table 6.3 shows the commands.

Usually, the ORDSYS user owns the image types if the installation is performed as outlined in the installation guide. By using the provided UDTs—ORDSYS, ORDIMGB, and ORDIMGF—and their contained methods, you greatly enhance the versatility of Oracle as far as image use.

Table 6.1 ORDIMGB and ORDIMGF TYPE attribute definitions.

Attribute	Datatype	Definition
CONTENT	BLOB	The **BLOB** value
HEIGHT	INTEGER	The image height in pixels
WIDTH	INTEGER	The image width in pixels
CONTENTLENGTH	INTEGER	Size of on-disk image
FILEFORMAT	VARCHAR2(64)	TIFF, JFIF, PCXF, PICT, RASF, CALS, BMPF, TGAF, JFIF
CONTENTFORMAT	VARCHAR2(64)	MONOCHROME, 4BITGRAYSCALE, 8BITGRAYSCALE, 1BITLUT, 2BITLUT, 4BITLUT, 8BITLUT, 16BITRGB, 24BITRGB, 32BITRGB, 24BITPLANER
COMPRESSIONFORMAT	VARCHAR2(64)	JPEG, SUNRLE, BMPRLE, TARGARLE, LZW, LZWHDIFF, FAX3, FAX4, HUFFMAN3, Packbits, GIFLZW.

Table 6.2 TYPE methods from image cartridge.

Method Name	Method Purpose
COPYCONTENT	Copies **BLOB** content.
SETPROPERTIES	Reads properties from **BLOB** file, and writes them into the **TYPE** attributes.
PROCESS	Performs various processing commands on the **BLOB** content (ORDIMGB only).
PROCESSCOPY	Performs a process, and copies the results to a second **BLOB**.

Table 6.3 Command inputs to the PROCESS method.

Command	Usage	Values
fileFormat	Change file format of image	GIFF, TIFF, PCXF, PICT, RASF,CALS, BMPF, TGAF, JFIF
contentFormat	Image/pixel/data format	MONOCHROME, RAW, 4BITGRAYSCALE, 4BITGRAYSCALE, 8BITGRAYSCALE, 8BITGRAYSCALE, 1BITLUT, 2BITLUT, 4BITLUT, 8BITLUT, 16BITRGB, 24BITRGB, 32BITRGB, 24BITPLANER
Scale	Scale factor (such as .5 or 2)	Positive FLOAT
xscale	X-axis scale factor	Positive FLOAT
yscale	Y-axis scale factor	Positive FLOAT
CompressionQuality	Compression quality HIGHCOMP	MAXCOMPRATIO, MAXINTEGRIT, LOWCOMP, MEDCOMP,
CompressionFormat	Compression type	JPEG, SUNRLE, BMPRLE, TARGARLE, LZW, LZWHDIFF, FAX3, FAX4, HUFFMAN3, Packbits, GIFLZW
byteOrder	Endian format	Intel, Motorola
bitOrder	Bits number 1-to-N or N-to-1	lsb, msb
bmpOrder	Bitmap order	NORMAL, INVERSE_DIB
bmpFormat	Bitmap format	WINDOWS, OS2
cut	Window to cut or crop	(Integer integer (origin.x origin.y width integer integer) limit < height) 65535

Practical Guide To

LOB Usage

- Creating **BLOB** And **CLOB** Datatypes

- Using **BLOB** And **CLOB** Datatypes

- Manipulating Internal **LOB** Datatypes

- Comparing Two **LOB**s

- Reading, Writing, And Appending **LOB** Values

- Searching **LOB**s

- Erasing **LOB** Values

- Confirming **LOB** Erasure Using **COMPARE**

- Using The **TRIM_LOB** Procedure

- Using The Server Image Cartridge

- Adding An Image Type To A Table

- Copying An Image Into An Image Type

- Setting An Image's Properties

- Using The **PROCESS** And **PROCESSCOPY** Methods On Image Types

Creating **BLOB** And **CLOB** Datatypes

BLOB and **CLOB** datatypes are created by the **CREATE** or **ALTER TABLE** or the **CREATE** or **ALTER TYPE** commands. In fact, you create them the same way as other nonsized datatypes, such as **DATE** and **LONG**, except for the **LOB** storage clause. You don't need the **LOB** storage clause if the maximum size of the **BLOB** doesn't exceed 4,000 bytes. You can store up to 4,000 bytes inline with the other data in the tablespace. If the length of the **BLOB** exceeds 4,000 bytes, it must be stored in either system-default storage (the same as the default for the table it resides in) or in an explicitly defined **LOB** storage area.

*I suggest that you always specify the **LOB** storage clause. If you force the system to do a default storage each time a **BLOB** or **CLOB** exceeds 4,000 bytes, you could cause datafile fragmentation and performance problems. The **LOB** storage clause gives the control to you instead of to the system.*

Listing 6.1 is an example of a table created using a **BLOB** datatype. It could just as easily have been a **CLOB**.

Listing 6.1   Example of the LOB storage clause and BLOB use in tables.

```
    CREATE TABLE internal_graphics (
     graphic_id number,
     graphic_desc varchar2(30),
     graphic_blob blob,
     graphic_type VARCHAR2(4))
  LOB (graphic_blob) store as glob_store (
  tablespace raw_data
  STORAGE (initial 100k next 100k pctincrease 0)
  CHUNK 4
  pctversion 10
  INDEX glob_index (
  TABLESPACE raw_index))
  TABLESPACE appl_data
  STORAGE (INITIAL 1M NEXT 1M PCTINCREASE 0)
 /
```

BLOBs and **CLOB**s are identical in creation and use. Their major difference is that **BLOB**s are used for binary data (much like **LONG RAW**), while **CLOB**s are used for single-byte character storage (such as **VARCHAR2**). The **TYPE** creation example in Listing 6.2 shows how to specify a **CLOB** for a **TYPE**.

Listing 6.2   Example use of CLOBs in a TYPE specification.

```
SQL> CREATE OR REPLACE TYPE clob_demo (
  2  clob_id       NUMBER,
  3  clob_value CLOB
  4 );

SQL> CREATE TABLE clob_table OF clob_demo
  5  LOB (clob_value) STORE AS clob_store (
  6  TABLESPACE raw_data
  7  STORAGE (INITIAL 100K NEXT 100K PCTINCREASE 0)
  8  CHUNK 4
  9  PCTVERSION 10
 10  INDEX clob_index (
 11  TABLESPACE raw_index))
 12  TABLESPACE appl_data
 12* STORAGE (INITIAL 1M NEXT 1M PCTINCREASE 0)
SQL> /
```

Notice that no **LOB** storage is specified when a **BLOB** or **CLOB** is used in a **TYPE** specification. The **LOB** storage clause is applied to the **BLOB** or **CLOB TYPE** only when it is used in a table.

Using **BLOB** And **CLOB** Datatypes

BLOBs and **CLOB**s are useless unless they are loaded. Essentially, you can load **BLOB**s and **CLOB**s into a database in two ways. The first method uses PL/SQL and the **DBMS_LOB** package and the **BFILE** datatype to transfer external **LOB** files into the database's internal **LOB** structures. The second method uses the Oracle Call Interface (OCI) to perform the same function. Let's look at the first method.

To load external **LOB** data into internal **LOB** storage using PL/SQL alone, you must first use a table containing **BFILE** locators for the files to allow Oracle to access them, as shown in Listing 6.3.

Listing 6.3   Example use of BFILE datatype in a table.

```
create table graphics_table (
  bfile_id number,
  bfile_desc varchar2(30),
  bfile_loc bfile,
  bfile_type varchar2(4))
  TABLESPACE appl_data
  storage (initial 1m next 1m pctincrease 0)
 /
```

Notice that no **LOB** storage clause is specified in Listing 6.3. This is because all that is stored in the database is a locator value for the **BFILE**, consisting of an internal **DIRECTORY** specification and a file name. The **BFILE** locators are loaded into the table using the **BFILENAME** function and a standard **INSERT** statement. Listing 6.4 shows an example of this process.

Listing 6.4   Example set of INSERT commands used to load BFILE locators manually.

```
SQL> INSERT INTO graphics_table
  2   VALUES(4,'April Book of Days
Woodcut',bfilename('GIF_FILES','APRIL.JPG'),'JPEG');

1 row created.

SQL> INSERT INTO graphics_table
  2   VALUES(8,'August Book of Days
Woodcut',bfilename('GIF_FILES','AUGUST.JPG'),'JPEG');

1 row created.

SQL> INSERT INTO graphics_table
  2   VALUES(13,'Benzene Molecule',bfilename('GIF_FILES','BENZNE.GIF'),'GIF');

1 row created.

    .
    .
    .

SQL> INSERT INTO graphics_table
  2   VALUES(30,'',bfilename('GIF_FILES','SHAPIROS.GIF'),'GIF');

1 row created.

SQL> INSERT INTO graphics_table
  2   VALUES(31,'',bfilename('GIF_FILES','SODF5.GIF'),'GIF');

1 row created.

SQL> INSERT INTO graphics_table
  2   VALUES(32,'',bfilename('GIF_FILES','WAVRA-CL.GIF'),'GIF');

1 row created.

SQL> commit;

Commit complete.
```

*Use a host command to perform a single-column directory listing into a file (for example, on NT: dir /B >file.lis), then use the **UTL_FILE** package to read the contents of the created file into the **DBMS_SQL** package. This builds the **INSERT** commands on the fly. An entire directory of **LOB** datafiles can be loaded at one time into a **BFILE** table and then into the internal **LOB** storage table. For an example, see Listing 6.5.*

Listing 6.5 Example procedure for loading BFILE locators based on an external file list.

```
CREATE  OR REPLACE PROCEDURE get_bfiles(
                                  bfile_dir in  VARCHAR2,
                                  bfile_lis in  VARCHAR2,
                                  bfile_int_dir VARCHAR2)
AS
 cur          INTEGER;
 bfile_int    VARCHAR2(100);
 sql_com      VARCHAR2(2000);
 file_proc    INTEGER;
 file_hand    utl_file.file_type;
 file_buff    VARCHAR2(1022);
 file_type    VARCHAR2(4);
BEGIN
 bfile_int:=UPPER(bfile_int_dir);
 file_hand:=utl_file.fopen(bfile_dir,bfile_lis,'R');
 LOOP
   BEGIN
   utl_file.get_line(file_hand,file_buff);
   cur:=dbms_sql.open_cursor;
   file_type:=SUBSTR(file_buff,INSTR(file_buff,'.')+1,3);
   file_type:=UPPER(file_type);
   IF file_type='GIF'
    THEN
        file_type:='GIF';
    ELSIF file_type='JPG'
    THEN file_type:='JPEG';
   END IF;
   sql_com:= 'INSERT INTO graphics_table '||CHR(10)||
            'VALUES (graphics_table_seq.NEXTVAL,'||CHR(39)||CHR(39)||
            ', bfilename('||
            CHR(39)||bfile_int||CHR(39)||','
            ||CHR(39)||file_buff||CHR(39)||
            ') ,'||CHR(39)||file_type||CHR(39)||')';
   dbms_output.put_line(sql_com);
   dbms_sql.parse(cur,sql_com,dbms_sql.v7);
   file_proc:=dbms_sql.execute(cur);
   dbms_sql.close_cursor(cur);
```

```
   EXCEPTION
    WHEN no_data_found THEN
    EXIT;
    END;
 END LOOP;
 utl_file.fclose(file_hand);
END;
/
```

Once the **BFILE** locators are set in the **BFILE** table, you can use the **DBMS_LOB** package to read the external **LOB** (**BFILE**) into an internal **LOB** (**BLOB**, **CLOB**, or **NCLOB**), as shown in Listing 6.6. The **SELECT** from the **temp_blob** table initializes the internal **LOB** values so they can be used; otherwise, an error will be returned.

Listing 6.6   Example procedure to load BFILE values into internal LOBs.
```
CREATE OR REPLACE PROCEDURE load_lob AS
   id          NUMBER;
   image1      BLOB;
   locator     BFILE;
   bfile_len   NUMBER;
   bf_desc     VARCHAR2(30);
   bf_name     VARCHAR2(30);
   bf_dir      VARCHAR2(30);
   bf_typ      VARCHAR2(4);
   ctr integer;
   CURSOR get_id IS
     SELECT bfile_id,bfile_desc,bfile_type FROM graphics_table;
BEGIN
  OPEN get_id;
LOOP
  FETCH get_id INTO id, bf_desc, bf_typ;
  EXIT WHEN get_id%notfound;
  dbms_output.put_line('ID: '||to_char(id));
  SELECT bfile_loc INTO locator FROM graphics_table WHERE bfile_id=id;
  dbms_lob.filegetname(locator,bf_dir,bf_name);
  dbms_output.put_line('Dir: '||bf_dir);
  dbms_lob.fileopen(locator,dbms_lob.file_readonly);
  bfile_len:=dbms_lob.getlength(locator);
  dbms_output.put_line('ID: '||to_char(id)||' length: '||to_char(bfile_len));
  SELECT temp_blob INTO image1 FROM temp_blob;
  bfile_len:=dbms_lob.getlength(locator);
  dbms_lob.loadfromfile(image1,locator,bfile_len,1,1);
  INSERT INTO internal_graphics VALUES (id,bf_desc,image1,bf_typ);
  dbms_output.put_line(bf_desc||' Length: '||TO_CHAR(bfile_len)||
  ' Name: '||bf_name||' Dir: '||bf_dir||' '||bf_typ);
  dbms_lob.fileclose(locator);
```

```
END LOOP;
END;
/
```

By enforcing a naming standard on the external **LOB** files, you could modify the loading procedure in Listing 6.6 to place **BLOB** types into **BLOB**s, **CLOB** types into **CLOB**s, and **NCLOB** types into **NCLOB**s, based on the file type values parsed from the file extensions in Listing 6.5. Between the procedure in Listing 6.5 and the one shown in Listing 6.6, the example tables in Listings 6.1 and 6.3 are populated with **LOB** values located in a specific directory.

Manipulating Internal **LOB** Datatypes

Once **LOB** datatypes (**BLOB**, **CLOB**) are loaded into a database, the **DBMS_LOB** package allows you to manipulate them. Additional manipulations are allowed via vendor-supplied data cartridge sets. You can also manipulate the **LOB** datatypes using the Oracle Call Interface. Table 6.4 shows the relationship between the OCI calls and **DBMS_LOB** procedures and functions.

The **DBMS_LOB** package works on the basis of the **LOB** locator, whether it is an external or internal **LOB**. Support for **NCLOB** datatypes seems to be severely lacking. If the OCI and **DBMS_LOB** objects listed in Table 6.4 support **NCLOB**s, this data is sorely lacking from the documentation.

You can perform the following actions against **BLOB**s and **CLOB**s using standard packages and OCI calls: **COMPARE** (two **LOB**s of the same type), **TRIM**, **COPY** (a

Table 6.4 OCI Calls and DBMS_LOB Procedures and Functions.

OCI Call	DBMS_LOB	Acts On
OCILobAppend	DBMS_LOB.APPEND()	BLOB, CLOB
OCILobCopy	DBMS_LOB.COPY()	BLOB,CLOB
OCILobErase	DBMS_LOB.ERASE()	BLOB,CLOB
OCILobFileClose	DBMS_LOB.FILECLOSE()	BFILE
OCILobFileCloseAll	DBMS_LOB.FILECLOSEALL()	BFILE
OCIFileExists	DBMS_LOB.FILE_EXISTS()	BFILE

(continued)

Table 6.4   OCI Calls and DBMS_LOB Procedures and Functions (continued).

OCI Call	DBMS_LOB	Acts On
OCILobFileGetName	DBMS_LOB.FILEGETNAME()	BFILE
OCILobFileIsOpen	DBMS_LOB.FILEISOPEN()	BFILE
OCILobFileOpen	DBMS_LOB.FILEOPEN()	BFILE
OCILobFileSetName	Use BFILENAME function	BFILE
OCILobGetLength	DBMS_LOB.GETLENGTH()	BLOB,CLOB,BFILE
OCILobLoadFromFile	DBMS_LOB.LOADFROMFILE()	ALL
OCILobRead	DBMS_LOB.READ()	BLOB,CLOB,BFILE
OCILobTrim	DBMS_LOB.TRIM()	BLOB,CLOB
OCILobWrite	DBMS_LOB.WRITE()	BLOB,CLOB
OCILobCharSetForm		CLOB,NCLOB
OCILobCharSetID		CLOB,NCLOB
OCILobEnableBuffering		BLOB,CLOB,NCLOB
OCILobDisableBuffering		BLOB,CLOB,NCLOB
OCILobFlushBuffer		BLOB,CLOB,NCLOB
OCILobIsEqual	Use PL/SQL equal operator	ALL
OCILobLocatorIsInit		ALL
OCILobLocatorSize		
	DBMS_LOB.COMPARE()	BLOB,CLOB,BFILE
	DBMS_LOB.INSTR()	BLOB,CLOB,BFILE
	DBMS_LOB.SUBSTR()	BLOB,CLOB,BFILE

LOB of one type to a **LOB** of the same type), **SUBSTRING**, **INSTRING** (for a given **LOB**), **EQUALITY** (of two **LOBs** of the same type), and **APPEND** (one **LOB** of a specific type to another **LOB** of the same type).

Comparing Two **LOBs**

The **DBMS_LOB.COMPARE** package allows comparison of two full **LOBs** or portions of two **LOBs**. You can specify the start byte and length to compare. If you do not specify, the start byte defaults to 1, and the length defaults to 4,294,967,295 bytes (4GB minus 1). Listing 6.7 shows how you can compare an external **BLOB** (the **BFILE**) and an internal **BLOB**. This listing uses **fileopen**, **loadfromfile**, **fileclose**, and **compare** components of the **DBMS_LOB** package.

Listing 6.7   Example of an anonymous PL/SQL block to compare two BLOBs—one from an external BFILE and one from an internal table.

```
DECLARE
bfile1        BFILE;
lob_1         BLOB;
lob_2         BLOB;
offset1       INTEGER:=1;
offset2       INTEGER:=2;
comp_length NUMBER;
match         INTEGER;
BEGIN
SELECT bfile_loc INTO bfile1 FROM graphics_table WHERE bfile_id=33;
dbms_lob.fileopen(bfile1,dbms_lob.file_readonly);
comp_length:=dbms_lob.getlength(bfile1);
SELECT temp_blob, temp_blob INTO lob_1,lob_2 FROM temp_blob;
dbms_lob.loadfromfile(lob_1,bfile1,comp_length,1,1);
SELECT graphic_blob INTO lob_2
 FROM internal_graphics
 WHERE graphic_id=33;
match:=dbms_lob.compare(lob_1,lob_2,comp_length,1,1);
IF match=0 THEN
  dbms_Output.put_line('Blobs match');
ELSE
  dbms_output.put_line('Blobs are not the same');
END IF;
dbms_lob.fileclose(bfile1);
END;
/
```

*Notice in Listing 6.7 the use of the **temp_blob** table. This table is my own creation and consists of:*

```
CREATE TABLE temp_blob(
    temp_blob  BLOB,
    temp_clob  CLOB,
    temp_nclob NCLOB);
```

*Into this table, I insert the empty **LOB** values:*

```
INSERT INTO temp_blob VALUES(
  empty_blob(),empty_clob(),empty_clob);
```

*You can use this table in place of the somewhat convoluted **INSERT/UPDATE** schemes used by Oracle documents to initialize the internal **BLOB**, **CLOB**, and **NCLOB** values, much the same as the **dual** table is used for **SYSDATE**, **USER**, and other **SELECT** commands. I suggest this table be created under the SYS user schema, with a public synonym and a public select grant.*

The **DBMS_LOB.COMPARE** component is a function that returns integer zero if the **LOB**s are identical, and a nonzero value if they are not. Additionally, a **NULL** value may be returned if an error occurs in the input values of the offsets or amount.

Reading, Writing, And Appending **LOB** Values

Before release 8.0.3, Oracle provided no simple way of copying a **LOB** from an external **BFILE** into an internal **LOB**. At times, a **LOB** will need to be read or written piecewise. The **read** and **write** components read in 32K (32,767 bytes, actually) chunks. The example code in Listing 6.8 uses the **read**, **write**, **copy**, **append**, **fileopen**, **fileclose**, **getlength**, and **filegetname** components of the **DBMS_LOB** package.

Listing 6.8   Example use of the read, write, copy, append, fileopen, fileclose, getlength, and filegetname components of the DBMS_LOB package.

```
DECLARE
  id         NUMBER;
  image1     BLOB;
  image2     BLOB;
  locator    BFILE;
  bfile_len  NUMBER;
  bf_desc    VARCHAR2(30);
```

```
    bf_name     VARCHAR2(30);
    bf_dir      VARCHAR2(30);
    get_buffer RAW(32767);
    amt         BINARY_INTEGER:=32767;
    i           INTEGER;
    pos         INTEGER;
    ctr         INTEGER;
    CURSOR get_id IS
      SELECT bfile_id,bfile_desc
      FROM graphics_table;
BEGIN
  OPEN get_id;
LOOP
  FETCH get_id INTO id, bf_desc;
  EXIT WHEN get_id%notfound;
  dbms_output.put_line('ID: '||to_char(id));
  SELECT bfile_loc INTO locator FROM graphics_table WHERE bfile_id=id;
  dbms_lob.filegetname(locator,bf_dir,bf_name);
  dbms_lob.fileopen(locator,dbms_lob.file_readonly);
  bfile_len:=dbms_lob.getlength(locator);
  dbms_output.put_line('ID: '||to_char(id)||' length: '||
                        to_char(bfile_len));
  i:=ceil(bfile_len/amt);
  SELECT temp_blob,temp_blob INTO image1,image2 FROM temp_blob;
  dbms_output.put_line('i='||to_char(i));
  pos:=1;
  FOR ctr IN 1..i loop
  dbms_lob.read(locator,amt,pos,get_buffer);
  dbms_output.put_line(TO_CHAR(pos));
  dbms_lob.write(image1,amt,1,get_buffer);
  IF ctr=1 THEN
    dbms_lob.copy(image2,image1,amt,1,1);
    ELSE
    dbms_lob.append(image2,image1);
  END IF;
  pos:=pos+amt;
  END LOOP;
  INSERT INTO internal_graphics VALUES (id,bf_desc,image1);
  dbms_output.put_line(bf_desc||' Length: '||TO_CHAR(bfile_len)||
  ' Name: '||bf_name||' Dir: '||bf_dir);
  dbms_lob.fileclose(locator);
END LOOP;
END;
/
```

Searching LOBs

Sometimes, you may want to return a subsection of a **LOB**, whether it is a selected portion of an image from a **BLOB** or a section of text from a **CLOB**. For example, you might want to do an image search to find a particular image or a document search for a specific phrase or word. The **DBMS_LOB** package is capable of searching for a substring, given a start byte (offset) and search pattern (up to 32,767 bytes). With this search capability, even nonconsecutive image sections can be portioned into a holding **BLOB** or **CLOB** and used as a search source for other **BLOB**s or **CLOB**s.

Of course, to do **BLOB** section searches, you must know the size in pixels for both the X and Y axes, as well as the compression format and the applicable offsets calculated for each **BLOB** subsection. **CLOB**s are more linear in nature than **BLOB**s, so a straight search from the start offset to the end of the amount to read can be used for comparison purposes as is.

For example, if an image application returns the two Points inside a 360 x 490 pixel image that correspond to the upper-left and lower-right corners of the desired subsection, then the corresponding image subsection will be a set of subsections parsed out of the image stream. A 360 x 490 pixel image can be stored in multiple compression formats, resulting in many different file sizes. You may have to store the exact subsection of the image as individual, compressed segments and search for each segment on an individual basis.

The displayed image sections would be captured as individual bit streams, and those individual sections would be compressed identically to the original file. Then, each segment would be stored into a holding area. Once these parse and save operations are complete, you could use procedures, such as those in Listing 6.9, to search specified **BLOB** or **BFILE** images for the parsed sections.

Listing 6.9   Example BLOB search procedures.

```
CREATE OR REPLACE PROCEDURE search_blob (
search_section IN RAW, searched_blob IN INTEGER, offset OUT INTEGER) AS
  temp_blob BLOB;
BEGIN
  SELECT graphic_blob INTO temp_blob
   FROM internal_graphics
   WHERE graphic_id=searched_blob;
  offset:=dbms_lob.instr(temp_blob, search_section, 1, 1);
END;
/
```

```
CREATE OR REPLACE PROCEDURE search_bfile (
search_section IN RAW, searched_bfile IN INTEGER, offset OUT INTEGER) AS
  comp_blob BLOB;
  temp_bfile BFILE;
  bfile_length NUMBER;
BEGIN
  SELECT temp_blob INTO comp_blob FROM temp_blob;
  SELECT bfile_loc INTO temp_bfile FROM graphics_table
   WHERE bfile_id = searched_bfile;
  dbms_lob.fileopen(temp_bfile,dbms_lob.file_readonly);
  offset:=dbms_lob.instr(temp_bfile, search_section, 1, 1);
  dbms_lob.fileclose(temp_bfile);
END;
/
```

Using the procedures in Listing 6.9, you can search either the table of **BFILE**s created in previous examples for a specified subsection of a **BLOB**, or the internally stored **BLOB** table values for a specified search subsection.

Let's look at an example search. To perform a search, select a section of a **BLOB** from the internal graphics table, and then search the external **BFILE** table for the external **BLOB** that contains the search subsection. This process is shown in Listing 6.10.

Listing 6.10 Example use of the search BLOB procedure that uses the INSTR search function.

```
DECLARE
  blob_section          RAW(2048);
  section_size      INTEGER:=2048;
  blb_id              INTEGER:=44;
  bfl_id                INTEGER;
  offset                INTEGER;
  temp_blob                BLOB;
  CURSOR get_bfiles IS
   SELECT bfile_id FROM graphics_table;
BEGIN
  SELECT graphic_blob INTO temp_blob FROM internal_graphics
   WHERE graphic_id=blb_id;
  blob_section:=dbms_lob.substr(temp_blob,section_size,223);
  OPEN get_bfiles;
  LOOP
   FETCH get_bfiles INTO bfl_id;
   EXIT WHEN get_bfiles%NOTFOUND;
   search_bfile(blob_section,bfl_id,offset);
```

```
    IF offset>0 THEN
      dbms_output.put_line('Found section in bfile_id:'||TO_CHAR(bfl_id)||
       ' at offset:'||TO_CHAR(offset));
    END IF;
  END LOOP;
END;
/
```

 ## Erasing **LOB** Values

Internal **LOB** values can be erased, while only *references* to external **BFILE**s can be
erased. Erasure of actual external files must be done at the operating-system level.
The **DBMS_LOB.ERASE** procedure erases internal **BLOB**s and **CLOB**s. Listing 6.11
shows an example of the use of the **DBMS_LOB.ERASE** package.

Listing 6.11   Example procedure to erase a BLOB.
```
CREATE OR REPLACE PROCEDURE erase_blob (
  blob_id IN INTEGER) AS
  blob_length2 NUMBER;
  blob_length   NUMBER;
  temp_blob     BLOB;
BEGIN
SELECT dbms_lob.getlength(graphic_blob),graphic_blob
 INTO blob_length,temp_blob
 FROM internal_graphics
 WHERE graphic_id=blob_id
 FOR UPDATE;
blob_length2:=dbms_lob.getlength(temp_blob);
dbms_output.put_line('Before BLOB Length: '||TO_CHAR(blob_length2));
dbms_lob.erase(temp_blob,blob_length,1);
blob_length2:=dbms_lob.getlength(temp_blob);
dbms_output.put_line('After BLOB Length: '||
 TO_CHAR(blob_length2)||' amount erased: '||TO_CHAR(blob_length));
COMMIT;
END;
/
```

Listing 6.12 shows how to use these procedures to erase a **BLOB**. Pay particular
attention to the before and after **BLOB** lengths.

Listing 6.12   Example output from the ERASE procedure.
```
Example Output from the ERASE Procedure:

SQL> set serveroutput on
SQL> @erase_blob
```

```
Procedure created.

SQL> execute erase_blob(33);
Before BLOB Length: 140725
After BLOB Length: 140725 amount erased: 140725

PL/SQL procedure successfully completed.
```

An erase operation does not change the size of the **BLOB**, only its contents. It places zero byte indicators into a **BLOB** and blanks into a **CLOB**.

Confirming **LOB** Erasure Using **COMPARE**

You can use the **DBMS_LOB.COMPARE** function to see if a **LOB** has been erased. For example, if you want to be sure that a **LOB** had been erased, you could compare it to a known copy.

The previous examples show a **BLOB** being erased from the **internal_graphics** table. To verify that, you can compare the erased **BLOB** to its original external file, as referenced in the **graphics_table BFILE** specification. Listing 6.13 shows an example PL/SQL anonymous block that uses the **COMPARE** function to compare the erased **BLOB** to its source **BFILE** external **BLOB**.

Listing 6.13   Example use of the COMPARE function to verify an erase operation.

```
DECLARE
comp_blob1      BLOB;
comp_blob2      BLOB;
blob_length     NUMBER;
comp_bfile      BFILE;
comp_res        NUMBER;
BEGIN
 SELECT bfile_loc INTO comp_bfile
  FROM graphics_table
  WHERE bfile_id = 33;
 dbms_lob.fileopen(comp_bfile);
 blob_length:=dbms_lob.getlength(comp_bfile);
 SELECT temp_blob INTO comp_blob1 FROM temp_blob FOR UPDATE;
 dbms_lob.loadfromfile(comp_blob1,comp_bfile,blob_length,1,1);
 SELECT graphic_blob INTO comp_blob2
  FROM internal_graphics
  WHERE graphic_id=33;
 comp_res:=dbms_lob.compare(comp_blob1,comp_blob2,blob_length,1,1);
```

```
  IF comp_res=0 THEN
   dbms_output.put_line('Blobs Match');
  ELSE
   dbms_output.put_line('Blobs Do not match');
  END IF;
  dbms_lob.fileclose(comp_bfile);
  COMMIT;
END;
```

Example execution of compare anonymous PL/SQL Block:

```
SQL> @comp_proc.sql
 27  /
Blobs Do not match

PL/SQL procedure successfully completed.
```

Notice that the **FOR UPDATE** clause on the **SELECT** statement pre-populates the **BLOB** with a **NULL** value from the **temp_blob** table. This is required for this type of operation. By specifying **FOR UPDATE**, you lock the row, preventing other users from changing the **LOB** value during the **COMPARE**.

Using The **TRIM_LOB** Procedure

If you want to reclaim the space from an erased **LOB**, use the **TRIM** procedure to trim the **LOB** back to zero length. Listing 6.14 is an example of this procedure.

Listing 6.14 An example run of the TRIM_LOB procedure.
```
CREATE OR REPLACE PROCEDURE trim_lob(blob_id IN INTEGER) AS
blob_loc BLOB;
blob_len NUMBER;
BEGIN
SELECT graphic_blob INTO blob_loc
  FROM internal_graphics
  WHERE graphic_id=blob_id FOR UPDATE;
dbms_lob.trim(blob_loc,0);
COMMIT;
SELECT dbms_lob.getlength(graphic_blob) INTO blob_len
   FROM internal_graphics
  WHERE graphic_id=blob_id;
dbms_output.put_line('BLOB Length: '||to_char(blob_len));
END;
```

```
Example execution of Procedure TRIM_LOB:
SQL> execute trim_lob(33);
BLOB Length: 0

PL/SQL procedure successfully completed.
```

Using The Server Image Cartridge

The Oracle8 Server Image Cartridge enhances Oracle's ability to handle and manipulate images. To add the data cartridge, execute ORDISPEC.SQL and ORDIBODY.PLB, located in the \orant\rdbms80\admin directory on NT 4 and the $ORACLE_HOME/rdbms/admin directory on Unix.

Adding An Image Type To A Table

To add an image type to a table, use the **ALTER TABLE** command:

```
ALTER TABLE graphics_table
ADD (enh_bfile ordsys.ordimgF);

-- or --

ALTER TABLE internal_graphics
ADD (enh_graphic ORDSYS.ORDIMGB);
```

Once you add **TYPE** to a table (or create the table with **TYPE** as an integral part), you can use the type's methods to perform changes and processes against the **BLOB** datatype contained in the table.

Copying An Image Into An Image Type

Once **TYPE** is part of a table, you can use the internal method **ORDSYS.COPY-CONTENT** to copy an image into the **TYPE** attribute, as shown in Listing 6.15.

Listing 6.15 Example procedure to load BFILE and BLOB data into image cartridge TYPEs.

```
DECLARE
  image1    ORDSYS.ORDIMGB;
  locator   ORDSYS.ORDIMGF;
  bfile_len NUMBER;
  bf_desc   VARCHAR2(30);
  bf_name   VARCHAR2(30);
  bf_dir    VARCHAR2(30);
```

```
BEGIN
  INSERT INTO graphics_table
    VALUES (graphics_table_seq.nextval, ' ',
    ORDSYS.ORDIMGF(bfilename('GIF_DIR','example.gif',
    NULL,NULL,NULL,NULL,NULL,NULL);
   SELECT enh_bfile INTO locator FROM graphics_table
    WHERE bfile_id=graphics_table_seq.curval FOR UPDATE;
   locator.setproperties;
   UPDATE enh_bfile SET enh_bfile=locator
     WHERE bfile_id=graphics_table_seq.curval;
  SELECT temp_ordtypb INTO image1 FROM temp_blob;
  locator.copycontent(image1.content);
  INSERT INTO internal_graphics
    VALUES (internal_graphics_seq.nextval,'',ORDSYS.ORDIMGB(image1));
  COMMIT;
END;
/
```

Setting An Image's Properties

Once a **BLOB** is loaded into either an ORDIMGB (**BLOB**) or ORDIMGF (**BFILE**)
TYPE specification, the properties are set using the **setproperties** method:

```
bfile_ordimgf_type.setproperties;
```

```
-- or --
```

```
BLOB_ordimgb_type.setproperties;
```

If you have defined **graphics_value** as an ORDIMGB **TYPE**

```
graphics_value   ORDSYS.ORDIMGB;
```

you can set the properties after loading the image into the **TYPE** by simply using the
METHOD invocation:

```
graphics_value.SetProperties;
```

Once the properties are set, you can query them using **TYPE** notation (the properties are read from the **BLOB** or **BFILE**, and each of the supported formats stores
information about itself internally in the file):

```
SELECT
graphics_value.width,graphics_value.height, graphics_file.fileFormat
FROM  graphics_table
WHERE graphics_id=1;
```

The values stored for each image are width, height, size, file type, and type of compression.

Using The **PROCESS** And **PROCESSCOPY** Methods On Image Types

The **PROCESS** and **PROCESSCOPY** methods execute different commands against an image and, optionally, copy it to a new location. For **BFILE** types, only **PROCESSCOPY** can be used, and even then, only after the **BFILE** content has been copied into an internal **BLOB**.

You might use **PROCESS** to convert the **BLOB** images stored in the example table, **internal_graphics**, from JPEG to GIF. This is demonstrated in Listing 6.16.

Listing 6.16   Example PL/SQL code to use the PROCESS method.
```
DECLARE
image1 ORDSYS.ORDIMGB;
image_id  NUMBER;
CURSOR get_image IS
  SELECT graphic_id, enh_graphic FROM
    FROM internal_graphics
    WHERE enh_graphic.fileformat='JPEG'
    FOR UPDATE;
BEGIN
  OPEN get_image;
  LOOP
    FETCH get_image INTO image_id, image1;
    EXIT WHEN get_image%NOTFOUND;
    image1.process('fileFormat=GIFF'', 'compressionFormat=BMPRLE')
    image1.setProperties;
    UPDATE  internal_graphics SET enh_graphic=image1
       WHERE graphic_id=image_id;
  END LOOP;
  COMMIT;
END;
```

Use of the **PROCESSCOPY** method is virtually identical to the use of the **PROCESS** method, except a destination **BLOB** is specified along with the command in the **CALLOUT** method.

PL/SQL Enhancements

In this chapter, we will examine the new Oracle8 PL/SQL enhancements. We have used several of these enhancements in previous chapters, so you will already be familiar with some enhancements, but others will be totally new.

Notes...

Chapter 7

Accessing Types And Collections

Collections (user-defined types, or UDTs) are type, **VARRAY**, and nested table definitions. By the strictest definitions, a type is not a collection unless it is a **VARRAY** or a nested table. These UDTs can be used either in a table creation or as internal data objects within PL/SQL. Past chapters have shown how to **INSERT**, **UPDATE**, and **DELETE** from table-based types. This chapter shows how to use collections in PL/SQL programming situations.

Object types (those created using **CREATE TYPE AS OBJECT**) must be created outside of PL/SQL as a stored type. This means they must be created from within a SQL*Plus, SVRMGR, or SQL*Worksheet session. Once the collection or object type exists, you can use it in declarations from within PL/SQL, exactly as an intrinsic scalar datatype.

Object Types And Methods

Oracle8 UDTs can contain methods. A method is an encapsulated PL/SQL routine that performs operations upon the specific type within which it is encapsulated. While a method is allowed to act on other types, this should be discouraged and all inter-type communication handled by an intermediate procedure or function. This requirement that a type's methods not directly change or read the contents of another type is in accordance with the basic tenets of object-oriented programming.

All methods (functions and procedures) have the intrinsic datatype **SELF**, which is implicitly declared whether or not you specify **SELF** in the parameter list. The **SELF** parameter always refers to the values of the object instance from which the method was invoked. For a function, the **SELF** variable defaults to **IN**; for a procedure, it defaults to **IN OUT**.

Methods can be overloaded just as functions and procedures. Method overloading consists of specifying multiple methods within the same object type that have the same name but differ in the number, datatype, or arrangement of their parameter lists. PL/SQL locates the proper method by examining the input parameters and comparing their order or type with the formal parameter list.

Object Types And *MAP* Or *ORDER* Methods

Each object type should have either a **MAP** or **ORDER** method specified (only one or the other) to tell PL/SQL how comparisons between instances of the object or comparisons with similar types should be resolved. A **MAP** method takes the value of the object instance and, based on conversion logic of one or more of the instance attributes, returns an integer value. An **ORDER** method can compare only two objects at a time (**SELF** and another instance of the same type).

If you are doing large-scale comparisons, use a **MAP** method, because it maps all of the values of the object at one time to an integer set and then uses the integer set to perform a comparison. An **ORDER** method is less efficient and should be used only if the majority of your comparisons are one-on-one. The **ORDER** method is less efficient, because it compares only two values at one time. Unless either a **MAP** or **ORDER** method is declared, an object type comparison can be done for equality only. Equality of two object types means they match exactly for all attributes.

Default Object Methods

By default, all object types have a **CONSTRUCTOR** method that is system-supplied and whose name is equivalent to the **TYPE** name. To populate an instance of an object type, the **CONSTRUCTOR** must be called explicitly. Collections (**VARRAY** and nested table) have several other default methods, called **COLLECTION** methods, discussed later in this chapter.

Functions And Purity

Methods that are functions must adhere to the following purity rules if they are to be used in a SQL statement:

1. They cannot insert into, update, or delete from a database table.

2. They cannot be executed remotely or in parallel if they read or write the values of packaged variables.

3. They cannot write the values of packaged variables unless called from a **SELECT**, **VALUES**, or **SET** clause.

4. They cannot call another method or subprogram that breaks one of these rules, nor can they reference views that break any of these rules. (Oracle replaces references to a view with a stored **SELECT** operation, which can include **FUNCTION** calls.)

Object Type Methods And Purity

Oracle cannot determine the purity of a method function except at compile time and only if the **PRAGMA RESTRICT_REFERENCES** precompiler option is declared to tell Oracle what you believe is the purity of the method function. This precompiler call is placed in the method header declaration in the **CREATE TYPE** command.

The **PRAGMA RESTRICT_REFERENCES** call has five possible arguments: **FUNCTION NAME**, **RNPS**, **WNPS**, **RNDS**, and **WNDS**. Of these arguments, **FUNCTION NAME** is required, as is at least one of the other arguments. The arguments have the following definitions:

- **FUNCTION NAME**—The name of the function for which the **PRAGMA** call is being made.

- **RNPS**—Tells the compiler that the function reads no package state (rules 2 and 4).

- **WNPS**—Tells Oracle the function writes no package state (rules 2, 3, and 4).

- **RNDS**—Tells Oracle the function reads no database state (rules 1 and 4).

- **WNDS**—Tells Oracle the function writes no database state (rules 1 and 4).

If for any reason the **PRAGMA** declaration is incorrect, the compiler will report this as an error, and the method, as well as its parent type, will be invalid.

Initialization Of Object Types

Before you can use an object type in a PL/SQL program, it must be initialized; otherwise, it is atomically **NULL**. An object type is initialized by calling its **CONSTRUCTOR** type with either actual default values or **NULL** values. An object type whose attributes are **NULL** can have its attributes assigned, whereas an object type that is atomically **NULL** cannot.

Object type attributes are accessed via dot notation. For example, if a **PICTURE** type has a **TITLE** attribute, the way to access this attribute would be **PICTURE.TITLE**.

Using **REF** Pointers

Object types can also reference object instances stored in object tables via a **REF** call. A **REF** call places the referenced object instance's **OID** value into the referring object attribute. The inverse of a **REF** call is a **DEREF** call, which returns the values stored at a **REF** location (the referenced object table's instance). Another call that is used with **REF** values is the **VALUE** call, which is supplied a table correlator (an object table alias) and returns the value of the object stored in that correlator location.

Collection Item Processing

You can manipulate a collection either as a set using the **THE** operator or as individual items using a collection index value. Both of the collection types—**VARRAY** and nested table—can have individual items selected via the use of an integer value that corresponds to that item's place in the collection. For example, to process the values in row 10 of the nested table called **addresses**, in the object table **employee**, the call would be **employee.addresses(10)**.

In addition to index-based addressing of collection items, each collection has an implicit set of **COLLECTION** methods, created when Oracle defines the type. These **COLLECTION** methods are:

- **EXISTS**—Determines if a particular row in a collection is populated. It is most useful with nested tables, which can be sparsely populated.

- **COUNT**—Determines the number of values in a **COLLECTION**. For a **nested table**, **COUNT** may not always equal **LAST**. For a **VARRAY**, which must be non-sparse, **COUNT** will always equal **LAST**.

- **LIMIT**—Gets the limit specified for a **VARRAY** collection type.

- **FIRST** and **LAST**—Retrieves the **FIRST** value index integer (will always be 1 for a **VARRAY**, but may not on a **nested table**) or **LAST** value index integer (will always equal **COUNT** for a **VARRAY**, but may not for a **nested table**).

- **PRIOR** and **NEXT**—Finds the **PRIOR** or **NEXT** populated value. These are most useful for a **nested table** collection, which can be sparse.

- **EXTEND**—Adds either **NULL** values or copies of existing values to the end of a collection. For **VARRAY**s, this cannot go beyond **LIMIT** in size.

- **TRIM**—Removes values from the end of a collection up to the value of **COUNT**.

- **DELETE**—Deletes either the entire collection, a range of elements (for a **nested table**), or a single element (for a **nested table**).

With these predefined method for the management and manipulation of collections, using PL/SQL is much easier. The Practical Guide in this chapter demonstrates techniques using these predefined collection methods.

Accessing External C Or 3GL Procedures

Oracle8 allows specification of **LIBRARY**s, which are pointers to external, sharable, or dynamic linked libraries (DLLs) of C routines. In the future, support for other 3GL type libraries is planned. **LIBRARY**s are just internal pointers to external locations and are created with the **CREATE LIBRARY** command.

Once a **LIBRARY** has been defined, Oracle processes (via PL/SQL procedures), can make calls to the functions stored in the external library file pointed to by the **LIBRARY** pointer. To accomplish this, the listener controller called **extproc** must start a Net8 process. The calls to external procedures are passed to **extproc**, which starts a second process for the user making the external call. This handles the passing of variables between the user's main process and the one running the external procedure.

This split of processes during external procedures allows isolation of the external procedure memory space to prevent accidental corruption of the user's memory space. This second process started for external procedure usage is active until the user signs out of Oracle. The **extproc** process may become multithreaded in the future, so be sure all external procedures are thread-safe.

PL/SQL and C have different datatype structures. A map must exist between C routine datatypes and the PL/SQL variable datatypes. External procedures cannot except **VARRAY**s, nested tables, **CURSOR VARIABLE**s, records, or object type instances. Another limitation is that PL/SQL variables support the concept of **NULL**, while C variables do not. Table 7.1 shows how PL/SQL variable datatypes map into C datatypes for use in external procedure calls.

Table 7.1 Datatype mapping between PL/SQL and C external procedures.

PL/SQL Type	Supported External Types	Default External Type
BINARY_INTEGER BOOLEAN PLS_INTEGER	CHAR, UNSIGNED_CHAR, SHORT, UNSIGNED SHORT, INT, UNSIGNED INT, LONG, UNSIGNED LONG, SB1, UB1, SB2, UB2, SB4, SIZE_T	INT
NATURAL, NATURALN, POSITIVE, POSITIVEN,SIGNTYPE	CHAR, UNSIGNED CHAR, SHORT, UNSIGNED SHORT, INT, UNSIGNED INT, LONG, UNSIGNED LONG, SB1, UB1, SB2, UB2, SB4, UB4, SIZE_T	
FLOAT, REAL	FLOAT	FLOAT
DOUBLE PRECISION	DOUBLE	DOUBLE
CHAR, CHARACTER, LONG, ROWID, VARCHAR, VARCHAR2	STRING	STRING
LONG RAW, LONG	RAW	RAW
BFILE, BLOB, CLOB	OCILOBLOCATOR	OCILOBLOCATOR

Calls made to external procedures may also have to specify properties associated with each of the variables being passed. These properties deal with **NULL** indication, lengths, and character-set information and are specified with the property specifiers: **INDICATOR**, **LENGTH**, **MAXLEN**, **CHARSETID**, and **CHARSETFORM**. Table 7.2 shows how these properties are defined.

External Procedure Guidelines

Currently, each user who calls an external procedure spawns an additional **extproc** operating-system level process that stays active until the user logs off of Oracle. You should, therefore, limit external procedure usage to functions that absolutely have to be that way for performance benefits. In the future, the **extproc** procedure may be multithreaded, so make sure any external procedures are thread-safe. Avoid using shared static values in particular.

Table 7.2 Property datatype mappings.

Property	C Parameter		PL/SQL Parameter	
	Allowed External Types	Default Type	Allowed Types	Modes
INDICATOR	SHORT, INT, LONG,	SHORT	all scalars	IN, IN OUT, OUT, RETURN
LENGTH	SHORT, UNSIGNED SHORT, INT UNSIGNED INT, LONG, UNSIGNED LONG	INT	CHAR, LONG RAW, RAW, VARCHAR2	IN, IN OUT, OUT, RETURN
MAXLEN	SHORT, UNSIGNED SHORT, INT UNSIGNED INT, LONG, UNSIGNED LONG	INT	CHAR, LONG RAW, RAW, VARCHAR2	IN OUT, OUT, RETURN
CHARSETID, CHARSETFORM	UNSIGNED SHORT, UNSIGNED INT, UNSIGNED LONG	UNSIGNED INT	CHAR, CLOB, VARCHAR2	IN, IN OUT, OUT, RETURN

Never write to **IN** parameters, overflow the capacity of **OUT** parameters, or read an **OUT** parameter or function result.

Always assign a value to an **IN OUT** and an **OUT** parameter and to function results; otherwise, you will go to the zombie process graveyard.

If the **WITH CONTEXT** and **PARAMETERS** clauses are used, you must specify the parameter **CONTEXT** to show the position of the context pointer in the parameter list. If the **PARAMETERS** clause is omitted, context is assumed to be the first parameter passed to the external procedure.

If the **PARAMETERS** clause is specified in a call to an external function, then the **RETURN** parameter (not **RETURN** property) is placed in the last position of the parameter list.

A one-to-one correspondence must exist between the parameter list passed and the formal parameter list for the external procedure. The datatypes must be compatible. No implicit conversion is done during an external procedure call.

If a parameter has **INDICATOR** or **LENGTH** specified for it, it is treated as the same mode as the corresponding formal parameter.

If a parameter has **MAXLEN**, **CHARSETID**, or **CHARSETFORM** specified, it is always treated as an **IN** parameter—even if **BY REF** is also specified.

If a parameter is of the types **CHAR**, **LONG RAW**, **RAW**, or **VARCHAR2**, the property **LENGTH** must be specified, and the length of the corresponding C external procedure parameter must be set to 0.

External Procedure Restrictions

External procedures have several restrictions that you need to be aware of. These restrictions are:

- This feature is available only on platforms that support DLLs (which includes the Sun operating system).

- Only routines callable from C code (not C++ code) are supported.

- You cannot pass PL/SQL cursor variables, records, collections, or instances of an object type to an external procedure.

- In the **LIBRARY** subclause, you cannot use a database link to specify a remote library.

- The Net8 listener must start an agent called **extproc** on the host that runs the Oracle Server.

- The maximum number of parameters that can be passed is 127. If **FLOAT** or **DOUBLE** datatypes are passed, this number drops. Treat each **FLOAT** or **DOUBLE** as two variable passes.

External procedure calls are a powerful new feature. Once the multithreading capability and ability to use some of the data collections and cursor variable passing is enabled, this feature will reach full potential.

Using OCI Calls In Oracle8

The Oracle Call Interface (OCI) allows use of the Oracle system at the application program interface level. This gives programmers a faster method of using Oracle features. Previous Oracle releases had limited capability in this area, but with Oracle8, the number and capabilities of the programs in the OCI have been greatly expanded.

These new features in OCI come at a price: Virtually all of the interface has been rewritten, all of the programs renamed, and all of the data structures revamped.

OCI Handles

OCI programs use handles to access storage areas allocated by the OCI library. These handles act as pointers to the storage areas and have no intrinsic value themselves. Table 7.3 lists the OCI handles used by the OCI programs to access these library structures.

Table 7.3   OCI handle types.

C Type	Description	Handle Type
OCIEnv	OCI Environment Handle	OCI_HTYPE_ENV
OCIError	OCI Error Handle	OCI_HTYPE_ERROR
OCISvcCtx	OCI Service Context Handle	OCI_HTYPE_SVCCTX
OCIStmt	OCI Statement Handle	OCI_HTYPE_STMT
OCIBind	OCI BIND Handle	OCI_HTYPE_BIND
OCIDefine	OCI Define Handle	OCI_HTYPE_DEFINE
OCIDescribe	OCI Describe Handle	OCI_HTYPE_DESCRIBE
OCIServer	OCI Server Handle	OCI_HTYPE_SERVER
OCISession	OCI User Session Handle	OCI_HTYPE_SESSION
OCITrans	OCI Transaction Handle	OCI_HTYPE_TRANS
OCIComplexObject	OCI Complex Object Retrieval (COR) Handle	OCI_HTYPE_COMPLEXOBJECT
OCISecurity	OCI Security Service Handle	OCI_HTYPE_SECURITY

Handles fall in a three-tier hierarchy: Environment at the top, BIND and define at the third tier beneath the statement handle, and the rest in the middle tier. With the exception of the environment handle, all user-allocated handles are allocated with the **OCIHandleAlloc()** call; the environment handle is allocated with the **OCIEnvInit()** call. All OCI applications must use the **OCIEnvInit()** call. Handles are freed with the **OCIHandleFree()** call.

OCI Descriptors And Locators

OCI also uses descriptors and locators. These, like handles, point to data structures that define specific data. Six descriptor locator types are allocated with the **OCIDescriptorAlloc()** call and released with the **OCIDescriptorFree()** call. The descriptor/locator constructs are shown in Table 7.4.

Notice in Table 7.4 that only **LOB**s have locators. This is because **LOB**s may be stored outside of the main table or even the entire database. The proper **OCILobLocator** is used with **OCI_DTYPE_LOB** or **OCI_DTYPE_FILE** OCI type constants. You must use **OCI_DTYPE_LOB** with **BLOB** or **CLOB** datatypes and **OCI_DTYPE_FILE** with **BFILE LOB**s.

OCI Operations

OCI programming follows a predefined set of operations:

- Initialization of an OCI process

- Allocation of handles and descriptors

Table 7.4   Listing of OCI descriptors/locators.

C Type	Description	OCI Type Constant
OCISnapshot	Snapshot Descriptor	OCI_DTYPE_SNAP
OCILobLocator	**LOB** Datatype Locator	OCI_DTYPE_LOB
OCILobLocator	**FILE** Datatype Locator	OCI_DTYPE_FILE
OCIParam	Read-only Parameter Descriptor	OCI_DTYPE_PARAM
OCIRowid	**ROWID** Descriptor	OCI_DTYPE_ROWID
OCIComplexObjectComp	Complex Object Descriptor	OCI_DTYPE_COMPLEX OBJECTCOMP

- Application initialization, connection, and authorization

- Process SQL statements

- Commit or rollback

- Terminate the application

- Release handles and descriptors

- Handle errors

Errors are handled by processing OCI return codes, which provide information on process state at termination. The OCI error codes are shown in Table 7.5.

OCIErrorGet() returns a single error at a time off of the error stack. Multiple calls should be made until no further errors are returned.

OCI Datatype Codes

Oracle datatypes are communicated to OCI through datatype codes. Conversions can be performed on returned data by specifying a different datatype code. Table 7.6 contains the internal Oracle datatypes and their lengths and datatype codes.

External datatypes are those used by your program. The external datatype code indicates to Oracle how a host variable represents data in your program. Table 7.7 shows

Table 7.5   Listing of OCI error codes.

OCI Return Code	Description
OCI_SUCCESS	The function completed successfully.
OCI_SUCCESS_WITH_INFO	The function completed successfully; a call to **OCIErrorGet()** will return additional diagnostic information, including warnings.
OCI_NO_DATA	The function completed; there is no further data.
OCI_ERROR	The function failed; a call to **OCIErrorGet()** will return additional information.
OCI_INVALID_HANDLE	An invalid handle was passed as a parameter; no further diagnostics are available.
OCI_NEED_DATA	The application must provide runtime data.

Table 7.6 Internal Oracle datatypes.

Internal Oracle Datatype	Maximum Internal Length	Datatype Code
VARCHAR2	4,000 bytes	1
NUMBER	21 bytes	2
LONG	2^31-1 bytes	8
ROWID	10 bytes	11
DATE	7 bytes	12
RAW	2,000 bytes	23
LONG RAW	2^31-1 bytes	24
CHAR	2,000 bytes	96
MLSLABEL	255 bytes	105
UDT	N/A	108
REF	N/A	111
CLOB	N/A	112
BLOB	N/A	113

how external datatypes map to external datatype codes, type of program variable, and OCI-defined constants.

About the only place that Oracle truly documents the format of the 7-byte date field (a date is only 7 bytes total length for the data part with one header byte, for a total of 8 bytes per date in internal format) is the OCI manual. A date is a 7-byte excess-100 notation value. Table 7.8 shows how a date is mapped into the 7 bytes.

Note that 17 (minute value) maps into 18. This is because it is an excess-1 notation for hours, minutes, and seconds (midnight is 1,1,1). A time of 3:00 p.m. maps to 12+3+1=16 (hours are 24-hour format). Dates before the common era (BCE) are less than 100. For Oracle, time begins at 01-JAN-4712 BCE.

OCI date entry does no validity checking, so the programmer is responsible for ensuring a valid date is entered.

Table 7.7 External datatypes and codes.

External Datatype Constant	Code	Program Variable	OCI ConstantSQLT
VARCHAR2	1	char(n)	SQLT_CHR
NUMBER	2	unsigned char[21]	SQLT_NUM
8-bit signed INTEGER	3	signed char	SQLT_INT
16-bit signed INTEGER	3	signed short signed int	SQLT_INT
32-bit signed INTEGER	3	signed int signed long	SQLT_INT
FLOAT	4	float double	SQLT_FLT
NULL-terminated STRING	5	char(n+1)	SQLT_STR
VARNUM	6	char[22]	SQLT_VNU
LONG	8	char[n]	SQLT_LNG
VARCHAR	9	char[n+sizeof(short integer)]	SQLT_VCS
ROWID (V7)	11	char[n]	SQLT_RID
DATE	12	char[7]	SQLT_DAT
VARRAW	15	unsigned char[n+sizeof(short integer)]	SQLT_VBI
RAW	23	unsigned char[n]	SQLT_BIN
LONG RAW	24	unsigned char[n]	SQLT_LBI
UNSIGNED INT	68	unsigned	SQLT_UIN
LONG VARCHAR	94	char[n+sizeof(short integer)]	SQLT_LVC
LONG VARRAW	95	unsigned char[n+sizeof(integer)]	SQLT_LVB
CHAR	96	char[n]	SQLT_AFC
CHARZ	97	char[n+1]	SQLT_AVC
ROWID descriptor (V8)	104	OCIRowid	SQLT_RDD

(continued)

Table 7.7 External datatypes and codes *(continued)*.

External Datatype Constant	Code	Program Variable	OCI ConstantSQLT
MLSLABEL	106	char[n]	SQLT_LAB
NAMED DATA TYPE	108	struct	SQLT_NTY
REF	110	OCIRef	SQLT_REF
Character LOB	112	OCILobLocator	SQLT_CLOB
Binary LOB	113	OCILobLocator	SQLT_BLOB
Binary FILE	114	OCILobLocator	SQLT_FILE
OCI string type	155	OCIString	SQLT_VST
OCI date type	156	OCIDate	SQLT_ODT

Table 7.8 Example date map into 7-byte internal format.

Byte	1	2	3	4	5	6	7
Meaning	Century	Year	Month	Day	Hour	Minute	Second
30-Nov-1992 3:17 PM	119	192	11	30	16	18	1

Allowed OCI Data Transformations

OCI allows specific data transformations between internal Oracle datatypes and external datatypes only. These conversions are shown in Table 7.9.

OCI maintains a typecode for each Oracle datatype. These typecodes are returned when a table is described via OCI calls. The typecodes map to the SQLT codes previously introduced. This allows the mapping and conversion between the two. Table 7.10 shows the relationships between Oracle type system typenames, typecodes, and the equivalent SQLT type.

Other datatypes, such as **ub2** or **sb4**, may show up in code. These are defined in the platform-specific oratypes.h file.

Table 7.9 Internal/External allowed datatype conversion chart for OCI.

External Datatypes	VARCHAR2	NUMBER	LONG	ROWID	DATE	RAW	LONG RAW	CHAR	MLSLABEL
1 VARCHAR	i/o	i/o	i/o	i/o	i/o	i/o	i/o	i/o	
2 NUMBER	i/o	i/o	i					i/o	
3 INTEGER	i/o	i/o	i					i/o	
4 FLOAT	i/o	i/o	i					i/o	
5 STRING	i/o	i/o	i/o	i/o	i/o	i/o	i/o	i/o	i/o
6 VARNUM	i/o	i/o	i					i/o	
7 DECIMAL	i/o	i/o	i					i/o	
8 LONG	i/o	i/o	i/o	i/o	i/o	i/o	i/o	i/o	i/o
9 VARCHAR	i/o	i/o	i/o	i/o	i/o	i/o	i/o	i/o	i/o
11 ROWID	i		i	i/o				i	
12 DATE	i/o		i		i/o			i/o	
15 VARRAW	i/o		i			i/o	i/o	i/o	
23 RAW	i/o		i			i/o	i/o	i/o	
24 LONG RAW	0		i			i/o	i/o	o	
68 UNSIGNED	i/o	i/o	i					i/o	
94 LONG VARCHAR	i/o	i/o	i/o	i/o	i/o	i/o	i/o	i/o	i/o
95 LONG VARRAW	i/o		i			i/o	i/o	i/o	
96 CHAR	i/o	i/o	i/o	i/o	i/o	i/o	i	i/o	i/o
97 CHARZ	i/o	i/o	i/o	i/o	i/o	i/o	i	i/o	i/o
104 ROWID DESC									
106 MSLABEL									i/o

i = input, i/o = input and output, o = output

Table 7.10 OCI_typecode to SQLT code mappings.

Oracle Type SystemTypename	Oracle Type System Typecode	SQLT Type
BFILE	OCI_TYPECODE_BFILE	SQLT_BFILE
BLOB	OCI_TYPECODE_BLOB	SQLT_BLOB
CHAR	OCI_TYPECODE_CHAR(n)	SQLT_AFC(n)
CLOB	OCI_TYPECODE_CLOB	SQLT_CLOB
COLLECTION	OCI_TYPECODE_NAMEDCOLLECTION	SQLT_NCO
DATE	OCI_TYPECODE_DATE	SQLT_DAT
DECIMAL	OCI_TYPECODE_DECIMAL(p)	SQL_NUM
DOUBLE	OCI_TYPECODE_DOUBLE	SQL_FLT(8)
FLOAT	OCI_TYPECODE_FLOAT(b)	SQLT_FLT(8)
INTEGER	OCI_TYPECODE_INTEGER	SQL_INT(i)
OBJECT	OCI_TYPECODE_OBJECT	SQLT_NTY
OCTET	OCI_TYPECODE_OCTET	SQLT)INT(1)
POINTER	OCI_TYPECODE_PTR	
RAW	OCI_TYPECODE_RAW	SQLT_LVB
REAL	OCI_TYPECODE_REAL	SQLT_FLT(4)
REF	OCI_TYPECODE_REF	SQLT_REF
SIGNED(8)	OCI_TYPECODE_SIGNED8	SQLT_INT(1)
SIGNED(16)	OCI_TYPECODE_SIGNED16	SQLT_INT(2)
SIGNED(32)	OCI_TYPECODE_SIGNED32	SQLT_INT(4)
SMALLINT	OCI_TYPECODE_SMALLINT	SQLT_INT(i)
TABLE	OCI_TYPECODE_TABLE	SQLT_TAB
UNSIGNED(8)	OCI_TYPECODE_UNSIGNED8	SQLT_UIN(1)

(continued)

Table 7.10   OCI_typecode to SQLT code mappings (continued).

Oracle Type SystemTypename	Oracle Type System Typecode	SQLT Type
UNSIGNED(16)	OCI_TYPECODE_UNSIGNED16	SQLT_UIN(2)
UNSIGNED(32)	OCI_TYPECODE_UNSIGNED32	SQLT_UIN(4)
VARRAY	OCI_TYPECODE_VARRAY	SQLT_NAR
VARCHAR	OCI_TYPECODE_VARCHAR(n)	SQLT_CHR(n)
VARCHAR2	OCI_TYPECODE_VARCHAR2(n)	SQLT_VCS(n)

n = size in integer, p = precision in digits, s = scale in digits, i = size in bytes, b = precision in binary digits.

Use Of SQL And PL/SQL In OCI

In the previous section, we discussed in general that the processing of OCI programs involves initialization of the environment and variables, and then the execution of SQL or PL/SQL statements. The execution of SQL or PL/SQL involves the use of several OCI calls to prepare, bind, execute, and retrieve results from the OCI/SQL operations.

Binding is a virtual requirement for using SQL in OCI calls. Editing and recompiling your OCI routine each time you want to change the variable parameters in your SQL or PL/SQL statements makes little sense. Instead, you bind the address of the parameter to a location in memory where the appropriate values for the parameters are placed at the start of operation or during operation. This allows the substitution to be dynamic in nature, but also allows the statements used to be parsed into the shared pool area of the SGA and reused without reparsing, adding to efficiency. Figure 7.1 shows the steps required to process SQL or PL/SQL code using the OCI.

*Versions of OCI prior to 8.x required an explicit parse step. In version 8.x, this is no longer required, because an implicit parse is done on execute. This means that all statements including DML and DDL must have an **EXECUTE** call.*

Improving Efficiency By Using Array Fetching With OCI

To improve efficiency and reduce Net8 round trips between a client and a server, you can set two attributes that enable array fetching during operations that fetch data from the server. By making calls to the **OCIAttrset()** call with values for the

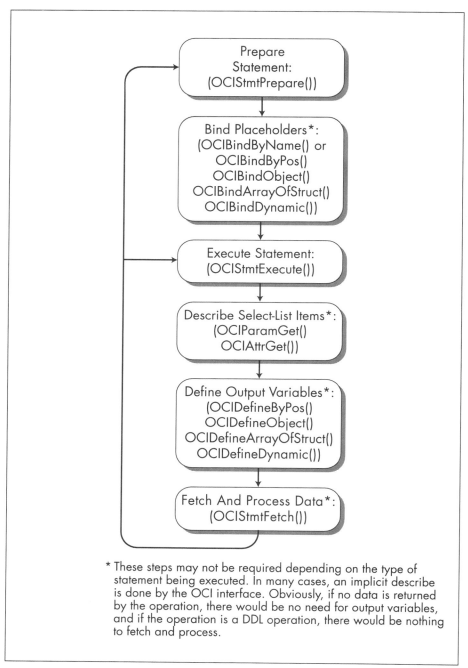

Prepare
Statement:
(OCIStmtPrepare())

Bind Placeholders*:
(OCIBindByName() or
OCIBindByPos()
OCIBindObject()
OCIBindArrayOfStruct()
OCIBindDynamic())

Execute Statement:
(OCIStmtExecute())

Describe Select-List Items*:
(OCIParamGet()
OCIAttrGet())

Define Output Variables*:
(OCIDefineByPos()
OCIDefineObject()
OCIDefineArrayOfStruct()
OCIDefineDynamic())

Fetch And Process Data*:
(OCIStmtFetch())

* These steps may not be required depending on the type of
statement being executed. In many cases, an implicit describe
is done by the OCI interface. Obviously, if no data is returned
by the operation, there would be no need for output variables,
and if the operation is a DDL operation, there would be nothing
to fetch and process.

Figure 7.1

Steps to execute SQL using the OCI.

oci_attr_prefetch_rows and **oci_attr_prefetch_memory** attributes, you can set the number of rows fetched with each call and the amount of memory to allocate for those rows. The controlling parameter is **oci_attr_prefetch_memory**, because you cannot fetch more rows than will fit in the allocated memory.

Another useful feature of OCI is the array interface, which allows passing of an entire array of input variables with a single OCI execute call. This greatly reduces Net8 round trips. To use the array interface, you bind arrays instead of single values to the placeholders.

 *In previous releases of Oracle (7.x), only **IN** variables needed to be initialized. With 8.x, both **IN** and **OUT** values need to be initialized, if only by setting the buffer length to 0 or the indicator value to -1.*

To bind scalar values or arrays of scalar values, use **OCIBindByName** or **OCIBindByPos** calls. Obviously, if you use a 10-place array for one of the scalar arrays, you should be sure to use a 10-place array for all of them that you bind. Binding a named datatype (**SQLT_NTY**) or a **REF** (**SQLT_REF**) requires two **BIND** calls: **OCIBindByName** or **OCIBindByPos**, and **OCIBindObject**.

To bind **LOB** data (**SQLT_BLOB**, **SQLT_CLOB**), you first allocate the **LOB** locator using **OCIDescriptorAlloc** and then bind its address (**OCILobLocator****) with **OCIBindByName** or **OCIBindByPos** using the appropriate **LOB** datatype. Binding an array of structures or static arrays requires two **BIND** calls: one to **OCIBindByName** or **OCIBindByPos**, and one to **OCIBindArrayOfStruc**. To do a piecewise insert of large objects, first call **OCIBindByName** or **OCIBindByPos**, and then call **OCIBindDynamic** to register piecewise callbacks. To bind **REF CURSOR** variables (**SQLT_RSET**), allocate a statement handle using **OCIStmt**, and then bind its address (**OCIStmt****) using the **SQLT_RSET** datatype.

Once the variables have been bound, they can be loaded into their respective memory addresses via C program reads and the SQL processed using the **OCIStmtExecute()** call. To get any data returned from the execute, the receiving memory areas must be identified and their names defined. This is most easily done via the **OCIDefineByPos()** or **OCIDefineByName()** calls after obtaining any required data about the returned values (such as type, length, etc.) with the **OCIParamGet()** and **OCIAttrGet()** calls. Advanced defines are accomplished via **OCIDefineArrayOfStruc()** for arrays and **OCIDefineDynamic()** for piecewise fetches.

If you do not take advantage of the implicit **DESCRIBE** or for some reason cannot use it, you will have to use the **OCIDescribeAny()** call after its handle has been allocated using **OCIHandleAlloc()**. Once this call has been processed, an attribute tree record about the described object is pointed to by the handle value. Once the attribute tree is created by the call to **OCIDescribeAny()**, subsequent calls to **OCIAttrGet()** and **OCIParmGet()** get their data from the tree and require no round trips to the host. **OCIDescribeAny()** works against top-level objects.

Using OCI With Oracle8 Object Types

To use OCI in the object environment of Oracle8, you must initialize it in object mode. In addition, you should use the object type translator (OTT) to generate a C struc header file for each object type that the OCI will use. In object mode, **SELECT**s will return **REF** values, which must then be pinned to get the values represented by the **REF**. These values will be placed in the client-side object buffer, where they can be modified. Once the modifications are complete, the object buffer is flushed back to the database on the server side. During **UPDATE** operations, you may want to lock an object instance. This is accomplished with the **OCIObjectLock()** call. All locks are released at the end of a transaction.

Oracle objects are either *persistent* or *transient*. Persistent objects are stored in the database and are either standalone or embedded into other objects. Transient objects are an instance of an object type created using the **OCIObjectNew()** call. They cannot be converted into persistent objects. Figure 7.2 shows the basic work flow for object-oriented OCI processes.

OCI can also create any object using the **OCIObjectNew()** call. This object can be either persistent or transient. If the object is to be persistent, the table in which it is to be stored must be specified using the **OCIObjectPinTable()** call. To create a transient object, use the **OCITypeBYName()** call to pass the type descriptor object for the type being created. To remove a transient object created by **OCIObjectNew()**, call the **OCIObjectFree()** routine. To delete a persistent object, use **OCIObject MarkDelete()**. Instances of an object can be copied using **OCIObjectCopy()**.

The Client-Side Object Cache

We have discussed the object cache in general terms, but what exactly is it? The object cache is a client-side memory structure used to hold fetched and pinned object instances. Only objects that can be referenced are pinned. If an instance is directly retrieved by value, it is not placed in the cache. Each initialized environment

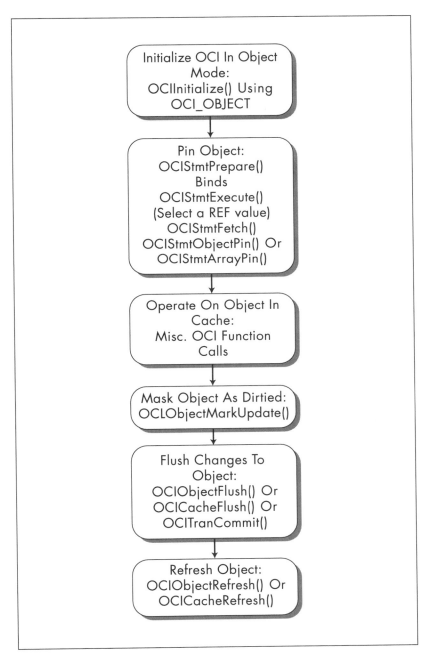

Figure 7.2

Example object OCI process work flow.

handle has one cache. Modifications to cache objects are not visible to other processes unless they are flushed from the cache.

Objects that are no longer needed can be freed, or unpinned, thus releasing their memory for reuse. The **OCIObjectUnpin()** call unpins individual object instances. The entire cache can be unpinned with the **OCICacheUnpin()** call. Pin duration can be set at the transaction level by setting the **oci_duration_trans** attribute or at the session level with the **oci_duration_session** attribute.

The object cache is controlled by two parameters that are passed to the OCI call initializing the environment handle: **oci_attr_cache_max_size** and **oci_attr_cache_opt_size**. If the memory used by the cache reaches or exceeds a calculated high-water mark based on **oci_attr_cache_max_size** and **oci_attr_cache_opt_size**, then objects with a pin count of 0 are aged out of the cache until **oci_attr_cache_opt_size** is reached or eligible objects no longer exist. The high-water level is calculated like this:

```
high_water (max cache size) =
oci_attr_cache_opt_size + oci_attr_cache_opt_size * (oci_attr_cache_max_size / 100)
```

The default value for **oci_attr_cache_max_size** is 10 percent. The default value for **oci_attr_cache_opt_size** is 200K.

Object Type Translator (OTT) Usage

We have looked at the object type translator in passing, but let's take a better look at just what it is and what it does. The OTT converts object definitions formed with **CREATE TYPE** commands into C language struc headers for use in C programs (usually ones using OCI calls). The OTT is a command-line level program, such as import and export.

The OTT program takes an **INTYPE** file and generates an **OUTTYPE** file, one or more C header files, and an optional implementation file:

```
ott user/password intype=intype.file outtype=outtype.file code= C|ANSI_C|KR_C
hfile=header.h
```

The **INTYPE** file contains instructions for the OTT program to use when translating the type(s) into header files. The **INTYPE** file can contain:

- **TYPE**—Tells which types from the database to translate.

- **TYPE x AS y**—Tells which name to use for the specified type.

- **VERSION**—Subclause under **TYPE** that tells version of **TYPE** to use—"$8.0", for example.

- **HFILE**—Subclause of **TYPE** that tells that this should go into the specified "xxx.h" file.

- **TRANSLATE x AS y**—Subclause of the **TYPE** command that identifies the attributes that need a name change during conversion to a header.

- **CASE**—Tells OTT whether the output should be in upper- or lowercase.

- **SCHEMA_NAMES**—Tells OTT whether to include schema names in the header file. Defaults to **ALWAYS**. The other values possible are **IF_NEEDED** and **FROM_INTYPE**.

Once the **TYPE** is translated into a header, the header is used in a C **include** command for the OCI program that needs to access that type.

Summary For OCI Section

This section covers only the high points of OCI usage. Oracle has documented all aspects of OCI usage in a two-volume set: *Programmer's Guide To The Oracle Call Interface, Release 8*, Volumes I and II, Part Number A54657-01, June 1997, by Phil Locke (primary author).

Before tackling a major OCI project (that is, any OCI project), you should review these two volumes. Oracle8 has 200 OCI calls, too many for me to cover in this book.

Using The Advanced Queuing Feature Of Oracle8

Oracle8's advanced queuing (AQ) option allows for disconnected/deferred messaging, persistent messages, message journaling and priority, and ordering of messages. The application uses database tables and external scheduling processes to maintain queue data. You use stored procedure calls to **ENQUEUE** and **DEQUEUE** messages.

The smallest level of the advanced queue process is the individual message. The queue tables hold messages that have been enqueued; exceptions are placed in exception queues. Agents (either producers or consumers) place messages in or remove them from the queue. Messages can be set to expire and "self-age" out of the queue.

Basic queuing involves a single producer and a single consumer. More complex schemes involve multiple producers and multiple consumers and may involve multiple uses of the same messages. Consumers are known as *subscribers* to a given queue. A producer can restrict the subscribers who can dequeue a message, based on a specified recipient list.

To use advanced queuing, you would follow the general process shown in Figure 7.3.

The CATQUEUE.SQL script builds the advanced queue option. It creates three special tables and builds the following packages:

- DBMSAQ.SQL, DBMSAQ.PLB—DBMS package specification for advanced queuing operations (**DBMS_AQ**).

  Procedures:

  ENQUEUE, DEQUEUE

- DBMSAQAD.SQL, PRVTADAQ.PLB—DBMS package specification for advanced queuing operations administration (**DBMS_AQADM**).

  Procedures:

  CREATE_QTABLE, CREATE_Q, DROP_Q,

  DROP_QTABLE, START_Q, STOP_Q, ALTER_Q,

  TEST_AC_DDL

- **DBMS_AQ_IMPORT_INTERNAL**

  Functions:

  AQ_TABLE_EXPORT_CHECK, AQ_EXPORT_CHECK

  Procedures:

  AQ_TABLE_DEFN_UPDATE, AQ_DEFN_UPDATE

Advanced queuing should be used where the following items are important:

- Ordering of messages (transactions—*a* comes before *b*, which comes before *c*).

- Sequence deviation.

- Correlation of discrete message events.

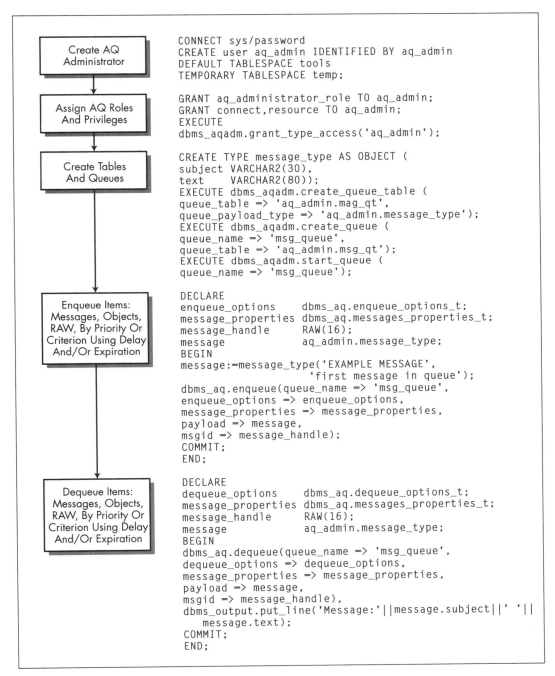

```
                            CONNECT sys/password
  ┌─────────────────┐       CREATE user aq_admin IDENTIFIED BY aq_admin
  │   Create AQ     │       DEFAULT TABLESPACE tools
  │  Administrator  │       TEMPORARY TABLESPACE temp;
  └─────────────────┘
           │               GRANT aq_administrator_role TO aq_admin;
  ┌─────────────────┐       GRANT connect,resource TO aq_admin;
  │  Assign AQ Roles│       EXECUTE
  │ And Privileges  │       dbms_aqadm.grant_type_access('aq_admin');
  └─────────────────┘
           │               CREATE TYPE message_type AS OBJECT (
  ┌─────────────────┐       subject VARCHAR2(30),
  │  Create Tables  │       text    VARCHAR2(80));
  │  And Queues     │       EXECUTE dbms_aqadm.create_queue_table (
  └─────────────────┘       queue_table => 'aq_admin.mag_qt',
           │               queue_payload_type => 'aq_admin.message_type');
           │               EXECUTE dbms_aqadm.create_queue (
           │               queue_name => 'msg_queue',
           │               queue_table => 'aq_admin.msg_qt');
           │               EXECUTE dbms_aqadm.start_queue (
           │               queue_name => 'msg_queue');

           │               DECLARE
  ┌─────────────────┐       enqueue_options      dbms_aq.enqueue_options_t;
  │ Enqueue Items:  │       message_properties dbms_aq.messages_properties_t;
  │Messages, Objects,│      message_handle      RAW(16);
  │RAW, By Priority Or│     message             aq_admin.message_type;
  │Criterion Using Delay│   BEGIN
  │ And/Or Expiration│      message:=message_type('EXAMPLE MESSAGE',
  └─────────────────┘                         'first message in queue');
           │               dbms_aq.enqueue(queue_name => 'msg_queue',
           │               enqueue_options => enqueue_options,
           │               message_properties => message_properties,
           │               payload => message,
           │               msgid => message_handle);
           │               COMMIT;
           │               END;

           │               DECLARE
  ┌─────────────────┐       dequeue_options      dbms_aq.dequeue_options_t;
  │ Dequeue Items:  │       message_properties dbms_aq.messages_properties_t;
  │Messages, Objects,│      message_handle      RAW(16);
  │RAW, By Priority Or│     message             aq_admin.message_type;
  │Criterion Using Delay│   BEGIN
  │ And/Or Expiration│      dbms_aq.dequeue(queue_name => 'msg_queue',
  └─────────────────┘       dequeue_options => dequeue_options,
                            message_properties => message_properties,
                            payload => message,
                            msgid => message_handle),
                            dbms_output.put_line('Message:'||message.subject||' '||
                              message.text);
                            COMMIT;
                            END;
```

Figure 7.3

Process for using the advanced queuing option.

- Time constraints on processing (*a* must be done before time *z* or not at all).

- Retention of messages is required (which transactions happened when).

- Message replies need to be queued/deferred.

- Exceptions need to be queued.

- The environment contains both transactional and nontransactional requests.

- The browsing of transactions (messages) may be required. (Has the Smith transaction processed yet?)

This advanced queuing model allows a better OLTP (Online Transaction Processing) modeling of real-world processes. Central to this concept is the **DBMS_AQ** package, which allows the queuing to take place. For security reasons, only **SYS** has initial execute privileges on the **DBMS_AQ** package. **AQ_USER_ROLE** can grant execute to other users as required.

The *ENQUEUE* Procedure

The **ENQUEUE** procedure has the following input and output parameters:

Input:

q_schema	**VARCHAR2** with a default of **NULL**
q_name	**VARCHAR2**
corrid	**VARCHAR2** with a default of **NULL**
transactional	**BOOLEAN** with a default of **TRUE**
priority	Positive integer with a default value of 1
delay	**DATE** with a default of **NULL**
expiration	**NATURAL** number with a default of 0 (zero)
relative_msgid	**NUMBER** with a default of **NULL**
seq_deviation	**CHAR** with a default of **A**
exception_queue_schema	**VARCHAR2** with a default of **NULL**

exception_queue	**VARCHAR2** with a default of **NULL**
reply_queue_schema	**VARCHAR2** with a default of **NULL**
reply_queue	**VARCHAR2** with a default of **NULL**
user_data	**RAW**/any object type

Output:

msgid	**RAW**

The purpose of the **ENQUEUE** procedure is to load a message into a queue specified by the user. The parameters for **ENQUEUE** have the following definitions:

- **q_schema**—Names the schema containing the queue table object. In 8.0.2, the schema must be specified. In later releases, it will default to the user's queue, if not specified.

- **q_name**—Names the queue table.

- **Corrid**—Identifies the correlation. This is optional but can be used to tell an application how to correlate this message with other messages.

- **Transactional**—Indicates whether the message being enqueued is part of the current transaction. **TRUE**, the default, means the operation is complete when the transaction commits. **FALSE** means the **ENQUEUE** is not part of the current transaction and is to be considered as a separate transaction. This inner transaction (the **ENQUEUE**) must complete before the outer transaction (the transaction that placed the **ENQUEUE**) can complete.

- **Priority**—Ranges from 1 to 100, with 100 being the highest priority. Messages with a higher priority are dequeued first, regardless of the order in which they were received in relation to lower-priority messages.

- **Delay**—Specifies a date calculation to be performed against the **ENQUEUE** time of the message before it is processed.

- **Expiration**—Specifies the expiration time in seconds for a message. If the message is not dequeued before this time limit expires, as measured from **ENQUEUE** time, then the message is placed in the exception queue and will be removed from the active queue.

- **relative_msgid**—Specifies the message ID, which must be processed before this message. This field is required if the **seq_deviation** is set to **B** for before.

- **seq_deviation**—Normally set to **A** for after, or normal processing. If set to **B**, then some value must be entered into the **relative_msgid** parameter to tell what message should be before this one. If **seq_deviation** is set to **T** (top), then this message is placed on top of the dequeue list ahead of any other message in this queue.

- **exception_queue_schema**—Identifies the schema where the exception queue table is stored. Each queue table has a default exception queue table (**aq$_<queuetable_name>$_E**). If this is left to **NULL**, the user's default schema is used.

- **exception_queue**—Identifies the exception queue table where excepted queue entries are placed for resolution. This defaults to **aq$_<queuetable_name>$_E** if not specified to some other value.

- **reply_queue_schema**—Specifies the schema where the **reply_queue** table resides. If not specified, it defaults to the user's default schema.

- **reply_queue**—Names the **reply_queue** table.

- **user_data**—Returns user data. It is a straight pass-through by the AQ processes. If it is non-**NULL**, the application must specify an **IN** parameter with the same type as the one defined for the queue; otherwise, an ORA-25221 error will be returned.

- **msgid**—Specifies a globally unique identifier for this message. The **msgid** serves as a handle for subsequent operations against this message.

The purpose of the **ENQUEUE** procedure is to place messages into the queue table.

The *DEQUEUE* Procedure

The **DEQUEUE** procedure has the following input and output parameters:

Input:

q_schema	**VARCHAR2** with a default of **NULL**
q_name	**VARCHAR2**

corrid	**VARCHAR2** with a default of **NULL**
deq_mode	**CHAR** with a default of **D**
wait_time	**NATURAL NUMBER** with a default of **0**
transactional	**BOOLEAN** with a default of **TRUE**

Output:

out_msgid	**NUMBER**
out_corrid	**VARCHAR2**
priority	Positive integer with a default value of **1**
delay	**DATE** with a default of **NULL**
retry	**NATURAL** number
exception_queue_schema	**VARCHAR2**
exception_queue	**VARCHAR2**
reply_queue_schema	**VARCHAR2** with a default of **NULL**
reply_queue	**VARCHAR2** with a default of **NULL**
user_data	**RAW**/any object type

The purpose of the **DEQUEUE** procedure is to unload a message from a queue specified by the user. The parameters for **DEQUEUE** have the following definitions:

- **q_schema**—Specifies the schema containing the queue table object. In 8.0.2, the schema must be specified. In later releases, it will default to the user's queue, if not specified.

- **q_name**—Specifies the queue table from which the message should be dequeued. Unless a specific **msgid** or **corrid** is specified, only messages ready to be dequeued will **DEQUEUE**.

- **msgid**—Specifies the message ID of the specific message (if any) to **DEQUEUE**.

- **corrid**—Specifies the user-supplied correlation identifier. AQ will retrieve the first available message with this **corrid**.

- **deq_mode**—Specifies execution of request and disposition of the message:

  D means dequeue and destroy.

  B means browse this message using consistent read; dequeue, but don't destroy.

  L means browse this message and lock it. This is a nondestructive dequeue and lock. To unlock, do a normal **DEQUEUE** against the message.

- **wait_time**—Specifies the number of seconds a **DEQUEUE** should wait if it finds no messages.

- **Transactional**—Indicates whether the message being dequeued is part of the current transaction. **TRUE**, the default, means the operation is complete when the transaction commits. **FALSE** means the **DEQUEUE** is not part of the current transaction and is to be considered a separate transaction. This transaction (the **ENQUEUE**) must complete before the outer (the transaction that placed the **ENQUEUE**) can complete.

- **out_msgid**—Returns the system-supplied identifier of the message that has been dequeued.

- **out_corrid**—Returns the application-supplied correlation identifier of the message.

- **Priority**—Returns the priority of the message. All messages must have priority.

- **Delay**—Returns the requested time delay of the dequeued message.

- **Expiration**—Returns the expiration time in seconds of a message.

- **Retry**—Returns the number of **DEQUEUE** operations performed on this message before it was successfully dequeued.

- **exception_queue_schema**—Returns the name of the schema where the **exception_queue** table is stored. Each queue table has a default exception queue table (**aq$_<queuetable_name>$_E**). If this is left to **NULL**, the user's default schema is used.

- **exception_queue**—Returns the name of the **exception_queue** table where excepted queue entries are placed for resolution. This defaults to **aq$_<queuetable_name>$_E** if not specified to some other value.

- **reply_queue_schema**—Returns the name of the schema where the **reply_queue** table resides. If not specified, it defaults to the user's default schema.

- **reply_queue**—Returns the name of the **reply_queue** table.

- **user_data**—Returns user data and is a straight pass-through by the AQ processes. If non-**NULL**, the application must specify an **IN** parameter with the same type as the one defined for the queue; otherwise, an ORA-25221 error will be returned.

The purpose of the **DEQUEUE** procedure is to remove messages from the queue table for processing.

Required init<SID>.ora Parameters

In order to work, the advanced queuing feature must have one queue process started. This is accomplished via the initialization parameter **AQ_TM_PROCESSES**. This parameter must be set to 1—and only 1—in 8.0.2, and the database must be shut down and restarted to turn advanced queuing on. Later releases promise to allow multiple queue processes.

DBMS_AQADM Procedure

The **DBMS_AQADM** package provides the administrative support packages for the advanced queuing option. Administrative support includes the building and dropping of queue tables and queues, as well as the stopping, starting, and altering of queues. The advanced queuing feature is new in Oracle8.

The CREATE_QTABLE Procedure

The **CREATE_QTABLE** procedure accepts the following input parameters:

q_schema	**VARCHAR2**
q_table	**VARCHAR2**
q_object_type_schema	**VARCHAR2** with a default of **NULL**
q_object_type	**VARCHAR2** with a default of **NULL**

object_type_format	**VARCHAR2** with a default of **U**
storage_space	**VARCHAR2** with a default of **NULL**
sort_list	**VARCHAR2** with a default of **NULL**
user_comment	**VARCHAR2** with a default of **NULL**
lob_storage	**VARCHAR2** with a default of **NULL**
lob_tspace	**VARCHAR2** with a default of **NULL**

The purpose of the **CREATE_QTABLE** procedure is to build a queue table and supporting query view for use by the advanced queuing option. Before a queue can be started, it must have a supporting queue table built by this procedure. The table will have a value of **aq$** as a prefix. A default ordering of the queue can be enforced by specifying a value for **sort_list**, which is a comma-separated list of **sort_column/sort_order** pairs.

The procedure's input parameters are defined as:

- **q_schema**—Specifies the schema in which the queue table is to be built.

- **q_table**—Specifies the queue table to be built. Because this is used for default naming of other objects, where prefixes and suffixes will be added, keep it to 25 characters at a maximum.

- **q_object_type_schema**—Specifies the schema to which the **q_object_type** belongs. It will default to the value of **q_schema**, if not specified.

- **q_object_type**—Specifies the object type of the user data stored (if any). If specified, the object type must exist when the table is created.

- **object_type_format**—Specifies whether the object type should be created **P** (packed) or **U** (unpacked). Unpacked is the default.

- **storage_space**—Specifies the storage parameters when the table is created. This parameter can be made up of any combinations of **PCTFREE**, **PCTUSED**, **INITRANS**, **MAXTRANS**, and a **STORAGE** clause.

- **sort_list**—A comma-separated list of column names and sort orders. This is used to specify the ordering of the queue. The allowed column names are: **msgid**, **priority**, and **enq_time**. Use **A** for ascending order and **D** for descending order. If not specified, the queue will be FIFO (first in first out, except for priority-coded messages).

- **user_comment**—A description of the table that will be added to the queue catalog.

- **lob_storage**—A list of storage parameters for the **LOB** column of the queue table.

- **lob_tspace**—Tablespace name for the **LOB** column of the queue table.

The **CREATE_QTABLE** procedure generates no documented exceptions.

The **CREATE_Q** Procedure

The **CREATE_Q** procedure has these input parameters:

q_schema	**VARCHAR2**
q_name	**VARCHAR2**
q_table	**VARCHAR2**
q_type	**VARCHAR2** with a default of **N**
max_retries	**NUMBER** with a default of **0**
retry_delay	**NUMBER** with a default of **0**
misc_tracking	**BOOLEAN** with a default of **FALSE**
retention	**BOOLEAN** with a default of **FALSE**
ret_time	**NATURAL** number with a default of **NULL**
comment	**VARCHAR2** with a default of **NULL**

The purpose of this procedure is to add the configuration information of a new queue into the catalog table **sys.aq$queues**. Once a queue is created, you can control it with the **start_q**, **stop_q**, and **alter_q** procedures. The **q_type** parameter controls whether a queue is a normal or an exception queue. Only dequeue operations are allowed on an exception queue.

The procedure's input parameters have the following definitions:

- **q_schema**—The schema to which the queue belongs.

- **q_name**—The name of the queue that is to be created.

- **q_table**—The name of the queue table that the queue is to use.

- **q_type**—The type of queue:

  N means the queue is normal; this is the default.

  E means this is an exception queue.

- **max_retries**— The number of times processing is retried after a failure ranges from 1 to 20. The default of 0 means no retries, and the parameter is ignored.

- **retry_delay**—The time in seconds to wait to retry this message execution after a transaction rollback. This defaults to 0, which means that the message should be retried as soon as possible. This parameter has no meaning if the value of **max_retries** is 0.

- **misc_tracking**—A **BOOLEAN TRUE** or **FALSE** that turns on or off tracking of miscellaneous queue events, not normally used.

- **retention**—If set to **TRUE**, all messages are retained in the queue. The default is **FALSE**, which tells AQ to destroy a message after a successful dequeue.

- **ret_time**—If specified, the number of days messages should be retained in the queue after successful execution. If retention is set to **TRUE**, then this value should be non-zero.

- **comment**—A user-entered comment that is stored in the queue catalog.

This procedure has no documented exceptions.

The *DROP_Q* Procedure

The **DROP_Q** procedure has two input parameters: **q_schema** (**VARCHAR2**) and **q_name** (**VARCHAR2**). The purpose of this procedure is to drop an existing queue. A queue must be stopped with the **stop_q** procedure before it can be dropped. If the queue has been stopped when **drop_q** is executed against it, it cleans up all queue entries and returns. If the queue hasn't been stopped, then a message giving a resource-busy error is returned.

The procedure input parameters are defined as:

- **q_schema**—The name of the schema to which the queue belongs.

- **q_name**—The name of the queue that should be dropped.

The *DROP_QTABLE* Procedure

The **DROP_QTABLE** procedure has three input parameters: **q_schema** (**VARCHAR2**), **q_table** (**VARCHAR2**), and **force** (**VARCHAR2** with a default value of **N**). The purpose of this procedure is to drop an existing queue table.

The procedure's input parameters are defined as:

- **q_schema**—The schema that the queue table to be dropped belongs to.

- **q_table**—The queue table to be dropped. A table of the same name is created as a repository for the queue messages.

- **force**—If the parameter is set to **N**, you must explicitly stop and drop all the queues that use the table before it can be dropped. If set to **Y**, then all queues are stopped and dropped internally.

This procedure has no documented exceptions.

The *START_Q* Procedure

The **START_Q** procedure has three input parameters: **q_name** (**VARCHAR2**), **ENQUEUE** (**BOOLEAN** with a default of **TRUE**), and **DEQUEUE** (**BOOLEAN** with a default of **TRUE**). The purpose of the procedure is to start a queue that has just been created or has been stopped via the **stop_q** command. Queues have to be started before they can be used. The parameters **ENQUEUE** and **DEQUEUE** enable and disable queuing of messages. By default, both enqueuing and dequeuing of messages are allowed.

The procedure's input parameters are defined as:

- **q_schema**—Specifies the schema that the queue belongs to.

- **q_name**—Specifies the queue to start.

- **ENQUEUE**—If **TRUE** (the default), allows queuing of messages to the queue. **FALSE** means no messages can be enqueued to the queue.

- **DEQUEUE**—If **TRUE** (the default), allows dequeuing of messages from the queue. **FALSE** means no messages can be dequeued from the queue.

The procedure has no documented exceptions.

The *STOP_Q* Procedure

The **STOP_Q** procedure has the following input parameters:

q_schema	**VARCHAR2**
q_name	**VARCHAR2**
ENQUEUE	**BOOLEAN** with a default of **TRUE**
DEQUEUE	**BOOLEAN** with a default of **TRUE**
wait	**BOOLEAN** with a default of **TRUE**

The purpose of the procedure is to stop processing on the specified queue. The procedure can selectively stop enqueues, dequeues, or both.

The procedure's input parameters are defined as:

- **q_schema**—The name of the schema that the queue belongs to.

- **q_name**—The name of the schema to operate against.

- **ENQUEUE**—**TRUE** stops enqueue processing (default). **FALSE** allows enqueues to continue.

- **DEQUEUE**—**TRUE** stops dequeue processing (default). **FALSE** allows dequeues to continue.

- **wait**—**TRUE** allows transactions currently using the queue to complete before the specified actions are taken. **FALSE** attempts to stop the queue. If no transactions are using the queue, it returns immediately; if transactions are using the queue, a resource-busy error is returned.

This procedure has no documented exceptions.

The *ALTER_Q* Procedure

The **ALTER_Q** procedure accepts the following input arguments:

q_schema	**VARCHAR2**
q_name	**VARCHAR2**

max_retries	**NUMBER**
retry_delay	**NUMBER**
retention	**BOOLEAN**

The purpose of the procedure is to alter the specified queue's characteristics. The procedure's input parameters have the same definitions as in the **CREATE_Q** procedure.

This procedure has no documented exceptions.

Summary For Advanced Queuing

Advanced queuing allows developers to use message-based processing for applications that require a discrete ordering of process steps. Examples would be in order processing, manufacturing, and any application where one step must not start (or perhaps complete) before another or where one set of processes may continue working after sending messages to other processes without waiting on the return. The *Oracle8 Server Application Developer's Guide, Release 8* (June 1997, Oracle Corporation) provides numerous excellent examples of various AQ methods.

Use Of Deferred Constraint Checking

Oracle8 introduced the concept of deferred constraint checking, which allows for deferring the enforcement of a particular constraint until the entire transaction is committed. This means, you can load parent and child tables with data, without the hassle of enabling or disabling constraints. Once an entire set of tables is loaded with data (assuming the data is fully checked for proper compliance with the constraints before it is loaded), then all referential integrity is verified at **COMMIT**.

Oracle8 has added the **defer_clause** to the **CREATE TABLE** command's **CONSTRAINT** option. The **defer_clause** is shown in Figure 7.4.

The **SET CONSTRAINT** command is used to alter a constraint's deferred status. The **SET CONSTRAINT** command has the following simple syntax:

```
SET CONSTRAINT(S)  constraint_list -- or -- ALL   IMMEDIATE -- or-- DEFERRED;
```

You cannot change a constraint's deferred status. It is either switched on or off. To change the basic defer setting, you must drop and re-create the constraint.

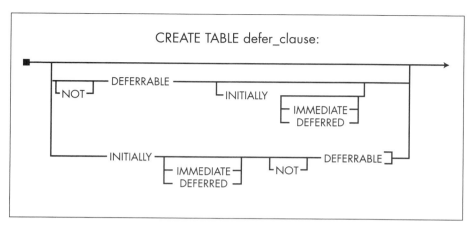

Figure 7.4

*Syntax for the **CREATE TABLE defer_clause**.*

Deferred constraints enhance the performance of bulk data loading and large transaction processing. The ability to switch the feature on and off—so that for normal transactions normal constraint checking is accomplished—is a powerful feature.

Practical Guide To

Use Of Oracle8 Collections And PL/SQL Features

- Access Of Types And Collections
- Using **CONSTRUCTOR** Methods
- Using The **THE** Keyword
- Using **REF** Values
- Example Of An External Procedure Call
- Using The OTT Program
- Creating A Deferred Constraint
- Using A Deferred Constraint

Access Of Types And Collections

Access of types and collections can be defined as selection, update to, and deletion of a type or collection.

The types used in this example are:

```
SQL> CREATE TYPE picture_part_v AS VARRAY(10)
  2  OF VARCHAR2(30);
  3  /

Type created.

SQL> CREATE TYPE artist_t AS OBJECT (
  2  last_name VARCHAR2(30),
  3  first_name VARCHAR2(30),
  4  middle_initial CHAR(1),
  5  ssn CHAR(11));
  6  /

Type created.

SQL> CREATE TYPE artist_list AS TABLE OF artist_t;
  2  /

Type created.

SQL> CREATE TYPE art_t AS OBJECT (
  2  picture_date DATE,
  3  picture_contents picture_part_v,
  4  artist artist_list);
  5  /

Type created.
```

This gives you a **VARRAY**, nested table, and a regular type rolled into a complex UDT called **art_t**. You can't do anything with this, however, until you use the UDT to create a table:

```
SQL> CREATE TABLE art OF art_t
  2  NESTED TABLE artist STORE AS artist_store;
Table created
```

Now you have an object table, **art**, composed of your complex UDT with its **VARRAY**, nested table, and **TYPE** definitions.

```
SQL> DESC art
   Name                                     Null?          Type
   ----------------------------------       ------------   ----------------
      PICTURE_DATE                                         DATE
      PICTURE_CONTENTS                                     PICTURE_PART_V
      ARTIST                                               ARTIST_LIST
```

To access the data stored in the table **art**, you first have to load the data into the table.

Using **CONSTRUCTOR** Methods

To load the types contained in **art**, use the **CONSTRUCTOR** methods created when the types themselves were created. These methods, named for the base types (**art_t**, **picture_part_v**, **artist_list**, and **artist_t**) are used to load the data into the **art** table:

```
SQL> INSERT INTO art VALUES (
  2    ART_T('18-sep-97',
  3    picture_part_v('DOG','CAT'','TREE'),
  4    ARTIST_LIST( ARTIST_T('Ault','Mike','R','222-33-4444').
  5                          ARTIST_T('Ault','Mike','R','111-22-3333')))
  6  );
1 row created
```

With this statement, you place a single value into the **picture_date** field of the first row of the **art** table, three values in the inline **VARRAY** structure **picture_contents**, and two values into the nested table structure (stored out of line in the **artist_store** storage table) **artist**.

What happens when you **SELECT** from **art**?

```
SQL> SELECT * FROM art

PICTURE_D
--------
PICTURE_CONTENTS
-----------------------------------------------------------------------------
ARTIST(LAST_NAME, FIRST_NAME, MIDDLE_INITIAL, SSN)
-----------------------------------------------------------------------------
18-SEP-97
PICTURE_PART_V('DOG', 'CAT', 'TREE')
ARTIST_LIST(ARTIST_T('Ault', 'Mike', 'R', '222-33-4444'), ARTIST_T('Ault', 'Susan',
'K', '111-22-3333'))
```

As you can see, you get back all the values that you put in. Using only SQL, you are limited to all or nothing from the **VARRAY** or nested table. To get individual values, you have to use PL/SQL. For example, to see the values stored in the **picture_contents VARRAY**, you would have to resort to PL/SQL:

```
SQL> SET SERVEROUTPUT ON
SQL> DECLARE
  2   artists artist_t;
  3   parts picture_part_v;
  4   ctr INTEGER;
  5   BEGIN
  6   SELECT picture_contents INTO parts FROM art WHERE picture_date='18-sep-97';
  7   FOR ctr IN 1..parts.last LOOP
  8   dbms_output.put_line('Picture part '||to_char(ctr)||':'||parts(ctr));
  9   END LOOP;
 10* END;
SQL> /
Picture part 1:DOG
Picture part 2:CAT
Picture part 3:TREE

PL/SQL procedure successfully completed.
```

What if you want to return a single row value from the table, based on a value stored in one of the collections? Because you didn't create a key value, the only way to identify a picture done by Susan is to report back the **picture_date**. Here's what you can do with your PL/SQL block to get this data:

```
SQL> SET SERVEROUTPUT ON
SQL> DECLARE
  2   artists artist_list;
  3   ctr INTEGER;
  4   pic_date DATE;
  5   CURSOR get_names IS
  6   SELECT picture_date,artist FROM art;
  7   BEGIN
  8   OPEN get_names;
  9   LOOP
 10   FETCH get_names INTO pic_date,artists;
 11   EXIT WHEN get_names%NOTFOUND;
 12    FOR ctr IN 1..artists.LAST LOOP
 13      IF artists(ctr).last_name='Ault' AND artists(ctr).first_name='Susan' THEN
 14     dbms_output.put_line('Picture Date '||to_char(pic_date,'DD-MON-YY'));
 15      END IF;
 16   END LOOP;
```

```
 17   END LOOP;
 18*  END;
SQL> /
Picture Date 18-SEP-97

PL/SQL procedure successfully completed.
```

If this seems incredibly complex in comparison with a simple join between a parent and child relational table, you are absolutely correct. You could have done the same with a single, fairly simple SQL **SELECT** statement in Oracle7.

In the previous examples, note the use of the **LAST** collection method to control the **LOOP** statements. This allows you to handle sparse arrays such as are found in nested tables. Using the **LAST** collection method also prevents overrun and exception problems when handling **VARRAY** types.

Using The **THE** Keyword

What if you want to update the values stored in a **VARRAY** or nested table? Oddly enough, you can do this with simple SQL. For this type of work, Oracle8 added the **THE** keyword. **THE** tells Oracle8 that it should expect a set of values to be returned. For example, suppose your artists change their last name to Smith. How would you update the nested table entries? Use the **THE** construct and a simple **UPDATE** command:

```
SQL> UPDATE
  2   THE
  3   ( SELECT artist FROM art a WHERE a.picture_date='18-sep-97'  ) artists
  4* SET artists.last_name='Smith'
SQL> /
2 rows updated.
SQL> commit;
Commit complete.
SQL> select artist from art;
ARTIST(LAST_NAME, FIRST_NAME, MIDDLE_INITIAL, SSN)
-----------------------------------------------------------------------------
ARTIST_LIST(ARTIST_T('Smith', 'Mike', 'R', '222-33-4444'), ARTIST_T('Smith',
'Susan', 'K', '111-22-3333'))
```

An **INSERT**, **UPDATE**, or **DELETE** command can use the same structure. Only **SELECT** is made to jump through the PL/SQL hoop.

Using **REF** Values

To implement one-to-many relationships in Oracle8 using objects, you use a **REF** value. A **REF** relationship is a one-to-one type of relationship. This is why it must point from the object table on the many side of the relation to the object table on the one side of the relation. A **REF** value is simply a pointer to the value of the related object table, essentially a copy of its **OID** value.

A **REF** can just be an **OID**, or it can include a **ROWID**. Using the **WITH ROWID** option allows a faster lookup of the related row. The disadvantage to using a **ROWID** in your **REF** is that doing an export and import operation requires a special **ANALYZE** command to verify that the **ROWID** values are reset properly.

Another problem with using **REF** values is that they are not automatically maintained. All **REF** type columns must be manually inserted either by SQL or via methods that you build into the type you use to build the object tables. I suggest using the latter method.

For an example of how the **REF** value is used, we will use a **purchase_orders** object table and its child object table **order_items**:

```
SQL> CREATE TYPE purchase_order_t AS OBJECT
  2  ( po_num number,
  3  po_date date,
  4  customer_name varchar2(30));
  5  /

Type created.

SQL> CREATE TYPE order_item_t AS OBJECT
  2  (po_ref REF purchase_order_t,
  3  line_no NUMBER,
  4  item_description VARCHAR2(60),
  5  item_number NUMBER,
  6  item_quantity NUMBER,
  7  item_price NUMBER
  8* );

Type created.

SQL> CREATE TABLE purchase_orders OF purchase_order_t;

Table created.
```

```
SQL> CREATE TABLE order_items OF order_item_t (
  2  SCOPE FOR (po_ref) IS purchase_orders);

Table created.

SQL> ALTER TABLE purchase_orders ADD CONSTRAINT
  2* PK_purchase_orders PRIMARY KEY (po_num)

Table altered.
```

First, we will demonstrate the manual method of **REF** population using SQL **INSERT** and **UPDATE** statements. Then, we will destroy the tables and re-create the types with intrinsic methods to do the job right:

```
SQL> INSERT INTO order_items (
  2  line_no,item_description,item_number,item_quantity, item_price)
  3  VALUES (
  4* 1,'Quarterly Update to modual 123.4',1,1,500)
  5  /

1 row created.

SQL> INSERT INTO order_items (
  2  line_no,item_description,item_number,item_quantity, item_price)
  3  VALUES (
  4* 2,'Quarterly Update to modual 123.5',1,1,200)
  5  /

1 row created.

SQL> INSERT INTO order_items (
  2  line_no,item_description,item_number,item_quantity, item_price)
  3  VALUES (
  4* 3,'Quarterly Update to modual 123.6',1,1,250)
SQL> /

1 row created.

SQL> update order_items set po_ref= (select ref(p) from purchase_orders p
  2* where po_num=1)
SQL> /

3 rows updated.

SQL> commit;

Commit complete.
```

Here is what the table looks like with the **REF** populated:

```
SQL> SELECT * FROM order_items;
PO_REF
-----------------------------------------------------------------------------
   LINE_NO ITEM_DESCRIPTION
--------- ------------------------------------------------------------
ITEM_NUMBER ITEM_QUANTITY ITEM_PRICE
---------- ------------- ----------
00002202085726D82E2C3A11D1AD680060972CFBA85726D82C2C3A11D1AD680060972CFBA8
         1 Quarterly Update to modual 123.4
         1             1        500

00002202085726D82E2C3A11D1AD680060972CFBA85726D82C2C3A11D1AD680060972CFBA8
         2 Quarterly Update to modual 123.5
         1             1        200

00002202085726D82E2C3A11D1AD680060972CFBA85726D82C2C3A11D1AD680060972CFBA8
         3 Quarterly Update to modual 123.6
         1             1        250


3 rows selected.
```

I don't know about you, but that long **OID** value means absolutely nothing to me. The return of the **REF** value will always default to the **OID** unless you specify the **DEREF** function. Of course, this also means you cannot use the **SELECT** * method of retrieving values generically; you must specify all columns. Here is an example using the **DEREF** function in a **SELECT**:

```
SQL> SELECT deref(po_ref),line_no,item_description,item_number,item_quantity,
item_price
  2 FROM order_items;

DEREF(PO_REF)(PO_NUM, PO_DATE, CUSTOMER_NAME)
-----------------------------------------------------------------------------
   LINE_NO ITEM_DESCRIPTION
--------- ------------------------------------------------------------
ITEM_NUMBER ITEM_QUANTITY ITEM_PRICE
---------- ------------- ----------
PURCHASE_ORDER_T(1, '18-SEP-97', 'RevealNet, Inc.')
         1 Quarterly Update to modual 123.4
         1             1        500

PURCHASE_ORDER_T(1, '18-SEP-97', 'RevealNet, Inc.')
         2 Quarterly Update to modual 123.5
         1             1        200
```

```
PURCHASE_ORDER_T(1, '18-SEP-97', 'RevealNet, Inc.')
        3 Quarterly Update to modual 123.6
            1           1          250
```

3 rows selected.

The second **SELECT** returns much more user-friendly information, even if the format is abominable. Why Oracle thinks we need to be reminded constantly of the type name in this fashion, cluttering up printouts, is beyond me. A quick perusal of the SQL*Plus manual shows no additional **SET** or **COLUMN** commands to alleviate this, so I guess Oracle is trying to force us into using **UTL_FILE** and PL/SQL for our reporting.

Another feature added to SQL and PL/SQL is the **VALUE** function. This is in no way related to the **VALUES** clause on an **UPDATE** statement. Its only function is to return the column values from an object type containing a **REF** in the parenthetically enclosed type format—not a particularly useful feature:

```
SQL> select value(p) from order_items p;

VALUE(P)(PO_REF, LINE_NO, ITEM_DESCRIPTION, ITEM_NUMBER, ITEM_QUANTITY, ITEM_PRI
--------------------------------------------------------------------------------
ORDER_ITEM_T(00002202085726D82E2C3A11D1AD680060972CFBA85726D82C2C3A11D1AD6800609
72CFBA8, 1, 'Quarterly Update to modual 123.4', 1, 1, 500)

ORDER_ITEM_T(00002202085726D82E2C3A11D1AD680060972CFBA85726D82C2C3A11D1AD6800609
72CFBA8, 2, 'Quarterly Update to modual 123.5', 1, 1, 200)

ORDER_ITEM_T(00002202085726D82E2C3A11D1AD680060972CFBA85726D82C2C3A11D1AD6800609
72CFBA8, 3, 'Quarterly Update to modual 123.6', 1, 1, 250)

3 rows selected
```

Here are the new type and table definitions with some basic **MAP** methods and a **GET_REF** method defined:

```
DROP TABLE order_items;
DROP TABLE purchase_orders;
drop type order_item_t;
drop type purchase_order_t;

CREATE or replace TYPE purchase_order_t AS OBJECT
    ( po_num INTEGER,
      po_date DATE,
```

```
    customer_name VARCHAR2(30),
    total_cost NUMBER,
    MAP MEMBER FUNCTION po_map RETURN INTEGER,
    PRAGMA RESTRICT_REFERENCES(po_map,WNPS,RNPS,WNDS,RNDS))
/

CREATE OR REPLACE TYPE BODY purchase_order_t AS
MAP MEMBER FUNCTION po_map RETURN INTEGER IS
BEGIN
 RETURN SELF.po_num;
END;
END;
/

CREATE TABLE purchase_orders OF purchase_order_t(
PRIMARY KEY(po_num))
/

CREATE OR REPLACE TYPE order_item_t AS OBJECT
    (po_ref REF purchase_order_t,
    line_no NUMBER,
    item_description VARCHAR2(60),
    item_number INTEGER,
    item_quantity NUMBER,
    item_price NUMBER,
    MAP MEMBER FUNCTION map_item RETURN INTEGER,
    PRAGMA RESTRICT_REFERENCES(map_item,WNDS,RNDS,WNPS,RNPS),
    MEMBER FUNCTION get_ref(po_no IN INTEGER)
    RETURN REF purchase_order_t,
    PRAGMA RESTRICT_REFERENCES(get_ref, WNDS)
        )
/

CREATE OR REPLACE TYPE BODY order_item_t AS
MAP MEMBER FUNCTION map_item RETURN INTEGER IS
BEGIN
RETURN item_number;
END;
MEMBER FUNCTION get_ref(po_no IN INTEGER)
RETURN REF purchase_order_t IS
po_ref REF purchase_order_t;
BEGIN
SELECT REF(p) INTO po_ref FROM purchase_orders p WHERE p.po_num=po_no;
RETURN po_ref;
END;
END;
/
```

```
CREATE TABLE order_items OF order_item_t(
SCOPE FOR (po_ref) IS purchase_orders)
/
```

You have now defined your types and a basic method to get **REF** values from one object table to another (although, I am not pleased with how this is implemented). You end up with one method, **GET_REF**, which is dependent on the table **purchase_orders** and the type **purchase_order_t**. This violates object-oriented programming methodologies, but I see no other way of doing this particular operation. Here is an example code run:

```
SQL> INSERT INTO purchase_Orders VALUES (1,'18-sep-97','RevealNet, Inc.',0);

SQL> DECLARE
  2   po_no integer:=1;
  3   BEGIN
  4    INSERT INTO order_items(
  5   line_no,
  6   item_description,
  7   item_number,
  8   item_quantity,
  9   item_price)
 10       VALUES (1,'Quarterly Update to modual 123.4',1,1,500);
 11   UPDATE order_items o SET o.po_ref=o.get_ref(po_no) WHERE o.line_no=1;
 12    INSERT INTO order_items(
 13   line_no,
 14   item_description,
 15   item_number,
 16   item_quantity,
 17   item_price)
 18       VALUES (2,'Quarterly Update to modual 123.5',1,1,200);
 19   UPDATE order_items o SET o.po_ref=o.get_ref(po_no) WHERE o.line_no=2;
 20    INSERT INTO order_items(
 21   line_no,
 22   item_description,
 23   item_number,
 24   item_quantity,
 25   item_price)
 26       VALUES (3,'Quarterly Update to modual 123.6',1,1,250);
 27   UPDATE order_items o SET o.po_ref=o.get_ref(po_no) WHERE o.line_no=3;
 28* END;
SQL> /

PL/SQL procedure successfully completed.

SQL> select * from order_items;
```

```
PO_REF
-------------------------------------------------------------------------------
  LINE_NO ITEM_DESCRIPTION
-------- ------------------------------------------------------------------
ITEM_NUMBER ITEM_QUANTITY ITEM_PRICE
----------- ------------- ----------
00002202085726D9622C3A11D1AD680060972CFBA85726D9512C3A11D1AD680060972CFBA8
        1 Quarterly Update to modual 123.4
        1             1        500

00002202085726D9622C3A11D1AD680060972CFBA85726D9512C3A11D1AD680060972CFBA8
        2 Quarterly Update to modual 123.5
        1             1        200

00002202085726D9622C3A11D1AD680060972CFBA85726D9512C3A11D1AD680060972CFBA8
        3 Quarterly Update to modual 123.6
        1             1        250


3 rows selected.
```

So, we have looked at **REF** values and shown how they are used in **REF**, **DEREF**, and **VALUE** statements. We have also shown the use of **REF** values for **INSERT** and **UPDATE** situations.

Example Of An External Procedure Call

External procedure calls invoke external C routines stored in the DLL format library location. This limits its usefulness to NT, Windows, or Sun platforms. As more users demand this functionality, Oracle will port it to more platforms.

To use the external library call, you must first use the **CREATE LIBRARY** call to create the external pointer to the location of the external DLL library file:

```
CREATE LIBRARY library_name {IS | AS} 'file_path';
```

```
Or in a real example:
```

```
CREATE LIBRARY geo_LIB is 'C:\USR\LIB\geo.DLL';
```

Once the library pointer is established, you can use calls to external procedures much the way the calls to internal procedures and functions are made. This is known as *registering* the external procedure:

```
EXTERNAL LIBRARY library_name
   [NAME external_procedure_name]
   [LANGUAGE language_name]
   [CALLING STANDARD {C | PASCAL}]
   [WITH CONTEXT]
   [PARAMETERS (external_parameter[, external_prameter]...)];

where external_parameter stands for
{  CONTEXT
 | {parameter_name | RETURN} [property] [BY_REF] [external_datatype]}
and property stands for
{INDICATOR | LENGTH | MAXLEN | CHARSETID | CHARSETFORM}
```

These are the parameters in the **EXTERNAL LIBRARY** definition:

- **LIBRARY**—Specifies a local alias library. (You cannot use a database link to specify a remote library.) The library name is a PL/SQL identifier. If you enclose the name in double quotes, it becomes case-sensitive. (By default, the name is stored in uppercase.) You must have EXECUTE privileges on the alias library.

- **NAME**—Specifies the external procedure to be called. If you enclose the procedure name in double quotes, it becomes case-sensitive. (By default, the name is stored in uppercase.) If you omit this subclause, the procedure name defaults to the uppercase name of the PL/SQL subprogram.

- **LANGUAGE**—Specifies the third-generation language in which the external procedure was written. Currently, only the language name C is allowed. If you omit this subclause, the language name defaults to C.

- **CALLING STANDARD**—Specifies the Windows NT calling standard (C or Pascal) under which the external procedure was compiled. (Under the Pascal Calling Standard, arguments are reversed on the stack and the called function must pop the stack.) If you omit this subclause, the calling standard defaults to C.

- **WITH CONTEXT**—Specifies that a context pointer will be passed to the external procedure. The context data structure is opaque to the external procedure but is available to service routines called by the external procedure.

- **PARAMETERS**—Specifies the positions and datatypes of parameters passed to the external procedure. It can also specify parameter properties, such as current length and maximum length, and the preferred parameter passing method (by value or by reference).

An example of the use of an external procedure follows. The function **GET_DIF** calculates the distance in miles between two locations specified by latitude and longitude X,Y pairs of data. The C data structure for this function is:

```
int c_get_dif(int x1_val, int y1_val, int x2_val, int y2_val);
```

To make this function callable, you need to register it. You have already created the **LIBRARY geo_lib** where the function **c_get_dif** is located, so let's look at the registration process:

```
CREATE FUNCTION GET_DIF (
-- find DISTANCE BETWEEN TWO SETS OF x and y COORDINATES
   x1 BINARY_INTEGER,
   y1 BINARY_INTEGER,
   X2 binary_integer,
   Y2 binary_integer)
RETURN BINARY_INTEGER AS EXTERNAL
   LIBRARY c_utils
   NAME "c_GET_DIF"  -- quotes preserve lower case
   LANGUAGE C;
```

Now that you have registered the external function **c_get_dif** as internal function **get_dif**, how do you use it?

You do not call an external procedure directly. Instead, you call the PL/SQL subprogram that registered the external procedure. Such calls, which you code in the usual way, can appear in:

- Anonymous blocks
- Standalone and packaged subprograms
- Methods of an object type
- Database triggers
- SQL statements (calls to packaged functions only)

*To call a packaged function from SQL statements, you must use the **PRAGMA RESTRICT_REFERENCES**, which asserts the purity level of the function (the extent to which the function is free of side effects). PL/SQL cannot check the purity level of the corresponding external routine. So, make sure the routine does not violate the **PRAGMA**. Otherwise, you might get unexpected results.*

In the next example, you call PL/SQL function **get_dif** from an anonymous block. PL/SQL passes the four integer parameters to external function **c_get_dif**, which returns the distance between the two coordinate pairs:

```
DECLARE
   D BINARY_INTEGER;
   X1 BINARY_INTEGER;
   Y1 BINARY_INTEGER;
   X2 BINARY_INTEGER;
   Y2 BINARY_INTEGER;
   ...
BEGIN
   ...
   D := GET_DIF(X1, Y2, X2, Y2);  -- call function
   IF d > 200 THEN ...
```

To call an external procedure, PL/SQL must know in which DLL it resides. PL/SQL looks up the alias library in the **EXTERNAL** clause of the subprogram that registered the external procedure, then Oracle looks up the DLL in the data dictionary.

Next, PL/SQL alerts a listener process, which, in turn, spawns (launches) a session-specific agent named **extproc**. Then, the listener hands over the connection to **extproc**. PL/SQL passes to **extproc** the name of the DLL, the name of the external procedure, and any parameters.

Then, **extproc** loads the DLL and runs the external procedure. **extproc** also handles service calls (such as raising an exception) and callbacks to the Oracle server. Finally, **extproc** passes to PL/SQL any values returned by the external procedure.

*The Net8 listener manager must start **extproc** on the machine that runs the Oracle server. Starting **extproc** on a different machine is not supported.*

After the external procedure completes, **extproc** remains active throughout your Oracle session. (When you log off, **extproc** is killed.) So, you incur the cost of spawning **extproc** only once, no matter how many calls you make. Still, you should call an external procedure only when the computational benefits outweigh the cost.

Using The OTT Program

The Oracle Type Translator (OTT) is a command-line program (on most platforms) that reads the Oracle data dictionary and, based on its internal algorithms, makes its best guess at the C header file needed to support the types that you want it to translate. Like all programs of this type, it can do only so much, but at least it will get you started and provide a template. I don't suggest that you always modify the C header it generates, but you should check it thoroughly to be sure that it is using appropriate conversion logic for your program. Don't assume that OTT always does the conversion 100 percent correctly.

The command for starting OTT is:

```
ott userid=bwzdglr/secureme intype=cnetin.typ outtype=cnetout.typ code=c
hfile=cnet.h
```

The input parameters were covered earlier in this chapter. Let's now look at some sample contents for the **INTYPE**, **OUTTYPE**, and **HFILE** files for a set of basic **TYPE** specifications.

The **INTYPE** file:

```
CASE=LOWER
TYPE CLIENT_SITES
  TRANSLATE lookup$ AS lookup
          site_id AS site
TYPE ADDRESSES
TYPE USERS
TYPE "ClientProfiles"
TYPE earnings_info_numbers AS ein
```

The first line, with the **CASE** keyword, indicates that generated C identifiers should be in lowercase. This **CASE** option is applied to only those identifiers not explicitly mentioned in the **INTYPE** file. Thus, **ADDRESSES** and **USERS** would always result in the C structures **ADDRESSES** and **USERS**, respectively. The members of these structures would be named in lowercase.

The lines that begin with the **TYPE** keyword specify which types in the database should be translated—in this case, the **CLIENT_SITES**, **ADDRESSES**, **USERS**, **ClientProfiles**, and **earnings_info_numbers**.

The **TRANSLATE...AS** keywords specify that the name of an object attribute should be changed when the type is translated into a C struct. In this case, the **LOOKUP$** attribute of the **CLIENT_SITES** type is translated to salary.

The **AS** keyword in the final line specifies that the name of an object type should be changed when it is translated into a struct. In this case, the **earnings_info_numbers** database type is translated into a struct called **ein**.

If **AS** is not used to translate a type or attribute name, the database name of the type or attribute will be used as the C identifier name—except that the **CASE** option will be observed, and any characters that cannot be mapped to a legal C identifier character will be replaced by an underscore. Reasons for translating a type or attribute name include:

- The name contains characters other than letters, digits, and underscores.

- The name conflicts with a C keyword.

- The type name conflicts with another identifier in the same scope. This may happen, for example, if the program uses two types with the same name from different schemas.

- The programmer prefers a different name.

Because of the hierarchical nature of Oracle **TYPE** structures, OTT may need to translate additional types that are not listed in the **INTYPE** file. OTT analyzes the types in the **INTYPE** file for type dependencies before performing the translation and translates other types as necessary. For example, if the **ADDRESSES** type were not listed in the **INTYPE** file, but the **USERS** type had an attribute of type **ADDRESS**, OTT would still translate **ADDRESS**, because it is required to define the **USERS** type.

A normal case-insensitive SQL identifier can be spelled in any combination of upper- and lowercase in the **INTYPE** file and is not quoted.

Use quotation marks, such as **TYPE "ClientProfiles"**, to reference SQL identifiers that have been created in a case-sensitive manner (e.g., **CREATE TYPE "ClientProfiles"**. Quotation marks can also be used to refer to a SQL identifier that is an OTT-reserved word (e.g., **TYPE "CASE"**). When a name is put into quotes for this reason, it must be uppercase if the SQL identifier was created in a case-insensitive manner (e.g., **CREATE TYPE CASE**). If an OTT-reserved word is used to refer to the name of a SQL identifier but is not in quotes, OTT will report a syntax error in the **INTYPE** file.

OTT takes the information it gleans from the data dictionary and creates the header file required to implement the structures in C. OTT uses the OCI datatype definitions, so the resulting header file is only usable through the OCI.

For example, for the following Oracle **TYPE** definition

```
CREATE TYPE employeeS AS OBJECT
(    name        VARCHAR2(30),
     empno       NUMBER,
     deptno      NUMBER,
     hiredate    DATE,
     salary$     NUMBER);
```

the OTT output, assuming **CASE=LOWER** and no explicit mappings of type or attribute names, is:

```
struct employees
{    OCIString * name;
     OCINumber empno;
     OCINumber department;
     OCIDate   hiredate;
     OCINumber salary_;
};

typedef struct emp_type emp_type;
struct employee_ind
{
     OCIInd _atomic;
     OCIInd name;
     OCIInd empno;
     OCIInd department;
     OCIInd hiredate;
     OCIInd salary_;
}
typedef struct employee_ind employee_ind;
```

The datatypes that are OCI-specific begin with **OCI**.

 ## Creating A Deferred Constraint

Use the **CREATE** or **ALTER TABLE** commands to create a deferred constraint. Once a constraint is created, its current **DEFER** status can change, but not its base status. To change a constraint's **DEFER** status, use the **SET CONSTRAINT** command. To change the base **DEFER** status of a constraint, it must be dropped and rebuilt with the new base state (it follows, then, that a constraint cannot be altered).

A constraint is either **DEFERRABLE** or **NOT DEFERRABLE**. The default is **NOT DEFERRABLE**. If a constraint is created as **DEFERRABLE**, it can be set as **INITIALLY DEFERRED** or **INITIALLY IMMEDIATE**. A constraint cannot be set to **NOT DEFERRABLE INITIALLY DEFERRED**.

A **DEFERRED** constraint is one that is checked only at the time of commit (at the end of the transaction). The **SET CONSTRAINT** command sets a constraint as either **IMMEDIATE** (where the constraint is checked for each operation) or **DEFERRED** (checked at the time of commit).

Here's an example to create an **INITIALLY DEFERRED DEFERRABLE** constraint:

```
SQL> CREATE TABLE purchase_orders
 2 (po_num NUMBER NOT NULL,
 3 po_type VARCHAR2(32),
 4 customer_code NUMBER,
 5 po_date DATE
 6 po_ship_date DATE,
 7 CONSTRAINT pk_purchase_orders
 8 PRIMARY KEY (po_num)
 9 USING INDEX PCTFREE 20
10 TABLESPACE raw_indexes
11 STORAGE (INITIAL 100k NEXT 100k PCTINCREASE 0)
12 /

Table created

SQL> CREATE table line_items
 2  (li_po_num NUMBER,
 3  line_number NUMBER,
 4  item_desc VARCHAR2(60),
 5  item_quantity NUMBER CONSTRAINT NN_line_items2_03 not null,
 6  item_price NUMBER    CONSTRAINT NN_line_items2_04 not null,
 7  CONSTRAINT pk_line_items PRIMARY KEY(line_number,li_po_num)
 8  USING INDEX PCTFREE 20 TABLESPACE raw_index
 9  STORAGE (INITIAL 100k NEXT 100k PCTINCREASE 0)
10  CONSTRAINT fk_line_items_01 FOREIGN KEY(li_po_num)
11  REFERENCES purchase_orders2(po_num)
12 INITIALLY DEFERRED DEFERRABLE)
SQL> /

Table created.
```

This example creates two tables: **purchase_orders** and **line_items**. It places a **NON-DEFERRABLE** primary key on **purchase orders** (remember, the default value for a constraint is **NONDEFERRABLE**) and a **DEFERRABLE** foreign key on **line_items** that is initially set to **DEFERRED**.

This means that you can load the **purchase_orders** and **line_items** tables with individual SQL*Loader streams, if you desire; via simultaneous SQL*Plus sessions via SQL scripts; or even manually, from two separate data-entry clerks—and not have to worry about synching up the primary and foreign key values until all data is entered and a commit ends the transactions.

Using A Deferred Constraint

Now that you have seen how to create a **DEFERRED** constraint, let's look at how they are used. Using the tables from the previous example, let's perform a test. In the first example, we will insert some records into the **line_items** table and attempt a commit:

```
SQL> desc line_items
 Name                            Null?     Type
 ------------------------------- --------  ----
 LI_PO_NUM                       NOT NULL  NUMBER
 LINE_NUMBER                     NOT NULL  NUMBER
 ITEM_DESC                                 VARCHAR2(60)
 ITEM_QUANTITY                   NOT NULL  NUMBER
 ITEM_PRICE                      NOT NULL  NUMBER

SQL> insert into line_items values (
  2   1,1,'Item1 for po 1',10,10.25);

1 row created.

SQL> insert into line_items values (
  2*  1,2,'Item2 for po 1',5,13.00)

1 row created.

SQL> insert into line_items values (
  2*  1,3,'Item3 for po 1',15,1.00)

1 row created.
```

```
SQL> commit;
commit
*
ERROR at line 1:
ORA-02091: transaction rolled back
ORA-02292: integrity constraint (SYSTEM.FK_LINE_ITEMS_01) violated - child record
found
```

So what happened? Just as we expected, the **DEFERRED** constraint allowed us to enter the values, but when we attempted to **COMMIT**, it was turned on and gave us a constraint violation. Now, do the same test, except this time, enter a record into the **purchase_orders** table that will provide the required primary key value:

```
SQL> insert into line_items values (
  2  1,1,'Item1 for po 1',10,10.25)
  3  /

1 row created.

SQL> insert into line_items values (
  2  1,2,'Item2 for po 1',5,13.00)
  3  /

1 row created.

SQL> insert into line_items values (
  2  1,3,'Item3 for po 1',15,1.00)
  3  /

1 row created.

SQL> insert into purchase_orders values
  2  ( 1,'In-store',1,'26-sep-97','27-sep-97')
  3  /

SQL> commit
  2  /

Commit complete.
```

Now that the primary key/foreign key relationship is filled in, when the **COMMIT** occurs and the **DEFERRED** constraint is activated, the records are committed. What if you wanted the checking to occur with a specific transaction? You would use the **SET CONSTRAINT** command to alter the deferrable state of the constraint. Here is an example:

```
SQL> SET CONSTRAINT FK_line_items_01 immediate;

Constraint set.

SQL> insert into line_items values
  2  (2,1,'Item1 for po 2',5,15.00);
insert into line_items values
            *
ERROR at line 1:
ORA-02291: integrity constraint (SYSTEM.FK_LINE_ITEMS_01) violated - parent key not
found
```

You can set the **DEFERRED** constraint to behave as a regular **NONDEFERRED** constraint when you wish. You can also return it to the **DEFERRED** state as shown here:

```
SQL> SET CONSTRAINT fk_line_items_01 deferred;

Constraint set.

SQL> insert into line_items values
  2  (2,1,'Item1 for po 2',5,15.00);

1 row created.

SQL> commit;
commit
*
ERROR at line 1:
ORA-02091: transaction rolled back
ORA-02292: integrity constraint (SYSTEM.FK_LINE_ITEMS_01) violated - child record
found
```

You still are not allowed to **COMMIT** until the parent record is present in the **purchase_orders** table.

The **DEFERRED** constraint allows for flexibility during complex inserts and large data loads. By enabling the defeat of constraints on a temporary basis, Oracle provides us with a powerful new tool.

The New Parallel And Distributed Features Of Oracle8

Oracle has called Oracle8 the "Parallel Everything" database. In this chapter, we will look at the expanded parallel capabilities of Oracle8 and discover that Oracle's claim isn't far off the mark. We will cover the requirements for parallel **INSERT**, **UPDATE**, and **DELETE** operations, and the enhancements to deferred transactions in light of parallel enhancements. We will also examine the new distributed features of Oracle8, including **LOB** support for distributed transactions.

Notes…

Chapter 8

Parallel Operations

Oracle8 supports numerous operations in parallel mode of operation. You must use the **ALTER SESSION ENABLE PARALLEL DML** command to set parallel mode; otherwise, the default nonparallel mode is used.

The parallel feature uses the concept of **DEGREE**, which is the number of parallel server processes that will be started for a particular operation. Normally, you determine the **DEGREE** of a parallel operation with the **PARALLEL** clause used for the table or index involved. For **UPDATE** and **DELETE** operations, you can use parallel features only against partitioned tables, and the **DEGREE** is set to the number of partitions.

The following operations can be executed using the parallel processing capabilities of Oracle8:

- Table scan
- Nested loop join
- Sort merge join
- Hash join
- **NOT IN** operations

- **GROUP BY**

- **SELECT DISTINCT**

- **UNION** and **UNION ALL**

- Aggregation

- PL/SQL functions called from SQL

- **ORDER BY**

- **CREATE TABLE...AS SELECT**

- **CREATE INDEX**

- **REBUILD INDEX** (for nonpartitioned indexes only)

- **REBUILD INDEX PARTITION**

- **MOVE PARTITION**

- **SPLIT PARTITION**

- **UPDATE** (partitioned tables only)

- **DELETE** (partitioned tables only)

- **INSERT...SELECT**

- **ENABLE CONSTRAINT** (the required table scan is parallelized)

- Star transformation

Parallel DML And DDL Operations

In comparison with previous releases where only full-table scans were parallelized, Oracle8 does seem, as Oracle says, "parallel everything." In this chapter, I refer to queries as queries; DML will involve only **INSERT**, **UPDATE**, and **DELETE** operations (sans query); and DDL will consist of everything that deals with the physical side of index and table build, rebuild, and drop.

The Oracle8 system can parallelize by these methods:

- Parallel server processes for inserts into nonpartitioned tables only

  - Nonpartitioned tables only

- Block ranges for scan operations, such as **SELECT**s and subqueries

  - Queries using table scans (including DML and DDL subqueries)

  - Move partition

  - Split partition

  - Rebuild index partition

  - **CREATE INDEX** (nonpartitioned index only)

  - **CREATE TABLE...AS SELECT** (nonpartitioned table only)

- Partitions for operations involving partitioned tables and indexes

  - **CREATE INDEX**

  - **CREATE TABLE...AS SELECT**

  - **UPDATE**

  - **DELETE**

  - **INSERT...SELECT**

  - **ALTER INDEX...REBUILD**

  - Queries using a range scan on a partitioned index

Parallel Query Coordinators And Servers

The system consists of a query coordinator (QC) and a set of query servers. The QC resolves all queries and decides whether the query should be split or left alone. The number of query servers is dynamic and controlled by the load as monitored by the QC. Oracle also uses dynamic partitioning for the CPUs and load balancing.

Under some parallel architectures, CPU A manages rows 1-10,000, CPU B manages 10,001-20,000, etc. If you need data from rows not managed by a specific CPU, it sits idle. On Oracle, all CPUs participate in a parallel operation, speeding up all operations.

The QC process breaks the query into parallel pieces, which are then sent to the query servers. The query servers perform their part of the transaction and return the results to the QC for assembly into the finished results. The QC handles the parsing of the statement.

The number of query servers the QC uses in processing a single query is the *parallelism* of the query. This is determined by:

- Hints specified in the query
- Table definition
- Initialization parameters

Generally speaking, the query must involve at least one full-table scan before it is considered for parallel processing. Once a statement is parsed and the execution plan determined, certain parts of the plan are candidates for parallel execution. These are:

- **AGGREGATE (GROUP BY)**
- **MERGE JOIN**
- **NESTED LOOPS**
- **SORT (GROUP BY)**
- **SORT (JOIN)**
- **SORT (ORDER BY)**
- **SORT (UNIQUE)**
- **TABLE ACCESS (FULL)**

The QC looks at partitioning requirements as well as execution plans. Based on partitioning requirements, the QC determines the order of operations. Each major operation, such as a full-table scan or merge join, may have multiple servers assigned to it; thus, each level of an execution plan may have its own degree of parallelization. Figure 8.1 shows how an example query would be broken into individual processes.

You can force parallelization through the **PARALLEL** hint:

```
>>--PARALLEL----(--alias_name------------------------------------------)------><
               |--table_name--|   |--,integer--| |--,integer--|
                                                 |--,DEFAULT--| |--,DEFAULT-|
                                                 |--,---------------|
```

An additional hint—**NOPARALLEL**—equates to a **PARALLEL** hint of:

```
/*+ PARALLEL (table_name, 1, 1) */
```

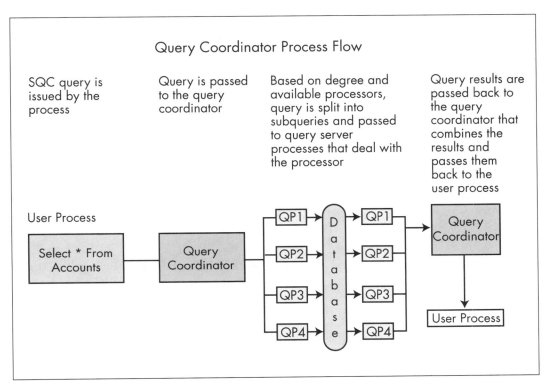

Figure 8.1

Parallel query process diagram.

In addition to hints, you can use the **PARALLEL** clause in the **CREATE TABLE**, **ALTER TABLE**, **CREATE CLUSTER**, and **ALTER CLUSTER** commands to create a table with a specific degree of parallelism.

```
>------PARALLEL----(--------DEGREE------integer--------)----------------------->
                   |             |--DEFAULT--------------------|        |

                   |--INSTANCES------integer-------------|
                   |-- DEFAULT---------------------|
>------NOPARALLEL--------------------------------------------------------------><
```

Within the **PARALLEL** clause, the **INSTANCES** parameter splits the table blocks among the SGAs of a set of parallel instances in the parallel server. The number of instances participating in this parallel caching activity is specified with the new initialization parameters, **PARALLEL_MAX_SERVERS** and **PARALLEL_DEFAULT_**

MAX_INSTANCES, or with the **ALTER SYSTEM** command options, **SET SCAN_INSTANCES** and **SET CACHE_INSTANCES**.

The following initialization parameters determine the number of query servers and when the servers are reduced in number:

- **PARALLEL_MAX_SERVERS**
- **PARALLEL_MIN_SERVERS**
- **PARALLEL_SERVER_IDLE_TIME**

If an insufficient number of servers is specified in the **PARALLEL_MAX_SERVERS** parameter, a new query will be processed sequentially.

The parallel query option is most beneficial for:

- Sequential Multiprocessing (SMP) or Massively Parallel Processing (MPP) systems
- Systems with high I/O bandwidth (many data files on many disks)
- Systems where CPU usage is generally less than 30 percent
- Systems with sufficient memory to support multiple sorts

The amount of memory consumed by sorts for a parallel query is the number of servers multiplied by the **SORT_AREA_SIZE** parameter. This is important when sizing your system memory.

The parallel query option is monitored through the view **V$PQ_SYSSTAT**.

When using the parallel load utility through SQL*Loader, disable the automatic indexing features and create the indexes in parallel. Then, enable the constraints for the indexes. This will dramatically increase the index build speeds for primary and unique key constraints.

In some cases, query servers may be allocated at up to two times the default degree of parallelism, to a single parallel operation if Oracle determines that it can do certain operations (such as a **SELECT** followed by an **ORDER BY**) using inter-operation parallelism and dynamic partitioning. The type of operation where inter-operation parallelism can be used is typified by a parent and child suboperation that can be performed concurrently. In the previous example, results from one parallel

SELECT can be sorted into order even while other sections of the operation are being performed; hence, inter-operation parallelism makes sense.

Determining Degree Of Parallelism

The default degree of parallelism is based on the following:

- The number of CPUs in the system.

- The number of Oracle parallel server instances.

- The number of disks (or files, if affinity information is not available).

- The number of partitions based on partition pruning.

- For parallel DML operations involving global partitioned indexes, the minimum number of transaction-free lists among all global indexes to be updated. This prevents self-deadlock.

For example, if a table has a default degree of parallelism of four, but the system has only two CPUs, then only two slaves will be assigned. If the system has 15 CPUs and the tables are spread across only 10 disks, then the default degree will be 10. The **PARALLEL** hint option can override the default degree. Table 8.1 summarizes the parallelization rules.

When using parallel DDL, such as in a **CREATE** situation, each parallel slave process will grab an extent the size of the **INITIAL** specification in the **STORAGE** clause. This means that for an **INITIAL** specification of 1MB and a degree of parallel setting of 5, at least 5MB of free space must be present in the tablespace where the table is being created. Each of the extents acquired in a parallel DDL operation will be trimmed by the final process, so the total required space will probably be less than the working space.

If the tablespace where the table being built in parallel is to reside has a value for **MINIMUM EXTENT** set to less than the free space in an extent used for parallel creation of a table, no trimming is performed, and the space is reserved for updates.

To speed recovery during parallel DML operations, set the initialization parameter **CLEANUP_ROLLBACK_ENTRIES** to a value approximately equal to the number of rollback entries required for the parallel processes (i.e., one per process assigned to the operation).

Parallel DML operations require more locks than do normal DML operations. The coordinator process requires one table lock SX, and one partition lock X per partition. Each

Table 8.1 Summary of parallel operations.

Parallel Operation	Clause	Hint	Declaration
Parallel query scan (partitioned or nonpartitioned table)		(1) PARALLEL	(2) of table
Parallel query index range scan (partitioned index)		(1)PARALLEL_INDEX	(2) of table
Parallel UPDATE/DELETE (partitioned table only)		(1) PARALLEL	(2) of table being updated or deleted from
INSERT operation of parallel INSERT...SELECT (partitioned)		(1) PARALLEL of insert	(2) of table being inserted into
SELECT operation of parallel CREATE TABLE...AS SELECT (partitioned or nonpartitioned table)		(1) PARALLEL of insert	Of selecting table
CREATE operation of parallel CREATE TABLE...AS SELECT (partitioned or nonpartitioned table)	(1)	Hint in select doesn't affect operation	
SELECT operation of parallel CREATE TABLE...AS SELECT (partitioned or non-partitioned)	(2)	(1) PARALLEL/ PARALLEL_INDEX	(3) of querying tables/ partitioned
Parallel CREATE INDEX (partitioned or nonpartitioned index)	(1)		
Parallel REBUILD INDEX (nonpartitioned only)	(1)		
REBUILD INDEX (partitioned index)	N/A	N/A	N/A
Parallel REBUILD INDEX partition	(1)		
Parallel MOVE/SPLIT partition	(1)		

1,2,3—Priorities if multiple PARALLEL declaration levels specified.

parallel server process requires one table lock SX, one partition lock **NULL**, and one partition wait lock X per partition.

The restrictions on parallel DML operations are as follows:

- **UPDATE** and **DELETE** operations are parallel only on partitioned tables.

- Global indexes are maintained by parallel **UPDATE** and **DELETE** operations only if they are nonunique. Local indexes are supported for parallel **UPDATE**, **DELETE**, and **INSERT** operations. For a parallel **INSERT** into a nonpartitioned table, there is no index maintenance.

- A parallel DML statement must be the first and only DML statement in a transaction (there must be intervening commits and **ALTER SESSION** statements for transactions involving multiple parallel DML statements).

- If the initialization parameter **ROW_LOCKING** is set to **INTENT**, then no **INSERT**, **UPDATE**, or **DELETE** operation can be performed in parallel.

- Replication functionality is not supported for parallel DML, because triggers are not supported for parallel DML operations. Any triggers must be disabled before parallel DML will work against a target table.

- The use of referential integrity, **DELETE CASCADE**, and deferred integrity prohibits the use of parallel DML. Referential integrity is not supported with direct-load **INSERT**.

- **NOT NULL** and **CHECK** constraints are supported.

- **UNIQUE** and **PRIMARY KEY** constraints allow parallel **UPDATE** only if the index is local.

- Generally speaking, **FOREIGN KEY** constraints prohibit the use of parallel DML.

- **DELETE CASCADE** is not supported for parallel **DELETE**.

- If a table has self-referential integrity, parallel DML operations are not supported.

- **DEFERRED** constraint operations will not use parallel DML processing.

- Use of **LOB**s, object columns, or index-organized tables prohibits the use of parallel DML.

- Parallel DML is not supported for distributed transactions.

- Clustered tables are not supported with parallel DML.

- Functions that read or write database or package state are not allowed in parallel DML statements.

Violation of any of these restrictions will result in the transaction being executed serially, with no warning that a violation occurred.

Even though some forms of replication aren't supported with parallel DML processes, the actual replication process itself can be made to use parallel update streams by selecting the appropriate checkboxes on the setup sheet for the advanced replication server setup. You must take into account the number of servers that will be required when setting up the number of parallel server slave processes.

Distributed Facilities Enhancements

Oracle8 has enhanced the performance and capabilities of the replication option in four ways:

- Application of parallel propagation

- Reduction of the amount of data replicated

- Internalization of triggers

- The use of separate database links for each replication group

Oracle replication supports the concept of a deferred transaction—one that for either process or timing reasons is delayed in its propagation to a replication site or back to a master site. Each transaction has a system commit number. A transaction may generate what is known as a dependent system commit number if that transaction updated data that is seen by the current transaction. Any transaction with a system commit number less than or equal to the dependent system commit number is propagated before the transaction with the dependent system commit number.

If there are no discernible dependencies, system commit numbers are processed in parallel. While the process that owns the dependent system commit number is waiting for the other transactions to process on the remote system(s), it is said to be *deferred*. The deferred transaction is stored within a deferred transaction job queue.

The SNP process on a system using replication periodically wakes up and flushes deferred jobs to the appropriate server. Oracle8 provides a means to view, execute, or remove deferred transactions. These are the same job queues set up for the **DBMS_JOB** processes. You may need to set up multiple job queues if your site uses advanced replication and also uses the job queues for other functions.

The setup and management of the entire advanced replication facility is beyond the scope of this book. This chapter's Practical Guide looks at managing the deferred transactions and any resulting error transactions. I suggest a complete review of Oracle's *Oracle8 Server Replication Manual* (Release 8.0, June 1997, Part No. A54651-01) before you tackle the setup and management of the advanced replication option.

This option requires less data propagation than prior releases in which entire rows were transferred, incurring a large overhead on network systems. Now, with the less-data-propagation feature, only the changed column and minimal key value data are transferred. The new initialization parameter **MIN_COMMUNICATION** turns this feature on. If you are using replication to previous releases, you cannot use this feature, and you should set **MIN_COMMUNICATION** to false. The following procedures use the less-data-propagation feature:

- **DBMS_REPCAT.CREATE_SNAPSHOT_REPOBJECT**

- **DBMS_REPCAT.GENERATE_REPLICATION_SUPPORT**

- **DBMS_REPCAT.REPLICATION_TRIGGER**

- **DBMS_REPCAT.GENERATE_SNAPSHOT_SUPPORT**

Another procedure, **SEND_AND_COMPARE_OLD_VALUES**, further reduces the amount of data needed to be sent by restricting transmission of old values to only those values needed to resolve conflicts.

Oracle8 introduced internalized triggers, which means that instead of a trigger being standard PL/SQL, it is stored as internalized C. These internalized triggers are functionally equivalent to after-row triggers. They become a part of the Oracle executable. Once generated, internal triggers do not have to be recompiled unless they are replaced by Oracle in an **UPDATE** or new release situation. This speeds execution of the trigger, thus increasing performance for the trigger-dependent replication process.

Oracle8 has also improved performance by improving the underlying streaming protocols, thus reducing round trips for both replications and snapshot processes. A specialized form of two-phase commit has also been incorporated to deal better with distributed transactions. This alternative two-phase commit stores redundant information at each site and exchanges this information as required to complete a transaction. These features are all automatic, requiring no action from the developer or user.

The security models for advanced replication have been streamlined to improve consistency, reliability, and simplicity. A single user can now act in the role of REPSYS and REPADMIN users. End users no longer require special privileges. Snapshot owners must exist at each site and have permission to replicate tables, propagate changes, and apply replicated updates. All transactions are executed or pushed by the propagator at each site. For each master site, one receiver user must be used.

In previous releases, you had to *quiesce* the entire replication environment for maintenance to one group. Now, because each group has its own link, quiescence is at the group level, leaving other replication groups on the same instance set operational.

Snapshot Enhancements To Oracle8

Oracle8 provides these significant enhancements to the snapshot process:

- Primary key snapshots

- Fast refresh for snapshots (enhanced)

- Snapshot registration at the master site (automatic)

- Updatable snapshots using **DEFERRED** constraints

- Subquery subsetting

- Indexes allowed on snapshot logs

Primary key snapshots allow reorganization of master tables while preserving the fast refresh capability. Standard, pre-Oracle8 snapshots required the **ROWID** for snapshot log entries. The new feature of Oracle8 allows primary key snapshots. As long as the entire primary key is included in the snapshot log, the table can be reorganized without performing a complete refresh of the snapshot.

A snapshot is automatically registered in Oracle8 at the master site when it is created or moved from one master site to another. When a snapshot is dropped, it is removed from registration. Registered snapshots are recorded in the **DBA_REGISTERED_ SNAPSHOTS** view.

*The **DBA_REGISTERED_SNAPSHOTS** view is owned by SYS, and no public synonyms are created. In order for other users to see the view easily, create a public synonym pointing to it.*

The **DBA_REGISTERED_SNAPHOTS** view can be joined to the **DBA_SNAPSHOTS** view to obtain data about refreshes.

To support fast refresh after a master table reorganization, Oracle8 provides two new procedures: **DBMS_SNAPSHOT.SNAPSHOT_BEGIN_TABLE_REORGANIZE** and (you guessed it) **DBMS_SNAPSHOT.SNAPSHOT_END_TABLE_REORGANIZE**. (Obviously, these Oracle developers never have to use the procedures they name. Wouldn't life be easier if they were named **DBMS_SNAPSHOT.BEGIN_TABLE_REORG** and **DBMS_SNAPSHOT.END_TABLE_REORG**?) The purpose of these procedures is to perform cleanup operations, verify the integrity of the logs and triggers that the fast refresh mechanism needs (not to mention deactivation and reactivation of the triggers), and invalidate the **ROWID** data stored in the snapshot log. The procedures accept the name of the master table to be reorganized.

An updatable snapshot may use constraints to verify data validity, uniqueness, or referential integrity; however, they must be deferred constraints so that they execute only on completion of the **UPDATE** transaction. Any triggers coded against the base table of the updatable snapshot must not fire until after the snapshot refresh (post-transaction trigger). Any triggers that fire during the refresh may get interesting results.

Another new feature of Oracle8 snapshots is called *subquery subsetting*. This can be used with only primary key snapshots. Essentially, subquery subsetting allows you to portion out sections of a large table—such as by territory, ZIP code, state, etc.—into a distributed database environment. The subquery must be a positive subset—that is, it must use **EXISTS** rather than **NOT**. An additional constraint on subquery subsets is that the **OR** predicate is not allowed for multitable subselects. The **AND** predicate, however, is allowed.

The final addition to the snapshot portion of the replication engine in Oracle8 is that you can assign indexes to the primary key of the snapshot log. This enhances the performance of the snapshot log when large amounts of update or insertion activity result in large snapshot logs.

Advanced Replication Support For **LOB**s

In Oracle8, advanced replication supports the replication of **LOB**s (**BLOB**s, **CLOB**s, and **NCLOB**s). **LONG** and **LONG RAW** are not supported for replication. To replicate

LOBs, all sites participating in the replication must be Oracle8 sites, the **MIN_COMMUNICATION** initialization parameter must be set to **TRUE** at all sites, and the **LOB** column cannot be used as a snapshot filter column. Any columns of **LONG** or **LONG RAW** type will be omitted from snapshot data, and any attempt to snapshot **BFILE** or UDT data will result in an error. Oracle supports only replication of piecewise changes to **LOB**s.

Advanced Replication Support For Partitioned Tables

Oracle8 supports the replication of partitioned tables and indexes. The replicated table or index will have the exact partitions of the master table or index. If a tablespace doesn't exist at the replication site, the default tablespace is used for that partition.

Advanced Replication Offline Instantiation

In a project I am a part of, several groups want information from a central database. To reduce contention for the data and improve performance for our standard users, we decided to use some form of replication mechanism. What was pulling us up short was how to start the snapshot process—one of the small tables has 2.6 million rows. The answer? Offline instantiation.

In short, *offline instantiation* is the process of cloning a set of already generated snapshots at multiple sites. The basic procedure involves creating the snapshot logs and snapshots at the master site using *loopback* database links (links that connect to the master site). You then export these snapshots and logs (created under a different owner than the base tables). At the new site, use the setup wizard from the replication manager to create the users and the required snapshot group (empty, of course). For each snapshot, use the **DBMS_OFFLINE_SNAPSHOT.BEGIN_LOAD** procedure to create the empty snapshots in the proper schema and object group, then import only the snapshot base tables from the export file(s). For each replicated schema and snapshot, use the **DBMS_OFFLINE_SNAPSHOT.END_LOAD** procedure to perform the required offline instantiation of the snapshots.

Oracle8 advanced replication (including snapshots) is a complex topic. To cover it completely would require a book by itself. Before beginning a project using advanced replication, read the appropriate Oracle Corporation manuals and practice on a test database. In the Practical Guide, I show techniques for using simple snapshots, but anything more complex is beyond the scope of this book.

Practical Guide To

Oracle8 Parallel Features

- Enabling Parallel DML
- Creating A Table Using The **PARALLEL** Clause
- Setting Up The Parallel Query Initialization Parameters
- Using The Parallel Hints
- Creating Snapshot Logs And Snapshots

Enabling Parallel DML

You enable parallel DML with a special **ALTER SESSION** command. This command has the following format:

```
>-------- ALTER SESSION ---------------------- PARALLEL DML ----;---->>
                                |--ENABLE--|
                                |--DISABLE--|
                                |--FORCE ----|
```

The options for the **ALTER SESSION** command are **ENABLE**, **DISABLE**, or **FORCE**. **ENABLE** tells Oracle that for this session, it should consider all DML statements for parallel execution if possible. **DISABLE** tells Oracle that no DML statements are to use parallel DML for this session. **DISABLE** is the default mode. **FORCE** tells Oracle to force parallel DML operations on all DML statements if no parallel DML restrictions are violated. If no **PARALLEL** clause is used and no **PARALLEL** hint is present, then Oracle uses a default level of parallelism—at least, this is what the documentation says. Let's test it. Because setting the value for **AUTOTRACE** and **EXPLAIN** at the session level doesn't give explain plans for **CREATE TABLE** commands, set **TRACE** so you can see what the optimizer does with **CREATE TABLE**, with **PARALLEL DML** disabled. Listing 8.1 shows an example session.

Listing 8.1   Example session to test parallel DDL.

```
SQL> ALTER SESSION DISABLE PARALLEL DML;

Session altered.

SQL> SET TIMING ON
SQL> ALTER SESSION SET SQL_TRACE=TRUE;

Session altered.

 real: 359
SQL> @create_par_dml
SQL> CREATE TABLE test_par_dml AS
  2  SELECT
  3  owner,
  4  table_name,
  5  column_name,
  6  data_type,
  7  data_type_mod,
  8  data_type_owner,
  9  data_length,
 10  data_precision,
```

```
  11   data_scale,
  12   nullable,
  13   column_id,
  14   default_length,
  15   num_distinct,
  16   low_value,
  17   high_value,
  18   density,
  19   num_nulls,
  20   num_buckets,
  21   last_analyzed,
  22   sample_size,
  23   character_set_name
  24   FROM sys.dba_tab_columns;

Table created.

 real: 5360

SQL> DROP TABLE test_par_dml;

Table dropped.

 real: 1203
SQL> ALTER SESSION ENABLE PARALLEL DML;

Session altered.

 real: 375
SQL> @create_par_dml
SQL> CREATE TABLE test_par_dml AS
   2   SELECT
   3   owner,
   4   table_name,
   5   column_name,
   6   data_type,
   7   data_type_mod,
   8   data_type_owner,
   9   data_length,
  10   data_precision,
  11   data_scale,
  12   nullable,
  13   column_id,
  14   default_length,
  15   num_distinct,
  16   low_value,
  17   high_value,
```

```
18   density,
19   num_nulls,
20   num_buckets,
21   last_analyzed,
22   sample_size,
23   character_set_name
24   FROM sys.dba_tab_columns;

Table created.

 real: 6422
SQL> DROP TABLE test_par_dml;

Table dropped.

 real: 953
```

Listing 8.2 shows the trace output, run through tkprof80 (tkprof80 is the Windows NT 4 version of the TKPROF utility. The TKPROF utility is used to format the contents of the Oracle trace files for human consumption). Notice that both of the statements resulted in identical traces (there was no separate output for **CREATE TABLE** with parallel DML enabled).

Listing 8.2   tkprof80 output from attempted parallel DML operations.
```
************************************************************************
CREATE TABLE test_par_dml AS
SELECT
owner,
table_name,
column_name,
data_type,
data_type_mod,
data_type_owner,
data_length,
data_precision,
data_scale,
nullable,
column_id,
default_length,
num_distinct,
low_value,
high_value,
density,
num_nulls,
num_buckets,
last_analyzed,
```

```
sample_size,
character_set_name
FROM sys.dba_tab_columns

call     count       cpu    elapsed       disk       query     current        rows
------   ------   -------   --------   --------   ---------   ---------   ---------
Parse        2      0.24       0.24          0           0           0           0
Execute      2      7.03       8.76          0       78258         228       20388
Fetch        0      0.00       0.00          0           0           0           0
------   ------   -------   --------   --------   ---------   ---------   ---------
total        4      7.27       9.00          0       78258         228       20388

Misses in library cache during parse: 2
Optimizer goal: CHOOSE
Parsing user id: 5  (SYSTEM)


Rows     Execution Plan
------   -------------------------------------------------
     0   CREATE TABLE STATEMENT   GOAL: CHOOSE
     0    LOAD AS SELECT
     0     FILTER
     0      NESTED LOOPS (OUTER)
     0       NESTED LOOPS (OUTER)
     0        NESTED LOOPS (OUTER)
     0         NESTED LOOPS (OUTER)
     0          NESTED LOOPS
     0           NESTED LOOPS
     0            TABLE ACCESS (FULL) OF 'USER$'
     0            TABLE ACCESS (BY INDEX ROWID) OF 'OBJ$'
     0             INDEX (RANGE SCAN) OF 'I_OBJ2' (UNIQUE)
     0           TABLE ACCESS (CLUSTER) OF 'COL$'
     0            INDEX (UNIQUE SCAN) OF 'I_OBJ#' (CLUSTER)
     0          TABLE ACCESS (CLUSTER) OF 'COLTYPE$'
     0         TABLE ACCESS (BY INDEX ROWID) OF 'HIST_HEAD$'
     0          INDEX (RANGE SCAN) OF 'I_HH_OBJ#_INTCOL#'
                    (NON-UNIQUE)
     0        TABLE ACCESS (BY INDEX ROWID) OF 'OBJ$'
     0         INDEX (RANGE SCAN) OF 'I_OBJ3' (NON-UNIQUE)
     0       TABLE ACCESS (CLUSTER) OF 'USER$'
     0        INDEX (UNIQUE SCAN) OF 'I_USER#' (CLUSTER)
     0      TABLE ACCESS (CLUSTER) OF 'TAB$'
     0       INDEX (UNIQUE SCAN) OF 'I_OBJ#' (CLUSTER)
```

****

In fact, the only way I could get the optimizer to use a parallel solution was to force the issue with a **PARALLEL** clause in the **CREATE TABLE** command:

```
SQL> @create_par_dml
SQL> CREATE TABLE test_par_dml PARALLEL (DEGREE DEFAULT) AS
  2    SELECT
  3    owner,
  4    table_name,
  5    column_name,
  6    data_type,
  7    data_type_mod,
  8    data_type_owner,
  9    data_length,
 10    data_precision,
 11    data_scale,
 12    nullable,
 13    column_id,
 14    default_length,
 15    num_distinct,
 16    low_value,
 17    high_value,
 18    density,
 19    num_nulls,
 20    num_buckets,
 21    last_analyzed,
 22    sample_size,
 23    character_set_name
 24    FROM sys.dba_tab_columns;

Table created.

  real: 9671
```

Here is the output from the **tkprof80** run against the trace file for the parallel
CREATE TABLE using the **EXPLAIN** option:

```
***********************************************************************

CREATE table test_par_dml PARALLEL (DEGREE DEFAULT) AS
SELECT
owner,
table_name,
column_name,
data_type,
data_type_mod,
data_type_owner,
data_length,
data_precision,
data_scale,
nullable,
```

```
column_id,
default_length,
num_distinct,
low_value,
high_value,
density,
num_nulls,
num_buckets,
last_analyzed,
sample_size,
character_set_name
FROM sys.dba_tab_columns
```

call	count	cpu	elapsed	disk	query	current	rows
Parse	1	0.13	0.30	0	0	0	0
Execute	1	1.26	8.73	0	912	373	10194
Fetch	0	0.00	0.00	0	0	0	0
total	2	1.39	9.03	0	912	373	10194

```
Misses in library cache during parse: 1
Optimizer goal: CHOOSE
Parsing user id: 5  (SYSTEM)
```

```
Rows      Execution Plan
------    ----------------------------------------------------
     0    CREATE TABLE STATEMENT   GOAL: CHOOSE
     0     LOAD AS SELECT [:Q4001]
              CREATE TABLE :Q4001 AS SELECT C0,C1,C2,C3,C4,C5,C6,C7,C8,C9,C10,
              C11,C12,C13,C14,C15,C16,C17,C18,C19,C20 FROM :Q4000
     0      FILTER [:Q4000]
     0       NESTED LOOPS (OUTER) [:Q3000]
              SELECT /*+ ORDERED NO_EXPAND USE_NL(A2) INDEX(A2) */ A1.C0,
              A1.C1,A1.C2,A1.C3,A1.C4,A1.C5,A1.C6,A1.C7,A1.C8,A1.C9,A1.C10,
              A1.C11,A1.C12,A1.C13,A1.C14,A1.C15,A1.C16,A1.C17,A1.C18,
              A1.C19,A1.C20,A1.C21(+),A1.C22(+),A1.C23,A1.C24,A1.C25(+),
              A1.C26,A1.C27,A1.C28,A1.C29,A1.C30,A1.C31,A1.C32,A1.C33,
              A1.C34(+),A1.C35,A1.C36,A1.C37,A1.C38(+),A2.ROWID,
              A2."USER#"(+),A2."NAME" FROM (SELECT /*+ ORDERED NO_EXPAND
              USE_NL(A4) INDEX(A4) */ A3.C0 C0,A3.C1 C1,A3.C2 C2,A3.C3 C3,
              A3.C4 C4,A3.C5 C5,A3.C6 C6,A3.C7 C7,A3.C8 C8,A3.C9 C9,A3.C10
              C10,A3.C11 C11,A3.C12 C12,A3.C13 C13,A3.C14 C14,A3.C15 C15,
              A3.C16 C16,A3.C17 C17,A3.C18 C18,A3.C19 C19,A3.C20 C20,
              A3.C21(+) C21,A3.C22(+) C22,A3.C23 C23,A3.C24 C24,A3.C25(+)
              C25,A3.C26 C26,A3.C27 C27,A3.C28 C28,A3.C29 C29,A3.C30 C30,
              A3.C31 C31,A3.C32 C32,A3.C33 C33,A3.C34(+) C34,A4.ROWID C35,
```

```
                    A4."OWNER#" C36,A4."NAME" C37,A4."OID$"(+) C38 FROM (SELECT
                    /*+ ORDERED NO_EXPAND USE_NL(A6) INDEX(A6) */ A5.CO CO,A5.C1
                    C1,A5.C2 C2,A5.C3 C3,A5.C4 C4,A5.C5 C5,A5.C6 C6,A5.C7 C7,
                    A5.C8 C8,A5.C9 C9,A5.C10 C10,A5.C11 C11,A5.C12 C12,A5.C13
                    C13,A5.C14 C14,A5.C15 C15,A5.C16 C16,A5.C17 C17,A5.C18 C18,
                    A5.C19 C19,A5.C20 C20,A5.C21(+) C21,A5.C22(+) C22,A5.C23 C23,
                    A6.ROWID C24,A6."OBJ#"(+) C25,A6."ROW_CNT" C26,A6."NULL_CNT"
                    C27,A6."TIMESTAMP#" C28,A6."SAMPLE_SIZE" C29,A6."DISTCNT"
                    C30,A6."LOWVAL" C31,A6."HIVAL" C32,A6."DENSITY" C33,
                    A6."INTCOL#"(+) C34 FROM (SELECT /*+ ORDERED NO_EXPAND
                    USE_NL(A8) */ A7.CO CO,A7.C1 C1,A7.C2 C2,A7.C3 C3,A7.C4 C4,
                    A7.C5 C5,A7.C6 C6,A7.C7 C7,A7.C8 C8,A7.C9 C9,A7.C10 C10,
                    A7.C11 C11,A7.C12 C12,A7.C13 C13,A7.C14 C14,A7.C15 C15,
                    A7.C16 C16,A7.C17 C17,A7.C18 C18,A7.C19 C19,A7.C20 C20,
                    A8."OBJ#"(+) C21,A8."COL#"(+) C22,A8."TOID" C23 FROM (SELECT
                    /*+ ORDERED NO_EXPAND USE_NL(A10) INDEX(A10) */ A9.CO CO,
                    A9.C1 C1,A9.C2 C2,A9.C3 C3,A9.C4 C4,A9.C5 C5,A9.C6 C6,
                    A10.ROWID C7,A10."OBJ#" C8,A10."COL#" C9,A10."NAME" C10,
                    A10."TYPE#" C11,A10."LENGTH" C12,A10."PRECISION#" C13,
                    A10."SCALE" C14,A10."NULL$" C15,A10."DEFLENGTH" C16,
                    A10."INTCOL#" C17,A10."PROPERTY" C18,A10."CHARSETID" C19,
                    A10."CHARSETFORM" C20 FROM (SELECT
0          NESTED LOOPS (OUTER) [:Q3000]
0           NESTED LOOPS (OUTER) [:Q3000]
0           NESTED LOOPS (OUTER) [:Q3000]
0            NESTED LOOPS [:Q3000]
0             NESTED LOOPS [:Q3000]
0              TABLE ACCESS (FULL) OF 'USER$' [:Q3000]
0              TABLE ACCESS (BY INDEX ROWID) OF 'OBJ$' [:Q3000]

0               INDEX (RANGE SCAN) OF 'I_OBJ2' (UNIQUE)
                    [:Q3000]
0             TABLE ACCESS (CLUSTER) OF 'COL$' [:Q3000]
0              INDEX (UNIQUE SCAN) OF 'I_OBJ#' (CLUSTER)
                    [:Q3000]
0            TABLE ACCESS (CLUSTER) OF 'COLTYPE$' [:Q3000]
0            TABLE ACCESS (BY INDEX ROWID) OF 'HIST_HEAD$' [:Q3000]

0              INDEX (RANGE SCAN) OF 'I_HH_OBJ#_INTCOL#'
                    (NON-UNIQUE) [:Q3000]
0           TABLE ACCESS (BY INDEX ROWID) OF 'OBJ$' [:Q3000]
0            INDEX (RANGE SCAN) OF 'I_OBJ3' (NON-UNIQUE) [:Q3000]
0          TABLE ACCESS (CLUSTER) OF 'USER$' [:Q3000]
0           INDEX (UNIQUE SCAN) OF 'I_USER#' (CLUSTER) [:Q3000]
0         TABLE ACCESS (CLUSTER) OF 'TAB$'
0          INDEX (UNIQUE SCAN) OF 'I_OBJ#' (CLUSTER)


*************************************************************************
```

Notice that parallel DDL/DML statements were used once the **PARALLEL** clause was added. You can tell that the optimizer used parallel mode when you see the **:Qxxxxx** table names. This actually means it took the output from that query process. The following command enables automatic tracing in Oracle.

```
SQL> ALTER SESSION SET SQL_TRACE=FALSE;

Session altered.

 real: 375
```

To ensure there are no barriers to parallel operations, let's analyze our new table:

```
SQL>  ANALYZE TABLE test_par_dml COMPUTE STATISTICS;

Table analyzed.

real:  1453
```

If you don't set your value for **LONG** when you use the **SET AUTOTRACE ON EXPLAIN** option, you will get errors:

```
SQL> set long 4000
```

Let's look at some example explain plans for various settings of the **PARALLEL DML** clause of the **ALTER SESSION** command, first using some simple **SELECT** statements. Turn **PARALLEL DML** on:

```
SQL> ALTER SESSION ENABLE PARALLEL DML;
SQL> SELECT count(*) FROM test_par_dml;

 COUNT(*)
--------
   10194

 real: 3578

Execution Plan
----------------------------------------------------------
   0      SELECT STATEMENT Optimizer=CHOOSE (Cost=14 Card=1)
   1    0   SORT (AGGREGATE)
   2    1     TABLE ACCESS* (FULL) OF 'TEST_PAR_DML' (Cost=14 Card=879 :Q80006)

   2 PARALLEL_TO_SERIAL            SELECT /*+ ROWID(A1) PIV_SSF */ COUNT(*)
                                             FROM "TEST_PAR_DML" A1
```

```
                              WHERE ROWID BETWEEN :B1
                              AND :B2
```

Now, **DISABLE** it. Logically from the definition, this should disable all DML processing:

```
SQL> ALTER SESSION DISABLE PARALLEL DML;

Session altered.

 real: 610
SQL> SELECT COUNT(*) FROM test_par_dml;

 COUNT(*)
--------
   10194

 real: 1703

Execution Plan
-----------------------------------------------------------
   0      SELECT STATEMENT Optimizer=CHOOSE (Cost=14 Card=1)
   1    0    SORT (AGGREGATE)
   2    1      TABLE ACCESS* (FULL) OF 'TEST_PAR_DML' (Cost=14 Card=879 :Q100006)

   2 PARALLEL_TO_SERIAL            SELECT /*+ ROWID(A1) PIV_SSF */ COUNT(*)
                                          FROM "TEST_PAR_DML" A1
                                          WHERE ROWID BETWEEN :B1
                                          AND :B2
```

What happened? The **PARALLEL** clause in the **CREATE TABLE** command is overriding the setting of the **ALTER SESSION** command. Now, turn off the **PARALLEL** clause for the table by setting the **DEGREE** to 1:

```
SQL> ALTER TABLE test_par_dml PARALLEL (DEGREE 1);

Table altered.

 real: 625
SQL>  select count(*) from test_par_dml;

 COUNT(*)
--------
   10194

 real: 2000
```

```
Execution Plan
---------------------------------------------------------
   0      SELECT STATEMENT Optimizer=CHOOSE
   1    0   SORT (AGGREGATE)
   2    1     TABLE ACCESS (FULL) OF 'TEST_PAR_DML'
```

This is more what you would expect. Now, try to force parallel DML, assuming it is possible:

```
SQL> ALTER SESSION FORCE PARALLEL DML;

Session altered.

 real: 610
SQL> select count(*) from test_par_dml;

 COUNT(*)
 --------
    10194

 real: 1938

Execution Plan
---------------------------------------------------------
   0      SELECT STATEMENT Optimizer=CHOOSE
   1    0   SORT (AGGREGATE)
   2    1     TABLE ACCESS (FULL) OF 'TEST_PAR_DML'
```

Yikes! It doesn't work. Let's look at some more parallel DML statements with this setting—for example, an **UPDATE**:

```
SQL> UPDATE test_par_dml SET density=2;

10194 rows updated.

 real: 12062

Execution Plan
---------------------------------------------------------
   0      UPDATE STATEMENT Optimizer=CHOOSE
   1    0   UPDATE OF 'TEST_PAR_DML'
   2    1     TABLE ACCESS (FULL) OF 'TEST_PAR_DML'
```

This doesn't work either. What if you **ROLLBACK** your changes and reset the **PARALLEL** clause for the table?

```
SQL> ROLLBACK;

Rollback complete.

 real: 5594
SQL> ALTER TABLE test_par_dml PARALLEL(DEGREE 2);

Table altered.

 real: 625
```

Now try **UPDATE** again:

```
SQL> UPDATE test_par_dml SET density=2;

10194 rows updated.

 real: 9797

Execution Plan
-----------------------------------------------------------
   0      UPDATE STATEMENT Optimizer=CHOOSE (Cost=14 Card=8796 Bytes=1
          14348)

   1   0    UPDATE OF 'TEST_PAR_DML'
   2   1      TABLE ACCESS* (FULL) OF 'TEST_PAR_DML' (Cost=14 Card=879
               :Q120006 Bytes=114348)

   2 PARALLEL_TO_SERIAL           SELECT /*+ ROWID(A1) */ A1.ROWID,A1."DENSITY
                                         " FROM "TEST_PAR_DML" A1
                                         WHERE ROWID BETWEEN
                                         :B1 AND :B2
```

Setting the **PARALLEL** state for the session doesn't really seem to have much effect, while the **PARALLEL** clause of the table does. Let's **ROLLBACK** and try something else.

```
SQL> ROLLBACK;

Rollback complete.

 real: 6000
```

Disable the **PARALLEL DML**, and try **UPDATE** with just the table **PARALLEL** clause in effect. By definition, it shouldn't do a **PARALLEL UPDATE** with the **PARALLEL DML** session mode turned off:

```
SQL> ALTER SESSION DISABLE PARALLEL DML;

Session altered.

 real: 610
SQL> UPDATE test_par_dml SET density=2;

10194 rows updated.

 real: 15984

Execution Plan
---------------------------------------------------------------
   0      UPDATE STATEMENT Optimizer=CHOOSE (Cost=14 Card=8796 Bytes=1
          14348)

   1    0   UPDATE OF 'TEST_PAR_DML'
   2    1     TABLE ACCESS* (FULL) OF 'TEST_PAR_DML' (Cost=14 Card=879
              :Q120006 Bytes=114348)

   2 PARALLEL_TO_SERIAL          SELECT /*+ ROWID(A1) */ A1.ROWID,A1."DENSITY
                                 " FROM "TEST_PAR_DML" A1
                                 WHERE ROWID BETWEEN
                                 :B1 AND :B2
```

This looks like the same explain plan as with **PARALLEL DML** turned on. Maybe it's that pesky **DEGREE 2**. Make it **DEFAULT** instead at the table level, and see if the **PARALLEL DML** clause has any effect at the session level:

```
SQL> ROLLBACK;

Rollback complete.

 real: 2421
```

First, set the **PARALLEL** clause of the table so **DEGREE** is set to **DEFAULT**:

```
SQL> ALTER TABLE test_par_dml PARALLEL(DEGREE DEFAULT);

Table altered.

 real: 610
```

Try your update with session-level **PARALLEL DML** turned off:

```
SQL> ALTER SESSION DISABLE PARALLEL DML;
```

```
SQL> UPDATE test_par_dml SET density=2;

10194 rows updated.

 real: 7828

Execution Plan
-----------------------------------------------------------
   0      UPDATE STATEMENT Optimizer=CHOOSE (Cost=14 Card=8796 Bytes=1
          14348)

   1   0    UPDATE OF 'TEST_PAR_DML'
   2   1      TABLE ACCESS* (FULL) OF 'TEST_PAR_DML' (Cost=14 Card=879
              :Q150006 Bytes=114348)

   2 PARALLEL_TO_SERIAL              SELECT /*+ ROWID(A1) */ A1.ROWID,A1."DENSITY
                                     " FROM "TEST_PAR_DML" A1
                                     WHERE ROWID BETWEEN
                                     :B1 AND :B2
```

Well, this looks like it used **PARALLEL DML** to me. Let's look at some other settings:

```
SQL> ROLLBACK;

Rollback complete.

 real: 2704
```

I think you know what this will look like, but let's do it just for completeness:

```
SQL> ALTER SESSION ENABLE PARALLEL DML;

Session altered.

 real: 594
SQL> UPDATE test_par_dml SET density=2;

10194 rows updated.

 real: 6000

Execution Plan
-----------------------------------------------------------
   0      UPDATE STATEMENT Optimizer=CHOOSE (Cost=14 Card=8796 Bytes=1
          14348)
```

```
    1    0    UPDATE OF 'TEST_PAR_DML'
    2    1        TABLE ACCESS* (FULL) OF 'TEST_PAR_DML' (Cost=14 Card=879
                  :Q150006 Bytes=114348)

    2 PARALLEL_TO_SERIAL              SELECT /*+ ROWID(A1) */ A1.ROWID,A1."DENSITY
                                             " FROM "TEST_PAR_DML" A1
                                             WHERE ROWID BETWEEN
                                             :B1 AND :B2


SQL> ROLLBACK;

Rollback complete.

 real: 5593
```

Again, I think we know the outcome here:

```
SQL> ALTER SESSION FORCE PARALLEL DML;

Session altered.

 real: 594
SQL>
SQL> UPDATE test_par_dml SET density=2;

10194 rows updated.

 real: 6344

Execution Plan
-----------------------------------------------------------
    0      UPDATE STATEMENT Optimizer=CHOOSE (Cost=14 Card=8796 Bytes=1
           14348)

    1    0    UPDATE OF 'TEST_PAR_DML'
    2    1        TABLE ACCESS* (FULL) OF 'TEST_PAR_DML' (Cost=14 Card=879
                  :Q150006 Bytes=114348)

    2 PARALLEL_TO_SERIAL              SELECT /*+ ROWID(A1) */ A1.ROWID,A1."DENSITY
                                             " FROM "TEST_PAR_DML" A1
                                             WHERE ROWID BETWEEN
                                             :B1 AND :B2


SQL> ROLLBACK;

Rollback complete.

 real: 5484
```

To summarize: On NT 4 with patch level 3 using Oracle 8.0.3 with two CPUs, the **ALTER SESSION...PARALLEL DML** option doesn't buy you much. At least on a single table test of **SELECT** and **UPDATE** commands, the **PARALLEL (DEGREE)** setting of the table involved overrode the **SET SESSION** command in every test. This may differ on other platforms.

Creating A Table Using The **PARALLEL** Clause

If you want a table to always be treated as a parallel operations-capable entity, you have to specify that fact using the **PARALLEL** clause of the **CREATE TABLE** command. The **PARALLEL** clause takes one of two options: either an integer value showing the level of parallelization or the keyword **DEFAULT**. Here is an example where the table is based on an existing table (actually a view) using the **DEFAULT** value for the **PARALLEL** clause:

```
SQL> @create_par_dml
SQL> CREATE TABLE test_par_dml PARALLEL (DEGREE DEFAULT) AS
  2  SELECT
  3  owner,
  4  table_name,
  5  column_name,
  6  data_type,
  7  data_type_mod,
  8  data_type_owner,
  9  data_length,
 10  data_precision,
 11  data_scale,
 12  nullable,
 13  column_id,
 14  default_length,
 15  num_distinct,
 16  low_value,
 17  high_value,
 18  density,
 19  num_nulls,
 20  num_buckets,
 21  last_analyzed,
 22  sample_size,
 23  character_set_name
 24  FROM sys.dba_tab_columns;

Table created.

real: 9671
```

Here is the output from the **tkprof80** run against the trace file for the parallel **CREATE TABLE** using the explain option:

```
***********************************************************************

CREATE table test_par_dml PARALLEL (DEGREE DEFAULT) AS
SELECT
owner,
table_name,
column_name,
data_type,
data_type_mod,
data_type_owner,
data_length,
data_precision,
data_scale,
nullable,
column_id,
default_length,
num_distinct,
low_value,
high_value,
density,
num_nulls,
num_buckets,
last_analyzed,
sample_size,
character_set_name
FROM sys.dba_tab_columns

call     count       cpu    elapsed       disk      query    current       rows
------   ------  --------  ---------- ----------  ---------- ---------- ----------
Parse        1      0.13       0.30          0          0          0          0
Execute      1      1.26       8.73          0        912        373      10194
Fetch        0      0.00       0.00          0          0          0          0
------   ------  --------  ---------- ----------  ---------- ---------- ----------
total        2      1.39       9.03          0        912        373      10194

Misses in library cache during parse: 1
Optimizer goal: CHOOSE
Parsing user id: 5  (SYSTEM)

Rows     Execution Plan
------   -------------------------------------------------------
    0    CREATE TABLE STATEMENT   GOAL: CHOOSE
    0     LOAD AS SELECT [:Q4001]
              CREATE TABLE :Q4001 AS SELECT C0,C1,C2,C3,C4,C5,C6,C7,C8,C9,C10,
                C11,C12,C13,C14,C15,C16,C17,C18,C19,C20 FROM :Q4000
```

```
0       FILTER [:Q4000]
0        NESTED LOOPS (OUTER) [:Q3000]
            SELECT /*+ ORDERED NO_EXPAND USE_NL(A2) INDEX(A2) */ A1.C0,
            A1.C1,A1.C2,A1.C3,A1.C4,A1.C5,A1.C6,A1.C7,A1.C8,A1.C9,A1.C10,
            A1.C11,A1.C12,A1.C13,A1.C14,A1.C15,A1.C16,A1.C17,A1.C18,
            A1.C19,A1.C20,A1.C21(+),A1.C22(+),A1.C23,A1.C24,A1.C25(+),
            A1.C26,A1.C27,A1.C28,A1.C29,A1.C30,A1.C31,A1.C32,A1.C33,
            A1.C34(+),A1.C35,A1.C36,A1.C37,A1.C38(+),A2.ROWID,
            A2."USER#"(+),A2."NAME" FROM (SELECT /*+ ORDERED NO_EXPAND
            USE_NL(A4) INDEX(A4) */ A3.C0 C0,A3.C1 C1,A3.C2 C2,A3.C3 C3,
            A3.C4 C4,A3.C5 C5,A3.C6 C6,A3.C7 C7,A3.C8 C8,A3.C9 C9,A3.C10
            C10,A3.C11 C11,A3.C12 C12,A3.C13 C13,A3.C14 C14,A3.C15 C15,
            A3.C16 C16,A3.C17 C17,A3.C18 C18,A3.C19 C19,A3.C20 C20,
            A3.C21(+) C21,A3.C22(+) C22,A3.C23 C23,A3.C24 C24,A3.C25(+)
            C25,A3.C26 C26,A3.C27 C27,A3.C28 C28,A3.C29 C29,A3.C30 C30,
            A3.C31 C31,A3.C32 C32,A3.C33 C33,A3.C34(+) C34,A4.ROWID C35,
            A4."OWNER#" C36,A4."NAME" C37,A4."OID$"(+) C38 FROM (SELECT
            /*+ ORDERED NO_EXPAND USE_NL(A6) INDEX(A6) */ A5.C0 C0,A5.C1
            C1,A5.C2 C2,A5.C3 C3,A5.C4 C4,A5.C5 C5,A5.C6 C6,A5.C7 C7,
            A5.C8 C8,A5.C9 C9,A5.C10 C10,A5.C11 C11,A5.C12 C12,A5.C13
            C13,A5.C14 C14,A5.C15 C15,A5.C16 C16,A5.C17 C17,A5.C18 C18,
            A5.C19 C19,A5.C20 C20,A5.C21(+) C21,A5.C22(+) C22,A5.C23 C23,
            A6.ROWID C24,A6."OBJ#"(+) C25,A6."ROW_CNT" C26,A6."NULL_CNT"
            C27,A6."TIMESTAMP#" C28,A6."SAMPLE_SIZE" C29,A6."DISTCNT"
            C30,A6."LOWVAL" C31,A6."HIVAL" C32,A6."DENSITY" C33,
            A6."INTCOL#"(+) C34 FROM (SELECT /*+ ORDERED NO_EXPAND
            USE_NL(A8) */ A7.C0 C0,A7.C1 C1,A7.C2 C2,A7.C3 C3,A7.C4 C4,
            A7.C5 C5,A7.C6 C6,A7.C7 C7,A7.C8 C8,A7.C9 C9,A7.C10 C10,
            A7.C11 C11,A7.C12 C12,A7.C13 C13,A7.C14 C14,A7.C15 C15,
            A7.C16 C16,A7.C17 C17,A7.C18 C18,A7.C19 C19,A7.C20 C20,
            A8."OBJ#"(+) C21,A8."COL#"(+) C22,A8."TOID" C23 FROM (SELECT
            /*+ ORDERED NO_EXPAND USE_NL(A10) INDEX(A10) */ A9.C0 C0,
            A9.C1 C1,A9.C2 C2,A9.C3 C3,A9.C4 C4,A9.C5 C5,A9.C6 C6,
            A10.ROWID C7,A10."OBJ#" C8,A10."COL#" C9,A10."NAME" C10,
            A10."TYPE#" C11,A10."LENGTH" C12,A10."PRECISION#" C13,
            A10."SCALE" C14,A10."NULL$" C15,A10."DEFLENGTH" C16,
            A10."INTCOL#" C17,A10."PROPERTY" C18,A10."CHARSETID" C19,
            A10."CHARSETFORM" C20 FROM (SELECT
0         NESTED LOOPS (OUTER) [:Q3000]
0          NESTED LOOPS (OUTER) [:Q3000]
0           NESTED LOOPS (OUTER) [:Q3000]
0            NESTED LOOPS [:Q3000]
0             NESTED LOOPS [:Q3000]
0              TABLE ACCESS (FULL) OF 'USER$' [:Q3000]
0              TABLE ACCESS (BY INDEX ROWID) OF 'OBJ$' [:Q3000]

0               INDEX (RANGE SCAN) OF 'I_OBJ2' (UNIQUE)
                   [:Q3000]
```

```
0          TABLE ACCESS (CLUSTER) OF 'COL$' [:Q3000]
0            INDEX (UNIQUE SCAN) OF 'I_OBJ#' (CLUSTER)
                [:Q3000]
0          TABLE ACCESS (CLUSTER) OF 'COLTYPE$' [:Q3000]
0          TABLE ACCESS (BY INDEX ROWID) OF 'HIST_HEAD$' [:Q3000]

0            INDEX (RANGE SCAN) OF 'I_HH_OBJ#_INTCOL#'
                (NON-UNIQUE) [:Q3000]
0          TABLE ACCESS (BY INDEX ROWID) OF 'OBJ$' [:Q3000]
0            INDEX (RANGE SCAN) OF 'I_OBJ3' (NON-UNIQUE) [:Q3000]
0          TABLE ACCESS (CLUSTER) OF 'USER$' [:Q3000]
0            INDEX (UNIQUE SCAN) OF 'I_USER#' (CLUSTER) [:Q3000]
0        TABLE ACCESS (CLUSTER) OF 'TAB$'
0          INDEX (UNIQUE SCAN) OF 'I_OBJ#' (CLUSTER)
```

****

Notice that parallel DDL/DML statements were used once the **PARALLEL** clause was added. You can tell that the optimizer used parallel mode when you see the **:Qxxxxx** table names. This actually means it took the output from that query process.

The use of the **DEFAULT** value in the **PARALLEL** clause tells Oracle to calculate the number of parallel query slaves based on table size and initialization parameter settings.

An example creating a regular table using the integer value for the **PARALLEL** clause follows:

```
CREATE TABLE test_par_clause (
col1 INTEGER NOT NULL,
col2 VARCHAR2(10),
col3 VARCHAR2(10),
col4 NUMBER(5,2))
PARALLEL (DEGREE 4)
TABLESPACE user_data
STORAGE (INITIAL 1M NEXT 1M PCTINCREASE 0 FREELISTS 12)
PCTFREE 10
PCTUSED 90
INITRANS 12
MAXTRANS 255
/
```

Notice in this more complete example that the parameters **FREELISTS** and **INITRANS** are related to the setting of the **PARALLEL** clause. The default level of **PARALLEL** is set to four (two per CPU). This means that you will use a default set of four parallel query slaves for parallel operations on this table. You can expect up to three simultaneous (no this isn't shown; I just happen to know this) processes that may be doing parallel operations, so you will have a minimum of 12 possible processes performing parallel operations—hence, the values of 12 for **FREELISTS** (if all three are doing updates) and 12 for **INITRANS**. If you really want this table to scream during parallel operations, you would make it a partitioned table spread across four disks.

Setting Up The Parallel Query Initialization Parameters

The initialization parameters are stored in the init<SID>.ora file, which is usually located in the \orant\dbs directory on NT and the $ORACLE_HOME/dbs file on Unix. I suggest placing them in a more OFA (optimal flexible architecture)-compliant structure on any platform to reduce the possibility that someone will edit the initORAPROD.ora file instead of the initORATEST.ora file if they are collocated. The parameters of concern for parallel query are these:

- **COMPATIBLE**—This determines the structure of your redo log files and directly determines which types of statements you can run. If **COMPATIBLE** is set to an earlier version (say 7.3.2), you will not be able to run any Oracle8 commands that depend on the new redo log format. I suggest it be set to a minimum of 8.0.0.

- **CPU_COUNT**—On virtually all platforms, this will automatically be set to the number of CPUs, but you should always check it anyway. (On HPUX, for example, this parameter was not being set correctly on some 7.x versions.) This parameter will be used in determining the minimum number of query servers if a default degree of parallelism is not specified. On most platforms, you will not be able to set this parameter. On those where it can be set, it must never be set higher than the number of CPUs you have.

- **DB_FILE_MULTIBLOCK_READ_COUNT**—This parameter tells Oracle how many blocks to read in one I/O pass. This is all well and good, except on many platforms, the Oracle system reads in 64K chunks, so this value—times the value of the **DB_BLOCK_SIZE** parameter— should be a multiple of 64K to be most efficient. If you set this parameter to greater than the maximum allowed I/O buffer size for your platform, the maximum will be used.

- **DB_FILE_SIMULTANEOUS_WRITES**—This parameter has a default of four and determines the number of simultaneous writes made to a specific database file. In striped environments, this should be set to the number of disks used in the stripe settings. For parallel query, it should be set to the degree of parallelism or the number of striped disks for the parallel operation table that is most used.

- **DML_LOCKS**—This parameter is set to the maximum number of concurrent transactions times the number of required DML locks (one per transaction per table DML is performed upon). So, if you plan parallel DML operations, boost this parameter accordingly. It defaults to 20, which for most environments falls woefully short of what is required. Start at 200, and adjust as needed.

- **ENQUEUE_RESOURCES**—This should be set to higher than **DML_LOCKS**+20. A minimum is one enqueue per table in the database.

- **HASH_AREA_SIZE**—This defaults to twice the size of **SORT_AREA_SIZE** and is the maximum amount of memory (in bytes) to be used in hash joins. It should be set to at least one-half the square root of the size of the smaller of the two tables in a join operation. If the smaller table is 36MB, then the appropriate size would be 3MB (specified in bytes). This should be set large, but not so large that you induce swapping or run out of memory.

- **OPTIMIZER_PERCENT_PARALLEL**—Set this parameter to 100. The default setting is 0, which will force the best serial plan to be used. A low value will favor *index* scan solutions, and a higher value will favor *table* scan solutions. A value of 100 will choose a parallel option unless a serial one can absolutely be shown to finish faster.

- **PARALLEL_MIN_SERVERS**—This is set to the minimum number of servers to have left operating after a parallel operation completes.

- **PARALLEL_MAX_SERVERS**—This should be set to the absolute maximum number of parallel query processes you expect to need in your environment. The minimum should be twice the number of CPUs times the number of concurrent users.

- **SHARED_POOL_SIZE**—This should have the component you specify for parallel query set to:

```
(3 * msgbuffer_size) * (CPUs + 2) * PARALLEL_MAX_SERVERS
```

  Remember that the shared pool has other areas to consider when sizing this parameter, as well as the PQO (parallel query option) area. The message buffer size is either 2K or 4K, depending on your platform. The size of the message buffer is documented in your platform-specific *Installation And Users Guide*. For Oracle Parallel Server (shared server), the formula becomes:

```
(4 * msgbuffer_size)*(CPUs_per_node*#nodes)+2) *  (PARALLEL_MAX_SERVERS *
#nodes)
```

- **ALWAYS_ANTI_JOIN**—This should be set to **HASH**, or processes involving **NOT IN** predicates will be evaluated serially instead of in parallel.

- **DB_BLOCK_SIZE**—Set this parameter to 8K or 16K. Set it at the time the database is created. It requires a re-creation of the database to change. Obviously, if you are worried about parallel operations, your database is large, and you do lots of large read-type operations. Larger values for **DB_BLOCK_SIZE** enhance large read performance.

- **DB_BLOCK_BUFFERS**—This should be set so that (**DB_BLOCK_BUFFERS** * **DB_BLOCK_SIZE**) + **SHARED_POOL_SIZE** account for about 60 percent of total physical memory. Also, be sure that the Unix-shared memory segment is sized to hold the total of these parameters plus the size of the redo log buffers and some miscellaneous overhead (add 10 to 15 percent).

- **SORT_DIRECT_WRITES**—Set this to **AUTO** so that if **SORT_AREA_SIZE** is greater than 10 times the block size, sorts will not be written through the buffer cache, increasing performance by up to a factor of 3.

- **SORT_READ_FAC**—The setting of this parameter depends on disk speed: The higher the speed, the higher you can set **SORT_READ_FAC**. This controls the number of blocks read from a temporary tablespace for a single read operation during a sort. Because sorts are the usual final step for a parallel DML operation, optimizing sorts to improve PQO performance makes sense.

Adjusting all of these parameters can be a challenge, but it is required if your parallel environment is to function optimally.

Using The Parallel Hints

You can control parallel activity with several hints. Hints are used in DML statements to force Oracle to take a specific optimization path. They give Oracle developers a club with which to beat sense into the sometimes overzealous cost-based optimizer. These are the parallel hints:

- **PARALLEL**—Tells Oracle to use parallel processing in the execution of this statement. The hint accepts multiple arguments, telling it not only to use parallel processes and how many but whether parallel instances should take part in the transaction.

- **NOPARALLEL**—Overrides any parallel processing, and forces serial mode processing.

- **APPEND**—Forces any data added to a table to be appended rather than taking advantage of any unused free space in already allocated blocks. The Oracle optimizer uses this as the default mode for parallel inserts.

- **NOAPPEND**—Overrides the default append mode for parallel inserts, and allows block free space to be used during parallel inserts.

- **PARALLEL_INDEX**— Tells Oracle how many servers should participate in the index scans for this query, insert, or update action. Generally used on parallel servers with partitioned indexes. This hint accepts up to four arguments: table name, index name, degree for table, and number of servers to participate in the transaction. Both numeric values can be replaced by the keyword **DEFAULT**, which tells Oracle to use the initialization and preset values to determine this value.

How are these hints used? Let's look at an example of each.

Example Use Of The *PARALLEL* Hint

The **PARALLEL** hint is used identically to other hints. For those of you who have never used hints, you place it into a comment inserted into the statement it applies to. The **clients** table, for example, is spread across five disks, and you have three parallel servers to throw at it to perform a large **SELECT** for a year-end report. Here's how can you tell Oracle this is what you want it to do:

```
SELECT /*+ FULL(clients) PARALLEL(clients,5,3) */ client_id, client_name,
client_adress FROM clients;
```

If you want the optimizer to determine the values for the number of query servers and instances, you can use the **DEFAULT** keyword:

```
SELECT /*+ FULL(clients) PARALLEL(clients,DEFAULT,DEFAULT) */ client_id,
client_name, client_adress FROM clients;
```

If a table alias is used in the statement, it must also be used in the hint. For example, if the **clients** and **addresses** tables were to be joined, and you wanted to force a full-table, parallel query scan of the **clients** table, you would use the following command:

```
SELECT /*+ FULL(a) PARALLEL(a,5,3) */  a.client_name, b.adress1, b.address2,
b.address3
FROM clients a, addresses b
WHERE a.address_id=b.address_id;
```

Example Use Of The *NOPARALLEL* Hint

If you do a large insert into a table specified as a parallel process table, each branch of the **INSERT** parallel process will be assigned its own segment in the table's tablespace. That segment will be the same size as the **NEXT** specification for the main table. After the **INSERT** query processes complete, the individual segments are merged and appended to the table. In many cases, the overall insert may be less than one **NEXT** value in size.

If you have limited space available in the tablespace that is the target of the insert, forcing serial execution may be wise. This forcing of serial behavior is what the **NOPARALLEL** hint was created for. Let's force serial behavior on a large update to the **clients** table.

First, you must be absolutely certain that the table will use a parallel path if you don't use the hint:

```
SQL> alter table clients parallel(degree default);

Table altered.
```

Test that it does, in fact, use a parallel path if you do not use the hint:

```
SQL> update clients set no_purchase='Y' where activity='N';

7612 rows updated.


Execution Plan
-----------------------------------------------------------
   0      UPDATE STATEMENT Optimizer=CHOOSE (Cost=6 Card=73 Bytes=1095)

   1   0    UPDATE OF 'CLIENTS'
   2   1      TABLE ACCESS* (FULL) OF 'CLIENTS' (Cost=6 Card=73 Bytes=1095) :Q36000

   2 PARALLEL_TO_SERIAL               SELECT /*+ ROWID(A1) */ A1.ROWID,A1."ACTIVITY"
                                      ,A1."NO_PURCHASE" FROM "CLIENTS" A1 WHERE
                                       ROWID BETWEEN :B1 AND :B2 AND A1."ACTIVITY"
                                      ='N'
```

Now, use the hint, and see what happens:

```
SQL>  update /*+ NOPARALLEL(clients) */ clients set no_purchase='Y' where
activity='N';
SQL> /

7612 rows updated.


Execution Plan
-----------------------------------------------------------
   0      UPDATE STATEMENT Optimizer=CHOOSE (Cost=11 Card=73 Bytes=1095)

   1   0    UPDATE OF 'CLIENTS'
   2   1      TABLE ACCESS (FULL) OF 'CLIENTS' (Cost=11 Card=73 Bytes=1095)
```

As you can see from this example, the hint forces a serial scan over a parallel scan.

Example Use Of The **NOAPPEND** Hint

Because **APPEND** is the normal mode of the parallel process for **INSERT** or **UP-DATE**, demonstrating the use of **NOAPPEND** is more important. In this example, you will do a bulk insert into the **clients** table from a specially prepared insert table called **new_clients**. You have enough room in your tablespace for the extents required for the new data, but not enough room for a large number of "temporary" parallel process extents. The command would be as follows:

```
INSERT /*+ NOAPPEND */ INTO clients SELECT * FROM new_clients;
```

The **NOAPPEND** hint made sure that any insert activity into the existing table was done against available space first, and new extents were appended as required. The next example demonstrates this using a table built as a copy of the DBA_TAB_COLUMNS view called **test_par_dml**. A second copy of the same view, called **test2**, will be used as a source for insert rows.

First, create the table **test_par_dml** using a canned script:

```
SQL> @create_par_dml

Table created.
```

Now, create freespace inside misc. blocks of the table:

```
SQL> DELETE FROM test_par_dml WHERE nullable='Y';

7628 rows deleted.

SQL> COMMIT;

Commit complete.
```

Here is the current count of blocks in the table:

```
SQL> SELECT COUNT(*) FROM dba_extents WHERE segment_name='TEST_PAR_DML';

 COUNT(*)
--------
        8
```

Now, be sure parallel processing will be used on the table:

```
SQL> ALTER TABLE test_par_dml PARALLEL (DEGREE 10);

Table altered.
```

Be sure parallel processing is turned on at the session level, even though in previous examples we proved this doesn't really affect processing of this type:

```
SQL> ALTER SESSION ENABLE PARALLEL DML;

Session altered.
```

Now, let's do some processing:

```
SQL> INSERT INTO test_par_dml SELECT * FROM test2;

10194 rows created.

SQL> COMMIT;

Commit complete.
```

How many extents did it take with parallel processing and **APPEND** as a default?

```
SQL>  SELECT COUNT(*) FROM dba_extents WHERE segment_name='TEST_PAR_DML';

 COUNT(*)
--------
      11
```

Now, do it all again using the **NOAPPEND** hint:

```
SQL> DROP TABLE test_par_dml;

Table dropped.

SQL> @create_par_dml

Table created.

SQL> ALTER TABLE test_par_dml PARALLEL (DEGREE 10);

Table altered.

SQL> DELETE FROM test_par_dml WHERE nullable='Y';

7628 rows deleted.

SQL> COMMIT;

Commit complete.

SQL> INSERT /*+ NOAPPEND(test_par_dml) */ INTO test_par_dml SELECT * FROM test2;

10194 rows created.

SQL> COMMIT;

Commit complete.
```

```
SQL> SELECT COUNT(*) FROM dba_extents WHERE segment_name='TEST_PAR_DML';

 COUNT(*)
--------
        9
```

By forcing the **INSERT** to use available free space, you saved the space required for two extents in this table.

Creating Snapshot Logs And Snapshots

Advanced replication is a complex topic with many facets, such as *n*-way, multimaster, master-slave, updatable snapshots, etc. I suggest reading the Oracle manual *Oracle8 Server Replication* (Release 8, June 1997, Part No. A54651-01) before attempting these advanced-level topics. In this section, I demonstrate the use of snapshots and snapshot logs. First, because they are required for fast refresh of snapshots, I show how to create a snapshot log, which is created on the master site, not the replication site.

Snapshots are asynchronous in nature. They reflect a table's or a collection's state at the time the snapshot was taken. A simple snapshot can be periodically refreshed by using either a snapshot log containing only the changed rows for the snapshot (fast refresh) or a totally new copy (complete refresh). In most cases, the fast refresh is quicker and just as accurate. It can be used only if the snapshot has a log that was created prior to the creation or last refresh of the snapshot. A complex snapshot requires a complete refresh. You can also allow the system to decide which to use— either a fast or complete refresh.

One problem with a snapshot log is that it keeps a copy of each and every change to a row. Therefore, if a row undergoes 200 changes between one refresh and the next, the snapshot log will have 200 entries that will be applied to the snapshot at refresh. This could lead to the refresh of the snapshot taking longer than a complete refresh. Examine each snapshot for the amount of activity it is seeing, and if this is occurring with any of them, eliminate the snapshot log or change the refresh mode to **COMPLETE**.

Because the snapshot log must be created prior to the snapshot itself for a simple snapshot, let's examine the administration of snapshot logs first.

Creating Snapshot Logs

A snapshot log is created for the master table of a snapshot. A simple snapshot has only one table. Creating a snapshot log for a complex snapshot does no good, because a complex snapshot requires a complete refresh that doesn't use a snapshot log. The user creating the snapshot must have the **CREATE TRIGGER** privilege on the table the log is being created for.

The **CREATE SNAPSHOT LOG** command is used to create a snapshot log. The format of the command is

```
>--CREATE SNAPSHOT LOG ON ---------------table----------------------------------->>
                          |-schema.-|
>------------------------------------------------------------------------------->>
   |- WITH -------------------------------------------------------|
                    |-PRIMARY KEY--------------------------------|
                    |-,ROWID------------------------------------|
                    |,filter column, filter column...--|
>------------------------------------------------------------------------------->>
   |- PCTFREE n -----------------------------|
   |- PCTUSED n-----------------------------|
   |- INITRANS n----------------------------|
   |- MAXTRANS n---------------------------|
   |- TABLESPACE tablespace------|
   |- STORAGE ( storage clause)-|
```

where the following holds true:

- **schema** is the schema in which to store the log. If not specified, this will default to the user's own schema.

- **table** is the table name to create the snapshot log for.

- **WITH** specifies what is recorded about the source table in the log— primary key, **ROWID**, or both. The columns listed as filter columns are used to tell Oracle to record changes to these columns.

- **PCTFREE**, **PCTUSED, INITRANS**, and **MAXTRANS** are the values for these parameters to use in creating the log file.

- **TABLESPACE** specifies the tablespace in which to create the snapshot log. This will default to the user's default tablespace if not specified.

- **STORAGE** is a standard storage clause.

The following example shows how the **CREATE SNAPSHOT LOG** command is used:

```
CREATE SNAPSHOT LOG ON  admin.personnel
   PCTFREE 10
   PCTUSED 70
```

```
TABLESPACE remote_admin_data
STORAGE ( INITIAL 50K NEXT 50K
    MINEXTENTS 1 MAXEXTENTS 50
    PCTINCREASE 0);
```

As noted, the **CREATE SNAPSHOT LOG** command creates an additional after-row trigger on the affected table.

Altering Snapshot Logs

Periodically, snapshot logs may need to be altered. Storage needs may change, or the storage dynamics may need to be altered on a snapshot log. These are accomplished by using the **ALTER SNAPSHOT LOG** command. The format for this command is

```
>--ALTER SNAPSHOT LOG ON -----------------table-------------------------------->>
                              |-schema.-|
>------------------------------------------------------------------------------>>
   |- ADD --------------------------------------------------|
                    |-PRIMARY KEY---------------|
                    |-,ROWID------------------------|
                    |,filter column, filter column...--|
>------------------------------------------------------------------------------>>
   |-  PCTFREE n -----------------|
   |-  PCTUSED n-----------------|
   |-  INITRANS n-----------------|
   |-  MAXTRANS n---------------|
   |-  STORAGE ( storage clause)-|
```

where:

- **schema** is the schema in which to store the log. If not specified, this will default to the user's own schema.

- **table** is the table name to alter the snapshot log for.

- **ADD** adds logging options, such as **ROWID**, or filter columns to the snapshot log profile.

- **PCTFREE**, **PCTUSED**, **INITRANS**, and **MAXTRANS** are the values for these parameters to use for the log file.

- **STORAGE** is a standard storage clause.

To change a snapshot log's location, you must use either an export/import or a drop/create of the snapshot log.

Dropping A Snapshot Log

A snapshot log is dropped using the **DROP SNAPSHOT LOG** command. The format for the command follows:

```
>--DROP SNAPSHOT LOG ON-------------------table------------------------>>
                                    |-schema.-|
```

Creating Snapshots

Once you have created any required snapshot logs, you can create the snapshots themselves. This is accomplished through the **CREATE SNAPSHOT** command. Snapshots can be simple or complex. A simple snapshot consists of either an entire single table or a simple **SELECT** of rows from a single table. A complex snapshot consists of joined tables, views, or grouped or complex **SELECT** statement queries. Build snapshots using the **CREATE SNAPSHOT** command:

```
>--   CREATE SNAPSHOT --------------------snapshot--------------------------->>
                      |-schema.-|
>----------------------------------------------------------------------------->>
    |-PCTFREE integer---------------------------------------|
    |-PCTUSED integer---------------------------------------|
    |-INITRANS integer--------------------------------------|
    |-MAXTRANS integer-------------------------------------|
    |-TABLESPACE tablespace------------------------|
    |-STORAGE storage_clause---------------------|
    |-CLUSTER cluster (column [, column] ...)----|
  >-- USING  ------------------------------------------------------------------>>
                        |-INDEX -------------------------------------------|
                        |                |-PCTFREE integer----|           |
                        |                |-PCTUSED integer----|           |
                        |                |-INITRANS integer ----|         |
                        |                |-MAXTRANS integer -|            |
                        |--   DEFAULT-- ROLLBACK SEGMENT-------------------------|
                        | |-MASTER--|                      |-rollback_segment-| |
                        | |-LOCAL----|                                          |
>--REFRESH ------------------------------------------------------------------>>
              |-FAST----------------------| |-START WITH date-| |-NEXT date-|
              |-COMPLETE------------------|
              |-FORCE---------------------|
              |-WITH ---------------------|
                              |-PRIMARY KEY-|
                              |-ROWID-----------|
>----------------------- AS subquery---------------------------------------><
    |-FOR UPDATE-|
```

The keywords and parameters for the **CREATE SNAPSHOT** command are:

- **schema**—Contains the snapshot. If you omit **schema**, Oracle creates the snapshot in your schema.

- **snapshot**—Specifies the name of the snapshot to be created. Oracle chooses names for the table, views, and index used to maintain the snapshot by adding a prefix and suffix to the snapshot name. To limit these names to 30 bytes and allow them to contain the entire snapshot name, limit your snapshot names to 19 bytes.

- **PCTFREE**, **PCTUSED**, **INITRANS**, and **MAXTRANS**—Establish values for the specified parameters for the internal table Oracle uses to maintain the snapshot's data.

- **TABLESPACE**—Specifies the tablespace in which the snapshot is to be created. If you omit this option, Oracle creates the snapshot in the default tablespace of the owner of the snapshot's schema.

- **STORAGE**—Establishes storage characteristics for the table Oracle uses to maintain the snapshot's data.

- **CLUSTER**—Creates the snapshot as part of the specified cluster. Because a clustered snapshot uses the cluster's space allocation, do not use the **PCTFREE**, **PCTUSED**, **INITRANS**, **MAXTRANS**, **TABLESPACE**, or **STORAGE** parameters with the **CLUSTER** option.

- **USING INDEX**—Specifies parameters for the index Oracle creates to maintain the snapshot. You can choose the values of the **INITRANS**, **MAXTRANS**, **TABLESPACE**, **STORAGE**, and **PCTFREE** parameters. For the **PCTFREE**, **PCTUSED**, **INITRANS**, and **MAXTRANS** parameters, specify the default storage and transaction attributes for the snapshot.

- **ROLLBACK SEGMENT**—Specifies the local snapshot and/or remote master rollback segments to be used during snapshot refresh.

- **DEFAULT**—Specifies that Oracle will choose which rollback segment to use.

- **MASTER**—Specifies the rollback segment to be used at the remote master for the individual snapshot.

- **LOCAL**—Specifies the rollback segment to be used for the local refresh group that contains the snapshot. If you do not specify **MASTER** or

LOCAL, Oracle uses **LOCAL** by default. If you do not specify **rollback_segment**, Oracle chooses the rollback segment to be used automatically. If you specify **DEFAULT**, you cannot specify **rollback_segment**.

- **REFRESH**—Specifies how and when Oracle automatically refreshes the snapshot:

    - **FAST**—Specifies a fast refresh or one using only the updated data stored in the snapshot log associated with the master table.

    - **COMPLETE**—Specifies a complete refresh or one that re-executes the snapshot's query.

    - **FORCE**—Specifies a fast refresh, if one is possible, or complete refresh, if a fast refresh is not possible. Oracle decides whether a fast refresh is possible at refresh time. If you omit the **FAST**, **COMPLETE**, and **FORCE** options, Oracle uses **FORCE** by default.

- **START WITH**—Specifies a date expression for the first automatic refresh time.

- **NEXT**—Specifies a date expression for calculating the interval between automatic refreshes. Both the **START WITH** and **NEXT** values must evaluate to a time in the future. If you omit the **START WITH** value, Oracle determines the first automatic refresh time by evaluating the **NEXT** expression when you create the snapshot. If you specify a **START WITH** value but omit the **NEXT** value, Oracle refreshes the snapshot only once. If you omit both the **START WITH** and **NEXT** values, or if you omit the **REFRESH** clause entirely, Oracle does not automatically refresh the snapshot.

- **WITH PRIMARY KEY**—Specifies that primary key snapshots are to be created. These snapshots allow snapshot master tables to be reorganized without impacting the snapshot's ability to continue to fast refresh. You can also define primary key snapshots as simple snapshots with subqueries.

- **WITH ROWID**—Specifies that **ROWID** snapshots are to be created. These snapshots provide backward compatibility with Oracle Release 7.3 masters. If you omit both **WITH PRIMARY KEY** and **WITH ROWID**, Oracle creates primary key snapshots by default.

- **FOR UPDATE**—Allows a simple snapshot to be updated. When used in conjunction with the replication option, these updates will be propagated to the master.

- **AS** subquery—Specifies the snapshot query. When you create the snapshot, Oracle executes this query and places the results in the snapshot. The select list can contain up to 1,000 expressions. The syntax of a snapshot query is described with the syntax description of subquery. The syntax of a snapshot query is subject to the same restrictions as a view query. For a list of these restrictions, see the **CREATE VIEW** command.

Snapshot Usage

The next example shows the use of the **CREATE SNAPSHOT** command for a simple snapshot. The following code segment uses the **CREATE SNAPSHOT** command with a complex snapshot. The sizing considerations should mirror those for the source table. If the source table is stable, you should use a large initial extent with smaller subsequent extents. Because snapshots will most likely be on slow growth tables, set **PCTINCREASE** to 0 in most cases:

```
CREATE SNAPSHOT new_drugs
PCTFREE 10 PCTUSED 70
TABLESPACE clinical_tests
STORAGE (INITIAL 50K NEXT 50K PCTINCREASE 0)
REFRESH
   START WITH ROUND(SYSDATE + 7) + 2/24
   NEXT NEXT_DAY(TRUNC(SYSDATE, 'TUESDAY') + 2/24
AS select * from appl_dba.test_drugs@kcgc;
```

In the snapshot shown in the previous example, the entire **test_drugs** table is used to create a snapshot from its location at a remote database identified in the **kcgc** connect string into the tablespace **clinical_trials** in the current database. It will be first refreshed in 7 days at 2:00 in the morning and, subsequently, at 7-day intervals on every Tuesday thereafter at 2:00 in the morning. Because no refresh mode is specified and it is a simple snapshot, if the table has a snapshot log, the fast mode will be used. If no snapshot log is available, then the complete mode will be used. If you specify the **FORCE** option, it will always try to do a fast refresh first.

```
CREATE SNAPSHOT trial_summary
PCTFREE 5 PCTUSED 60
TABLESPACE clinical_tests
STORAGE (INITIAL 100K NEXT 50K PCTINCREASE 0)
REFRESH COMPLETE
   START WITH ROUND(SYSDATE + 14) + 6/24
   NEXT NEXT_DAY(TRUNC(SYSDATE, 'FRIDAY') + 19/24
```

```
AS
select td.drug_name, s.trial_number, dr.doctor_id,
 s.comment_line,s.comment
from
   appl_dba. test_drugs@kcgc td,
   appl_dba.trial_doctors@kcgc dr,
   appl_dba.trial_summaries@kcgc s
where
   td.drug_id = s.drug_id and
   s.trial_id = dr.trial_id and
   s.doctor_id = dr.doctor_id;
```

The script shown here produces a complex snapshot called **trial_summary** with data from the **test_drugs**, **trial_doctors**, and **trial_summaries** tables in the database specified in the connect string **kcgc**. The snapshot is refreshed using the complete mode, because it is a complex query and is created in the **clinical_tests** tablespace of the local database.

Altering A Snapshot

A snapshot is altered using the **ALTER SNAPSHOT** command. You may alter such items as storage and space usage parameters, type, and frequency of refresh. The format for this command is

```
>--ALTER SNAPSHOT ---------------------snapshot-------------------------------->>
                    |-schema.-|
>----------------------------------------------------------------------------->>
    |- PCTFREE integer-----------------------------------------|
    |- PCTUSED integer-----------------------------------------|
    |- INITRANS integer----------------------------------------|
    |- MAXTRANS integer---------------------------------------|
    |- TABLESPACE tablespace------------------------------|
    |- STORAGE storage_clause----------------------------|
    |- CLUSTER cluster (column [, column] ...)----|
  >--  USING  -------------------------------------------------------------->>
                    |-INDEX ----------------------------------------------------|
                    |       |- PCTFREE integer----|                             |
                    |       |- PCTUSED integer----|                             |
                    |       |-INITRANS integer ----|                            |
                    |       |-MAXTRANS integer -|                     |         |
                    |-- DEFAULT---- ROLLBACK SEGMENT------------------------------|
                    |   |-MASTER--|                       |-rollback_segment-| |
>--REFRESH ----------------------------------------------------------------->>
            |-FAST--------------------------|  |-START WITH date-| |-NEXT date-|
            |-COMPLETE------------------|
            |-FORCE--------------------------|
            |-WITH PRIMARY KEY--------|
```

where:

- **schema** is the schema in which to store the log. If not specified, this will default to the user's own schema.

- **table** is the table name to create the snapshot log for.

- **PCTFREE**, **PCTUSED**, **INITRANS**, and **MAXTRANS** are the values for these creation parameters to use for the created log file.

- **STORAGE** is a standard storage clause.

- **REFRESH** specifies the refresh mode:

  - **FAST** uses a **SNAPSHOT LOG**. It is the default mode.

  - **COMPLETE** re-performs the subquery and is the only valid mode for a complex snapshot.

  - **FORCE** causes the system to first try a **FAST**, and if this is not possible, then a **COMPLETE**.

- **START WITH** specifies the date for the first refresh.

- **NEXT** specifies either a date or a time interval for the next refresh of the snapshot. **START WITH** and **NEXT** values are used to determine the refresh cycle for the snapshot. If just **START WITH** is specified, only the initial refresh is done. If both are specified, the first is done on the **START WITH** date, and the **NEXT** is evaluated against the **START WITH** to determine future refreshes. If just the **NEXT** value is specified, it computes based on the date the snapshot is created. If neither is specified, the snapshot is not automatically refreshed.

Dropping A Snapshot

A snapshot is dropped using the **DROP SNAPSHOT** command. The command's format follows:

```
>----DROP SNAPSHOT ------------------------snapshot--------------------------->>
                         |-schema.-|
```

When a snapshot is dropped, if it has a snapshot log associated with it, only the rows required for maintaining that snapshot are dropped. Dropping a master table upon which a snapshot is based doesn't drop the snapshot. Any subsequent refreshes will fail, however.

Chapter 9

The Oracle8 Data Dictionary

*Oracle8 has expanded the data dictionary to include coverage for **TYPEs**, **REFs**, **LOBs**, objects—in short, all of its new features. In addition, Oracle has expanded coverage for existing objects since version 7.3. This chapter looks at the components of the data dictionary, and the Practical Guide shows how these components can make both the DBA's and developer's jobs easier.*

Notes…

Chapter

9

The Oracle Instance

Oracle is more than a collection of programs that ease data access. It can be compared with an operating system that overlays the operating system of the computer on which it resides. Oracle has its own file structures, buffer structures, global areas, and tunability above and beyond those provided within the operating system. It controls its own processes, records, and consistencies and cleans up after itself.

Oracle, as it exists on your system (with the exception of DOS or OS/2), consists of executables, five to nine detached processes, a global memory area, datafiles, and maintenance files. It can be as small as a couple of megabytes or as large as a massive globe-spanning construction of gigabytes.

Previous chapters address the concept of a *database instance*, defined as the system global area (SGA) and process set that make up an invocation of Oracle. Notice that this definition does not mention disk files. This exclusion of disk files from the concept of an instance shows the separation between the concept of an Oracle database (defined as the datafiles and instances that make up an entire interrelated implementation of Oracle) and an Oracle instance (the SGA and process set). Each database may have several instances associated with it; it has only one set of database files, however. Figures 9.1 and 9.2 show diagrams of a typical Oracle7 and Oracle8 environment. You may want to refer to these diagrams as you read the next sections.

Let's first look at a typical Oracle system operating in the Unix environment.

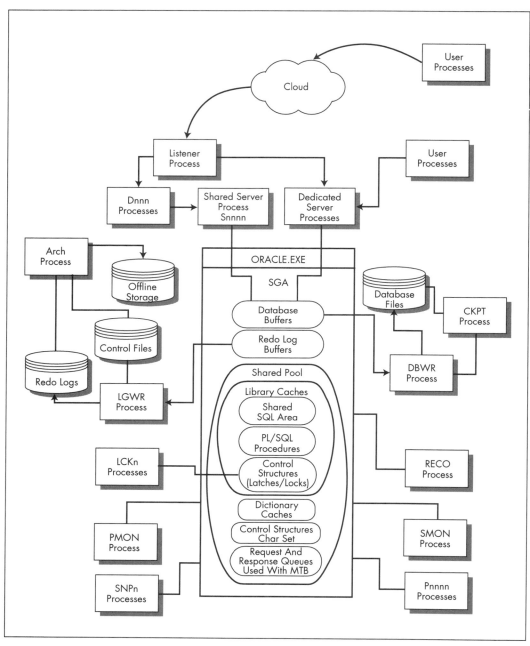

Figure 9.1

Oracle7 SGA structure.

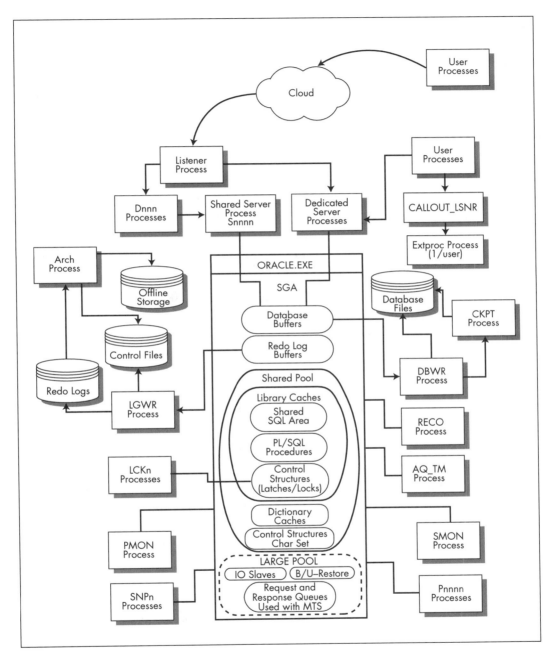

Figure 9.2

Oracle8 SGA structure.

Oracle Processes

Oracle7 has a minimum of eight detached processes running on Unix. For Oracle8, this jumps to nearly a dozen. Four of these are the base Oracle processes started every time Oracle is started up on a system. The additional processes may be started if the database is using archiving or TCP/IP, or is being run in parallel and/or distributed mode. The Oracle job queues, snapshot processes, advanced queuing options, and callout processes all add to the process count.

Under NT, three processes start: one base Oracle process, ORACLE80.EXE; a Net8 process, called TNSLSNR90.EXE, if SQL*Net is to be used; and an additional Oracle process called STRTDB80.EXE that was used to start the Oracle instance. Under NT, seven threads are spun off of the main ORACLE80.EXE process. These would be separate processes on Unix for a base Oracle8 instance with no additional processes allocated. The usual names for the Oracle processes on Unix and VMS operating systems are listed here:

- *DBWR (dirty buffer writer)*—Handles data transfer from the buffers in the SGA to the database files. If a buffer in the SGA is modified, it is considered "dirty." The DBWR process cleans the SGA by writing these dirty buffers to the disk system. If the buffer region controlled by the initialization parameter **DB_BLOCK_BUFFERS** is too small, DBWR may have to work harder to keep the SGA clean, as well as spend time swapping buffers aged by the LRU (least recently used) algorithm back to disk. This causes a low value for a statistic known as *hit ratio*.

  The LRU process uses latches to handle the marking and tracking of blocks as they age in and out of the SGA. The number of LRU latches is controlled by the **DB_BLOCK_LRU_LATCHES** initialization parameter, which defaults to the number of CPUs. Usually, the number of **DB_BLOCK_LRU_LATCHES** is sufficient. The number of DBWR processes is controlled by the **DB_WRITERS** (pre-Oracle8) or **DBWR_IO_SLAVES** (post-Oracle8) initialization parameter; if your system uses asynchronous disk I/O, you should not use this parameter. If your system doesn't use asynchronous I/O, however, then setting the **DB_WRITERS** or **DBWR_IO_SLAVES** parameter to the number of disks used by Oracle will enhance performance.

- *LGWR (log writer)*—Transfers data from the redo log buffers to the redo log database files. The LGWR process writes all redo entries that have been copied into the buffer since the last time it wrote. LGWR is kicked off by the following actions:

- A commit record when a transaction is committed

- An internal timer every three seconds

- The redo log buffer when it is one-third full

- DBWR writes modified buffers to the disk system

The LGWR process writes to all redo logs in a single group in a simultaneous write operation. If a single log in a group is damaged, the error is logged in the LGRW trace file and the instance alert log; no error is written to the user process. If all redo logs in a log group are damaged or unwritable, the archiver stops and issues an error. Previous to Oracle8, only one LGWR process was allowed. Now, the **LGWR_IO_SLAVES** parameter can be set on platforms that do not support asynchronous I/O to simulate it to disks. The parameter value should be equal to the number of logs in a redo group.

- *SMON (system monitor)*—Performs instance recovery on instance startup and is responsible for cleaning up temporary segments. In a parallel environment, this process recovers failed nodes. SMON also coalesces contiguous free extents in tablespaces where the default storage clause value for the **PCTINCREASE** parameter is greater than 0.

- *PMON (process monitor)*—Recovers user processes that have failed, then cleans up the cache. It recovers the resources from a failed process. In a multithreaded server (MTS) environment, PMON also detects and restarts any dispatcher or server processes that may have died prematurely (not those that Oracle killed itself).

- *ARCH (archiver process)*—Writes the redo log datafiles that are filled into the archive log datafiles. It is active only if archive logging is in effect.

- *RECO (distributed transaction)*—Resolves recoverer failures involving distributed transactions. When RECO reestablishes connections between servers involved in in-doubt transactions, it automatically resolves those transactions. RECO is created only if the instance has the distributed option and the initialization parameter **DISTRIBUTED_TRANSACTIONS** is set to greater than 0.

- *LCKn (lock process)*—Provides inter-instance locking in an Oracle7 or Oracle8 parallel server environment. A maximum of 10 LCK*n* processes (0 through 9) can be set up on any one instance, but one is usually sufficient.

- *Dnnn (dispatcher)*—Allows multiple processes to share a finite number of Oracle7 or Oracle8 process servers. It queues and routes process requests to the next available server. The dispatcher processes are used only with multithreaded servers. The dispatcher process is called by the listener (Net8/SQL*Net) process and then dispatches the process handed it by the listener to a server process. The dispatcher and server processes are controlled via the MTS parameters in the initialization file, such as **MTS_SERVERS**, **MTS_MAX_SERVERS**, **MTS_MAX_DISPATCHERS**, **MTS_DISPATCHERS**, **MTS_LISTENER_ADDRESS** (be careful with this one if you have multiple instances; specifying an incorrect address that points to a different database may make an instance unreachable), **MTS_MULTIPLE_LISTENERS**, **MTS_RATE_LOG_SIZE**, **MTS_RATE_SCALE**, and **MTS_SERVICE** (usually same as the instance name). A new parameter, **LOCAL_LISTENER**, if set, will override other listener settings, so take great care with its use.

- *Snnn (servers)*—Makes all the required calls to the database to resolve a user's requests. It returns results to the D*nnn* process that calls it.

- *Listener (Net8 or SQL*Net server)*—Runs if you are running SQL*Net or Net8 (Oracle's network communications layer), usually only one per node. If you use external procedure calls, an additional listener process that deals only with external procedure calls must be started with a separate call to the lsnrctl program.

- *CKPxx*—Starts the checkpoint process that optimizes the checkpoint operation for Oracle logging in Oracle7. In Oracle8, it is automatically started. Checkpoints update all headers for all files used by all tablespaces and the controlfile. The checkpoint process does not write blocks to disk; it just updates header records.

- *Snpxx*—Starts snapshot and job process queues when configured in the initialization file to do so using the **JOB_QUEUE_PROCESSES** parameter.

- *Aq_tnxx (advanced queuing)*—Starts only if configured to do so in the initialization file with the **AQ_TM_PROCESSES** parameter. Version

8.0.3 allows only one process, but later releases should allow more. Setting this value to greater than 1 will result in an error.

- *EXTPROC*—Specifies the callout queues. Each session performing callouts will have one. I hope that Oracle will multithread these processes; otherwise, the callout feature could be unusable in a large multiuser environment. As of the 8.0.2 beta version, this also was not working with environments where a multithreaded server was enabled. This functionality has been promised in 8.0.3.

- *Pxxxx*—Specifies parallel DML/query processes. For each operation involving parallel operations (**INSERT**, **UPDATE**, **DELETE**), multiple *Pxxxx* processes may be started. On some platforms, parallel DML/query operations can result in large numbers of zombie processes, so be careful using it. The number of parallel DML/query processes are controlled with the initialization parameters **PARALLEL_MAX_SERVERS**, **PARALLEL_MIN_SERVERS**, **PARALLEL_SERVER_IDLE_ TIME**, and for parallel recovery operations, **RECOVERY_ PARALLELISM**.

On a Unix system, this additional process may be present:

- *ARCHMON (archive monitor)*—Monitors the archive process and writes the redo logs to the archives. It requires a dedicated window or terminal on BSD (Berkeley Standard Distribution) systems.

On multiuser-capable systems, each user process may spawn several subprocesses, depending on the type of activities being done by that process. Depending on how Oracle is configured, a single parallel query may start dozens of query slave processes for a single user.

 When specifying semaphores on a Unix system, always allow for many more than the base number of Oracle processes if you are using the Oracle parallel query option.

The global memory area, or SGA, is an area of CPU memory reserved for Oracle use only. It contains buffers that are used to speed transaction throughput and help maintain the system integrity and consistency. No data is altered directly on the disk; it all passes through the SGA. The size and configuration of the SGA are defined by a file called the initialization file, or INIT.ORA, which can contain information on each type of buffer or shared pool area in the SGA.

Shared programs also make up a typical instance. These can be as few as one (e.g., the Oracle kernel) or as complex as the entire tool set. Placing the tool set into shared memory (on VMS) reduces the memory requirements for each user.

As I said before, you can view Oracle as an operating system that overlays your existing operating system. It has structures and constructs that are unique to it alone. The major area of an Oracle installation is, of course, the database. To access an Oracle database, you must first have at least one *instance* of Oracle assigned to that database. An instance consists of the subprocesses, global area, and related structures that are assigned to it. Multiple instances can attach to a single database. Many of an instance's and database's characteristics are determined when they are created. A single VMS, NT, or Unix platform can have several instances in operation simultaneously. On VMS and some Unix systems, they can be attached to their own database, or they may share one.

Oracle Memory Structures

The previous sections deal with physical Oracle processes, but what do these processes interact with? Some, such as DBRW and LGWR, interact on one side with the disks that actually store the data in quasi-permanent form. Other processes, such as servers and dispatchers, interact with user processes. What is the glue that holds these diverse process structures together? As Figures 9.1 and 9.2 show earlier in this chapter, this glue is the SGA, which is made up of several areas of buffers and caches:

- *Database buffer cache*—Controlled by initialization parameters **DB_ BLOCK_SIZE** and **DB_BLOCK_BUFFERS**.

- *Redo log buffer cache*—Controlled by initialization parameter **LOG_ BUFFER**. The Oracle8 documentation says a value of 65,536 or higher would not be unreasonable, but I suggest sizes of 1MB or more if you have large redo logs (larger than 5MB).

- *Shared and large pools*—Controlled by the initialization parameters **SHARED_ POOL_SIZE**, **SHARED_POOL_RESERVED_SIZE**, and **SHARED_POOL_ RESERVED_MIN_ALLOC** for a non-MTS (multithreaded server) shared pool. The shared pool contains dictionary and library caches and control structures. It may also be used for sort area allocation.

  For a shared pool where MTS is being used, two new parameters (as of Oracle8) specify a special area known as the **LARGE_POOL**, which is used for session memory and I/O buffers for backup. The new parameters are:

- **LARGE_POOL_MIN_ALLOC**, whose minimum value is 16K and maximum value is around 64MB.

- **LARGE_POOL_SIZE**, with a minimum value of 300K or **LARGE_POOL_MIN_ALLOC**—whichever is larger—and a maximum value that is operation-system specific, but generally 2GB or larger.

The more ad hoc query operations you have that do not use bind variables that your database users create, the larger your shared pool will have to be. Oracle's default size is usually too small for a modern database. I suggest making the shared pool at least 20MB and maybe up to 40MB, depending on user load and transaction types. The library area contains the shared SQL area, PL/SQL packages and procedures, and the control areas.

Outside of the SGA are the sort areas, software code areas, and program global areas (PGAs). The sort areas are controlled by the initialization parameters **SORT_AREA_SIZE** and **SORT_AREA_RETAINED_SIZE**. If MTS is being used, the sort area is taken from the SGA. Only one area of **SORT_AREA_SIZE** is ever allocated to a single process. If additional area is required, the sort is performed as a disk sort.

Software code areas are controlled by the operating system. Oracle code area sizes depend on the size of the programs themselves and vary by release. If possible, you should place Oracle code in a shared memory area, so multiple copies are not required to be in memory for each user on the system.

PGA is a memory region that contains data and control information for a single user process. If an instance is not running the MTS, then the PGA contains the stack space and session information. If the instance is running MTS, then the PGA contains only the stack space; the session information moves into the SGA. Shared SQL areas are always in the SGA, not the PGA, with or without the MTS server running. The PGA size is somewhat controlled by the initialization parameters **OPEN_LINKS**, **DB_FILES**, and **LOG_FILES**.

The Concept Of **ROWID**s In Oracle7 And Oracle8

Oracle used the concept of the **ROWID** in Oracle7 and earlier releases to uniquely identify each row in each table in the database. This was represented as the pseudocolumn **ROWID** in Oracle7 and earlier releases. Hence, unknown to many DBAs and developers, even nonunique identified tables that violate third-normal form always had unique identifiers that could be used for removing duplicates and other unique-identifier-required operations: the **ROWID** column. Of course, views don't have **ROWID**s.

In Oracle8, the concept of **ROWID** is still with us, but the format has been expanded. We'll discuss the **DBMS_ROWID** set of Oracle-provided packages that let you manipulate **ROWID** between the old and new formats, and to piece out as well as build **ROWID**s.

This chapter examines the Oracle7 **ROWID** concepts, and Oracle8 **ROWID** concepts are presented in the next chapter.

Oracle7 **ROWID** Format

ROWID in Oracle7 is a **VARCHAR2** representation of a binary value shown in hexadecimal format as

```
bbbbbbbb.ssss.ffff
```

where **bbbbbbbb** is the block ID, **ssss** is the sequence in the block, and **ffff** is the file ID.

This **ROWID** is a pseudo-column (meaning the **DESCRIBE** command won't show it) in each table (and cluster). **ROWID** is always unique, except in the case of cluster tables that have values stored in the same block. This makes **ROWID** handy for doing entry comparisons in tables that may not have a unique key, especially when you want to eliminate or show duplicates before creating a unique or primary key. In *Oracle Performance Tuning* by Mark Gurry and Peter Corrigan (O'Reilly & Associates, 1993), a simple query for determining duplicates using **ROWID** is shown:

```
DELETE FROM emp E
WHERE E.rowid > ( SELECT MIN (x.rowid)
            FROM emp X
                    WHERE X.emp_no = E.emp_no );
```

Of course, any operation where you can do a **SELECT**, **UPDATE**, or **DELETE** based on exact **ROWID** values will always outperform virtually any other similar operation using standard column value logic. The file ID portion of the **ROWID** points to the file with that number, which happens to be the same number given the datafile in the **DBA_DATA_FILES** view. The **ROWID** pseudo-column is one that any DBA should be aware of and use to advantage. Oracle has expanded the **ROWID** concept in Oracle8.

The **ROWID** Concept In Oracle8

Oracle8 introduced the concept of **OBJECTS**. These **OBJECTS** have identifiers that now are added to the **ROWID**, giving an **EXTENDED ROWID** format that is 10 bytes long rather than 6 bytes, as was the norm in Oracle7. The Oracle8 **ROWID** is a **VARCHAR2** representation of a base 64 number (remember that base 64 starts at *B*, not *A*; *A* designates 0). The **ROWID** is displayed as

```
000000.FFF.BBBBBB.SSS
```

where **OOOOOO** is the data object number, **FFF** is the relative file number, **BBBBBB** is the block number, and **SSS** is the slot number.

An example of the new **ROWID** would be

```
AAAAVJAAEAAAABEAAA
```

where **AAAAVJ** is the data object number, **AAE** is the relative file number, **AAAABE** is the block number, and **AAA** is the slot number.

The new parts of **ROWID** are the object number and the relative file number. Multiple files can have the same relative file number because Oracle assigns the number based on tablespace. This means that these numbers are only unique per tablespace, which indicates that you cannot derive an absolute address directly from the new **ROWID**. The new **ROWID** addressing schema is tablespace relative.

The new **ROWID** contains the data object number, which increments when an object's version changes. The version changes whenever a table is truncated or a partition is moved. The data object number is not related to the object identifier.

ROWID can be easily manipulated with the **DBMS_ROWID** package. If you have used **ROWID** in your Oracle7 application (which Oracle has repeatedly said not to do, but some people never listen…), then you will have to familiarize yourself with this package.

Old **ROWID**s (called restricted **ROWID**s) will be automatically converted to the new format if:

- You use export/import to move data.

- You use the migration utility.

If you have used **ROWID**s in your application and store them as columns in other tables, then you will have to manually change these columns to the new format using the **DBMS_ROWID** package. If a column in a table has been designated as a datatype of **ROWID**, it will be altered to accept the new format during migration, but this will not affect the data in the column.

The Concept Of Object Identifiers (**OID**s) In Oracle8

Each object in Oracle8 (i.e., table, cluster, etc.) has a 16-byte object identifier (**OID**). It is guaranteed to be globally unique across all databases in your environment. It is a 16-byte base 64 number that allows for some ridiculously high number of objects to be identified—in the peta- region of countability (a petillion?). The maximum is 2^{128} (340,283,266,920,938,463,463,374,607,431,768,211,456).

The **OID** is used to construct **REF**s for nested tables. In some statements involving nested tables, if you don't specifically tell Oracle to bring back the **UNREF** value (i.e., translate the **OID** and get the data), you will get a 42- to 46-byte **REF** number returned, as useful as that sounds. The number itself is simply an identifier and contains no "intelligence," such as would be in a **ROWID**. The **REF** value can vary in size from 42 through 46 bytes of internal storage.

The Oracle-Provided **DBMS_ROWID** Package

The **DBMS_ROWID** package provides procedures to create **ROWID**s and to interpret their contents between the change from Oracle7 to Oracle8 format. Execution privilege is granted to **PUBLIC** for **DBMS_ROWID**. Procedures in this package run under the caller security. Beginning with Oracle8, two types of **ROWID** are available:

- *Restricted*—Oracle7 and earlier

- *Extended*—Oracle8 and later

These are equated to two constants for use in identifying specific operations in this package:

- **ROWID_TYPE_RESTRICTED**   0

- **ROWID_TYPE_EXTENDED**   1

Two additional constants are defined for use when verifying **ROWID** state:

- **ROWID_IS_VALID**   constant integer := 0
- **ROWID_IS_INVALID**   constant integer := 1

The **ROWID_CREATE** Function

The **ROWID_CREATE** function constructs a **ROWID** from its constituents:

- **ROWID_TYPE**—Type (restricted/extended) number
- **OBJECT_NUMBER**—Data object number (**ROWID_OBJECT_UNDEFINED** for restricted) (number)
- **RELATIVE_FNO**—Relative file number (number)
- **BLOCK_NUMBER**—Block number in this file (number)
- **FILE_NUMBER**—File number in this block (number)

The function returns a valid **ROWID**. It asserts purity, so it can be used in packages outside of its parent package.

The **ROWID_INFO** Procedure

The **ROWID_INFO** procedure breaks a specified **ROWID** into its components and returns them. The procedure has the following input and output parameters:

- Input

  ROWID_IN—**ROWID** to be interpreted (**ROWID**)

- Output

  ROWID_TYPE—Type (restricted/extended) (number)

  OBJECT_NUMBER—Data object number **ROWID_OBJECT_UNDEFINED** for restricted(number)

  RELATIVE_FNO—Relative file number (number)

  BLOCK_NUMBER—Block number in this file (number)

  FILE_NUMBER—File number in this block (number)

This procedure asserts purity.

The **ROWID_TYPE** Function

The **ROWID_TYPE** function accepts a single input parameter—**ROW_ID** (**ROWID**). The function returns the type of a **ROWID** (number corresponding to restricted/extended). The input is defined as:

- **ROW_ID—ROWID** to be interpreted.

The function's number return is defined as:

- **ROWID_TYPE_RESTRICTED**   0
- **ROWID_TYPE_EXTENDED**   1

The function asserts purity, so it can be used in packages outside of its parent package.

The **ROWID_OBJECT** Function

The **ROWID_OBJECT** function accepts a single input parameter—**ROW_ID** (**ROWID**). The function extracts the data object number from the input **ROWID** and returns it as a number. The **ROWID_OBJECT_UNDEFINED** is returned for restricted **ROWID**s. The function asserts purity, so it can be used in packages other than its parent package.

The **ROWID_RELATIVE_FNO** Function

The **ROWID_RELATIVE_FNO** function accepts a single input parameter—**ROW_ID** (**ROWID**). The function extracts the relative file number from this **ROWID** and returns it as a number. The function asserts purity, so it can be used in packages outside of its parent package.

The **ROWID_BLOCK_NUMBER** Function

The **ROWID_BLOCK_NUMBER** function accepts a single input parameter—**ROW_ID** (**ROWID**). The function extracts the block number from this **ROWID** and returns it as a number. The function asserts purity, so it can be called from a package other than its parent package.

The **ROWID_ROW_NUMBER** Function

The **ROWID_ROW_NUMBER** function accepts a single input parameter—**ROW_ID** (**ROWID**). The function extracts the row number from this **ROWID** and returns a number. The function asserts purity, so it can be called from packages outside of its parent package.

The **ROWID_TO_ABSOLUTE_FNO** Function

The **ROWID_TO_ABSOLUTE_FNO** function accepts three input parameters—**ROW_ID** (**ROWID**), **SCHEMA_NAME** (**VARCHAR2**), and **OBJECT_NAME** (**VARCHAR2**). The function extracts the relative file number from this data and returns a number. The function asserts purity, so it can be used in packages outside of its parent package.

The **ROWID_TO_EXTENDED** Function

The **ROWID_TO_EXTENDED** function accepts the following input parameters:

- **OLD_ROWID** (**ROWID**)
- **SCHEMA_NAME** (**VARCHAR2**)
- **OBJECT_NAME** (**VARCHAR2**)
- **CONVERSION_TYPE** (**INTEGER**)

The parameters have the following definitions:

- **OLD_ROWID**—**ROWID** to be converted
- **SCHEMA_NAME**—Name of the schema that contains the table (optional)
- **OBJECT_NAME**—Table name (optional)
- **CONVERSION_TYPE**—**ROWID_CONVERT_INTERNAL/EXTERNAL_CONVERT_EXTERNAL** (whether **OLD_ROWID** was stored in a column of **ROWID** type or the character string)

The function translates the restricted **ROWID** that addresses a row in a given table to the extended format. The function asserts purity, so it can be used in packages outside of its parent package.

The **ROWID_TO_RESTRICTED** Function

The **ROWID_TO_RESTRICTED** function accepts two input parameters—**OLD_ROWID** (**ROWID**) and **CONVERSION_TYPE** (**NUMBER**). These parameters are defined as:

- **OLD_ROWID**—**ROWID** to be converted into the old style restricted **ROWID**.

- **CONVERSION_TYPE**—This **IN** parameter determines whether the conversion process returns an internal or external representation of the **ROWID** once it is converted. If the value **ROWID_CONVERT_INTERNAL** is used, the function returns an internal format (**ROWID**) **ROWID** value. If the input parameter is **EXTERNAL_CONVERT_EXTERNAL**, then the value returned is a **VARCHAR2** format instead of a **ROWID** format.

 *The Oracle documentation is incorrect for this function in that it specifies only one input. The file **DBMSUTIL.SQL** package header specification shows two input parameters.*

This function translates the extended **ROWID** into a restricted format and returns it as a **ROWID** in either internal (**ROWID**) or external (**VARCHAR2**) format.

The **ROWID_VERIFY** Function

The **ROWID_VERIFY** function accepts the following input parameters:

- **ROWID_IN** (**ROWID**)
- **SCHEMA_NAME** (**VARCHAR2**)
- **OBJECT_NAME**(**VARCHAR2**)
- **CONVERSION_TYPE** (**INTEGER**)

The function verifies the **ROWID**. It returns **ROWID_VALID** or **ROWID_INVALID** value, depending on whether or not a given **ROWID** is valid. The function's input parameters are defined as:

- **ROWID_IN**—**ROWID** to be verified
- **SCHEMA_NAME**—Name of the schema that contains the table
- **OBJECT_NAME**—Table name
- **CONVERSION_TYPE**—**ROWID_CONVERT_INTERNAL/ EXTERNAL_CONVERT_EXTERNAL** (whether **OLD_ROWID** was stored in a column of **ROWID** type or the character string)

The function asserts purity, so it can be used in packages outside of its parent package.

Oracle Metadata—The **K** And **X$** Structs

The base level of the Oracle metadata consists of C structs that the actual executables use. These structs are normally not visible to users and must be accessed through a circuitous route by defining a view against them. Oracle versions 7.3 and 8.x have a view that lists these tables (at least most of the ones that interest us). It is called **GV_$FIXED_TABLE**. This view lists only the table names. Any structural data must be dug out by hand or by looking at related structures, such as the **GV_$** views. A related view, called **GV_$FIXED_VIEW_DEFINITION**, provides details of the **GV_$** tables that give insights into the actual structure of the **K** and **X$** tables. The **GV_$FIXED_VIEW_DEFINITION** view gives the actual text for the creation of the **GV_$** views. The contents of the **GV_$FIXED_VIEW_DEFINITION** view for version 8.0.3 of Oracle are listed in its appendices.

Oracle Metadata—The **XXX$** Tables

The first physical implementation of the data dictionary is what is known as the **XXX$** table. A few new tables don't follow this convention. Some examples of the dollar tables include **COL$**, **AUD$**, and **TAB$**. Descriptions of these tables are available in the appendices for version 8.0.3 of Oracle.

These tables can be difficult to view at times, because most of the information is encoded in numeric or integer codes that must be translated. In addition, you usually need joins between multiple tables to get a complete picture. The **DBA**, **ALL**, and **USER** views are based on the **XXX$** tables and give a more user-friendly look at the data they contain. To get a good picture of the values for the codes listed in the **XXX$** tables, look at the definitions for the **DBA** views as listed in the **DBA_VIEWS** view. The listings of the view definitions for version 8.0.3 of Oracle are shown in its appendices.

Oracle Metadata—The **GV$** And **V$** Views And Tables

The **K** and **X$** tables can be impossible to understand without months or even years of study. They contain columns whose names usually start with **kma** or **kgl** or some other combination of letters followed by equally cryptic sets of letters and numbers. No doubt, they give a clear picture of what the column is to the person or team that developed the tables, but they give nothing away to the uninitiated. To overcome this, Oracle provided the **GV$** and **V$** views for a user-friendly look at these underlying structs.

The **V$** views are simply copies of the **GV$** views with the data segregated for the current instance. The **GV$** views provide information on all instances in a parallel server environment. For a nonparallel server environment (i.e., 90 percent of Oracle customers), the **GV$** and **V$** views will vary only in that the **GV$** views will have a column, such as **INST#**, that contains a value of 1.

The **GV$** and **V$** views are important, because they are not static views. They allow you to monitor the current conditions of the database and change when the database changes. This means, you can monitor a session as it progresses through a transaction or watch as resources are used and released.

Oracle Metadata—The **DBA**, **ALL**, And **USER** Views

The workhorses of the data dictionary are the **DBA**, **ALL**, and **USER** views. The **DBA** views give you a complete look at the particular objects the views monitor. For example, the **DBA_TABLES** view lists all tables in the database. The **ALL** views provide each user with a look at the objects the view monitors that the user has access (permission) to. For example, the **ALL_TABLES** view is a subselect against the **DBA** views that restricts the data according to the various permissions and grants held by the current user. The **USER** views show only the objects that the particular user has created or owns. For example, the **USER_TABLES** view shows only the tables in the current schema.

Practical Guide To

The Oracle Data Dictionary

- Monitoring The Oracle Processes On NT
- Monitoring The Oracle Processes On Unix
- Monitoring The MTS Process
- Monitoring Average Wait Time For MTS
- Monitoring The SGA And Shared Pool
- Using The Data Dictionary To Monitor Database Objects

Monitoring The Oracle Processes On NT

At times, you need to know how many processes Oracle is using. On NT, this task is made easy with built-in monitoring tools.

NT provides two levels of monitoring: course and fine. Course-level monitoring begins with the Ctrl+Alt+Del combination of key strokes, which will take you to the Windows NT security panel. The panel has the following buttons:

- Lock_workstation
- Logoff
- Shut Down
- Change Password
- Task Manager
- Cancel

Click on the Task Manager button, which takes you to a multipage window containing the following page tabs:

- Applications
- Processes
- Performance

The last two of these pages have data that will interest you if you are monitoring the Oracle8 processes. For example, the Processes page shows you the currently running processes, their memory usage, PID, CPU percentage, and CPU time. Say that you get a call from several users saying the database is not responding. You can quickly go to this screen and see if the problem is with the TNSLSNR80.EXE image.

You can also pinpoint problems from the Processes page by looking at the values for CPU percentage of use and CPU time. If a particular process indicates excessive use of resources in these areas, then something may be wrong with that process. This page also allows privileged users to terminate processes.

The Performance page contains a graph for each CPU, showing percentage busy, a combined CPU usage graph, and a memory usage graph set. Charts at the bottom of the page indicate Totals for handles, threads, and processes, physical memory usage statistics, commit charge data, and kernel memory statistics.

For fine-level monitoring on NT, use the Start button to show the program's menu item. From Programs, select the Administrative Tools (Common) menu item, and, from the resulting display, select Performance Monitor.

The Performance Monitor is a user-configurable monitoring tool that allows selection from the following levels of monitoring:

- Browser
- Cache
- FTP server
- Gopher server
- HTTP service
- Internet Information Services global
- Logical disk
- Memory
- NBT connection
- NetBEUI
- And many, many others

Of particular interest to system administrators and DBAs are the areas dealing with disk, CPU, memory, server work queues, servers, and threads. Under each of these, you can select multiple parameters for monitoring via graphs. For example, you could choose threads and then select, by thread, the parameters to monitor. This would allow you to monitor all Oracle-related threads to find a problem child. Of course, in a large environment with hundreds of users, this might prove a challenge. If faced with this type of monitoring, third-party tools are sometimes the answer. On the CD-ROM included with this book is the Q product from Savant Corporation. It is well-suited to this type of task.

You can also have multiple Performance Monitor sessions running simultaneously to monitor different aspects of system performance—for example, one to monitor problem threads, one to monitor CPU activity, and another to monitor disk I/O. Another nice feature of the NT Performance Monitor is the ability to save settings, log findings, and export charts.

Monitoring The Oracle Processes On Unix

On Unix, you monitor Oracle processes from the command line via the **ps** command. You can perform additional monitoring for system resource usage with the **ipcs -b** command, which will show the current memory and semaphore usage for all processes.

Using the **ps** command, you usually filter the results with a pipe through **grep** or, maybe, **awk**. An example is shown in Listing 9.1.

Listing 9.1   Example output from the ps -ef|grep command construct.

```
a1244157:oracle ps -ef|grep oracle
  oracle 25999     1  0   Oct 07 ?            2:37 ora_arch_ORCNETP1
  oracle 26016     1  0   Oct 07 ?            0:01 ora_s009_ORCNETP1
  oracle 22137     1  0   Oct 09 ?            0:00 ora_pmon_ORCNETT2
  oracle 26019     1  0   Oct 07 ?           18:57 ora_d001_ORCNETP1
  oracle 26011     1  0   Oct 07 ?            0:06 ora_s004_ORCNETP1
  oracle 26818     1  0   Oct 09 ?            0:00 ora_s004_ORCNETT3
  oracle 22147     1  0   Oct 09 ?           12:43 ora_snp0_ORCNETT2
  oracle 26010     1  0   Oct 07 ?            1:19 ora_s003_ORCNETP1
  oracle 26806     1  0   Oct 09 ?            0:02 ora_dbwr_ORCNETT3
  oracle 26004     1  0   Oct 07 ?            0:01 ora_reco_ORCNETP1
  oracle 22589 25997  0   Oct 10 ?            2:39 ora_snp0_ORCNETP1
  oracle 26035     1  0   Oct 07 ?            5:59 ora_p001_ORCNETP1
  oracle 26828     1  0   Oct 09 ?            0:00 ora_d005_ORCNETT3
  oracle 26812     1  0   Oct 09 ?            0:00 ora_snp0_ORCNETT3
     .
     .
     .
```

Oracle's **ps -ef|grep** command will produce a list of all processes with **oracle** in the name. By setting this **grep** value to the name of your instance, you can get all of the current processes that are connected to your database. For example, if the database is called ORCNETP1, the command would be as shown in Listing 9.2.

Listing 9.2   Example use of the ps -ef|grep command for a single instance name.

```
a1244157:oracle ps -ef|grep ORCNETP1
  oracle 25999     1  0   Oct 07 ?            2:37 ora_arch_ORCNETP1
  oracle 26016     1  0   Oct 07 ?            0:01 ora_s009_ORCNETP1
  oracle 26019     1  0   Oct 07 ?           18:57 ora_d001_ORCNETP1
  oracle 26011     1  0   Oct 07 ?            0:06 ora_s004_ORCNETP1
  oracle 26010     1  0   Oct 07 ?            1:19 ora_s003_ORCNETP1
  oracle 26004     1  0   Oct 07 ?            0:01 ora_reco_ORCNETP1
  oracle 22589 25997  0   Oct 10 ?            2:39 ora_snp0_ORCNETP1
```

```
oracle 26035      1  0   Oct 07 ?          5:59 ora_p001_ORCNETP1
oracle 25998      1  0   Oct 07 ?         10:57 ora_dbwr_ORCNETP1
oracle 26028      1  0   Oct 07 ?          2:11 ora_d008_ORCNETP1
oracle 26023      1  0   Oct 07 ?          2:26 ora_d003_ORCNETP1
oracle 13334 25997 0   Oct 08 ?        384:19 ora_s000_ORCNETP1
oracle 26013      1  0   Oct 07 ?          0:01 ora_s006_ORCNETP1
oracle 26012      1  0   Oct 07 ?          0:00 ora_s005_ORCNETP1
oracle 26025      1  0   Oct 07 ?          1:56 ora_d005_ORCNETP1
oracle 26034      1  0   Oct 07 ?          5:24 ora_p000_ORCNETP1
oracle 26017      1  0   Oct 07 ?         34:01 ora_d000_ORCNETP1
oracle 26002      1  0   Oct 07 ?          0:23 ora_smon_ORCNETP1
oracle 26000      1  0   Oct 07 ?         15:10 ora_lgwr_ORCNETP1
oracle 26022      1  0   Oct 07 ?          3:38 ora_d002_ORCNETP1
oracle 26001      1  0   Oct 07 ?          8:36 ora_ckpt_ORCNETP1
oracle 26015      1  0   Oct 07 ?          0:00 ora_s008_ORCNETP1
oracle 25997      1  0   Oct 07 ?          0:01 ora_pmon_ORCNETP1
oracle 26026      1  0   Oct 07 ?          1:08 ora_d006_ORCNETP1
oracle 26030      1  0   Oct 07 ?          0:00 ora_d010_ORCNETP1
oracle 26027      1  0   Oct 07 ?          1:29 ora_d007_ORCNETP1
oracle 26024      1  0   Oct 07 ?          1:06 ora_d004_ORCNETP1
oracle 26006      1  0   Oct 07 ?         72:48 ora_snp1_ORCNETP1
oracle 12823 25997 0   Oct 09 ?         36:18 ora_s001_ORCNETP1
oracle 26014      1  0   Oct 07 ?          0:00 ora_s007_ORCNETP1
oracle 26029      1  0   Oct 07 ?          1:08 ora_d009_ORCNETP1
oracle  7069 25997 0   Oct 08 ?          9:33 ora_s002_ORCNETP1
oracle 27257 27123 0 20:47:02 pts/5      0:00 grep ORCNETP1
```

Of course, if all you are interested in is a gross count of the number of processes, add a second pipe to the **wc** command, using the **-l** modifier:

```
a1244157:oracle  ps -ef|grep ORCNETP1|wc -l
                 33
```

To monitor the resource usage as far as semaphores and memory, use the **ipcs -b** command shown in Listing 9.3.

Listing 9.3 Example output from the ipcs -b command.

```
a1244157:oracle ipcs -b
IPC status from <running system> as of Sat Oct 11 20:47:38 1997
T     ID    KEY       MODE      OWNER     GROUP QBYTES
Message Queues:
q      0 0x00044eff -Rrw-rw-rw-  bscalog  bscalog  4096
T     ID    KEY       MODE      OWNER     GROUP SEGSZ
Shared Memory:
m  23003 0x010083c4 --rw-rw-rw-  root     root   1132
m  56004 0x010081c0 --rw-rw-rw-  root     root    760
```

```
m    5005 0x08001cf6 --rw-r----    oracle    dba750215168    <---- Value for instance 1
m    1006 0x64747336 --rw-rw-rw-   oracle    dba     4096
m    1007 0x13e6bd75 --rw-rw-rw-   root      other   34368
m    9008 0x08c015bf --rw-r----    oracle    dba251584512    <---- Value for instance 2
m    3009 0x088015bc --rw-r----    oracle    dba251584512    <---- Value for instance 3
T    ID   KEY        MODE          OWNER     GROUP NSEMS
Semaphores:
s2228227 0x810083c4 --ra-ra-ra-    root      root       2
s2883588 0x810081c0 --ra-ra-ra-    root      root       2
s 327685 00000000   --ra-r----     oracle    dba      300      <---- Value for instance 1
s  65542 00000000   --ra-ra-ra-    oracle    dba       25
s  65543 0x13e6bd75 --ra-ra-ra-    root      other      1
s 589832 00000000   --ra-r----     oracle    dba      200      <---- Value for instance 2
s 196617 00000000   --ra-r----     oracle    dba      200      <---- Value for instance 3
```

The output from the **ipcs -b** command can be confusing if all instances on the machine are the same size and have the same process count assigned.

I suggest setting the process counts differently for each instance you create on the same Unix platform. By comparing the value of the initialization parameter **PROCESSES** *to the value for the number of semaphores assigned, you can easily determine the identity of each Oracle instance in the output of the* **ipcs** *command. The order of entries in the two sections of the* **ipcs** *output correspond on a one-to-one basis.*

In one situation, the use of the **ipcs -b** command solved a particularly perplexing problem. On a version 7.2.3 database, I had an abnormal termination of the **PMON** process caused by an improperly set semaphore value for the Unix kernel. This resulted in an internal pipe break, which left the Oracle instance in a hung state. I couldn't shut it down, I couldn't log in—in short, I was sunk. I killed all the Oracle processes and eliminated the sgadef.ora files by hand, and I still couldn't log in, even as connect internal via SVRMGRL. A run of the **ipcs -b** command showed that even though I had killed all Oracle processes for the instance, because of the broken pipe, the kernel hadn't released the semaphores and memory segments assigned to the problem instance.

Armed now with the identifiers (the ID column) for both the memory and semaphore latches, I ran the **ipcrm** command to release these bound resources. The format for the command is:

```
$ ipcrm -m id#   <---- To release the memory segments held by the latch id
                      specified
$ ipcrm -s id#   <------ To release semaphores held by the latch id specified
```

Note that in the **ipcs -b** command, the value for the identifier column is not the same for memory and semaphores, so the input to the **ipcrm** command will be different for each type of release.

Once the memory segments and semaphores were released, the broken pipe was deleted, and I could restart the instance.

As a DBA, you will often hear the question, "Is the database up?", or, if you have more than one instance running, "Are the databases up?" One way to answer is to do a **ps -ef|grep smon**. This will tell you which databases have active **SMON** processes and should therefore be "up." Listing 9.4 shows the results of the **ps -ef|grep smon** command execution.

Listing 9.4 Example use of the ps -ef|grep SMON command to show active instances.

```
a1244157:oracle ps -ef|grep smon
  oracle 26810    1  0   Oct 09 ?        0:07 ora_smon_ORCNETT3
  oracle 26002    1  0   Oct 07 ?        0:23 ora_smon_ORCNETP1
  oracle 22145    1  0   Oct 09 ?        0:07 ora_smon_ORCNETT2
  oracle 27701 27123  0 21:13:48 pts/5   0:00 grep smon
```

Of course, the output from the **ps -ef|grep smon** command isn't particularly attractive. You could create a short shell script to dress up the output, as shown in Listing 9.5.

Listing 9.5 Shell script to show active instances.

```
    rm -f proc.lis
    rm -f dbs.lis
    touch dbs.lis
    touch proc.lis
    ps -ef|grep smon>>proc.lis
            cat proc.lis | while read LINE2
            do
                command='echo $LINE2 | awk -F: 'BEGIN { FS = " " }
                        { print substr($9,10)}' -'
                if [ "$command" = "" ] ; then
                    command='echo $LINE2 | awk -F: 'BEGIN { FS = " " }
                        { print substr($8,10)}' -'
                if
                test_it='echo $LINE2 | awk -F: 'BEGIN { FS = " " }
                        { print substr($8,1)}' -'
            if [ "$test_it" != "grep" ] ; then
                        command='Database: '$command' is up'
                        echo $command>>dbs.lis
            if
            done
```

```
more dbs.lis
rm -f dbs.lis
```

The Unix operating system provides many ways to monitor processes. Some plat-forms support the **top** command, which shows processes ranked in order of resource usage with the highest users first. Several third-party vendor packages are available for monitoring Unix system resources.

 ## Monitoring The MTS Process

The multithreaded server processes require monitoring. If you use a product, such as the Q diagnostic tool included on the companion CD-ROM, this becomes a fairly trivial task. If you must resort to manual monitoring, however, be prepared to use the data dictionary and other internal sources of information.

The multithreaded server consists of sets of dispatchers and servers, which are used by multiple protocols, such as TCP/IP, NetBIOS, named pipes, IPX, etc. Knowing the details about the internal operations—such as average queue wait times, how busy dispatchers are at any given time, or how long the average wait queue has be-come—is important.

Monitoring Average Wait Time For MTS

The data dictionary table of interest for monitoring the average wait time for MTS queues is the **V$QUEUE** dynamic performance view. The **totalq** and **wait** columns provide average wait time for the queue. Listing 9.6 shows an example report for this value.

Listing 9.6   Example SQL report to check average MTS queue wait time.
```
rem Name: mts_awt.sql
rem Function: Generate Average wait time report for dispatchers
rem History: MRA Revealnet script
COLUMN awt FORMAT A30 HEADING 'Average Wait Time per Request'
SET FEEDBACK OFF VERIFY OFF LINES 78 PAGES 58
START title80 'Dispatcher Average Wait Time'
SPOOL rep_out\&&db\mts_awt.lis
SELECT
   DECODE (TOTALQ,0, 'No Requests',
   (wait/totalq)*100||'Seconds Request Wait') awt
FROM
   v$queue
```

```
WHERE
  type = 'COMMON';
SPOOL OFF
SET FEEDBACK ON VERIFY ON LINES 80 PAGES 22
PAUSE Press enter to continue
```

Example Execution:

```
Date: 10/11/97                                          Page:   1
Time: 09:42 PM          Dispatcher Average Wait Time    SYSTEM
                            ORCNETP1 database

Average Wait Time per Request
-----------------------------
1.20554735 Seconds Request Wait

Press enter to continue
```

An excessive wait time may indicate a need for more dispatchers. If, on the other hand, you have relatively few waits, you may have too many dispatchers set up.

Another concern is how busy the dispatchers are. A query to the **V$DISPATCHER** dynamic performance table (DPT) will tell you. Listing 9.7 shows an example SQL report generating a percent busy report for MTS dispatchers.

Listing 9.7   Example MTS dispatcher percent busy report.

```
rem Name: mts_disp.sql
rem Function: Generate percent busy report for dispatchers
rem History: MRA Revealnet script
COLUMN protocol FORMAT A9 HEADING 'Dispatcher|Protocol'
COLUMN busy FORMAT 999.99 HEADING 'Percent|Busy'
SET FEEDBACK OFF VERIFY OFF LINES 78 PAGES 58
START title80 'Dispatcher Status'
SPOOL rep_out\&&db\mts_disp.lis
SELECT network protocol,
    (SUM(busy)/(SUM(busy)+SUM(idle)))*100 busy
FROM v$dispatcher
GROUP BY network;
SPOOL OFF
SET FEEDBACK ON VERIFY ON
TTITLE OFF
```

Example Report Output:

```
Date: 10/11/97                                          Page:   1
Time: 09:48 PM             Dispatcher Status            SYSTEM
                            ORCNETP1 database
```

```
Dispatcher  Percent
Protocol    Busy
--------    ------
ipc          .00
tcp         1.00
```

Again, if the dispatchers are extremely busy, the Oracle system will automatically start up more dispatchers—up to the value of **MTS_MAX_DISPATCHERS**. If you are nearing your maximum number of dispatchers and your percent busy is still high, increase the value of the **MTS_MAX_DISPATCHERS** parameter.

Listing 9.8 shows the average wait time for each type of dispatcher. This type of report is generated from the **v$queue** and **v$dispatcher** dynamic performance tables.

Listing 9.8   Example SQL report for determining MTS dispatcher wait by protocol.

```
rem Name: mts_wait.sql
rem Function: Generate wait time report for dispatchers
rem History: MRA Revealnet script
COLUMN network FORMAT A9 HEADING 'Protocol'
COLUMN aw FORMAT A30 HEADING 'Average Wait Time %'
SET FEEDBACK OFF VERIFY OFF LINES 78 PAGES 58
START title80 'Dispatcher Wait Times'
SPOOL rep_out\&&db\mts_wait.lis
SELECT
    NETWORK,
    DECODE (SUM(totalq),0,'No responses',
    SUM(wait)/SUM(totalq)*100||'Seconds Wait Per response') aw
FROM v$queue q, v$dispatcher d
WHERE q.type = 'DISPATCHER' AND
    q.paddr = d.paddr
GROUP BY network;
SPOOL OFF
SET FEEDBACK ON VERIFY ON
TTITLE OFF


Example Report Output:

Date: 10/11/97                                          Page:   1
Time: 09:49 PM            Dispatcher Wait Times     SYSTEM
                          ORCNETP1 database

Protocol  Average Wait Time %
--------  ------------------------------
ipc       No responses
tcp       3.2958 Seconds Wait Per response
```

As with the other monitoring scripts discussed, if the average wait time gets too high (i.e., your users start complaining), increase the number of dispatchers for that particular protocol.

The MTS server is a complex process. By monitoring the different aspects of the dispatchers and queues, you can get a better idea of when you need to add more dispatchers, reduce the number of dispatchers, or look to other ways to tune your system.

Monitoring The SGA And Shared Pool

Other than looking at the "outside" of the SGA from the operating system with the methods described in previous sections, the only way to look at the internals of the SGA is through the various **V$** and **DBA** views that Oracle provides. The Q tool from Savant on the enclosed CD-ROM is an excellent third-party tool to look at the SGA in almost realtime, though you may want to use hard-copy reports for documentation purposes. Let's examine a few reports.

Monitoring The Overall SGA For Set Sizes

The **V$SGA** DPT provides a look at all of the fixed SGA component sizes. A simple query against this view will tell you how your overall SGA is configured. Listing 9.9 shows this type of query.

Listing 9.9   Example query of the V$SGA   DPT.
```
SQL> select * from v$sga
NAME                      VALUE
-------------------- --------
Fixed Size                46136
Variable Size          13048308
Database Buffers       32768000
Redo Buffers            1048576
```

In most cases, you will want a deeper level of information than a simple **V$SGA** query provides. Listing 9.10 shows an example report that uses the **V$SGASTAT** DPT to generate a report on all used areas in the SGA and their sizes. You can use this type of report in conjunction with other reports and data to tune the various SGA components.

Listing 9.10   Example SGA component report.

```
rem   Name:      sgastat.sql
rem
rem   FUNCTION: Report on the various SGA components
rem             and their sizes
rem
rem
COLUMN sum_bytes NEW_VALUE divide_by NOPRINT
COLUMN percent FORMAT 999.99999
SET PAGES 60 LINES 80 FEEDBACK OFF VERIFY OFF
BREAK ON REPORT
COMPUTE SUM OF bytes ON REPORT
COMPUTE SUM OF percent ON REPORT
SELECT SUM(value) sum_bytes FROM sys.v_$sga;
START title80 'SGA Component Sizes Report'
SPOOL rep_out\&db\sga_size
SELECT a.name,a.bytes,a.bytes/&divide_by*100  Percent
FROM sys.v_$sgastat a
ORDER BY bytes DESC
/
SPOOL OFF
PAUSE Press Enter to continue
```

Example output from report:

```
Date: 10/12/97
Time: 11:44 AM           SGA Component Sizes Report
                            ORTEST1 database


NAME                         BYTES    PERCENT
-------------------------- --------- ----------
db_block_buffers          32768000  69.85139
free memory                7113664  15.16416
db_block_buffers           1664000   3.54714
log_buffer                 1048576   2.23524
sql area                    850372   1.81273
library cache               646104   1.37730
dictionary cache            386828    .82460
KQLS heap                   366756    .78181
db_block_hash_buckets       312468    .66609
PL/SQL DIANA                273332    .58266
sessions                    245180    .52265
event statistics per sess   187680    .40008
miscellaneous               164412    .35048
transactions                108864    .23206
enqueue_locks                88752    .18919
PL/SQL MPCODE                87892    .18736
processes                    80400    .17139
ktlbk state objects          53928    .11496
kxfp buffer su               51608    .11001
fixed_sga                    46136    .09835
SYSTEM PARAMETERS            43980    .09375
```

```
db_handles                      42000      .08953
branches                        30480      .06497
character set memory            28220      .06016
state objects                   28100      .05990
db_files                        24636      .05252
DML locks                       23200      .04946
transaction_branches            22816      .04864
enqueue_resources               19080      .04067
table columns                   18620      .03969
LRMPD SGA Table                 17528      .03736
network connections             16700      .03560
node map                        16384      .03493
log_buffer                      16384      .03493
KGFF heap                        9512      .02028
kxfp subheap                     3704      .00790
PLS non-lib hp                   2096      .00447
KGK heap                         1972      .00420
fixed allocation callback         576      .00123
table definiti                     80      .00017
                              --------   ----------
sum                          46911020   100.00000
Press Enter to continue
```

Notice that the total here is not the same as the total for the SGA area's query in Listing 9.8. This shows that some of the SGA is not being used.

Monitoring The Shared Pool

Next to the database buffer's section, the shared pool will be the second largest area of the SGA (for most application environments). The script shown in Listing 9.11 details the various parts of the shared pool and their sizes. The report also shows the percentage of the shared pool that is used.

Listing 9.11   Example report to show shared pool components.

```
SET ECHO OFF
COLUMN dbname NEW_VALUE db NOPRINT
SELECT name dbname FROM v$database;
SPOOL rep_out/&&db/pool_est
/*
**********************************************************
*                                                        *
* TITLE       : Shared Pool Estimation                   *
* CATEGORY    : Information, Utility                      *
* SUBJECT AREA : Shared Pool                              *
* DESCRIPTION  : Estimates shared pool utilization        *
*   based on current database usage. This should be      *
*   run during peak operation, after all stored          *
*   objects, i.e., packages and views, have been loaded. *
*                                                        *
*                                                        *
**********************************************************/
```

```
Rem If running MTS uncomment the mts calculation and output
Rem commands.
SET SERVEROUTPUT ON;
DECLARE
        object_mem NUMBER;
        shared_sql NUMBER;
        cursor_mem NUMBER;
        mts_mem NUMBER;
        used_pool_size NUMBER;
        free_mem NUMBER;
        pool_size VARCHAR2(512); -- same as V$PARAMETER.VALUE
BEGIN
-- Stored objects (packages, views)
SELECT SUM(sharable_mem) INTO object_mem FROM v$db_object_cache;
-- Shared SQL -- need to have additional memory if dynamic SQL used
SELECT SUM(sharable_mem) INTO shared_sql FROM v$sqlarea;
-- User Cursor Usage -- run this during peak usage.
--   assumes 250 bytes per open cursor, for each concurrent user.
SELECT SUM(250*users_opening) INTO cursor_mem FROM v$sqlarea;
-- For a test system -- get usage for one user, multiply by # users
-- SELECT (250 * value) bytes_per_user
-- FROM v$sesstat s, v$statname n
-- WHERE s.statistic# = n.statistic#
-- AND n.name = 'opened cursors current'
-- AND s.sid = 25;   -- where 25 is the sid of the process
-- MTS memory needed to hold session information for shared server users
-- This query computes a total for all currently logged on users (run
--   multiply by # users.
--SELECT SUM(value) INTO mts_mem FROM v$sesstat s, v$statname n
--        WHERE s.statistic#=n.statistic#
--        AND n.name='session uga memory max';
-- Free (unused) memory in the SGA: gives an indication of how much memory
-- is being wasted out of the total allocated.
SELECT bytes INTO free_mem FROM v$sgastat
        WHERE name = 'free memory';
-- For non-MTS add up object, shared sql, cursors and 20% overhead.
used_pool_size := ROUND(1.2*(object_mem+shared_sql+cursor_mem));
-- For MTS mts contribution needs to be included (comment out previous line)
-- used_pool_size := round(1.2*(object_mem+shared_sql+cursor_mem+mts_mem));
SELECT value INTO pool_size FROM v$parameter WHERE name='shared_pool_size';
-- Display results
dbms_output.put_line ('Obj mem:  '||TO_CHAR (object_mem) || ' bytes');
dbms_output.put_line ('Shared sql:  '||TO_CHAR (shared_sql) || ' bytes');
dbms_output.put_line ('Cursors:  '||TO_CHAR (cursor_mem) || ' bytes');
-- dbms_output.put_line ('MTS session: '||TO_CHAR (mts_mem) || ' bytes');
dbms_output.put_line ('Free memory: '||TO_CHAR (free_mem) || ' bytes ' || '(' ||
TO_CHAR(ROUND(free_mem/1024/1024,2)) || 'MB)');
dbms_output.put_line (
```

```
 'Shared pool utilization (total):  '|| TO_CHAR(used_pool_size) || ' bytes '||
  '(' || TO_CHAR(ROUND(used_pool_size/1024/1024,2)) || 'MB)');
dbms_output.put_line ('Shared pool allocation (actual):  '|| pool_size ||' bytes '
|| '(' ||
TO_CHAR(ROUND(pool_size/1024/1024,2)) || 'MB)');
dbms_output.put_line ('Percentage Utilized:  '||TO_CHAR (ROUND(used_pool_size/
pool_size*100)));
end;
/
SPOOL OFF
CLEAR COLUMNS
SET ECHO ON
```

Example of the report output:

```
DOC>*************************************************************
DOC>*                                                          *
DOC>* TITLE       : Shared Pool Estimation                     *
DOC>* CATEGORY    : Information, Utility                        *
DOC>* SUBJECT AREA : Shared Pool                               *
DOC>* DESCRIPTION  : Estimates shared pool utilization         *
DOC>*  based on current database usage. This should be         *
DOC>*  run during peak operation, after all stored             *
DOC>*  objects, i.e., packages and views have been loaded.*
DOC>*                                                          *
DOC>*                                                          *
DOC>*************************************************************/
Obj mem:  681898 bytes
Shared sql:  1576354 bytes
Cursors:  1000 bytes
Free memory: 6497436 bytes (6.2MB)
Shared pool utilization (total):  2711102 bytes (2.59MB)
Shared pool allocation (actual):  10000000 bytes (9.54MB)
Percentage Utilized:  27
```

Based on the results shown in Listing 9.11, if this were for an operating system and the report were run under full-load conditions, it would tell us that we need to reduce the shared pool, because only 27 percent of the pool was being used.

Another aspect of the shared pool is how the memory is really being used. The report shown in Listing 9.12 shows how to use a view of the **v$sqlarea** and **dba_users** data dictionary objects to provide a summary of the memory usage in the shared pool by user.

Listing 9.12 Example report to summarize SQL area use per user.

```
rem
rem FUNCTION: Generate a summary of SQL Area Memory Usage
rem FUNCTION: uses the sql_summary view.
rem           showing user SQL memory usage
```

```
rem   The sql_summary view is constructed using this query:
rem
rem   create view sql_summary as select username, sharable_mem,
rem   persistent_mem, runtime_mem
rem   from sys.v$sqlarea a, dba_users b
rem where a.parsing_user_id = b.user_id
rem
rem sqlsum.sql
rem
COLUMN areas                                              HEADING Used|Areas
COLUMN sharable          FORMAT 999,999,999              HEADING Shared|Bytes
COLUMN persistent        FORMAT 999,999,999              HEADING Persistent|Bytes
COLUMN runtime           FORMAT 999,999,999              HEADING Runtime|Bytes
COLUMN username                                           HEADING "User" FORMAT a15
START title80 "Users SQL Area Memory Use"
SPOOL rep_out\&db\sqlsum
SET PAGES 59 LINES 80
BREAK ON report
COMPUTE SUM OF sharable ON REPORT
COMPUTE SUM OF persistent ON REPORT
COMPUTE SUM OF runtime ON REPORT
SELECT
   username, SUM(sharable_mem) Sharable, SUM( persistent_mem) Persistent,
   SUM( runtime_mem) Runtime , COUNT(*) Areas
FROM
    sql_summary
GROUP BY
   username
ORDER BY 2;
SPOOL OFF
PAUSE Press enter to continue
CLEAR COLUMNS
CLEAR BREAKS
SET PAGES 22 LINES 80
TTITLE OFF
```

Example results from the report:

```
Date: 10/12/97                                            Page:   1
Time: 11:57 AM           Users SQL Area Memory Use        SYSTEM
                          ORTEST1 database

                 Shared      Persistent     Runtime     Used
User             Bytes       Bytes          Bytes       Areas
-------------- ------------ ------------ ------------ --------
SYSTEM           751,574       17,284      103,184       34
SYS            1,233,434       77,944      350,744      171
               ------------ ------------ ------------
sum            1,985,008       95,228      453,928
```

The report in Listing 9.12 solved an interesting problem on a recent project. During the course of the day, performance would be fine following a restart, but would get steadily worse as the day progressed until it became virtually unsatisfactory by mid-day. A look at the Q monitor showed that the shared pool was filling and staying full, and we weren't getting any ORA-4031 errors. Sounds great, right? Well, the report from Listing 9.12 showed we had several users with more than 900 SQL areas assigned to them, and, overall, the system had to examine well over 10,000 assigned SQL areas for each new piece of SQL that was generated.

To see why each user had so many SQL area assignments, we ran the companion report in Listing 9.13. We found that each query being issued by the third-party graphical user interface was not using bind variables, which resulted in multiple nearly identical SQL areas per user that varied only by the query field value. We instituted an automatic procedure that flushed the shared pool based on a ratio value between memory used for SQL areas and available memory. This solved the performance problem. We loaded the procedure into the job queue and fired it off every hour.

Listing 9.13 Report to show a user's SQL areas in the shared pool.

```
rem
rem FUNCTION: Generate a report of SQL Area Memory Usage
rem              showing SQL Text and memory categories
rem
rem sqlmem.sql
rem
COLUMN sql_text       FORMAT a40    HEADING Text word_wrapped
COLUMN sharable_mem                 HEADING Shared|Bytes
COLUMN persistent_mem               HEADING Persistent|Bytes
COLUMN parse_calls                  HEADING Parses
COLUMN users          FORMAT a15    HEADING "User"
COLUMN executions                   HEADING "Executions"
START title132 "Users SQL Area Memory Use"
SPOOL rep_out\&db\sqlmem
SET LONG 1000 PAGES 59 LINES 132
BREAK ON users
COMPUTE SUM OF sharable_mem ON users
COMPUTE SUM OF persistent_mem ON users
COMPUTE SUM OF runtime_mem ON users
SELECT
  username users, sql_text, Executions, parse_calls, sharable_mem, persistent_mem
FROM
  sys.v_$sqlarea a, dba_users b
```

```
WHERE
   a.parsing_user_id = b.user_id
   AND b.username LIKE UPPER('%&user_name%')
ORDER BY 1;
SPOOL OFF
PAUSE Press enter to continue
CLEAR COLUMNS
CLEAR COMPUTES
CLEAR BREAKS
SET PAGES 22 LINES 80
```

Example Report Output:

```
Enter value for user_name: SYSTEM

Date: 10/12/97
Time: 11:56 AM                              Users SQL Area Memory Use
                                               ORTEST1 database

                                                                     Shared Persistent
User            Text                     Executions   Parses    Bytes     Bytes
--------------  ------------------------ ----------   --------  --------  ----------
SYSTEM          DECLARE job BINARY_INTEGER := :job;       18       18     10495        468
                next_date DATE := :mydate;  broken
                BOOLEAN := FALSE; BEGIN hitratio;
                :mydate := next_date; IF broken THEN :b
                := 1; ELSE :b := 0; END IF; END;

                INSERT INTO HIT_RATIOS VALUES (           18       18      8927        560
                :b1,:b2,:b3,:b4,:b5,:b6,0,0,:b7   )

                SELECT BYTES   FROM V$SGASTAT  WHERE       2        2     22914        508
                NAME = 'free memory'

                SELECT COUNT(*)   FROM V$SESSION  WHERE   18       18     52997        484
                USERNAME IS NOT NULL

                SELECT DECODE('A','A','1','2') FROM DUAL   2        2      5597        468
                SELECT NAME,VALUE   FROM V$SYSSTAT        18       18     13515        532
                WHERE NAME = 'consistent gets'

                SELECT NAME,VALUE   FROM V$SYSSTAT        18       18     14173        532
                WHERE NAME = 'db block gets'

                SELECT NAME,VALUE   FROM V$SYSSTAT        18       18     13906        532
                WHERE NAME = 'physical reads'

                SELECT SUM(250 * USERS_OPENING )   FROM    2        2     50554        496
                V$SQLAREA
```

You should also monitor the other sections of the shared pool, such as the library cache, data dictionary cache, and object cache. Listing 9.14 shows a report to monitor the library cache.

Listing 9.14   Example report for the library cache area of the shared pool.

```
rem
rem Title: libcache.sql
rem
rem FUNCTION: Generate a library cache report
rem
COLUMN namespace                          HEADING "Library Object"
COLUMN gets                               HEADING "Gets"
COLUMN gethitratio       FORMAT 999.99    HEADING "Get Hit%"
COLUMN pins                               HEADING "Pins"
COLUMN pinhitratio       FORMAT 999.99    HEADING "Pin Hit%"
COLUMN reloads                            HEADING "Reloads"
COLUMN invalidations                      HEADING "Invalidations"
COLUMN db                FORMAT a10
SET PAGES 58 LINES 80
START title80 "Library Caches Report"
DEFINE output = rep_out\&db\lib_cache
SPOOL &output
SELECT
   namespace,
   gets,
   gethitratio*100 gethitratio,
   pins,
   pinhitratio*100 pinhitratio,
   reloads,
   invalidations
FROM
   v$librarycache
/
SPOOL OFF
PAUSE Press enter to continue
SET PAGES 22 LINES 80
TTITLE OFF
UNDEF output
```

Example Report Output:

```
Date: 10/12/97                                      Page:   1
Time: 12:05 PM            Library Caches Report       SYSTEM
                          ORTEST1 database


Library Object      Gets Get Hit%    Pins Pin Hit%  Reloads Invalidations
--------------  -------- --------  -------- --------  -------- -------------
SQL AREA           14383   98.44     33594    98.74       10             2
TABLE/PROCEDURE     3134   93.33      3602    89.28        0             0
BODY                  45   86.67        45    86.67        0             0
TRIGGER                0  100.00         0   100.00        0             0
INDEX                 27     .00        27      .00        0             0
CLUSTER              190   97.37       258    98.06        0             0
```

```
OBJECT            0   100.00      0   100.00      0           0
PIPE              0   100.00      0   100.00      0           0
```

Press enter to continue

For library caches that are frequently used—that is, they exhibit a high number for gets (the number of requests for this item) and pins (a pin is when an item is found already in the memory catch)—the **Hit%** columns should be in the 80- to 90-percent range. If the **Hit%** for the busy areas show lower than 80 to 90 percent, then increase the size of the shared pool.

Another area that should be periodically monitored is the data dictionary cache. Listing 9.15 shows an example report.

Listing 9.15   Example data dictionary cache report.

```
REM
REM NAME      : DD_CACHE.SQL
REM FUNCTION : GENERATE REPORT ON DATA DICTIONARY CACHE CONDITION
REM USE      : FROM SQLPLUS
REM Limitations  : None
REM Revisions:
REM Date       Modified By  Reason For change
REM 21-AUG-1991   MIKE AULT INITIAL CREATE
REM 27-NOV-1991   MIKE AULT ADD % CALCULATION TO REPORT
REM 28-OCT-1992   MIKE AULT ADD CALL TO TITLE PROCEDURE
REM 21-Jun-1997   MIKE AULT Updated to ORACLE8
REM SET FLUSH OFF
REM SET TERM OFF
SET PAGESIZE 59
SET LINESIZE 79
COLUMN parameter FORMAT A20
COLUMN type FORMAT A10
COLUMN percent FORMAT 999.99 HEADING "%";
START title80 "DATA DICTIONARY CACHE STATISTICS"
SPOOL rep_out/&db/ddcache.lis
SELECT
   parameter,
   type,
   gets,
   getmisses,
   ( getmisses / gets * 100) percent,
   count,
   usage
FROM
   v$rowcache
```

```
WHERE
   gets > 100 AND
   getmisses > 0
ORDER BY parameter;
SPOOL OFF
```

Example Report Output:

```
Date: 10/12/97                                              Page:   1
Time: 12:06 PM          DATA DICTIONARY CACHE STATISTICS    SYSTEM
                              ORTEST1 database

PARAMETER               TYPE        Gets GETMISSES      %    COUNT   USAGE
--------------------    ----------  ----     ----     ----   ----    ----
dc_free_extents         PARENT     10943      307     2.81     58      48
dc_histogram_defs       PARENT       436      436   100.00    438     436
dc_object_ids           PARENT       314       40    12.74     91      89
dc_objects              PARENT      2806      144     5.13    194     193
dc_rollback_segments    PARENT      3197        7      .22     24       8
dc_segments             PARENT       300      131    43.67    138     124
dc_tablespaces          PARENT       281        2      .71      6       2
dc_used_extents         PARENT       293      148    50.51     52      19
dc_user_grants          SUBORDINATE  257        7     2.72      8       7
dc_usernames            PARENT       147        4     2.72     21       4
dc_users                PARENT       424       11     2.59     25      11
```

Again, if the overall percentage seems low for a majority of the rows in the report in Listing 9.15, then you should increase the size of the shared pool.

The object cache of the shared pool (not to be confused with the client size object cache) can also be monitored via reports against the **V$DB_OBJECT_CACHE** DPT. Listing 9.16 shows an example of this type of report.

Listing 9.16 Example report for the object cache of the shared pool.

```
rem
rem FUNCTION: Report Stored Object Statistics
rem
COLUMN owner         FORMAT a11      HEADING Schema
COLUMN name          FORMAT a30      HEADING Object|Name
COLUMN namespace                     HEADING Name|Space
COLUMN type                          HEADING Object|Type
COLUMN kept          FORMAT a4       HEADING Kept
COLUMN sharable_mem  FORMAT 999,999  HEADING Shared|Memory
COLUMN executions    FORMAT 999,999  HEADING Executes
SET LINES 132 PAGES 47 FEEDBACK OFF
@title132 'Oracle Objects Report'
BREAK ON owner ON namespace ON type
SPOOL rep_out/&db/o_stat
SELECT
   owner,
   namespace,
```

```
   type,
   name,
   sharable_mem,
   loads,
   executions,
   locks,
   pins,
   kept
FROM
  v$db_object_cache
WHERE
  type NOT IN ('NOT LOADED','NON-EXISTENT')
  AND executions>0
ORDER BY owner,namespace,type,executions DESC;
SPOOL OFF
SET LINES 80 PAGES 22 FEEDBACK ON
CLEAR COLUMNS
CLEAR BREAKS
TTITLE OFF
```

Example Report Output:

Schema	Name Space	Object Type	Object Name	Shared Memory	LOADS	Executes	LOCKS	Pins	Kept
SYS	BODY	PACKAGE BODY	DBMS_APPLICATION_INFO	2,753	1	37	1	0	NO
			DBMS_OUTPUT	6,835	1	27	1	0	NO
			STANDARD	23,736	1	8	1	0	NO
			DBMS_DDL	9,668	1	1	0	0	NO
			DBMS_UTILITY	16,740	1	1	0	0	NO
	TABLE/PROCEDURE	PACKAGE	DBMS_APPLICATION_INFO	12,545	1	38	1	0	NO
			DBMS_OUTPUT	13,607	1	30	1	0	NO
			DBMS_STANDARD	14,041	1	19	0	0	NO
			STANDARD	165,108	1	8	1	0	NO
			DBMS_DDL	1,780	1	1	0	0	NO
			DBMS_UTILITY	21,636	1	1	0	0	NO
		SEQUENCE	IDGEN1$	855	1	2,227	3	0	NO
			AUDSES$	855	1	4	0	0	NO
		TABLE	USER$	1,741	1	10	0	0	YES
			OBJ$	2,484	1	9	0	0	YES
			FET$	2,484	1	7	0	0	YES
			IND$	2,484	1	7	0	0	YES
			JOB$	1,412	1	7	0	0	NO
			DUAL	1,104	1	6	0	0	NO
			SEG$	1,660	1	6	0	0	YES
			DEPENDENCY$	1,419	1	6	0	0	NO

If an object shows an excessive number of loads, consider pinning it (if possible) into the shared pool using the **DBMS_SHARED_POOL** package that Oracle provides.

The report in Listing 9.16 shows "good" objects, but what about objects that possibly have problems? The report in Listing 9.17 shows how you can track down these "bad" objects.

Listing 9.17 Example report on "bad" objects.

```
rem
rem FUNCTION: Report on "bad" objects
rem
rem
COLUMN owner          FORMAT a10      HEADING Schema
COLUMN name           FORMAT a30      HEADING Object|Name
COLUMN namespace                      HEADING Name|Space
COLUMN type                           HEADING Object|Type
COLUMN kept           FORMAT a4       HEADING Kept
COLUMN sharable_mem   FORMAT 999,999  HEADING Shared|Memory
COLUMN executions     FORMAT 9,999    HEADING Executes
SET LINES 132 PAGES 47 FEEDBACK OFF
@title132 'Oracle Objects Report'
BREAK ON owner ON namespace ON type
SPOOL rep_out/&db/o_stat2
SELECT
   owner,
   namespace,
   type,
   name,
   sharable_mem,
   loads,
   executions,
   locks,
   pins,
   kept
FROM
   v$db_object_cache
WHERE
   type IN ('NOT LOADED','NON-EXISTENT')
ORDER BY owner,namespace,type,executions desc;
SPOOL OFF
CLEAR COLUMNS
CLEAR BREAKS
SET LINES 80 PAGES 22 FEEDBACK ON
```

```
Date: 10/12/97                                                   Page:   1
Time: 12:12 PM              Oracle Objects Report               SYSTEM
                             ORTEST1 database
```

Schema	Name Space	Object Type	Object Name	Shared Memory	LOADS	Executes	LOCKS	Pins	Kept
SYS	BODY	NOT LOADED	DBMS_STANDARD	0	1	20	0	0	NO
	TABLE/PROCEDURE	NOT LOADED	DBA_OBJECTS	0	0	0	0	0	NO
			ORDER_OBJECT_BY_DEPENDENCY	0	0	0	0	0	NO
			DBA_TAB_PARTITIONS	0	0	0	0	0	NO
			DBMS_JOB	0	0	0	0	0	NO
			DBMS_SESSION	0	0	0	0	0	NO
			X$STANDARD	0	0	0	0	0	NO
			DBMS_SQL	0	0	0	0	0	NO
			DBA_IND_PARTITIONS	0	0	0	0	0	NO
SYSTEM	TABLE/PROCEDURE	NON-EXISTENT	DBMS_OUTPUT	626	1	0	0	0	NO
			DUAL	523	1	0	0	0	NO
			V$ROWCACHE	529	1	0	0	0	NO
			DBA_USERS	528	1	0	0	0	NO
			V$LIBRARYCACHE	533	1	0	0	0	NO

You should examine the objects in the report in Listing 9.17 for possible problems or pinning.

You can monitor the latch area of the shared pool with the **V$LATCHNAME** and **V$LATCH** DPTs. Listing 9.18 shows an example report for monitoring latches.

Listing 9.18   Example report for latch monitoring.

```
rem
rem NAME        : LATCH_CO.SQL
rem FUNCTION    : Generate latch contention report
rem USE         : From SQLPlus or other front end
rem Limitations : None
rem
COLUMN name    FORMAT A30
COLUMN ratio   FORMAT 999.999
SET PAGES 58 NEWPAGE 0
START title80 "LATCH CONTENTION REPORT"
SPOOL rep_out\&db\latchs
SELECT a.name,100.*b.sleeps/b.gets ratio FROM
v$latchname a, v$latch b WHERE
a.latch# = b.latch# AND b.sleeps > 0;
SPOOL OFF
PAUSE PRESS RETURN TO CONTINUE
CLEAR COLUMNS
TTITLE OFF
SET PAGES 22


Example Report Output:

Date: 10/12/97                                        Page:   1
Time: 12:17 PM            LATCH CONTENTION REPORT     SYSTEM
                             ORTEST1 database
```

```
NAME                             RATIO
-------------------------------- --------
messages                            .001
library cache                       .001

2 rows selected.
```

The ratio in the report in Listing 9.18 should be lower than 0.1; otherwise, you need to adjust the initialization parameters that control the latches showing the bad ratio.

You can generate a report that shows buffer contention using the **V$WAITSTAT** DPT. The report is shown in Listing 9.19.

Listing 9.19 Example contention report.

```
REM
REM CONTEND.SQL
REM FUNCTION: SHOWS WHERE POSSIBLE CONTENTION FOR RESOURCES
REM             IN BUFFER BUSY WAITS USE TO PINPOINT ADDITIONAL
REM             TUNING AREAS.
REM
REM CALLED FROM STATUS
REM
SET VERIFY OFF FEEDBACK OFF
SET PAGES 58
SET LINES 79
START title80 "AREA OF CONTENTION REPORT"
DEFINE output = 'rep_out\&db\contend'
SPOOL &output
SELECT
    class, SUM(count) total_waits, SUM(time) total_time
FROM
    v$waitstat
GROUP BY class;
SPOOL OFF
PAUSE PRESS RETURN TO CONTINUE
SET VERIFY ON FEEDBACK ON PAGES 22 LINES 80
TTITLE OFF


Example Report Output:

Date: 10/12/97                                        Page:   1
Time: 12:18 PM          AREA OF CONTENTION REPORT     SYSTEM
                           ORTEST1 database

CLASS                TOTAL_WAITS TOTAL_TIME
------------------   ---------- ----------
bitmap block               0          0
bitmap index block         0          0
data block                 4          4
```

```
extent map              0        0
free list               0        0
save undo block         0        0
save undo header        0        0
segment header          0        0
sort block              0        0
system undo block       0        0
system undo header      0        0
undo block              0        0
undo header             0        0
unused                  0        0

PRESS RETURN TO CONTINUE
```

If a buffer area shows a number of waits, you need to increase the portion of the SGA that holds it. The values shown for **undo** deal with rollback segments, and, thus, they aren't used for tuning the SGA. You can adjust the other areas using initialization and table setup parameters.

Using The Data Dictionary To Monitor Database Objects

You can also use the data dictionary to monitor database objects, such as users, tables, and indexes. These are considered "physical" database objects, because they are persistent in nature—unlike the transient entries in the **V$** table entries. Generally speaking, the values for persistent objects stay the same unless explicitly altered by a user or automated Oracle system process. First, we will examine a report on users. Listing 9.20 shows just such a report.

Listing 9.20   Example user report.

```
REM
REM NAME         : USER8.SQL
REM FUNCTION     : GENERATE USER_REPORT
REM USE          : CALLED BY USER_REPORT.COM
REM Limitations : None
REM
set pagesize 58   linesize 131
rem
COLUMN username                  FORMAT a10 HEADING User
COLUMN account_status            FORMAT a10 HEADING Status
COLUMN default_tablespace        FORMAT a15 HEADING Default
COLUMN temporary_tablespace      FORMAT a15 HEADING "Temporary"
COLUMN granted_role              FORMAT a21 HEADING Roles
COLUMN default_role              FORMAT a10 HEADING Default?
COLUMN admin_option              FORMAT a7  HEADING Admin?
COLUMN profile                   FORMAT a15 HEADING 'Users Profile'
rem
```

```
START title132 'ORACLE USER REPORT'
DEFINE output = rep_out\&db\usr_rep
BREAK ON username SKIP 1 ON account_status ON default_tablespace ON
temporary_tablespace ON profile
SPOOL &output
rem
SELECT
  username, account_status,
  default_tablespace, temporary_tablespace, profile,
  granted_role, admin_option, default_role
FROM
  sys.dba_users a, sys.dba_role_privs b
WHERE
    a.username = b.grantee
ORDER BY
  username,account_status, default_tablespace,
  temporary_tablespace,profile, granted_role;
rem
SPOOL OFF
SET TERMOUT ON FLUSH ON FEEDBACK ON VERIFY ON
CLEAR COLUMNS
CLEAR BREAKS
PAUSE Press enter to continue
```

Example Report Output:

```
Date: 10/12/97                                                      Page:   1
Time: 5:17 PM                     ORACLE USER REPORT                SYSTEM
                                  ORTEST1 database


User       Status    Default      Temporary       Users Profile   Roles                    Admin?  Default?
---------- --------- ------------ --------------- --------------- ----------------------- ------ ----------
BFILE_DBO  OPEN      RAW_DATA     TEMPORARY_DATA  DEFAULT         CONNECT                  NO     YES
                                                                  RESOURCE                 NO     YES

DBSNMP     OPEN      SYSTEM       SYSTEM          DEFAULT         CONNECT                  NO     YES
                                                                  RESOURCE                 NO     YES
                                                                  SNMPAGENT                NO     YES

MIGRATE    OPEN      SYSTEM       SYSTEM          DEFAULT         DBA                      NO     YES
                                                                  RESOURCE                 NO     YES

ORDSYS     OPEN      SYSTEM       SYSTEM          DEFAULT         CONNECT                  NO     YES
                                                                  RESOURCE                 NO     YES

SYS        OPEN      SYSTEM       TEMPORARY_DATA  DEFAULT         AQ_ADMINISTRATOR_ROLE    YES    YES
                                                                  AQ_USER_ROLE             YES    YES
                                                                  CONNECT                  YES    YES
                                                                  DBA                      YES    YES
                                                                  DELETE_CATALOG_ROLE      YES    YES
                                                                  EXECUTE_CATALOG_ROLE     YES    YES
```

					EXP_FULL_DATABASE		YES	YES
					IMP_FULL_DATABASE		YES	YES
					RECOVERY_CATALOG_OWNER		YES	YES
					RESOURCE		YES	YES
					SELECT_CATALOG_ROLE		YES	YES
					SNMPAGENT		YES	YES
SYSTEM	OPEN	USER_DATA	TEMPORARY_DATA	DEFAULT	DBA		YES	YES
TELE_DBA	OPEN	SCOPUS_DATA	TEMPORARY_DATA	DEFAULT	CONNECT		NO	YES
					RESOURCE		NO	YES

```
24 rows selected.
```

The report shown in Listing 9.20 documents how all users on your system are configured. This report can provide a handy lookup resource when you can't get to the terminal to run Oracle Enterprise Manager.

The next set of objects we will consider is tables. Of course, Oracle8 has partitioned tables and index-only tables, as well as normal tables. Let's look at a couple of reports used to document these different table configuration types. Listing 9.21 shows a generic report for all tables that are referenced in the **DBA_TABLES** view.

Listing 9.21 Example generic table report.

```
REM
REM NAME        : TABLE.SQL
REM FUNCTION    : GENERATE TABLE REPORT
REM Limitations : None
clear COLUMNs
COLUMN owner            FORMAT a15  HEADING 'Table | Owner'
COLUMN table_name                   HEADING Table
COLUMN tablespace_name  FORMAT A15  HEADING Tablespace
COLUMN pct_increase                 HEADING 'Pct|Increase'
COLUMN init                         HEADING 'Initial|Extent'
COLUMN next                         HEADING 'Next|Extent'
COLUMN partitioned      FORMAT a4   HEADING 'Par?'
COLUMN iot_type         FORMAT a4   HEADING 'Iot?'
COLUMN nested           FORMAT a5   HEADING 'Nest?'
BREAK ON owner ON tablespace_name
SET PAGES 48 LINES 132
START TITLE132 "ORACLE TABLE REPORT"
SPOOL rep_out\&db\tab_rep
SELECT
  owner,
  tablespace_name,
  table_name,
  initial_extent Init,
```

```
   next_extent Next,
   pct_increase,
   partitioned,
   DECODE(iot_type,NULL,'No','Yes') iot_type,
   nested
FROM
   sys.dba_tables
WHERE
   owner NOT IN  ('SYSTEM','SYS')
ORDER BY
   owner,
   tablespace_name,
   table_name;
SPOOL OFF
CLEAR COLUMNS
PAUSE Press enter to continue
SET PAGES 22 LINES 80
TTITLE OFF
CLEAR COLUMNS
CLEAR BREAKS
```

Example Report Output:

Table Owner	Tablespace	Table	Initial Extent	Next Extent	Pct Increase	Par?	Iot?	Nest?
BFILE_DBO	RAW_DATA	TEMP_BLOB	20480	20480	50	NO	No	NO
	SCOPUS_DATA	GRAPHICS_TABLE	1048576	1048576	0	NO	No	NO
		INTERNAL_GRAPHICS	1048576	1048576	0	NO	No	NO
MIGRATE	SYSTEM	FET$	12288	32768	50	NO	No	NO
		TS$	12288	32768	50	NO	No	NO
TELE_DBA	SCOPUS_DATA	ACCOUNT_EXECS	12288	12288	0	NO	No	NO
		ADDRESSES	209715200	104857600	0	NO	No	NO
		AUDIT_RECORDS	12288	12288	0	NO	No	NO
		BATCH_CONTROL	20480	14729216	50	NO	No	NO
		BATCH_CONTROL2	20971520	5242880	0	NO	No	NO
		BILLINGS	20480	20480	50	NO	No	NO
		CIRCUIT_ID_INFO	209715200	104857600	0	YES	No	NO
		CLIENTPROFILES	53248	53248	0	NO	No	NO
		CLIENTS	209715200	104857600	0	YES	No	NO
		COMPANY	20480	20480	50	NO	No	NO
		CONTRACTS_STORE	12288	12288	0	NO	No	YES
		DUNS_TRACKING_RECORDS	12288	12288	0	NO	No	NO
		EARNINGS_INFO_NMBRS	209715200	104857600	0	YES	No	NO
		EMPLOYEES	20480	20480	0	NO	No	NO
		FRANCHISE_CODES	78643200	10485760	0	NO	No	NO
		HOUSES	20480	20480	50	NO	No	NO
		INTERACTION_LOG	32768	32768	0	NO	No	NO
		INTERACTION_LOG_ACTIVITY	12288	12288	0	NO	No	NO

```
LOOKUPS                      12288     12288      0    NO   Yes   NO
PLAN_TABLE                   20480     20480     50    NO   No    NO
PRICE_ADJUST                 20480     20480     50    NO   No    NO
PURCHASE_ORDERS              20480     20480     50    NO   No    NO
ROOMS                        20480     20480     50    NO   No    NO
SIC_CODES               104857600 104857600      0    NO   No    NO
SYSTEM_USER_PROFILES         12288     12288      0    NO   No    NO
TEMP_BATCH                   20480   9818112     50    NO   No    NO
TEST4                       102400      4096     50    NO   No    NO
TESTIE                       57344     57344     32    NO   No    NO
TKP_EXAMPLE                  20480     20480     50    NO   No    NO
TKP_EXAMPLE2                 20480     49152     50    NO   No    NO
UPDATE_TABLES                12288     12288      0    NO   No    NO
USERPROFILES                 53248     53248      0    NO   No    NO
USERS                   209715200 104857600      0    NO   No    NO
SQL> spool off
```

The output of the report from Listing 9.21 provides a hard-copy document showing how each table in the database was built and whether it is a regular, partitioned, index-only, or nested table. You may want to know more about partitioned tables and index-only tables than is shown in this report. Listing 9.22 shows an example partitioned table report.

Listing 9.22   Example partitioned table report.

```
rem
rem Name: tab_part.sql
rem Function : Report on partitioned table structure
rem History: MRA 6/13/97 Created
rem
COLUMN table_owner        FORMAT a10 HEADING 'Owner'
COLUMN table_name         FORMAT a15 HEADING 'Table'
COLUMN partition_name     FORMAT a15 HEADING 'Partition'
COLUMN tablespace_name    FORMAT a15 HEADING 'Tablespace'
COLUMN high_value         FORMAT a10 HEADING 'Partition|Value'
COLUMN logging            FORMAT a3  HEADING 'Log'
SET LINES 78
START title80 'Table Partition Files'
BREAK ON table_owner ON table_name
SPOOL rep_out/&&db/tab_part.lis
SELECT
   table_owner,
   table_name,
   partition_name,
   high_value,
   tablespace_name,
   logging
FROM sys.dba_tab_partitions
ORDER BY table_owner,table_name
/
SPOOL OFF
```

Example report output:

```
Date: 06/14/97                                                Page:   1
Time: 08:51 PM            Table Partition Files           SYSTEM
                          ORTEST1 database


                                        Partition
Owner       Table            Partition  Value    Tablespace      LOG
----------  ---------------  ---------------  ----------  --------------  --
SYSTEM      PART_TAB_TEST    TEST_P1      10       RAW_DATA        YES
                             TEST_P2      20       RAW_DATA        YES
                             TEST_P3      30       RAW_DATA        YES

3 rows selected.
```

With the report in Listing 9.22, you now have hard-copy documentation of your partitioned tables. This is just a general report and can be expanded as you see fit—for example, to add storage information.

You may also be interested in nested tables. Listing 9.23 shows a report for nested table values.

Listing 9.23 Example report to document nested tables.

```
rem
rem NAME: tab_nest.sql
rem PURPOSE: Report on Nested Tables
rem HISTORY: MRA 6/14/97 Created
rem
COLUMN owner                FORMAT a10 HEADING 'Owner'
COLUMN table_name           FORMAT a20 HEADING 'Store Table'
COLUMN table_type_owner     FORMAT a10 HEADING 'Type|Owner'
COLUMN table_type_name      FORMAT a15 HEADING 'Type|Name'
COLUMN parent_table_name    FORMAT a25 HEADING 'Parent|Table'
COLUMN parent_table_column  FORMAT a15 HEADING 'Parent|Column'
SET PAGES 58 LINES 132 VERIFY OFF FEEDBACK OFF
START title132 'Nested Tables'
BREAK ON owner
SPOOL rep_out\&db\tab_nest.lis
SELECT
   owner,
   table_name,
   table_type_owner,
   table_type_name,
   parent_table_name,
   parent_table_column
FROM sys.dba_nested_tables
ORDER BY owner;
SPOOL OFF
```

Example Report Output:

```
Date: 10/12/97                                                        Page:   1
Time: 6:04 PM                   Nested Tables                         SYSTEM
                               ORTEST1 database


                        Type      Type           Parent                   Parent
Owner     Store Table   Owner     Name           Table                    Column
--------- ------------- --------- -------------- ------------------------ --------------

SYSTEM    ARTIST_STORE  SYSTEM    ARTIST_LIST    ART                      ARTIST
TELE_DBA  CONTRACTSV8   TELE_DBA  CONTRACT_LIST  EARNINGS_INFO_NUMBERSV8  CONTRACTS
          CIRCUITSV8    TELE_DBA  CIRCUIT_LIST   EARNINGS_INFO_NUMBERSV8  CIRCUITS
          ADDRESSESV8   TELE_DBA  ADDRESS_LIST   CLIENTSV8                ADDRESSES
          X4            TELE_DBA  TESTEE         TESTIE                   X3
```

With the report in Listing 9.23, you have a map showing how your nested tables, their parent tables, and base types were configured.

The final type of reporting against Oracle8 tables we will look at is a column list for our tables. Listing 9.24 is an example report to show the columns assigned to tables.

Listing 9.24   Example report on table columns.

```
rem
rem tab_col.sql
rem
rem FUNCTION: Report on Table and View Column Definitions
rem
rem MRA 9/18/96
rem MRA 6/14/97 Added table level selectivity
rem
COLUMN owner        FORMAT a10  HEADING Owner
COLUMN table_name   FORMAT a30  HEADING "Table or View Name"
COLUMN COLUMN_name  FORMAT a32  HEADING "Table or View COLUMN"
COLUMN data_type    FORMAT a15  HEADING "Data|Type"
COLUMN data_length              HEADING Length
COLUMN nullable     FORMAT a5   HEADING Null?
BREAK ON owner ON table_name SKIP 1
SET LINES 132 PAGES 48 FEEDBACK OFF VERIFY OFF
START title132 "Table Columns Report"
SPOOL rep_out/&db/tab_col
SELECT
   a.owner,
   table_name||' '||object_type table_name,
   column_name,
   data_type,
   data_length,
   DECODE(nullable,'N','NO','YES') nullable
FROM
   dba_tab_columns a, dba_objects b
```

```
WHERE
   a.owner not in ('SYS','SYSTEM') AND
   a.owner=UPPER('&owner') AND
   a.owner=b.owner AND
   a.table_name LIKE UPPER('%&table%') AND
   a.table_name=b.object_name AND
   object_type IN ('TABLE','VIEW','CLUSTER')
ORDER BY
   owner,
   object_type,
   table_name,
   column_id
/
SPOOL OFF
TTITLE OFF
SET LINES 80 PAGES 22 FEEDBACK ON VERIFY ON
```

Example Report Output:

```
Date: 10/12/97                                                Page:  1
Time: 6:13 PM               Table Columns Report             SYSTEM
                              ORTEST1 database


                                                   Data
Owner      Table or View Name    Table or View Column    Type        Length  Null?
---------  -----------------     --------------------    --------    ------  -----
BFILE_DBO  GRAPHICS_TABLE TABLE  BFILE_ID               NUMBER          22    NO
                                 BFILE_DESC             VARCHAR2        30    YES
                                 BFILE_LOC              BFILE          530    YES
                                 BFILE_TYPE             VARCHAR2         4    YES

           INTERNAL_GRAPHICS TABLE  GRAPHIC_ID          NUMBER          22    NO
                                 GRAPHIC_DESC           VARCHAR2        30    YES
                                 GRAPHIC_BLOB           BLOB          4000    YES
                                 BLOB_TYPE              VARCHAR2         4    YES

           TEMP_BLOB TABLE       TEMP_BLOB              BLOB          4000    YES
                                 TEMP_CLOB              CLOB          4000    YES
                                 TEMP_NCLOB             NCLOB         4000    YES
```

Using the descriptions of the data dictionary tables and views located in the appendix, you should be able to modify these example reports to give any combination on data about tables available in the data dictionary.

Another set of objects that needs reports is indexes. With indexes, you are interested in physical storage, key usage, and partition, as well as bitmap indication. Listing 9.25 shows a basic index report on physical storage.

Listing 9.25 Example index general report.

```
rem
rem NAME: ind_rep.sql
rem FUNCTION: Report on indexes
rem HISTORY: MRA 6/14/97 Creation
rem
COLUMN owner      FORMAT a8 HEADING 'Index|Owner'
COLUMN index_name         FORMAT a27 HEADING 'Index'
COLUMN index_type         FORMAT a6  HEADING 'Type|Index'
COLUMN table_owner        FORMAT a8  HEADING 'Table|Owner'
COLUMN table_name         FORMAT a24 HEADING 'Table Name'
COLUMN table_type         FORMAT a10 HEADING 'Table|Type'
COLUMN uniqueness         FORMAT a1  HEADING 'U|n|i|q|u|e'
COLUMN tablespace_name FORMAT a13 HEADING 'Tablespace'
COLUMN column_name        FORMAT a25 HEADING 'Col. Name'
SET PAGES 58 LINES 130 FEEDBACK OFF VERIFY OFF
BREAK ON owner
START title132 'Expanded Index Report'
SPOOL rep_out\&db\ind_exp.lis
SELECT
   a.owner,
   a.index_name,
   a.index_type,
   a.table_owner,
   a.table_name,
   a.table_type,
   DECODE
   (a.uniqueness, 'UNIQUE', 'U','NONUNIQUE','N') uniqueness,
   a.tablespace_name,
   b.column_name
FROM
   dba_indexes a, dba_ind_columns b
WHERE
   owner LIKE UPPER('%&owner%')
   AND a.owner=b.index_owner(+)
   AND a.index_name=b.index_name(+)
ORDER BY
   owner, index_type;
SPOOL OFF
```

Example report output:

```
Date: 06/15/97                                                        Page:   1
Time: 11:54 PM          Index Columns by Owner and Table Name       SYSTEM
                               ORTEST1 database

                                                                        U
                                                                        N
                                                                        I
```

Object Owner	Type	Object Name	Index Name	QUE	Column Name	Part
TELE_DBA	TABLE	ACCOUNT_EXECS	PK_ACCOUNT_EXECS	U	CLIENTS_ID	NO
					ACCOUNT_EXECS_ID	NO
			FK_ACCOUNT_EXECS_1	N	AE_USERID	NO
			FK_ACCOUNT_EXECS_2		CLIENTS_ID	NO
		ADDRESSES	PK_ADDRESSES	U	ADDRESSES_ID	NO
			FK_ADDRESSES_1	N	USERID	NO
			FK_ADDRESSES_2		CLIENTS_ID	NO
			FK_ADDRESSES_3		EARNINGS_INFO_NMBRS_ID	NO
		ADDRESS_TEST	SYS_C00800	U	SYS_NC_OID$	NO
		AUDIT_RECORDS	PK_AUDIT_RECORDS	U	EARNINGS_INFO_NMBRS_ID	NO
					AUDIT_RECORDS_ID	NO
			FK_AUDIT_RECORDS_1	N	EARNINGS_INFO_NMBRS_ID	NO
		CIRCUIT_ID_INFO	PK_CIRCUIT_ID_INFO	U	CIRCUIT_ID_INFO_ID	NO
		CLIENTPROFILES	PK_CLIENTPROFILES	U	CLIENTPROFILES_ID	NO
			FK_CLIENTPROFILES_1	N	CLIENTS_ID	NO
		CLIENTS	PK_CLIENTS	U	CLIENTS_ID	NO
			UK_CLIENTS		DUNS_NO	NO
		CLIENTSV8	OID_CLIENTSV8	U	SYS_NC_OID$	NO
			PK_CLIENTSV8		CLIENTS_ID	NO
			SYS_C00900		SYS_NC0000400005$	NO
		COMPANY	TEST_INDEX	N	"COMPANY_ADDRESS"."ZIP_CODE"	NO
		CONTRACTS	PK_CONTRACTS	U	EARNINGS_INFO_NMBRS_ID	NO
					CONTACTS_ID	NO
			FK_CONTRACTS_1	N	EARNINGS_INFO_NMBRS_ID	NO

Notice that the report in Listing 9.25 doesn't list storage data. You can easily obtain that information from the **DBA_INDEXES** view, if desired. As with partitioned tables, partitioned indexes require a report to document partition location and values that were used to set the partitions. Listing 9.26 shows this type of report.

Listing 9.26 Example partitioned index report.

```
rem
rem Name: ind_part.sql
rem Function : Report on partitioned index structure
rem History: MRA 6/14/97 Created
rem
COLUMN index_owner      FORMAT a10 HEADING 'Owner'
COLUMN index_name       FORMAT a15 HEADING 'Index'
COLUMN partition_name   FORMAT a15 HEADING 'Partition'
COLUMN tablespace_name  FORMAT a15 HEADING 'Tablespace'
COLUMN high_value       FORMAT a10 HEADING 'Partition|Value'
SET LINES 78
START title80 'Index Partition Files'
BREAK ON index_owner ON index_name
SPOOL rep_out/&&db/ind_part.lis
SELECT
   index_owner,
   index_name,
   partition_name,
   high_value,
   tablespace_name,
   logging
FROM sys.dba_ind_partitions
ORDER BY index_owner,index_name
/
SPOOL OFF
```

Example report output:

```
Date: 06/14/97                                         Page:   1
Time: 08:51 PM            Index Partition Files        SYSTEM
                          ORTEST1 database

                                      Partition
Owner      Index            Partition Value    Tablespace      LOG
---------- ---------------  --------------- ---------- -------------- ---
SYSTEM     PART_IND_TEST    TEST_I_P1        10        RAW_INDEX       YES
                            TEST_I_P2        20        RAW_INDEX       YES
                            TEST_I_P3        30        RAW_INDEX       YES
```

3 rows selected.

To demonstrate what storage information you can pull from the data dictionary on partitioned indexes (and tables, for that matter), Listing 9.27 shows an example partitioned index storage report.

Listing 9.27   Example partitioned index storage report.

```
rem
rem NAME: ind_pstor.sql
rem FUNCTION: Provide data on partitioned index storage characteristics
rem HISTORY: MRA 6/13/97 Created
rem
COLUMN owner             FORMAT a6      HEADING 'Owner'
COLUMN index_name        FORMAT a14     HEADING 'Table'
COLUMN partition_name    FORMAT a9      HEADING 'Partition'
COLUMN tablespace_name   FORMAT a11     HEADING 'Tablespace'
COLUMN pct_free          FORMAT 9999    HEADING '%|Free'
COLUMN ini_trans         FORMAT 9999    HEADING 'Init|Tran'
COLUMN max_trans         FORMAT 9999    HEADING 'Max|Tran'
COLUMN initial_extent    FORMAT 9999999 HEADING 'Init|Extent'
COLUMN next_extent       FORMAT 9999999 HEADING 'Next|Extent'
COLUMN max_extent                       HEADING 'Max|Extents'
COLUMN pct_increase      FORMAT 999     HEADING '%|Inc'
COLUMN distinct_keys     FORMAT 9999999 HEADING '#Keys'
COLUMN clustering_factor FORMAT 999999  Heading 'Clus|Fact'
SET LINES 130
START title132 'Index Partition File Storage'
BREAK ON index_owner on index_name
SPOOL rep_out/&&db/ind_pstor.lis
SELECT
   index_owner,
   index_name,
   tablespace_name,
   partition_name,
   pct_free,
   ini_trans,
   max_trans,
   initial_extent,
   next_extent,
   max_extent,
   pct_increase,
   distinct_keys,
   clustering_factor
FROM sys.dba_ind_partitions
ORDER BY index_owner,index_name
/
SPOOL OFF

Example Report Output:

Date: 06/15/97                                                          Page:   1
Time: 12:00 PM             Index Partition File Storage                 SYSTEM
                                ORTEST1 database
```

INDEX_OWNER	Table	Tablespace	Partition	% Free	Init Tran	Max Tran	Init Extent	Next Extent	Max Extents	% Inc	#Keys	Clus Fact
SYSTEM	PART_IND_TEST	RAW_DATA	TEST_I_P1	10	2	255	20480	20480	249	50	0	0
		RAW_DATA	TEST_I_P2	10	2	255	20480	20480	249	50	0	0
		RAW_DATA	TEST_I_P3	10	2	255	20480	20480	249	50	0	0

```
3 rows selected.
```

For a final index report, we will use an anonymous PL/SQL script to generate a list of the primary/foreign key relationships. Listing 9.28 shows how a report of this type is constructed.

Listing 9.28   Example PL/SQL report on index primary/foreign keys.

```
REM   FUNCTION: SCRIPT FOR DOCUMENTING DATABASE PRIMARY/FOREIGN KEYS
REM
REM   FUNCTION: This script must be run by the constraint owner.
REM
REM   FUNCTION: This script is intended to run with Oracle7 or Oracle8.
REM
REM FUNCTION: Running this script will document the primary key - foreign key
REM FUNCTION: constraints in the database
REM
REM
REM Only preliminary testing of this script was performed.  Be sure to test
REM it completely before relying on it.
REM
REM MRA 6/14/97 Verified for Oracle8
REM
SET ARRAYSIZE 1 VERIFY OFF  FEEDBACK OFF TERMOUT OFF ECHO OFF PAGESIZE 0 LONG 4000
SET TERMOUT ON
SELECT 'Creating constraint documentation script...' FROM dual;
SET TERMOUT OFF
CREATE TABLE cons_temp (owner VARCHAR2(30),
        constraint_name VARCHAR2(30),
        constraint_type VARCHAR2(11),
        search_condition VARCHAR2(2000),
        table_name VARCHAR2(30),
        referenced_owner VARCHAR2(30),
        referenced_constraint VARCHAR2(30),
        delete_rule VARCHAR2(9),
        constraint_columns VARCHAR2(2000),
        con_number NUMBER);
TRUNCATE TABLE cons_temp;
--
```

```
DECLARE

    CURSOR cons_cursor IS
      SELECT owner,
    constraint_name,
            DECODE(constraint_type,'P','Primary Key',
                                    'R','Foreign Key',
                                    'U','Unique',
                                    'C','Check',
                                    'D','Default'),
          search_condition,
          table_name,
          r_owner,
          r_constraint_name,
          delete_rule
      FROM user_constraints
      WHERE owner NOT IN ('SYS','SYSTEM')
      ORDER BY owner;
--
    CURSOR cons_col (cons_name IN VARCHAR2) IS
    SELECT
      owner,
      constraint_name,
      column_name
      FROM user_cons_columns
      WHERE owner NOT IN ('SYS','SYSTEM') AND
    constraint_name = UPPER(cons_name)
      ORDER BY owner, constraint_name, position;

    CURSOR get_cons (tab_nam IN VARCHAR2) IS
    SELECT DISTINCT
      owner,table_name,constraint_name,constraint_type
    FROM cons_temp
    WHERE table_name=tab_nam
    AND constraint_type='Foreign Key'
    ORDER BY owner,table_name,constraint_name;
      CURSOR get_tab_nam IS
    SELECT distinct table_name
    FROM cons_temp
    WHERE constraint_type='Foreign Key'
    ORDER BY table_name;
--
    tab_nam    user_constraints.table_name%TYPE;
    cons_owner    user_constraints.owner%TYPE;
    cons_name user_constraints.constraint_name%TYPE;
    cons_type VARCHAR2(11);
    cons_sc    user_constraints.search_condition%TYPE;
```

```
      cons_tname   user_constraints.table_name%TYPE;
      cons_rowner user_constraints.r_owner%TYPE;
      cons_rcons   user_constraints.r_constraint_name%TYPE;
      cons_dr    user_constraints.delete_rule%TYPE;
      cons_col_own user_cons_columns.owner%TYPE;
      cons_col_nam user_cons_columns.constraint_name%TYPE;
      cons_column user_cons_columns.column_name%TYPE;
      cons_tcol_name user_cons_columns.table_name%TYPE;
      all_columns  VARCHAR2(2000);
      counter    INTEGER:=0;
      cons_nbr   INTEGER;

BEGIN
   OPEN cons_cursor;
   LOOP
      FETCH cons_cursor INTO  cons_owner,
          cons_name,
          cons_type,
          cons_sc,
          cons_tname,
          cons_rowner,
          cons_rcons,
          cons_dr;
      EXIT WHEN cons_cursor%NOTFOUND;
   all_columns :='';
   counter := 0;
   OPEN cons_col (cons_name);
   LOOP
      FETCH cons_col  INTO
            cons_col_own,
            cons_col_nam,
            cons_column;
   EXIT WHEN cons_col%NOTFOUND;
      IF cons_owner = cons_col_own AND cons_name=cons_col_nam
      THEN
         counter := counter+1;
         IF counter = 1 THEN
         all_columns := all_columns||cons_column;
         ELSE
         all_columns := all_columns||', '||cons_column;
         END IF;
      END IF;
   END LOOP;
   CLOSE cons_col;
   INSERT INTO cons_temp VALUES (cons_owner,
                cons_name,
                cons_type,
                cons_sc,
```

```
                  cons_tname,
                  cons_rowner,
                  cons_rcons,
                  cons_dr,
              all_columns,
              0);
     COMMIT;
     END LOOP;
     CLOSE cons_cursor;
     COMMIT;
BEGIN
 OPEN get_tab_nam;
LOOP
  FETCH get_tab_nam INTO tab_nam;
  EXIT WHEN get_tab_nam%NOTFOUND;
/*sys.dbms_output.put_line(tab_nam);*/
  OPEN get_cons (tab_nam);
  cons_nbr:=0;
  LOOP
    FETCH get_cons INTO cons_owner,
        cons_tname,
        cons_name,
        cons_type;
    EXIT WHEN get_cons%NOTFOUND;
    cons_nbr:=cons_nbr+1;
/*     sys.dbms_output.put_line('cons_nbr='||cons_nbr);*/
/*sys.dbms_output.put_line(cons_owner||'.'||cons_name||' '||cons_type);*/
    UPDATE cons_temp SET con_number=cons_nbr WHERE
  constraint_name=cons_name AND
  constraint_type=cons_type AND
  owner=cons_owner;
  END LOOP;
  CLOSE get_cons;
  COMMIT;
END LOOP;
CLOSE get_tab_nam;
COMMIT;
END;
END;
/
CREATE index pk_cons_temp ON cons_temp(constraint_name);
CREATE index 1k_cons_temp2 ON cons_temp(referenced_constraint);
SET FEEDBACK OFF PAGES 0 TERMOUT OFF ECHO OFF
SET VERIFY OFF
SET PAGES 48 LINES 132
COLUMN pri_own FORMAT a10 HEADING 'Pri Table|Owner'
COLUMN for_own FORMAT a10 HEADING 'For Table|Owner'
```

```
COLUMN pri_tab FORMAT a25 HEADING 'Pri Table|Name'
COLUMN for_tab FORMAT a25 HEADING 'For Table|Name'
COLUMN pri_col FORMAT a25 HEADING 'Pri Key|Columns' WORD_WRAPPED
COLUMN for_col FORMAT a25 HEADING 'For Key|Columns' WORD_WRAPPED
START title132 'Primary Key - Foreign Key Report'
SPOOL rep_out\&db\pk_fk
BREAK ON pri_own ON pri_tab ON for_own ON for_tab
SELECT
   b.owner pri_own,
   b.table_name pri_tab,
   RTRIM(b.constraint_columns) pri_col,
   a.owner for_own,
   a.table_name for_tab,
   RTRIM(a.constraint_columns) for_col
FROM
   cons_temp a,
   cons_temp b
WHERE
   a.referenced_constraint=b.constraint_name
ORDER BY
   b.owner,b.table_name,a.owner,a.table_name;
SPOOL OFF
DROP table cons_temp;
SET VERIFY ON FEEDBACK ON TERMOUT ON PAGESIZE 22 LINES 80
CLEAR COLUMNS
CLEAR BREAKS
TTITLE OFF
```

Example Report Output:

```
Date: 06/14/97                                                      Page:   1
Time: 11:31 AM            Primary Key - Foreign Key Report          TELE_DBA
                                ORTEST1 database


Pri Table  Pri Table        Pri Key               For Table For Table        For Key
Owner      Name             Columns               Owner     Name             Columns
---------- ---------------- --------------------- --------- ---------------- ---------------
TELE_DBA   CLIENTS          CLIENTS_ID            TELE_DBA  ACCOUNT_EXECS    CLIENTS_ID
                            CLIENTS_ID                      ADDRESSES        CLIENTS_ID
                            CLIENTS_ID                      CLIENTPROFILES   CLIENTS_ID
                            CLIENTS_ID                      EARNINGS_INFO_NMBRS CLIENTS_ID
                            CLIENTS_ID                      FRANCHISE_CODES  CLIENTS_ID
                            CLIENTS_ID                      INTERACTION_LOG  CLIENTS_ID
                            CLIENTS_ID                      SIC_CODES        CLIENTS_ID
                            CLIENTS_ID                      USERS            CLIENTS_ID
           EARNINGS_INFO_NMBRS EARNINGS_INFO_NMBRS_ID TELE_DBA ADDRESSES     EARNINGS_INFO_NMBRS_ID
                            EARNINGS_INFO_NMBRS_ID          AUDIT_RECORDS    EARNINGS_INFO_NMBRS_ID
                            EARNINGS_INFO_NMBRS_ID          CIRCUIT_ID_INFO  EARNINGS_INFO_NMBRS_ID
                            EARNINGS_INFO_NMBRS_ID          CONTRACTS        EARNINGS_INFO_NMBRS_ID
                            EARNINGS_INFO_NMBRS_ID          DUNS_TRACKING_RECORDS EARNINGS_INFO_NMBRS_ID
```

The information in the report generated by the script in Listing 9.28 is difficult to get at with normal SQL—hence, the use of PL/SQL. Again, you can use the table and view listings in the appendix to generate reports on any index attributes that you desire.

New in Oracle8 is the concept of types. Because types are the new atomic-level construct for the object implementations in Oracle8, let's examine a report to document the types in your Oracle8 database. The script in Listing 9.29 shows a report for types.

Listing 9.29   Example types report.

```
rem
rem NAME: types.sql
rem FUNCTION: Provide basic report of all database types
rem HISTORY : MRA 6/15/97 Created
rem
COLUMN owner        FORMAT a10      HEADING 'Type|Owner'
COLUMN type_name    FORMAT a30      HEADING 'Type|Name'
COLUMN typecode     FORMAT a27      HEADING 'Type|Code'
COLUMN predefined FORMAT a3         HEADING Pre?
COLUMN incomplete FORMAT a3         HEADING Inc?
COLUMN methods      FORMAT 9999999 HEADING '#|Methods'
COLUMN attributes FORMAT 999999    HEADING '#|Attrib'
SET LINES 130 PAGES 58 VERIFY OFF FEEDBACK OFF
BREAK ON owner
START title132 'Database Types Report'
SPOOL rep_out\&db\types.lis
SELECT
   DECODE(owner, NULL,'SYS-GEN',owner) owner,
   type_name,
   typecode,
   attributes,
   methods,
   predefined,
   incomplete
FROM dba_types
ORDER BY owner, type_name;
SPOOL OFF

Example Report Output:

Date: 10/12/97                                        Page:  1
Time: 08:11 PM         Database Types Report          SYSTEM
                         ORTEST1 database
```

Type Owner	Type Name	Type Code	Attrib	# Methods	# Pre	Inc
ORDSYS	ORDIMGB	OBJECT	7	4	NO	NO
	ORDIMGF	OBJECT	7	3	NO	NO
SYS	AQ$_AGENT	OBJECT	3	0	NO	NO
	AQ$_DEQUEUE_HISTORY	OBJECT	7	0	NO	NO
	AQ$_DEQUEUE_HISTORY_T	COLLECTION	0	0	NO	NO
	AQ$_DUMMY_T	OBJECT	1	0	NO	NO
	AQ$_HISTORY	COLLECTION	0	0	NO	NO
	AQ$_RECIPIENTS	COLLECTION	0	0	NO	NO
	AQ$_SUBSCRIBERS	COLLECTION	0	0	NO	NO
	KOKED	OBJECT	2	0	YES	NO
	KOTAD	OBJECT	15	0	YES	NO
	KOTMD	OBJECT	7	0	YES	NO
	KOTMI	OBJECT	1	0	YES	NO
	KOTTB	OBJECT	10	0	YES	NO
	KOTTD	OBJECT	10	0	YES	NO
	ORDIMGB	OBJECT	7	4	NO	NO
	ORDIMGF	OBJECT	7	3	NO	NO
	SIC_T	OBJECT	0	0	NO	YES
SYS-GEN	BFILE	BFILE	0	0	YES	NO
	BINARY ROWID	BINARY ROWID	0	0	YES	NO
	BLOB	BLOB	0	0	YES	NO
	CANONICAL	CANONICAL	0	0	YES	NO
	CFILE	CFILE	0	0	YES	NO
	CHAR	CHAR	0	0	YES	NO
	CLOB	CLOB	0	0	YES	NO
	CONTIGUOUS ARRAY	CONTIGUOUS ARRAY	0	0	YES	NO
	DATE	DATE	0	0	YES	NO
	DECIMAL	DECIMAL	0	0	YES	NO
	DOUBLE PRECISION	DOUBLE PRECISION	0	0	YES	NO
	FLOAT	FLOAT	0	0	YES	NO
	INTEGER	INTEGER	0	0	YES	NO

You might want to have a record of the attributes included in your types. The script in Listing 9.30 shows a report for an individual user's types and their attributes.

Listing 9.30 Example user's types report.

```
rem
rem User Types Report
rem Function: generate a list of User Types and Attributes for
rem the current user.
rem History: Created 10/12/97 MRA
rem
COLUMN attr_name FORMAT a27 HEADING Attribute
COLUMN type_name FORMAT a15 HEADING Name
COLUMN attr_type_name FORMAT a10 HEADING Datatype
COLUMN length FORMAT 9,999
COLUMN precision FORMAT 999,999
COLUMN scale FORMAT 9,999
BREAK ON type_name
```

```
SET ECHO OFF PAGES 58 LINES 79
START title80 "User Type Report"
SPOOL rep_out\&db\type
SELECT
   type_name,
   attr_name,
   attr_type_name,
   length,
   precision,
   scale
FROM
   user_type_attrs
ORDER BY type_name
/
SPOOL OFF
SET PAGES 22
```

Example Report Output:

```
Date: 08/17/97                                              Page:   1
Time: 02:35 PM                    User Type Report          SYSTEM
                                  ORTEST1 database


Name            Attribute                    Datatype   LENGTH  PRECISION    SCALE
--------------  ---------------------------  ---------- ------  ---------    ------
ADDRESS_T       STREET                       VARCHAR2       30
                CITY                         VARCHAR2       30
                STATE                        CHAR            2
                ZIP                          CHAR            5
COMPANY_T       COMPANY_NAME                 VARCHAR2       32
                COMPANY_BUSINESS             VARCHAR2       32
                COMPANY_CONTACT              NAME_T
                CONTACT_HOME                 VARCHAR2       20
DEPENDENT_T     RELATION                     VARCHAR2       10
                NAME                         NAME_T
                AGE                          NUMBER
DEPT_T          DNAME                        VARCHAR2      100
                ADDRESS                      VARCHAR2      200
DOC_T           DOC_ID                       INTEGER
                NAME                         VARCHAR2      512
                AUTHOR                       VARCHAR2       60
                URL                          VARCHAR2    2,000
                PUBLICATION_YEAR             INTEGER
EMPLOYEE_T      EMPLOYEE_ID                  INTEGER
                NAME                         NAME_T
                DEPENDENTS                   DEPENDENT_
                                             LIST

EMP_T           EMPLOYEE_ID                  INTEGER
                NAME                         NAME_T
                BIRTHDATE                    DATE
                HIREDATE                     DATE
                ADDRESS                      ADDRESS_T
                DEPENDENTS                   DEPENDENT_
                                             LIST
```

```
NAME_T          FIRST_NAME              VARCHAR2     32
                LAST_NAME               VARCHAR2     32
                MIDDLE_INITIAL          VARCHAR2      3
ROOM            LNGTH                   NUMBER
                WIDTH                   NUMBER
ROOM_T          LNGTH                   NUMBER
                WIDTH                   NUMBER
                HEIGHT                  NUMBER
SITE_T          SITE_ID                 INTEGER
                COMPANY                 COMPANY_T
                ADDRESS                 ADDRESS_T
                EMPLOYEE_ID_R           EMP_T
TEST3           TYPE_PASSED             VARCHAR2      8

40 rows selected.
```

Another vital part of types is their included methods. Listing 9.31 provides a report of the methods included in a user's type definitions.

Listing 9.31 Example type method report.

```
rem
rem NAME typ_meth.sql
rem FUNCTION : Create a report of type methods
rem HISTORY: MRA 6/16/97 Created
rem
COLUMN owner          FORMAT a10      HEADING 'Owner'
COLUMN type_name      FORMAT a13      HEADING 'Type|Name'
COLUMN method_name    FORMAT a17      HEADING 'Method|Name'
COLUMN method_type                    HEADING 'Method|Type'
COLUMN parameters     FORMAT 99999    HEADING '#|Param'
COLUMN results        FORMAT 99999    HEADING '#|Results'
COLUMN method_no      FORMAT 999999   HEADING 'Meth.|Number'
BREAK ON owner ON type_name
SET LINES 80 PAGES 58 VERIFY OFF FEEDBACK OFF
START title80 'Type Methods Report'
SPOOL rep_out\&db\typ_meth.lis
SELECT
   owner,
   type_name,
   method_name,
   method_no,
   method_type,
   parameters,
   results
FROM dba_type_methods
ORDER BY owner, type_name;
SPOOL OFF
```

```
Example Report Output:

Date: 06/16/97                                                Page:  1
Time: 12:43 AM                 Type Methods Report            SYSTEM
                                ORTEST1 database


            Type        Method              Meth.   Method    #        #
Owner       Name        Name                Number  Type      Param    Results
----------  ----------- ------------------  ------- ------    ------   -------
TELE_DBA    CLIENT_T    DO_SOUNDEX             1     PUBLIC     3        0
            EARNING_T   GET_CLIENT_ID_REF      1     PUBLIC     3        0
```

The actual text of each method for a type is also stored and can be retrieved similarly to how the text of used shared SQL areas was retrieved in a previous example.

I have attempted to show the diversity of information stored in the data dictionary of an Oracle8 database instance. Virtually any data used to create users, tables, tablespaces, etc. can be retrieved and viewed. In addition to static values, the dynamic performance tables give current information concerning all phases of database performance.

Chapter 10 looks at how the DPTs and other Oracle8 data dictionary constructs can tune an Oracle instance for optimal performance.

Chapter 10

Tuning Oracle Applications

This chapter examines the various methods for application tuning. It covers the Oracle tools TKPROF, Explain Plan, and the new automated features of the SQL*Plus engine, useful for tuning Oracle application statements.

Notes...

Chapter

10

The Oracle Tuning Process

The number and complexity of databases and the tools for monitoring and tuning Oracle databases has exploded since I wrote my first book in 1994. At that time, a database of a couple of hundred megabytes was considered large, and a database in the gigabyte range was considered the purview of legacy mainframes.

This is not the case anymore. With Oracle8, the size a database can reach is virtually unlimited—in the pedabyte range (more than a human mind can store well into old age). Obviously, this explosion in the number and size of Oracle databases (now databases in the hundreds of gigabytes are common) has led to differences in tuning methodology.

On top of it all, Oracle has added advanced replication, queuing, multithreaded server, parallel query, parallel server—indeed, parallel everything. This chapter looks at a majority of these issues, but I caution you, this is not a database-tuning book. Back around Oracle version 7.1.16 or so, that topic became far too complex for a single chapter in a single book. You can now find books of more than 800 pages devoted solely to tuning Oracle. I will, however, cover the major application statement tuning aspects.

In an analogy that still holds true, the Oracle object-relational database management system (ORDBMS) has been compared with an operating system that overlays

437

a computer's existing operating system. The Oracle ORDBMS handles its own buffering, caching, and file management within pseudo-disks known as *tablespaces*. All of these internal Oracle functions can add to or detract from performance. Both Oracle7 and Oracle8 provide numerous tuning options to optimize these functions.

The *Oracle7 Server Tuning*, release 7.3, manual provides guidelines to tuning the various functions within Oracle. The *Oracle8 Server Tuning*, release 8.0, Part No. A54638-01, June 1997 (or most current), manual provides insight into the various aspects of tuning Oracle8 databases. In most cases, the tuning that applies to Oracle7 will also apply to Oracle8. Where differences exist, this chapter points them out.

Tuning Oracle is a three-part process—design, implementation, and tuning—in which the old 80/20 rule applies: 80 percent of the performance gains will be accomplished through 20 percent of the work, as shown in Figure 10.1. With Oracle, this 20 percent corresponds to the first part of the process—application design.

Simply by using proper design concepts and then properly optimizing a table layout, you can realize immense performance gains. The proper design of any system starts with appropriate business, or system, rules.

The designers of your system have to be familiar with Oracle; they can't design in a vacuum. If the designers aren't aware of Oracle features and strengths, how can they take advantage of them? In one project I worked on, the designers did not use

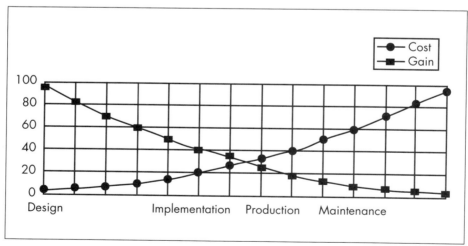

Figure 10.1

Generalized cost-benefit graph for tuning.

functions, packages, or procedures because they weren't aware of them. In another, all of the referential integrity (RI) was done through triggers, again, because the designers weren't aware of the way Oracle did RI.

Once the Oracle system is designed, based on sound business rules and Oracle-based design practices, the second phase of the process begins: The application developers implement the Oracle-based design using Oracle-based development practices. Again, spend the time to find, and the cash to hire, experienced Oracle developers. Believe me, the time you save from having to redo code, correct mistakes, and teach Oracle to off-the-shelf developers will more than equal the dollars to hire qualified people in the first place. Experience with Sybase or INGRES database systems doesn't qualify a developer to develop in Oracle. While the concepts are similar among database systems, the execution in many cases is far different. Ask yourself, do you want to pay for learning-curve time?

Proper specification of business rules, application of the rules to a design, and implementation of the design using Oracle-savvy developers will give you 80 percent of your database performance. Developers must be familiar with Oracle application statement tuning. It is their responsibility, not the DBA's.

All of your developers should be familiar with Explain Plan, TKPROF, and the strengths and weaknesses of cost- and rule-based optimizers. Provide good tools to good people, and you will be amazed at the results. Many tools that automatically analyze code are now available. Some, such as those offered by Precise Inc., will even suggest alternative, better-performing ways to do a particular piece of code. A demo copy of the Precise software set is provided on the attached CD-ROM.

In some cases, merely adding a hint, analyzing a table, or changing the structure of a query will improve a statement's performance by an order of magnitude. Imagine what performance gains can be made over an entire application. In one case, adding a simple index changed a 4-hour process into less than 10 seconds. The mere act of analyzing a recently loaded table may translate into hours of saved processing time.

After you have seen 80 percent of your performance gains through proper design and implementation, you can achieve the remaining 20 percent through tuning the structures and processes that make up the Oracle system. This is the DBA's job. Reducing disk, memory, and I/O contention and improving sort and checkpoint speed will all improve performance. Of course, if all of these functions were really out-of-tune, database performance may show more than a 20-percent gain.

Unfortunately, DBAs are usually not hired until too late—after the programmer (who got to be DBA because no one else wanted the job) has made a complete mess of the project. Indeed, usually by the time a true DBA is hired, a project is only weeks away from production. Then, Oracle and the DBA are blamed for poor performance. Chapter 11 covers tuning database internals.

Application Tuning

Application tuning is a complex concept. It involves both the design (logical, as well as physical) and execution of an application. Depending on how your company is organized, you may or may not have any control over application development. If you have no control, try to show management the value you can add by providing application-tuning skills and tools to the developers.

The best approach is to send each developer to the application-tuning class provided by Oracle Corporation for the particular release of Oracle you are using. If your company cannot send them to training, see if you can sponsor a workshop where the application tuning concepts can be presented to the developers.

The application tuning part of the process involves several steps:

1. Proper specification of system or business rules

2. Proper logical design

    a. Normalization of data

    b. Denormalization of selected tables for performance

3. Proper physical layout of application areas

    a. Placement of tables in multiple tablespaces

    b. Placement of indexes away from tables

    c. Placement of other database objects

4. Tuning of application statements

    a. Determination of index requirements

    b. Proper use, and non-use, of indexes

    c. Query tuning—the use of TKPROF and Explain Plan

5. Tuning of Oracle internals and processes

   a. SGA

   b. Shared pool and large pool

   c. Parallel query

   d. MTS

   e. Archive logging

   f. Latches and locks

6. Application processing scheduling

   a. Concurrent processes

   b. Batch jobs

Steps 1 through 4 will be discussed in this chapter. Steps 5 and 6 will be discussed in later chapters.

Proper Specification Of System Or Business Rules

You will probably be hired well after the system or business rules have been specified. If you are fortunate enough to come on board before that point, try to have as much input as possible. You need to ensure that the rules make sense from a database point of view. If a rule can't be clearly understood, it can't be clearly programmed into a database.

You have to ensure that a proper balance is struck between too amorphous a set of rules—where anything that can store data (up to and including a leaky bucket) will meet them—and rules that are so specific they tell you what color shoes to wear when tuning the database. A rule should give the *requirement*, not the *solution*.

If possible, the DBA should have the right to inspect the rules and ask for clarifications where needed. After all, the database will probably outlast the managers and designers who build it.

Proper Logical Design

Logical design is no more than applying the rules of normalization to a data model and knowing when to break the rules through de-normalization for performance reasons.

Normalization

Simply stated, a fully normalized design is one in which all attributes for a specific entity relate to the entity's unique identifier—and only to the entity's unique identifier. In other words, they relate to the whole key and nothing but the key. Of course, with the new type structures in Oracle, the normalization rules must be bent. The wise course is still to ensure that each type used in an object specification is normalized. Wherever possible, eliminate redundant data storage.

Denormalization

Sometimes, for performance of special reports or frequently run important queries, you may want to denormalize a table or tables in your design. Denormalization is the process by which columns from multiple tables are combined into a single table to speed queries on the data contained in those columns. In cases where the data from two or more tables is accessed repeatedly for reports or special queries, denormalization will speed access.

Clustering the tables may sometimes be better than denormalizing them. This will depend on how often the tables are to have update or insert activity. The more frequent the update to a set of tables, the poorer candidates they are for clustering.

Denormalization involves redundant storage of database information. If you use denormalization, be sure that your application performs updates to all of the data-storage locations. The major problems with denormalized data are update, delete, and insert anomalies. In Oracle7, Oracle suggests using database-stored triggers to handle the possible storage problems brought on by denormalization. Build stored triggers for each redundant field so that an update, delete, or insert activity must affect all values in the database. In Oracle8, type methods and procedures should be used to ensure redundant data is kept in sync.

Assistance From CASE Tools

A good computer-aided software engineering (CASE) tool can assist developers and DBAs in checking logical design. Oracle offers the Designer/Developer/2000 tool set. Another product that supports Oracle8 and type usage is the Rational Rose tool set from Rational Software. A demo set of these tools for Oracle7 and C++ is provided on the enclosed CD-ROM. Oracle8 is supported by the actual program set from Rational. The company plans an Oracle8 demo set for early 1998, so watch its Web site at **www.rational.com**.

Proper Physical Design

Physical design involves the tables themselves. As the DBA, you are concerned with the type, table, index, cluster, sizing, and storage parameters. This section looks at these issues and provides some guidelines to their proper use.

Sizing

Use of the sizing formulas provided in the various Oracle8 manuals should provide you with detailed sizing data for the database objects. Be sure that you have sized the tables for at least a year's worth of activity (unless, of course, the application's expected lifetime is less than a year). If the amount of storage used is not of prime consideration, oversizing is better than undersizing. Whenever possible, you don't want dynamic space extension in database objects. In fact, sizing rows to take up equal fractions of an Oracle block may have advantages.

Dynamic space extension is the process by which a database object grows past its initial settings. If the database objects have been created too small, this can result in the Swiss-cheese type of tablespace fragmentation that is detrimental to performance. Generally speaking, you want as few extensions per table as possible (except in the case of partitioned tables or indexes).

Use Of A Test Database

You should create a small test database loaded with test data that represents what you expect the data in the real database to look like. To get good sizing estimates, load into the test database at least 10 percent of the data (or a representative sample if the database is so large that 10 percent would qualify as a VLDB (Very Large Database) in its own right) you expect in the final database. Run the various sizing reports and check the database objects for dynamic extension.

Once you are satisfied that the best sizing parameters have been used, determine the sizing parameters for your production installation. This involves deriving the ratio of how much data is expected in the actual table against how much was loaded into the test database table. This number is then applied to the sizing numbers from the test database.

Key Sizing Parameters

The **INITIAL**, **NEXT**, and **PCTINCREASE** values are the key sizing parameters. If you are dealing with legacy systems where a great deal of existing data is to be loaded, make the initial extent large enough to handle this existing data *plus a year's worth* of additional data. Make the next parameter big enough to deal with an additional year's worth of expected entries for the table. If you aren't sure what the data-entry requirements will be that far in the future, perform a SWAG (scientific wild-assed guess) and use the **PCTINCREASE** parameter to take up the slack.

Remember, the **PCTINCREASE** is an incrementally applied value. The first extent added after the one that uses the **NEXT** parameter will be (1+**PCTINCREASE**/100) times larger than the **NEXT** parameter. The next extent after that one will be another (1+**PCTINCREASE**/100) times larger, and so on. This factor is applied to the size of only the previous extent generated. In previous versions of Oracle, the factor was applied via formula, so a seemingly minor increase in the factor could result in a catastrophically large next extent.

The actual value for the **INITIAL** and **NEXT** extent values should be carefully calculated to allow as close as possible to an even number of entries per extent for the table. For some fixed-length entries, this is easy. For entries that vary in length, it will require a careful determination of the average row length. The calculations in the Oracle8 manuals will help determine sizing requirements of tables and indexes. To facilitate the DBWR and other processes, and make extent reuse easier, some experts say to make table extents a standard size. Most feel this wastes more space than it saves.

Table Placement

Read the manual's sections concerning the Optimal Flexible Architecture (OFA). By applying these principles, you can easily accomplish file placement. Generally, you want to distribute an Oracle database across as many drives as possible. Ideally, one table per tablespace and one tablespace per driveset would give the ultimate performance.

Of course, few, if any, of us can afford such an extensive disk array as would be required in this scenario, nor would any of us wish to manage an environment this complex. The next best option is to spread the disk I/O across available platters as evenly as possible. With the widespread acceptance of RAID technologies of various denominations (0,1, 0+1, 0+1+5), this concept tends to blur as the concept of *disk* morphs into *disk array*. Most RAID implementations will balance I/O across the platters, especially if you use RAID 1 (striping). The wise course is still to place indexes on one disk array controller and tables on another. The file-spreading rules now are applied over disk arrays or controllers instead of just disks.

You should place high-volume, high-activity files in their own tablespaces on their own disks if possible. Low-volume, low-activity tables, such as static look-up tables, can be placed together in a single tablespace, preferably away from the high-volume tables. Other database tables, such as redo logs, rollback segments, and system tablespaces, should be placed to reduce disk farm contention and maximize dependability and recoverability. A few general rules follow (remember, an array is controlled by a single controller):

- *Place redo logs and archive files on separate platters or arrays*—Because one is a backup to the other, this only makes sense.

- *Place redo logs and rollback segments on different platters or arrays*—Both of these tend to be high activity, so separation reduces disk contention.

- *Separate the system tablespace from other application tablespaces if possible*—The system tablespace is called by all others, so separation reduces contention.

- *Run exports to a separate drive or array from archive logs*—These provide two of the three legs of recovery: archives, exports and system backups. Separation of each from the other improves recoverability.

- *Place archive logs away from active disks or arrays, preferably on their own platter*—These files can be large and numerous. If you don't have adequate space for storing these archive files, the database will stop.

Table Striping

As DBA, you will make decisions about striping of tables. Large tables may exceed the storage capacity of a single disk. In other cases, you may want to place a table across several disks to optimize performance. Under Oracle7, you can accomplish this in the following manner:

1. Determine the size of each table fragment. Try to make each the same size.

2. Create a tablespace that has datafiles spread across the platters. The datafiles should each be sized to hold one table fragment:

```
CREATE TABLESPACE ACCOUNT_SPREAD
DATAFILE ('/oracle01/ORTEST1/data/account_file1.dbf' SIZE 500M REUSE,
 '/oracle02/ORTEST1/data/account_file2.dbf' SIZE 500M REUSE,
 '/oracle03/ORTEST1/data/account_file3.dbf' SIZE 500M REUSE)
ONLINE;
```

3. Create the table in the tablespace from Step 2 with *X* initial extents, each the same size as the datafiles from Step 2:

```
CREATE TABLE accounts(acct_no number CONSTRAINT pk_acct PRIMARY KEY,
    acct_name varchar2(32) CONSTRAINT nn_act_name NOT NULL,
     acct_size number,
     acct_desc  varchar2(64))
PCTFREE 5   PCTUSED 90
TABLESPACE ACCOUNT_SPREAD
STORAGE (INITIAL 495M    NEXT 495M
        MINEXTENTS 3    MAXEXTENTS 3
        PCTINCREASE 0)
```

4. Load the data into the table, using either SQLLOADER or **IMPORT**.

If you choose to spread a table in this manner, try to sort the data before it is loaded. If the data is already loaded into existing tables, use a query to load the data that presorts the records. If the data is in flat files or another database, use operating system utilities or existing database reporting capabilities to sort the data. This will improve the data's accessibility to your users once it is loaded into the spread data table.

Data partitioning under Oracle7 is virtually impossible unless you create individual tables for each partition. Later versions of Oracle7 allow for a partitioned view where, if proper criteria are met, a set of related partitioned tables can look like one table.

With Oracle8, you can easily accomplish data partitioning with the **PARTITION** clause of the **CREATE TABLE** command. The major advantage of the new partitioning in Oracle8 is that it is by ranges of data instead of a hit-or-miss separation.

The **CREATE INDEX** command also has a **PARTITION** clause. Placing the partitions on individual disks or arrays enhances performance. You can simply spread data in multiple equal-sized extents, or you can specify data ranges for each partition. You can partition both indexes and tables, if desired. By default, a partitioned table has indexes that are partitioned the same, up to and including the tablespace locations. If you are using partitioned tables, be sure to specify the locations for your index partitions. Only standard relational-style tables can be partitioned in version 8.0.3 of Oracle; they cannot include collections, nested tables, or **VARRAY**s.

Tuning Application Query Statements

Tuning application queries is a complex topic. Such factors as index use, index non-use, order of query **WHERE** clauses, and Oracle optimizer settings can all affect query performance. In addition, the number of data dictionary caches and database buffers also affect query performance, as does the sort area size.

Use Of TKPROF To Tune Statements

Oracle provides two tools to tune SQL statements, TKPROF and Explain Plan. TKPROF uses the Oracle **TRACE** facility to give statistics and query plans on all statements executed while the session is in trace mode. Explain Plan is used on any query at any time. SQL*Plus now also allows tracing to be done automatically. Use the **SET AUTOTRACE ON EXPLAIN** command to turn Explain Plan on at the session level. A second command, **SET TIMING ON**, displays execution time for a specific query or operation. Listing 10.1 is an example of the use of the **SET AUTOTRACE** and **SET TIMING** commands. The time is expressed in realtime, not CPU time. The units are milliseconds.

Listing 10.1   Example use of the trace and timing features of SQL*Plus.

```
SQL>  set timing on autotrace on explain
SQL> select count(*) from dba_tables;

 COUNT(*)
--------
     355


 real: 1219

Execution Plan
----------------------------------------------------------
   0        SELECT STATEMENT Optimizer=CHOOSE
   1     0   SORT (AGGREGATE)
   2     1    NESTED LOOPS
   3     2     NESTED LOOPS
   4     3      NESTED LOOPS (OUTER)
   5     4       NESTED LOOPS (OUTER)
   6     5        NESTED LOOPS
   7     6         TABLE ACCESS (FULL) OF 'OBJ$'
   8     6         TABLE ACCESS (CLUSTER) OF 'TAB$'
   9     8          INDEX (UNIQUE SCAN) OF 'I_OBJ#' (CLUSTER)
  10     5         INDEX (UNIQUE SCAN) OF 'I_OBJ1' (UNIQUE)
  11     4        TABLE ACCESS (CLUSTER) OF 'SEG$'
  12    11         INDEX (UNIQUE SCAN) OF 'I_FILE#_BLOCK#' (CLUSTER)
  13     3       TABLE ACCESS (CLUSTER) OF 'TS$'
  14    13        INDEX (UNIQUE SCAN) OF 'I_TS#' (CLUSTER)
  15     2      TABLE ACCESS (CLUSTER) OF 'USER$'
  16    15       INDEX (UNIQUE SCAN) OF 'I_USER#' (CLUSTER)
```

PreciseSQL from Precise Software allows you to take any SQL query and, as long as it functions as it is, optimize the code by showing alternative statement structures and relative associated costs. PreciseSQL also allows you to specify schema changes, such as the addition of indexes, and shows the results of these actions on all current SQL area statements. The enclosed CD-ROM provides a demo copy of PreciseSQL for your review.

The **TRACE** facility allows Oracle to keep an execution log of each session. These logs track a number of statistics for analyzing performance of your applications. TKPROF translates the trace logs into a readable format. Listing 10.2 shows two queries that differ only in the structure of the **WHERE** clause.

Listing 10.2   Example queries.

```
Query 1:
SELECT C.OWNER, C.TABLE_NAME, C.CONSTRAINT_NAME,
CC.COLUMN_NAME, R.TABLE_NAME REF_TABLE,
RC.COLUMN_NAME REF_COLUMN
FROM DBA_CONSTRAINTS C, DBA_CONSTRAINTS R, DBA_CONS_COLUMNS CC, DBA_CONS_COLUMNS RC
WHERE C.R_CONSTRAINT_NAME = R.CONSTRAINT_NAME
AND C.R_OWNER = R.OWNER AND C.CONSTRAINT_NAME = CC.CONSTRAINT_NAME
AND C.OWNER = CC.OWNER AND R.CONSTRAINT_NAME = RC.CONSTRAINT_NAME
AND R.OWNER = RC.OWNER AND CC.POSITION = RC.POSITION
AND C.CONSTRAINT_TYPE = 'R' AND C.OWNER <> 'SYS'
AND C.OWNER <> 'SYSTEM'
ORDER BY C.OWNER, C.TABLE_NAME, C.CONSTRAINT_NAME, CC.POSITION

Query 2:
SELECT C.OWNER, C.TABLE_NAME, C.CONSTRAINT_NAME,
CC.COLUMN_NAME, R.TABLE_NAME REF_TABLE,
RC.COLUMN_NAME REF_COLUMN
FROM DBA_CONSTRAINTS C, DBA_CONSTRAINTS R, DBA_CONS_COLUMNS CC, DBA_CONS_COLUMNS RC
WHERE C.CONSTRAINT_TYPE = 'R'
AND C.OWNER NOT IN ('SYS','SYSTEM')
AND C.R_OWNER = R.OWNER
and C.R_CONSTRAINT_NAME = R.CONSTRAINT_NAME
AND C.CONSTRAINT_NAME = CC.CONSTRAINT_NAME
AND C.OWNER = CC.OWNER
AND R.CONSTRAINT_NAME = RC.CONSTRAINT_NAME
AND R.OWNER = RC.OWNER
AND CC.POSITION = RC.POSITION
ORDER BY C.OWNER, C.TABLE_NAME, C.CONSTRAINT_NAME, CC.POSITION
```

You execute TKPROF by either moving to the directory where the trace files are located (the value of the initialization parameter **user_dump_destination** gives this information) or moving the trace file to a work directory and executing the **TKPROF** command against it:

```
tkprof input output explain=user/password sort=(sort options)
```

Both of the queries are complex queries against views. They both retrieve the same information from the database. Close examination reveals that the only difference between them is the order of the **WHERE** clause columns. Listing 10.3 shows the results of analyzing the previous queries with the TKPROF tool. As you can see, the second query performs better. This is because the most restrictive columns come first, thus reducing the volume of subsequent merges and sorts.

The explain plan generated is huge, because this is a multitable and multiview join. Unfortunately, a query against views that are not owned by the user running TKPROF cannot be run through the Explain Plan option. Therefore, if the queries you analyze involve views from multiple owners, an Explain Plan output will not be available.

Listing 10.3   TKPROF results from queries in Listing 10.2.
```
*****************************************************************************
select c.owner,c.table_name,c.constraint_name,
cc.column_name,r.table_name ref_table,
rc.column_name ref_column
from dba_constraints c, dba_constraints r, dba_cons_columns cc,
dba_cons_columns rc
where c.r_constraint_name=r.constraint_name
and c.r_owner=r.owner and c.constraint_name=cc.constraint_name
and c.owner=cc.owner and r.constraint_name=rc.constraint_name
and r.owner=rc.owner and cc.position=rc.position
and c.constraint_type='R' and c.owner<>'SYS'
and c.owner<>'SYSTEM'
order by c.owner, c.table_name, c.constraint_name,cc.position
```

call	count	cpu	elapsed	disk	query	current	rows
Parse	1	2.67	2.67	0	0	0	0
Execute	1	0.00	0.00	0	0	0	0
Fetch	3	0.52	0.52	0	6737	2	21
total	5	3.19	3.19	0	6737	2	21

```
Misses in library cache during parse: 0
Optimizer goal: CHOOSE
Parsing user id: SYS
```

```
Rows      Execution Plan
------    -------------------------------------------------------
    0     SELECT STATEMENT    GOAL: CHOOSE
    0      SORT (ORDER BY)
    0       NESTED LOOPS (OUTER)
    0        NESTED LOOPS
    0         NESTED LOOPS
    0          NESTED LOOPS
    0           NESTED LOOPS (OUTER)
    0            NESTED LOOPS (OUTER)
    0             NESTED LOOPS
    0              NESTED LOOPS
    0               NESTED LOOPS
    0                NESTED LOOPS
    0                 NESTED LOOPS
    0                  NESTED LOOPS
    0                   NESTED LOOPS (OUTER)
    0                    NESTED LOOPS (OUTER)
    0                     NESTED LOOPS
    0                      NESTED LOOPS
    0                       NESTED LOOPS
    0                        NESTED LOOPS
    0                         NESTED LOOPS
    0                          NESTED LOOPS
    0                           NESTED LOOPS (OUTER)
    0                            NESTED LOOPS
    0                             NESTED LOOPS
    0                              NESTED LOOPS
    0                               TABLE ACCESS
                                       (FULL) OF 'OBJ$'
    0                               TABLE ACCESS
                                       (CLUSTER) OF 'CCOL$'
    0                                INDEX
                                       (UNIQUE SCAN) OF 'I_COBJ#' (CLUSTER)
    0                               INDEX (UNIQUE
                                       SCAN) OF 'I_CDEF1' (UNIQUE)
    0                               TABLE ACCESS (BY
                                       INDEX ROWID) OF 'COL$'
    0                               INDEX (UNIQUE
                                       SCAN) OF 'I_COL3' (UNIQUE)
    0                               TABLE ACCESS
                                       (CLUSTER) OF 'ATTRCOL$'
    0                               TABLE ACCESS (BY
                                       INDEX ROWID) OF 'CON$'
    0                               INDEX (UNIQUE SCAN)
                                       OF 'I_CON2' (UNIQUE)
```

```
0                          TABLE ACCESS (CLUSTER)
                              OF 'USER$'
0                          INDEX (UNIQUE SCAN)
                              OF 'I_USER#' (CLUSTER)
0                        TABLE ACCESS (BY INDEX
                            ROWID) OF 'USER$'
0                        INDEX (UNIQUE SCAN) OF
                            'I_USER1' (UNIQUE)
0                      TABLE ACCESS (BY INDEX
                          ROWID) OF 'CON$'
0                      INDEX (UNIQUE SCAN) OF
                          'I_CON1' (UNIQUE)
0                    TABLE ACCESS (BY INDEX ROWID)
                        OF 'CDEF$'
0                    INDEX (UNIQUE SCAN) OF
                        'I_CDEF1' (UNIQUE)
0                    TABLE ACCESS (BY INDEX ROWID)
                        OF 'OBJ$'
0                    INDEX (UNIQUE SCAN) OF
                        'I_OBJ1' (UNIQUE)
0                  TABLE ACCESS (BY INDEX ROWID) OF
                      'CON$'
0                  INDEX (UNIQUE SCAN) OF
                      'I_CON2' (UNIQUE)
0                TABLE ACCESS (CLUSTER) OF 'USER$'
0                INDEX (UNIQUE SCAN) OF 'I_USER#'
                    (CLUSTER)
0              TABLE ACCESS (BY INDEX ROWID) OF
                  'USER$'
0              INDEX (UNIQUE SCAN) OF 'I_USER1'
                  (UNIQUE)
0            TABLE ACCESS (BY INDEX ROWID) OF
                'USER$'
0            INDEX (UNIQUE SCAN) OF 'I_USER1'
                (UNIQUE)
0          TABLE ACCESS (BY INDEX ROWID) OF 'CON$'
0          INDEX (UNIQUE SCAN) OF 'I_CON1'
              (UNIQUE)
0        TABLE ACCESS (BY INDEX ROWID) OF 'CON$'
0        INDEX (UNIQUE SCAN) OF 'I_CON1' (UNIQUE)
0        INDEX (UNIQUE SCAN) OF 'I_CDEF1' (UNIQUE)
0      TABLE ACCESS (BY INDEX ROWID) OF 'CDEF$'
0      INDEX (UNIQUE SCAN) OF 'I_CDEF1' (UNIQUE)
0      TABLE ACCESS (BY INDEX ROWID) OF 'OBJ$'
0      INDEX (UNIQUE SCAN) OF 'I_OBJ1' (UNIQUE)
0    TABLE ACCESS (BY INDEX ROWID) OF 'CON$'
0    INDEX (UNIQUE SCAN) OF 'I_CON2' (UNIQUE)
```

```
     0           TABLE ACCESS (CLUSTER) OF 'USER$'
     0              INDEX (UNIQUE SCAN) OF 'I_USER#' (CLUSTER)
     0            TABLE ACCESS (BY INDEX ROWID) OF 'CCOL$'
     0              INDEX (RANGE SCAN) OF 'I_CCOL2' (UNIQUE)
     0           INDEX (UNIQUE SCAN) OF 'I_OBJ1' (UNIQUE)
     0          TABLE ACCESS (BY INDEX ROWID) OF 'COL$'
     0            INDEX (UNIQUE SCAN) OF 'I_COL3' (UNIQUE)
     0          TABLE ACCESS (CLUSTER) OF 'ATTRCOL$'
```

****

```
select c.owner,c.table_name,c.constraint_name,
cc.column_name,r.table_name ref_table,
rc.column_name ref_column
from dba_constraints c, dba_constraints r, dba_cons_columns cc,
dba_cons_columns rc
where c.constraint_type='R'
and c.owner not in ('SYS','SYSTEM')
and c.r_owner=r.owner
and c.r_constraint_name=r.constraint_name
and c.constraint_name = cc.constraint_name
and c.owner=cc.owner
and r.constraint_name=rc.constraint_name
and r.owner=rc.owner
and cc.position=rc.position
order by c.owner, c.table_name, c.constraint_name,cc.position
```

call	count	cpu	elapsed	disk	query	current	rows
Parse	1	0.02	0.01	0	0	0	0
Execute	1	0.00	0.00	0	0	0	0
Fetch	3	0.51	0.52	0	6737	2	21
total	5	0.53	0.53	0	6737	2	21

Misses in library cache during parse: 1
Optimizer goal: CHOOSE
Parsing user id: SYS

```
Rows      Execution Plan
------    -------------------------------------------------------
     0    SELECT STATEMENT   GOAL: CHOOSE
     0     SORT (ORDER BY)
     0      NESTED LOOPS (OUTER)
     0       NESTED LOOPS
     0        NESTED LOOPS
     0         NESTED LOOPS
```

```
0             NESTED LOOPS (OUTER)
0            NESTED LOOPS (OUTER)
0           NESTED LOOPS
0          NESTED LOOPS
0         NESTED LOOPS
0        NESTED LOOPS
0       NESTED LOOPS
0      NESTED LOOPS
0     NESTED LOOPS
0      NESTED LOOPS (OUTER)
0       NESTED LOOPS (OUTER)
0        NESTED LOOPS
0         NESTED LOOPS
0          NESTED LOOPS
0           NESTED LOOPS
0            NESTED LOOPS
0             NESTED LOOPS
0              NESTED LOOPS (OUTER)
0               NESTED LOOPS
0                NESTED LOOPS
0                 NESTED LOOPS
0                  TABLE ACCESS
                       (FULL) OF 'OBJ$'
0                  TABLE ACCESS
                       (CLUSTER) OF 'CCOL$'
0                    INDEX
                       (UNIQUE SCAN) OF 'I_COBJ#' (CLUSTER)
0                    INDEX (UNIQUE
                       SCAN) OF 'I_CDEF1' (UNIQUE)
0                  TABLE ACCESS (BY
                       INDEX ROWID) OF 'COL$'
0                    INDEX (UNIQUE
                       SCAN) OF 'I_COL3' (UNIQUE)
0                  TABLE ACCESS
                       (CLUSTER) OF 'ATTRCOL$'
0                  TABLE ACCESS (BY
                       INDEX ROWID) OF 'CON$'
0                  INDEX (UNIQUE SCAN)
                       OF 'I_CON2' (UNIQUE)
0                  TABLE ACCESS (CLUSTER)
                       OF 'USER$'
0                  INDEX (UNIQUE SCAN)
                       OF 'I_USER#' (CLUSTER)
0                  TABLE ACCESS (BY INDEX
                       ROWID) OF 'USER$'
0                  INDEX (UNIQUE SCAN) OF
                       'I_USER1' (UNIQUE)
```

```
0                          TABLE ACCESS (BY INDEX
                             ROWID) OF 'CON$'
0                        INDEX (UNIQUE SCAN) OF
                           'I_CON1' (UNIQUE)
0                       TABLE ACCESS (BY INDEX ROWID)
                           OF 'CDEF$'
0                      INDEX (UNIQUE SCAN) OF
                         'I_CDEF1' (UNIQUE)
0                     TABLE ACCESS (BY INDEX ROWID)
                         OF 'OBJ$'
0                    INDEX (UNIQUE SCAN) OF
                       'I_OBJ1' (UNIQUE)
0                   TABLE ACCESS (BY INDEX ROWID) OF
                       'CON$'
0                  INDEX (UNIQUE SCAN) OF
                     'I_CON2' (UNIQUE)
0                 TABLE ACCESS (CLUSTER) OF 'USER$'
0                INDEX (UNIQUE SCAN) OF 'I_USER#'
                   (CLUSTER)
0               TABLE ACCESS (BY INDEX ROWID) OF
                   'USER$'
0              INDEX (UNIQUE SCAN) OF 'I_USER1'
                 (UNIQUE)
0             TABLE ACCESS (BY INDEX ROWID) OF
                 'USER$'
0            INDEX (UNIQUE SCAN) OF 'I_USER1'
               (UNIQUE)
0           TABLE ACCESS (BY INDEX ROWID) OF 'CON$'
0          INDEX (UNIQUE SCAN) OF 'I_CON1'
             (UNIQUE)
0         TABLE ACCESS (BY INDEX ROWID) OF 'CON$'
0          INDEX (UNIQUE SCAN) OF 'I_CON1' (UNIQUE)
0         INDEX (UNIQUE SCAN) OF 'I_CDEF1' (UNIQUE)
0        TABLE ACCESS (BY INDEX ROWID) OF 'CDEF$'
0         INDEX (UNIQUE SCAN) OF 'I_CDEF1' (UNIQUE)
0        TABLE ACCESS (BY INDEX ROWID) OF 'OBJ$'
0         INDEX (UNIQUE SCAN) OF 'I_OBJ1' (UNIQUE)
0        TABLE ACCESS (BY INDEX ROWID) OF 'CON$'
0         INDEX (UNIQUE SCAN) OF 'I_CON2' (UNIQUE)
0       TABLE ACCESS (CLUSTER) OF 'USER$'
0        INDEX (UNIQUE SCAN) OF 'I_USER#' (CLUSTER)
0       TABLE ACCESS (BY INDEX ROWID) OF 'CCOL$'
0        INDEX (RANGE SCAN) OF 'I_CCOL2' (UNIQUE)
0      INDEX (UNIQUE SCAN) OF 'I_OBJ1' (UNIQUE)
0     TABLE ACCESS (BY INDEX ROWID) OF 'COL$'
0      INDEX (UNIQUE SCAN) OF 'I_COL3' (UNIQUE)
0    TABLE ACCESS (CLUSTER) OF 'ATTRCOL$'
```

****

This example shows that seemingly innocuous queries can produce absolutely hideous query plans if the queries are against views. As you can see, the rearrangement of the **WHERE** clause has reduced the CPU and elapsed statistics for the parse phase of the query processing. Getting valid results may be difficult unless your data sets are large or your processor is slow.

To use the TKPROF tool and get timing results, you must set the **TIMED_STATISTICS** parameter in the INIT.ORA file to **TRUE**. To limit the size of the generated trace file, set the INIT.ORA parameter **MAX_DUMP_FILE_SIZE** to the desired file-size limit. If you want the files to be created in other than the **ORA_INSTANCE**, **ORA_TRACE**, or **$ORACLE_HOME** directory, set **USER_DUMP_DEST** to the desired file location. For these parameters to take effect, the instance has to be shut down and restarted. Once testing is finished, reset the **TIMED_STATISTIC** parameter to **FALSE**; otherwise, you will experience a performance hit because of continuous statistics collection.

Setting **TIMED_STATISTICS** to **TRUE** will allow individual users to set the **SQL_TRACE** value for their process to **TRUE**. This will then generate a trace file in the **ORA_TRACE** or selected directory. Users should then execute the statements from within SQL*Plus. To take advantage of the **TRACE** facility in SQL*Plus, use the **ALTER SESSION** command. For example:

```
ALTER SESSION SET SQL_TRACE TRUE;
```

Use Of TKPROF

Once the SQL statements or forms have been run, exit SQL*Plus or the forms-based application and look for the trace file that corresponds to the PID of the process that generated it. For example, if the PID in Oracle is 263, the trace file name (on NT) will be Ora00263.trc. On your system, the file name may be different. Usually, the name will contain the PID. If you try to look at this file without processing through TKPROF, you will receive little benefit. TKPROF formats the trace files into a user-readable form.

Invoke TKPROF using this syntax:

```
>--tkprof -- trace_file -- output_file --------------------------------------->>
                            |----SORT =-------------------------------------|
                            |        v--------,--------------|        |
                            |--(---- option -------------)--|
```

```
>----------------------------------------------------------------------->>
   |-- PRINT = integer --|        |--INSERT = filename --|    |-- SYS = YES|NO ----|
>----------------------------------------------------------------------->>
   |------------------------------------------------EXPLAIN = user/password------|
          |-- TABLE = schema.table ------|
>------------------------------------------------------------------------><
        |-- RECORD = filename----|
```

If you invoke the **TKPROF** command with no arguments, online help is displayed.

Use the following arguments with **TKPROF**:

- *Trace file*—Specifies the input file, a trace file containing statistics produced by the SQL trace facility. This file can be either a trace file produced for a single session or a file produced by concatenating individual trace files from multiple sessions.

- *Output file*—Specifies the file to which TKPROF writes its formatted output.

- *AGGREGATE*—If you specify **AGGREGATE=NO**, then TKPROF does not aggregate multiple users of the same SQL text.

- *EXPLAIN*—Determines the execution plan for each SQL statement in the trace file and writes these execution plans to the output file. TKPROF determines execution plans by issuing the **EXPLAIN PLAN** command after connecting to Oracle with the user and password specified in this parameter. The specified user must have **CREATE SESSION** system privileges. TKPROF will take longer to process a large trace file if the **EXPLAIN** option is used.

- *TABLE*—Specifies the schema and name of the table into which TKPROF temporarily places execution plans before writing them to the output file. If the specified table already exists, TKPROF deletes all rows in the table, uses it for the **EXPLAIN PLAN** command (which writes more rows into the table), and then deletes those rows. If this table does not exist, TKPROF creates it, uses it, and then drops it. The specified user must be able to issue **INSERT**, **SELECT**, and **DELETE** statements against the table. If the table does not already exist, the user must also be able to issue **CREATE TABLE** and **DROP TABLE** statements. For the privileges to issue these statements, see the Oracle8 *Server SQL Reference*. This option allows multiple individuals to run TKPROF concurrently with the same user in the **EXPLAIN** value.

These individuals can specify different **TABLE** values and avoid destructively interfering with each other's processing on the temporary plan table.

If you use the **EXPLAIN** parameter without the **TABLE** parameter, TKPROF uses the table **prof$plan_table** in the schema of the user specified by the **EXPLAIN** parameter. If you use the **TABLE** parameter without the **EXPLAIN** parameter, TKPROF ignores the **TABLE** parameter.

- *INSERT*—Creates a SQL script that stores the trace file statistics in the database. TKPROF creates this script with the name filename3. This script creates a table and inserts a row of statistics for each traced SQL statement into the table.

- *SYS*—Enables and disables the listing of SQL statements issued by the user SYS or recursive SQL statements into the output file. The default value of **YES** causes TKPROF to list these statements. The value of **NO** causes TKPROF to omit them. Note that this parameter does not affect the optional SQL script. The SQL script always inserts statistics for all traced SQL statements, including recursive SQL statements.

- *SORT*—Sorts the traced SQL statements in descending order of the specified sort option before listing them into the output file. If more than one option is specified, the output is sorted in descending order by the sum of the values specified in the sort options. If you omit this parameter, TKPROF lists statements into the output file in order of first use.

The sort options are as follows:

- *PRSCNT*—Number of times parsed.

- *PRSCPU*—CPU time spent parsing.

- *PRSELA*—Elapsed time spent parsing.

- *PRSDSK*—Number of physical reads from disk during parse.

- *PRSMIS*—Number of consistent mode block reads during parse.

- *PRSCU*—Number of current mode block reads during parse.

- *PRSMIS*—Number of library cache misses during parse.

- **EXECNT**—Number of executes.

- **EXECPU**—CPU time spent executing.

- **EXEELA**—Elapsed time spent executing.

- **EXEDSK**—Number of physical reads from disk during execute.

- **EXEQRY**—Number of consistent mode block reads during execute.

- **EXECU**—Number of current mode block reads during execute.

- **EXEROW**—Number of rows processed during execute.

- **EXEMIS**—Number of library cache misses during execute.

- **FCHCNT**—Number of fetches.

- **FCHCPU**—CPU time spent fetching.

- **FCHELA**—Elapsed time spent fetching.

- **FCHDSK**—Number of physical reads from disk during fetch.

- **FCHQRY**—Number of consistent mode block reads during fetch.

- **FCHCU**—Number of current mode block reads during fetch.

- **FCHROW**—Number of rows fetched.

- **PRINT**—Lists only the first integer sorted SQL statements into the output file. If you omit this parameter, TKPROF lists all traced SQL statements. Note that this parameter does not affect the optional SQL script, which always inserts statistics for all traced SQL statements.

- **RECORD**—Creates a SQL script with the specified file name with all of the nonrecursive SQL in the trace file. This can replay the user events from the trace file.

The **EXPLAIN** Option Of TKPROF

To use the **EXPLAIN** option, you must have resource privilege on a tablespace, so you can create the necessary tables. The command is issued at the operating-system level. You can split the command on multiple lines: In VMS, place a dash at the end of each line; in Unix, you simply place a forward slash (/) character at the end of the line to be continued.

This command generates a file named to whatever you specified the output file to be. If you include the **SORT** qualifier, the output will be sorted accordingly. If you include the **EXPLAIN** qualifier, a temporary table will be created in the user's default tablespace, and the various SQL statements will be "explained" in accordance with the formats of the **EXPLAIN PLAN** command.

TKPROF Statistics

Each line of statistics will correspond to either the parse, execute, or fetch part of the query operation. These parts of a query are defined as:

- *Parse*—The query is translated into an execution plan. If the user doesn't have the proper security or table authorization or the objects in the query don't exist, this step will catch it as well.

- *Execute*—The execution plan is executed against the ORDBMS.

- *Fetch*—In this final step, all rows that satisfy the query are retrieved from the database.

For each step, the following parameters are traced:

- *Count*—The number of times this step was repeated.

- *CPU*—The total CPU time for the step in hundredths of a second.

- *Elapsed*—The total elapsed time for the step in hundredths of a second.

- *Disk*—The total number of database blocks read from disk for the step.

- *Query*—The number of buffers retrieved in a consistent read mode.

- *Current*—The number of buffers retrieved in current mode.

- *Rows*—The number of rows processed during the SQL statement execution step.

Practical Guide To

Tuning Application Statements

- TKPROF Example Tuning Session
- Using The Cost-Based Optimizer
- Example Of Proper Index Use
- Optimizers And **ANALYZE**
- Other Application Tuning Tips
- Using Standalone Explain Plan
- Using The UTLSIDXS Utility
- Using Hints To Force Behavior

TKPROF Example Tuning Session

This section looks at some example outputs from TKPROF using **EXPLAIN**. We will run through some tuning scenarios on an example query. The descriptions for tables being used for these examples are shown in Listing 10.4.

Listing 10.4 Structures of tables used in TKPROF examples.

```
DESC TKP_EXAMPLE
Name                            Null?     Type
------------------------------- --------  ----
USERNAME                        NOT NULL  VARCHAR2(30)
USER_ID                         NOT NULL  NUMBER
PASSWORD                                  VARCHAR2(30)
ACCOUNT_STATUS                  NOT NULL  VARCHAR2(32)
LOCK_DATE                                 DATE
EXPIRY_DATE                               DATE
DEFAULT_TABLESPACE              NOT NULL  VARCHAR2(30)
TEMPORARY_TABLESPACE            NOT NULL  VARCHAR2(30)
CREATED                         NOT NULL  DATE
PROFILE                         NOT NULL  VARCHAR2(30)
EXTERNAL_NAME                             VARCHAR2(4000)

Record count for TKP_EXAMPLE: 21


DESC TKP_EXAMPLE2
Name                            Null?     Type
------------------------------- --------  ----
OWNER                                     VARCHAR2(30)
OBJECT_NAME                               VARCHAR2(128)
OBJECT_TYPE                               VARCHAR2(15)
TABLESPACE_NAME                           VARCHAR2(30)

Record count for TKP_EXAMPLE2: 5113
```

In the first examples, let's look at the TKPROF output from a query using these tables without indexes. Of course, what we expect is that the ORDBMS will do full-table scans no matter how complex the query. Remember, doing a full-table scan isn't always bad; it depends entirely upon the selectivity of your query. If you are returning only a few rows, you are well-advised to use an index. The old rule of thumb is if your query returns less than 10 to 15 percent of rows in the table, use an index.

With the new parallel capabilities in Oracle7 and Oracle8, full-table scans may actually be the fastest method to return data for a broader range of queries. To quote Michael

Abby, Author, Lecturer, and Consultant, in a speech during the 1997 IOUG-A Alive! in Dallas, Texas, "Table Scan is no longer a four-letter word." The **SELECT** statement in Listing 10.5 is a two-table join, stripping out system tables from the two tables in Listing 10.4. Experienced system managers will recognize these tables as copies of portions of the **DBA_USERS**, **DBA_OBJECTS**, and **DBA_TABLES** views. They were created using the **CREATE TABLE** command with the **AS** clause. Listing 10.5 shows an example TKPROF output from a query against these tables with no indexes.

Listing 10.5 Query against example tables with no indexes.

```
select
     username,
     default_tablespace,
     tablespace_name,
     object_name
from
     tkp_example, tkp_example2
where
     username != 'SYS' and
     username != 'SYSTEM' and
     default_tablespace=tablespace_name and
     owner=username
```

call	count	cpu	elapsed	disk	query	current	rows
Parse	1	0.01	0.01	0	0	0	0
Execute	1	0.00	0.00	0	0	0	0
Fetch	57	0.22	0.22	0	28	6	849
total	59	0.23	0.23	0	28	6	849

```
Misses in library cache during parse: 1
Optimizer goal: CHOOSE
Parsing user id: 5  (SYSTEM)
```

Rows	Execution Plan
0	SELECT STATEMENT GOAL: CHOOSE
849	MERGE JOIN
5113	SORT (JOIN)
5113	TABLE ACCESS (FULL) OF 'TKP_EXAMPLE2'
19	SORT (JOIN)
21	TABLE ACCESS (FULL) OF 'TKP_EXAMPLE'
22	

As you can see, the performance isn't as bad as we thought it might be. Even with stripping out the system tables and other objects, 849 rows were still returned. As expected, the query performed two full-table scans. But what are **MERGE JOIN**, **SORT(JOIN)**, etc.? These are part of the execution plan that the parse step generated. In addition to the information presented in Listing 10.5, Oracle8's TKPROF provides the number of misses in the library cache during the parse step, and Oracle7 added a **ROWS** column to the query plan. Table 10.1 lists the possible outputs from the **EXPLAIN** portion of the TKPROF output.

Table 10.1 Possible query plan parts.

Action	What It Means
AND-EQUAL	If the **WHERE** clause contains references to unique indexed columns only, the system will choose to use the **ROWID**s from the indexes to perform the table intersections. This is faster than a full-table scan type of intersection.
CONNECT-BY	Shows up only in queries that use a **CONNECT** clause. When a **CONNECT-BY** is executed, it forces a tree-walk of the table structure to perform the operation.
CONCATENATION	A full union of two or more tables. For small tables, it won't hurt; for large tables, it can kill you.
COUNT	This action happens if the query uses the **COUNT** aggregate to return the number of rows. The **STOPKEY** value, if returned, shows that a **ROWNUM** was used to limit the number of returns.
FILTER	A process by which rows not meeting the selection criteria are removed from the returned set of values.
FIRST ROW	Only the first row of a query was returned. It shows activity with a cursor.
FOR UPDATE	The query operation involved a possible update situation (such as in a form of **SELECT...FOR UPDATE**). This indicates that the rows involved were write-locked during the operation.
INDEX	A query used an index to resolve the (**UNIQUE** or **RANGE SCAN**) needed values. The **UNIQUE** qualifier shows that the index was scanned for specific unique values. The **RANGE** qualifier shows that a specific range of values was searched, such as that specified in a **BETWEEN** or less-than/greater-than construct. The **RANGE SCAN** may also have the **DESCENDING** qualifier.

(continued)

Table 10.1 Possible query plan parts (continued).

Action	What It Means
INTERSECTION	The query retrieved the rows from the tables in the query that were common to each of the tables based on the conditions in the **WHERE** clause. The rows are sorted.
MERGE JOIN (OUTER)	Two sorted sets of operations were joined to resolve the query. The **OUTER** qualifier shows that an outer join was performed.
MINUS	An **INTERSECTION** type operation was performed, but instead of similar rows being returned, only rows that didn't match the specified criteria were returned.
NESTED LOOPS (OUTER)	For each of the first child operations, one or more of the other child operations that follow it were performed. The **OUTER** qualifier signifies that an outer join was performed between the results.
PROJECTION	A subset of a table's columns was returned.
REMOTE	A retrieval from other than the current database was performed to resolve the query.
SEQUENCE	A sequence was accessed during a query.
SORT	A query used one of the ordering clauses (**UNIQUE, GROUP BY, JOIN**). The type of clause will be listed as a **ORDER BY, AGGREGATE** qualifier.
TABLE ACCESS (by ROWID)	A table access was performed. Some queries **FULL, CLUSTER, HASH** can be resolved by an index scan only. The type of access performed is shown by the included qualifier. **ROWID** is generally the fastest form of table access and shows an index scan was also used.
UNION	A retrieval of unique rows from each table was performed with the duplicates removed from the output.
VIEW	The query accessed a view to resolve the query.

Let's look at this first query's **EXPLAIN** output.

Execution plan:

- **MERGE JOIN**—Shows that the results from the following operations are merged.

- **SORT (JOIN)**—Shows that the results are sorted before being passed to the **MERGE**.

- **TABLE ACCESS (FULL)** of **tkp_example2**—Indicates the full table was scanned.

- **SORT (JOIN)**—Shows that the results are sorted before being passed to the **MERGE**.

- **TABLE ACCESS (FULL)** of **tkp_example**—Indicates the full table was scanned.

What does this tell us? First, both tables were fully scanned to retrieve the rows that met the **WHERE** clause's criteria. Next, the results from each were sorted. Finally, the results were merged based on the selection criteria. Can these results be improved upon for this type of query? Let's add some indexes (shown in Listing 10.6) and find out.

I've tried to ensure that the indexes have high selectivity and that columns most accessed in the tables are the leading portion of one or more indexes. Let's reissue the **SELECT** from Listing 10.5 and see what happens.

Listing 10.6 Indexes added to tables from Listing 10.4.

```
SQL> CREATE  UNIQUE INDEX TKP_EXP_INDEX

   2  ON TKP_EXAMPLE(
     USERNAME,
     DEFAULT_TABLESPACE,
     TEMPORARY_TABLESPACE);

SQL> CREATE  UNIQUE INDEX TKP_EXP_INDEX2
   2  ON TKP_EXAMPLE(
       TEMPORARY_TABLESPACE,
       USERNAME,
       DEFAULT_TABLESPACE);

SQL> CREATE  UNIQUE INDEX TKP_EXP_INDEX3

   2  ON TKP_EXAMPLE(
       DEFAULT_TABLESPACE,
       TEMPORARY_TABLESPACE,
       USERNAME);
```

```
SQL> CREATE UNIQUE INDEX TKP_EXP2_INDEX ON
  2 TKP_EXAMPLE2(
     OWNER,
     OBJECT_NAME
     OBJECT_TYPE);

SQL> CREATE UNIQUE INDEX TKP_EXP2_INDEX2 ON
  2 TKP_EXAMPLE2(
     OWNER,
     TABLESPACE_NAME,
     OBJECT_NAME,
     OBJECT_TYPE);

SQL> CREATE UNIQUE INDEX TKP_EXP2_INDEX3 ON
  2 TKP_EXAMPLE2(
     TABLESPACE_NAME,
     OWNER,
     OBJECT_NAME,
     OBJECT_TYPE);
```

Listing 10.7 shows the result of a query using the indexes.

Listing 10.7 The results on the query from Listing 10.5, with indexes.

call	count	cpu	elapsed	disk	query	current	rows
Parse	1	0.00	0.00	0	0	0	0
Execute	1	0.00	0.00	0	0	0	0
Fetch	57	0.38	0.38	0	6932	3	849
total	59	0.38	0.38	0	6932	3	849

```
Misses in library cache during parse: 0
Optimizer goal: CHOOSE
Parsing user id: 5  (SYSTEM)

Rows     Execution Plan
-------  ---------------------------------------------------
     0   SELECT STATEMENT   GOAL: CHOOSE
   849   NESTED LOOPS
  5113    TABLE ACCESS (FULL) OF 'TKP_EXAMPLE2'
  2738    INDEX (RANGE SCAN) OF 'TMP_EXP_INDEX' (UNIQUE)
```

As you can see, the indexes didn't improve performance; in fact, they made it worse. A key indicator that something is wrong is that the current parameter jumped by several orders of magnitude. This is an example of a query that returns more than 15 percent of a table.

How can you restore performance? If you use the **NOT IN** or **LIKE** clause instead of the comparison operators (!=, =), are indexes used? Look at the same query, with the **NOT** clause replacing != in the **SELECT** statement. Listing 10.8 shows the TKPROF results from this query. Did performance improve? No. In fact, the results are almost identical—even down to the execution plan. **NOT** and != are treated identically.

Listing 10.8   Results of replacing != with a NOT IN.

```
select
        username,
        default_tablespace,
        tablespace_name,
        object_name
from
        tkp_example, tkp_example2
where
        username not in ('SYS','SYSTEM') and
        default_tablespace=tablespace_name and
        owner=username
```

call	count	cpu	elapsed	disk	query	current	rows
Parse	1	0.01	0.01	0	0	0	0
Execute	1	0.00	0.00	0	0	0	0
Fetch	57	0.33	0.33	0	6932	3	849
total	59	0.34	0.34	0	6932	3	849

```
Misses in library cache during parse: 1
Optimizer goal: CHOOSE
Parsing user id: 5  (SYSTEM)

Rows     Execution Plan
-------  -----------------------------------------------------
      0  SELECT STATEMENT   GOAL: CHOOSE
    849   NESTED LOOPS
   5113    TABLE ACCESS (FULL) OF 'TKP_EXAMPLE2'
   2738    INDEX (RANGE SCAN) OF 'TMP_EXP_INDEX' (UNIQUE)
```

Why are the results the same for the queries in Listings 10.7 and 10.8? In the query in Listing 10.8, the controlling table is **tkp_example2**. The **NOT** doesn't affect the **tkp_example2** table, which was already using a full-table scan. What happens if you replace the = operator with a **LIKE** statement? Listing 10.9 shows the results.

Listing 10.9   Results of replacing = with LIKE.

```
select
        username,
        default_tablespace,
        tablespace_name,
        object_name
from
        tkp_example, tkp_example2
where
        username not in ('SYS','SYSTEM') and
        default_tablespace like tablespace_name and
        owner like username
```

call	count	cpu	elapsed	disk	query	current	rows
Parse	1	0.00	0.00	0	0	0	0
Execute	1	0.00	0.00	0	0	0	0
Fetch	57	0.56	0.56	1	6932	3	849
total	59	0.56	0.56	1	6932	3	849

```
Misses in library cache during parse: 1
Optimizer goal: CHOOSE
Parsing user id: 5  (SYSTEM)
```

```
Rows      Execution Plan
-------   --------------------------------------------------
      0   SELECT STATEMENT    GOAL: CHOOSE
    849     NESTED LOOPS
   5113       TABLE ACCESS (FULL) OF 'TKP_EXAMPLE2'
  19866       INDEX (RANGE SCAN) OF 'TMP_EXP_INDEX3' (UNIQUE)
```

Even by replacing = with **LIKE**, you have not forced full-table scans, and performance still isn't as good as it is with the original nonindexed tables. The index scanned was changed from **tkp_exp_index** to **tkp_exp_index3**. The performance is still poor, because for each row of the **tkp_example2** table, there is a scan of the **tkp_exp_index3** index, with the scan's rejecting tables owned by SYS and SYSTEM. Notice the increase in CPU and elapsed time. This increase is a result of the increased number of index scans.

To achieve the results from the first query, supposedly you can defeat the use of indexes by adding a 0 to a number column or concatenating a **NULL** to a character column. Let's see if we can get back to the performance we want to achieve. First, take a look at Listing 10.10.

Listing 10.10 Use of NULL concatenation to defeat indexes.

```
select
        username,
        default_tablespace,
        tablespace_name,
        object_name
from
        tkp_example, tkp_example2
where
        username not in ('SYS','SYSTEM') and
        default_tablespace||''=tablespace_name and
        owner||''=username
```

call	count	cpu	elapsed	disk	query	current	rows
Parse	1	0.00	0.00	0	0	00	
Execute	1	0.00	0.00	0	0	0	0
Fetch	54	0.51	0.51	0	10101	3	849
total	56	0.51	0.51	0	10101	3849	

```
Misses in library cache during parse: 0
Optimizer goal: CHOOSE
Parsing user id: 5  (SYSTEM)
```

Rows	Execution Plan
0	SELECT STATEMENT GOAL: CHOOSE
849	NESTED LOOPS
5113	TABLE ACCESS (FULL) OF 'TKP_EXAMPLE2'
8531	INDEX (RANGE SCAN) OF 'TMP_EXP_INDEX' (UNIQUE)

Listing 10.10 still uses the index. Notice in the last section of the **WHERE** clause that the order compares **OWNER** to **USERNAME**. This causes the **tkp_example2** table to drive the query. If you switch the order of this comparison, you can use the shorter table **tkp_example** instead of **tkp_example2**. The index is still used, but the shorter table significantly reduces the query execution time. Listing 10.11 demonstrates this.

Listing 10.11 Results of switching the WHERE order.

```
select
        username,
        default_tablespace,
        tablespace_name,
        object_name
```

```
from
        tkp_example, tkp_example2
where
        username not in ('SYS','SYSTEM') and
        default_tablespace||''=tablespace_name and
        username||''=owner
```

call	count	cpu	elapsed	disk	query	current	rows
Parse	1	0.00	0.00	0	0	0	0
Execute	1	0.00	0.00	0	0	0	0
Fetch	54	0.03	0.14	9	101	3	810
total	56	0.03	0.14	9	101	3	810

As you can see, performance is back to the levels you had before you created the indexes. Did the use of **NULL** concatenation really affect performance for this query? Leaving the **WHERE** clause the same, go back to the standard comparison, and see if the results change. Listing 10.12 shows this new query.

Listing 10.12 Effects of the switched WHERE clause and no NULL concatenation.

```
select
        username,
        default_tablespace,
        tablespace_name,
        object_name
from
        tkp_example, tkp_example2
where
        username not in ('SYS','SYSTEM') and
        default_tablespace=tablespace_name and
        username=owner
```

call	count	cpu	elapsed	disk	query	current	rows
Parse	1	0.01	0.01	0	0	0	0
Execute	1	0.00	0.00	0	0	0	0
Fetch	57	0.35	0.35	0	6932	3	849
total	59	0.36	0.36	0	6932	3	849

```
Misses in library cache during parse: 1
Optimizer goal: CHOOSE
Parsing user id: 5  (SYSTEM)
```

```
Rows       Execution Plan
-------    ------------------------------------------------------
      0    SELECT STATEMENT    GOAL: CHOOSE
    849      NESTED LOOPS
   5113        TABLE ACCESS (FULL) OF 'TKP_EXAMPLE2'
   2738        INDEX (RANGE SCAN) OF 'TMP_EXP_INDEX' (UNIQUE)
```

The results look virtually identical to those we had before we switched the **WHERE** clause. For this type of statement, the best course is to defeat as many indexes as possible and force execution driven by the shortest table.

Using The Cost-Based Optimizer

In Oracle7 and Oracle8, the cost-based optimizer is also available. To use this optimizer, you should analyze all tables in the application that contain data. For larger tables, consider sampling only about 20 percent of the rows. For small tables, analyze the entire table. The example here will analyze the entire table. Using the worst-performing query, from Listing 10.9, we will see what results we get with the optimizer using cost- instead of rule-based optimization. Listing 10.13 shows the results from using cost-based optimization.

Listing 10.13   Example using the cost-based optimizer.
```
select
        username,
        default_tablespace,
        tablespace_name,
        object_name
from
        tkp_example, tkp_example2
where
        username not in ('SYS','SYSTEM') and
        default_tablespace like tablespace_name and
        owner like username
```

call	count	cpu	elapsed	disk	query	current	rows
Parse	1	0.01	0.01	0	0	0	0
Execute	1	0.00	0.00	0	0	0	0
Fetch	57	0.55	0.55	0	588	57	849
total	59	0.56	0.56	0	588	57	849

```
Misses in library cache during parse: 1
Optimizer goal: CHOOSE
Parsing user id: 5  (SYSTEM)


Rows     Execution Plan
-------  --------------------------------------------------
      0  SELECT STATEMENT    GOAL: CHOOSE
    849    NESTED LOOPS
     22      INDEX GOAL: ANALYZED (RANGE SCAN) OF 'TMP_EXP_INDEX' (UNIQUE)
  97147    TABLE ACCESS    GOAL: ANALYZED (FULL) OF 'TKP_EXAMPLE2'
```

The cost-based optimizer does a good job of performing optimization if its statistics are good. The performance here is similar to mid-range performance; notice, however, that the table scans of **tkp_example2** were excessive.

Again, this underscores the need to understand the application, the size and use of its tables, and how its indexes are constructed. If the DBA doesn't understand the application, the tuning of the application should be the developer's job, with the DBA assisting. Even though the cost-based optimizer improved performance, it still didn't do as good a job as an experienced DBA and the rule-based optimizer for this query.

Example Of Proper Index Use

When do indexes do any good? If the query returns a small percentage of the table values, an index will improve performance. An example of a restricted query with no index is shown in Listing 10.14.

Listing 10.14   Restricted query with full-table scans (no indexes).

```
select
        username,
        default_tablespace,
        tablespace_name,
        object_name
from
        tkp_example,
        tkp_example2
where
        username='SYSTEM' and
        default_tablespace=tablespace_name and
        owner=username
```

```
call      count    cpu   elapsed    disk    query    current       rows
------    ------  ------  --------  ------  --------  ----------  ----------
Parse         1    0.00     0.00        0         0           0           0
Execute       1    0.00     0.00        0         0           0           0
Fetch         2    0.16     0.16        0        28           6          25
------    ------  ------  --------  ------  --------  ----------  ----------
total         4    0.16     0.16        0        28           6          25
```

```
Misses in library cache during parse: 1
Optimizer goal: CHOOSE
Parsing user id: 5  (SYSTEM)
```

```
Rows       Execution Plan
-------    ---------------------------------------------------------
      0    SELECT STATEMENT   GOAL: CHOOSE
     25     MERGE JOIN
   5113      SORT (JOIN)
   5113       TABLE ACCESS (FULL) OF 'TKP_EXAMPLE2'
      1      SORT (JOIN)
     21       TABLE ACCESS (FULL) OF 'TKP_EXAMPLE'
```

Does adding indexes improve query performance? Look at Listing 10.15.

Listing 10.15 Same query as Listing 10.14, but using indexes.

```
select
        username,
        default_tablespace,
        tablespace_name,
        object_name
from
        tkp_example,
        tkp_example2
where
        username='SYSTEM' and
        default_tablespace=tablespace_name and
        owner=username
```

```
call      count    cpu   elapsed    disk    query    current       rows
------    ------  ------  --------  ------  --------  ----------  ----------
Parse         1    0.00     0.00        0         0           0           0
Execute       1    0.00     0.00        0         0           0           0
Fetch         2    0.00     0.00        0         5           0          25
------    ------  ------  --------  ------  --------  ----------  ----------
total         4    0.00     0.00        0         5           0          25
```

```
Misses in library cache during parse: 0
Optimizer goal: CHOOSE
Parsing user id: 5  (SYSTEM)

Rows     Execution Plan
-------  -------------------------------------------------------
      0  SELECT STATEMENT   GOAL: CHOOSE
     25  NESTED LOOPS
      2    INDEX (RANGE SCAN) OF 'TKP_EXP_INDEX' (UNIQUE)
     26    INDEX (RANGE SCAN) OF 'TKP_EXP2_INDEX3' (UNIQUE)
```

The performance gains in Listing 10.15, even for these small tables, is rather large—especially considering the number of rows processed per step. An additional indicator of problems with a query is a high current-to-rows ratio. If this value exceeds 15, the query needs tuning.

What has this exercise taught you? First, statement tuning is complex. The optimizer built in to the SQL processor makes choices based on built-in optimization rules, which, in turn, are based on statement rank for the rule-based optimizer, or on cost for the cost-based optimizer. At times, the Oracle cost-based optimizer doesn't always use the right index or truly optimize the statement.

For unrestricted queries that return most, if not all, of the values in a table or group of tables, use methods to restrict the use of indexes as much as possible. With unrestricted queries, start the **WHERE** clause by restricting the values to be retrieved as much as possible and as rapidly as possible. Try to get full-table scans on small tables first, and use their results to search other tables.

There is some debate as to whether placing the small table as the controlling table does really improve performance. If the small table can be completely cached in memory, driving from the larger table may make sense. This is because multiblock reads can be used rather than random reads, which may reread the same block several times. This would have the effect of reducing time-consuming physical block reads for the query. Because this will be application and index controlled, in situations where this happens, use TKPROF to find out the facts before simply following a possibly outmoded rule.

Indexing Guidelines

For restricted queries that retrieve a small percentage of the table's entries, create indexes that will assist the query. The guidelines for indexing columns follow.

Create indexes for columns that:

- are used frequently in **WHERE** clauses
- are used frequently in **MIN** or **MAX** selects
- are used to join tables
- have high selectivity

Remember, you can concatenate two low-selectivity columns to form a higher-selectivity index than either column has singly.

Don't create indexes for columns that:

- don't have high selectivity
- have columns in small tables (fewer than five blocks)
- have columns that are frequently modified

Remember, you never get something for nothing. The more indexes you have, the longer the inserts, updates, and deletes will take. Optimizing queries doesn't gain you much if you pay a stiff penalty for update activity.

Concatenated indexes are used only when the predicate value is equality (i.e., e.jobname = f.jobname). The full key is used only if all the concatenated values are referenced in the **WHERE** clause. If the concatenated key is used, only the leading edge of the columns are used. The new index type, bitmapped, should be used on low-cardinality data where possible, if that data is frequently accessed

It would be wonderful if the rules for optimizing your tables, indexes, and queries could be simply stated and listed and you could be guaranteed that your application would run as hoped if they were followed. Unfortunately, this is not the case. Just when you think you have the proper cast on optimization, Oracle will release a new version that throws a monkey wrench into your logic and makes you start again. As a DBA, you will have to keep abreast of changes to Oracle and filter the new ways of optimization down to the developers.

Query Paths And Ranks

The paths a query can take are ranked according to speed—the lower the rank, the higher the speed. The paths for the rule-based optimizer are shown in Table 10.2.

Table 10.2   Path ranks used by the rule-based optimizer.

Rank	Path
1	Single row by **ROWID**
2	Single row by cluster join
3	Single row by hash cluster key with unique or primary key
4	Single row by unique or primary key
5	Cluster join
6	Hash cluster key
7	Indexed cluster key
8	Composite index
9	Single-column index
10	Bounded range search on indexed columns
11	Unbounded range search on indexed columns
12	Sort-merge join
13	**MAX** or **MIN** on indexed column
14	**ORDER BY** indexed columns
15	Full-table scan

Optimizers And **ANALYZE**

Under Oracle7, the optimizer uses cost-based optimization if any table in the query has been analyzed. However, through the use of hints, it can be forced to use rule-based optimization. Cost-based optimization assigns a cost to each possible execution path, based on data distribution statistics for the objects used in the SQL statement being optimized. These statistics are loaded into the various object tables and views using the **ANALYZE** command.

Use Of **ANALYZE**

For various applications, you must run the **ANALYZE** command periodically, perhaps based on table growth. In systems using similar schemes, the analyzer had to be run for each 30-percent change in a table's contents. Note that this is for a change in contents, not just size. If a table has a fairly constant size, but its contained data is altered frequently, thus affecting the row size and index structure, then **ANALYZE** needs to be run on it as well. You can build a simple script using dynamic SQL that will analyze all the tables for a specific user. The script will resemble one of those in Listing 10.16.

Listing 10.16   Scripts to analyze tables and schemas.

Script to create a procedure for single table analysis:

```
CREATE OR REPLACE PROCEDURE analyze_table(table_name in VARCHAR2) AS
CURSOR get_index(tab_name varchar2) IS
    SELECT index_name FROM user_indexes
    WHERE table_name=tab_name;
i_name         index_stats.name%TYPE;
i_stats index_stats%ROWTYPE;
cur1 INTEGER;
cur2 INTEGER;
processed INTEGER;
com_strng VARCHAR2(90);
BEGIN
    com_strng:='ANALYZE TABLE '||table_name||' ESTIMATE STATISTICS SAMPLE 15
PERCENT';
    cur1:=dbms_sql.open_cursor;
    dbms_sql.parse(cur1,com_strng,dbms_sql.v7);
    processed:=dbms_sql.execute(cur1);
    dbms_sql.close_cursor(cur1);
    OPEN get_index(table_name);
    FETCH get_index INTO i_name;
    LOOP
            EXIT WHEN get_index%NOTFOUND;
            cur2:=dbms_sql.open_cursor;
            com_strng:='ANALYZE INDEX '||i_name||' VALIDATE STRUCTURE';
            dbms_sql.parse(cur2,com_strng,dbms_sql.v7);
            processed:=dbms_sql.execute(cur2);
            dbms_sql.close_cursor(cur2);
            INSERT INTO ind_stat_tab SELECT * FROM index_stats;
    END LOOP;
END;
/

Script to use DBMS_UTILITY package to analyze all schema in the database:

SET HEADING OFF VERIFY OFF PAGES 0 FEEDBACK OFF
TTITLE OFF
SPOOL analz_sch.sql
```

```
SELECT DISTINCT 'EXECUTE dbms_utility.analyze_schema('||chr(39)||
owner||chr(39)||','||chr(39)||'&METHOD'||chr(39)||','||&NUM_OF_ROWS||',
&PERCENT_TO_USE);'
FROM dba_tables WHERE owner NOT IN ('SYS','SYSTEM')
/
SPOOL OFF
SPOOL analz_sch.log
SET ECHO ON
START analz_sch.sql
SET ECHO OFF
SPOOL OFF
```

Procedure to analyze tables when contents increase/decrease >30%:

```
CREATE OR REPLACE PROCEDURE check_tables (owner_name in varchar2) AS

CURSOR get_tab_count (own varchar2) IS
        SELECT table_name, nvl(num_rows,1)
        FROM dba_tables
        WHERE owner = upper(own);

tab_name   VARCHAR2(32);
rows     INTEGER;
string VARCHAR2(255);
cur      INTEGER;
ret      INTEGER;
row_count INTEGER;
com_string   VARCHAR2(255);

BEGIN
OPEN get_tab_count (owner_name);
LOOP
        FETCH get_tab_count INTO tab_name, rows;
        IF rows=0 THEN
          rows:=1;
        END IF;
EXIT WHEN get_tab_count%NOTFOUND;
dbms_output.put_line('Table name: '||tab_name||' rows: '||to_char(rows));
com_string :=
        'SELECT COUNT(*) from '||tab_name;
   cur := dbms_sql.open_cursor;
   dbms_sql.parse(cur,com_string,dbms_sql.v7);
   dbms_sql.define_column(cur,1,row_count);
   ret := dbms_sql.execute(cur);
   IF dbms_sql.fetch_rows(cur)>0 THEN
    dbms_sql.column_value(cur,1,row_count);
   END IF;
   dbms_sql.close_cursor(cur);
```

```
        IF row_count=0 THEN
            row_count:=1;
        END IF;
dbms_output.put_line('Row count for '||tab_name||': '||TO_CHAR(row_count));
dbms_output.put_line('Ratio: '||to_char(row_count/rows));
        IF ABS((row_count/rows))>1.42 THEN
            string :=
    'ANALYZE TABLE '||tab_name||' ESTIMATE STATISTICS SAMPLE 20 PERCENT';
            cur := dbms_sql.open_cursor;
            dbms_sql.parse(cur,string,dbms_sql.v7);
            ret := dbms_sql.execute(cur)   ;
            dbms_sql.close_cursor(cur);
            dbms_output.put_line(' Table: '||tab_name||' had to be analyzed.');
        END IF;
END LOOP;
CLOSE get_tab_count;

EXCEPTION
    WHEN OTHERS THEN
        raise_application_error(-20002,'Error in analyze: '||to_char(sqlcode)||' on
'||tab_name,TRUE);
        IF dbms_sql.is_open(cur) THEN
          dbms_sql.close_cursor(cur);
        END IF;
END;
/
```

The DBA needs to watch the growth of the main tables in an application. The reports provided in the Visual Dictionary Lite program on the enclosed CD-ROM should provide the necessary data. If the DBA isn't using an automated script, such as the one in Listing 10.16, once the required threshold for percent change is reached, the **ANALYZE** command should be run. The **ANALYZE** command format follows:

```
>---- ANALYZE--TABLE ------------------- table---- COMPUTE ----------STATISTICS;->
          |- INDEX ----|  |-schema.-||-index--|  |--ESTIMATE - SAMPLE  n--------|
          |-CLUSTER-|                |-cluster-|                      |--ROWS--|
                                                                  |-PERCENT--|
```

Where:

COMPUTE   Calculates statistics on all rows, this may take a long period of time.

ESTIMATE   Calculates statistics based on the **SAMPLE** clause. If you don't
            specify the number of rows or a value for **PERCENT** 1064 rows
            are sampled. If over 50 percent of the table is specified he entire
            table is computed.

The results are loaded into the SYS tables **dba_tables**, **dba_indexes**, or **dba_clusters** and can be examined via the **DBA**, **USER**, or **ALL** views. For an excellent discussion of how Oracle7 uses cost-based optimization, read Chapter 13 of the *Oracle7 Server Concepts Manual*. Note that detailed index statistics are loaded into the **INDEX_STATS** single-row view for each index analyzed. If you want this data preserved, you will need to analyze and then pull the statistics out of the **INDEX_STATS** view into a temporary table.

Other Application Tuning Tips

There are probably as many tuning tips for various Oracle application problems as there are leaves in a b-tree index for a million row table, here are a few of the heavy-hitters:

- *Use PL/SQL to speed processing*—A PL/SQL statement is parsed once and allows loop processing. This reduces re-parsing. The statements in a PL/SQL block are passed at the same time, reducing the number of ORDBMS calls.

- *Use sequence generators*—Sequence numbers are cached, speeding access to numbers used for keys or in applications for tracking entries. This eliminates the SQL calls used in a trigger that calls up the current **MAX** value and then increments it by 1.

- *Use clusters for frequently joined tables*—However, if the tables are frequently updated, clustering can have a negative effect on performance. Use the TKPROF tool to check a test database that is clustered versus one that is not clustered.

- *Use array processing in applications where multiple values are required*—This will reduce ORDBMS calls.

Using Standalone Explain Plan

The Explain Plan program can be used in standalone fashion without the TKPROF application. To use Explain Plan in this way, you must create a plan table in your tablespace. You can do so with the supplied SQL script UTLXPLAN.SQL, which is located in the directory pointed at by the ORA_RDBMS logical in VMS, or in the oracle/rdbms/admin directory on most Unix systems.

The UTLXPLAN.SQL procedure creates the **plan_table**. As an alternative, you can create a table with any name you choose, but the table must have the columns and datatypes shown in Listing 10.17.

Listing 10.17   Contents of the Explain Plan table.

Characteristics of file to hold EXPLAIN PLAN output:

```
CREATE TABLE plan_table
    (statement_id      VARCHAR2(30),
    timestamp          DATE,
    remarks            VARCHAR2(80),
    operation          VARCHAR2(30),
    options            VARCHAR2(30),
    object_node        VARCHAR2(128),
    object_owner       VARCHAR2(30),
    object_name        VARCHAR2(30),
    object_instance    NUMERIC,
    object_type        VARCHAR2(30),
    optimizer          VARCHAR2(255),
    search_columns     NUMERIC,
    id                 NUMERIC,
    parent_id          NUMERIC,
    position           NUMERIC,
    partition_start    NUMERIC,
    partition_stop     NUMERIC,
    partition_id       NUMERIC,
    cost               NUMERIC,
    cardinality        NUMERIC,
    bytes              NUMERIC,
    other_tag          VARCHAR2(255)
    other              LONG);
```

The **plan_table** used by the **EXPLAIN PLAN** command contains the following columns:

- **statement_id**—The value of the option **statement_id** parameter specified in the **EXPLAIN PLAN** statement.

- **timestamp**—The date and time when the **EXPLAIN PLAN** statement was issued.

- **remarks**—Any comment (up to 80 bytes) you wish to associate with each step of the Explain Plan. If you need to add or change a remark on any row of the **plan_table**, use the **update**.

- **operation**—The name of the internal operation performed in this step. In the first row generated for a statement, the column contains one of the following values:

  DELETE STATEMENT

  INSERT STATEMENT

  SELECT STATEMENT

  UPDATE STATEMENT

- **options**—A variation on the operation described in the **operation** column.

- **object_node**—The name of the database link used to reference the object (a table name or view name). For local queries using the parallel query option, this column describes the order in which output from operations is consumed.

- **object_owner**—The name of the user who owns the schema containing the table or index.

- **object_name**—The name of the table or index.

- **object_instance**—A number corresponding to the ordinal position of the object as it appears in the original statement. The numbering proceeds from left to right, outer to inner, with respect to the original statement text. Note that view expansion will result in unpredictable numbers.

- **object_type**—A modifier that provides descriptive information about the object. For example, **NON-UNIQUE** for indexes.

- **optimizer**—The current mode of the optimizer.

- **search_columns**—Not currently used.

- **id**—A number assigned to each step in the execution plan.

- **parent_id**—The ID of the next execution step that operates on the output of the ID step.

- **position**—The order of processing for steps that all have the **parent_id**.

- **partition_start**—The **START** partition of a range of accessed partitions.

- **partition_stop**—The **STOP** partition of a range of accessed partitions.

- **partition_id**—The step that has computed the pair of values of the **partition_start** and **partition_stop** columns.

- **cost**—The cost of the operation as estimated by the optimizer's cost-based approach. For statements that use the rule-based approach, this column is **NULL**. Cost is not determined for table-access operations. The value of this column does not have any particular unit of measurement; it is merely a weighted value used to compare costs of execution plans.

- **cardinality**—The estimate by the cost-based approach of the number of rows accessed by the operation.

- **bytes**—The estimate by the cost-based approach of the number of bytes accessed by the operation.

- **other**—Other information specific to the execution step that a user may find useful.

- **other_tag**—Describes the contents of the **other** column. See Table 10.3 for more information on the possible values for this column.

Table 10.3 describes the values that may appear in the **other_tag** column.

The TKPROF section lists each combination of **OPERATION** and **OPTION** values produced by the **EXPLAIN PLAN** command and its meaning within an execution plan.

When TKPROF is run using the **EXPLAIN** option, the table is created and dropped automatically. If it is created for use in Explain Plan, it is permanent. The table should have the **DELETE** command issued against it between runs of Explain Plan, or duplicate rows will be inserted into the table and into any output generated, based on the table. Note that both the Precise tool and the Q diagnostic tool included on the enclosed CD-ROM will do Explain Plans of statements. The Precise tool is designed particularly to optimize SQL code.

Once this table is generated, the user issues the **EXPLAIN PLAN** command from within SQL*Plus to generate output to the table. The **EXPLAIN PLAN** command format is

Table 10.3 Values in the other_tag column.

other_tag Text	Interpretation
(blank)	Serial execution.
serial_from_remote	Serial execution at a remote site.
serial_to_parallel	Serial execution; output of step is partitioned or broad cast to parallel query servers.
parallel_to_parallel	Parallel execution; output of step is repartitioned to second set of parallel query servers.
parallel_to_serial	Parallel execution; output of step is returned to serial "query coordinator" process.
parallel_combined_with_parent	Parallel execution; output of step goes to next step in same parallel process. No interprocess communication to parent.
parallel_combined_with_child	Parallel execution; input of step comes from prior step in same parallel process. No interprocess communication from child.

```
EXPLAIN PLAN [SET STATEMENT_ID = 'descriptor']
               [INTO table]
FOR SQL statement;
```

where:

- **descriptor** is a short name to identify the SQL statement. If not specified, the entire statement will be used as the identifier.

- **table** is where it is named, if other than the **plan_table** is used.

- **SQL statement** is the SQL statement to analyze.

An example of the use of the **EXPLAIN PLAN** command is shown in Listing 10.18.

Listing 10.18 Example use of the EXPLAIN PLAN command.
```
SQL> explain plan
  2  set statement_id='EXP PLAN EXAMPLE'
  3  for
  4  select t.owner,t.table_name,t.tablespace_name,
```

```
 5    i.index_name,i.tablespace_name
 6    from tkp_example t, tkp_example2 i
 7    where
 8    t.table_name=i.table_name and
 9    t.owner not in ('SYS','SYSTEM')
10*
```

Explained.

To get the results of the **EXPLAIN PLAN** command, the table **plan_table**, or what-ever table was specified in the **EXPLAIN PLAN** command, must be queried. Let's look at a simple query of this table for the previous SQL statement. The query and its output are shown in Listing 10.19.

Listing 10.19 Example output from query of the plan_table.
```
SQL> column position format 99999999
SQL> column object_name format a12
SQL> column options format a7
SQL> column operation format a15
SQL> select operation, options, object_name, id,  parent_id,
  2  position
  3  from plan_table
  4  where statement_id='EXP PLAN EXAMPLE'
  5* order by id
```

OPERATION	OPTIONS	OBJECT_NAME	ID	PARENT_ID	POSITION
SELECT STATEMENT			0		
MERGE JOIN			1	0	1
SORT	JOIN		2	1	1
TABLE ACCESS	FULL	TKP_EXAMPLE2	3	2	1
SORT	JOIN		4	1	2
TABLE ACCESS	FULL	TKP_EXAMPLE	5	4	1

```
6 rows selected
```

While this type of query will provide useful information, it leaves the logical ar-rangement of the information retrieved to the user. With use of the padding options and connect features available in SQL, you can generate a pseudo-execu-tion plan comparable to the one generated in TKPROF. The query used for this and the output generated in place of the tabular information in Listing 10.19 are shown in Listing 10.20.

Listing 10.20 shows the result of using the **LEVEL** clause to format the query output.

Listing 10.20   SQL statement to generate an execution plan from the plan_table.

```
SQL> column query_plan format a60
SQL> select lpad(' ',2*level)||operation||' '||object_name query_plan
  2    from plan_table where statement_id is not null
  3    connect by prior id=parent_id
  4    start with id=0;

QUERY_PLAN
------------------------------------------------------------
  SELECT STATEMENT
    MERGE JOIN
      SORT
        TABLE ACCESS TKP_EXAMPLE2
      SORT
        TABLE ACCESS TKP_EXAMPLE

6 rows selected.
```

This new format shown in Listing 10.20 is easier to understand. The TKPROF output for each statement also needs to be reviewed, as was shown in the first part of this chapter. Just because index, rather than table, scans are used doesn't mean the query executed faster. If the index is neither bitmapped nor selective, its use can actually slow a query rather than speed it up. In one case, an index with poor selectivity (low cardinality) forced full-index scans of a more selective index, generating poor performance. Removal of the poor index resulted in a severalfold increase in query speed.

Remember that these plans need to be read from the bottom up—for example, in the plan in Listing 10.20, the **tkp_example** table is accessed and all rows that don't have the OWNER SYS or SYSTEM are retrieved. Then, the **tkp_example2** table is accessed and for each row in the **tkp_example** table, all rows that have matches in the **table_name** column are selected. The results for both accesses are then sorted and merged to form the final output.

The Oracle8 table also has columns to document if partitions are being used, and this data can be added to the select if desired, as well as a number of other columns that you may find useful.

Using The UTLSIDXS Utility

Another tuning tool provided with Oracle is UTLSIDXS. This utility consists of three scripts: UTLSIDXS.SQL, UTLOIDXS.SQL, and UTLDIDXS.SQL under Oracle7 and

Oracle8. These scripts are located in the directory specified in the ORA_RDBMS logical under VMS, in the oracle/rdbms/admin directory on most Unix systems, and in the x:\orant\rdbms80\admin directory on NT 4 (replace the *x* with the drive letter where you installed Oracle). These scripts provide detailed statistics on indexes used for a specific table. The basic scripts haven't changed that much since 1992, with the changes that did occur happening in 1994.

The scripts provide the following functionality:

- *UTLSIDX.SQL*—Starts the UTLOIDXS.SQL script on multiple tables and columns. It requires the input of the table name and the column name. Its main use is to provide the selectivity information on key candidates.

- *UTLOIDXS.SQL*—Called by UTLSIDXS.SQL.

- *UTLDIDXS.SQL*—Run after UTLOIDXS.SQL. It takes the same arguments as UTLSIDX.SQL and can take **%** as a wild-card value. UTLDIDXS.SQL generates a report based on the statistics. The report is shown only on screen. For hard-copy output, you must modify the script to add **SPOOL** and **SPOOL OFF** statements.

Before you can use the scripts, the tables and columns must exist. The scripts are generally used on single-column indexes. To run the scripts on a concatenated index, create a test table consisting of a single column that simulates the concatenated index as a single column. For example, if your index is on **po_num**, **po_date**, create a test table that concatenates these into a single column:

```
CREATE TABLE test_index AS SELECT po_num||po_date  po_ind FROM purchase_order;
```

Once you have created the test table, you run the script the same as if you were analyzing a normal single-column index candidate. This is essentially a three-step process:

1. Choose the candidate columns from the table.

2. Log on to SQL*Plus, and run UTLSIDXS.SQL for entire applications and UTLOIDXS.SQL for single tables, giving UTLOIDXS.SQL the table and column name.

3. Use UTLDIDXS.SQL to generate a report on the index candidate(s).

Listing 10.21 shows an example run of UTLSIDXS, including an example UTLDIDXS report.

Listing 10.21   Example use of UTLSIDXS, UTLOIDXS, and UTLDIDXS.

```
SQL> @c:\orant\rdbms80\admin\utloidxs tkp_example owner


TKP_EXAMPLE OWNER


SQL> @c:\orant\rdbms80\admin\utldidxs tkp_example owner


TAB_NAME                           COL_NAME
------------------------------     -------------------------------
TKP_EXAMPLE                        OWNER


TABLE_NAME     COLUMN_NAME    STAT_NAME                     STAT_VALUE
-------------- -------------- --------------------------    ------------
TKP_EXAMPLE    OWNER          Rows - Null                         0.00
TKP_EXAMPLE    OWNER          Rows - Total                    1,366.00
TKP_EXAMPLE    OWNER          Rows per key - avg                341.50
TKP_EXAMPLE    OWNER          Rows per key - dev                251.68
TKP_EXAMPLE    OWNER          Rows per key - max                658.00
TKP_EXAMPLE    OWNER          Rows per key - min                 42.00
TKP_EXAMPLE    OWNER          Total Distinct Keys                 4.00
TKP_EXAMPLE    OWNER          db_gets_per_key_hit               240.55
TKP_EXAMPLE    OWNER          db_gets_per_key_miss              480.61


TABLE_NAME     COLUMN_NAME    BADNESS    KEYS_COUNT   ROW_PERCENT   KEY_PERCENT
-------------- -----------    ---------  ----------   -----------   -----------
TKP_EXAMPLE    OWNER             658          1          48.17         25.00
TKP_EXAMPLE    OWNER             335          1          24.52         25.00
TKP_EXAMPLE    OWNER             331          1          24.23         25.00
TKP_EXAMPLE    OWNER              42          1           3.08         25.00


SQL> @c:\orant\rdbms80\admin\utloidxs tkp_example object_name


TKP_EXAMPLE     OBJECT_NAME


SQL> @c:\orant\rdbms80\admin\utldidxs tkp_example object_name


TAB_NAME                           COL_NAME
------------------------------     -------------------------------
TKP_EXAMPLE                        OBJECT_NAME


TABLE_NAME     COLUMN_NAME    STAT_NAME                     STAT_VALUE
-----------    -------------- --------------------------    ------------
TKP_EXAMPLE    OBJECT_NAME    Rows - Null                        0.00
TKP_EXAMPLE    OBJECT_NAME    Rows - Total                   1,366.00
```

```
TKP_EXAMPLE   OBJECT_NAME   Rows per key - avg                       1.24
TKP_EXAMPLE   OBJECT_NAME   Rows per key - dev                       0.47
TKP_EXAMPLE   OBJECT_NAME   Rows per key - max                       3.00
TKP_EXAMPLE   OBJECT_NAME   Rows per key - min                       1.00
TKP_EXAMPLE   OBJECT_NAME   Total Distinct Keys                  1,102.00
TKP_EXAMPLE   OBJECT_NAME   db_gets_per_key_hit                      1.04
TKP_EXAMPLE   OBJECT_NAME   db_gets_per_key_miss                     1.41
```

TABLE_NAME	COLUMN_NAME	BADNESS	KEYS_COUNT	ROW_PERCENT	KEY_PERCENT
TKP_EXAMPLE	OBJECT_NAME	3	19	4.17	1.72
TKP_EXAMPLE	OBJECT_NAME	2	226	33.09	20.51
TKP_EXAMPLE	OBJECT_NAME	1	857	62.74	77.77

As you can see from examining the UTLDIDXS reports, **owner** would not make a good index. It has a low selectivity, and its **db_gets_per_key_hits** is 50-percent lower than its **db_gets_per_key_misses**—which means it misses a row twice as much as it finds it. This is further witnessed by its high "badness" (a relative term that shows how well the column will act as an index) of 143 and low **keys_count**, where the badness is low (badness ratings are summarized by the number of keys that exhibit that amount of badness). On the other hand, **table_name** makes a good index because of its high selectivity, its nearly unity hit/miss ratio, and its low badness ratings. How often, however, will you look for a table strictly by its name? What would the performance be if you made a concatenated index of both **owner** and **table_name**? Listing 10.22 shows an example.

Listing 10.22   Example test of a pseudo-concatenated index.

```
SQL> REM CONCAT_INDEX is a table made by selecting
SQL> REM "owner||object_name||object_type"
SQL> REM into the column ONE_COL. The column values are selected from SQL> REM
TKP_EXAMPLE. It demonstrates the performance of a concatenated SQL> REM index on
these three columns.
SQL>
SQL> create table concat_index as
  2  select owner||object_name||object_type one_col
  3* from tkp_example

SQL> @c:\orant\rdbms80\admin\utloidxs concat_index one_col

CONCAT_INDEX     ONE_COL

SQL> @c:\orant\rdbms80\admin\utldidxs concat_index one_col
```

TAB_NAME	COL_NAME
CONCAT_INDEX	ONE_COL

TABLE_NAME	COLUMN_NAME	STAT_NAME	STAT_VALUE
CONCAT_INDEX	ONE_COL	Rows - Null	0.00
CONCAT_INDEX	ONE_COL	Rows - Total	1,366.00
CONCAT_INDEX	ONE_COL	Rows per key - avg	1.00
CONCAT_INDEX	ONE_COL	Rows per key - dev	0.00
CONCAT_INDEX	ONE_COL	Rows per key - max	1.00
CONCAT_INDEX	ONE_COL	Rows per key - min	1.00
CONCAT_INDEX	ONE_COL	Total Distinct Keys	1,366.00
CONCAT_INDEX	ONE_COL	db_gets_per_key_hit	1.00
CONCAT_INDEX	ONE_COL	db_gets_per_key_miss	1.00

TABLE_NAME	COLUMN_NAME	BADNESS	KEYS_COUNT	ROW_PERCENT	KEY_PERCENT
CONCAT_INDEX	ONE_COL	1	1,366	100.00	100.00

By making the same comparisons as with either **owner** or **object_name**, this new concatenated index would perform better than either of the previous single-column indexes. It has the added benefit of allowing you to search on **owner** with no performance penalties. In fact, for a simple query, looking for **owner**'s and **object_name**'s performance should be much better because it can be resolved completely in the index.

Using Hints To Force Behavior

One important feature of Oracle is its ability to issue hints to the optimizer. In Oracle7 and Oracle8, you can tell the optimizer directly to use a specific type of action for your queries. This gives the DBA or application developer more control than was possible in earlier versions. Let's look at how this feature is used.

Hints are enclosed within comments to the SQL commands **DELETE**, **SELECT**, or **UPDATE** or are designated by two dashes and a plus sign. To show the format, only the **SELECT** statement will be used, but the format is identical for all three commands:

```
SELECT              /*+ hint --or-- text */
statement body
```

or

```
SELECT              --+ hint --or-- text
statement body
```

where:

- /* is the comment delimiter.

- + tells Oracle a hint follows; it must come immediately after the /*.

- **hint** is one of the allowed hints.

- **text** is the comment text.

Table 10.4 lists Oracle's hints.

Our dilemma in the first part of this chapter with the stubborn index usage could have been easily solved using hints. You must know the application to be tuned. The DBA can provide guidance to developers, but in all but the smallest development projects, a DBA cannot know everything about each application. The responsibility for application tuning rests solely on the developer's shoulders with help and guidance from the DBA.

Table 10.4 Oracle hints and their meanings.

Hint	Meaning
+	Must be immediately after comment indicator; tells Oracle this is a list of hints.
ALL_ROWS	Use the cost-based approach for best throughput.
CHOOSE	Default. If statistics are available, will use cost; if not, rule.
FIRST_ROWS	Use the cost-based approach for best response time.
RULE	Use rule-based approach. This cancels any other hints specified for this statement. This is not available after Oracle7.
Access method hints:	
CLUSTER(table)	Tells Oracle explicitly to do a cluster scan to access the table.
FULL(table)	Tells the optimizer to do a full scan of the specified table.

(continued)

Table 10.4   Oracle hints and their meanings *(continued).*

Hint	Meaning
HASH(table)	Tells Oracle explicitly to choose the hash access method for the table.
HASH_AJ(table)	Transforms a **NOT IN** subquery to a hash anti-join.
ROWID(table)	Forces a **ROWID** scan of the specified table.
INDEX(table [index])	Forces an index scan of the specified table using the specified index(s). If a list of indexes is specified, the optimizer chooses the one with the lowest cost. If no index is specified, the optimizer chooses the available index for the table with the lowest cost.
INDEX_ASC (table [index])	Same as **INDEX**, except it performs an ascending search of the index chosen. This is functionally identical to the **INDEX** statement.
INDEX_DESC(table [index])	Same as **INDEX**, except it performs a descending search. If more than one table is accessed, this is ignored.
INDEX_COMBINE(table index)	Combines the bitmapped indexes on the table if the cost shows that to do so would give better performance.
INDEX_FFS(table index)	Performs a fast full-index scan rather than a table scan.
MERGE_AJ (table)	Transforms a **NOT IN** subquery into a merge anti-join.
USE_CONCAT	Forces combined **OR** conditions in the **WHERE** clause to be transformed into a compound query using the **UNION ALL** set operator.
AND_EQUAL(table index index [index index index])	This hint causes a merge on several single column indexes. Two must be specified; five can be.
Hints for join orders:	
ORDERED	This hint forces tables to be joined in the order specified. If you know table X has fewer rows, then ordering it first may speed execution in a join.
STAR	Forces the largest table to be joined last using a **nested_loops** join on the index.

(continued)

Table 10.4 Oracle hints and their meanings _(continued)_.

Hint	Meaning
Hints for join operations:	
NO_MERGE (table)	Causes Oracle to join each specified table with another row source without a sort-merge join.
USE_HASH (table)	Causes Oracle to join each specified table with another row source with a hash join.
USE_NL(table)	Forces a nested loop using the specified table as the controlling table.
USE_MERGE(table,[table,...])	Forces a sort-merge-join operation of the specified tables.
Hints for parallel operations:	
APPEND	Specifies that data is to be or not to be.
NOAPPEND	Appended to the end of a file rather than into existing free space. Use only with **INSERT** commands.
NOPARALLEL (table)	Specifies the operation is not to be done in parallel.
PARALLEL(table, instances)	Specifies the operation is to be done in parallel.
PARALLEL_INDEX	Allows parallelization of a fast full-index scan on any index.
Other hints:	
CACHE	Specifies that the blocks retrieved for the table in the hint are placed at the most recently used end of the LRU list when the table is full-table scanned.
NOCACHE	Specifies that the blocks retrieved for the table in the hint are placed at the least recently used end of the LRU list when the table is full-table scanned.
PUSH_SUBQ	Causes nonmerged subqueries to be evaluated at the earliest possible point in the execution plan.

Chapter 11

Database Internals Tuning

Database internals tuning is a complex topic. Every time you think you have Oracle internals figured out, Oracle slips in some new features, takes old ones away, or, just for some perverse form of fun, changes the structures of tried-and-true tables and views. Actually, it is all a secret plot by senior Oracle DBAs and Oracle to maintain job security.

Notes…

Chapter

11

The Internal Tuning Process

This chapter covers one of the more challenging and critical aspects of the DBA's job: analyzing, diagnosing, and fixing performance problems of database internals. Chapter 10 discussed application tuning. Most of the performance gains in an application result from proper database configuration and application tuning. Where you are most vulnerable, however, is in the area of internals tuning. Squeezing that last bit of performance from the database seems to be the one area managers like to focus on (they forget the part about application tuning and now expect you to work miracles) when problems show up.

Once the application is tuned, the DBA's job really begins. Now, you can begin tuning the Oracle system itself to take advantage of the tuned application from Chapter 10. This step of the tuning process is typically a five-part process:

1. *Review and set all initialization parameters for your application and operating system*—
   This step involves reading the operating system's specific release manual and
   database readme files for any new, changed, or improved initialization parameters. Using your knowledge of the number of users, size of the system memory,
   number and configuration of disks, sizing of tables, and other system and application parameters, you must do your best to set all of the initialization parameters
   that will help your system perform better.

2. *Tune memory allocation*—This requires an operating database against which you run various performance-monitoring scripts and tools. Then, you read-just the initialization parameters.

3. *Eliminate I/O bottlenecks*—The third step requires monitoring your disk assets and their performance. Your system administrator will be critical to assuring the success of this step. If you were able to have a hand in designing the system layout, you won't have much I/O-related tuning. Inherited databases (especially those from after-market products) usually require extensive file movements and optimizations, so this step could actually give the most performance gains.

   In one system I inherited, a well-meaning DBA had rebuilt the application indexes by disabling and then reenabling the primary keys, without specifying the location for the indexes. Of course, you will remember what this causes: It results in all of the indexes being placed in the same tablespace as the data tables. Simply moving the indexes to their (empty) tablespace resulted in a performance gain of more than 300 percent (one 30-minute query dropped to less than 1 minute). I was an instant hero. What this anecdote should tell you is this: Carefully examine any inherited database for badly placed indexes, tablespaces, rollback segments, and redo logs. Just putting everything where it should be can provide dramatic improvement in performance for poorly laid-out systems.

4. *Tune resource contention*—Step 4 involves more monitoring with tools or scripts. Contention for system resources (latches, rollbacks, logs, memory, etc.) can be a real performance drain. Always review the alert log for all databases you inherit; they will tell you if there are some forms of contention, such as for redo logs. The scripts that follow in this chapter will help determine if there are other types of contention.

5. *Tune sorts, freelists, and checkpoints*—This step involves monitoring system statistics on a running application. Numerous tools, as well as the scripts included with this section, can tell you if you have problems with sorts, freelists, and checkpoints. Tuning sorts is especially important in DSS and reporting databases. In one case, a 10-minute sort dropped to less than 1 minute by bumping up the **SORT_AREA_SIZE** parameter from 2MB to 3MB, thus preventing disk sorts.

Each of the following sections handles a specific area with reports and scripts to help you monitor your database.

As previously stated, Step 1 involves a review of the initialization parameters. These are documented in the *Oracle8 Server Reference*, Release 8.0, June 1997, Part No. A54645-01.

The INIT<sid>.ORA (Initialization File) Parameters

The most important file as far as database setup and operation is the INIT<sid>.ORA, or initialization file. This file contains the assignments for the database initialization parameters.

Version 7.3 of Oracle has 154 initialization parameters; version 8.0.2 has 184. Table 11.1 is a list of the INIT.ORA parameters, their default values, and descriptions.

Table 11.1 Oracle7 and Oracle8 initialization parameters.

Name	Value	Description
spin_count	2000	amount to spin waiting for a latch
processes	50	user processes
sessions	60	user and system sessions
timed_statistics	FALSE	maintain internal timing statistics
timed_os_statistics*	off	maintain internal OS statistics
resource_limit	FALSE	master switch for resource limit
license_max_sessions	0	maximum number of nonsystem user sessions allowed
license_sessions_warning	0	warning level for number of nonsystem user sessions
lm_procs*	72	number of client processes configured for the lock manager
lm_ress*	6000	number of resources configured for the lock manager
lm_locks*	12000	number of locks configured for the lock manager
parallel_transaction_resource_timeout*	300	global parallel transaction resource deadlock timeout in seconds
cpu_count	1	number of CPUs for this instance
instance_groups*		list of instance group names
event		debug event control - default null string
shared_pool_size	6500000	size in bytes of shared pool
shared_pool_reserved_size	325000	size in bytes of reserved area of shared pool

*New for Oracle8   (continued)

Table 11.1 Oracle7 and Oracle8 initialization parameters (continued).

Name	Value	Description
shared_pool_reserved_min_alloc	5K	minimum allocation size in bytes for reserved area of shared pool
large_pool_size*	0	size in bytes of the large allocation pool
largpool_min_alloc*	16K	minimum allocation size in bytes for the large allocation pool
pre_page_sga	FALSE	pre-page sga for process
lock_name_space*		lock name space used for generating lock names for standby/clone
enqueue_resources	155	resources for enqueues
nls_language		AMERICAN NLS language name
nls_territory		AMERICA NLS territory name
nls_sort		NLS linguistic definition name
nls_date_language		NLS date language name
nls_date_format		NLS Oracle date format
nls_currency		NLS local currency symbol
nls_numeric_characters		NLS numeric characters
nls_iso_currency		NLS ISO currency territory name
disk_asynch_io	TRUE	use asynch I/O for random access devices
tape_asynch_io*	TRUE	use asynch I/O requests for tape devices
dbwr_io_slaves*	0	DBWR I/O slaves
lgwr_io_slaves*	0	LGWR I/O slaves
arch_io_slaves*	0	ARCH I/O slaves
backup_io_slaves*	0	BACKUP I/O slaves
io_min_servers*	2	minimum I/O slaves per instance
db_file_name_convert		datafile name convert pattern and string for standby/clone database
(db_file_standby_name_convert V7)		
log_file_name_convert		logfile name convert pattern and string for standby/clone database
(log_file_standby_name_convert V7)		
db_block_buffers	200	number of database blocks cached in memory
db_block_checksum	FALSE	store checksum in db blocks and check during reads
db_block_size	2048	size of database block in bytes
db_block_checkpoint_batch	8	max number of blocks to checkpoint in a DB Writer I/O
db_block_lru_statistics (slow)	FALSE	maintain buffer cache LRU hits-by-position statistics
db_block_lru_extended_statistics	0	maintain buffer cache LRU statistics for last N blocks discarded
db_block_lru_latches	1	number of LRU latches
max_commit_propagation_delay	90000	max age of new snapshot in .01 seconds

*New for Oracle8

(continued)

Table 11.1 Oracle7 and Oracle8 initialization parameters *(continued)*.

Name	Value	Description
compatible software	8.0.0.0	Database will be completely compatible with this version
compatible_no_recovery		database will be compatible unless crash or media recovery is needed
log_archive_start	FALSE	start archival process on SGA initialization
log_archive_buffers	4	number of buffers to allocate for archiving
log_archive_buffer_size	127	size of each archival buffer in logfile blocks
log_archive_dest	%RDBMS80%\	archival destination text string
log_archive_duplex_dest*		duplex archival destination text string
log_archive_min_succeed_dest*	1	minimum number of archive destinations that must succeed
log_archive_format	ARC%S.%T	archival destination format
log_buffer	8192	redo circular buffer size
log_checkpoint_interval	10000	redo blocks checkpoint threshold
log_checkpoint_timeout	0	maximum time interval between checkpoints in seconds
log_block_checksum	FALSE	calculate checksum for redo blocks when writing
log_small_entry_max_size	80	redo entries larger than this will acquire the redo copy latch
log_simultaneous_copies	2	number of simultaneous copies into redo buffer of copy latches
db_files	1024	max allowable number of db files
db_file_simultaneous_writes	1	max simultaneous (overlapped) writes per db file
db_file_multiblock_read_count	8	db block to be read each I/O
log_files	255	max allowable log files
parallel_server*	FALSE	if TRUE, startup in parallel server mode
gc_lck_procs	1	number of background parallel server lock processes to start
gc_releasable_locks	0	releasable locks (DFS)
gc_rollback_locks		undo locks (DFS)
gc_files_to_locks		mapping between file numbers and hash buckets (DFS)
thread	0	redo thread to mount
freeze_DB_for_fast_ instance_recovery*	FALSE	freeze database during instance recovery
checkpoint_process	FALSE	create a separate checkpoint process
log_checkpoints_to_alert	FALSE	log checkpoint begin/end to alert file

*New for Oracle8

(continued)

Table 11.1 Oracle7 and Oracle8 initialization parameters *(continued)*.

Name	Value	Description
recovery_parallelism	0	number of server processes to use for parallel recovery
control_file_record_keep_time*	7	control file record keep time in days
temporary_table_locks	60	temporary table locks
dml_locks	100	dml locks—one for each table modified in a transaction
row_locking		always use row-locking
serializable	FALSE	serialize transactions
delayed_logging_block_cleanouts	TRUE	turn on delayed-logging block cleanouts feature
instance_number	0	instance number
spread_extents*	TRUE	should extents be spread across files in the tablespace
max_rollback_segments	30	max number of rollback segments in SGA cache
transactions	66	max number of concurrent active transactions
transactions_per_rollback_segment	11	number of active transactions per rollback segment
rollback_segments		undo segment list
cleanup_rollback_entries	20	number of undo entries to apply per transaction cleanup
transaction_auditing*	TRUE	transaction auditing records generated in the redo log
discrete_transactions_enabled	FALSE	enable OLTP mode
sequence_cache_entries	10	number of sequence cache entries
sequence_cache_hash_buckets	10	number of sequence cache hash buckets
row_cache_cursors	10	number of cached cursors for row cache management
os_roles	FALSE	retrieve roles from the operating system
max_enabled_roles	20	max number of roles a user can have enabled
remote_os_authent	FALSE	allow nonsecure remote clients to use auto-logon accounts
remote_os_roles	FALSE	allow nonsecure remote clients to use OS roles
O7_DICTIONARY_ACCESSIBILITY*	TRUE	version 7 Dictionary Accessibility Support
remote_login_passwordfile	SHARED	password file usage parameter
dblink_encrypt_login	FALSE	enforce password for distributed login always be encrypted
license_max_users	0	max number of named users that can be created in the database
db_domain	WORLD	directory part of global database name stored with CREATE DATABASE

*New for Oracle8

(continued)

Table 11.1   Oracle7 and Oracle8 initialization parameters (continued).

Name	Value	Description
global_names	FALSE	enforce that database links have same name as remote database
distributed_lock_timeout	60	number of seconds a distributed transaction waits for a lock
distributed_transactions	16	max number of concurrent distributed transactions
max_transaction_branches	8	max number of branches per distributed transaction
distributed_recovery_connection_ hold_time*	200	number of seconds RECO holds outbound connections open
commit_point_strength*	1	bias this node has toward not preparing in a two-phase commit
mts_service*		service supported by dispatchers
mts_dispatchers		specifications of dispatchers
mts_servers*	0	number of servers to start up
mts_max_servers*	0	max number of servers
mts_max_dispatchers	0	max number of dispatchers
mts_listener_address	(address= (protocol=ipc) (key=%s))	address(es) of network listener
mts_multiple_listeners	FALSE	are multiple listeners enabled?
open_links	4	max number open links per session
open_links_per_instance*	4	max number open links per instance
close_cached_open_cursors	FALSE	close cursors cached by PL/SQL at each commit
fixed_date		fixed SYSDATE value
audit_trail	NONE	enable system auditing
sort_area_size	655326	size of in-memory sort work area
sort_area_retained_size	0	size of in-memory sort work area retained between fetch calls
sort_direct_writes	AUTO	use direct write
sort_write_buffers	2	number of sort direct write buffers
sort_write_buffer_size	32768	size of each sort direct write buffer
sort_spacemap_size	512	size of sort disk area space map
sort_read_fac	20	multiblock read factor for sort
db_name		database name specified in CREATE DATABASE
open_cursors	50	max number of cursors per process
ifile		include file in INIT.ORA
sql_trace		FALSE enable SQL trace
os_authent_prefix	OPS$	prefix for auto-logon accounts
optimizer_mode	CHOOSE	optimizer mode (either RULE or CHOOSE)
sql92_security	FALSE	require select privilege for searched update/delete

*New for Oracle8

(continued)

Table 11.1 Oracle7 and Oracle8 initialization parameters (continued).

Name	Value	Description
blank_trimming	FALSE	blank trimming semantics parameter
always_anti_join	NESTED_LOOPS	always use this anti-join when possible
partition_view_enabled	FALSE	enable/disable partitioned views
b_tree_bitmap_plans*	FALSE	enable the use of bitmap plans for tables w. only b-tree indexes
star_transformation_ enabled*	FALSE	enable the use of star transformation
serial_reuse*	DISABLE	reuse the frame segments
cursor_space_for_time	FALSE	use more memory in order to get faster execution
session_cached_cursors	0	number of cursors to save in the session cursor cache
text_enable	FALSE	enable text searching
remote_dependencies_mode	TIMESTAMP	remote-procedure-call dependencies mode parameter
utl_file_dir		utl_file accessible directories list
plsql_v2_compatibility*	FALSE	PL/SQL version 2.x compatibility flag
job_queue_processes	0	number of job queue processes to start
job_queue_interval	60	wake-up interval in seconds for job queue processes
job_queue_keep_connections	FALSE	keep network connections between execution of jobs
snapshot_refresh_processes	1	number of job queue processes to start
snapshot_refresh_interval	60	wakeup interval in seconds for job queue processes
snapshot_refresh_keep_connections	FALSE	keep network connections between execution of jobs
optimizer_percent_parallel	0	optimizer percent parallel
optimizer_search_limit	5	optimizer search limit
parallel_min_percent	0	minimum percent of threads required for parallel query
parallel_default_max_ instances	0	default maximum number of instances for parallel query
cache_size_threshold	80	maximum size of table or piece to be cached (in blocks)
create_bitmap_area_size	8388608	size of create bitmap buffer for bitmap index
bitmap_merge_area_size	1048576	maximum memory allowed for BITMAP MERGE
parallel_min_servers	0	minimum parallel query servers per instance
parallel_max_servers	5	maximum parallel query servers per instance
parallel_server_idle_time	5	idle time before parallel query server dies
allow_partial_sn_results*	FALSE	allow partial results when processing gv$ views
parallel_instance_group*		instance group to use for all parallel operations

*New for Oracle8

(continued)

Table 11.1 Oracle7 and Oracle8 initialization parameters (continued).

Name	Value	Description
ops_admin_group*		instance group to use for global v$ queries
hash_join_enabled	TRUE	enable/disable hash join
hash_area_size	0	size of in-memory hash work area
hash_multiblock_io_count	8	number of blocks hash join will read/write at once
background_dump_dest	%RDBMS80%\ trace	detached process dump directory
user_dump_dest	%RDBMS80%\ trace	user process dump directory
max_dump_file_size	102400	maximum size (blocks) of dump file
oracle_trace_enable	FALSE	Oracle TRACE instance wide enable/disable
oracle_trace_facility_path	%OTRACE80%\ ADMIN\FDF\	Oracle TRACE facility path
oracle_trace_collection_path	%OTRACE80%\ ADMIN\CDF\	Oracle TRACE collection path
oracle_trace_facility_name	oracled	Oracle TRACE default facility name
oracle_trace_collection_name		Oracle TRACE default collection name
oracle_trace_collection_size	5242880	Oracle TRACE collection file max. size
object_cache_optimal_size	102400 cache in bytes	optimal size of the user session's object
object_cache_max_size_percent*	10	percentage of maximum size over optimal of the user session's object
session_max_open_files*	0	maximum number of open files allowed per session
aq_tm_processes*	0	number of AQ Time Managers to start

*New for Oracle8

The Oracle7 initialization parameters shown in Table 11.2 are invalid for use with Oracle8.

The DBA should review the applicable administrator's and tuning guides before modifying any INIT.ORA parameters.

The Undocumented Initialization Parameters (_*)

In addition to the Oracle-documented initialization parameters, every version of Oracle has varying numbers of undocumented initialization parameters. These un-documented parameters are usually used only in emergencies and should be used only under the direction of a senior DBA or Oracle support. Listing 11.1 shows a script for getting the undocumented initialization parameters out of an Oracle 7.2 instance and then out of a 7.3 or 8.0.2 instance.

Table 11.2 Invalid initialization parameters for use with Oracle8.

NAME	VALUE	DESCRIPTION
gc_segments	10	number of segment headers
gc_tablespaces	5	number of tablespaces
gc_rollback_segments	20	number of undo Segments
gc_db_locks	200	number of DB locks (DFS)
gc_save_rollback_locks	20	number of save Undo locks in (DFS)
gc_freelist_groups	50	number of freelist groups locks in (DFS)

Listing 11.1 Scripts for documenting undocumented initialization parameters (pre-7.3 and post-7.3).

```
REM Script for getting undocumented init.ora
REM parameters from a 7.2 instance
REM MRA - Revealnet 2/23/97
REM
COLUMN parameter FORMAT a40
COLUMN value FORMAT a30
COLUMN ksppidf HEADING 'Is|Default'
SET FEEDBACK OFF VERIFY OFF PAGES 55
START title80 'Undocumented Init.ora Parameters'
SPOOL rep_out/&db/undoc
SELECT  ksppinm "Parameter",
  ksppivl "Value",
  ksppidf
FROM x$ksppi
WHERE ksppinm LIKE '/_%' escape '/'
/
SPOOL OFF
TTITLE OFF

REM Script for getting undocumented init.ora
REM parameters from a 7.3 or 8.0.2 instance
REM MRA - Revealnet 4/23/97
REM
COLUMN parameter    FORMAT a37
COLUMN description  FORMAT a30 WORD_WRAPPED
COLUMN "Session Value" FORMAT a10
COLUMN "Instance Value" FORMAT a10
SET LINES 100
```

```
SET PAGES 0
SPOOL undoc.lis
SELECT
  a.ksppinm  "Parameter",
  a.ksppdesc "Description",
  b.ksppstvl "Session Value",
  c.ksppstvl "Instance Value"
FROM
  x$ksppi a,
  x$ksppcv b,
  x$ksppsv c
WHERE
  a.indx = b.indx
  AND a.indx = c.indx
  AND a.ksppinm LIKE '/_%' escape '/'
/
SPOOL OFF
SET LINES 80 PAGES 20
CLEAR COLUMNS
```

The output for an Oracle 7.2 database looks like Table 11.3.

The undocumented parameters for 7.3 are listed in Table 11.4. Note that the descriptions for the parameters are available starting with Oracle 7.3.

Table 11.5 shows the list of undocumented initialization parameters for Oracle8.

Table 11.3 Undocumented initialization parameters for Oracle 7.2 not included in Oracle 7.3 and 8.0.2.

Date: 03/04/97		Page: 1
Time: 03:47 PM	Undocumented Init.ora Parameters ORCNETD1 database	SYS
Parameter Is	Value	Default Is
_latch_spin_count (7.3 — _spin_count)	100	TRUE
_trace_instance_termination	FALSE	TRUE
_wakeup_timeout	100	TRUE
_lgwr_async_write	TRUE	TRUE

Table 11.4 Undocumented initialization parameters for Oracle 7.3 not included in 8.0.2.

Parameter Name	Parameter Description	Default Value
_standby_lock_name_space	lock name space used for generating lock names for standby database	
_enable_dba_locking	enable persistent locking	FALSE

Table 11.5 Undocumented initialization parameters for 8.0.2.

Parameter Name	Description	Default	Instance
_trace_files_public	create publicly accessible trace files	FALSE	FALSE
_max_sleep_holding_latch	max time to sleep while holding a latch	4	4
_max_exponential_sleep	max sleep during exponential backoff	0	0
_latch_wait_posting	post sleeping processes when free latch	1	1
_latch_recovery_alignment	align latch recovery structures 80	80	
_session_idle_bit_latches	one latch per session or a latch per group of sessions	0	0
_lm_dlmd_procs*	number of background lock manager daemon processes to start	1	1
_lm_xids*	number of transaction IDs configured for the lock manage	79	79
_lm_groups*	number of groups configured for the lock manager	20	20
_lm_domains*	number of groups configured for the lock manager	2	2
_lm_non_fault_tolerant*	disable lock fault-tolerance mode manager	FALSE	FALSE
_lm_statistics*	enable lock manager statistics collection	FALSE	FALSE
_single_process	run without detached processes	FALSE	FALSE
_number_cached_attributes	maximum number of cached	10	10
_debug_sga	debug SGA	FALSE	FALSE
_test_param_1	test parameter 1	25	25
_test_param_2	test parameter 2		
_test_param_3	test parameter 3		
_messages	message queue resources - dependent on number of processes and number of buffers	200	200
_enqueue_locks	locks for managed enqueues	1481	1481
_enqueue_hash	enqueue hash table length	265	265
_enqueue_debug_multi_instance	debug enqueue multi-instance	FALSE	FALSE
_enqueue_hash_chain_latches	enqueue hash chain latches	2	2

* Indicates that this parameter is Oracle8 only

(continued)

Table 11.5 Undocumented initialization parameters for 8.0.2 (continued).

Parameter Name	Description	Default	Instance
_trace_buffers_per_process	trace buffers per process	0	0
_trace_block_size	trace block size	2048	2048
_trace_archive_start	start trace process on SGA initialization	FALSE	FALSE
_trace_flushing	TRWR should try to keep tracing buffers clean	FALSE	FALSE
_trace_enabled	should tracing be enabled at startup	TRUE	TRUE
_trace_events	turns on and off trace events		
_trace_archive_dest	trace archival destination	%RDBMS80%\ TRACE.DAT	%RDBMS80%\ TRACE.DAT
_trace_file_size	trace file size	10000	10000
_trace_write_batch_size	trace write batch size	32	32
_io_slaves_disabled*	do not use I/O slaves	FALSE	FALSE
_open_files_limit*	limit on number of files opened by I/O subsystem	4294967294	4294967294
_controlfile_enqueue_timeout	control file enqueue timeout in seconds (true only when debugging)	900	900
_db_block_cache_protect	protect database blocks	FALSE	FALSE
_db_block_hash_buckets	number of database block hash buckets	2000	2000
_db_block_no_idle_writes	disable periodic writes of buffers when idle	FALSE	FALSE
_db_handles	systemwide simultaneous buffer operations	420	420
_db_handles_cached	buffer handles cached each process	3	3
_wait_for_sync	wait for sync on commit MUST BE ALWAYS TRUE	TRUE	TRUE
_db_block_max_scan_cnt	maximum number of buffers to inspect when looking for free	0	0
_db_writer_scan_depth	number of LRU buffers for dbwr to scan when looking for dirty buffers	0	0
_db_writer_scan_depth_increment	add to dbwr scan depth when dbwr is behind	0	0
_db_writer_scan_depth_decrement	subtract from dbwr scan depth when dbwr is working too hard	0	0
_db_large_dirty_queue	number of buffers that force dirty queue to be written	0	0
_db_block_write_batch	number of blocks to group in each DB Writer IO	0	0
_db_block_cache_clone	always clone data blocks on get (for debugging)	FALSE	FALSE
_db_block_cache_map*	map/unmap and track reference counts on blocks (for debugging)	0	0

* Indicates that this parameter is Oracle8 only

(continued)

Table 11.5 Undocumented initialization parameters for 8.0.2 *(continued)*.

Parameter Name	Description	Default	Instance
_db_block_max_cr_dba	maximum allowed number of CR buffers per dba	10	10
_db_block_low_priority_batch_size*	percentage of write batch used for 20 low-priority ckpts	20	
_db_block_med_priority_ batch_size*	percentage of write batch used for medium-priority ckpts	40	40
_db_block_med_priority_batch_size*	percentage of write batch used for high-priority ckpts	40	40
_minimum_giga_scn	minimum SCN to start with in 2^30 units	0	0
_log_checkpoint_recovery_check	number of redo blocks to verify after checkpoint	0	0
_log_io_size	automatically initiate log write if this manyredo blocks in buffers	0	
_log_buffers_debug	debug redo buffers (slows things down)	FALSE	FALSE
_log_debug_multi_instance	debug redo multi-instance code FALSE	FALSE	
_log_entry_prebuild_threshold	redo entries larger than this will be prebuilt before getting logged	0	0
_disable_logging	disable logging	FALSE	FALSE
_db_no_mount_lock	do not get a mount lock	FALSE	FALSE
_cr_deadtime*	global cache lock CR deadlock timeout in seconds	6 6	
_gc_class_locks*	set locks for the minor classes (DFS)	0	0
_defer_pings*	if TRUE, defer pings (DFS)	FALSE	FALSE
_upconvert_from_ast*	if TRUE, attempt to up-convert from an AST (DFS)	FALSE FALSE	
_save_escalates*	if TRUE, save escalates from basts (DFS)	TRUE	TRUE
_defer_time*	how long to defer a ping (DFS) 100	100	
_log_blocks_during_backup	log block images when changed during backup	TRUE TRUE	
_allow_resetlogs_corruption	allow resetlogs even if it will cause corruption	FALSE FALSE	
_corrupt_blocks_on_stuck_recovery	number of times to corrupt a block when media recovery stuck	0	
_log_space_errors	should we report space errors to alert log	TRUE	TRUE
_bump_highwater_mark_count	how many blocks should we allocate per freelist on advancing HWM	0	0
_rollback_segment_initial	starting undo segment number	1	1
_rollback_segment_count	number of undo segments	0	0
_offline_rollback_segments	offline undo segment list		
_corrupted_rollback_segments	corrupted undo segment list		
_small_table_threshold	threshold level of table size for forget-bit enabled during scan	160	160
_release_insert_threshold	maximum number of unusable blocks to unlink from freelist	5	5

* Indicates that this parameter is Oracle8 only

(continued)

Table 11.5 Undocumented initialization parameters for 8.0.2 (continued).

Parameter Name	Description	Default	Instance
_walk_insert_threshold	maximum number of unusable blocks to walk across freelist	0	0
_reuse_index_loop	number of blocks being examined for index block reuse	5	5
_row_cache_instance_locks	number of row cache instance locks	100	100
_row_cache_buffer_size	size of row cache circular buffer	200	200
_kgl_multi_instance_lock	whether KGL to support multi-instance locks	TRUE	TRUE
_kgl_multi_instance_pin	whether KGL to support multi-instance pins	TRUE	TRUE
_kgl_multi_instance_invalidation	whether KGL to support imulti-instance nvalidations	TRUE	TRUE
_kgl_latch_count	number of library cache latches	0	0
_kgl_bucket_count	index to the bucket count array	0	0
_passwordfile_enqueue_timeout	password file enqueue timeout in seconds	900	900
_mts_load_constants	server load balancing constants (S,P,D,I)	3,0.75,0.2 5,0.1	3,0.75,0.2 5,0.1
_mts_fastpath	dispatcher network fastpath	TRUE	TRUE
_mts_listener_retry	listener connection retry rate (secs)	120	120
_all_shared_dblinks*	treat all dblinks as shared		
_init_sql_file	file containing SQL statements to execute upon database creation	%RDBMS80%\ ADMIN\SQL. BSQ	%RDBMS80%\ ADMIN\SQL. BSQ
_shared_session_sort_fetch_buffer	size of in-memory merge buffer for mts or xa fetch calls	0	0
_optimizer_undo_changes	undo changes to query optimizer	FALSE	FALSE
_sql_connect_capability_table	SQL Connect Capability Table (testing only)		
_sql_connect_capability_override	SQL Connect Capability Table override	0	0
_always_star_transformation*	always favor use of star transformation	FALSE	FALSE
_parallel_server_sleep_time	sleep time between dequeue timeouts (in 1/100ths)	10	10
_dynamic_stats_threshold*	delay threshold (in 1/100ths) between sending statistics message	6000	6000
_parallel_min_message_pool	minimum size of shared pool memory to reserve for pq servers	64440	64440
_affinity_on*	enable/disable affinity at runtime	TRUE	TRUE
_cursor_db_buffers_pinned*	additional number of buffers a cursor can pin at once	78	78
_disable_ntlog_events*	disable logging to NT event log	FALSE	FALSE
_oracle_trace_events	Oracle TRACE event flags		
_oracle_trace_facility_version	Oracle TRACE facility version		
_no_objects*	no object features are used	FALSE	FALSE

* Indicates that this parameter is Oracle8 only

Note in Table 11.5 that each undocumented parameter begins with an underscore (_) character. For those of you who have been around awhile, you will also notice some of these "undocumented" parameters used to be documented. You may have seen some of them used, such as **_OFFLINE_ROLLBACK_SEGMENTS**; others you will never use or see used. You should be aware that there are more parameters than those listed in a user's manual. You may need to prompt Oracle support if you see one (such as **_CORRUPTED_ROLLBACK_SEGMENTS**) that may just be helpful in a sticky situation.

Step 2 will involve tuning memory allocations; Oracle has provided a script set to help with this and other tuning steps. This script set—UTLBSTAT/UTLESTAT—is covered in Chapter 12.

For more information on tuning in general, the following additional reading is suggested:

- *Oracle7 Server Tuning*, Release 7.3, Oracle Corp., Part No. A32537-1, June 1996.

- *Oracle7 Server Administrator's Guide*, Release 7.3, Chapter 21, Oracle Corp., Part No. A32535-1, February 1995.

- *Oracle7 Server Application Developer's Guide*, Appendix B, Oracle Corp., Part No. 6695-70-1292, December 1992.

- *Performance Tuning With BSTAT/ESTAT*, Powell, K., Oracle Corp., 1991 IOUG proceedings in Miami, Florida.

- *Tuning Oracle*, Corey, Michael J., Abbey, Michael, and Dechichio Jr., Daniel J., Oracle Press, Osborne McGraw-Hill, 1995.

Practical Guide To

Internals Tuning

- Tools For Tuning Memory Contention
- Tools For Tuning I/O Contention
- Tuning To Prevent Contention
- Tools For Additional Tuning Concerns
- New Oracle Tuning Options

Tools For Tuning Memory Contention

Memory contention will make the best-tuned application perform poorly. If the application is constantly having to go to disk to get data dictionary and actual data, performance will suffer. If you will remember, the SGA is divided into three major areas: the shared pool under Oracle7, the redo log buffer, and the database buffers. Oracle8 adds an area to the SGA: the large pool, for databases using the multithreaded server and Net8.

Tuning The Shared Pool

Missing a get on the data dictionary or shared pool area of the SGA is more costly than missing a get on a data buffer or waiting for a redo buffer. Therefore, we will look at a SQL script that allows the DBA to look at the current status of the data dictionary or shared pool area. This SQL script is shown in Listing 11.2.

Listing 11.2   Script to generate data dictionary cache statistics report.

```
REM
REM NAME                   : DD_CACHE.SQL
REM FUNCTION               : GENERATE REPORT ON DATA DICTIONARY CACHE CONDITION
REM USE                    : FROM SQLPLUS
REM Limitations            : None
REM Revisions:
REM Date                   Modified By          Reason For Change
REM 21-AUG-1991            MIKE AULT            INITIAL CREATE
REM 27-NOV-1991            MIKE AULT            ADD % CALCULATION TO REPORT
REM 28-OCT-1992            MIKE AULT            ADD CALL TO TITLE PROCEDURE
REM 21-Jun-1997            MIKE AULT            Updated to ORACLE8REM SET FLUSH
OFF
REM SET TERM OFF
SET PAGESIZE 59
SET LINESIZE 79
COLUMN parameter FORMAT A20
COLUMN type FORMAT a10
COLUMN percent FORMAT 999.99 HEADING "%";
START title80 "DATA DICTIONARY CACHE STATISTICS"
SPOOL rep_out/&db/ddcache.lis
SELECT
        parameter,
        type,
        gets,
        getmisses,
        ( getmisses / gets * 100) percent,
        count,
        usage
```

```
FROM
        v$rowcache
WHERE
        gets > 100 AND
        getmisses > 0
ORDER BY parameter;
SPOOL OFF
```

Notice that the script selects only statistics that have been used more than 100 times
and have had getmisses occur. Obviously, if the parameter has had no getmisses, it
should be satisfactory. The factor of 100 gets was selected to ensure that the parameter has had enough activity to generate valid statistics.

You might also notice that the percentage of misses is automatically calculated and
reported for each parameter. If you desire, you could use the percent value to generate a decoded value of **RAISE** if the percentage is greater than 10, or **LOWER** if the
value is less than a predetermined value. An example of this script's output is shown
in Table 11.6.

In reviewing this report, check the following items:

- *Review* **count** *and* **usage** *columns*—If **usage** is equal to **count**, the cache
  area is being fully used. If **usage** is consistently low compared with
  count, consider reducing the INIT.ORA parameter that controls the
  caches (**SHARED_POOL_SIZE**).

Table 11.6 Example data dictionary cache report.

Date: 06/21/97 Time: 05:04 PM	DATA DICTIONARY CACHE STATISTICS SYSTEM ORTEST1 database					Page: 1
PARAMETER	**TYPE**	**GETS**	**GETMISSES**	**%**	**COUNT**	**USAGE**
dc_free_extents	PARENT	8845	29	.33	44	29
dc_object_ids	PARENT	193	22	11.40	72	71
dc_objects	PARENT	407	64	15.72	121	113
dc_rollback_segments	PARENT	4386	7	.16	9	8

- If **count** and **usage** are equal and % is greater than 10, consider increasing the INIT.ORA parameter that controls the caches (**SHARED_POOL_SIZE**).

Because you are concerned with an aggregate look at the cache area performance, you can substitute the following query into the report to give you an overall health indicator:

```
SELECT (SUM(getmisses) / SUM(gets)) 'DD CACHE MISS RATIO'
FROM V$ROWCACHE;
```

This substitution simplifies the report into:

```
Date: 06/21/97                                              Page:   1
Time: 04:39 PM              DD Cache Hit Ratio              SYSTEM
                             ORTEST1 database


RATIO
--------
.01141403

1 row selected.
```

Tuning The Library Cache

An additional area of the shared pool deals with the tuning of the library cache. The library cache is used to store information concerning the shared objects. These consist mainly of the **SQL AREA**, **TABLE/PROCEDURE**, **BODY**, and **TRIGGER** type objects. These areas are monitored via the **v$librarycache** table. This table has the columns: **namespace**, **gets**, **gethitratio**, **pins**, **pinhitratio**, **reloads**, and **invalidations**.

namespace refers to the type of object. **pins** refers to the number of times the object was executed. **reloads** shows the number of library cache misses on execution steps. If the ratio of reloads to pins exceeds 1 percent, you should increase the **SHARED_POOL_SIZE** parameter. This can be determined by a simple query:

```
SELECT (SUM(reloads)/SUM(pins)) * 100 'Miss %'
FROM v$librarycache;
```

To fully use the higher value for **SHARED_POOL_SIZE**, you may also want to increase the number of cursors available to each user. This is accomplished via the **OPEN_CURSORS** INIT.ORA parameter.

You can realize additional gains by making your SQL statements identical, not just in content, but in form as well—right down to the spaces, capitalization, and punctuation. This will allow the SQL statements to share the shared SQL area. You can standardize queries by using views to replace them and encapsulating standard reports into PL/SQL. I suggest using the new UTLFILE package to generate output directly to files from PL/SQL. Listing 11.3 is a report on the library caches.

Listing 11.3 Script to report on library cache health.

```
rem Title: libcache.sql
rem FUNCTION: Generate a library cache report
COLUMN namespace                                    HEADING "Library Object"
COLUMN gets                                           HEADING "Gets"
COLUMN gethitratio       FORMAT 999.99   HEADING "Get Hit%"
COLUMN pins                                            HEADING "Pins"
COLUMN pinhitratio       FORMAT 999.99   HEADING "Pin Hit%"
COLUMN reloads                                       HEADING "Reloads"
COLUMN invalidations                            HEADING  "Invalidations"
COLUMN db                      FORMAT a10
SET PAGES 58 LINES 80
START title80 "Library Caches Report"
DEFINE output = rep_out\&db\lib_cache
SPOOL &output
SELECT
        namespace,gets,
        gethitratio*100 gethitratio,
        pins,
        pinhitratio*100 pinhitratio,
        reloads,invalidations
FROM
        v$librarycache
/
SPOOL OFF
PAUSE Press enter to continue
SET PAGES 22 LINES 80
TTITLE OFF
UNDEF output
```

Table 11.7 shows what the output for the script in Listing 11.3 should look like.

If your **gethitratio** (Get Hit%) or **pinhitratio** (Pin Hit%) falls below 70 to 80 percent for objects with high values for gets and pins, you should increase your **SHARED_POOL_SIZE** parameter. If you see excessive reloads, you will also want to increase the **SHARED_POOL_SIZE**. Invalidations should not occur in a production environment but are probably going to be seen frequently under development. This

Table 11.7 Library cache report.

Date: 06/21/97 Time: 05:24 PM			Library Caches Report ORTEST1 database			Page: 1 SYSTEM
Library Object	**Gets**	**GetHit%**	**Pins**	**Pin Hit%**	**Reloads**	**Invalidations**
SQL AREA	890	90.34	2466	93.03	0	0
TABLE/PROCEDURE	557	80.79	905	80.99	0	0
BODY	12	75.00	12	75.00	0	0
TRIGGER	0	100.00	0	100.00	0	0
INDEX	27	.00	27	.00	0	0
CLUSTER	114	95.61	156	96.79	0	0
OBJECT	0	100.00	0	100.00	0	0
PIPE	0	100.00	0	100.00	0	0

rule may not hold true for an application that requires frequent flushes of the shared pool to accommodate excessive ad hoc query usage.

Monitoring And Tuning The Shared SQL Area

The shared SQL area contains the Pcode versions of all of the current SQL commands that haven't been aged out of the shared pool. Numerous statistics are available via the **v$sqlarea** DPT. The test of SQL statements in the shared pool can be retrieved (at least the first tens of bytes) from the **v$sqltext** DPT. The script in Listing 11.4 produces a report that displays the SQL statements in the SQL area with the most disk reads (these will probably be the ones you will want to review and tune).

Listing 11.4 Script to monitor SQL area disk reads by script.

```
rem Name: sqldrd.sql
rem Function: retrun the sql statements from the shared area with
rem Function: highest disk reads
rem History: Presented in paper 35 at IOUG-A 1997, converted for
rem use 6/24/97 MRA
rem
```

```
DEFINE access_level = 1000 (NUMBER)
COLUMN parsing_user_id              FORMAT 9999999        HEADING 'User Id'
COLUMN executions                   FORMAT 9999            HEADING 'Exec'
COLUMN sorts                        FORMAT 99999           HEADING 'Sorts'
COLUMN command_type                 FORMAT 99999           HEADING 'CmdT'
COLUMN disk_reads                         FORMAT 999,999,999 HEADING 'Block Reads'
COLUMN sql_text                           FORMAT a40              HEADING
'Statement' WORD_WRAPPED
SET LINES 130 VERIFY OFF FEEDBACK OFF
START title132 'SQL Statements With High Reads'
SPOOL rep_out/&db/sqldrd.lis
SELECT
        parsing_user_id, executions,
        sorts,command_type,
        disk_reads,sql_text
FROM
        v$sqlarea
WHERE
        disk_reads > &&access_level
ORDER BY
        disk_reads;
SPOOL OFF
SET LINES 80 VERIFY ON FEEDBACK ON
```

The report shows the actual SQL statements that have a high value for number of reads stored in the SGA. The report's output is shown in Table 11.8.

This example report used a size of 10 for read's limit. Usually, disk reads are in the range specified by the **DEFINE** statement.

You might also be interested in the amount of memory used by a single user. This could point to someone who is using too much ad hoc query type SQL and not enough packages, procedures, and functions. The script in Listing 11.5 gives this information.

Listing 11.5   SQL area memory summary report and supporting view.

```
rem
rem FUNCTION: Generate a summary of SQL Area Memory Usage
rem FUNCTION: uses the sqlsummary view.
rem          showing user SQL memory usage
rem
rem sqlsum.sql
rem
COLUMN areas                                 HEADING Used|Areas
COLUMN sharable        FORMAT 999,999,999    HEADING Shared|Bytes
COLUMN persistent      FORMAT 999,999,999    HEADING Persistent|Bytes
```

```
COLUMN runtime          FORMAT 999,999,999     HEADING Runtime|Bytes
COLUMN username         FORMAT A15             HEADING "User"
START TITLE80 "USERS SQL AREA MEMORY USE"
SPOOL rep_out\&db\sqlsum
SET PAGES 59 LINES 80
BREAK ON REPORT
COMPUTE SUM OF sharable ON REPORT
COMPUTE SUM OF persistent ON REPORT
COMPUTE SUM OF runtime ON REPORT
SELECT
        username,
        SUM(sharable_mem) Sharable,
        SUM( persistent_mem) Persistent,
        SUM( runtime_mem) Runtime ,
        COUNT(*) Areas
FROM
        sql_summary
GROUP BY
        username
ORDER BY
        2;
SPOOL OFF
PAUSE Press enter to continue
CLEAR COLUMNS
CLEAR BREAKS
SET PAGES 22 LINES 80
TTITLE OFF

The report uses the following view:

CREATE OR REPLACE VIEW sql_summary AS
SELECT username, sharable_mem, persistent_mem, runtime_mem
FROM sys.v_$sqlarea a, dba_users b
WHERE a.parsing_user_id = b.user_id;
```

The output from the SQL summary report is shown in Table 11.9.

Judging from the report in Table 11.9, I don't really have any problems in ORTEST1, because the shared pool is 12MB and I am using a total of less than 2MB.

If you detect a user that seems to be using more than his or her share of the shared pool, you can run the script in Listing 11.6 to see exactly what that user has been executing. From the results of the script, you might be able to help the user optimize the processing (or want to take a two-by-four to the user's back side).

Table 11.8 Example output from SQL disk read script.

SQL Statements With High Reads
ORTEST1 database

User Id	Exec	Sorts	CmdT	Block Reads	Statement
0	403	0	3	11	select f.file#, f.block#, f.ts#, f.length from fet$ f, ts$ t where t.ts#=f.ts# and t.dflextpct!=0
0	11	0	3	11	select order#,columns,types from access$ where d_obj#=:1
0	12	0	3	12	select /*+ index(idl_ub1$ i_idl_ub11) +*/ piece#,length,piece from idl_ub1$ where obj#=:1 and part=:2 and version =:3 order by piece#
5	34	0	3	13	SELECT NAME,VALUE FROM V$SYSSTAT WHERE NAME = 'db block gets'
0	12	0	3	14	select /*+ index(idl_ub2$ i_idl_ub21) +*/ piece#,length,piece from idl_ub2$ where obj#=:1 and part=:2 and version =:3 order by piece#
0	17	0	3	27	select file#, block#, ts# from seg$ where type# = 3
0	1	1	3	79	select distinct d.p_obj#,d.p_timestamp from sys.dependency$ d, obj$ o where d.p_obj#>=:1 and d.d_obj#=o.obj# and o.status!=5
5	34	0	47	90	DECLARE job BINARY_INTEGER := :job; next_date DATE := :mydate; broken BOOLEAN := FALSE; BEGIN hitratio; :mydate := next_date; IF broken THEN :b := 1; ELSE :b := 0; END IF; END;

Table 11.9 Example output from the SQL summary report.

Date: 06/25/97 Time: 12:10 AM		Users SQL Area Memory Use ORTEST1 database			Page: 1 SYSTEM
User	**Shared Bytes**	**Persistent Bytes**	**Runtime Bytes**	**Used Areas**	
SYS	546,933	42,196	140,108	63	
SYSTEM	580,693	13,172	83,180	24	
sum	1,127,626	55,368	223,288		

2 rows selected.

Listing 11.6 Script to show shared memory usage for a user (or users).

```
rem
rem FUNCTION: Generate a report of SQL Area Memory Usage
rem              showing SQL Text and memory catagories
rem
rem sqlmem.sql
rem
COLUMN sql_text        FORMAT a40    HEADING Text word_wrapped
COLUMN sharable_mem                  HEADING Shared|Bytes
COLUMN persistent_mem                HEADING Persistent|Bytes
COLUMN parse_calls                   HEADING Parses
COLUMN users           FORMAT a15    HEADING "User"
COLUMN executions                    HEADING "Executions"
START title132 "Users SQL Area Memory Use"
SPOOL rep_out\&db\sqlmem
SET LONG 1000 PAGES 59 LINES 132
BREAK ON users
COMPUTE SUM OF sharable_mem ON users
COMPUTE SUM OF persistent_mem ON users
COMPUTE SUM OF runtime_mem ON users
SELECT username users, sql_text, Executions, parse_calls, sharable_mem,
persistent_mem
FROM sys.v_$sqlarea a, dba_users b
WHERE a.parsing_user_id = b.user_id
AND b.username LIKE UPPER('%&user_name%')
ORDER BY 1;
SPOOL OFF
PAUSE Press enter to continue
```

```
CLEAR COLUMNS
CLEAR COMPUTES
CLEAR BREAKS
SET PAGES 22 LINES 80
```

The report output in Table 11.10 shows the actual SQL areas used by the SYSTEM user. The variable statements that begin with a colon (such as **:b1** in the second SQL statement) are called bind variables. You should use these variables whenever possible for any SQL statements that may be reused. If you place actual values into the commands instead of bind variables, each command issued will get its own SQL area and result in overuse of the SQL area and performance degradation.

Oh, before you email me: Yes, I am aware the totals in Table 11.10 are incorrect, as is the count of rows; I truncated this report so it would fit here; the original is three pages long.

Table 11.10 Example output from the SQL memory usage for a user report.

Date: 06/25/97 Time: 12:21 AM	Users SQL Area Memory Use ORTEST1 database				Page:1 SYSTEM
User	**Text**	**Exec**	**Parses**	**Shared Bytes**	**Persist Bytes**
SYSTEM	DECLARE job BINARY_INTEGER := :job; next_date DATE := :mydate; broken BOOLEAN := FALSE; BEGIN hitratio; :mydate := next_date; IF broken THEN :b := 1; ELSE :b := 0; END IF; END;	34	34	10207	460
	INSERT INTO HIT_RATIOS VALUES (:b1,:b2,:b3,:b4,:b5,:b6,0,0,:b7)	34	34	8931	552
	SELECT parsing_user_id, executions, sorts,command_type, disk_reads,sql_text FROM v$sqlarea WHERE disk_reads >10	1	1	50861	744
	SELECT parsing_user_id, executions, sorts,command_type, disk_reads,sql_text FROM v$sqlarea WHERE disk_reads >100	1	1	51150	744

(continued)

Table 11.10 Example output from the SQL memory usage for a user report _(continued)._

User	Text	Exec	Parses	Shared Bytes	Persist Bytes
SELECT	parsing_user_id, executions,	2	2	52384	748
	sorts,command_type, disk_reads,sql_text FROM v$sqlarea WHERE disk_reads > 10 ORDER BY disk_reads				
	SELECT parsing_user_id, executions, sorts,command_type, disk_reads,sql_text FROM v$sqlarea WHERE disk_reads > 1000 ORDER BY disk_reads	3	3	52234	748
	SELECT COUNT(*) FROM V$SESSION WHERE USERNAME IS NOT NULL	34	34	51205	476
	SELECT DECODE('A','A','1','2') FROM DUAL	3	3	7485	460
	SELECT NAME,VALUE FROM V$SYSSTAT WHERE NAME = 'consistent gets'	34	34	13099	524
	SELECT NAME,VALUE FROM V$SYSSTAT WHERE NAME = 'db block gets'	34	34	13713	524
	SELECT NAME,VALUE FROM V$SYSSTAT WHERE NAME = 'physical reads'	34	34	13666	524
	SELECT TO_CHAR(SYSDATE,'DD-MON-YY') FROM DUAL	34	34	5656	460
	SELECT TO_CHAR(SYSDATE,'HH24') FROM DUAL	34	34	4935	460
	SELECT TO_CHAR(SYSDATE,'MM/DD/YY') TODAY, TO_CHAR(SYSDATE,'HH:MI AM') TIME, name`ll' database' DATABASE, rtrim(name) passout, user passout2 FROM	1	1	32736	680
***************					
sum				663349	14044

25 rows selected.

The final step in tuning the shared pool is to determine if some objects should be pinned. Pinning is the process of telling the Oracle LRU algorithm that certain objects in the shared pool are hands off. You accomplish pinning by using the **DBMS_SHARED_POOL.KEEP** procedure. I have seen several questions on online forums about determining the size of objects in the shared pool and keeping the LRU algorithm from forcing objects out of the shared pool. The **DBMS_SHARED_POOL** package provides procedures to facilitate these actions.

The **DBMS_SHARED_POOL.SIZES** procedure searches the shared pool for any objects larger than the size in kilobytes of the argument it is passed. Generally, the larger the size, the more likely the object is a package and you will want to keep it in the pool. Smaller objects tend to be individual queries and can be aged out of the pool. The use of **DBMS_SHARED_POOL.SIZES** is shown in Listing 11.7.

Listing 11.7   Example of the use of the DBMS_SHARED_POOL.SIZES procedure.

```
SQL> set serveroutput on size 4000;
SQL> execute sys.dbms_shared_pool.sizes(10);
SIZE(K) KEPT    NAME
------ ------   --------------------------------------------------------
139             SYS.STANDARD                    (PACKAGE)
56              SYS.DBMS_SHARED_POOL            (PACKAGE BODY)
31              SELECT TO_CHAR(SHARABLE_MEM / 1000 ,'999999') SZ,DECODE(KEPT_VE
                RSIONS,0,' ',RPAD('YES(' || TO_CHAR(KEPT_VERSIONS) |
                | ')' ,6)) KEEPED,RAWTOHEX(ADDRESS) || ',' || TO_CHAR(HASH
                _VALUE)  NAME,SUBSTR(SQL_TEXT,1,354) EXTRA   FROM V$SQLAREA
                WHERE SHARABLE_MEM > :b1 * 1000   UNION SELECT TO_CHAR(SH
                ARABLE_MEM / 1000 ,'999999') SZ,DECODE(KEPT,'YES','YES
                (004D7F84,2008220828)     (CURSOR)
30              SYS.STANDARD                    (PACKAGE BODY)
27              SYS.DBMS_SHARED_POOL            (PACKAGE)
17              SYS.V$SQLAREA           (VIEW)
16              SYS.V$DB_OBJECT_CACHE   (VIEW)
15              insert into idl_ub2$(obj#,part,version,piece#,length,piece) val
                ues(:1,:2,:3,:4,:5,:6)
                (0027BA44,-512326869)     (CURSOR)
PL/SQL procedure successfully completed.
```

The **set serveroutput on size 4000** command in Listing 11.7 limits the size of the output buffer to 4,000 bytes. The **set serveroutput** command is required. Perhaps in the future, if we all bug Oracle for an enhancement, it will incorporate the **UTIL_FILE** and just generate a report listing we can peruse as desired. As you can see from

Listing 11.7, one large package is in shared memory. Listing 11.8 shows the results of issuing a **keep** against this package to retain it.

Listing 11.8 Example use of the DBMS_SHARED_POOL.KEEP packaged procedure.

```
SQL> execute dbms_shared_pool.keep('sys.standard');
PL/SQL procedure successfully completed.
SQL> execute dbms_shared_pool.sizes(130);
SIZE(K) KEPT    NAME
------  ------  ----------------------------------------------------------
139     YES     SYS.STANDARD         (PACKAGE)
PL/SQL procedure successfully completed.
```

By issuing **keep**s against large packages to hold them in memory, you can mitigate shared-pool fragmentation that results in the ORA-04031 error. By pinning the packages so they don't age out, you can prevent smaller queries, cursors, and procedures from taking their areas. Then, when the packages are reloaded, you see an ORA-04031 as the package seeks a large enough group of areas in which to install itself. Under Oracle8, this is supposed to be eliminated because of the way the shared memory area is now used. For those of you still on previous Oracle7 versions, I have included on the enclosed CD-ROM some scripts that check for a set of packages you specify, and if they aren't pinned, load and pin them. This set of scripts is in the **dbms_revealnet.sql** package included in the Visual Dictionary Lite program on the CD-ROM.

Tuning The Buffer Cache

The buffer cache is the area in memory where data is stored from data tables, indexes, rollback segments, clusters, and sequences. By ensuring that enough buffers are available for storage of these data items, you can speed execution by reducing required disk reads.

The statistics **db block gets**, **consistent gets** (their sum is logical reads), and **physical reads** from the **v$sysstat** table show the relationship between *logical*, or cache, hits and *physical*, or disk, hits, while retrieving data. The statistic called **hit ratio** is determined by the simple formula:

```
logical reads = db_block_gets+consistent_gets
hit ratio(%) = ((logical reads - physical reads) / logical reads) * 100
```

If the hit ratio is less than 80 to 90 percent in a loaded and running database, this indicates that insufficient buffers are allocated. If the hit ratio is less than 80 to 90 percent, increase the INIT.ORA parameter **DB_BLOCK_BUFFERS**.

Monitoring Hit Ratio

A PL/SQL procedure that can be used to periodically load hit ratio, usage, and number of users into a table for later review is shown in Listing 11.10. The script can be run hourly, every half hour, every four hours—in short, at whatever period of time the DBA decides to monitor for, with minor changes. The short script in Listing 11.9 runs the hit ratio procedure either manually or by using a call to SQL*Plus scheduled in a cron or queued procedure. This can provide valuable information about peak usage times and the hit ratio at those peak times. By adding columns, you can measure other statistics if desired. A script more suited for this is shown later in this section.

A common mistake many DBAs make is to monitor only the cumulative hit ratio. Remember, all of the statistics are cumulative; therefore, any ratios or calculated values will be cumulative in nature unless you do as the UTLBSTAT/UTLESTAT reports do and use a holding table for the statistics and then monitor over discrete time periods, calculating deltas and applying the ratios to the deltas.

For an instantaneous or period hit ratio, you must create a table to store this information. Its structure is:

```
create table hit_ratios (
                CHECK_DATE          DATE,
                CHECK_HOUR          NUMBER,
                DB_BLOCK_GETS       NUMBER,
                CONSISTENT          NUMBER,
                PHY_READS           NUMBER,
                HITRATIO            NUMBER,
                PERIOD_HIT_RATIO    NUMBER,
                PERIOD_USAGE        NUMBER,
                USERS               NUMBER)
storage (initial 10k next 10k pctincrease 0);
```

In addition, you should create a unique index on **CHECK_DATE**, **CHECK_HOUR** to prevent duplicate entries. Listing 11.9 shows a script used to run the hit ratio PL/SQL procedure.

Listing 11.9   SQL script used to run hit ratio PL/SQL procedure.

```
REM
REM NAME                     :RUN_B_HRATIO.SQL
REM PURPOSE                  :RUN PL/SQL PROCEDURE TO LOAD HIT RATIO AND USAGE DATA
REM USE                       :FROM RUN_B_HRATIO.COM
REM Limitations              : None
REM Revisions:
```

```
REM   Date                        Modified By      Reason For change
REM   10-JUL-1992        M. AULT           INITIAL CREATE
REM   22-Jun-1997
EXECUTE hitratio;
EXIT
```

The procedure in Listing 11.10 can be scheduled using the Oracle job queues to run hourly. If you want it to run with more or less frequency, you must modify the PL/SQL procedure. If you decide to run the script on a manual basis only as needed, the command is executed in the SQL*Plus environment. Therefore, you need to build a small file consisting of an **EXECUTE** command. This file is what is actually run by the batch scheduling program. The file should look something like the script in Listing 11.11.

Listing 11.10   PL/SQL procedure to monitor period hit ratio.

```
CREATE OR REPLACE PROCEDURE HITRATIO IS
  c_date DATE;
  c_hour NUMBER;
  h_ratio NUMBER;
  con_gets NUMBER;
  db_gets NUMBER;
  p_reads NUMBER;
  stat_name CHAR(64);
  temp_name CHAR(64);
  stat_val NUMBER;
  users  NUMBER;
BEGIN
  SELECT TO_CHAR(sysdate,'DD-MON-YY') INTO c_date FROM DUAL;
  SELECT TO_CHAR(sysdate,'HH24') INTO c_hour FROM DUAL;
  SELECT
        name, value
  INTO
        temp_name, stat_val
  FROM
        v$sysstat
  WHERE
        NAME = 'db block gets';
  db_gets:=stat_val;
  dbms_output.put_line(temp_name||'='||to_char(db_gets));
  SELECT
        name, value
  INTO
        temp_name, stat_val
  FROM
        v$sysstat
```

```
WHERE
        name = 'consistent gets';
con_gets:=stat_val;
dbms_output.put_line(temp_name||'='||to_char(con_gets));
SELECT
        name, value
INTO
        temp_name, stat_val
FROM
        v$sysstat
WHERE
        name = 'physical reads';
p_reads:=stat_val;
dbms_output.put_line(temp_name||'='||to_char(p_reads));
SELECT COUNT(*)
INTO users
FROM v$session
WHERE username IS NOT NULL;
dbms_output.put_line('Users='||to_char(users));
  H_RATIO := (((DB_GETS+CON_GETS-p_reads)/(DB_GETS+CON_GETS))*100);
dbms_output.put_line('h_ratio='||to_char(h_ratio));
  INSERT INTO  hit_ratios
    VALUES (c_date,c_hour,db_gets,con_gets,p_reads,h_ratio,0,0,users);
COMMIT;
UPDATE hit_ratios SET period_hit_ratio =
  (SELECT ROUND(((((h2.consistent-h1.consistent)+(h2.db_block_gets-
h1.db_block_gets)-
      (h2.phy_reads-h1.phy_reads))/((h2.consistent-h1.consistent)+
      (h2.db_block_gets-h1.db_block_gets)))*100,2)
   FROM hit_ratios h1, hit_ratios h2
   WHERE h2.check_date = hit_ratios.check_date
    AND h2.check_hour = hit_ratios.check_hour
    AND ((h1.check_date = h2.check_date AND h1.check_hour+1 = h2.check_hour)
    OR(h1.check_date+1 = h2.check_date AND h1.check_hour = '23' AND
h2.check_hour='0')))
 WHERE period_hit_ratio = 0;
 COMMIT;
 UPDATE hit_ratios SET period_usage =
  (SELECT ((h2.consistent-h1.consistent)+(h2.db_block_gets-h1.db_block_gets))
   FROM hit_ratios h1, hit_ratios h2 where h2.check_date = hit_ratios.check_date
    AND h2.check_hour = hit_ratios.check_hour
    AND ((h1.check_date = h2.check_date AND h1.check_hour+1 = h2.check_hour)
    OR (h1.check_date+1 = h2.check_date
    AND h1.check_hour = '23' and h2.check_hour='0')))
 WHERE period_USAGE = 0;
 COMMIT;
 EXCEPTION
   WHEN ZERO_DIVIDE THEN
```

```
    INSERT INTO  hit_ratios  VALUES
(c_date,c_hour,db_gets,con_gets,p_reads,0,0,0,users);
    COMMIT;
END;
/
```

The procedure in Listing 11.10 is designed for hourly monitoring of the hit ratio.
Once the script completes, it is rescheduled to run the next hour. Of course, the job
is easier if you use the **DBMS_JOB** package to allow Oracle to execute the procedure
automatically. The script in Listing 11.11 demonstrates how this is done. To use a job
queue, the initialization parameters **JOB_QUEUE_PROCESSES** and **JOB_QUEUE_
INTERVAL** have to be set and the instance restarted. The hit ratio for the previous
hour is calculated, as are the cumulative hit ratio and usage as a function of read/
write activity.

**Listing 11.11   Example PL/SQL script to submit hit ratio procedure to job
                 queue.**
```
DECLARE
jobno NUMBER;
BEGIN
dbms_job.submit (jobno, 'HITRATIO;',sysdate,'sysdate+1');
dbms_output.put_line(TO_CHAR(jobno));
END;
Note: You must put a semicolon at the end of the "HITRATIO" statement.
```

Some example results, generated by the script in Listing 11.12, are shown in Table
11.11. Using the **DECODE** and **PAD** statements, you can plot the hit ratio data as a
graph on any printer. This program is shown in Listing 11.13.

Listing 11.12   Script to generate hit ratio and usage report.
```
REM
REM NAME   :HRSUMM.SQL
REM FUNCTION:GENERATE SUMMARY REPORT OF PERIOD HIT RATIOS AND USAGE
REM FUNCTION:BETWEEN TWO DATES
REM USE :FROM SQLPlus
REM Limitations   : None
REM Revisions:
REM  Date Modified By  Reason For change
REM  10-JUL-1992 M.AULT  INITIAL CREATE
REM  23-Jun-1997 M.AULT     Verify against 8
REM
SET VERIFY OFF PAGES 58 NEWPAGE 0
START title80 "HIT RATIO AND USAGE FOR &&CHECK_DATE1 TO &&CHECK_DATE2"
DEFINE output = rep_out/&db/hrsumm.lis
```

```
SPOOL &output
SELECT
        check_date,
        check_hour,
        period_hit_ratio,
        period_usage,
        users
FROM
        hit_ratios
WHERE
        check_date BETWEEN '&&check_date1' AND '&&check_date2'
ORDER BY
        check_date,check_hour;
SPOOL OFF
PAUSE Press return to continue
```

Table 11.11   Example output of periodic hit ratio report.

Date: 06/23/97 Time: 05:59 AM	HIT RATIO AND USAGE FOR 22-jun-97 TO 23-jun-ORTEST1 database			Page: 1 SYSTEM
CHECK_DAT	CHECK_HOUR	PERIOD_HIT_RATIO	PERIOD_USAGE	USERS
----------------	----------------	------------------------	--------------------	--------
22-JUN-97	13			1
22-JUN-97	15			2
22-JUN-97	16	97.76	2098	2
22-JUN-97	17	100	1066	2
22-JUN-97	18	100	1098	2
22-JUN-97	19	100	1067	2
22-JUN-97	20	100	1096	2
22-JUN-97	21	100	1066	2
22-JUN-97	22	100	1096	2
22-JUN-97	23	100	1067	2
23-JUN-97	0	100	1096	2
23-JUN-97	1	100	1073	2
23-JUN-97	2	100	1096	2
23-JUN-97	3	100	1067	2
23-JUN-97	4	100	1324	2
23-JUN-97	5	100	1067	2

16 rows selected.

Note: The 100 hit ratios are not because I am the perfect DBA; they are a result of the way the system treats purely internal (**V$**) requests and an artifact of the calculation process.

The problem with sporadic monitoring of hit ratios is that the DBA may catch the system at a low point, or just when the database usage has switched from one user to another on a different application. All of this can contribute to incorrect hit ratio results. The use of a periodic script to monitor hit ratio tends to even out these fluctuations and provide a better look at the statistic.

Another problem with looking at the hit ratio as it is described in the Oracle manuals is that you are looking at a running average, a cumulative value. This will result in low readings when the database is started and high readings after it has been running. Graphs generated using modifications to the script in Listing 11.13, showing actual periodic hit ratio and cumulative hit ratio, are shown in Tables 11.12 and 11.13.

Listing 11.13   SQL script to generate a 132-column hit ratio graph.

```
REM
REM NAME       :HRATIO_REPORT.SQL
REM PURPOSE:CREATE PLOT OF PERIOD HIT RATIO FOR 1 DAY
REM USE         :FROM STATUS_REPORTS.COM
REM Limitations : None
REM Revisions:
REM  Date              Modified By         Reason For change
REM  10-JUL-1992          M. AULT       INITIAL CREATE
REM           23-Jun-1997 M. Ault       Verify for 8
REM
rem host SET TERM/WID=132 REM: For VMS only, won't work under Unix
set lines 131 newpage 0 VERIFY OFF pages 180 space 0 feedback off column hr format
99
start title132 "Period HR for &&check_date1 TO &&check_date2"
define output = 'rep_out/&db/phrgrph.lis'
spool &output
select
    check_hour hr,
    decode(round(period_hit_ratio),0,'o',null) zchk0,
    decode(round(period_hit_ratio),1,'o',null) chk1,
    decode(round(period_hit_ratio),2,'o',null) chk2,
    decode(round(period_hit_ratio),3,'o',null) chk3,
    decode(round(period_hit_ratio),4,'o',null) chk4,
    decode(round(period_hit_ratio),5,'o',null) chk5,

       .
       .
       .

    decode(round(period_hit_ratio),94,'o',null) chk94,
    decode(round(period_hit_ratio),95,'o',null) chk95,
    decode(round(period_hit_ratio),96,'o',null) chk96,
    decode(round(period_hit_ratio),97,'o',null) chk97,
    decode(round(period_hit_ratio),98,'o',null) chk98,
```

```
      decode(round(period_hit_ratio),99,'o',null) chk99,
      decode(round(period_hit_ratio),100,'o',null) chk100
from hit_ratios
WHERE CHECK_DATE BETWEEN '&&CHECK_DATE1' AND '&&CHECK_DATE2'
order by CHECK_DATE,check_hour;
spool off
PAUSE 'PRESS RETURN TO CONTINUE'
rem host SET TERM/WID=80  rem: Only for VMS, will not work on UNIX
```

For the cumulative graph, **hit_ratio**, instead of **period_hit_ratio**, is fed into the **DECODE** statements. You can use this technique to plot just about any data set if you normalize the numbers to between 0 and 100. As you can see, the cumulative hit ratio graph stayed fairly constant for the period, while the actual, or period, hit ratio varied between 18.78 and 92.95 percent. In fact, the cumulative hit ratio will reach a steady, slowly increasing value, shortly after startup.

If your hit ratio for periods of high usage is below 70 to 90 percent, increase the **DB_BLOCK_BUFFERS** INIT.ORA parameter. As you can see from Table 11.11, when

Table 11.12 Graph of periodic hit ratio for 18 May, 1993.

Date: 06/05/93	"Your Company Name"	Page: 1
Time: 03:52 PM	Period HR by hour for 18-may-93 "Your" Database	DEV_DBA

```
HRZCCCCCCCCCCCCCCCCCCCCCCCCCCCCCCCCCCCCCCCCCMCCCCCCCCCCCCCCCCCCCCCCCCCCCECCCCCCCCC
                                o
 1                              o
 2                              o
 3                              o
 4                              o
 5                              o
 6                              o
 7                              o
 8                        o
 9                          o
10                                                          o
11
12                     o
13                                                  o
14              o
15              o
16              o
17               o
18              o
19              o
20              o
21              o
22              o
23              o
23                                                      o
```

Table 11.13   Graph of cumulative hit ratio for 18 May, 1993.

Date: 06/05/93	"Your Company Name"	Page: 1
Time: 03:52 PM	Period HR by hour for 18-may-93 "Your" Database	DEV_DBA

```
HRZCCCCCCCCCCCCCCCCCCCCCCCCCCCCCCCCCCCCCMCCCCCCCCCCCCCCCCCCCCCCCCCCCCCCCCCNCC
 1                                                              o
 2                                                              o
 3                                                              o
 4                                                              o
 5                                                              o
 6                                                             o
 7                                                             o
 8                                                             o
 9                                                             o
10                                                           o
11                                                          o
12                                                              o
13                                                             o
14                                                            o
15                                                            o
16                                                            o
17                                                            o
18                                                           o
19                                                           o
20                                                           o
21                                                           o
22                                                           o
```

database usage was minimal, the hit ratio hovered at 18 to 20 percent; once usage increased above 10,000 to 20,000, the hit ratio leapt to greater than 90 percent, as would be expected.

If **DB_BLOCK_BUFFERS** is set too high, you may run out of PAD area under VMS or exceed shared memory size for your instance on Unix. Another possible result is that the entire Oracle process could be swapped out because of memory contention with other processes. In either case, it is not a desirable condition. To avoid exceeding your PAD or shared memory areas, be sure you set these values high when creating the instance. To avoid swapping, know how much memory you are able to access; your system administrator can tell you this.

Use Of *x$cbrbh* And *x$cbcbh* Tables

Oracle provides a virtual table owned by the SYS user to provide information on the effects of adding buffers to the buffer cache. This is the **x$cbrbh** table. This table has two columns: **indx** and **count**. You activate the table by setting the value of the initialization parameter **DB_BLOCK_LRU_EXTENDED_STATISTICS** to a nonzero value, indicating the number of buffers you wish to add. The value you set this parameter to will determine the number of rows in the **x$cbrbh** table. There is one row for each additional buffer.

Once **DB_BLOCK_LRU_EXTENDED_STATISTICS** is set, the database will have to be shut down and restarted. This parameter should not be left enabled, as it will cause a performance hit. The magnitude of the performance hit is directly proportional to the number of additional buffers about which data is collected .

There are two methods for reviewing the statistics collected in **v$cbrbh**. The first is to select the sum of the values of **count** over a specific interval:

```
SELECT SUM(count) "interval total"
                FROM v$kcbrbh
                WHERE indx BETWEEN ( interval start, interval end);
```

The second, which is the suggested method, gives more detailed information. It provides summation over several intervals and gives the DBA more detail upon which to base the choice of number of buffers to add:

```
SELECT
    50 * TRUNC(indx/50)+1||' to '||50 * (TRUNC(indx/50)+1) "interval",
    SUM(count) "Buffer Cache Hits"
FROM  sys.x$kcbrbh
GROUP BY TRUNC(indx/50);
```

The output from the above **SELECT** looks like the following:

Interval	Buffer Cache Hits
1 to 50	17350
51 to 100	9345
101 to 150	404
151 to 200	19568

You can change the value of 50 to any appropriate value. The output of this report shows the interval and the expected increase in buffer cache hits that could be expected from adding that many buffers to the cache. These examples show that adding 50, 100, or 200 buffers would significantly add to the number of hits. Adding 150 buffers would add very few hits. Therefore, add 50, 100, or 200 buffers, but not 150.

The script shown in Listing 11.14 gives a more refined report.

Listing 11.14 More detailed report of Data Dictionary cache increment results.

```
rem   ********************************************************************
rem
rem   NAME: SGA_INC.sql
rem
rem   HISTORY:
rem   Date            Who                       What
rem   --------        ----------------          -----------------------------------
rem   10/25/92        Cary Millsap              Creation
rem   01/07/93        Michael Brouillette       Switched to title80
rem   06/05/93        Mike Ault                 Added capability to use interval
rem
rem   FUNCTION: Examine the statistice in the X$KCBRBH table with the
rem   intent to increase the size of the SGA.
rem
rem   ********************************************************************
COLUMN bufval NEW_VALUE nbuf NOPRINT
COLUMN thits NEW_VALUE tot_hits NOPRINT
SELECT  value   bufval
FROM   v$parameter
WHERE
   LOWER(name) = 'db_block_lru_extended_statistics';
SELECT SUM(count)  thits FROM v$kcbrbh;
START title80 "Prospective Hits if &nbuf Cache Buffers were Added"
COLUMN interval   FORMAT            a20 JUSTIFY c HEADING 'Buffers'
COLUMN cache_hits FORMAT 999,999,990 JUSTIFY c HEADING -
   'Cache Hits that would have been|gained by adding Buffers'
COLUMN cum FORMAT 99.99 HEADING 'Percent of Gain'
SET TERMOUT OFF FEEDBACK OFF VERIFY OFF ECHO OFF
SPOOL rep_out/&db/sga_inc.lis
SELECT
lpad(TO_CHAR((&nbuf/&incr)*TRUNC(indx/(&nbuf/&&incr))+1,'999,990'),8)||' to '||
LPAD(TO_CHAR((&nbuf/&&incr)*(TRUNC(indx/(&nbuf/&&incr))+1),'999,990'),8)
interval,
   SUM(count) cache_hits, SUM(count)/&tot_hits * 100 cum
FROM v$kcbrbh
GROUP BY
   TRUNC(indx/(&nbuf/&&incr));
SPOOL OFF
SET TERMOUT ON FEEDBACK 15 VERIFY ON
UNDEF NBUF
```

The report in Listing 11.14 prompts for the value to increment the summation by and then generates a report that also lists the percentage gain for each increment.

Of course, the analysis of the buffer cache may indicate that the buffers have been over-allocated. The **x$kcbcbh** table provides data on the results of removing buffers from the buffer cache. The current buffer cache has a row in the table for each buffer configured in the SGA. The collection of statistics is enabled by setting **DB_BLOCK_LRU_STATISTICS** to **TRUE**, then shutting down and restarting the database. This data collection causes a performance hit; its severity is proportional to the number of current buffers in the buffer cache. Once data collection is complete, the **DB_BLOCK_LRU_STATISTICS** parameter should be set to **FALSE**.

The methods for reviewing data in the **x$kcbcbh** table are similar to those used for the **x$kcbrbh** table. You can select for a specific interval, or gather summation for ranges of buffers.

To determine the results from having, say, only 100 buffers in the cache, perform the following **SELECT**:

```
SELECT SUM(count) "Hit Misses"
                FROM x$kcbcbh
                WHERE indx >= 100;
```

To summarize data over intervals of buffers, you could use a **SELECT** similar to the following:

```
SELECT 10*TRUNC(indx/10)+1||' to '||10*(TRUNC(indx/10)+1) "Interval",
SUM(copunt) 'Buffer Hits'
FROM x$kcbcbh
WHERE indx > 0
GROUP BY TRUNC(indx/10);
```

The results will look like the following:

Interval	Buffer Hits
1 to 10	2500
11 to 20	1345
21 to 30	1097
31 to 40	896
41 to 50	110

In this case, if the number of buffers were reduced by 10, there would be few hits lost. If anything greater than 10 were dropped, significant losses in hits would occur. Therefore, drop only 10 buffers in this situation.

A more detailed report is generated with the script in Listing 11.15.

Once the buffer cache is tuned, you have completed the tuning of memory. The next step is to tune I/O contention.

Listing 11.15   Example of buffer cache decrement detailed report script.

```
rem   ****************************************************************
rem   NAME: SGA_DEC.sql
rem
rem   HISTORY:
rem   Date              Who                    What
rem   --------          ------------------     ------------------------
rem   10/25/92          Cary Millsap           Creation
rem   01/07/93          Michael Brouillette    Switched to title80
rem   06/05/93          Mike Ault              Added selectable ranges
rem   FUNCTION: Examine statistics in the X$KCBCBH table with intent to
rem            shrink the SGA.
rem   ****************************************************************
COLUMN bufval NEW_VALUE nbuf NOPRINT
COLUMN thits NEW_VALUE tot_hits NOPRINT
SELECT value  bufval
FROM v$parameter
WHERE
  LOWER(name) = 'db_block_buffers';
SELECT SUM(count) thits
FROM x$kcbhcbh;
START title80 "Lost Hits if &nbuf Cache Buffers were Removed"
COLUMN interval    FORMAT           a20 JUSTIFY c HEADING 'Buffers'
COLUMN cache_hits FORMAT 999,999,990 JUSTIFY c HEADING -
  'Hits that would have been lost|had Cache Buffers been removed'
COLUMN cum FORMAT 99.99 'Percent of loss'
SET TERMOUT OFF FEEDBACK OFF VERIFY OFF ECHO OFF
SPOOL rep_out/&db/sga_dec.lis
SELECT
  LPAD(to_char(&&incr*trunc(indx/&&incr)+1,'999,990'),8)||' to '||
  LPAD(to_char(&&incr*(trunc(indx/&&incr)+1),'999,990'),8) interval,
  SUM(count)  cache_hits,
  SUM(count)/&tot_hits * 100 cum
FROM x$kcbcbh
WHERE indx > 0
GROUP BY
  TRUNC(indx/&&incr) ;
SPOOL OFF
SET TERMOUT ON FEEDBACK 15 VERIFY ON
```

 ## Tools For Tuning I/O Contention

Once the shared SQL areas and buffer caches have been tuned, you must turn your attention to the I/O performance of the disks and files associated with the Oracle system to realize further performance gains.

Tuning I/O To Avoid Bottlenecks

Once the application and memory areas have been tuned, the next performance bottleneck can be the disk subsystem. This system is tuned by tuning the input and output processes that Oracle uses, reducing contention for disk resources, and reducing or eliminating dynamic space allocation within database data files.

Tuning The DBWR Process

The DBWR process manages the buffer cache. In this capacity, it writes filled buffers from the buffer cache in the SGA to the disks. Obviously, a properly tuned DBWR process will be the first step in tuning I/O for the Oracle system. The DBWR process, as described in the section on UTLBSTAT and UTLESTAT, uses the hidden INIT.ORA parameters **_DB_BLOCK_WRITE_BATCH** and **_DB_BLOCK_MAX_SCAN_CNT** to determine when it should write used, or dirty, buffers to the disk, thus freeing them for further use. DBWR triggers on the following conditions:

- A user process writes a used buffer to the dirty buffer list and finds it is **_DB_BLOCK_WRITE_BATCH** / 2 long.

- A user process searches **_DB_BLOCK_MAX_SCAN_CNT** buffers without finding a clean one.

- DBWR has been inactive for three seconds.

- When a checkpoint occurs, LGWR signals DBWR, triggering it to write.

The DBWR writes out **_DB_BLOCK_WRITE_BATCH** buffers each time it is triggered. If there aren't that many buffers in the dirty buffer list, the buffers on the LRU list are written until **_DB_BLOCK_WRITE_BATCH** buffers are written.

DBWR is monitored using the statistic **free buffer waits** (available from the **v$sysstat** table), which should be as low as possible and should remain at a slowly increasing value. What this means for your system you have to decide. I suggest using a method similar to that shown in the previous section to follow the delta values for this statistic. If you see spikes when database activity is high, consider the following:

- If your system doesn't support asynchronous I/O, use more db writers by setting the initialization parameter **DB_WRITERS** (pre-Oracle8) or **DBWR_IO_SLAVES** (for Oracle8) equal to the number of disks used by Oracle.

- If your system supports asynchronous I/O, you can set the **ASYNC_IO** initialization parameter to **TRUE**.

If setting **DB_WRITERS**, **DBWR_IO_SLAVES**, or **ASYNC_IO** doesn't help reduce the spikes on free buffer waits, verify that **_DB_BLOCK_MAX_SCAN_CNT** is set at 30 or greater. Normally, the default value of 30 is fine for this parameter. If you are dissatisfied with the performance of DBWR, try increasing the INIT.ORA parameter **_DB_BLOCK_WRITE_BATCH** first. This improves DBWR's ability to use operating system facilities to write to multiple disks and write adjacent blocks in a single I/O operation. Increasing the number of db block buffers may also be in order if DBWR performance is poor.

Disk Contention

Once DBWR is tuned, you need to look at disk contention. Disk contention happens when users attempt to read the same disk at the same time, or in some cases, access a different disk through the same controller path at the same time. This is prevented by spreading Oracle-related files across several platters or sets of platters—the more the better. The new RAID options don't relieve the DBA of file-placement concerns. You should be sure that the RAID volumes are properly set. I had one system where a system administrator set up multiple RAID 5 volumes using two disks for each volume (a hint: the 5 is a meaningful number for RAID 5).

The DBA can monitor disk activity by looking at the statistics for disk I/O stored in the database virtual tables. Using the hit ratio scripts from the previous section as a model, the DBA should be able to devise a periodic monitoring script that calculates periodic disk usage as well as the cumulative figures already stored in the virtual tables. The script in Listing 11.16 shows how to access the SYS tables for this cumulative information.

For periodic measurements, simply perform the **SELECT** shown in Listing 11.16 as part of an update to a DBA-created table. In addition to the disk information, append a date and time stamp; then, the table can be used to perform periodic disk I/O calculations, just as did the **hit_ratios** table in the previous pages. Instead of indexing by only date and hour, index by date, hour, and file name.

Listing 11.16   SQL script for report on disk activity.

```
REM
REM NAME       :FILE_EFF.SQL
REM PURPOSE :GENERATE FILE IO EFFICIENCIES REPORT
REM USE            :FROM STATUS_REPORTS.COM
REM Limitations :MUST BE RUN FROM ORACLE DBA ACCOUNT
REM Revisions:
REM Date                    Modified By         Reason For change
REM 10-JUL-1992             M. AULT             INITIAL CREATE
```

```
REM 07-JUN-1993          M.AULT              Added reads to writes, reformatted
REM 23-Jun-1997          M.Ault              kcffio went away, rewrote to use
REM                                          existing views/tables
SET PAGES 58 NEWPAGE 0
SET LINES 131
COLUMN eff    FORMAT A6                            HEADING '% Eff'
COLUMN rw FORMAT 9,999,999 HEADING 'Phys Block|read/writes'
COLUMN ts FORMAT A22                          HEADING 'Tablespace Name'
COLUMN name FORMAT A40                          HEADING 'File Name'
start title132 "FILE IO EFFICIENCY"
BREAK ON ts
DEFINE OUTPUT = 'rep_out/&db/file_io.lis'
spool &OUTPUT
SELECT
    f.tablespace_name ts,
     f.file_name name,
    v.phyreads+v.phywrts rw,
    TO_CHAR(DECODE(v.phyblkrd,0,null,
    ROUND(100*(v.phyrds+v.phywrts)/(v.phyblkrd+v.phyblkwrt),2))) eff
FROM dba_data_files f, v$filestat v
WHERE f.file_id=v.file#
ORDER BY 1,file#;
SPOOL OFF
PAUSE Press return to continue
```

This is a cumulative report that gives information based on I/O since the Oracle instance was started. The report generated (shown in Table 11.14) lists physical block reads and efficiency (the efficiency number measures the percentage of time Oracle asked for and got the right block the first time; this is a function of the type of table scan and indexing).

Some points to notice about the example report in Table 11.14 are:

- The SYSTEM areas in general have relatively low efficiency. This is a result of indexes and tables being mixed together in the SYSTEM area. A classic case on Oracle's part of "Do what we say, not what we do."

- If your temporary tablespace (TEMP in the example) shows an efficiency number, someone is using it for real, instead of temporary, tables.

- Rollback efficiency should always be 100 percent; if not, someone is using the rollback area for tables.

Table 11.14 Example of the output of file I/O efficiency report.

Date: 06/23/97	Page: 1		
Time: 11:30 AM	FILE IO EFFICIENCY ORCNETT3 database		SYS
Tablespace Name	File Name	Phys Block read/writes	% Eff
RBS	/oracle04/ORCNETT3/data/rbs01.dbf	3,728	100
APPL_DATA	/oracle05/ORCNETT3/data/APLDAT01_ORCNETT3.dbf	10	100
	/oracle05/ORCNETT3/data/APLDAT02_ORCNETT3.dbf	427	100
	/oracle05/ORCNETT3/data/APLDAT03_ORCNETT3.dbf	10	100
	/oracle05/ORCNETT3/data/APLDAT04_ORCNETT3.dbf	1	100
	/oracle05/ORCNETT3/data/APLDAT05_ORCNETT3.dbf	4	100
	/oracle05/ORCNETT3/data/APLDAT06_ORCNETT3.dbf	223	100
APPL_INDEX	/oracle06/ORCNETT3/data/APLIND01_ORCNETT3.dbf	15	100
	/oracle06/ORCNETT3/data/APLIND02_ORCNETT3.dbf	494	100
	/oracle06/ORCNETT3/data/APLIND03_ORCNETT3.dbf	166	100
	/oracle06/ORCNETT3/data/APLIND04_ORCNETT3.dbf	51	100
SYSTEM	/oracle00/ORCNETT3/data/system01.dbf	2,552	65.71
TEMP	/oracle01/ORCNETT3/data/temp01.dbf	0	
	/oracle01/ORCNETT3/data/temp02.dbf	0	
TOOLS	/oracle02/ORCNETT3/data/tools01.dbf	2,710	88.28
USERS	/oracle03/ORCNETT3/data/user01.dbf	23	100

16 rows selected.

- Index tablespaces should always show high efficiencies; if they don't, then either the indexes are bad or someone is using the index areas for normal tables.

- An attempt should be made to even out I/O. In the example, too much I/O is being done on **oracle04**; some of these data files should be spread to other disks.

- This report shows total I/O for the time frame beginning with the Oracle system startup. The results could be stored for two or more dates and times and then subtracted to show the disk I/O for a selected period of time. Use UTLBSTAT/UTLESTAT for this type of measurement.

By producing this report before and after an application test run, you can develop an idea of the disk I/O profile for the application. With this profile, combined with information concerning the maximum I/O supported by each disk, or each controller, you can determine how best to split out the application's files among disks.

For more detailed information and further reading, take a look at the following:

- *Oracle7 Server Tuning*, Release 7.3, Part No. A32537-1, Oracle Corp., June 1996.

- *Oracle7 Server Administrators Guide*, Release 7.3, Part No. A32535-1, Oracle Corp., February 1996.

- *Oracle8 Server Tuning*, Release 8.0-Beta2, Part No. A50660-1, Oracle Corp., February 1997.

- *Tuning Oracle*, Oracle Press, Osborne-Mcgraw-Hill, Corey, Michael J., Abbey, Michael, and Dechichio Jr., Daniel, 1995.

- *Oracle Performance Tuning*, Gurry, Mark, Corrigan, Peter, Second Edition, O'Reilly and Associates Inc., November 1996.

- *The Key 20 Scripts For The DBA To Ensure Sleep Is Not Just A Dream*, Trezzo, Joseph C., TUSC, Paper 35, IOUG-A Alive!, Dallas, Texas, Spring 1997.

- *Tuning An Oracle RDBMS, One View*, Osborn, Paul, Menlo Software, Paper 15, IOUG-A Alive!, Dallas, Texas, Spring 1997.

- *Quick Impact Tuning For The DBA And Developer*, Niemiec, Richard J., Paper 136, TUSC, IOUG-A Alive!, Dallas, Texas, Spring 1997.

Tuning To Prevent Contention

Contention occurs when a number of users attempt to access the same resource at the same time. This can occur for any database object, but is most noticeable when the contention is for rollback segments, redo logs, latches, or locks. Under Oracle7, you can also experience contention with the processes involved with the multi-threaded server.

To correct contention, you must first realize that it is occurring. The two scripts shown in Listing 11.17 can be used to monitor for contention.

Listing 11.17   SQL and PL/SQL scripts to generate contention statistics.

```
REM
REM NAME    : DO_CALSTAT.SQL
REM FUNCTION :Generate calculated statisitics report using
REM FUNCTION :just_statistics procedure
REM USE          :FROM STATUS.SQL or SQLPLUS
```

```
REM Limitations              :
REM Revisions:
REM Date                     Modified By              Reason For change
REM 05-MAY-1992              Mike Ault   Initial Creation
REM 23-JUN-1997               Mike Ault   Updated to V8
REM
SET PAGES 58  NEWPAGE 0
EXECUTE just_statistics
START title80 "CALCULATED STATISTICS REPORT"
DEFINE output = rep_out\&db\cal_stat.lis
SPOOL &output
SELECT * FROM dba_temp;
SPOOL OFF


Listing of just_statistics - The called PL/SQL procedure

CREATE OR REPLACE PROCEDURE just_statistics AS
    start_date      DATE;
    dd_ratio        NUMBER := 0;
    r_calls         NUMBER := 0;
    h_ratio         NUMBER := 0;
    suhw_cont       NUMBER := 0;
    subw_cont       NUMBER := 0;
    uhw_cont        NUMBER := 0;
    ubw_cont        NUMBER := 0;
    db_gets         NUMBER := 0;
    con_gets        NUMBER := 0;
    p_reads         NUMBER := 0;
    suh_waits       NUMBER := 0;
    sub_waits       NUMBER := 0;
    uh_waits        NUMBER := 0;
    ub_waits        NUMBER := 0;
    u_calls         NUMBER := 0;
    calls_u         NUMBER := 0;
    rlog_wait       NUMBER := 0;
    stat_name       VARCHAR2(64);
    temp_name       VARCHAR2(64);
    stat_val        NUMBER := 0;
    temp_value      NUMBER := 0;
    version         varchar2(9);
CURSOR get_latch IS
  SELECT a.name,100.*b.sleeps/b.gets
  FROM v$latchname a, v$latch b
  WHERE a.latch# = b.latch# and b.sleeps > 0;
CURSOR get_totals IS
  SELECT object_type,count(*)
  FROM dba_objects
  WHERE owner not IN ('SYS','SYSTEM')
```

```
    GROUP BY object_type
    ORDER BY object_type;
CURSOR get_stat(stat IN VARCHAR2) IS
  SELECT name,value
  FROM  v$sysstat
  WHERE name = stat;
CURSOR get_count(stat IN VARCHAR2) IS
  SELECT class,"COUNT"
  FROM v$waitstat
  WHERE class = stat_name;
BEGIN
  DELETE dba_temp;
BEGIN
DBMS_REVEALNET.STARTUP_DATE(start_date);
  IF start_date IS NOT NULL THEN
   INSERT INTO dba_temp VALUES
   'Startup Date:'||TO_CHAR(start_date,'dd-mon-yy hh24:mi:ss'),0,1);
  ELSE
   INSERT INTO dba_temp values ('Startup Date: unknown',0,1);
  END IF;
END;
BEGIN
  stat_name := 'recursive calls';
         OPEN get_stat(stat_name);
         FETCH get_stat INTO temp_name, r_calls;
         CLOSE get_stat;
EXCEPTION
    WHEN NO_DATA_FOUND THEN
CLOSE get_stat;
END;
BEGIN
  stat_name := 'DATA DICTIONARY MISS %';
  SELECT
    stat_name,(SUM(getmisses)/SUM(gets))*100 INTO temp_name,dd_ratio
  FROM v$rowcache;
  INSERT INTO dba_temp VALUES (stat_name, dd_ratio,17);
EXCEPTION
    WHEN NO_DATA_FOUND THEN
     INSERT INTO dba_temp VALUES (stat_name,0,17);
    COMMIT;
END;
BEGIN
  stat_name := 'user calls';
         OPEN  get_stat(stat_name);
         FETCH get_stat INTO temp_name, u_calls;
         CLOSE get_stat;
```

```
EXCEPTION
    WHEN NO_DATA_FOUND THEN
CLOSE get_stat;
END;
BEGIN
  stat_name := 'db block gets';
        OPEN get_stat(stat_name);
        FETCH get_stat INTO temp_name, db_gets;
        CLOSE get_stat;
EXCEPTION
    WHEN NO_DATA_FOUND THEN
CLOSE get_stat;
END;
BEGIN
  stat_name := 'consistent gets';
        OPEN get_stat(stat_name);
        FETCH get_stat INTO temp_name, con_gets;
        CLOSE get_stat;
EXCEPTION
    WHEN NO_DATA_FOUND THEN
CLOSE get_stat;
END;
BEGIN
  stat_name := 'physical reads';
        OPEN get_stat(stat_name);
        FETCH get_stat INTO temp_name, p_reads;
        CLOSE get_stat;
EXCEPTION
    WHEN NO_DATA_FOUND THEN
CLOSE get_stat;
END;
BEGIN
  stat_name := 'system undo header';
        OPEN get_count(stat_name);
        FETCH get_count INTO temp_name, suh_waits;
        CLOSE get_count;
EXCEPTION
    WHEN NO_DATA_FOUND THEN
CLOSE get_count;
END;
BEGIN
  stat_name := 'system undo block';
        OPEN get_count(stat_name);
        FETCH get_count INTO temp_name, sub_waits;
        CLOSE get_count;
EXCEPTION
    WHEN NO_DATA_FOUND THEN
```

```
CLOSE get_count;
END;
BEGIN
  stat_name := 'undo header';
          OPEN get_count(stat_name);
          FETCH get_count INTO temp_name, uh_waits;
          CLOSE get_count;
EXCEPTION
    WHEN NO_DATA_FOUND THEN
CLOSE get_count;
END;
BEGIN
  stat_name := 'undo block';
          OPEN get_count(stat_name);
          FETCH get_count INTO temp_name, ub_waits;
          CLOSE get_count;
EXCEPTION
    WHEN NO_DATA_FOUND THEN
CLOSE get_count;
END;
BEGIN
    calls_u := (r_calls/u_calls);
    h_ratio := ((db_gets+con_gets)/(db_gets+con_gets+p_reads));
    suhw_cont  := (suh_waits/(db_gets+con_gets)*100);
    subw_cont  := (sub_waits/(db_gets+con_gets)*100);
    uhw_cont   := (uh_waits/(db_gets+con_gets)*100);
    ubw_cont   := (ub_waits/(db_gets+con_gets)*100);
    stat_name := 'RECURSIVE CALLS PER USER';
  INSERT INTO dba_temp VALUES (stat_name, calls_u,18);
    stat_name := 'CUMMULATIVE HIT RATIO';
  INSERT INTO dba_temp VALUES (stat_name, H_RATIO,2);
    stat_name := 'SYS UNDO HDR WAIT CONTENTION %';
  INSERT INTO dba_temp VALUES (stat_name, suhw_cont,3);
    stat_name := 'SYS UNDO BLK WAIT CONTENTION %';
  INSERT INTO dba_temp VALUES (stat_name, subw_cont,3);
    stat_name := 'UNDO HDR WAIT CONTENTION %';
  INSERT INTO dba_temp VALUES (stat_name, uhw_cont,3);
    stat_name := 'UNDO BLK WAIT CONTENTION %';
  INSERT INTO dba_temp VALUES (stat_name, ubw_cont,3);
    stat_name := 'freelist';
          OPEN get_count(stat_name);
          FETCH get_count INTO temp_name, stat_val;
          CLOSE get_count;
  stat_name := 'FREE LIST CONTENTION RATIO';
    INSERT INTO dba_temp VALUES (stat_name, stat_val/(db_gets+con_gets),18);
```

```
EXCEPTION
    WHEN ZERO_DIVIDE THEN
        INSERT INTO dba_temp VALUES (stat_name,0,32);
        CLOSE get_count;
    COMMIT;
    WHEN NO_DATA_FOUND THEN
        INSERT INTO dba_temp VALUES (stat_name,0,32);
        CLOSE get_count;
    COMMIT;
END;
BEGIN
version:=DBMS_REVEALNET.RETURN_VERSION;
IF substr(version,1,5) in ('7.2.3','7.3.0','7.3.1','7.3.2','7.3.3','8.0.0',
'8.0.0','8.0.1','8.0.2', '8.0.3') THEN
  stat_name := 'LATCH MISS %';
        SELECT (1-((SUM(sleeps)+SUM(immediate_misses))/(
        SUM(gets)+SUM(immediate_misses)+SUM(immediate_gets)))*100) INTO stat_val
        FROM v$latch;
    INSERT INTO dba_temp VALUES (stat_name, stat_val,4);
END IF;
EXCEPTION
    WHEN NO_DATA_FOUND THEN
        INSERT INTO dba_temp VALUES (stat_name,0,4);
    COMMIT;
END;
BEGIN
  stat_name := 'ROLLBACK WAIT %';
        SELECT (SUM(waits)/SUM(gets))*100 INTO stat_val
        FROM v$rollstat;
    INSERT INTO dba_temp VALUES (stat_name, stat_val,5);
EXCEPTION
    WHEN NO_DATA_FOUND THEN
        INSERT INTO dba_temp VALUES (stat_name,0,5);
    COMMIT;
END;
BEGIN
  stat_name := 'LIBRARY RELOAD %';
        SELECT SUM(reloads)/SUM(pins)*100   INTO stat_val
        FROM v$librarycache;
    INSERT INTO dba_temp VALUES (stat_name, stat_val,5);
EXCEPTION
    WHEN NO_DATA_FOUND THEN
        INSERT INTO dba_temp VALUES (stat_name,0,5);
    COMMIT;
END;
```

```
BEGIN
  stat_name := 'table fetch by rowid';
        OPEN get_stat(stat_name);
        FETCH get_stat INTO temp_name, stat_val;
        CLOSE get_stat;
    INSERT INTO dba_temp VALUES (stat_name, stat_val,9);
EXCEPTION
    WHEN NO_DATA_FOUND THEN
        INSERT INTO dba_temp VALUES (stat_name,0,9);
CLOSE get_stat;
    COMMIT;
END;
BEGIN
  stat_name:='NON-INDEX LOOKUP RATIO';
  SELECT a.value/(a.value+b.value) INTO stat_val
  FROM v$sysstat a, v$sysstat b
  WHERE a.name='table scans (long tables)'
  AND b.name='table scans (short tables)';
  INSERT INTO dba_temp VALUES (stat_name, stat_val,8);
EXCEPTION
    WHEN NO_DATA_FOUND THEN
        INSERT INTO dba_temp VALUES (stat_name,0,8);
        CLOSE get_stat;
    COMMIT;
END;
BEGIN
  stat_name := 'table fetch continued row';
        OPEN get_stat(stat_name);
        FETCH get_stat INTO temp_name, stat_val;
        CLOSE get_stat;
    INSERT INTO dba_temp VALUES (stat_name, stat_val,14);
EXCEPTION
    WHEN NO_DATA_FOUND THEN
        INSERT INTO dba_temp VALUES (stat_name,0,14);
        CLOSE get_stat;
    COMMIT;
END;
BEGIN
  stat_name := 'sorts (memory)';
        OPEN get_stat(stat_name);
        FETCH get_stat INTO temp_name, stat_val;
        CLOSE get_stat;
    INSERT INTO dba_temp VALUES (stat_name, stat_val,15);
EXCEPTION
    WHEN NO_DATA_FOUND THEN
        INSERT INTO dba_temp VALUES (stat_name,0,15);
        CLOSE get_stat;
    COMMIT;
END;
```

```
BEGIN
  stat_name := 'sorts (disk)';
        OPEN get_stat(stat_name);
        FETCH get_stat INTO temp_name, stat_val;
        CLOSE get_stat;
  INSERT INTO dba_temp VALUES (stat_name, stat_val,16);
EXCEPTION
    WHEN NO_DATA_FOUND THEN
        INSERT INTO dba_temp VALUES (stat_name,0,16);
        CLOSE get_stat;
    COMMIT;
END;
BEGIN
  stat_name := 'redo log space requests';
        OPEN get_stat(stat_name);
        FETCH get_stat INTO temp_name, stat_val;
        CLOSE get_stat;
  INSERT INTO dba_temp VALUES (stat_name, stat_val,6);
EXCEPTION
    WHEN NO_DATA_FOUND THEN
        INSERT INTO dba_temp VALUES (stat_name,0,6);
        CLOSE get_stat;
    COMMIT;
END;
BEGIN
  stat_name := 'redo log space wait time';
        OPEN get_stat(stat_name);
        FETCH get_stat INTO temp_name, stat_val;
        CLOSE get_stat;
  INSERT INTO dba_temp VALUES (stat_name, stat_val, 6);
EXCEPTION
    WHEN NO_DATA_FOUND THEN
        INSERT INTO dba_temp VALUES (stat_name,0,6);
        CLOSE get_stat;
    COMMIT;
END;
BEGIN
  stat_name := 'TOTAL ALLOCATED MEG';
        SELECT SUM(BYTES)/1048576 INTO stat_val
        FROM dba_data_files WHERE
        STATUS = 'AVAILABLE';
  INSERT INTO dba_temp VALUES (stat_name, stat_val,25);
EXCEPTION
    WHEN NO_DATA_FOUND THEN
        INSERT INTO dba_temp VALUES (stat_name,0,25);
    COMMIT;
END;
```

```
BEGIN
  stat_name := 'TOTAL USED MEG';
        SELECT SUM(BYTES)/1048576 INTO stat_val
        FROM dba_extents;
  INSERT INTO dba_temp VALUES (stat_name, stat_val,26);
EXCEPTION
    WHEN NO_DATA_FOUND THEN
        INSERT INTO dba_temp VALUES (stat_name,0,26);
    COMMIT;
END;
BEGIN
  stat_name := 'TOTAL SGA SIZE';
        SELECT stat_name, SUM(b.value) INTO temp_name, stat_val
        FROM v$sga b;
  INSERT INTO dba_temp VALUES (stat_name, stat_val,31);
EXCEPTION
    WHEN NO_DATA_FOUND THEN
        INSERT INTO dba_temp VALUES (stat_name,0,31);
    COMMIT;
END;
BEGIN
OPEN get_latch;
LOOP
        FETCH get_latch INTO stat_name,stat_val;
        EXIT WHEN get_latch%NOTFOUND;
        INSERT INTO dba_temp VALUES (stat_name, stat_val,33);
END LOOP;
        CLOSE get_latch;
        COMMIT;
END;
BEGIN
OPEN get_totals;
LOOP
        FETCH get_totals INTO stat_name,stat_val;
        EXIT WHEN get_totals%NOTFOUND;
        INSERT INTO dba_temp VALUES (stat_name, stat_val,34);
END LOOP;
        CLOSE get_totals;
        COMMIT;
END;
  COMMIT;
END;
```

The first section of Listing 11.17 shows the SQL script used to call and run the PL/SQL script located in the second section of the listing. This script retrieves contention and database health-related statistics, and calculates other statistics based upon those it retrieves. An example of the report generated by these two scripts is shown in Table 11.15. The calls to the **dbms_revealnet** package shouldn't worry you; this package is on the CD-ROM included with the book.

The statistics calculated in Table 11.15 are shown in uppercase. The "raw" values are reported in lowercase. What is this report telling us? Let's look at each of the statistics:

- *Startup Date: 22-jun-97 19:09:38*—This is self-explanatory; it is the startup time for this instance. I report it because the statistics are cumulative, so if you run the report immediately upon startup, the results will be skewed. This is a quick check that the numbers will be valid.

- *CUMMULATIVE HIT RATIO*—As the name implies, this is the total cumulative hit ratio since the instance was started. Normally, it should rise to a maximum value and stay near there. If the maximum is much less than 0.90, you should look at increasing **DB_BLOCK_BUFFERS**.

- *SYS UNDO HDR WAIT CONTENTION %*—This is the contention for the system rollback segment. It is basically information only. If you see contention for the system rollback segment, too many people have access to SYS, SYSTEM, and INTERNAL, because these are the only users that should be using the system rollback segment.

- *UNDO BLK WAIT CONTENTION %*—This statistic shows contention for rollback segment blocks. If it reaches whole numbers, you should look at increasing the number of rollback segments.

- *UNDO HDR WAIT CONTENTION %*—This statistic shows contention for rollback segments. If you are getting rollback segment wait activity, then you need either more rollback segments or more extents in the existing rollbacks.

- *SYS UNDO BLK WAIT CONTENTION %*—See the previous entry for the system rollback segment.

- *LATCH MISS%*—This statistic shows if you are experiencing latch contention. If it reaches 5 to 10 percent, look into the CONTEND.SQL report to see which latches are causing the contention. Usually, you can fix this by increasing the **SHARED_POOL_SIZE** initialization parameter.

Table 11.15 Example of calculated statistics report.

Date: 06/23/97	Page:	1
Time: 01:46 PM	CALCULATED STATISTICS REPORT	SYSTEM
	ORCNETD1 database	

NAME	VALUE
Startup Date: 22-jun-97 19:09:38	0
CUMMULATIVE HIT RATIO	.94986157
SYS UNDO HDR WAIT CONTENTION %	0
UNDO BLK WAIT CONTENTION %	0
UNDO HDR WAIT CONTENTION %	0
SYS UNDO BLK WAIT CONTENTION %	0
LATCH MISS %	.99029399
ROLLBACK WAIT %	0
LIBRARY RELOAD %	.09405527
redo log space requests	1
redo log space wait time	79
NON-INDEX LOOKUPS RATIO	.00130208
table fetch by rowid	1756693
table fetch continued row	6311
sorts (memory)	6307
sorts (disk)	12
DATA DICTIONARY MISS %	.45421233
RECURSIVE CALLS PER USER	1.4314641
FREELIST CONTENTION RATIO	0
TOTAL ALLOCATED MEG	19228
TOTAL USED MEG	7303.5547
TOTAL SGA SIZE	251581848
cache buffers chains	1.469E-05
library cache	.02203606
virtual circuit queues	.00136422
virtual circuit buffers	.00383542
shared pool	.08755574
cache buffers lru chain	.00758422
row cache objects	.00045992
DATABASE LINK	1
FUNCTION	46
INDEX	804
PACKAGE	11
CLUSTER	1

(continued)

Table 11.15   Example of calculated statistics report (continued).

NAME	VALUE
PACKAGE BODY	11
PROCEDURE	317
SEQUENCE	190
SYNONYM	1697
TABLE	781
TRIGGER	272
VIEW	249

41 rows selected.

- *ROLLBACK WAIT %*—This statistic is related to the UNDO statistics. If it gets into the whole percentages, look at increasing rollback segments or number of extents.

- *LIBRARY RELOAD %*—This statistic shows how much the library cache is having to reload. This indicates the **SHARED_POOL_SIZE** parameter needs to be increased to prevent premature aging of objects.

- *redo log space requests*—This statistic shows that contention for redo logs is occurring. If you get values for this parameter, you may need to increase the number of redo log groups.

- *redo log space wait time*—This statistic goes hand-in-hand with redo log space requests. You must have the **TIMED_STATISTICS** initialization parameter set to **TRUE** to get meaningful values.

- *NON-INDEX LOOKUPS RATIO*—This calculated statistic gives the ratio of table scans (long tables) to the sum of table scans (long tables), plus table scans (short tables) based on the assumption that indexes will be much smaller than the tables they serve. More indexes will represent short tables. The ratio is a quick means to tell if you have enough (and proper) indexes.

- *table fetch by rowid*—This tells the number of times a value was retrieved using the fetch by **ROWID** access path.

- *table fetch continued row*—This statistic indicates that chained rows exist in the database. If it is greater than 10 percent of the table fetches total (table fetch by rowid + table fetch continued row), then you need to look at your high update tables where you have **VARCHAR2** values. Analyze these tables for chained rows.

- *sorts (memory)*—This statistic tells you how many memory sorts are being done. Memory sorts are good.

- *sorts (disk)*—This tells you how many disk sorts are being done. Generally speaking, disk sorts are bad and should be avoided. If you get sorts (disk), increase your **SORT_AREA_SIZE** initialization parameter.

- *DATA DICTIONARY MISS %*—This statistic tells you the health of the data dictionary caches. If this value should increase to more than 10 percent, increase the **SHARED_POOL_SIZE** initialization parameter.

- *RECURSIVE CALLS PER USER*—This is a calculated ratio of total recursive calls against total cumulative users. This statistic tells you on average the number of times the database is having to search outside of the data dictionary and buffers for data and if dynamic space management is occurring. If this statistic stays above 10, then look at increasing your **DB_BLOCK_BUFFERS** and adjusting your table storage parameters.

- *FREELIST CONTENTION RATIO*—This statistic shows that contention for table or index freelists is occurring. If this statistic reaches 0.1, look at rebuilding tables and indexes with more freelists.

- *TOTAL ALLOCATED MEG*—This calculated statistic tells how much physical disk area has been allocated to Oracle.

- *TOTAL USED MEG*—This statistic tells how much of the allocated space is being used by object extents. This doesn't mean the space is filled with data; it just means the space has been grabbed by an object.

- *TOTAL SGA SIZE*—This is a summation of the **v$sga** DPT.

The following parameters are latches that are showing contention. If the contention is higher than 0.1, consider increasing the **SHARED_POOL_SIZE** initialization parameter:

- cache buffers chains

- library cache

- virtual circuit queues

- virtual circuit buffers

- shared pool

- cache buffers lru chain

- row cache objects

The following statistics show the total number of the particular type of object in the database:

- DATABASE LINK

- FUNCTION

- INDEX

- PACKAGE

- CLUSTER

- PACKAGE BODY

- PROCEDURE

- SEQUENCE

- SYNONYM

- TABLE

- TRIGGER

- VIEW

Buffer Contention

If you think there may be contention for buffers, as shown by the buffer busy waits statistic mentioned in previous sections, you can run the report in Listing 11.18 to show possible areas of contention.

Listing 11.18   SQL script for report to show possible contention areas.

```
REM
REM NAME: CONTEND.SQL
REM FUNCTION: Shows where possible contention for resources
REM           in buffer busy waits use to pinpoint additional
REM           tuning areas.
REM
REM USE: Called from status
REM
SET VERIFY OFF FEEDBACK OFF
SET PAGES 58
SET LINES 79
START title80 "AREA OF CONTENTION REPORT"
DEFINE output = 'rep_out\&db\contend'
SPOOL &output
SELECT
        class,
        SUM(count) total_waits,
        SUM(time) total_time
FROM
        v$waitstat
GROUP BY
        class;
SPOOL OFF
PAUSE Press return to continue
SET VERIFY ON FEEDBACK ON PAGES 22 LINES 80
TTITLE OFF
```

The output from Listing 11.18 is shown in Table 11.16.

The report in Table 11.16 covers the following types of blocks in the buffer cache:

- *data block*—Shows waits for blocks in the data buffer cache.

- *freelist*—Shows waits for freelists (freelist contention).

- *system undo header*—Shows waits for header blocks of the system rollback segment.

- *system undo block*—Shows waits for buffers containing other than header blocks for the system rollback segment.

- *undo header*—Shows waits for buffers containing nonsystem rollback segment header blocks.

- *undo blocks*—Shows waits for buffers containing other than header blocks for the nonsystem rollback segments.

Table 11.16 Example output from CONTEND.SQL script.

Date: 06/13/97 Time: 08:05 AM	AREA OF CONTENTION REPORT ORCNETP1 database		Page: 1 SYSTEM
CLASS	**TOTAL_WAITS**	**TOTAL_TIME**	
data block	27	23	
freelist	0	0	
save undo block	0	0	
save undo header	0	0	
segment header	0	0	
sort block	0	0	
system undo block	0	0	
system undo header	0	0	
undo block	0	0	
undo header	4	1	

- *segment header, save undo header, save undo block,* and *sort block*—Not used by DBAs for tuning.

The statistic with the highest value is the area where you should concentrate your tuning efforts. In the example report (no statistic is actually high enough to warrant action), the initialization parameter **DB_BLOCK_BUFFERS** could be increased to reduce data-block buffer contention.

If rollback contention is indicated ("undo" statistics), increase the number of rollback segments. Contention is indicated when any one area shows greater than a 1 percent value for the calculation:

```
parameter / (db block gets + consistent gets)
```

Latch Contention

The next type of contention deals with latches. The script in Listing 11.19 generates a report of latch contention. The script restricts output to only those latches that exhibit a greater than zero timeout value. Obviously, if a latch shows zero timeouts, there is no contention for that latch. This restriction greatly reduces the amount of information you have to review.

Listing 11.19   SQL script to generate latch contention report.

```
REM
REM NAME         : LTCH7_CO.SQL
REM FUNCTION     : Genereate latch contention report
REM USE          : From SQLPlus or other front end
REM Limitations  : None
REM
COLUMN name      FORMAT A30
COLUMN ratio1    FORMAT 999.999
COLUMN ratio2    FORMAT 999.999
SET PAGES 58 NEWPAGE 0
START title80 "LATCH CONTENTION REPORT"
SPOOL rep_out\&db\latchs
SELECT
  a.name,
  100.*b.misses/b.gets ratio1
  100.*b.immediate_misses/(b.immediate_gets+b.immediate_misses) ratio2
FROM
  v$latchname a, v$latch b
WHERE
        a.latch# = b.latch# AND b.misses > 0;
SPOOL OFF
PAUSE PRESS RETURN TO CONTINUE
CLEAR COLUMNS
TTITLE OFF
SET PAGES 22
```

The output from the report in Listing 11.19 is shown in Table 11.17.

This report is much easier to look at than many tools' monitor screens, such as the Oracle Performance Pack. The suggested calculations are done behind the scenes, and you can tell at a glance if any latches are suffering from contention. Notice that all of these values are fractional percentages. If these values get up into whole percentages, reduce contention by increasing the **SHARED_POOL_SIZE** parameter under Oracle7 or Oracle8.

Some latches may not have exact correspondences (i.e., **redo_copy**, **redo_allocation**, etc.). These are discussed in the section on UTLBSTAT and UTLESTAT in Chapter 12.

The following latches are the major ones the DBA needs to be concerned about; the others shouldn't require tuning:

Table 11.17 Example report generated by LATCH_CO.SQL.

Date: 06/23/97	Page: 1		
Time: 03:40 PM	LATCH CONTENTION REPORT		SYSTEM
	ORCNETD1 database		

NAME	RATIO1	RATIO2
session allocation	.0034	.0000
messages	.0005	.0000
cache buffers chains	.0000	
cache buffers lru chain	.0082	
row cache objects	.0006	
shared pool	.0740	.0000
library cache	.0107	
virtual circuit buffers	.0021	.0000
virtual circuit queues	.0007	.0000
virtual circuits	.0003	.0000

10 rows selected.

- *cache buffers chain*—This latch indicates user processes are waiting to scan the SGA for block access. To tune this latch, adjust **DB_BLOCK_BUFFERS**.

- *cache buffers LRU chains*—This latch indicates waits when a user attempts to scan the LRU chain that contains all the used blocks in the database buffers. To reduce waits on this latch, increase **DB_BLOCK_BUFFERS** or **_DB_BLOCK_WRITE_BATCH**.

- *enqueues*—This latch is controlled by the INIT.ORA parameter **ENQUEUE_RESOURCES**. If the ratio of timeouts to total exceeds 1 percent in Oracle7, increase **ENQUEUE_RESOURCES**.

- *redo allocation*—This latch controls the allocation of space in the redo buffer. There is only one allocation latch per instance in Oracle7. To reduce contention for this latch, reduce the value of the INIT.ORA parameter **LOG_SMALL_ENTRY_MAX_SIZE** on multi-CPU systems to force use of a redo copy latch. On single-CPU systems, the value of **CPU_COUNT** in the INIT.ORA file is set to 0; this indicates no redo copy latches are allowed. Setting the **CPU_COUNT** to 1 and **LOG_**

SIMULTANEOUS_COPIES to 2 is not recommended by Oracle for single-CPU machines, even though two redo copy latches are allowed per CPU. In the example report, 90 uses of the redo copy latch are shown, even though the CPU count for the computer was set to 0, indicating there are redo copy latches even on single-CPU machines.

- *redo copy*—This latch is used when an entry's size exceeds **LOG_SMALL_ ENTRY_SIZE** and use of a redo copy latch is forced. This happens on both single- and multi-CPU computers. On multi-CPU computers, you can reduce redo copy latch contention by increasing **LOG_ SIMULTANEOUS_COPIES** to twice the value of **CPU_COUNT**. The **LOG_SMALL_ENTRY_MAX_SIZE** parameter specifies the maximum size of a redo entry that can be copied on the redo allocation latch. On single CPU systems, changing **LOG_SIMULTANEOUS_COPIES** and **LOG_SMALL_ENTRY_MAX_SIZE** has no effect.

- *row cache objects*—This latch shows waits for the user processes attempting to access the cached data dictionary values. To reduce contention for this latch, you should tune the shared SQL area. This will be covered in a later section.

The rest of the latches shouldn't require tuning. If excessive contention is shown for them, contact the Oracle support group.

Tools For Additional Tuning Concerns

Once you have tuned memory, I/O, and contention, you still need to consider a couple of minor items. These items will improve performance, but any improvement would be masked by the other tuning areas if they are not taken care of first. This is why these are addressed last. The final tuning areas concern sorts, freelists, and checkpoints.

Sorts, Freelists, And Checkpoints

You need to monitor sorts, freelists, and checkpoints on a regular basis and tune them as needed to get peak performance from the database. Improvement of sort speed provides obvious benefits. Freelists provide information on the free blocks inside database tables. An insufficient number of freelists can have an impact on performance. Checkpoints are writes from buffers to disk. If excessive, they can adversely affect performance; if insufficient, recovery from disasters can be impeded.

Tuning Oracle Sorts

Sorts are done when Oracle performs operations that retrieve information and require the information retrieved to be an ordered set—in other words, sorted. Sorts are done when the following operations are performed:

- Index creation

- **GROUP BY** or **ORDER BY** statements

- Use of the distinct operator

- Join operations

- Use of the union, intersect, and minus set operators

Each of these operations requires a sort. There is one main indicator that your sorts are going to disk, and, therefore, your sort area in memory is too small. This area is defined by the initialization parameter **SORT_AREA_SIZE** in both Oracle7 and Oracle8.

The primary indicator is the sorts (disk) statistic shown in Table 11.15. If this parameter exceeds 10 percent of the sum of sorts (memory) and sorts (disk), increase the **SORT_AREA_SIZE** parameter. Large values for this parameter can induce paging and swapping, so be careful you don't over-allocate. This area is allocated either directly from memory to each user, or, if the multithreaded server is used, a section of the shared pool is allocated to each user. In Oracle8, an extra shared area called the large pool is used (if it has been initialized).

Under Oracle7 and Oracle8, the **SORT_AREA_SIZE** parameter controls the maximum sort area. The sort area will be dynamically reallocated down to the size specified by the initialization parameter **SORT_AREA_RETAINED_SIZE**.

In version 7.2 and later, the initialization parameters **SORT_DIRECT_WRITES**, **SORT_WRITE_BUFFER_SIZE**, and **SORT_WRITE_BUFFERS** control how needed disk sorts are optimized. By specifying **SORT_DIRECT_WRITES** to **TRUE**, you can improve your sort times by severalfold, because this forces writes direct to disk rather than using the buffers. The **SORT_WRITE_BUFFER_SIZE** parameter should be set such that **SORT_WRITE_BUFFERS** * **SORT_WRITE_BUFFER_SIZE** is as large as you dare have it be on your system and still not get swapping. **SORT_WRITE_BUFFERS** is a value from 2 through 8, and the **SORT_WRITE_BUFFER_SIZE** is set between 32K and 64K. Therefore, the maximum size this can be is 8*64K = 512K, or half a megabyte.

Additional sort parameters include **SORT_READ_FAC** and **SORT_SPACEMAP_SIZE**. **SORT_READ_FAC** assists with sort merges. Set this to between 25 and 100 percent of the value of the **_DB_BLOCK_MULTIBLOCK_READ_COUNT** parameter. The **SORT_SPACEMAP_SIZE** parameter, if set correctly, helps with actions, such as index builds. The suggested setting is

```
((total sort bytes/(SORT_AREA_SIZE)) + 64
```

where:

total sort bytes = (number of records in sort) * (average row length + (2 * no_of_columns))

Setting it higher temporarily, however, isn't harmful and can speed the index build appreciably.

For standard sorts, you should set the **SORT_AREA_SIZE** to the average sort size for your database. The temporary tablespace's initial and next default storage parameter should be set to the value of **SORT_AREA_SIZE**. For use with parallel query sorts, a temporary tablespace should be spread (striped) across as many disks as the degree of parallelism.

Reducing Freelist Contention

As was stated earlier, a freelist is a list of data blocks that are free for use. Every table has one or more freelists. This is determined by the storage clause parameter **FREE_LISTS** and **FREE_LIST_GROUPS**. **FREE_LISTS** has its default value set to 1. The maximum value of **FREE_LISTS** is block-size dependent and should be set to the number of simultaneous update processes that will be inserting into or updating the table. The setting of this parameter at the time the table is created determines the number of freelists for the table. The **FREE_LIST_GROUPS** parameter is used in parallel server (not parallel query!) installations only and should be set equal to the number of instances accessing the table. Both parameters apply to tables; only **FREE_LISTS** applies to indexes.

Under Oracle7, each table specifies its own number of freelists with the **FREELISTS** parameter of the **CREATE TABLE** command. This parameter will default to 1 if not specified.

Freelist contention is shown by contention for data blocks in the buffer cache. If you get contention (as shown in the report in Table 11.17) under the data block area, this can also indicate there aren't enough freelists.

Tuning Checkpoints

Checkpoints provide for rolling forward after a system crash. Data is applied from the time of the last checkpoint forward from the redo entries. Checkpoints also provide for reuse of redo logs. When a redo log is filled, the LGWR process automatically switches to the next available log. All data in the now-inactive log is written to disk by an automatic checkpoint. This frees the log for reuse or archiving.

Checkpoints occur when a redo log is filled, when the INIT.ORA parameter **LOG_CHECKPOINT_INTERVAL** is reached (total bytes written to a redo log), or the elapsed time has reached the INIT.ORA parameter **LOG_CHECKPOINT_TIMEOUT**, expressed in seconds or every three seconds, or when an **ALTER SYSTEM** command is issued with the **CHECKPOINT** option specified under Oracle7.

While frequent checkpoints will reduce recovery time, they will also decrease performance. Infrequent checkpoints will increase performance but increase required recovery times. To reduce checkpoints to happen only on log switches, set **LOG_CHECKPOINT_INTERVAL** to be larger than your redo log size, and set **LOG_CHECKPOINT_TIMEOUT** to 0.

If checkpoints still cause performance problems, under Oracle7 set the INIT.ORA parameter **CHECKPOINT_PROCESS** to **TRUE** to start the CKPT process running; for Oracle8, this process starts automatically. This will free the LGWR from checkpoint and increase performance. The INIT.ORA parameter **PROCESSES** may also have to be increased.

New Oracle Tuning Options

Later versions of Oracle7 and Oracle8 have numerous new tuning areas and capabilities. Histograms, anti-joins, hash-joins (not to mention using bitmapped indexes and partitioned tables and indexes)—all of these can increase the performance of Oracle.

Use Of Histograms

Histograms help optimize queries and other actions against data that is not uniformly distributed about a mean. The common term for poorly distributed data is *skewed data*. In particular, especially in earlier versions of Oracle7, the cost-based optimizer would go out to lunch if you handed it skewed data. A cost is associated with histograms, so they should be used only for badly skewed data. Histograms are static and must be periodically renewed, just like table statistics.

Histograms should not be used if:

- All predicates on the column use bind variables.

- The column data is uniformly distributed.

- The column is not used in **WHERE** clauses of queries.

- The column is unique and is used only with equality predicates.

Histograms are created in *bands* of value ranges. For example, if the data in your **test_result** table's **measurement** column is skewed into six general ranges, then you would want to create six bands of history:

```
ANALYZE TABLE test_result
COMPUTE STATISTICS FOR COLUMNS measurement SIZE 6;
```

Hisotogram statistics are stored in the **DBA_**, **USER_**, and **ALL_ HISTOGRAMS** views. Additional row statistics appear in the **USER_TAB_COLUMNS**, **ALL_TAB_ COLUMNS**, and **DBA_TAB_COLUMNS** views.

New Types Of Joins

Two new types of joins became available in the later versions of Oracle7 and Oracle8:

- *Hash join*—The hash join has nothing to do with hash clusters or the **TABLE ACCESS HASH** method. A hash join compares two tables in memory. The first table is full-table scanned, and a hashing function is applied to the data in memory. Then, the second table is full-table scanned, and the hashing function is used to compare the values. Matching values are returned to the user. The user usually has nothing to do with this process, which is completely optimizer controlled. It can be used only by the cost-based optimizer. Generally, hash joins will gain something for you only if you are using parallel query. The optimizer will use hash joins for small tables that can be scanned quickly. To use hash joins, the **HASH_JOIN_ENABLED** initialization parameter must be set to **TRUE**.

Several HASH parameters affect how hash joins are used:

- **HASH_JOIN_ENABLED**—Set to **TRUE** to use hash joins.

- **HASH_AREA_SIZE**—Large value reduces cost of hash joins, so they are used more frequently (set to half the square root of the size of the smaller of the two objects, but not less than 1MB). Suggested range is between 8MB and 32MB.

- **HASH_MULTIBLOCK_IO_COUNT**—Large value reduces the cost of hash joins, so they are used more frequently. Suggested size is 4.

- *Anti-joins*—To use anti-joins, you must set the initialization parameter **ALWAYS_ANTI_JOIN** to **HASH** or **MERGE**. This causes the **NOT IN** clause in queries always to be resolved using a parallel hash or parallel-merge anti-join. If the **ALWAYS_ANTI_JOIN** parameter is set to anything other than **HASH** or **MERGE**, the **NOT IN** will be evaluated as a correlated subquery. You can force Oracle to perform a specific query as an anti-join by using the **MERGE_AJ** or **HASH_AJ** hints.

Multitier Statement Tuning

Oracle is being used more and more in multitier client-server applications. If you don't take care when designing the queries used in these client-server applications, your performance will be terrible. You want the server still to do the processing of the result set and just pass the result set back to the client. An improper query can return the entire contents of the source tables to your PC and expect the PC to process the data—something you don't want in most situations. The bane of many networks is excessive packet traffic soaking up bandwidth.

To prevent bandwidth absorption, you want to encapsulate SQL statements as much as possible. Some general rules to follow when designing applications for client-server systems are listed here. How you accomplish this is generally easy, although for specific applications it can be complex, and in an ad hoc environment, impossible:

- *Push processing to the server, pull results back*—This is accomplished by use of views and using PL/SQL encapsulation. If you issue

```
SELECT * FROM EMP WHERE DEPTNO=10;
```

in an ad hoc query, chances are the contents of **EMP** may get passed back to you to be processed. If, however, a server view is created

```
CREATE VIEW EMP10 AS SELECT * FROM EMP WHERE DPTNO=10;
```

and then you issue

```
SELECT * FROM EMP10;
```

you get the same result set, but it is processed on the server and passed back to you.

- *Use views to prebuild queries*—We have already discussed this trick. Essentially, if you have a standard data set that is selected against repeatedly, then create a view to preprocess this data set and select against the view. This ensures that processing is pushed to the server and not to the client.

If you have several related commands, encapsulate them in a PL/SQL block, rather than issue each individual command. A PL/SQL block is treated as a single statement by Net8, so a single packet set is used to transfer it to the server, greatly reducing network travel. Let's look at an example.

You have a status report that selects several statistics into a temporary table and then generates a report. Right now, the script to run this report looks like this:

```
INSERT INTO dba_temp
   SELECT name, value, 1
   FROM v$sysstat
   WHERE name='consistent gets';
INSERT INTO dba_temp
   SELECT name, value, 2
   FROM v$sysstat
   WHERE name='physical reads';
INSERT INTO dba_temp
   SELECT name, value, 3
   FROM v$sysstat
   WHERE name='db block gets';
INSERT INTO dba_temp
   SELECT 'Hit Ratio',(a.value+b.value)-c.value/(a.value+b.value)
   FROM v$sysstat a, v$sysstat b, v$sysstat c
       WHERE a.name='consistent gets' and
       b.name='db block gets' and
       c.name='physical reads';
SELECT * FROM DBA_TEMP;
```

So, you have five calls to the database, five parses, and five statements stored in the shared pool. This is not very efficient, and the network round trips can be significant. Let's see if we can write a PL/SQL routine to perform this (at least the initial processing):

```
CREATE OR REPLACE PROCEDURE hitratio
p_reads number;
db_gets number;
con_gets number;
h_ratio number;
param varchar2(32);
CURSOR get_param (stat_name varchar2) IS
SELECT value FROM v$sysstat WHERE name=stat_name;
PROCEDURE write_it (stat_name VARCHAR2,p_value NUMBER,
reporder INTEGER) IS
                  BEGIN
                  INSERT INTO dba_temp
                  VALUES (stat_name, p_value, reporder);
                  END;
BEGIN
   param:='consistent gets';
   OPEN get_param(param);
   FETCH get_param INTO con_gets;
   CLOSE get_param;
   write_it(param, con_gets, 1);
   param:='db block gets';
   OPEN get_param(param);
   ETCH get_param INTO db_gets;
   write_it(param, db_gets, 2);
   param:='physical reads';
   OPEN get_param(param);
   FETCH get_param INTO p_reads;
   write_it(param, p_reads, 3);
   h_ratio:=((con_gets+db_gets)-p_reads)/(con_gets+db_reads);
   param:='Hit Ratio';
   write_it(param, h_ratio, 4);
   COMMIT:
END;
```

Once this procedure is compiled on the server, the SQL script becomes:

```
EXECUTE hitratio;
ELECT * FROM dba_temp;
```

Now you have reduced the round trips to two, and because the stored procedure is on the server, you may not even have to parse the statement. All of the actions between **BEGIN** and **END** are treated as a single transaction. If you make the call to **dba_temp** a call to a view, you can be sure that any processing is done for that table on the server. There is also a method to use the UTLFILE package to output directly to a file on a client, but it would result in more net round trips in this situation.

More complex processing using variables could be done using the **DBMS_SQL** package and dynamic SQL.

- *Use MTS only when your number of connections exceeds 50 to 100 users—* The multithreaded server allows for large numbers of users to connect through a limited number of database connections. This is great for large environments where it would be impossible for everyone to connect if they had to use individual connect processes. Unless you normally run with at least 50 to 100 concurrent processes accessing Oracle at the same time, MTS can hurt your performance. Use of parallel query will just about guarantee that you should use MTS.

In a test using a multi-gigabyte database and 10 users, a standard set of queries generated more than 200 separate processes using dedicated connections. Some queries required more than 30 minutes to complete. We switched on MTS and ran the same queries. None took more than 5 minutes using MTS, the SGA usage (it had been running 100 percent for db block buffers) dropped to 75 percent (as shown by the Q monitor system from Savant), and log-in times dropped to 0 (under a dedicated server, we saw up to 5-minute delays logging in to the machine), an E6000 from Sun with 9 CPUs, 3GB of memory, and a 600GB disk farm using RAID0-1 and RAW disks. Access was over a normal Ethernet-type network from PC clients using TCP/IP protocols.

MTS is a queuing system for database connections. It allows multiple users to share the same single connection to the database by a time-sharing mechanism. If only 5 to 10 users are connecting, they may actually see delays in statement execution and processing due to this queuing mechanism.

- *Use PL/SQL blocks, stored procedures, and functions on both client and server—* Always look at multistep SQL scripts, whether they are standalone or embedded in an application, and ask yourself if they could be changed into a stored procedure, function, or anonymous PL/SQL block. Even with 3GL programs running from a client to a database server, if you encapsulate the SQL with **BEGIN-END** block construction (assuming this can be done; some statements can't be done this way), then they will be passed as a single network transaction to the server.

As was previously demonstrated, a complex set of SQL statements can be converted into a PL/SQL procedure or function, and the procedure or function stored on the server, allowing a simple **EXECUTE** or direct function call. For example, about the only way to get the bytes of a table's records from SQL is to issue a **SUM(BYTES)** type statement against the table's entry in **DBA_EXTENTS**. If you want to include a count of the rows in a report, you either have to **ANALYZE** the table and pull the count from out of **DBA_TABLES** as a join, or do the **SELECT COUNT** into a local variable. This results in more network round trips and server work. If you create a function that does this type of operation for you, then you can issue the call to the function directly from a **BEGIN-END** block or even from the **SELECT** itself. For example:

```
CREATE OR REPLACE FUNCTION get_sum(table_name VARCHAR2)
RETURN NUMBER AS
sum_bytes NUMBER;
BEGIN
  SELECT SUM(bytes) INTO sum_bytes FROM dba_extents
  WHERE segment_name=UPPER(table_name) AND
    segment_type=ëTABLEí;
  RETURN sum_bytes;
END;
```

Using this function (compiled and stored on the server), you can now select the sum of bytes used by any table, just as a regular column:

```
SELECT table_name, get_sum(table_name) tab_size FROM dba_tables;
```

Such techniques as this can substantially reduce network traffic. Use of functions and procedures forces processing to the server and returns only results to the client. Your goal as a DBA tuning in a multitier environment is to pack as much content into each piece of network traffic as possible. To do so, you have to move more into the Object Paradigm by passing messages (such as a procedure or function call) rather than an entire procedural structure, such as a SQL routine. This also ensures proper use of the shared pool and SGA resources, because multiple "almost virtually" identical statements won't end up being stuffed into your SGA.

Chapter 12

The Oracle-Supplied Scripts And Their Uses

Oracle provides many useful utility scripts for DBAs and developers. In this chapter, we will discuss several of these scripts and show examples of their use.

Notes…

Chapter 12

Oracle Utility Scripts

Oracle provides a number of utility scripts that help both developers and DBAs tune not only statements but also the entire database system. Generally, the scripts are located in the $ORACLE_HOME/rdbms/admin directory on Unix hosts and x:\orant\rdbms80\admin on NT hosts. On other machines, look in the Oracle top-level directory, and find the rdbms subdirectory; the admin directory will be located there. Everyone—especially DBAs—should be familiar with the scripts located in this directory. On my NT 4 box with Oracle version 8.0.3 loaded, 267 scripts are located in the d:\orant\rdbms80\admin directory.

Don't let the large number of scripts in the admin subdirectory throw you—many you will never use. For example, of all of the scripts that start with "CAT", you will be concerned with only CATBLOCK.SQL; of all the scripts beginning with "DBMS" or "PRVT", you need concern yourself with only DBMSPOOL.SQL or PRVTPOOL.SQL.

Several scripts begin with "UTL". Many of these are useful utilities; however, a few you *do not* have to worry about: UTLRAW.SQL, UTLHTTP.SQL, USERLOCK.SQL, UTLMAIL.SQL, UTLPG.SQL, and UTLFILE.SQL—all of which run automatically when a database is built by using the CATPROC.SQL script and shouldn't have to be run again. This chapter addresses several of the remaining UTL scripts.

A Quick Overview Of The UTL* Scripts

Most of the scripts that a DBA or developer will use will come from the UTL* family. These scripts and their uses follow:

- *UTLBSTAT.SQL and UTLESTAT.SQL*—Assist the DBA with tuning the database internals. These scripts take a beginning snapshot (BSTAT) and ending snapshot (ESTAT) of database statistics and generate a set of differences reports.

- *UTLCHAIN.SQL*—Creates the default table for storage of chained row information generated from the **ANALYZE TABLE...LIST CHAINED ROWS** command.

- *UTLCONST.SQL*—A script that must be run from the user SYS or INTERNAL to check that date constraints are valid.

- *UTILDIDXS.SQL, UTLOIDXS.SQL, and UTLSIDXS.SQL*—Test table columns for their suitability for indexes. These scripts were demonstrated in Chapter 10.

- *UTLDTREE.SQL*—Generates a dependency tree graph of an object's dependent objects. It creates two tables, **deptree** and **ideptree**, that store information about the dependency data for a specified object.

- *UTLEXCPT.SQL*—Creates the exceptions table for use when you create constraints and may have exceptions. The table stores the table name, owner, and constraint generating the exception along with the **ROWID**s of any excepted rows.

- *UTLLOCKT.SQL*—Creates a lock-wait graph tree used to diagnose system locking problems.

- *UTLPWDMG.SQL*—Sets up password management for Oracle8 servers. It sets the default password resource limits and creates the default password verification algorithm.

- *UTLSAMPL.SQL*—Builds user SCOTT/TIGER.

- *UTLTKPRF.SQL*—Grants public access to all views used by the TKPROF facility, which is discussed in Chapter 10.

- *UTLVALID.SQL*—Creates the default table (**invalid_rows**) for the output from the **ANALYZE...VALIDATE** command for partitioned tables.

- *UTLXPLAN.SQL*—Creates the **plan_table** used by the **EXPLAIN PLAN** command and the **EXPLAIN** option of TKPROF.

Some Other Scripts Of Interest

Several of the DBMS* and CAT* scripts should be run manually. Generally speaking, these scripts are run automatically at database creation and do not need to be run again unless you are updating your copy of Oracle. Some of these useful scripts, however, do not run automatically:

- *DBMSPOOL.SQL and PRVTPOOL.PLB*—Create the **DBMS_SHARED_POOL** package useful for DBAs (which must be run if you are going to use the scripts in the Visual Dictionary Lite program, because DBMS_REVEALNET.SQL requires **DBMS_SHARED_POOL** and many of the scripts depend on **DBMS_REVEALNET**). The package contains the procedures:

  - **SIZES**—Shows the sizes of objects in the shared pool greater than a specified minimum size.

  - **KEEP**—Used to "keep" (or pin) objects in the shared pool. It is useful for larger objects. Changes in how Oracle stores objects in the shared pool may render this obsolete.

  - **UNKEEP**—Used to "unkeep" objects that have been kept.

  - **ABORTED_REQUEST_THRESHOLD**—Sets the minimum size in bytes of a request that will not attempt to free space in the shared pool.

- *CATPARR.SQL*—Usually runs only if you are going to run parallel server; however, it creates several useful views for peering into the SGA buffers.

- *CATBLOCK.SQL*—Creates several useful views for system locks. The WAITERS.SQL and BLOCKERS.SQL scripts in the Visual Dictionary Lite script set depend on this script being run to create the required views.

Practical Guide To

The Oracle Utility Scripts

- Using UTLBSTAT/UTLESTAT
- Using UTLCONST
- Using UTLDTREE
- Using UTLLOCKT

Using UTLBSTAT/UTLESTAT

After shutting down the database, set the **TIMED_STATISTICS** parameter of the initialization file to **TRUE**, and then restart the database. The script UTLBSTAT is run from the SQLDBA, SVRMGR, or the SQL worksheet under the SYS user after the database has reached equilibrium (i.e., after the database has been started and the buffers and caches have stabilized). If you don't wait until the database has reached a steady state condition, the statistics will reflect "startup noise" from the various process startups and will not give a true baseline. Once UTLBSTAT has been run, the application you wish to test is then run through its paces.

When you are satisfied that the application has been fully wrung out under as close as possible to actual running conditions (a 1-user test of a 20-user application isn't going to tell you much), the UTLESTAT script is run, again from SQLDBA, SVRMGR, or the SQL worksheet from the SYS user. The UTLESTAT script calculates various statistics for the database and generates several reports that you can use for tuning. Let's look at these reports and see how they can help with the various aspects of tuning. These reports cover virtually every aspect of internals and general database tuning.

 The first line of both reports is a connect internal. If you are using password files (such as on NT), then you must either edit the file to include the password or remove this line and just log in before you run it. Sometimes, trying to "help" Oracle makes our jobs harder.

UTLESTAT Library Cache Report

The first report is for the library cache. Pay attention to the hit ratios, reloads, and invalidations. Essentially, the hit ratios should be as close as possible to 1; values less than 0.80 are too low (assuming the gets and pins have significantly high values). The reloads should be as close as possible to 0, as should the invalidations. If the caches aren't big enough, and a statement needs to be parsed, Oracle will age out an old statement if it can't find room. If the statement that was aged from the cache is then needed again, it has to be reloaded. This is not good. Invalidations happen when a table, index, procedure, or other object becomes invalid. Usually, invalidations don't happen in a production environment, but can be significant in a development arena.

An environment where invalidations may be high would be one where periodic flushes of the shared pool are required because of excessive ad hoc queries. If your system suffers from overstuffing of the shared SQL area of the shared pool because of poor ad hoc SQL practices (such as non-use of bind variables), then you may see excessive invalidations.

As far as tuning for latches, this is actually simple: increase the size of the initialization parameter **SHARED_POOL_SIZE**, which will automatically increase the sizes of the cache regions on the next startup of the database.

Table 12.1 shows the library cache report.

UTLESTAT Session Statistics Report

The next report is session-based statistics. An example report is shown in Table 12.2.

The important statistics from the report in Table 12.2 are:

- *Consistent changes*—This is the number of times a block was changed and/or rollback had to be read for a transaction to have consistent reads. A high figure could indicate long-running updates during prime usage times.

- *Consistent gets*—If a block is acquired in a consistent mode, this increments. The statistic is incremented for each block read in a full-table

Table 12.1   Library cache report from UTLESTAT.SQL.

LIBRARY	GETS	GETHIT RATIO	PINS	PINHIT RATIO	RELOADS	INVALIDA-TIONS
BODY	8	1	8	1	0	0
CLUSTER	7	1	11	1	0	0
INDEX	0	1	0	1	0	0
OBJECT	0	1	0	1	0	0
PIPE	0	1	0	1	0	0
SQL AREA	434	.963	1432	.977	0	9
TABLE/ PROCED	42	.905	104	.942	0	0
TRIGGER	0	1	0	1	0	0

8 rows selected.

Table 12.2 Session statistics report from UTLESTAT.SQL.

Statistic	Total	Per Transact	Per Logon	Per Second
CPU used by this session	19092	19092	4773	12.81
CPU used when call started	5694	5694	1423.5	3.82
DBWR buffers scanned	145100	145100	36275	97.38
DBWR free buffers found	144985	144985	36246.25	97.31
DBWR lru scans	2902	2902	725.5	1.95
DBWR make free requests	2900	2900	725	1.95
DBWR summed scan depth	145100	145100	36275	97.38
DBWR timeouts	486	486	121.5	.33
SQL*Net roundtrips to/from	129	129	32.25	.09
background timeouts	1493	1493	373.25	1
buffer is not pinned count	968	968	242	.65
buffer is pinned count	123553	123553	30888.25	82.92
bytes received via SQL*Net	10389	10389	2597.25	6.97
bytes sent via SQL*Net to c	5700	5700	1425	3.83
calls to get snap shot scn:	576	576	144	.39
calls to kcmgas	44	44	11	.03
calls to kcmgcs	8	8	2	.01

(continued)

Table 12.2   Session statistics report from UTLESTAT.SQL *(continued).*

Statistic	Total	Per Transact	Per Logon	Per Second
calls to kcmgrs	835	835	208.75	.56
change write time	4	4	1	0
cleanouts only – consistent	71	71	17.75	.05
cluster key scan block gets	544	544	136	.37
cluster key scans	288	288	72	.19
commit cleanout failures: b	72	72	18	.05
commit cleanouts	102	102	25.5	.07
commit cleanouts successful	30	30	7.5	.02
consistent gets	124351	124351	31087.75	83.46
cursor authentications	8	8	2	.01
db block changes	1197	1197	299.25	.8
db block gets	10806	10806	2701.5	7.25
deferred (CURRENT) block cl	9	9	2.25	.01
enqueue releases	356	356	89	.24
enqueue requests	350	350	87.5	.23
execute count	576	576	144	.39
free buffer requested	108001	108001	27000.25	72.48
immediate (CR) block cleanout	71	71	17.75	.05
immediate (CURRENT) block c	5	5	1.25	0

(continued)

Table 12.2 Session statistics report from UTLESTAT.SQL *(continued).*

Statistic	Total	Per Transact	Per Logon	Per Second
logons cumulative	4	4	1	0
logons current	1	1	.25	0
messages received	2977	2977	744.25	2
messages sent	2977	2977	744.25	2
no work - consistent read g	123549	123549	30887.25	82.92
opened cursors cumulative	422	422	105.5	.28
opened cursors current	2	2	.5	0
parse count (hard)	16	16	4	.01
parse count (total)	433	433	108.25	.29
parse time cpu	21	21	5.25	.01
parse time elapsed	27	27	6.75	.02
physical reads	117581	117581	29395.25	78.91
physical writes	9845	9845	2461.25	6.61
process last non-idle time	912827947	912827947	228206986.75	612636.21
recursive calls	6931	6931	1732.75	4.65
recursive cpu usage	147	147	36.75	.1
redo blocks written	334	334	83.5	.22
redo entries	689	689	172.25	.46
redo size	144528	144528	36132	97
redo small copies	229	229	57.25	.15
redo synch time	4	4	1	0

(continued)

Table 12.2 Session statistics report from UTLESTAT.SQL (continued).

Statistic	Total	Per Transact	Per Logon	Per Second
redo synch writes	3	3	.75	0
redo wastage	11864	11864	2966	7.96
redo write time	326	326	81.5	.22
redo writes	45	45	11.25	.03
session connect time	912827947	912827947	228206986.75	612636.21
session logical reads	125436	125436	31359	84.19
session pga memory	5725488	5725488	1431372	3842.61
session pga memory max	13293956	13293956	3323489	8922.12
session uga memory	54552	54552	13638	36.61
session uga memory max	163460	163460	40865	109.7
sorts (disk)	2	2	.5	0
sorts (memory)	14	14	3.5	.01
sorts (rows)	6723541	6723541	1680885.25	4512.44
table fetch by rowid	43	43	10.75	.03
table scan blocks gotten	80	80	20	.05
table scan rows gotten	53	53	13.25	.04
table scans (short tables)	14	14	3.5	.01
total file opens	14	14	3.5	.01
user calls	125	125	31.25	.08
user commits	1	1	.25	0
write requests	47	47	11.75	.03

78 rows selected.

scan and by the height of any indexes that are scanned. The statistic increments for each block read in an index-only read as well.

- *db block changes*—This is the total number of used, or dirty, blocks in the buffer cache. The term *dirty* means the block has been changed. Even if multiple rows in a block are changed, this counts only as one block change. This statistic will also indicate the amount of redo used for the BSTAT/ESTAT period.

- *db block gets*—This indicates the number of blocks read for update. Updates are made to temporary segment headers, rollback segments, index segments, as well as extent allocation or high-water-mark update.

- *DBWR checkpoints*—If this number gets to be excessive, you should consider starting up a checkpoint process using the **CHECKPOINT_PROCESSES** initialization parameter to relieve the DBWR process of the checkpoint duties. If for some reason you don't want another process, adjust the **LOG_CHECKPOINT_INTERVAL** and **LOG_CHECKPOINT_TIMEOUT** initialization parameters to reduce the number of checkpoints. The size of your redo logs also has an effect on the checkpoint frequency. Generally speaking, you want a checkpoint only at log-switch time; therefore, set **LOG_CHECKPOINT_TIMEOUT** to 0, which actually means infinite, and **LOG_CHECKPOINT_INTERVAL** to a size larger than your redo log size in blocks.

- *DBWR timeouts*—Every three seconds, the DBWR scans the buffer cache looking for dirty buffers to write—not really important for database tuning.

- *DBWR make free requests*—This statistic can be used to determine if **DB_BLOCK_BUFFERS** is tuned correctly. If you increase **DB_BLOCK_BUFFERS** and this statistic decreases substantially, you need more buffers. It increments each time a request is made to the buffer cache to cleanup, so more data can be loaded (i.e., not enough free space was available without removing items from the least-used side of the LRU list).

- *DBWR free buffers found*—This statistic shows the number of times that DBWR found free buffers on the LRU list. Free buffers can either be clean (they don't have to be written to disk) or dirty (they do have to be written before they can be used again). To find the percentage of buffers that were clean, calculate:

```
(DBWR free buffers found / DBWR make free requests) * 100
```

- *Free buffer waits*—This statistic shows the number of times a free buffer was requested and none was available. If this statistic shows excessive values (i.e., it continues to increase after startup and during application activity), you need to increase **DB_BLOCK_BUFFERS**.

- *Physical reads and writes*—These tell how many times the database reads from or writes to the disks. Each is incremented only once for each read or write, regardless of the number of blocks read or written in the read or write operation (one increment for each **DB_FILE_MULTIBLOCK_ READ_COUNT**).

- *Recursive calls*—This statistic tells you the number of times the database had to use dynamic extension and make recursive calls to the library caches. If this parameter seems excessive, check your object sizing and increase **SHARED_POOL_SIZE**.

- *Redo log space requests*—This statistic tells you that a session or process had to wait for a redo log. It can indicate that you have redo logs that are too small or that you don't have enough redo log groups. Usually, this is caused by the logs filling faster than the log writer can write them to disk. Ideally, this statistic should be as close to 0 as possible (on many of the systems I manage, it is at 0, so it can be done).

- *Sorts(disk)*—This indicates that the size of a sort exceeded **SORT_ AREA_SIZE**, and the sort had to be completed using the temporary tablespace for the user. Ideally, this should be 0. If you see a ratio of

```
(sorts(disk)/(sorts(memory)+sorts(disk))
```

that is greater than 0.01, increase your **SORT_AREA_SIZE**. However having said this, let me also tell you that **SORT_AREA_SIZE** for non-MTS systems is assigned to each user when he or she logs in to Oracle, so you may have to make a tradeoff between disk sorts and **SORT_ AREA_SIZE** on memory-poor systems. In MTS systems, the **SORT_ AREA_SIZE** comes out of the shared pool on Oracle7 systems and, if it is configured, the large pool on Oracle8 systems, so be sure to size these areas for the number of users you expect.

- *Table fetch continued row*—This indicates row chaining if it is greater than 0. If it is small in comparison to "table fetch by rowid," then don't worry; but if it exceeds one to two percent, you should consider evaluating all tables with **VARCHAR2** variables for row chaining. Also, adjust **PCTFREE** to a higher value for affected tables. If you use **LONG** values, you may want to increase the size of your database blocks (**DB_BLOCK_SIZE**), but, remember, to do so, you must rebuild the entire database.

- *Table scans (short tables)*—This tells the number of rows read from a table whose size was smaller than **_SMALL_TABLE_THRESHOLD**. (Yes, the leading underscore is part of the parameter; in earlier versions, this was a documented parameter, but in later versions of Oracle7 and Oracle8, it is undocumented.) This defaults to 10 percent of the allocated **DB_BLOCK_BUFFERS**, so if you have set **DB_BLOCK_BUFFERS** at 20,000, any table of fewer than 2,000 blocks in size would count as a small table. I would suggest setting it to the size of your most-used index, if you explicitly size it.

- *Table scans (long tables)*—This tells the number of rows read from a table whose size was larger than **_SMALL_TABLE_THRESHOLD**. This size defaults to 10 percent of the allocated size of the **DB_BLOCK_BUFFERS** size in blocks. If you specify 20,000 **DB_BLOCK_BUFFERS**, scans of any table of fewer than 2,000 blocks will be treated as a small table scan. I would suggest setting it to the size of your most-used index, if you explicitly size it. This allows you to do a quick and dirty calculation of the ratio of index scans to full-table scans to determine index efficiency.

- *Hit ratio*—This is not a reported calculation but is a calculable one from statistics in the ESTAT/BSTAT report. Essentially, the hit ratio you calculate tells how efficiently you are using your database buffers. A high hit ratio (near 1) is what you want. Any hit ratio less than 95 percent for an OLTP environment or 85 percent for batch applications should be investigated. The calculation is:

```
hit ratio = ((consistent gets+db block gets) - physical reads)/
consistent gets+db block gets
```

So, from the example report:

- consistent gets = 124,351

- db block gets = 10,806

- physical reads = 117,581

- hit ratio = ((124,351 + 10,806) - 117,581) / (124,351 + 10,806)

- hit ratio = 0.13

Based on this information, the instance this report was run on probably needs more **DB_BLOCK_BUFFERS**.

Appendix C of the *Oracle8 Server Reference Manual* (Release 8.0, Part no. A50665-1, January 23, 1987) has detailed descriptions of all of the other statistics in this report.

UTLESTAT Average Dirty Buffer Write Queue Report

The next report shows the average length of the dirty buffer write queue. If this is larger than the value of

```
(db_files * db_file_simultaneous_writes)/2
```

or

```
1/4 of db_block_buffers
```

(whichever is smaller), and there is a platform-specific limit on the write batch size (normally 1,024 or 2,048 buffers), increase **DB_FILE_SIMULTANEOUS_WRITES** or **DB_FILES**. Also, check for disks that are doing many more I/Os than other disks and look at spreading their database files over more drives. Table 12.3 shows an example of this report.

Table 12.3   Average write queue length report from UTLESTAT.SQL.

Average Write Queue Length
0
1 row selected.

UTLESTAT Systemwide Wait Events (Non-Background) Report

The next report shows systemwide wait events for non-background processes (PMON, SMON, etc.). Times are in hundredths of seconds. Each one of these is a context switch that costs CPU time. By looking at the Total Time, you can often determine the bottleneck that processes are waiting for. This shows the total time spent waiting for a specific event and the average time per wait on that event. The example report shows that the SQL*Net wait was the most significant; however, the SQL*Net event waits will probably always be the largest, so you should probably disregard this event and look at the next largest, which in this case is the "db file scattered read." This could indicate disk contention or excessive full-table scans are occurring. Table 12.4 shows an example of this report.

UTLESTAT Systemwide Wait Events (Background) Report

The next report shows systemwide wait events for background processes (PMON, SMON, etc.). If excessive waits are shown in these processes, you should tune the

Table 12.4 Wait event report for non-background processes from UTLESTAT.SQL.

Event Name	Count	Total Time	Avg Time
SQL*Net message from client	157	257932	1642.88
db file scattered read	5629	23374	4.15
db file sequential read	18505	17284	.93
rdbms ipc reply	33	61	1.85
direct path write	16	28	1.75
control file sequential read	11	13	1.18
log file sync	3	4	1.33
file identify	3	2	.67
SQL*Net break/reset to client	6	0	0
file open	28	0	0
SQL*Net message to client	158	0	0
11 rows selected.			

process. The "rdbms ipc message" event waits are an indication that this system was mostly idle. The timer waits show that the processes were idle as well. Generally, timer and message waits of this type are normal and can be disregarded. Some amount of read/write waits can be expected as well. For a detailed discussion of all wait events, see the *Oracle8 Server Reference Manual*, Release 8.0. Table 12.5 shows an example of this report.

UTLESTAT Latch Statistics

The next report deals with latch statistics. Latch contention will show up as a large value for the "latch-free" event in the wait events. Sleeps should be low. The hit ratio should be high (near or equal to 1). Most latch contention problems (depending on the latch) are resolved by increasing the **SHARED_POOL_SIZE** initialization parameter. Table 12.6 shows an example of this report.

UTLESTAT No-Wait Gets Latch Report

The next report shows statistics on no-wait gets of latches. A no-wait get does not wait for the latch to become free; it immediately times out. As long as the hit ratio is near 1, there is no problem. If the hit ratio drops below 0.9 (indicating processes are missing gets), increase the **SHARED_POOL_SIZE** parameter. An example of this report is shown in Table 12.7.

Table 12.5   Wait event report for background processes from UTLESTAT.SQL.

Event Name	Count	Total Time	Avg Time
rdbms ipc message	4460	775075	173.78
pmon timer	496	148800	300
smon timer	4	120000	30000
log file parallel write	45	326	7.24
db file parallel write	47	45	.96
db file sequential read	15	21	1.4
db file scattered read	5	14	2.8
log file sync	1	0	0
8 rows selected.			

Table 12.6 Latch report from UTLESTAT.SQL.

LATCH_NAME	GETS	MISSES	HIT_RATIO	SLEEPS	SLEEPS/MISS
Active checkpoint	495	0	1	0	0
Checkpoint queue l	108448	0	1	0	0
Token Manager	653	0	1	0	0
cache buffer handl	51	0	1	0	0
cache buffers chai	492336	0	1	0	0
cache buffers lru	111063	0	1	0	0
dml lock allocatio	253	0	1	0	0
enqueue hash chain	692	0	1	0	0
enqueues	1001	0	1	0	0
ktm global data	4	0	1	0	0
library cache	5974	0	1	0	0
library cache load	12	0	1	0	0
list of block allo	87	0	1	0	0
loader state objec	4	0	1	0	0
messages	12006	3	1	0	0
modify parameter v	4	0	1	0	0
multiblock read ob	11272	0	1	0	0
ncodef allocation	23	0	1	0	0
process allocation	4	0	1	0	0
redo allocation	1325	0	1	0	0
row cache objects	3472	0	1	0	0
sequence cache	9	0	1	0	0

(continued)

Table 12.6 Latch report from UTLESTAT.SQL (continued).

LATCH_NAME	GETS	MISSES	HIT_RATIO	SLEEPS	SLEEPS/MISS
session allocation	55	0	1	0	0
session idle bit	258	0	1	0	0
session switching	23	0	1	0	0
shared pool	895	0	1	0	0
sort extent pool	8	0	1	0	0
system commit numb	923	0	1	0	0
transaction alloca	139	0	1	0	0
undo global data	283	0	1	0	0
user lock	10	0	1	0	0

31 rows selected.

Table 12.7 NOWAIT GETS latches report from UTLESTAT.SQL.

LATCH_NAME	NOWAIT_GETS	NOWAIT_MISSES	NOWAIT_HIT_RATIO
cache buffers chai	384761	0	1
cache buffers lru	18031	0	1
process allocation	4	0	1
redo copy	538	0	1

4 rows selected.

UTLESTAT Buffer Busy Waits Report

If the value for "buffer busy wait" in the wait event statistics is high, this report will identify which class of blocks has high contention. If the "undo header" waits are high, then add more rollback segments. If the "segment header" waits are high, then adding freelists might help. Check **v$session_wait** to get the addresses of the actual blocks experiencing contention. The report shows only those classes with counts

Table 12.8 Class value table for blocks.

CLASS	ADJUST
bitmap block	BITMAP_MERGE_AREA_SIZE
bitmap index block	BITMAP_MERGE_AREA_SIZE
data block	DB_BLOCK_BUFFERS
extent map	Freelists
freelist	Freelists
save undo block	Not used
save undo header	Not used
segment header	Add more freelists
sort block	SORT_AREA_SIZE
system undo block	System-owned rollback segment
system undo header	System-owned rollback segment
undo block	All other rollback segments
undo header	All other rollback segments unused

greater than 0. The possible classes are as shown in Table 12.8. An example of the buffer busy waits report is shown in Table 12.9.

UTLESTAT Rollback Segment Statistics Report

The next report deals with rollback segment statistics (**UNDO_SEGMENTS**). High waits for **trans_tbl** implies you should add rollback segments. Excessive shrinks may indicate that your rollback extent sizes are too small and the rollbacks should be rebuilt. The report output should be similar to Table 12.10.

UTLESTAT Initialization Parameter Report

The initialization parameter report is informational and not used for tuning purposes. It shows the initialization parameters currently in effect that are set to other than their default values. An example report is shown in Table 12.11.

Table 12.9 Buffer busy waits report from UTLESTAT.SQL.

CLASS	COUNT	TIME
0 rows selected.		

Table 12.10 Rollback segment statistics report from UTLESTAT.SQL.

UNDO SEGMENT	TRANS_TBL GETS	TRANS_TBL WAITS	UNDO_BYTES WRITTEN	SEGMENT SIZE_BYTES	XACTS	SHRINKS	WRAPS
0	5	0	0	978944	0	0	0
2	161	0	44780	3190784	0	0	0
3	5	0	0	2125824	0	0	0
4	5	0	0	2125824	0	0	0
5	5	0	0	2125824	0	0	0
6	5	0	0	2125824	0	0	0
6 rows selected.							

Note: Report has been reformatted to fit page.

UTLESTAT Data Dictionary Cache Report

The dictionary cache statistics (a part of the shared pool) are shown in the next report. The **GET_MISS** and **SCAN_MISS** statistics should be very low compared with the requests. The **CUR_USAGE** statistic is the number of entries in the cache that are being used. If the **GET_MISS** and **SCAN_MISS** statistics are high compared with requests, increase the **SHARED_POOL_SIZE** parameter. Add up the **GET_REGS** and **GET_MISS** columns, and determine the ratio. If the overall ratio of **GET_MISSES** to **GET_REGS** is greater than 10 percent, increase the **SHARED_POOL_SIZE** parameter.

An example report is shown in Table 12.12. For a quick look at an overall statistic for this, use the following query of the **v$rowcache** table:

```
SELECT (SUM(getmisses) / SUM(gets)) 'DD CACHE MISS RATIO'
FROM V$ROWCACHE;
```

Table 12.11   Initialization parameter report from UTLESTAT.SQL.

NAME	VALUE
background_dump_dest	c:\oracle1\ortest1\admin\bdump
checkpoint_process	TRUE
control_files	C:\ORACLE1\ORTEST1\CONTROL\ctl1ORTEST1
db_block_size	4096
db_files	100
db_name	ORTEST1
dml_locks	200
ifile	c:\oracle1\ortest1\admin\pfile\initorte
log_archive_start	TRUE
log_buffer	1048576
log_checkpoint_interval	100000
max_dump_file_size	102400
processes	100
remote_login_passwordfile	SHARED
rollback_segments	rb1, rb2, rb3, rb4, rb5
sequence_cache_entries	100
sequence_cache_hash_buckets	89
shared_pool_size	10000000
sort_area_retained_size	2097152
sort_area_size	8388608
text_enable	TRUE
timed_statistics	TRUE
user_dump_dest	c:\oracle1\ortest1\admin\udump

23 rows selected.

Table 12.12 Data dictionary cache report from UTLESTAT.SQL.

NAME	GET_REQS	GET_MISS	SCAN_REQ	SCAN_MIS	MOD_REQS	COUNT	CUR_USAG
dc_tablespaces	72	1	0	0	0	8	4
dc_free_extents	310	67	33	0	165	63	34
dc_segments	43	4	0	0	35	53	41
dc_rollback_seg	56	0	0	0	0	10	8
dc_used_extents	66	33	0	0	66	50	32
dc_users	31	0	0	0	0	21	14
dc_user_grants	20	0	0	0	0	21	14
dc_objects	33	3	0	0	0	222	214
dc_usernames	9	1	0	0	0	20	4
dc_object_ids	14	1	0	0	0	132	130
dc_profiles	3	0	0	0	0	3	1
dc_histogram_de	73	73	0	0	73	77	73

12 rows selected.

UTLESTAT Tablespace I/O Summary Report

The next report shows a summary of I/O operations over tablespaces. If your application is spread over several tablespaces, this report can help show "hot" tablespaces that should, perhaps, have tables moved out into other tablespaces on separate disks or arrays. In this case, the index tablespaces were hit the hardest, so if you were approaching a read/write limit on the disks where they were located, I would consider moving some of the indexes or, perhaps, partitioning them. An example output from this report is shown in Table 12.13.

UTLESTAT Disk I/O Spread Report

I/O should be spread evenly across drives. A big difference between **PHYS_READS** and **PHYS_BLKS_READ** implies that table scans are going on. If the I/O is concentrated into specific datafiles, consider spreading the datafile contents by physically moving the contents or partitioning tables or indexes. Index-only tables and

Table 12.13 Tablespace I/O report from UTLESTAT.SQL.

TABLE_SPACE	READS	BLKS_READ	READ_TIME	WRITES	BLKS_WRT	WRITE_TIME	MEGABYTES
RAW_DATA	0	0	0	0	0	0	734
RAW_INDEX	6774	6774	11394	0	0	0	524
ROLLBACK_DATA	20	20	31	29	29	29	524
SCOPUS_DATA	5632	90016	23400	0	0	0	2096
SCOPUS_INDEX	10944	10944	3828	0	0	0	1048
SYSTEM	107	119	259	83	83	85	52
TEMPORARY_DATA	670	9718	1816	621	9733	28	629
USER_DATA	0	0	0	0	0	0	10

8 rows selected.

bitmapped indexes can also reduce I/O loads on a system. In this case, most of the I/O again is in the index datafiles. The report is shown in Table 12.14.

UTLESTAT Time And Version Reports

The final two reports are informational and tell you the times that BSTAT and ESTAT were run and the version information for the instance. An example of their format is shown in Tables 12.15 and 12.16.

Using UTLCONST

The UTLCONST.SQL script is used from the SYS or INTERNAL user to verify all date-based constraints. Essentially, it reads the format of the existing constraint, re-creates it under a different name, and checks for any errors when the constraint is created. If no errors are received, then it assumes that the constraint is functional. The new constraint that the procedure creates is then dropped, and the old constraint is either left as is (if there are no problems) or marked as invalid and listed in the report. Listing 12.1 shows an example run of the script.

Listing 12.1 Example run of the UTLCONST.SQL script.

```
SQL> @d:\orant8\rdbms80\admin\utlconst.sql
Session altered.
```

```
Checking for bad date constraints
Finished checking -- All constraints OK!
PL/SQL procedure successfully completed.
no rows selected
```

Listing 12.1 indicates the database doesn't have any invalid date constraints. You can query the table **c$def** to get more information about any constraints reported as being bad.

Using UTLDTREE

The UTLDTREE.SQL script creates the **deptree_temptab** table, two views (**deptree** and **ideptree**), and a procedure (**deptree_fill**). The **deptree_fill** procedure accepts

Table 12.14   Datafile/disk I/O report from UTLESTAT.SQL.

TABLESPACE	FILE_NAME	PHYS READS	PHYS BLKS READ	READ TIME	PHYS WRITES	PHYS BLKS WRT	WRITE_ TIME	MEGABYTE
RAW_DATA	E:\ORTEST1\RAW01.DBF	0	0	0	0	0	0	73
RAW_INX	C:\ORTEST1\RAW_I1.DBF	6774	6774	11394	0	0	0	524
RBK_DATA	C:\ORTEST1\RBS1.DBF	20	20	31	29	29	29	524
APPL_DATA	D:\ORTEST1\APLDAT1.DBF	0	0	0	0	0	0	524
APPL_DATA	D:\ORTEST1\APLDAT2.DBF	3197	51111	13483	0	0	0	524
APPL_DATA	D:\ORTEST1\APLDAT3.DBF	1786	28531	7369	0	0	0	524
APPL_DATA	E:\ORTEST1\APLDAT4.DBF	649	10374	2548	0	0	0	524
APPL_INX	E:\ORTEST1\APLIDX2.DBF	6430	6430	2212	0	0	0	524
APPL_INX	F:\ORTEST1\APLIDX1.DBF	4514	4514	616	0	0	0	524
SYSTEM	C:\ORTEST1\SYSTEST.ORA	107	119	259	83	83	85	52
TEMP	F:\ORTEST1\TMP1.DBF	670	9718	1816	621	9733	28	629
USER	C:\ORTEST1\USR1.DBF	0	0	0	0	0	0	10

12 rows selected.

Note: Report has been reformatted to fit page.

Table 12.15 UTLBSTAT/UTLESTAT start and stop times report.

START_TIME	END_TIME
19-jun-97 17:00:25	19-jun-97 17:25:15
1 row selected.	

Table 12.16 Instance version data report from UTLESTAT.SQL.

BANNER
Oracle8 Server Release 8.0.2.0.1 - Beta
PL/SQL Release 3.0.2.0.1 - Beta
CORE Version 4.0.2.0.1 - Production
TNS for 32-bit Windows: Version 3.0.2.0.0 - Beta
NLSRTL Version 3.3.0.0.1 - Beta
5 rows selected.

three arguments—type, schema, and name—where type is the type of object, schema is the owner, and name is the object name.

The example in Listing 12.2 was selected for brevity. I first ran the example using the **col$** table and ended up with a four-page report, including some cursor definitions. You will get cursor definitions only if you run the script from the SYS user.

Listing 12.2 Example run of UTLDTREE.SQL.

```
SQL> @d:\orant\rdbms80\admin\utldtree
drop sequence deptree_seq
              *
ERROR at line 1:
ORA-02289: sequence does not exist

Sequence created.

drop table deptree_temptab
           *
ERROR at line 1:
ORA-00942: table or view does not exist
```

```
Table created.

Procedure created.

drop view deptree
*
ERROR at line 1:
ORA-00942: table or view does not exist

SQL>
SQL> REM This view will succeed if current user is sys.  This view shows
SQL> REM which shared cursors depend on the given object.  If the current
SQL> REM user is not sys, then this view will get an error either about lack
SQL> REM of privileges or about the non-existence of table x$kglxs.
SQL>
SQL> set echo off

View created.

SQL>
SQL> REM This view will succeed if current user is not sys.  This view
SQL> REM does *not* show which shared cursors depend on the given object.
SQL> REM If the current user is sys then this view will get an error
SQL> REM indicating that the view already exists (since prior view create
SQL> REM will have succeeded).
SQL>
SQL> set echo off
create view deptree
           *
ERROR at line 1:
ORA-00955: name is already used by an existing object

drop view ideptree
*
ERROR at line 1:
ORA-00942: table or view does not exist

View created.


SQL> execute deptree_fill('TABLE','SYS','AUD$');

PL/SQL procedure successfully completed.

SQL> select * from deptree order by nested_level
  2  ;
```

```
NESTED_LEVEL  TYPE            SCHEMA      NAME                           SEQ#
------------  --------------  ----------  ------------------------  ----------
           0  TABLE           SYS         AUD$        0
           1  VIEW            SYS         DBA_AUDIT_TRAIL                  111
           2  VIEW            SYS         USER_AUDIT_TRAIL                 112
           2  VIEW            SYS         DBA_AUDIT_SESSION                116
           2  VIEW            SYS         DBA_AUDIT_STATEMENT              117
           2  VIEW            SYS         DBA_AUDIT_OBJECT                 118
           2  VIEW            SYS         DBA_AUDIT_EXISTS                 119
           3  VIEW            SYS         USER_AUDIT_SESSION               113
           3  VIEW            SYS         USER_AUDIT_OBJECT                115
           3  VIEW            SYS         USER_AUDIT_STATEMENT             114

10 rows selected.


SQL> select * from ideptree

DEPENDENCIES
---------------------------------------------------------------------------
TABLE SYS.AUD$
   VIEW SYS.DBA_AUDIT_TRAIL
   VIEW SYS.USER_AUDIT_TRAIL
   VIEW SYS.USER_AUDIT_SESSION
   VIEW SYS.USER_AUDIT_STATEMENT
   VIEW SYS.USER_AUDIT_OBJECT
   VIEW SYS.DBA_AUDIT_SESSION
   VIEW SYS.DBA_AUDIT_STATEMENT
   VIEW SYS.DBA_AUDIT_OBJECT
   VIEW SYS.DBA_AUDIT_EXISTS

10 rows selected.
```

 ## Using UTLLOCKT

The UTLLOCKT.SQL script prints the sessions in the system that are waiting for locks, and the locks for which they wait. The script generates a tree-structured-format report. If a session ID is printed immediately below and to the right, then it is waiting for that session. The session IDs printed at the left-hand side of the page are the sessions for which everyone is waiting.

For example, in the printout in Table 12.17, session 9 is waiting for session 8; 7 is waiting for 9; and 10 is waiting for 9. This example was taken from the online script header for UTLLOCKT.SQL.

Table 12.17   Example output from the UTLLOCKT.SQL script.

WAITING_SESSION	TYPE	MODE REQUESTED	MODE HELD	LOCK ID1	LOCK ID2
8	NONE	None	None	0	0
9	TX	Share(S)	Exclusive (X)	65547	16
7	RW	Exclusive (X)	S/Row-X (SSX)	33554440	2
10	RW	Exclusive (X)	S/Row-X (SSX)	33554440	2

The lock information to the right of the session ID describes the lock that the session is waiting for (not the lock it is holding).

Note that this is a script, not a set of view definitions. **CONNECT-BY** is used in the implementation, and, therefore, a temporary table is created and dropped, because you cannot do a join in a **CONNECT-BY**.

This script has two small disadvantages:

- One, a table is created when this script is run. To create a table, you must acquire a number of locks. This might cause the session running the script to get caught in the lock problem it is trying to diagnose.

- Two, if a session waits on a lock held by more than one session (share lock) then the wait-for graph is no longer a tree, and the **CONNECT-BY** will show the session (and any sessions waiting on it) several times.

With the use of UTLLOCKT.SQL and the other utility scripts provided by Oracle, tuning and troubleshooting can be greatly simplified. I am a firm believer in not reinventing wheels, and Oracle has provided several rather nice ones in the UTL* series of scripts. Use them.

Using Java With Oracle8 SQL And PL/SQL

The other chapters in this book deal with many diverse topics, but most of them are "server-centric"—that is, dealing with the current database or server. This chapter deals with the new kid on the block—the Web. Oracle8 is one of the few Web-ready databases. With the new Web server from Oracle, new Java connectivity options, and new stored procedures, Oracle8 promises to blow open the Web (either intra- or inter-) for Oracle applications.

Notes…

Chapter 13

Java, PL/SQL, And SQL

Java, an interpreted, platform-independent language, was only recently introduced to the computing world. In a few short years, it has risen from total obscurity (indeed, nonexistence) to a preeminent position in the hierarchy of programming languages. This book is not intended as a primer for Java. We will examine a few examples using JDBC (Java Database Connectivity) and JSQL (an alpha release of the Oracle PRO*JAVA product offering) against an Oracle8 database. JDK (Java Developers Kit) 1.1.4, JDBC, and JSQL are all included on the enclosed CD-ROM. For more detailed looks at Java and JDBC, I suggest the following books:

- *SQL Database Programming With Java*, Bill McCarty, The Coriolis Group, 1998.

- *Java In A Nutshell*, David Flanagan, O'Reilly, May 1997.

- *Java Database Programming*, Brian Jepson, John Wiley and Sons, 1997.

- *Laura Lemay's Java 1.1 Interactive Course*, Laura Lemay, Charles Perkins, Michael Morrison, and Daniel Groner, Waite Group Press, 1997.

Java owes its platform independence to the fact that it is interpreted and not compiled. Essentially, the machine-level code for a Java script (Java bytecode) is not generated until runtime, so the script is downloaded from the Web to the local machine.

This means that as long as a Java interpreter has been written for the operating system your users are on, the Java applet (a standalone section of Java code that is treated as an object) that you write on your PC will run on it. This is synonymous to the Basic language in the early days of programming. You have to wonder, if machines had been as fast back in the early days of Basic—making interpreted languages possible for use in production-level systems— would other languages, such as FORTRAN, COBOL, and even C, have been pursued as readily?

Java was initially built to be a toolkit language for small device programming (i.e., that Java-enabled cappuccino machine). This meant that it had to be highly portable—hence, its emergence as a language of choice for Web applications. Now, extensions, such as JDBC (a takeoff on ODBC—Open Database Connectivity) and JSQL (Java SQL), place Java firmly as a prime candidate for use in company intranet databases and for Web databases as the language to use for your interface between HTML pages and database servers.

Of course, Java with the various extensions, such as JDBC and JSQL, can also be used as a standalone language with or without HTML wrapping. JavaScript also will play a part in the development of the entire Java paradigm.

Figure 13.1 shows how these various components fit together. JSQL is passed through a Java precompiler and then, using JDBC connections possible through a Web server, communicates with the Oracle8 database either on the same server or on an entirely different server.

Because of security features of Java, if it is used to access databases on other servers, it is not allowed to rely on such objects as external shared libraries, such as DLLs. Therefore, there are two modes for using the JDBC component:

- The first relies on external ODBC/JDBC communication libraries.

- The second, known as a "thin" connection, uses internalized drivers, allowing it to access remote databases.

Because Java is in its youth, it is still undergoing many changes and improvements. This can sometimes lead to difficulties as classes are *deprecated* (this means made obsolete, dropped, or changed); the **www.javasoft.com** Web page will provide the latest copy of the JDK, at least until the language is officially "mature." The version provided on the enclosed CD-ROM is 1.1.4; additionally, the JDK 1.0 version is provided in case your system browsers can't support the newer version. I suggest you obtain the latest copies of the various browsers and be sure that they are Java-compliant,

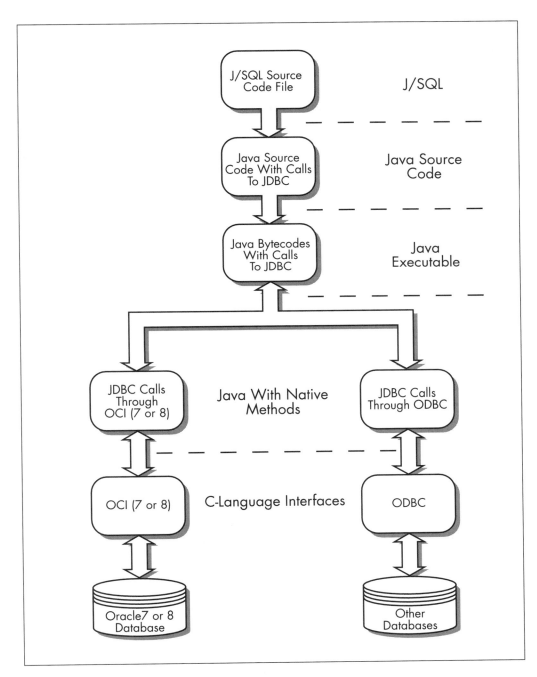

Figure 13.1

Java, JDBC, JSQL, and Oracle8 relationships.

or the examples in this book may not function without modification (beyond user name, password, and connection data).

The JDBC and JSQL extensions are available from the **www.oracle.com** Web page; if you buy this book after mid-1998, I suggest downloading the latest copies from that Web page. I will endeavor to keep the CD-ROM current, but this may not always be possible.

In Oracle8, Java is attractive because of the capability to directly map Oracle8 types into Java types (or classes, as they are called in Java).

A Comparison With Java

Java is one of the few truly object-oriented languages. Because it comes closest to the "ideal" object language, let's compare how Java does types with how Oracle has implemented them. Java types, or classes, are usually implemented as C++ strucs, except that a single object file serves as the interface definition and implementation for a type.

Attributes of a Java object and internal methods are accessed via the dot notation, the same as in Oracle8, as you shall see in this chapter's Practical Guide. Java does all referencing for you—there is no manipulation of pointers. Oracle8 uses references, and you can manipulate them. A major difference between Java and Oracle8 is that no objects in Java are persistent, while types and objects created by them can be persistent in Oracle—or, if they are used in the context of PL/SQL, they don't have to be. Therefore, Oracle8 (and to a limited extent, Oracle 7.3) is more flexible than Java as far as typing.

Java allows forward reference, as does Oracle8. This eliminates the header requirements of some languages, such as C and C++. Java allows definition of variables anywhere in the program body; Oracle8 (in PL/SQL) doesn't. Both Java and Oracle8 in PL/SQL allow method (procedure/function) overloading. This means that multiple methods, procedures, or functions can be declared with the same name but different argument types. This allows the same method to be called for various data types. The Java or Oracle8 engine chooses the proper method, procedure, or function to use based on the data type of the argument.

Let's look at a simple class/type definition in both Java and Oracle8.

An Example Class/Type Definition In Both Java And Oracle8

I will use a simple **Room** class/type definition, introduced in Chapter 4, to demonstrate. In Java, this definition looks like Listing 13.1.

Listing 13.1 Example class definition in Java.

```
public class Room {
        public double l, w;      //The length and width of the room
        public double h;          //The height of the room

//Methods that return the square feet and cubic feet of the room
public double square_feet() { return l * w; }
public volume() { return l * w * h; }
}
```

The class definition in Listing 13.1 can store a room's height, width, and length and contains methods for calculating its square feet and cubic feet. What would the same definition look like in Oracle8? Look at Listing 13.2.

Listing 13.2 Example OBJECT type definition in Oracle8.

```
CREATE TYPE room_T AS OBJECT (
lngth NUMBER,
width NUMBER,
height NUMBER,
MEMBER FUNCTION square_foot RETURN NUMBER,
pragma RESTRICT_REFERENCES(square_foot, WNDS, WNPS),
MEMBER FUNCTION volume RETURN NUMBER,
pragma RESTRICT_REFERENCES(VOLUME, wnds, wnps));
create type body ROOM_t as
member function SQUARE_FOOT return number is
begin
return LNGTH * WIDTH;
end;
member function VOLUME return number is
begin
return LNGTH * WIDTH * HEIGHT;
end;
end;
```

The major difference between Listings 13.1 and 13.2 is that the actual methods are declared in a separate code section under Oracle8. Take a look at how Java and Oracle8 access and use classes/types and methods.

Java And Oracle8's Use Of Classes/Types

Now that you have seen a basic example of how types and classes look in Oracle8 and Java, let's look at how they are used. Listing 13.3 shows how Java would use the class created in Listing 13.1.

Listing 13.3   Example using Java class and method.

```
Room LivingRoom = new Room();
double area;
LivingRoom.w = 10;
LivingRoom.l = 20;
area = LivingRoom.square_foot();
```

Notice how once you create an instance of **Room**, you can then call methods (**area**) that are part of the class by simply using the instance name you created and the method name using dot notation (**LivingRoom.area**). How would this look in Oracle8? Listing 13.4 shows the same process in Oracle8 SQL and PL/SQL.

In PL/SQL (persistent), first create an object table from type **room**.

Listing 13.4   Example in PL/SQL using types and method access.

```
CREATE TABLE rooms (room varchar2(20), room_dimensions room_T);
INSERT INTO rooms VALUES ('LivingRoom',room_dimensions(10,20,16));

DECLARE
area NUMBER;
volume NUMBER;
roomtemp room_t;
BEGIN
SELECT room_dimensions INTO roomtemp
FROM rooms r WHERE room='LivingRoom';
area:=roomtemp.square_foot();
volume:=roomtemp.volume();
dbms_output.put_line('Square feet='||TO_CHAR(area));
dbms_output.put_line('Volume='||TO_CHAR(volume));
END;
In PL/SQL (non-persistent):
DECLARE
LivingRoom room_T:=ROOM_T(0,0,0);
area number;
BEGIN
LivingRoom.lngth := 10;
LivingRoom.width := 20;
area := LivingRoom.square_foot();
END;
```

As you can see, for nonpersistent values (Java and PL/SQL), you can use virtually identical code. For persistent objects (PL/SQL), you need to create the storage area and then use data-access methods to perform operations. The Oracle8 and Java methods can be accessed in virtually identical ways.

A Closer Look At Java

Java uses the object-oriented concepts of inheritance, polymorphism, and classes. It is one of the few truly object-oriented languages and looks similar to C++. However, much of the "fat" in C++ has been pared away, leaving a lean, mean programming language.

Java is case-sensitive. This means if a method is named **DBATempSelect**, that is how it must be referred to from that point on. This seems to be a carry-over from Java's Sun-Unix beginnings. I know I would never have multiple objects with only a capital letter or so difference between their names. How about you? If a method, class, or variable name is shown a specific way, then it must be used that way. Remember this fact when dealing with the Java documentation.

I suggest that you purchase a good Java book (or two, or three). To develop the examples in the Practical Guide for this chapter, I used more than $300 worth of after-market books. Java is young enough that no one reference has yet evolved to provide insight into the use of Java with databases, with images, and the use of Java, JDBC, and JSQL. Each book seems to have pieces of the puzzle but not the complete picture. Two good references I used in building the examples are:

- *The Java Tutorial—Object-Oriented Programming For The Internet*, Mary Campione, Kathy Walrath, Addison-Wesley Publishing, 1996.

- *Graphic Java1.1—Mastering The AWT*, 2nd Edition, David M. Geary, Sun MicroSystems, Prentice-Hall Publishing, 1997.

In spite of all of these references, I still had to email other Coriolis authors with a question about a problem that the Java virtual machine beat me up over for a couple of days. Using the most current versions of the JDK and class libraries is critical. Make sure your references are as current as possible.

One problem that you will encounter if you use outdated libraries is called *deprecation*. This is the process by which old versions of Java classes are marked so that the Java compiler warns you that they are no longer actively supported. While many books tell you about this, they don't tell you how to fix the problem when it happens. I ended up doing a Web search to find data on which methods have been deprecated and which new methods have replaced them. You can find this information at **http:/ /java.sun.com/products/jdk/1.1/docs/guide/awt/DeprecatedMethods.html** for the AWT module. Other deprecated methods for other classes of objects are stored in similar structures on the same site.

In Java, there are already several major classes with many subclasses beneath them. Some examples of the major classes are: **awt**, **io**, **lang**, **applet**, **net**, and **utl**. Some examples (from the **awt** superclass) of subclasses are: **peer**, **image**, **graphics**, and **component**, just to name a few. The section of the earlier mentioned LeMay book on the **awt** package of classes takes 165 pages to cover just the basics of the package definition. Of course, each class and subclass may have many methods (usually 8 to 10), including constructor methods; and, because Java supports inheritance, any subclass inherits behaviors from the superclass it is a part of. All of this inheritance can lead to great confusion when you are trying to find out exactly how to make an instance of class X perform operation Y.

Scripts And Applets

As in PL/SQL, in Java you can have standalone programs called *scripts* (anonymous PL/SQL blocks in PL/SQL) and class and method declarations called *applets* (stored procedures, functions in PL/SQL). In addition, classes can be rolled up into packages just like individual procedures, and functions can be rolled up into packages in PL/SQL. A class definition, as shown earlier, is virtually identical in both languages.

Java code is stored in files just like the code from other languages. The name of the file must match, both in content and format, the name of the class contained within the file. A Java file usually ends with the .java extension. All Java code must be passed through the Java compiler and be made into a bytecode module with a suffix of class before it can be used. The Java compiler, called *javac*, is included with JDK114.exe on the CD-ROM. The compiler must be run from a command-line session (i.e., MS-DOS) on Windows 95 or NT platforms. The Java compiler has the following command-line options:

- -classpath path—Specifies the path javac uses to look up classes needed to run javac or being referenced by other classes you are compiling. Overrides the default or the **CLASSPATH** environment variable if it is set. Directories are separated by semicolons. It is often useful for the directory containing the source files to be on the class path. You should always include the system classes at the end of the path. For example:

```
javac -classpath .;C:\users\dac\classes;C:\tools\java\classes ...
```

- -d directory— Specifies the root directory of the class file hierarchy. In other words, this is essentially a destination directory for your compiled classes. For example,

```
javac -d C:\users\dac\classes MyProgram.java
```

causes the class files for the classes in the MyProgram.java source file to be saved in the directory C:\users\dac\classes. If your class is in the package demos\awt, the class files would be placed in directory C:\users\dac\classes\demos\awt.

Note that the -d and -classpath options have independent effects. The compiler reads only from the class path, and writes only to the destination directory. It is often useful for the destination directory to be on the class path. If the -d option is not specified, the source files should be stored in a directory hierarchy that reflects the package structure, so the resulting class files can be easily located.

- -encoding encoding name—Specifies the source file encoding name, such as EUCJIS\SJIS. If this option is not specified, the platform default converter is used.

- -g—Enables generation of debugging tables. These tables contain information about line numbers and local variables—information used by Java debugging tools. By default, only line numbers are generated, unless optimization (-O) is turned on.

- -deprecation—Enables deprecation warnings. The compiler will emit a warning for each use of a deprecated member or class (unless the deprecated member or class is also being compiled or recompiled). A class or member is deprecated if it contains a documentation comment with the tag **@deprecated**.

- -nowarn—Turns off warnings. If used, the compiler does not print out any warnings.

- -O—Optimizes compiled code by inlining static, final, and private methods. Note that your classes may get larger in size.

- -verbose—Causes the compiler and linker to print out messages about what source files are being compiled and what class files are being loaded.

- -depend—Causes recompilation of class files on which the source files given as command-line arguments recursively depend. Without this option, only files that are directly depended on and missing or out-of-date will be recompiled. Recompilation does not extend to missing or out-of-date files depended on only by already up-to-date class files.

- -Jjavaoption—Passes through the string **javaoption** as a single argument to the Java interpreter, which runs the compiler. The argument should not contain spaces. Multiple argument words must all begin with the prefix -J, which is stripped. This is useful for adjusting the compiler's execution environment or memory usage.

Example: Compiling One Or More Classes

In this example, the source files are located at c:\jdk\src\java\awt*.java. Change the directory holding the class or classes you want to compile. Then, run javac, supplying one or more class names:

```
% cd c:\jdk\src\java\awt
% javac Button.java Canvas.java
```

This compiles the two classes.

Environmental Variables

Two environmental variables—**PATH** and **CLASSPATH**—will affect the operation of your Java programs, such as java, javac, and appletviewer:

- **CLASSPATH**—Used to provide the system a path to user-defined classes. Directories are separated by semicolons. For example:

  ```
  .;C:\users\dac\classes;C:\tools\java\classes
  ```

- **PATH**—Used to tell the operating system which path to traverse to search for executables.

On Unix, these variables can be set in the .profile file for each user or through a global setup .profile (the file name may differ depending on the shell you use under Unix). On a Windows 95 platform, a simple addition to the autoexec.bat file in the boot directory is all that is required; on Windows NT, you can use the autoexec.bat method added to a trip through the registry editor. Getting the various browsers to recognize new **CLASSPATH** variables can be difficult; I would suggest getting some expert help to add this data to your browser path.

The Java Interpreter

Once Java code has been compiled, it is executed by the Java Virtual Machine (JVM), using the **java** command. For example, **java DBATempSelect** would load and run the **DBATempSelect.class** file into the Java interpreter and execute it. The Java interpreter has the following command-line options:

- -debug—Allows the Java debugger (jdb) to attach itself to this Java session. When **-debug** is specified on the command line, Java displays a password that must be used when starting the debugging session.

- -classpath path—Specifies the path Java uses to look up classes. Overrides the default or the **CLASSPATH** environment variable, if it is set. Directories are separated by colons. Thus, the general format for path is: .:<your_path>. For example:

   C:\xyz\classes;C:\usr\local\java\classes

- -mx x—Sets the maximum size of the memory allocation pool (the garbage collected heap) to x. The default is 16MB of memory. X must be greater than or equal to 1,000 bytes. The maximum memory size must be greater than or equal to the startup memory size (specified with the **-ms** option, default 16MB). By default, x is measured in bytes. You can specify x in either kilobytes or megabytes by appending the letter k for kilobytes or the letter m for megabytes.

- -ms x—Sets the startup size of the memory allocation pool (the garbage collected heap) to x. The default is 1MB of memory. x must be greater than 1,000 bytes. The startup memory size must be less than or equal to the maximum memory size (specified with the **-mx** option; default 16MB). By default, x is measured in bytes. You can specify x in either kilobytes or megabytes by appending the letter k for kilobytes or the letter m for megabytes.

- -noasyncgc—Turns off asynchronous garbage collection. When activated, no garbage collection takes place unless it is explicitly called or the program runs out of memory. Normally, garbage collection runs as an asynchronous thread in parallel with other threads.

- -noclassgc—Turns off garbage collection of Java classes. By default, the Java interpreter reclaims space for unused Java classes during garbage collection.

- -prof—Starts the Java runtime, with Java profiling enabled. By default, this puts profile results in the file .\java.prof. This option works only with java_g and javaw_g.

- -prof: file—Starts the Java runtime, with Java profiling enabled. This form of the flag allows the user to specify a different output file for the profile information. For example, the flag **-prof:myprog.prof** enables profiling and puts the profile results in the file myprog.prof rather than in the default file .\java.prof. This option works only with java_g and javaw_g.

- -version—Prints the build version information.

- -help—Prints a usage message.

- -ss x—Each Java thread has two stacks: one for Java code and one for C code. The **-ss** option sets the maximum stack size that can be used by C code in a thread to x. Every thread that is spawned during the execution of the program passed to Java has x as its C stack size. The default units for x are bytes. The value of x must be greater than or equal to 1,000 bytes. You can modify the meaning of x by appending either the letter k for kilobytes or the letter m for megabytes. The default stack size is 128 kilobytes (-ss 128k).

- -oss x—Each Java thread has two stacks: one for Java code and one for C code. The **-oss** option sets the maximum stack size that can be used by Java code in a thread to x. Every thread that is spawned during the execution of the program passed to Java has x as its Java stack size. The default units for x are bytes. The value of x must be greater than or equal to 1,000 bytes. You can modify the meaning of x by appending either the letter k for kilobytes or the letter m for megabytes. The default stack size is 400 kilobytes (-oss 400k).

- -t—Prints a trace of the instructions executed (java_g only).

- -v, -verbose—Causes Java to print a message to stdout each time a class file is loaded.

- -verify—Performs bytecode verification on the class file. Beware, however, that Java **-verify** does not perform a full verification in all situations. Any code path that is not actually executed by the interpreter is not verified. Therefore, Java **-verify** cannot be relied upon to certify class files unless all code paths in the class file are actually run.

- -verifyremote—Runs the verifier on all code that is loaded into the system via a classloader; **-verifyremote** is the default for the interpreter.

- -noverify—Turns verification off.

- -verbosegc—Causes the garbage collector to print out messages whenever it frees memory.

- -DpropertyName=newValue—Redefines a property value. **propertyName** is the name of the property whose value you want to change, and **newValue** is the value to change it to. For example, the command line % **java -Dawt.button.color=green ...** sets the value of the property **awt.button.color** to "green". Java accepts any number of **-D** options on the command line.

A Quick Look At Java Fundamentals

All Java code begins with the **import** section. The **import** section of a Java script or applet tells the compiler what class packages you are using in the code body. If a class package is used in the code body and it has not been imported, you will receive an error, and your code will not run.

Following the **import** section, each set of Java code will usually have either a **class** definition with an **init()** module or a **main()** declaration. Following these major Java sections will be the methods that define the functionality of the script or applet. Each script or applet can have multiple methods. As in all languages, watch your parentheses in Java—they are especially important because they define the context of your variable definitions. Generally speaking, variables are downwardly referenceable, but are not upwardly referenceable unless they have been globally defined in the **class** definition or at the highest level of the script. An applet must have an **init()** method, while an application or script will have a **main()** method.

In Listing 13.6, notice the line:

```
public static void main (String args[])
```

It tells you that this piece of code is not an applet that could be run via an HTML call from a Web page. This type of script must be run from the **java** (note the lowercase designation; this is a reference to the java.exe program). The name of a method includes the method type, return type, and the method name, as well as a list of any variables that must be passed to the method. In the case of **public static void main (String args[])**, the method type is **public,** meaning it can be accessed externally to the class; the return type is **static void**, which means there is no return type; the method name is **main**, and the argument passed is a string (character) type called **args[]** (the [] indicates that it is a string array).

Applets include the line:

```
public class <class_name> extends java.applet.Applet
```

and the call:

```
public void init ()
```

Applets are run from either a Java-enabled Web browser or from the appletviewer.exe program. The appletviewer program is included in the JDK release on the CD-ROM included with this book.

 *If a class is imported, then only the class path following the imported section of the class path needs to be included in internal references. For example, if the import line for the applet class is **import java.applet.***, this indicates that everything after **java.applet** in the class hierarchy is to be included. This inclusion means you can now refer to **java.applet.Applet** as just **Applet** in code references.*

Overriding Methods In Java

Frequently, you will need to add functionality to a Java method or fill in a method stub. A good example of a situation where an override of a method is required is the **paint(Graphics g)** method used in graphics work. As it exists, the **paint(Graphics g)** method is just a stub, or, if you prefer, a null method. Usually, you must add functionality to the **paint(Graphics g)** method to make graphics work properly. For example, the simplest form of this method override would be a call to the method that is used to draw graphics with a default location specification. Location specifications for graphics are in pixels and correspond roughly to the resolution of your monitor driver (for example, 1,024×768 pixels); the location is a (x,y) data point. The simplest override method for the **paint(Graphics g)** method would look like Listing 13.5.

Listing 13.5 Example of method overriding.
```
public void paint (Graphics g)
 {
g.drawImage(imagename,0,0,this);
 }
```

Methods, such as **paint()**, **update()**, and **repaint()**, will usually be overridden to generate desired behaviors. Other methods—again, mostly related to graphics generation—such as **getPreferredSize()**, are usually overridden as required. I suggest reading up on the method before deciding to override it.

JSQL, JDBC, And Java
The previous examples didn't deal with Java against persistent objects. To use Java against persistent objects in Oracle8, you will have to use the JDBC or JSQL protocols.

The JDBC protocol sets up a predefined set of classes that allows access to SQL databases. The proper classes must be invoked against the proper database (be it SQL Server, Oracle, or whatever).

JSQL
The JSQL protocol is actually a pre-interpreter for Java scripts that adhere to the JSQL coding standards. A properly coded Java applet or script is fed into the JSQL pre-interpreter, which converts all embedded SQL calls into something standard Java interpreters can understand. The pre-interpreted JSQL code is then used identically to standard Java applets or scripts. Listing 13.6 shows **DBATempSelect.jsql**, which uses JSQL with code borrowed unmercifully from the **TestInstallJSQL.jsql** routine supplied with the JSQL release. Listing 13.7 shows the same code after being passed through the JSQL precompiler. Notice that all Java commands, just like all PL/SQL commands, must end with a semicolon unless they encapsulate other code sections.

Listing 13.6 Example DBATempSelect JSQL code.
```
/* Import J/SQL Context and SQL Exceptions classes. Any method
containing SQL.exec clauses needs access to these classes.
The JSQLContext class provides the means of associating an actual
database with the program's SQL constructs.
The SQLException comes from JDBC. SQL.exec clauses result in
calls to JDBC, so methods containing SQL.exec clauses must either
catch or throw SQLException.
*/
```

```
import oracle.jsql.JSQLContext ;
import java.sql.SQLException ;
// cursor for the select
SQL.cursor(MyCurs (String NAME));
class DBATempSelect {
/* This attribute holds the J/SQL Context object associated with
an instance of this class.
   */
JSQLContext context = null ;
/* The constructor method takes a J/SQL context as an argument
so objects of this type have a value for the getContext
method to return.
   */
DBATempSelect(JSQLContext context) { this.context = context  ; }
/* This class uses SQL.exec clauses that do not specify an
explicit context identifier. Therefore, it must have a
getContext method.
   */
JSQLContext getContext() { return context ; }
//Main method
public static void main (String args[])
  {
/* This variable holds the new J/SQL context created below by
connecting to the database. It then serves as an argument to
    */
JSQLContext context = null  ;
context = ConnectionManager.newContext();
//Run the example
DBATempSelect ti = new DBATempSelect(context);
try {
ti.runExample();
} catch (SQLException e) {
System.err.println("Error running the example: " + e);
    }
//Close the connection
try {
context.close() ;
} catch (SQLException e) {
System.err.println("Error closing the connection: " + e) ;
    }
} //End of method main
//Method that runs the example
void runExample() throws SQLException
  {
//Issue SQL command to clear the DBA_TEMP table
SQL.exec ( DELETE FROM DBA_TEMP ) ;
SQL.exec ( BEGIN dbms_revealnet.just_statistics; END; );
```

```
MyCurs curs = SQL.exec((MyCurs) SELECT rpad(NAME,40)||
to_char(VALUE,'99,999,999,999.99999') name FROM DBA_TEMP );
while (curs.next()) {
System.out.println(curs.NAME());
    }
  }
}
```

So, what exactly is going on with the code in Listing 13.6? As stated earlier, the first section (disregarding the comments) is the **import** section:

```
import oracle.jsql.JSQLContext ;
import java.sql.SQLException ;
```

These **import** calls load the classes related to the JSQL and JDBC features. By default, all Java scripts and applets load the **java.lang.*** set of classes, which form the core of the Java language.

The next section of code in Listing 13.6 invokes JSQL-specific calls to create cursors and cursor contexts:

```
// define a cursor
SQL.cursor(MyCurs (String NAME));
class DBATemp {
JSQLContext context = null ;
// get context
DBATempSelect(JSQLContext context) { this.context = context  ; }
JSQLContext getContext() { return context ; }
```

These commands that define cursors and context can be likened to the cursor definition statements in PL/SQL. Notice that the definitions in the cursor definition section contain no statement definitions (**SELECT**, **INSERT**, **UPDATE**); these come later.

The next section of Listing 13.6 is the definition of the **main()** section of this Java script. Generally, the **main()** section does little processing; instead, it acts as a traffic director and initializer:

```
// Create main unit
public static void main (String args[])
  {
JSQLContext context = null   ;
context = ConnectionManager.newContext();
//Run the example
```

```
DBATempSelect ti = new DBATempSelect(context);
try {
ti.runExample();  // This is a method that actually does the work
} catch (SQLException e) {
System.err.println("Error running the example: " + e);
    }
//Close the connection
try {
context.close() ;
} catch (SQLException e) {
System.err.println("Error closing the connection: " + e) ;
    }
  }
// End of method main
```

In this **main()** section, you set up the context (make the Oracle connection), run the example through a call to another method (**runExample**), and close the connection by closing the context. Notice the exception traps. Most methods will "throw" exceptions if they are fairly complex. Always check for any exceptions that you expect. In the **main()** method, look for the **SQLException**, and take action based on receiving it within the **catch {}** definition. In this case, when you receive an exception, you print a simple error message using the **System.err.println** method, which is predefined and just prints the error to the screen.

The final section of the script in Listing 13.6 actually defines the SQL statements that are to be run and then executes them within the predefined context:

```
// Method that runs the example
void runExample() throws SQLException
  {
//Issue SQL command to clear the DBA_TEMP table
SQL.exec ( DELETE FROM dba_temp );
SQL.exec ( BEGIN dbms_revealnet.just_statistics; END;);
MyCurs curs = SQL.exec((MyCurs) SELECT RPAD(name,40)||
TO_CHAR(value, '99,999,999,999.9999') name FROM dba_temp);
while (curs.next()) {
System.out.println(curs.NAME());
    }
  }
```

The calls to the **SQL.exec** method execute the contained statements in the current context. The values are returned, and then the **while (curs.next()) {}** loop processes the results using the **System.out.println()** method to display them on screen.

Listing 13.7 shows the same code as in Listing 13.6, only this code has been passed through the JSQL precompiler.

Listing 13.7 Example output from the JSQL precompiler.

```
//  DO NOT EDIT THIS FILE - it is machine generated.
/* Import J/SQL Context and SQL Exceptions classes. Any method
containing SQL.exec clauses needs access to these classes.
The JSQLContext class provides the means of associating an actual
database with the program's SQL constructs.
The SQLException comes from JDBC. SQL.exec clauses result in
calls to JDBC, so methods containing SQL.exec clauses must either
catch or throw SQLException.
*/
import oracle.jsql.JSQLContext ;
import java.sql.SQLException ;
// cursor for the select

// SQL.cursor(MyCurs (String NAME))
/**
·        A strongly typed J/SQL-generated cursor
 **/
class MyCurs
extends oracle.jsql.JSPCursorImpl
{
/**
·        J/SQL-private method to be used only by J/SQL-generated code
 **/
public MyCurs(java.sql.ResultSet resultSet, oracle.jsql.JSPGettable parent)
throws java.sql.SQLException
{
super(1, resultSet, parent);
jSQLBind(jSQLFindColumn("NAME"), m_NAME = new oracle.jsql.StringOut());
}
/**
·        Creates a new strongly typed cursor for the given ResultSet.
·        For each column-attribute of the cursor, there must be a column
·        in the ResultSet with the same name and a compatible type.
·        @param resultSet the data used to populate the cursor
·        @exception java.sql.SQLException
·        if resultSet and cursor are incompatible
 **/
public MyCurs(java.sql.ResultSet resultSet)
throws java.sql.SQLException
{
this(resultSet, null);
}
/**
```

```
    •       @return an InOutHolder which can be used to pass a MyCurs
    •       cursor to J/SQL operations as an in-out parameter.<P>
    •       Note: this is only useful for JDBC drivers which support
    •       passing and retrieving ResultSets as SQL values
  **/
static public oracle.jsql.ObjectInOut newInOutHolder()
{
return new MyCurs$InOut();
}
/**
    •       @return an OutHolder which can be used to pass a MyCurs
    •       cursor to J/SQL operations as an out parameter.<P>
    •       Note: this is only useful for JDBC drivers which support
    •       passing and retrieving ResultSets as SQL values
  **/
static public oracle.jsql.ObjectOut newOutHolder()
{
return ((oracle.jsql.ObjectOut)(newInOutHolder()));
}
/**
    •       Advances the cursor to the first and only row
    •       @return this
    •       @exception java.sql.SQLException
    •       if cursor does not contain exactly one row
    •       or next() has previously been called
  **/
public MyCurs singleton()
throws java.sql.SQLException
{
jSQLSingleton();
return this;
}
/**
    •       J/SQL-private method to be used only by J/SQL-generated code
  **/
static public MyCurs jSQLCast(Object curs)
{
return ((MyCurs)(curs));
}
private oracle.jsql.StringOut m_NAME;
/**
    •       @return the value of the current row's "NAME" column
    •       @exception java.util.IndexOutOfBoundsException
    •       if cursor contains no rows or next() has not been called
  **/
public String NAME()
{
```

```
jSQLCheckBounds();
return m_NAME.value;
}
}
;
class DBATempSelect {
/* This attribute holds the J/SQL Context object associated with
an instance of this class.
  */
JSQLContext context = null ;
/* The constructor method takes a J/SQL context as an argument
so objects of this type have a value for the getContext
method to return.
  */
DBATempSelect(JSQLContext context) { this.context = context  ; }
/* This class uses SQL.exec clauses that do not specify an
explicit context identifier. Therefore, it must have a
getContext method.
  */
JSQLContext getContext() { return context ; }
//Main method
public static void main (String args[])
  {
/* This variable holds the new J/SQL context created below by
connecting to the database. It then serves as an argument to
  */
JSQLContext context = null  ;
context = ConnectionManager.newContext();
//Run the example
DBATempSelect ti = new DBATempSelect(context);
try {
ti.runExample();
} catch (SQLException e) {
System.err.println("Error running the example: " + e);
  }
//Close the connection
try {
context.close() ;
} catch (SQLException e) {
System.err.println("Error closing the connection: " + e) ;
  }
} //End of method main
//Method that runs the example
void runExample() throws SQLException
  {
//Issue SQL command to clear the DBA_TEMP table
```

```
// SQL.exec ( DELETE FROM DBA_TEMP )
getContext().jSQLStatement(DBATempSelect$JSQLStmts.m_stmts[0]).jSQLExec() ;

// SQL.exec ( BEGIN dbms_revealnet.just_statistics; END; )
getContext().jSQLStatement(DBATempSelect$JSQLStmts.m_stmts[1]).jSQLExec();
MyCurs curs =
// SQL.exec((MyCurs) SELECT rpad(NAME,40)||
to_char(VALUE,'99,999,999,999.99999') name FROM DBA_TEMP )
MyCurs.jSQLCast(getContext().jSQLStatement
(DBATempSelect$JSQLStmts.m_stmts[2]).jSQLExec(0, MyCurs.newOutHolder()));
while (curs.next()) {
System.out.println(curs.NAME());
    }
  }
}


// ADDITIONAL machine generated classes

/**
 *       GENERATED CLASS FOR J/SQL INTERNAL USE ONLY
 **/
class MyCurs$InOut
extends oracle.jsql.ObjectInOut
{
MyCurs$InOut()
{
super();
}
public void jSQLSet(oracle.jsql.JSPGettable gettableObject, int pos)
throws java.sql.SQLException
{
java.sql.ResultSet rs = gettableObject.getResultSet(pos);
value = (rs == null) ? null : new MyCurs(rs, gettableObject);
}
}
/**
 * GENERATED CLASS FOR J/SQL INTERNAL USE ONLY
 **/
class DBATempSelect$JSQLStmts
{
static final oracle.jsql.JSPStmtInfo[] m_stmts = {
new oracle.jsql.JSPStmtInfo("DELETE FROM DBA_TEMP", 0),
new oracle.jsql.JSPStmtInfo("BEGIN dbms_revealnet.just_statistics; END;", 0),
new oracle.jsql.JSPQueryInfo("SELECT rpad(NAME,40)||
to_char(VALUE,\'99,999,999,999.99999\') name FROM DBA_TEMP", 1)
};
}
```

As you can see from Listing 13.7, the level of complexity of the code increases substantially after passing through the precompiler. The output from the Java script in Listing 13.7 is shown in Listing 13.8.

Listing 13.8 Example output from DBATempSelect.jsql.

```
C:\ jsql DBATempSelect.jsql
C:\ javac DBATempSelect.java
C:\ java DBATempSelect
Startup Date: 09-nov-1997 16:52:30                    .00000
Data Dictionary Miss Percent                         4.32038
RECURSIVE CALLS PER USER                            25.08757
CUMULATIVE HIT RATIO                                  .73678
UNDO HDR WAIT CONTENTION                              .03869
Latch Miss%                                           .89742
table fetch by rowid                       1,259,777.00000
Non-Index Lookups Ratio                              .11672
table fetch continued row                        516.00000
sorts (memory)                                12,590.00000
sorts (disk)                                      45.00000
redo log space requests                       21,661.00000
redo log space wait time                   2,154,537.00000
TOTAL ALLOCATED MEG                            21,255.00000
TOTAL USED MEG                                12,302.74219
TOTAL SGA SIZE                           237,398,464.00000
cache buffers lru chain                              .05110
shared pool                                          .01259
parallel query stats                                8.64198
CLUSTER                                             1.00000
FUNCTION                                           50.00000
INDEX                                             955.00000
PACKAGE                                            16.00000
PACKAGE BODY                                       17.00000
PROCEDURE                                         332.00000
SEQUENCE                                          155.00000
SYNONYM                                         1,797.00000
TABLE                                             765.00000
TRIGGER                                           274.00000
VIEW                                              233.00000
```

The JSQL precompiler has multiple command-line options, shown in Table 13.1.

JDBC

For local and remote database monitoring, the JDBC package of classes provides for interface through the normal ODBC interface to the Oracle data sources. A simple JDBC Java script is shown in Listing 13.9.

Table 13.1 Table of JSQL command-line options.

Command Format: jsql [-option[-option]] file.jsql

Name	Type	Default	Description
Help	none	none	Shows descriptions of options.
Version	none	none	Shows the build version.
Dir	string		The directory for the generated files.
Props	file name	none	The name of a property file from which to load options.
Jdbc	string	java.sql	The location of the JDBC package.
Warn	string	nulls precision	Enable or disable warning messages. Possible values are none, all, nulls, nonulls, precision, noprecision, verbose, noverbose.
Jsql	string	oracle.jsql	The location of the JSQL runtime package.
Driver	string-list	none	Name of JDBC driver class.
Context	string-list	none	Java expression used to retrieve a JSQLContext object for a SQL [.<tag>].exec(...) call. Optionally tagged with context.
Connection	string-list	none	Connection string for accessing the database in order to perform semantic analysis. Optionally tagged with context.
User	string-list	none	User/password string for connecting to the database in order to perform semantic analysis. Optionally tagged with context.

Listing 13.9 Example script that uses the JDBC connection classes.

```
import oracle.jsql.JSQLContext ;          // Get JDBC driver data
import java.sql.*;                        // Ditto
class TestInstallJDBC {                   // Define class name
  public static void main
    (String args[]) throws SQLException   // define main() section
```

```
  {
    Connection conn=null;;                          // Establish connection context
    PreparedStatement ps=null;                      // Establish statement context
    ResultSet rs=null;                              // Establish result set context
    conn = ConnectionManager.newConnection();       // Pass the connection context
    ps = conn.prepareStatement("SELECT rpad(NAME,40)|':        // Load statement
    ||to_char(VALUE,'999,999,999.999') FROM DBA_TEMP order by rep_order");
    rs = ps.executeQuery();                         // Execute statement
    while (rs.next()) {                             // Process results
      System.out.println(rs.getString(1));         // Print to stdout()
    }
  }
}
```

Of course, if you look closely at the code in Listing 13.9, you'll see it actually makes a call to a class called **ConnectionManager** that does the work of connection. This class definition is shown in Listing 13.10.

Listing 13.10 Example of the ConnectionManager class.

```
import java.sql.SQLException;                       // These get JDBC Classes
import java.sql.DriverManager;
import java.sql.Connection;
import oracle.jsql.JSQLContext ;
public class ConnectionManager {                    // Define class name
static public String DRIVER = null ;        //JDBC Driver class
static public String DBURL  = null ;  //Database URL
  static public String UID    = null ;  //User ID for database account
  static public String PWD    = null ;  //Password for database account
static {
DRIVER = "oracle.jdbc.driver.OracleDriver" ;
DBURL  = "jdbc:oracle:thin:@90.31.28.18:1521:ORTEST1" ;
    UID    = "system" ;
    PWD    = "not_password" ;
  }
static public Connection newConnection()  // Establish connection context
  {
Connection conn = null;                             // Disconnect if needed
if (UID== null || PWD==null || DBURL==null || DRIVER==null)  // Verify inputs
    {
System.err.println (
"Please edit the ConnectionManager.java file to assign " +
"non-null values to the static string variables " +
"DBURL, DRIVER, UID, and PWD. Then recompile and try again." ) ;
System.exit(1) ;
    }
  try {
```

```
Class.forName( DRIVER );                              // Load driver
} catch (ClassNotFoundException exception) {
System.err.println( "Could not load driver: " + DRIVER ) ;
System.err.println(exception) ;
System.exit(1) ;
    }
try {
conn = DriverManager.getConnection (DBURL, UID, PWD);     // Establish connect
} catch (SQLException exception) {
System.out.println("Error: could not get a connection");
System.err.println(exception) ;
System.exit(1);
    }
return conn;                                          // return context to calling application
   }
static public JSQLContext newContext()
   {
// one way to construct a JSQLContext object is to provide
// an open JDBC Connection object.
return new JSQLContext (newConnection() ) ;
   }
}
```

Notice that Listing 13.10 uses the **thin** client connection. Other possible values include **oci7** and **oci8**. The only valid driver for access of remote databases is **thin**. The difference between the **thin** type of driver and the **oci7** or **oci8** driver is that the **thin** driver is internally implemented, while the others depend on externally defined dynamic link libraries (DLLs). This dependence on external files in the **oci7** and **oci8** drivers results in a security violation for remote database access attempts through JDBC, if they are used for that purpose. The **thin** client is usually used in applets.

To access PL/SQL from within Java, either the entire PL/SQL script is passed as a single argument, or, an execute call is made against a prebuilt PL/SQL stored procedure or function. Obviously, the latter is the option of choice, because it will reduce the number of network roundtrips required to perform the same function, thereby improving performance. Listing 13.11 shows execution of a PL/SQL script and then a query against the results of that procedure execution using a JDBC-based Java applet. This script performs the same function as the DBATempSelect.jsql script shown in Listing 13.7. The actual PL/SQL procedure being executed, **DBMS_REVEALNET.JUST_STATISTICS**, is included on the CD-ROM.

Listing 13.11 Example execution of a stored procedure and select using JDBC connection.

```
/*
This sample applet executes a stored procedure and
selects the results from the database
 */

// Import the JDBC classes
import java.sql.*;

// Import the java classes used in applets
import java.awt.*;
import java.io.*;
import java.util.*;
import oracle.jdbc.driver.*;
import java.awt.event.*;

// Define Applet Name
public class DBATempApplet extends java.applet.Applet
implements ActionListener
{
// The driver to load
static final String driver_class = "oracle.jdbc.driver.OracleDriver";

// The connect string
static final String connect_string =
"jdbc:oracle:thin:system/not_pword@90.10.100.1:1521:ortest1";
// This is the kind of string you would use if going through the
// Oracle8 connection manager which lets you run the database on a
// different host than the Web Server.  See the online documentation
// for more information.
/* static final String connect_string = "jdbc:oracle:thin:system/not_pword@
(description=(address_list=(address=(protocol=tcp)
(host=g1028018)(port=1521))(address=(protocol=tcp)))
(source_route=yes)(connect_data=(sid=ORTEST2)))";*/

// The statement and query we will execute
static final String query = "SELECT rpad(NAME,40)||': '||
to_char(VALUE,'999,999,999.999') FROM DBA_TEMP order by rep_order";

// The button to push for executing the query
Button execute_button;

// The place where to dump the query result
TextArea output;
Font outputFont = new  Font("Courier", Font.PLAIN, 12);
// The connection to the database
Connection conn;
```

```
// Create the User Interface
public void init ()
   {
this.setLayout (new BorderLayout ());
Panel p = new Panel ();
p.setLayout (new FlowLayout (FlowLayout.LEFT));
execute_button = new Button ("Test JDBC");
execute_button.addActionListener(this);
p.add (execute_button);
this.add ("North", p);
output = new TextArea (30, 60);
output.setFont(outputFont);
this.add ("Center", output);
   }

// Do the work
public void actionPerformed(ActionEvent event)
{
Object source = event.getSource() ;
if (source == execute_button)
   {
try
   {
// Clear the output area
output.setText (null);

// See if we need to open the connection to the database
if (conn == null)
      {
// Load the JDBC driver
output.append ("Loading JDBC driver " + driver_class + "\n");
Class.forName (driver_class);

// Connect to the database
output.append ("Connecting to " + connect_string + "\n");
conn = DriverManager.getConnection (connect_string);
output.append ("Connected\n");
      }

// Create a statement
Statement stmt = conn.createStatement ();

// Execute the statement and query
output.append("Executing stored procedure" + "\n");
OracleCallableStatement cstmt =
(OracleCallableStatement)
conn.prepareCall ("begin dbms_revealnet.just_statistics; end;");
```

```
cstmt.execute ();
output.append("Executing query " + query + "\n");
ResultSet rset = stmt.executeQuery (query);
// Dump the result
while (rset.next ())
output.append(rset.getString (1) + "\n");

// We're done
output.append("done.\n");
      }
catch (Exception e)
      {
// Oops
output.append("Error: " + e.getMessage () + "\n");
      }
    }
  }
}
```

Of course, because this is an applet, you need to use an HTML wrapper and run it using either a browser, such as Netscape or Internet Explorer, or use the appletviewer executable supplied in the JDK114.exe package. All applet examples shown have been tested using the appletviewer. Listing 13.12 is an example HTML wrapper used for testing applets.

Listing 13.12 Example HTML wrapper for applet testing.
```
<!DOCTYPE HTML PUBLIC "-//W3C//DTD HTML 3.2//EN">
<HTML>
<HEAD>
<TITLE></TITLE>
<META NAME="Author" CONTENT="">
<META NAME="GENERATOR" CONTENT="Mozilla/3.01Gold (Win95; I) [Netscape]">
</HEAD>
<BODY>
<APPLET CODE=DBATempApplet.class WIDTH=600 HEIGHT=560>
</APPLET>
</BODY>
</HTML>
```

The supplied applet viewer, appropriately named *appletviewer*, has the following command-line options:

- -debug—Starts the applet viewer in the Java debugger, jdb, thus allowing you to debug the applets in the document.

- -encoding encoding name—Specifies the input HTML file encoding name.

- -J javaoption—Passes through the string **javaoption** as a single argument to the Java interpreter, which runs the compiler. The argument should not contain spaces. Multiple argument words must all begin with the prefix **-J**, which is stripped. This is useful for adjusting the compiler's execution environment or memory usage.

Let's dissect the example shown in Listing 13.11 to see what is really happening. As with all Java code, the first section holds the **import** commands:

```
// Import the JDBC classes
import java.sql.*;

// Import the java classes used in applets
import java.awt.*;
import java.io.*;
import java.util.*;
import oracle.jdbc.driver.*;
import java.awt.event.*;
```

This important section includes the **sql**, **awt**, **io**, **util**, **awt.event**, and **oracle.jdbc.driver** classes. You could have used the **java.awt.*** class call just to load the **awt** class and all of its subclasses, but by including the import of **java.awt.event.***, it allows you to shorten any calls to the **event** subclasses. The full specification of the **oracle.jdbc.driver.*** class path also allows you to shorten calls to any of its subclasses.

The next session declares items that will be globally available to all subclasses and methods defined in the code section:

```
// Define Applet Name
public class JdbcApplet extends java.applet.Applet
implements ActionListener
{
// The driver to load
static final String driver_class = "oracle.jdbc.driver.OracleDriver";

// The connect string
static final String connect_string =
"jdbc:oracle:thin:system/not_pword@90.10.100.1:1521:ortest1";
// This is the kind of string you would use if going through the
// Oracle8 connection manager which lets you run the database on a
// different host than the Web Server.  See the online documentation
```

```
// for more information.
/* static final String connect_string = "jdbc:oracle:thin:system/not_pword@
(description=(address_list=(address=(protocol=tcp)(host=g1028018)
(port=1521))(address=(protocol=tcp)))(source_route=yes)
(connect_data=(sid=ORTEST2)))";*/

// The statement and query we will execute
static final String query = "SELECT rpad(name,40)||': '||
to_char(value,'999,999,999.999') FROM dba_temp order by rep_order";

// The button to push for executing the query
Button execute_button;

// The place where to dump the query result
TextArea output;
Font outputFont = new  Font("Courier", Font.PLAIN, 12);
// The connection to the database
Connection conn;
```

In this section, notice that you begin with a class declaration:

```
public class DBATempApplet extends java.applet.Applet
```

If you had included an import of **java.applet.***, this could have been shortened to:

```
public class DBATempApplet extends Applet
```

Also notice that there is no closing "}". This is because this is the "wrapper" method for everything that follows; its finishing "}" is at the end of the entire set of code. The line

```
implements ActionListener
```

tells the Java system that there will be components, such as buttons, that it has to "listen" for operations of, such as pushes, clicks, or other types of actions.

Next, you define some **String** variables—**driver_class, connect_string**, and **query**—which will be used in other sections. The **Button execute_button;** declaration tells Java you are implementing an abstract windows toolkit (**awt**) feature known as a button. As its name implies, a button object appears as a button on your user interface. The listener you implement will watch the button for activities, such as a mouse click on the button.

The next line

```
TextArea output;
```

defines another **awt** feature known as a **TextArea**. This area holds the results of the query operation. The line

```
Font ouptutFont = new Font("Courier", font.PLAIN, 12);
```

tells Java to initialize a font with the specified characteristic. The font created in this section can be attached to any text object, such as **output**, to tell Java how to display the textual content of **output**. The final line

```
Connection conn;
```

creates a **Connection** object from the database interface set of classes. This **conn** object will be used to control the connection to the database in later sections.

The next section is the **init()** section, usually used to lay out the user interface:

```
// Create the User Interface
public void init ()
   {
this.setLayout (new BorderLayout ());
Panel p = new Panel ();
p.setLayout (new FlowLayout (FlowLayout.LEFT));
execute_button = new Button ("Test JDBC");
execute_button.addActionListener(this);
p.add (execute_button);
this.add ("North", p);
output = new TextArea (30, 60);
output.setFont(outputFont);
this.add ("Center", output);
   }
```

In the first line

```
this.setLayout(new BorderLayout(());
```

the Java **awt** interface is instructed to use a border type layout for **this** object. A border layout has five possible locations: East, West, North, South, and Center. Other types of layout are Grid, Flow, or Card (of course, more may be added before you read this). The next line

```
Panel p = new Panel ();
```

tells the **awt** interface that you want to create a container called a **Panel**. Containers are used to hold other objects. For example, the container **p** is used to hold the button called **execute_button** and the text area called **output**. These objects are added to the container **p** by the **add** method of the **Panel** class. Notice the line

```
execute_button.addActionListener(this);
```

which immediately follows the line

```
execute_button = new Button("Test JDBC");
```

which creates a new instance of the **execute_button** with the label **"Test JDBC"**. The **this** value tells the Java compiler to apply the referenced method to the object that was last defined or to the current context. Also notice the line

```
output.setFont(outputFont);
```

which adds the font defined earlier to the text area **output**.

The next section from Listing 13.11 defines the required actions to be taken based on output from the action listener you defined and attached to the **execute_button**:

```
// Do the work
public void actionPerformed(ActionEvent event)
{
Object source = event.getSource() ;
if (source == execute_button)
    {
try
    {
// Clear the output area
output.setText (null);

// See if we need to open the connection to the database
if (conn == null)
    {
// Load the JDBC driver
output.append ("Loading JDBC driver " + driver_class + "\n");
Class.forName (driver_class);

// Connect to the database
output.append ("Connecting to " + connect_string + "\n");
conn = DriverManager.getConnection (connect_string);
output.append ("Connected\n");
    }

// Create a statement
Statement stmt = conn.createStatement ();
```

```
// Execute the statement and query
output.append("Executing stored procedure" + "\n");
OracleCallableStatement cstmt =
(OracleCallableStatement)
conn.prepareCall ("BEGIN dbms_revealnet.just_statistics; END;");
cstmt.execute ();
output.append("Executing query " + query + "\n");
ResultSet rset = stmt.executeQuery (query);
// Dump the result
while (rset.next ())
output.append(rset.getString (1) + "\n");

// We're done
output.append("done.\n");
        }
catch (Exception e)
        {
// Oops
output.append("Error: " + e.getMessage () + "\n");
        }
    }
  }
```

This section has but one action to look for—a simple interaction, such as a mouse click on the button object. The lines

```
public void actionPerformed(ActionEvent event)
{
Object source = event.getSource() ;
if (source == execute_button)
```

instruct the Java compiler that this is an **ActionEvent** response method. The second line in the method

```
Object source = event.getSource();
```

tells the compiler to get any information about an event and place it in the **source** object. The next line then checks this **source** object for the source of the event. In this case, it is checked to see if the source is the **execute_button**. If so, then the actions specified in the following {} section are taken.

The next section of Listing 13.11 begins with the **try** keyword, which tells the compiler that what follows may throw some exceptions. The use of **try** is required inside of an applet whenever an exception could be thrown; if you do not use **try**, you will receive a compiler error.

```
try
    {
// Clear the output area
output.setText (null);

// See if we need to open the connection to the database
if (conn == null)
        {
// Load the JDBC driver
output.append ("Loading JDBC driver " + driver_class + "\n");
Class.forName (driver_class);

// Connect to the database
output.append ("Connecting to " + connect_string + "\n");
conn = DriverManager.getConnection (connect_string);
output.append ("Connected\n");
        }

// Create a statement
Statement stmt = conn.createStatement ();

// Execute the statement and query
output.append("Executing stored procedure" + "\n");
OracleCallableStatement cstmt =
(OracleCallableStatement)
conn.prepareCall ("BEGIN dbms_revealnet.just_statistics; END;");
cstmt.execute ();
output.append("Executing query " + query + "\n");
ResultSet rset = stmt.executeQuery (query);
// Dump the result
while (rset.next ())
output.append(rset.getString (1) + "\n");

// We're done
output.append("done.\n");
        }
```

This section begins by clearing the **output** object by setting its value to null with the **output.settext(null);** method. Next, you see if the **conn** object has been initialized using a test to see if it is null:

```
if (conn == null).
```

If the connection object **conn** is null, the applet loads the driver using the **Class.forName(driver_class);** method. If you will remember, you set the **driver_class** string value in one of the first sections. Notice that you use the line:

```
output.append ("Loading JDBC driver " + driver_class + "\n");
```

to notify the user by outputting to the **output** object, which is a text area displayed on the **Panel** object **p**.

The actions that occur in the section involve the actual connection to the database. The line

```
conn = DriverManager.getConnection (connect_string);
```

executes the method that performs the actual connection to the database. Again, the **append** method is used to report on status to the user. Once the connection is established, you can create a statement context using:

```
OracleCallableStatement cstmt =
(OracleCallableStatement)
conn.prepareCall ("BEGIN dbms_revealnet.just_statistics; END;");
cstmt.execute ();
```

These code lines create and issue the call to execute the stored procedure **dbms_revealnet.just_statistics**. The next set of code lines

```
ResultSet rset = stmt.executeQuery (query);
// Dump the result
while (rset.next ())
output.append(rset.getString (1) + "\n");
```

execute the query that you placed into the **query** String object and return the results using the lines:

```
while (rset.next ())
output.append(rset.getString (1) + "\n");
```

The rest of the code is used to catch any exceptions that are thrown by the code using the **catch** method:

```
catch (Exception e)
     {
// Oops
output.append("Error: " + e.getMessage () + "\n");
     }
```

In this code, you just report the actual error text back to the user and exit. The output from this applet is shown in Figure 13.2.

As you can see from Figure 13.2, the output using the appletviewer and applet code is generally much nicer to look at. Not only does it have the look and feel of other GUI applications we are used to, it provides added features, such as scroll bars for the viewing of results in the text area.

Using JSQL, JDBC, and Java, you can build complex applications. The Practical Guide will look at displaying images, selecting data from the database, inputting values into an applet, and selecting **BLOB** data from the database based on the input values.

The examples in the Practical Guide will build on the objects built in Chapter 6 on **LOB**s. A convenient source of **LOB** data for test purposes is the Web itself. A simple search using a search tool, such as Yahoo!, will give you plenty of listings where image

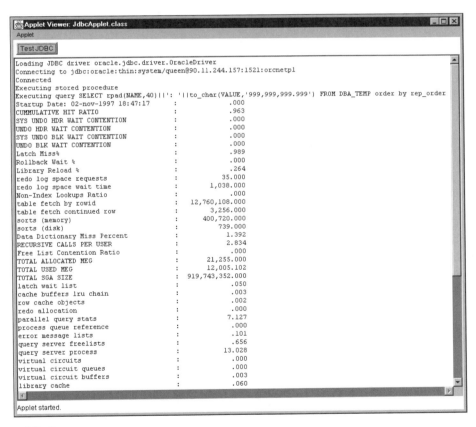

Figure 13.2

Example output from the DBATempApplet.java applet.

data is downloadable. On most browsers, you can download most graphics you view on the Web with a simple click of the right-hand button on the mouse.

One interesting application for Java applets and HTML-enabled Web pages is remote database monitoring. With a properly configured Web page, you can quickly review status data for all of your company's intranet-linked database servers. The Practical Guide shows a primitive monitoring screen for some basic statistics.

Practical Guide To

Using Java With SQL And PL/SQL

- Creating A Generic Connection Manager Class
- Fetching A **BLOB** From The Database Using Java
- Creating A Simple Application Using Oracle8, **BLOB**s, And Java
- Additional Java Reading

Creating A Generic Connection Manager Class

In previous examples in this chapter, I showed connections to the Oracle8 database that were static in nature—that is, they always connected to the same user and database. What if you want to connect to other databases or use other users than were specified in the static connections? Using the type of connections shown so far, you would have to create a connection manager class for each user—obviously, not a satisfactory solution.

Let's examine a method to create a generic connection manager class that will allow you to specify the database you want to connect to, along with a user name and password pair for connection to the database.

Here are the steps for using an Oracle JDBC driver from a Java program:

1. Load the JDBC classes by including the statement:

    ```
    import java.sql.* ;
    ```

2. Load the driver by including the statement:

    ```
    Class.forName ("oracle.jdbc.driver.OracleDriver")
    ```

3. Connect to the database by including the statement:

    ```
    DriverManager.getConnection (arguments)
    ```

4. Issue queries and receive results using standard JDBC syntax.

If you wish to use JDBC **thin** in an applet in a browser that supports only JDK 1.0.2 (Netscape Navigator 3, for example), change the first two steps to:

```
import jdbc.sql.* ;
Class.forName ("oracle.jdbc.dnlddriver.OracleDriver") ;
```

The method **getConnection** has three different forms. They differ only in the parameter arguments:

- The simplest form is **getConnection ("URL")**.

  The URL is of the form

  ```
  jdbc:oracle:drivertype:user/password@database
  ```

  where **drivertype** is **oci8**, **oci7**, or **thin**.

Choose between **oci8** and **oci7** on the basis of your client program version. Use **oci8** with OCI (Oracle Call Interface) 8 and **oci7** with OCI 7. Either of these can access both Oracle7 and Oracle8 servers. Use **thin** in an applet. For example:

```
getConnection ("jdbc:oracle:oci8:scott/tiger@database");
```

The **@database** phrase is optional, if a default database is associated with the installation. If you specify it, it must be one of the following:

- A SQL*Net name-value pair.

- For JDBC OCI drivers—An entry in the tnsnames.ora file.

- For JDBC **thin**—A string of the form host:port:sid.

- The second form of **getConnection** call breaks URL into three string arguments. For example:

```
getConnection ("jdbc:oracle:oci8:","scott","tiger");
```

Or, if you specify the database explicitly:

```
getConnection ("jdbc:oracle:oci8:@database","scott","tiger");
```

- The third form of **getConnection** relies on a **Properties** object. For example:

```
java.util.Properties info = new java.util.Properties();
info.addProperty ("user", "scott");
info.addProperty ("password","tiger");
getConnection ("jdbc:oracle:oci8:",info);
```

Oracle JDBC drivers support other properties as well. Table 13.2 provides a complete list.

You can implement the generic connection module using either of two basic methods:

- The first is to use a window (or in this case, a **Frame**) class object to get the desired inputs from the user, and then call the connection class with the results.

Table 13.2 JDBC driver property values.

Property Name	Short Name	Type	Description	Equivalent to
user	N/A	String	The user name for logging into the database	N/A
password	N/A	String	The password name for logging into the database	N/A
database	Server	String	The connect string for the database	N/A
defaultRowPrefetch	Prefetch	Integer	The default row prefetch	**setDefaultRowPrefetch**
remarksReporting	Remarks	Boolean	True If **getTables** and **getColumns** should report **TABLE_REMARKS**	**setRemarksReporting**

- The other is just to place the arguments as required inputs to the **ConnectionManager** class and require the developers of the user application using the class to provide input values.

Let's use the first method and provide a window class object to gather the input from the user and then make the connection. Listing 13.13 shows the code to implement the required program.

Listing 13.13 Example applet using generic login window.

```
import java.applet.*;
import java.sql.*;
import java.awt.*;
import java.awt.event.*;
import java.util.*;
public class DBATempSelect extends Applet
implements ActionListener
{
Frame theFrame = new Frame();
Frame logFrame = new Frame();
Panel mainPanel = new Panel();
Panel loginPanel = new Panel();
Panel buttonPanel = new Panel();
TextField theStatus = new TextField(64);
TextArea  theResult = new TextArea(15,60);
```

```
static TextField theSource = new TextField(32);
Button doConnect = new Button("Connect");
Button qryButton = new Button ("Do Query");
Button stopdamnit = new Button ("Quit");
Panel[] thePanel = new Panel[4];
static TextField theUser = new TextField(32);
static TextField thePassword = new TextField(32);
Button btnOK = new Button("OK");
Button btnCancel = new Button("Cancel");
Button btnQuit = new Button("Quit");
boolean statusOK = false;
String theURL;
Statement theStatement;
ResultSet rs;
Connection theConnection;
public void init( )
  {
theFrame.setTitle("Simple Query");
theFrame.add("Center",mainPanel);
mainPanel.setLayout(new BorderLayout());
mainPanel.add("North",theSource);
mainPanel.add("South",theStatus);
theResult.setFont(new Font("Courier", Font.PLAIN, 12));
mainPanel.add("Center", theResult);
mainPanel.add("North",buttonPanel);
buttonPanel.setLayout(new GridLayout(1,3));
buttonPanel.add("North", doConnect);
doConnect.addActionListener(this);
buttonPanel.add("North", qryButton);
qryButton.addActionListener(this);
buttonPanel.add("North", stopdamnit);
stopdamnit.addActionListener(this);
logFrame.setTitle("Login Frame");
setFont(new Font("Courier", Font.PLAIN, 12));
loginPanel.setLayout(new GridLayout(4, 1));
for (int i = 0; i < 3; i++)
    {
thePanel[i] = new Panel( );
thePanel[i].setLayout(new BorderLayout( ));
    }
thePanel[0].add("West", new Label("URL:         ",Label.RIGHT));
thePanel[0].add("Center",theSource);
loginPanel.add(thePanel[0]);
thePanel[1].add("West", new Label("User:        ",Label.RIGHT));
thePanel[1].add("Center", theUser);
loginPanel.add(thePanel[1]);
thePanel[2].add("West", new Label("Password:    ",Label.RIGHT));
```

```
thePanel[2].add("Center", thePassword);
loginPanel.add(thePanel[2]);
thePanel[3] = new Panel( );
thePanel[3].setLayout(new FlowLayout( ));
thePanel[3].add(btnOK);
thePanel[3].add(btnCancel);
thePanel[3].add(btnQuit);
loginPanel.add(thePanel[3]);
btnOK.addActionListener(this);
btnCancel.addActionListener(this);
btnQuit.addActionListener(this);
logFrame.setLayout(new BorderLayout());
logFrame.add("Center",loginPanel);
logFrame.validate();
logFrame.pack();
logFrame.setVisible(false);
theFrame.pack();
theFrame.setVisible(true);
   }
public void actionPerformed(ActionEvent event)
 {
Object source = event.getSource( );
theStatus.setText("Status: OK");
if (source == doConnect)
    {
logFrame.setVisible(true);
theSource.requestFocus();
openConnection();
    }
if (source == qryButton) doQuery();
if (source == btnOK)
    {
logFrame.setVisible(false);
statusOK=true;
    }
if (source == btnQuit)
    {
blankText();
logFrame.setVisible(false);
statusOK=false;
    }
if (source == stopdamnit) System.exit(0);
 }
public boolean openConnection()
 {
try
    {
```

```
theStatus.setText("Status: OK");
if (statusOK==true)
    {
String driver_class = "oracle.jdbc.driver.OracleDriver";
Class.forName (driver_class);
if (theConnection != null) theConnection.close( );
/*System.out.println(getURL() + ":" + getUser() + ":" + getPassword());*/
theConnection =
DriverManager.getConnection("jdbc:oracle:thin:@" + getURL( ),
getUser( ),
getPassword( ));
logFrame.setVisible(false);
blankText();
    }
return true;
    }
catch (NullPointerException n)
    {
theStatus.setText("Error:" + n);
    }
catch (Exception t)
    {
theStatus.setText("Status: Login Dialog " + t);
    }
return false;
 }
public void doQuery()
 {
/*System.out.println("Got to doQuery");*/
try
    {
theResult.setText("");
/*System.out.println("First Try at connection");*/
theStatement = theConnection.createStatement();
rs = theStatement.executeQuery("SELECT rpad(NAME,40)||': '||
to_char(VALUE,'999,999,999.999')" +
"FROM DBA_TEMP order by rep_order");
while (rs.next())
    {
theResult.append(rs.getString(1)+"\n");
    }
    }
catch(SQLException sqlex)
    {
theStatus.setText("Error: " + sqlex.getMessage( ));
    }
 }
```

```
public void requestClose()
 {
setVisible(false);
try
   {
if (theConnection != null) theConnection.close();
   }
catch(SQLException sql) { ; }
 }
public boolean getStatus( )   { return statusOK; };
public String getURL( )       { return theSource.getText( ); }
public String getUser( )      { return theUser.getText( ); }
public String getPassword( ) { return thePassword.getText( ); }
public void blankText ()
 {
theSource.setText("");
theUser.setText("");
thePassword.setText("");
 }
}
```

Don't let the length of the code upset you. I realize that logging in to SQL*Plus and doing a **SELECT** might seem easier (heck, it is easier), but the purpose of this applet is to run through a Web browser, which would be impossible to do with SQL*Plus. In addition, this code executes only a single SQL command and returns the results to the user—not very useful in the long run and not very flexible. I am not attempting to demonstrate the versatility of SQL with this example, merely to show how to set up a login dialog window using Java, so the same applet can be used against multiple databases. Figure 13.3 shows an example of the output from this applet run through the appletviewer interface.

The screen shot in Figure 13.4 shows the applet running in appletviewer with the Login Frame activated by a mouse click on the Connect button. To log in to the system of choice, the user fills in the text areas on the Login Frame. For example, to log in to the TEST instance on node 90.10.100.1 using port 1521 user SYSTEM with a password of SYSTEM_TEST, the Login Frame would look like Figure 13.4. Once the data is filled in, the user clicks on the OK button.

The applet will issue the select against the **DBA_TEMP** table and display the results once the Do Query button is clicked on after a connection is established. The results will look like Figure 13.5 (assuming the user has created the **DBA_TEMP** table and has executed the **DBMS_REVEALNET.JUST_STATISTICS** procedure).

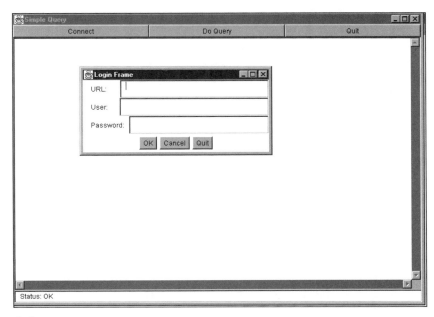

Figure 13.3

Example run of DBATempSelect.java applet.

Figure 13.4

Example filled-in Login Frame dialog window.

Of course, clicking on the Cancel button in the Login Frame exits to the Simple Query frame, and clicking on the Quit button in the Simple Query frame exits the applet. To make the applet more useful, a query entry box could be added to allow ad hoc query of the selected database. (For excellent examples of this type of application, refer to McCarty's book, mentioned in the beginning of this chapter.)

How is all this accomplished? Let's examine the code and see what is happening under the hood. First, the import section:

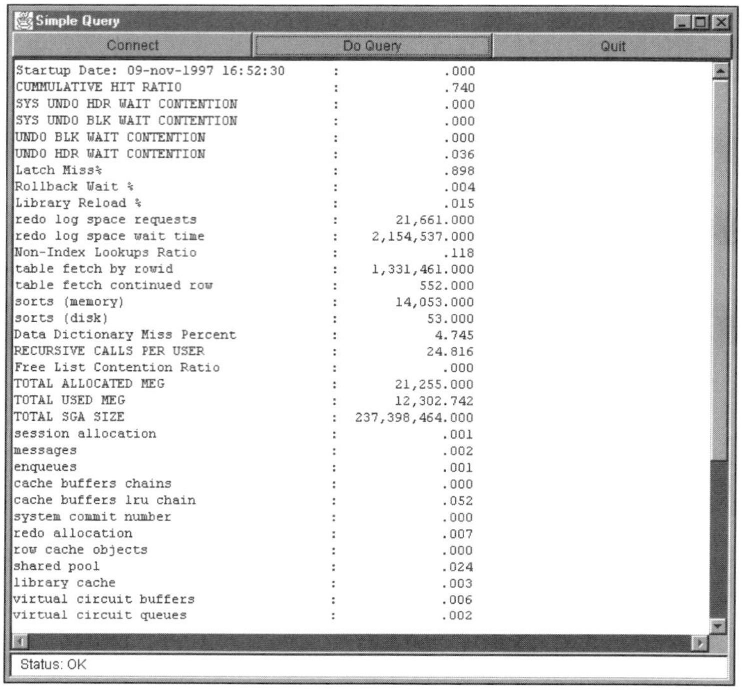

Figure 13.5

Results of clicking on the Do Query button.

```
import java.applet.*;
import java.sql.*;
import java.awt.*;
import java.awt.event.*;
import java.util.*;
```

As I have said before, the import section loads classes from the class libraries that the Java script, applet, or application requires. If you know that a specific class or method set is required for your Java, specify exactly up to that point in the **import** command. For example, the line

```
import java.applet.*;
```

allows us simply to say

```
public class DBATempSelect extends Applet
```

instead of

```
public class DBATempSelect extends java.applet.Applet
```

The **awt** class controls the window and container classes, the **sql** class controls the JDBC classes, and the **util** class contains many useful Java utility classes.

The next section sets up the global variables and definitions, as well as the name for the Java class (script, applet, or application) you are creating:

```
public class DBATempSelect extends Applet
implements ActionListener
{
Frame theFrame = new Frame();
Frame logFrame = new Frame();
Panel mainPanel = new Panel();
Panel loginPanel = new Panel();
Panel buttonPanel = new Panel();
TextField theStatus = new TextField(64);
TextArea  theResult = new TextArea(15,60);
static TextField theSource = new TextField(32);
Button doConnect = new Button("Connect");
Button qryButton = new Button ("Do Query");
Button stopdamnit = new Button ("Quit");
Panel[] thePanel = new Panel[4];
static TextField theUser = new TextField(32);
static TextField thePassword = new TextField(32);
Button btnOK = new Button("OK");
Button btnCancel = new Button("Cancel");
Button btnQuit = new Button("Quit");
boolean statusOK = false;
String theURL;
Statement theStatement;
ResultSet rs;
Connection theConnection;
```

Notice in the first lines, the snippet:

```
implements ActionListener
```

This is required, because you will be using controls (buttons, in this case) that will require listeners. Listeners listen for actions, such as mouse clicks, keystrokes, mouse movements, and window openings and closings, and then allow you to test for the action and take any required program steps. In this section, you have also declared the **Frame**, **Panel**, **Text**, **Button**, and other objects you will use globally in the program.

The next section sets up the parameters for the GUI. Here you define **Frame** (window) layouts, add components to each other, and specify component characteristics, such as fonts and sizes:

```
public void init( )
   {
theFrame.setTitle("Simple Query");
theFrame.add("Center",mainPanel);
mainPanel.setLayout(new BorderLayout());
mainPanel.add("North",theSource);
mainPanel.add("South",theStatus);
theResult.setFont(new Font("Courier", Font.PLAIN, 12));
mainPanel.add("Center", theResult);
mainPanel.add("North",buttonPanel);
buttonPanel.setLayout(new GridLayout(1,3));
buttonPanel.add("North", doConnect);
doConnect.addActionListener(this);
buttonPanel.add("North", qryButton);
qryButton.addActionListener(this);
buttonPanel.add("North", stopdamnit);
stopdamnit.addActionListener(this);
logFrame.setTitle("Login Frame");
setFont(new Font("Courier", Font.PLAIN, 12));
loginPanel.setLayout(new GridLayout(4, 1));
for (int i = 0; i < 3; i++)
    {
thePanel[i] = new Panel( );
thePanel[i].setLayout(new BorderLayout( ));
    }
thePanel[0].add("West", new Label("URL:          ",Label.RIGHT));
thePanel[0].add("Center",theSource);
loginPanel.add(thePanel[0]);
thePanel[1].add("West", new Label("User:         ",Label.RIGHT));
thePanel[1].add("Center", theUser);
loginPanel.add(thePanel[1]);
thePanel[2].add("West", new Label("Password:     ",Label.RIGHT));
thePanel[2].add("Center", thePassword);
loginPanel.add(thePanel[2]);
thePanel[3] = new Panel( );
thePanel[3].setLayout(new FlowLayout( ));
thePanel[3].add(btnOK);
thePanel[3].add(btnCancel);
thePanel[3].add(btnQuit);
loginPanel.add(thePanel[3]);
btnOK.addActionListener(this);
btnCancel.addActionListener(this);
btnQuit.addActionListener(this);
```

```
logFrame.setLayout(new BorderLayout());
logFrame.add("Center",loginPanel);
logFrame.validate();
logFrame.pack();
logFrame.setVisible(false);
theFrame.pack();
theFrame.setVisible(true);
    }
```

This section's name tells us this code is probably from an applet; a **void init()** section is usually (but not always) a part of an applet object. Generally speaking, an applet will not have a **main(String args[])** section. This section also implements the required action listeners by adding them to the components that need them. For example,

```
btnOK.addActionListener(this);
```

adds an action listener to the **btnOK** button component. In a later section, you will check if this listener has registered an action and execute other actions as required. Note the use of a "vector" of panel objects (as denoted by **thePanel[ ]**) in this section. This allows a loop to be used to assign the button layout values.

The next section uses the listeners to tell the program what actions to take based upon whether specific buttons are clicked on by the mouse.

```
public void actionPerformed(ActionEvent event)
  {
Object source = event.getSource( );
theStatus.setText("Status: OK");
if (source == doConnect)
     {
logFrame.setVisible(true);
theSource.requestFocus();
openConnection();
     }
if (source == qryButton) doQuery();
if (source == btnOK)
     {
logFrame.setVisible(false);
statusOK=true;
     }
if (source == btnQuit)
     {
blankText();
logFrame.setVisible(false);
```

```
statusOK=false;
     }
if (source == stopdamnit) System.exit(0);
 }
```

The example applet has five possible actions. Each consists of a click action against the buttons you have defined (**doConnect**, **qryButton**, **btnOK**, and **stopdamnit**). The code takes actions based on which button has been activated. Notice the line

```
theSource.requestFocus();
```

that follows the

```
if (source == doConnect)
```

This tells the Java system to place the cursor or action focus on the object to which the **requestFocus()** is attached—in this case, the **theSource** text field. Another technique used here is the **setVisible()** method invocation. As you can probably guess, the **setVisible()** method makes a component either visible (if set to true) or invisible (if set to false). The **stopdamnit** button invokes the **System.exit(0)** method, which exits the applet and returns control to the operating system with a status of 0.

The next section of the applet opens the connection to the selected database. In the method shown in the first part of the chapter (**ConnectionManager**), we discussed this type of method:

```
public boolean openConnection()
 {
try
   {
theStatus.setText("Status: OK");
if (statusOK==true)
     {
String driver_class = "oracle.jdbc.driver.OracleDriver";
Class.forName (driver_class);
if (theConnection != null) theConnection.close( );
/*System.out.println(getURL() + ":" + getUser() + ":" + getPassword());*/
theConnection =
DriverManager.getConnection("jdbc:oracle:thin:@" + getURL( ),
getUser( ),
getPassword( ));
logFrame.setVisible(false);
blankText();
     }
```

```
return true;
    }
catch (NullPointerException n)
    {
theStatus.setText("Error:" + n);
    }
catch (Exception t)
    {
theStatus.setText("Status: Login Dialog " + t);
    }
return false;
 }
```

What is different about **openConnection()** is that it is generic in nature in comparison with the **ConnectionManager()** method. What I mean by generic is that it allows connection to any Oracle database that you want to specify using the **thin** driver. Notice how you use calls to the "get" methods (shown later) to "scrape" the values for URL, User, and Password from the Login Window. The complete URL is usually required for the **thin** driver. If you are connecting to a local database, you should use the **oci7** or **oci8** drivers, which will shorten the required URL to only the instance name as it is listed in the **tnsnames.ora** file from Net8 or SQL*Net.

Once you have established a connection to the database, the next section will allow you to run the canned query against the **DBA_TEMP** table:

```
public void doQuery()
 {
/*System.out.println("Got to doQuery");*/
try
    {
theResult.setText("");
/*System.out.println("First Try at connection");*/
theStatement = theConnection.createStatement();
rs = theStatement.executeQuery("SELECT rpad(NAME,40)||
': '||to_char(VALUE,'999,999,999.999')" +
"FROM DBA_TEMP order by rep_order");
while (rs.next())
        {
theResult.append(rs.getString(1)+"\n");
        }
    }
catch(SQLException sqlex)
    {
theStatus.setText("Error: " + sqlex.getMessage( ));
    }
 }
```

The commented lines (those surrounded by the /* and */ delimiters) allowed trouble-shooting during the creation of the applet by sending output lines to the stdout device (the screen). Any call to **System.out.println()** will send output to the stdout device. If, instead of a canned query, a string value containing an input query is placed in the line

```
rs = theStatement.executeQuery("SELECT rpad(NAME,40)||': '||
to_char(VALUE,'999,999,999.999')" +
"FROM DBA_TEMP order by rep_order");
```

the specified query would have been run. You can get quite elegant in your queries by using the specialized classes available to fetch metadata information from the database. By using the metadata information, you can lay out the output from a query on the fly. For more information on the use of the metadata classes and complex query usage, I again suggest Carter's *SQL Database Programming With Java*, Coriolis Group Books. Notice how the query results are appended to the **theResult -TextArea** object using the line:

```
theResult.append(rs.getString(1)+"\n");
```

The final sections of the applet are utility methods:

```
public void requestClose()
 {
setVisible(false);
try
   {
if (theConnection != null) theConnection.close();
   }
catch(SQLException sql) { ; }
 }
public boolean getStatus( )  { return statusOK; };
public String getURL( )      { return theSource.getText( ); }
public String getUser( )     { return theUser.getText( ); }
public String getPassword( ) { return thePassword.getText( ); }
public void blankText ()
 {
theSource.setText("");
theUser.setText("");
thePassword.setText("");
 }
```

You can use the **requestClose()** method to close a window by setting its visible setting to false using the **setVisible()** method. The **getURL()**, **getUser()**, and **getPassword()**

methods scrape the values for the URL, user name, and password from the Login Frame entry areas. The final method, **blankText()**, resets the text fields to blank.

You can use this type of applet for generic connection and running a canned query against Oracle data sources. With a few minor modifications, an applet based on these methods can provide the capability to perform ad hoc queries.

Fetching A **BLOB** From The Database Using Java

Oracle8 introduced **BLOB**s. While Oracle8 allows selection of **BLOB** identifiers, manipulation of **BLOB** contents, and moving external **BLOB**s to internal storage, you cannot display image **BLOB**s using the standard Oracle8 query tools, such as SQL*Plus. Java allows selection of **BLOB** data (using the JSQL interface) and the display of this data as images (GIFF or JPEG format). The applet in Listing 13.14 shows a basic technique for retrieving a **BLOB** from the database, writing the **BLOB** to a temporary file, and then displaying the **BLOB**.

When combined with the methods shown in Chapter 6 to store **BLOB** data in the database, these methods make possible many useful applications, such as online catalogs, photo and image databases, or even video or audio libraries.

Listing 13.14   Java applet to read a BLOB image from the database and display it on screen.

```
import java.awt.Graphics;
import java.awt.Image;
import java.awt.*;
import java.awt.event.*;
import java.applet.*;
import java.sql.*;
import java.io.*;
import java.util.*;
// Importing the Oracle Jdbc driver package makes the code more readable
import oracle.jdbc.driver.*;

public class DisplayImage extends java.applet.Applet
implements ActionListener
{
Image theImage;
String showImage;
// The button to push for showing the graphic
Button execute_button;
TextField  theStatus  = new TextField(64);
Font  theFixedFont = new Font("Courier",Font.PLAIN,12);
//
```

```
public void init( )
   {
// Load the Oracle JDBC driver
try
   {
Class.forName ("oracle.jdbc.driver.OracleDriver");
   }
catch (ClassNotFoundException c)
   {
handleError(c);
   }
try
   {
// Connect to the database
Connection conn =
DriverManager.getConnection (
    "jdbc:oracle:oci8:TEST", "graphics_dba", "graphics1");
// Create a Statement
Statement stmt = conn.createStatement ();
// Select the lob
ResultSet rset = stmt.executeQuery (
"select graphic_blob from internal_graphics where graphic_id=6");
if (rset.next ())
   {
OracleBlob blob = ((OracleResultSet)rset).getBlob (1);
dumpBlob(conn,blob);
   }
   }
catch (SQLException sql)
   {
handleError(sql);
   }
catch (IOException e)
   {
handleError(e);
   }
catch (Exception s)
   {
handleError(s);
   }
   {
this.setLayout (new BorderLayout ());
Panel p = new Panel ();
p.setLayout (new FlowLayout (FlowLayout.LEFT));
execute_button = new Button ("Show Image");
execute_button.addActionListener(this);
p.add (execute_button);
```

```java
this.add ("North", p);
add(theStatus, "South");
theStatus.setEditable(false);
theImage = getImage(getCodeBase(),"theImage.gif");
    }
  }
public void actionPerformed(ActionEvent event)
 {
Object source = event.getSource();
if (source == execute_button)
        {
showImage = "true";
repaint();
        }
 }
public void paint(Graphics theGraphic)
 {
if (showImage != null) {
int iwidth = theImage.getWidth(this);
int iheight = theImage.getHeight(this);
int xpos = 375;
theGraphic.drawImage(theImage, xpos, 10, iwidth, iheight, this);}
String showImage = null;
 }
public void handleError(Throwable t)
{
theStatus.setText("Error: " + t.getMessage( ));
t.printStackTrace( );
}
// Utility function to dump Blob contents
static void dumpBlob (Connection conn, OracleBlob blob)
throws Exception
  {
OracleCallableStatement cstmt1 =
(OracleCallableStatement)
conn.prepareCall ("begin ? := dbms_lob.getLength (?); end;");
OracleCallableStatement cstmt2 =
(OracleCallableStatement)
conn.prepareCall ("begin dbms_lob.read (?, ?, ?, ?); end;");

cstmt1.registerOutParameter (1, Types.NUMERIC);
cstmt1.setBlob (2, blob);
cstmt1.execute ();
long length = cstmt1.getLong (1);
long i=0;
int chunk=100;
FileOutputStream file = new FileOutputStream ("theImage.gif");
```

```
while (i < length)
    {
cstmt2.setBlob (1, blob);
cstmt2.setLong (2, chunk);
cstmt2.registerOutParameter (2, Types.NUMERIC);
cstmt2.setLong (3, i+1);
cstmt2.registerOutParameter (4, Types.VARBINARY);
cstmt2.execute ();
long read_this_time = cstmt2.getLong (2);
byte [] bytes_this_time = cstmt2.getBytes (4);
        {
// Put into file
file.write (bytes_this_time);
i += read_this_time;
/*      System.out.print ("Read " + i + " bytes of " + length + "\n");*/
        if ((i + read_this_time)>length) chunk = (int) (length-i);
        }
    }
      file.close();
    cstmt1.close ();
    cstmt2.close ();
  }
}
```

Because we have discussed the import and GUI setup sections of applets, we will dispense with discussing them again and get right to the interesting sections—those dealing with the fetch, placement in the temporary file, and display of the **BLOB**. The first section will be the **init()** section. Unlike previous sections, this **init()** actually sees some processing.

The first part of the **init()** method establishes the Oracle connection. Note the use of the **oci8** driver, which tells us that this applet is designed to be used by an application running on the same server as the database. We know this because the **oci8** driver calls a dynamic link library that will cause a security violation if used to call a database not resident on the applet's server.

```
public void init( )
  {
    // Load the Oracle JDBC driver
    try
    {
    Class.forName ("oracle.jdbc.driver.OracleDriver");
    }
```

```
  catch (ClassNotFoundException c)
  {
   handleError(c);
  }
 try
{
  // Connect to the database
  Connection conn =
    DriverManager.getConnection ("jdbc:oracle:oci8:TEST",
       "graphics_dba", "graphics1"); // note use of oci8
  // Create a Statement
  Statement stmt = conn.createStatement ();
  // Select the lob
  ResultSet rset = stmt.executeQuery (
     "select graphic_blob from internal_graphics where graphic_id=6");
  if (rset.next ())
  {
    OracleBlob blob = ((OracleResultSet)rset).getBlob (1);
    dumpBlob(conn,blob);
  }
}
  catch (SQLException sql)
  {
   handleError(sql);
  }
  catch (IOException e)
  {
   handleError(e);
  }
  catch (Exception s)
  {
   handleError(s);
  }
  {
  this.setLayout (new BorderLayout ());
  Panel p = new Panel ();
  p.setLayout (new FlowLayout (FlowLayout.LEFT));
  execute_button = new Button ("Show Image");
  execute_button.addActionListener(this);
  p.add (execute_button);
  this.add ("North", p);
  add(theStatus, "South");
  theStatus.setEditable(false);
  theImage = getImage(getCodeBase(),"theImage.gif");
  }
}
```

Notice in the code snippet that the **SELECT** command is a fixed **SELECT**—that is, it will always fetch the **BLOB** with the ID value of 6. The last example in the chapter will show a more useful form of this routine.

Next, notice that an Oracle-specific method, **getBlob**, fetches the **BLOB** value from the database. Remember, a **BLOB** value is just a pointer to the actual **BLOB**, whether it is stored internally as a **BLOB**, **CLOB**, or **NCLOB** or external to the database as a **BFILE**. This means that you cannot use a **BLOB**, **CLOB**, **NCLOB**, or **BFILE** directly in an application. They must first be translated into the actual **BLOB** by transversing the identifier. In this applet, this is accomplished by calls to the **dumpBlob()** method. Once you have translated the **BLOB** identifier into an actual image using the **dumpBlob()** method, read the resulting image from the disk file into which it was placed, using the line:

```
theImage = getImage(getCodeBase(),"theImage.gif");
```

This uses a call to the **getImage()** Image class method to read the image from the holding file (theImage.gif) at the location specified by **getCodeBase()**, which retrieves the value set in the HTML file for the variable CODEBASE. The HTML file acts as a wrapper for the applet. Once the image is read into the internal **Image** class, the code invokes the method (**repaint()**) that displays it onto your graphics area.

The next section we will discuss is the **getBlob()** method, which takes the **BLOB** identifier and a connection value and uses the Oracle8 stored procedure from the **DBMS_LOB** package actually to read the **BLOB** and place the image data into a holding file:

```
// Utility function to dump Blob contents
  static void dumpBlob (Connection conn, OracleBlob blob)
    throws Exception
  {
    OracleCallableStatement cstmt1 =
      (OracleCallableStatement)
        conn.prepareCall ("begin ? := dbms_lob.getLength (?); end;");
    OracleCallableStatement cstmt2 =
      (OracleCallableStatement)
        conn.prepareCall ("begin dbms_lob.read (?, ?, ?, ?); end;");

    cstmt1.registerOutParameter (1, Types.NUMERIC);
    cstmt1.setBlob (2, blob);
    cstmt1.execute ();
    long length = cstmt1.getLong (1);
```

```
     long i=0;
     int chunk=100;
     FileOutputStream file = new FileOutputStream ("theImage.gif");
     while (i < length)
     {
       cstmt2.setBlob (1, blob);
       cstmt2.setLong (2, chunk);
       cstmt2.registerOutParameter (2, Types.NUMERIC);
       cstmt2.setLong (3, i+1);
       cstmt2.registerOutParameter (4, Types.VARBINARY);
       cstmt2.execute ();
       long read_this_time = cstmt2.getLong (2);
       byte [] bytes_this_time = cstmt2.getBytes (4);
       {
       // Put into file
       file.write (bytes_this_time);
       i += read_this_time;
/*       System.out.print ("Read " + i + " bytes of " + length + "\n");*/
       if ((i + read_this_time)>length) chunk = (int) (length-i);
       }
     }
       file.close();
     cstmt1.close ();
     cstmt2.close ();
   }
```

The **dumpBlob()** method uses the JDBC Oracle implementation to prepare and execute the calls to the database. The following code snippet shows the Oracle-specific
calls:

```
OracleCallableStatement cstmt1 =
    (OracleCallableStatement)
      conn.prepareCall ("begin ? := dbms_lob.getLength (?); end;");
  OracleCallableStatement cstmt2 =
    (OracleCallableStatement)
      conn.prepareCall ("begin dbms_lob.read (?, ?, ?, ?); end;");
```

The question marks in the calls to the **prepareCall()** method mark locations where
variables are written. These variables are written using code similar to the following
code lines:

```
    cstmt1.registerOutParameter (1, Types.NUMERIC);
    cstmt1.setBlob (2, blob);
    cstmt1.execute ();
```

The first call to the **registerOutParameter** for **cstmt1** registers the first question mark in the line

```
("begin ? := dbms_lob.getLength (?); end;");
```

as a value that is returned (**dbms_lob.getLength()** is a function and must return a value) and sets its type as **NUMERIC**. The call to **setBlob()** registers the second (as shown by the 2) question mark as an input to the function in **cstmt1**, setting it to the actual **BLOB** identifier. The last statement in the snippet executes the statement **cstmt1** after making the substitutions. This call to **dbms_lob.getLength()** returns the length of the **BLOB**. You must know the length before you can retrieve the **BLOB** using **dbms_lob.read()**, as overruns of the **BLOB** boundaries are not permitted and will result in an error if they happen.

The next section in **dumpBlob()** uses repeated calls to the **dbms_lob.read()** Oracle8 procedure to read the **BLOB** values piecewise. Once the pieces are placed in memory using the **getBytes()** method, calls to the **write()** method of the Java **File** class place the bytes into the designated file. To create a file, you should use more advanced streaming methods (as demonstrated in *Graphic Java 1.1—Mastering The AWT*, 2nd Edition, David M. Geary, The SunSoft Press, 1997).

```
      long length = cstmt1.getLong (1);
      long i=0;
      int chunk=100;
      FileOutputStream file = new FileOutputStream ("theImage.gif");
      while (i < length)
      {
        cstmt2.setBlob (1, blob);
        cstmt2.setLong (2, chunk);
        cstmt2.registerOutParameter (2, Types.NUMERIC);
        cstmt2.setLong (3, i+1);
        cstmt2.registerOutParameter (4, Types.VARBINARY);
        cstmt2.execute ();
        long read_this_time = cstmt2.getLong (2);
        byte [] bytes_this_time = cstmt2.getBytes (4);
        {
        // Put into file
        file.write (bytes_this_time);
        i += read_this_time;
/*        System.out.print ("Read " + i + " bytes of " + length + "\n");*/
        if ((i + read_this_time)>length) chunk = (int) (length-i);
        }
      }
```

One technique to take note of in this code snippet is the calculation:

```
if ((i + read_this_time)>length) chunk = (int) (length-i);
```

This calculation prevents the loop from reading past the end of the **BLOB** and generating an exception. This would cause the transaction to be backed out, and you would get only a partial (if any) image transferred into your file.

Once the image file is created and the **BLOB** has been completely transferred, the file and the Oracle statements are closed:

```
    file.close();
    cstmt1.close ();
    cstmt2.close ();
  }
```

The next section we are interested in is the **paint()** method. As discussed in previous sections, the **paint()** method is always overridden to give desired graphics behavior. The call to the **repaint()** method actually calls the **paint()** method, invoking it using the current graphic context (hence, no **Graphic** class is passed to **paint()** from **repaint()**). A control break is set, using the **showImage** string to prevent the graphic from being painted until you click on the **execute_button** Button control.

```
public void paint(Graphics theGraphic)
  {
        if (showImage != null) {
        int iwidth = theImage.getWidth(this);
        int iheight = theImage.getHeight(this);
        int xpos = 375;
        theGraphic.drawImage(theImage, xpos, 10, iwidth, iheight, this);}
        String showImage = null;
  }
```

In **paint(Graphics theGraphic)**, you use the image methods **getWidth()** and **getHeight()** to get the size of the image stored in the graphic file and then draw it using the **Graphic** class method **drawImage()**.

The final section we will look at in this example is the **actionPerformed(ActionEvent event)** method call. In this applet, this method is very short, because you set up only one button, the execute_button, whose sole function is to invoke the **repaint()** method to force the graphics context to be displayed; otherwise, it would stay invisible in the background. Notice how the **showImage** string value is set to true so that **paint()** will be called:

```
public void actionPerformed(ActionEvent event)
  {
     Object source = event.getSource();
      if (source == execute_button)
         {
             showImage = "true";
             repaint();
         }
  }
}
```

Once the graphic is displayed, this applet is finished. While it is not a very useful applet in the grand scheme of things, the techniques shown, combined with live query, can produce a useful application, as we shall see in the next section.

Creating A Simple Application Using Oracle8, **BLOB**s, And Java

Up to this point, we have been dealing with fixed-query applications—either a single table or single value were selected from the database and displayed for the user. In this final example, we will combine many of the techniques covered thus far and add a live query (a query built from user input). The example will provide a list of graphics stored in the database, available to the user on request. The user can enter an index value, which is then used to query the database and pull up the requested graphic for display. This application, combined with some of the techniques shown in Chapter 6, allow the building of a simple graphics storage and retrieval application capable of being used on the Internet or an intranet.

From the description, you can see that this application is actually a combination of two of the applets we have already seen: a canned query return and a **BLOB** retrieval display. This application combines the two into a single applet and adds the capability to specify the graphic returned. Listing 13.15 shows the complete application.

Listing 13.15 Full code for graphics retrieval applet.
```
/* This applet demonstrates advanced Lob support in the oci8 driver
 */
import java.awt.Graphics.*;
import java.awt.Image.*;
import java.awt.*;
import java.awt.event.*;
import java.applet.*;
import java.sql.*;
```

```java
import java.io.*;
import java.util.*;
// Import the Oracle Jdbc driver package to make the code more readable

import oracle.jdbc.driver.*;
// Define the class as an extension of the Applet calss
public class DisplayImage2 extends java.applet.Applet
implements ActionListener
{

// Set up global variables
MediaTracker theTracker = null;
String blob_id;
Image theImage;
Graphics theGraphic;

// The buttons to push for showing the graphic, cancel
Button show_button;
Button cancel_button;
Button execute_button;

// The text fields for status and blob id input
Canvas blobCanvas = new drawCanvas();
TextField  theStatus  = new TextField(64);
TextField  getblobid  = new TextField(4);
TextArea   output      = new TextArea();
Font outputFont = new  Font("Courier", Font.PLAIN, 12);

// The sequence value for the image file
static String inc_value;
// The global panels and frame definitions
Frame imageFrame = new Frame("Blob Retrieval Window");
Panel queryPanel = new Panel ();
Panel statusPanel = new Panel ();
Panel buttonPanel = new Panel ();
Panel blobPanel = new Panel();

// The Applets main section init() to set up screen
public void init( )
 {

// Create the User Interface
// Setup Query Panel

queryPanel.setLayout (new BorderLayout ( ));
execute_button = new Button ("Get BLOBs");
```

```
execute_button.addActionListener(this);
queryPanel.add ("North", execute_button);
output = new TextArea (22, 40);
output.setFont(outputFont);
queryPanel.add ("Center", output);

// Setup buttonPanel
buttonPanel.setLayout (new GridLayout (1,3));
show_button = new Button ("Show");
show_button.addActionListener(this);
buttonPanel.add("North", show_button);
cancel_button = new Button ("Cancel");
cancel_button.addActionListener(this);
buttonPanel.add("North", cancel_button);
buttonPanel.add("West", new Label("Enter Blob ID:", Label.RIGHT));
buttonPanel.add("Center", getblobid);

// Setup Blob Panel
blobPanel.setLayout (new BorderLayout());
blobPanel.add("East", blobCanvas);
blobPanel.add("North", buttonPanel);
this.validate();
// Setup Status Panel

statusPanel.setLayout (new BorderLayout ( ));
statusPanel.add("South", theStatus);

// Set text editable status
theStatus.setEditable(false);
getblobid.setEditable(true);

//Setup Master Layout
imageFrame.setLayout (new BorderLayout( ));
imageFrame.add("West", queryPanel);
imageFrame.add("South", statusPanel);
imageFrame.add("East", blobPanel);
imageFrame.pack();
imageFrame.setVisible(true);
theTracker = new MediaTracker(this);
 }

// What to do when buttons pushed
public void actionPerformed(ActionEvent event)
 {

// Get event
Object source = event.getSource();
```

```
// Determine type of event and take action
if (source == execute_button)
    {
try
      {
// Clear the output area
output.setText (null);
// open the connection to the database
Class.forName ("oracle.jdbc.driver.OracleDriver");
// Connect to the database
Connection conn =
DriverManager.getConnection ("jdbc:oracle:oci8:TEST",
    "graphics_dba", "graphics1");
// Create a Statement
Statement stmt = conn.createStatement ();
// Create a statement
// Execute the statement and query
output.append("Blobs Available to View" + "\n");
ResultSet rset = stmt.executeQuery ("SELECT rpad(to_char(graphic_id),5)||
': '||rpad(graphic_desc,30)||' : '||rpad(graphic_type,10)
FROM internal_graphics order by graphic_id");
// Dump the result
while (rset.next ()) output.append(rset.getString (1) + "\n");
      }
catch (Exception e)
      {
handleError(e);
      }
getblobid.requestFocus();
    }
if (source == show_button)
    {
blob_id = getblobid.getText();
theStatus.setText("Looking For BLOB :" + blob_id);
// Load the Oracle JDBC driver
try
      {
theStatus.setText("Logging On");
Class.forName ("oracle.jdbc.driver.OracleDriver");
// Connect to the database
Connection conn =
DriverManager.getConnection ("jdbc:oracle:oci8:TEST",
    "graphics_dba", "graphics1");
theStatus.setText("Connection Established");
// Create a Statement
Statement stmt = conn.createStatement ();
// Get increment value for temp file
```

```
       ResultSet inc = stmt.executeQuery (
          "select to_char(image_seq.nextval) from dual");
       if (inc.next ())
       inc_value = inc.getString (1);
       // Select the lobs
       theStatus.setText("Fetching BLOB :" + blob_id);
       ResultSet rset = stmt.executeQuery (
          "select graphic_blob from internal_graphics where graphic_id=" + blob_id);
             //
       if (rset.next ())
                {
       OracleBlob blob = ((OracleResultSet)rset).getBlob (1);
       theStatus.setText("Placing Blob in Temp File");
       dumpBlob(conn,blob);
       theStatus.setText("Showing Image");
       getblobid.setText("");
       theImage = getImage(getCodeBase(),"images/theImage" + inc_value + ".gif");
       theTracker = new MediaTracker(this);
       theTracker.addImage(theImage, 0);
       try {
       theTracker.waitForID(0);
                   }
       catch (InterruptedException e) { }
       blobPanel.setVisible(false);
       repaint();
       blobPanel.setVisible(true);
       getblobid.requestFocus();
             }
           }
       catch (ClassNotFoundException c)
           {
       handleError(c);
           }
       catch (SQLException sql)
           {
       handleError(sql);
           }
       catch (Exception s)
           {
       handleError(s);
           }
        }
       if (source == cancel_button) System.exit(0);
        }

       // Override of paint() with canvas to do exactly what we want
       class drawCanvas extends Canvas
        {
```

```java
int iWidth = 480;
int iHeight = 500;
public void paint(Graphics theGraphic)
    {

Dimension minSize = getPreferredSize();
if (theTracker != null)
      {
if (theTracker.isErrorAny())
       {
theGraphic.setColor(Color.red);
theGraphic.drawString("Image Error",60,10);
return;
       }
if (theTracker.checkAll(true))
        {
iWidth = theImage.getWidth(this);
iHeight = theImage.getHeight(this);
if (iHeight>480)
         {
iWidth=iWidth/2;
iHeight=iHeight/2;
         }
if (iWidth>500)
         {
iWidth=iWidth/2;
iHeight=iHeight/2;
         }
int xpos = 60;
minSize = getPreferredSize();
theGraphic.drawImage(theImage, xpos, 20, iWidth, iHeight, this);
        }
else
        {
theGraphic.setColor(Color.green);
theGraphic.drawString("Image loading ....", 60,10);
repaint(100);
        }
      }
    }
public Dimension getPreferredSize()
   {
/*System.out.println(iWidth + " x " + iHeight);*/
return new Dimension (iWidth,iHeight);
   }
  }
```

```
// Since JAVA doesn't clean up graphics context, do it in an override
// of destroy()
public void destroy()
  {
theGraphic.dispose();
System.gc();
  }

// Utility to handle exceptions cleanly
public void handleError(Throwable t)
  {
theStatus.setText("Error: " + t.getMessage( ));
t.printStackTrace( );
  }

// Utility function to dump Blob contents
static void dumpBlob (Connection conn, OracleBlob blob)
throws Exception
  {
OracleCallableStatement cstmt1 =
(OracleCallableStatement)
conn.prepareCall ("begin ? := dbms_lob.getLength (?); end;");
OracleCallableStatement cstmt2 =
(OracleCallableStatement)
conn.prepareCall ("begin dbms_lob.read (?, ?, ?, ?); end;");
cstmt1.registerOutParameter (1, Types.NUMERIC);
cstmt1.setBlob (2, blob);
cstmt1.execute ();
long length = cstmt1.getLong (1);
long i=0;
int chunk=100;
FileOutputStream file = new FileOutputStream (
   "images/theImage" + inc_value+ ".gif");
while (i < length)
    {
cstmt2.setBlob (1, blob);
cstmt2.setLong (2, chunk);
cstmt2.registerOutParameter (2, Types.NUMERIC);
cstmt2.setLong (3, i+1);
cstmt2.registerOutParameter (4, Types.VARBINARY);
cstmt2.execute ();
long read_this_time = cstmt2.getLong (2);
byte [] bytes_this_time = cstmt2.getBytes (4);
      {
// Put into file
file.write (bytes_this_time);
i += read_this_time;
```

```
/*      System.out.print ("Read " + i + " bytes of " + length + "\n");*/
        if ((i + read_this_time)>length) chunk = (int) (length-i);
        }
    }
file.close();
cstmt1.close ();
cstmt2.close ();
    }
}
```

To give you an idea about what the different sections do, look at Figure 13.6, which shows the **BLOB** retrieval application as it looks when it is first started. Notice the five main panels: the two top button panels, the central query and BLOB display panels, and the bottom status display panel. All of these panels are attached to a main frame component.

Figure 13.7 shows the results of a mouse click on the Get BLOBs button. The click of the button institutes a query of the **internal_graphics** table showing the index value,

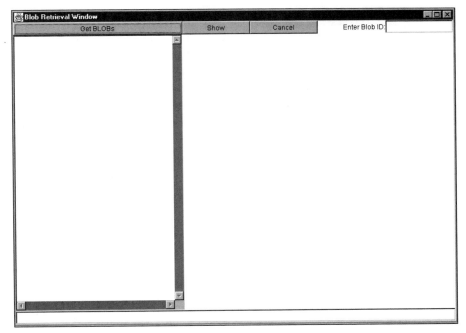

Figure 13.6

BLOB retrieval application at startup.

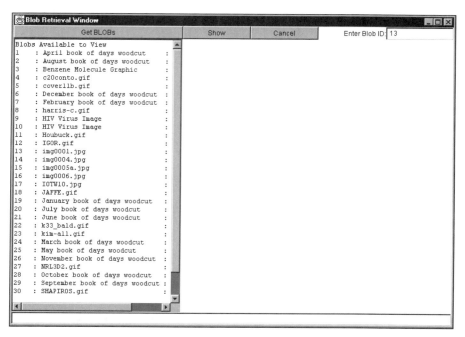

Figure 13.7

BLOB *retrieval application with **BLOB** data displayed.*

description, and type of each **BLOB** stored in the database. This **internal_graphics** table should look familiar from Chapter 6; it is the table used to demonstrate the loading of **BLOB**s from **BFILE** values using PL/SQL and **DBMS_LOB**. Notice how the **awt** panel component automatically adds scroll bars to text regions as needed. Also, notice in the Enter BLOB ID textbox, we have entered a **BLOB** ID from the display on the right, but have not yet clicked on the Show button.

Figure 13.8 shows the results from clicking on the Show button. This initiates the query to get the **BLOB** locator from the database. Use the **BLOB** locator to retrieve the actual image data from the database using the **DBMS_LOB** package, and place the result in one of the temporary files in a rotating pool. Finally, the image is displayed on the graphic canvas, a part of the right panel.

How is all of this accomplished? A look at the import section shows we are using the same mix of classes used for the first version of the applet, DisplayImage.java, used in a previous example. A look at the global variables shows we are initializing a new class called **MediaTracker**, but more about this in a minute. We are also initializing

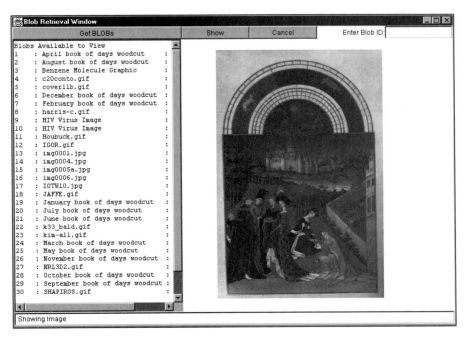

Figure 13.8

BLOB *retrieval application after the Show button is clicked.*

many more buttons and panels. Because this is the most complex applet we have
built, that only makes sense. Another new item is the canvas, used to draw on from
within an applet or application. A canvas is usually attached to another object, or
container if you prefer, such as panels, frames, windows, or even buttons.

```
// Set up global variables
MediaTracker theTracker = null;  → Note new Class, MediaTracker
String blob_id;
Image theImage;
Graphics theGraphic;

// The buttons to push for showing the graphic, cancel
Button show_button;
Button cancel_button;
Button execute_button;

// The text fields for status and blob id input
Canvas blobCanvas = new drawCanvas();  → Note new object, a Canvas
TextField  theStatus  = new TextField(64);
TextField  getblobid  = new TextField(4);
```

```
TextArea    output    = new TextArea();
Font outputFont = new  Font("Courier", Font.PLAIN, 12);

// The sequence value for the image file
static String inc_value;
// The global panels and frame definitions
Frame imageFrame = new Frame("Blob Retrieval Window");
Panel queryPanel = new Panel ();
Panel statusPanel = new Panel ();
Panel buttonPanel = new Panel ();
Panel blobPanel = new Panel();
```

These initial definitions are not all of the components we will be using. These are
only the ones that are used in multiple methods within DisplayImage2.java. The
init() method defines the rest of the user interface components:

```
public void init( )
 {

// Create the User Interface
// Setup Query Panel

queryPanel.setLayout (new BorderLayout ( ));
execute_button = new Button ("Get BLOBs");
execute_button.addActionListener(this);
queryPanel.add ("North", execute_button);
output = new TextArea (22, 40);
output.setFont(outputFont);
queryPanel.add ("Center", output);

// Setup buttonPanel
buttonPanel.setLayout (new GridLayout (1,3));
show_button = new Button ("Show");
show_button.addActionListener(this);
buttonPanel.add("North", show_button);
cancel_button = new Button ("Cancel");
cancel_button.addActionListener(this);
buttonPanel.add("North", cancel_button);
buttonPanel.add("West", new Label("Enter Blob ID:", Label.RIGHT));
buttonPanel.add("Center", getblobid);

// Setup Blob Panel
blobPanel.setLayout (new BorderLayout());
blobPanel.add("East", blobCanvas);
blobPanel.add("North", buttonPanel);
this.validate();
// Setup Status Panel
```

```
statusPanel.setLayout (new BorderLayout ( ));
statusPanel.add("South", theStatus);

// Set text editable status
theStatus.setEditable(false);
getblobid.setEditable(true);

//Setup Master Layout
imageFrame.setLayout (new BorderLayout( ));
imageFrame.add("West", queryPanel);
imageFrame.add("South", statusPanel);
imageFrame.add("East", blobPanel);
imageFrame.pack();
imageFrame.setVisible(true);
theTracker = new MediaTracker(this);
 }
```

Other than this section being a bit more lengthy, there is really nothing much new, except for the addition of the **MediaTracker** with this line of code:

```
theTracker = new MediaTracker(this);
```

This line attaches the media listener to the **imageFrame** component's **blobPanel**. The **blobPanel** contains the **blobCanvas** drawing component. Another method used before, but not commented on, is **pack()**. The **pack()** method makes a component just big enough to hold its components. It can cause problems with graphic elements if the graphic element isn't initialized. This is especially true of the **Canvas** class of objects (more on this later).

The next section of code determines which actions are taken when the buttons are clicked using the mouse buttons:

```
public void actionPerformed(ActionEvent event)
 {

// Get event
Object source = event.getSource();
// Determine type of event and take action
if (source == execute_button)
   {
try
     {
// Clear the output area
output.setText (null);
// open the connection to the database
```

```
Class.forName ("oracle.jdbc.driver.OracleDriver");
// Connect to the database
Connection conn =
DriverManager.getConnection ("jdbc:oracle:oci8:TEST",
    "graphics_dba", "graphics1");
// Create a Statement
Statement stmt = conn.createStatement ();
// Create a statement
// Execute the statement and query
output.append("Blobs Available to View" + "\n");
ResultSet rset = stmt.executeQuery ("SELECT rpad(to_char(graphic_id),5)||
    ': '||rpad(graphic_desc,30)||' : '||rpad(graphic_type,10)
    FROM internal_graphics order by graphic_id");
// Dump the result
while (rset.next ()) output.append(rset.getString (1) + "\n");
      }
catch (Exception e)
      {
handleError(e);
      }
getblobid.requestFocus();
   }
if (source == show_button)
   {
blob_id = getblobid.getText();
theStatus.setText("Looking For BLOB :" + blob_id);
// Load the Oracle JDBC driver
try
      {
theStatus.setText("Logging On");
Class.forName ("oracle.jdbc.driver.OracleDriver");
// Connect to the database
Connection conn =
DriverManager.getConnection (
    "jdbc:oracle:oci8:TEST", "graphics_dba", "graphics1");
theStatus.setText("Connection Established");
// Create a Statement
Statement stmt = conn.createStatement ();
// Get increment value for temp file
ResultSet inc = stmt.executeQuery (
    "select to_char(image_seq.nextval) from dual");
if (inc.next ())
inc_value = inc.getString (1);
// Select the lobs
theStatus.setText("Fetching BLOB :" + blob_id);
ResultSet rset = stmt.executeQuery (
    "select graphic_blob from internal_graphics where graphic_id=" + blob_id);
      //
```

```
if (rset.next ())
        {
OracleBlob blob = ((OracleResultSet)rset).getBlob (1);
theStatus.setText("Placing Blob in Temp File");
dumpBlob(conn,blob);
theStatus.setText("Showing Image");
getblobid.setText("");
theImage = getImage(getCodeBase(),"images/theImage" + inc_value + ".gif");
theTracker = new MediaTracker(this);
theTracker.addImage(theImage, 0);
try {
theTracker.waitForID(0);
            }
catch (InterruptedException e) { }
blobPanel.setVisible(false);
repaint();
blobPanel.setVisible(true);
getblobid.requestFocus();
        }
      }
catch (ClassNotFoundException c)
      {
handleError(c);
      }
catch (SQLException sql)
      {
handleError(sql);
      }
catch (Exception s)
      {
handleError(s);
      }
   }
if (source == cancel_button) System.exit(0);
 }
```

Rather than using a more modular approach (which, by the way, I tried, but it ended up more complex than I liked), I decided to integrate the operations into the **actionPerformed(ActionEvent event)** module.

In this case, if the **execute_button** (**Get BLOBs**) is clicked, the code to retrieve the contents of the **internal_graphics** table is activated. There is nothing new in this section, other than the query being different. The code closely resembles the first example, with one exception: Because I have only one set of graphics in one database, I left out the generic connection sections. Notice that at the end of the process of retrieving the **BLOB** data, I place the focus of input into the **getblobid** text area, so the user doesn't have to manually select the area using a mouse action.

The next action item is the **show_button** (**Show**). If the **show_button** is clicked, the value from the **getblobid** region is scraped from the screen using a **getText()** method call. This **getblobid** value will be used in a query to get the **BLOB** of choice. First, reconnect (if needed) to the database and get the next sequence value from a database-maintained sequence called **image_seq**. This sequence is set to cycle from 1 through 32 forever and allows you to randomly associate the graphic with one of the 32 temporary image files. This could probably be done with fewer files, but 32 seemed like a good idea because I had 32 graphics in the database.

I found that if I attempted to use a single temporary image file, the graphic context would not remap (display). I assume that because Java saw I was using the same file name, it meant I wanted the same graphic. This behavior even persisted if I used a **dispose()** method and a **System.gc()** call (**dispose()** is supposed to destroy the graphic context, and the **System.gc()** call initiates a garbage cleanup). Use of multiple temp files corrected this rather annoying feature of Java. Once you have the temporary file, you can proceed to **SELECT** the **BLOB** id from the **internal_graphics** table and pass this information to the **dumpBlob()** method. Also, notice that you must create a new instance of tracker at the start of the run, or any error returned will be carried into the next cycle of operation ad infinitum.

Once control returns from the **dumpBlob()** method, the image is retrieved from the temporary file and the **MediaTracker** object is attached to the process retrieving the image from the file. The **MediaTracker** object follows the progress of the image load into memory and, if there is a problem, reports it back to the process. The **MediaTracker** is useful in situations where images are being transferred from one net location to another to prevent draw and paint routines from attempting to draw incomplete graphics. Once a graphics context is assigned, the control is returned immediately. Without the call to the **MediaTracker**, the image might not be complete before operations using it begin.

The next set of commands kept me up several nights trying to figure them out. When I first wrote the application, I could get the graphics to display only by collapsing and reinitializing the window using the frame interface with mouse clicks—hardly what I wanted:

```
blobPanel.setVisible(false);
repaint();
blobPanel.setVisible(true);
getblobid.requestFocus();
```

The act of making the **blobPanel** invisible, then doing the call to **repaint()** and making the panel visible, fixed the problem.

As a final step in the process, I return focus to the **getblobid** text area, again for user convenience. Once a graphic context is initialized, it will remain in memory, cluttering things up until a **dispose()** is issued against it. Using appletviewer in an MS-DOS window on NT 4, I was able only to display about two to three images before the process locked and required a destructive drop using the Task Manager. With the addition of the **dispose** method call in the overridden **destroy()** method call, this increased to 12 to 13, and with a final call to garbage collection (**System.gc()**), I was finally able alternatively to retrieve and display an unlimited number of images:

```
public void destroy()
  {
theGraphic.dispose();
System.gc();
  }
```

In this applet, the **paint()** routine is encapsulated in an overridden **Canvas** class definition. The **paint()** routine has been expanded to include a call to the **getPreferredSize()** overridden method to get an initialization set of dimensions set by globally declaring the **iWidth** and **iHeight** integer values and using these as a return value set whenever the **getPreferredSize()** routine is called. With the returned values tied to **iWidth** and **iHeight** when you reset these to the actual and adjusted width and height of the graphic, any calls to **getPreferredSize()** return the proper value. Notice we use a new class, the **Dimension** class, to set up our **iWidth** and **iHeight** values into the **minSize()** calls. Notice how the value of **theTracker** (the **MediaTracker** object) verifies if the image is properly loaded:

```
class drawCanvas extends Canvas
  {
int iWidth = 480;
int iHeight = 500;
public void paint(Graphics theGraphic)
    {
```

```
Dimension minSize = getPreferredSize();
if (theTracker != null)
        {
if (theTracker.isErrorAny())
          {
theGraphic.setColor(Color.red);
theGraphic.drawString("Image Error",60,10);
return;
          }
if (theTracker.checkAll(true))
          {
iWidth = theImage.getWidth(this);
iHeight = theImage.getHeight(this);
if (iHeight>480)
            {
iWidth=iWidth/2;
iHeight=iHeight/2;
            }
if (iWidth>500)
            {
iWidth=iWidth/2;
iHeight=iHeight/2;
            }
int xpos = 60;
minSize = getPreferredSize();
theGraphic.drawImage(theImage, xpos, 20, iWidth, iHeight, this);
          }
else
          {
theGraphic.setColor(Color.green);
theGraphic.drawString("Image loading ....", 60,10);
repaint(100);
          }
        }
    }
public Dimension getPreferredSize()
    {
/*System.out.println(iWidth + " x " + iHeight);*/
return new Dimension (iWidth,iHeight);
    }
```

The **dumpBlob** method is identical to the one discussed in the previous example, so I won't cover it again. Its general process is to connect to the database using a passed-in connection context. With the passed-in **BLOB** locator, use the **DBMS_LOB getlength()** and **read()** procedures to read the image stored in the **BLOB** locator location and place it into a temporary file, passing control back to the calling process.

In the applets we have discussed, the general usage of Java, JDBC, and JSQL has been demonstrated along with the more general use of **java.awt**, **java.io**, **java.util**, **java.applet**, and several other classes of objects. By using the techniques as demonstrated, the reader should be able to use Java to access virtually any data in an Oracle database.

Additional Java Reading

Java Sourcebook—A Complete Guide To Creating Java Applets For The Web, Ed Anuff, John Wiley and Sons, 1996.

The Java Tutorial—Object–Oriented Programming For The Internet, Mary Campione, Kathy Walrath, Addison-Wesley, 1996.

Java In A Nutshell—A Desktop Quick Reference, 2nd Edition, David Flanagan, O'Reilly, 1997.

Graphic Java 1.1—Mastering The AWT, 2nd Edition, David M. Geary, Sunsoft Press (Prentice-Hall) Java Series, 1997.

Java Database Programming—Master Next Generation Web Database Techniques, Brian Jepson, John Wiley and Sons, 1997.

Laura Lemay's Java 1.1 Interactive Course—A Web-based Learning Center, Laura Lemay, Charles Perkins, Michael Morrison, Danial Groner, Waite Group Press, 1997.

SQL Database Programming With Java, Bill McCarty, The Coriolis Group, 1998.

Oracle Databases On The Web, Robert Papaj, Donald Burleson, The Coriolis Group, 1997.

www.javasoft.com

www.oracle.com

CompuServe JAVASoft Forum

Appendix

The Oracle8 Data Dictionary Tables And Views

During development, monitoring, and tuning efforts, the tables and views of the Oracle8 data dictionary need to be accessed and used for status checking, type checking, transaction state verification, and dozens of other reasons. This appendix lists the most current definitions of the objects contained in the Oracle8 data dictionary for version 8.0.3 available at the time of publication.

Notes…

Appendix

Data Dictionary $ Tables

Probably the most often used tables in the data dictionary are the $ tables. These tables are called $ (dollar) tables, because they used to end with a dollar sign (Oracle recently moved away from this convention, but a majority of the tables still end in a dollar sign, and I still call them that). The $ tables are one step up from the K and X$ C language strucs that are the heart of any Oracle system. This appendix will not cover the K and X$ strucs, because they are usually not used in DBA or developer work. For a glimpse at how the K and X$ strucs look, examine the definitions for the **GV$** fixed views contained in one of the next sections.

The dollar tables are built by several scripts, but the core set of tables is created by the sql.bsq script located in the $ORACLE_HOME/rdbms/admin directory on Unix and under the X:\orant\RDBMS80\ADMIN (where *X* is the disk where the ORANT subdirectory resides) on NT 4.

Descriptions Of Data Dictionary $ Tables

The **ACCESS$** table contains information concerning resources currently being accessed, giving dependency and column information.

Listing A.1   Description of the data dictionary table ACCESS$.

Name	Null?	Type
D_OBJ#	NOT NULL	NUMBER
ORDER#	NOT NULL	NUMBER
COLUMNS		RAW(126)
TYPES	NOT NULL	NUMBER

The **ARGUMENT$** table contains information on stored procedure arguments.

Listing A.2   Description of the data dictionary table ARGUMENT$.

Name	Null?	Type
OBJ#	NOT NULL	NUMBER
PROCEDURE$		VARCHAR2(30)
OVERLOAD#	NOT NULL	NUMBER
POSITION#	NOT NULL	NUMBER
SEQUENCE#	NOT NULL	NUMBER
LEVEL#	NOT NULL	NUMBER
ARGUMENT		VARCHAR2(30)
TYPE#	NOT NULL	NUMBER
CHARSETID		NUMBER
CHARSETFORM		NUMBER
DEFAULT#		NUMBER
IN_OUT		NUMBER
LENGTH		NUMBER
PRECISION#		NUMBER
SCALE		NUMBER
RADIX		NUMBER
DEFLENGTH		NUMBER
DEFAULT$		LONG

The **ATEMPTAB$** table is used internally and never contains data.

Listing A.3 Description of the data dictionary table ATEMPTAB$.

Name	Null?	Type
ID		NUMBER

The **ATTRCOL$** table contains information about user-defined type attributes.

Listing A.4 Description of the data dictionary table ATTRCOL$.

Name	Null?	Type
OBJ#	NOT NULL	NUMBER
INTCOL#	NOT NULL	NUMBER
NAME	NOT NULL	VARCHAR2(4000)

The **ATTRIBUTE$** table contains information about attributes as they are used in other objects. Attribute size and precision data is kept here.

Listing A.5 Description of the data dictionary table ATTRIBUTE$.

Name	Null?	Type
TOID	NOT NULL	RAW(16)
VERSION#	NOT NULL	NUMBER
NAME	NOT NULL	VARCHAR2(30)
ATTRIBUTE#	NOT NULL	NUMBER
ATTR_TOID	NOT NULL	RAW(16)
ATTR_VERSION#	NOT NULL	NUMBER
PROPERTIES	NOT NULL	NUMBER
CHARSETID		NUMBER
CHARSETFORM		NUMBER
LENGTH		NUMBER
PRECISION#		NUMBER
SCALE		NUMBER
SPARE1		NUMBER
SPARE2		NUMBER
SPARE3		NUMBER

The **AUD$** table is used by the system auditing to track all audited actions. This table will need to be periodically purged of old records if auditing is used.

Listing A.6 Description of the data dictionary table AUD$.

Name	Null?	Type
SESSIONID	NOT NULL	NUMBER
ENTRYID	NOT NULL	NUMBER
STATEMENT	NOT NULL	NUMBER
TIMESTAMP#	NOT NULL	DATE
USERID		VARCHAR2(30)
USERHOST		VARCHAR2(2000)
TERMINAL		VARCHAR2(2000)
ACTION#	NOT NULL	NUMBER
RETURNCODE	NOT NULL	NUMBER
OBJ$CREATOR		VARCHAR2(30)

```
OBJ$NAME                        VARCHAR2(128)
AUTH$PRIVILEGES                 VARCHAR2(16)
AUTH$GRANTEE                    VARCHAR2(30)
NEW$OWNER                       VARCHAR2(30)
NEW$NAME                        VARCHAR2(128)
SES$ACTIONS                     VARCHAR2(19)
SES$TID                         NUMBER
LOGOFF$LREAD                    NUMBER
LOGOFF$PREAD                    NUMBER
LOGOFF$LWRITE                   NUMBER
LOGOFF$DEAD                     NUMBER
LOGOFF$TIME                     DATE
COMMENT$TEXT                    VARCHAR2(4000)
SPARE1                          VARCHAR2(255)
SPARE2                          NUMBER
OBJ$LABEL                       RAW(255)
SES$LABEL                       RAW(255)
PRIV$USED                       NUMBER
```

The **AUDIT$** table tells what auditing options are turned on.

Listing A.7   Description of the data dictionary table AUDIT$.

Name	Null?	Type
USER#	NOT NULL	NUMBER
OPTION#	NOT NULL	NUMBER
SUCCESS		NUMBER
FAILURE		NUMBER

The **AUDIT_ACTIONS** table lists available audit codes.

Listing A.8   Description of the data dictionary table AUDIT_ACTIONS.

Name	Null?	Type
ACTION	NOT NULL	NUMBER
NAME	NOT NULL	VARCHAR2(27)

The **BOOTSTRAP$** table is used internally by Oracle.

Listing A.9   Description of the data dictionary table BOOTSTRAP$.

Name	Null?	Type
LINE#	NOT NULL	NUMBER
OBJ#	NOT NULL	NUMBER
SQL_TEXT	NOT NULL	VARCHAR2(4000)

The **CCOL$** table contains information on all constraint columns in the database.

Listing A.10   Description of the data dictionary table CCOL$.

Name	Null?	Type
CON#	NOT NULL	NUMBER
OBJ#	NOT NULL	NUMBER
COL#	NOT NULL	NUMBER
POS#		NUMBER
INTCOL#	NOT NULL	NUMBER
SPARE1		NUMBER
SPARE2		NUMBER
SPARE3		NUMBER
SPARE4		VARCHAR2(1000)
SPARE5		VARCHAR2(1000)
SPARE6		DATE

The **CDEF$** table contains information on all constraints defined in the database.

Listing A.11   Description of the data dictionary table CDEF$.

Name	Null?	Type
CON#	NOT NULL	NUMBER
OBJ#	NOT NULL	NUMBER
COLS		NUMBER
TYPE#	NOT NULL	NUMBER
ROBJ#		NUMBER
RCON#		NUMBER
RRULES		VARCHAR2(3)
MATCH#		NUMBER
REFACT		NUMBER
ENABLED		NUMBER
CONDLENGTH		NUMBER
CONDITION		LONG
INTCOLS		NUMBER
MTIME		DATE
DEFER		NUMBER
SPARE1		NUMBER
SPARE2		NUMBER
SPARE3		NUMBER
SPARE4		VARCHAR2(1000)
SPARE5		VARCHAR2(1000)
SPARE6		DATE

The **CLU$** table contains information about all clusters defined in the database.

Listing A.12   Description of the data dictionary table CLU$.

Name	Null?	Type
OBJ#	NOT NULL	NUMBER
DATAOBJ#		NUMBER
TS#	NOT NULL	NUMBER
FILE#	NOT NULL	NUMBER
BLOCK#	NOT NULL	NUMBER
COLS	NOT NULL	NUMBER
PCTFREE$	NOT NULL	NUMBER
PCTUSED$	NOT NULL	NUMBER
INITRANS	NOT NULL	NUMBER
MAXTRANS	NOT NULL	NUMBER
SIZE$		NUMBER
HASHFUNC		VARCHAR2(30)
HASHKEYS		NUMBER
FUNC		NUMBER
EXTIND		NUMBER
FLAGS		NUMBER
DEGREE		NUMBER
INSTANCES		NUMBER
AVGCHN		NUMBER
SPARE1		NUMBER
SPARE2		NUMBER
SPARE3		NUMBER
SPARE4		NUMBER
SPARE5		VARCHAR2(1000)
SPARE6		VARCHAR2(1000)
SPARE7		DATE

The **COL$** table contains information on all columns contained in the database.

Listing A.13   Description of the data dictionary table COL$.

Name	Null?	Type
OBJ#	NOT NULL	NUMBER
COL#	NOT NULL	NUMBER
SEGCOL#	NOT NULL	NUMBER
SEGCOLLENGTH	NOT NULL	NUMBER
OFFSET	NOT NULL	NUMBER
NAME	NOT NULL	VARCHAR2(30)
TYPE#	NOT NULL	NUMBER
LENGTH	NOT NULL	NUMBER
FIXEDSTORAGE	NOT NULL	NUMBER
PRECISION#		NUMBER
SCALE		NUMBER
NULL$	NOT NULL	NUMBER

```
DEFLENGTH                               NUMBER
DEFAULT$                                 LONG
INTCOL#                   NOT NULL NUMBER
PROPERTY                  NOT NULL NUMBER
CHARSETID                               NUMBER
CHARSETFORM                             NUMBER
SPARE1                                  NUMBER
SPARE2                                  NUMBER
SPARE3                                  NUMBER
SPARE4                                  VARCHAR2(1000)
SPARE5                                  VARCHAR2(1000)
SPARE6                                  DATE
```

The **COLLECTION$** table contains information on all collections (**VARRAY** and nested table) in the database.

Listing A.14   Description of the data dictionary table COLLECTION$.

```
Name                              Null?     Type
------------------------------ -------- ----
TOID                              NOT NULL RAW(16)
VERSION#                          NOT NULL NUMBER
COLL_TOID                         NOT NULL RAW(16)
COLL_VERSION#                     NOT NULL NUMBER
ELEM_TOID                         NOT NULL RAW(16)
ELEM_VERSION#                     NOT NULL NUMBER
PROPERTIES                        NOT NULL NUMBER
CHARSETID                                  NUMBER
CHARSETFORM                                NUMBER
LENGTH                                     NUMBER
PRECISION                                  NUMBER
SCALE                                      NUMBER
UPPER_BOUND                                NUMBER
SPARE1                                     NUMBER
SPARE2                                     NUMBER
SPARE3                                     NUMBER
```

The **COLTYPE$** table contains information about the column types for the tables in the database. It is a link table to other tables containing only references to other tables.

Listing A.15 Description of the data dictionary table COLTYPE$.

Name	Null?	Type
OBJ#	NOT NULL	NUMBER
COL#	NOT NULL	NUMBER
INTCOL#	NOT NULL	NUMBER
TOID	NOT NULL	RAW(16)
VERSION#	NOT NULL	NUMBER
PACKED	NOT NULL	NUMBER
INTCOLS		NUMBER
INTCOL#S		RAW(2000)
FLAGS		NUMBER

The **COM$** table stores all comments registered against tables or columns in the database.

Listing A.16 Description of the data dictionary table COM$.

Name	Null?	Type
OBJ#	NOT NULL	NUMBER
COL#		NUMBER
COMMENT$		VARCHAR2(4000)

The **CON$** table contains the constraint names with a link to the owning schema. This table stores the values for the **CON#** identifier used in other tables in the data dictionary to refer to this constraint.

Listing A.17 Description of the data dictionary table CON$.

Name	Null?	Type
OWNER#	NOT NULL	NUMBER
NAME	NOT NULL	VARCHAR2(30)
CON#	NOT NULL	NUMBER
SPARE1		NUMBER
SPARE2		NUMBER
SPARE3		NUMBER
SPARE4		VARCHAR2(1000)
SPARE5		VARCHAR2(1000)
SPARE6		DATE

The **DBMS_ALERT_INFO** table is created by the DBMSALRT.SQL script rather than SQL.BSQ. The table is also used by the **DBMS_ALERT** package to register alerts.

Listing A.18   Description of the data dictionary table DBMS_ALERT_INFO.

Name	Null?	Type
NAME	NOT NULL	VARCHAR2(30)
SID	NOT NULL	VARCHAR2(30)
CHANGED		VARCHAR2(1)
MESSAGE		VARCHAR2(1800)

The **DBMS_LOCK_ALLOCATED** table is created by the DBMSLOCK.SQL script and is used to track user-created locks.

Listing A.19   Description of the data dictionary table DBMS_LOCK_ ALLOCATED.

Name	Null?	Type
NAME	NOT NULL	VARCHAR2(128)
LOCKID		NUMBER(38)
EXPIRATION		DATE

The **DEFROLE$** table tracks users' default roles.

Listing A.20   Description of the data dictionary table DEFROLE$.

Name	Null?	Type
USER#	NOT NULL	NUMBER
ROLE#	NOT NULL	NUMBER

The **DEPENDENCY$** table is used to track object dependencies. The table gives parent (**P_**) and dependent (**D_**) objects and the dependency order (**ORDER#**).

Listing A.21   Description of the data dictionary table DEPENDENCY$.

Name	Null?	Type
D_OBJ#	NOT NULL	NUMBER
D_TIMESTAMP	NOT NULL	DATE
ORDER#	NOT NULL	NUMBER
P_OBJ#	NOT NULL	NUMBER
P_TIMESTAMP	NOT NULL	DATE
D_OWNER#	NOT NULL	NUMBER
PROPERTY	NOT NULL	NUMBER

The **DIR$** table is used to track the definitions of directories used with the **BFILE LOB** identifiers for externally stored **LOB** objects.

Listing A.22 Description of the data dictionary table DIR$.

```
Name                                  Null?     Type
------------------------------------- --------- ----
OBJ#                                  NOT NULL  NUMBER
AUDIT$                                NOT NULL  VARCHAR2(38)
OS_PATH                                         VARCHAR2(4000)
```

The **DUAL** table contains a single column and a single value. The **DUAL** column is used for **SELECT** operations where system variables, such as **SYSDATE**, **USER**, or constants are being used—for example, **SELECT sysdate FROM dual;**. It has no other purpose and should *never* contain more than one entry.

Listing A.23 Description of the data dictionary table DUAL.

```
Name                                  Null?     Type
------------------------------------- --------- ----
DUMMY                                           VARCHAR2(1)
```

The **DUC$** table is used to track packages and their contained procedures.

Listing A.24 Description of the data dictionary table DUC$.

```
Name                                  Null?     Type
------------------------------------- --------- ----
OWNER                                 NOT NULL  VARCHAR2(30)
PACK                                  NOT NULL  VARCHAR2(30)
PROC                                  NOT NULL  VARCHAR2(30)
FIELD1                                          NUMBER
OPERATION#                            NOT NULL  NUMBER
SEQ                                   NOT NULL  NUMBER
COM                                             VARCHAR2(80)
```

The **ERROR$** table tracks errors that occur during procedure, package, trigger, and other stored object creation activities. The **SHOW ERR** command references this table.

Listing A.25 Description of the data dictionary table ERROR$.

```
Name                                  Null?     Type
------------------------------------- --------- ----
OBJ#                                  NOT NULL  NUMBER
SEQUENCE#                             NOT NULL  NUMBER
LINE                                  NOT NULL  NUMBER
POSITION#                             NOT NULL  NUMBER
TEXTLENGTH                            NOT NULL  NUMBER
TEXT                                  NOT NULL  VARCHAR2(4000)
```

The **EXPACT$** table is used by the export process to control export actions. Usually, end users do not use this table.

Listing A.26   Description of the data dictionary table EXPACT$.

Name	Null?	Type
OWNER	NOT NULL	VARCHAR2(30)
NAME	NOT NULL	VARCHAR2(30)
FUNC_SCHEMA	NOT NULL	VARCHAR2(30)
FUNC_PACKAGE	NOT NULL	VARCHAR2(30)
FUNC_PROC	NOT NULL	VARCHAR2(30)
CODE	NOT NULL	NUMBER
CALLORDER		NUMBER
CALLARG		VARCHAR2(1)
OBJ_TYPE	NOT NULL	NUMBER
USER_ARG		VARCHAR2(2000)

The **FET$** table contains data on free extents for the entire database. Its opposite is the **UET$** table, which tracks used extents.

Listing A.27   Description of the data dictionary table FET$.

Name	Null?	Type
TS#	NOT NULL	NUMBER
FILE#	NOT NULL	NUMBER
BLOCK#	NOT NULL	NUMBER
LENGTH	NOT NULL	NUMBER

The **FILE$** table contains information on all datafiles defined in the database.

Listing A.28   Description of the data dictionary table FILE$.

Name	Null?	Type
FILE#	NOT NULL	NUMBER
STATUS$	NOT NULL	NUMBER
BLOCKS	NOT NULL	NUMBER
TS#		NUMBER
RELFILE#		NUMBER
MAXEXTEND		NUMBER
INC		NUMBER
CRSCNWRP		NUMBER
CRSCNBAS		NUMBER
OWNERINSTANCE		VARCHAR2(30)
SPARE1		NUMBER
SPARE2		NUMBER
SPARE3		VARCHAR2(1000)
SPARE4		DATE

The **HISTGRM$** table contains information about all histograms defined in the database.

Listing A.29   Description of the data dictionary table HISTGRM$.

Name	Null?	Type
OBJ#	NOT NULL	NUMBER
COL#	NOT NULL	NUMBER
ROW#		NUMBER
BUCKET	NOT NULL	NUMBER
ENDPOINT	NOT NULL	NUMBER
INTCOL#	NOT NULL	NUMBER
SPARE1		NUMBER
SPARE2		NUMBER

The **HIST_HEAD$** table contains the data collected for histograms in the database.

Listing A.30   Description of the data dictionary table HIST_HEAD$.

Name	Null?	Type
OBJ#	NOT NULL	NUMBER
COL#	NOT NULL	NUMBER
BUCKET_CNT	NOT NULL	NUMBER
ROW_CNT	NOT NULL	NUMBER
CACHE_CNT		NUMBER
NULL_CNT		NUMBER
TIMESTAMP#		DATE
SAMPLE_SIZE		NUMBER
MINIMUM		NUMBER
MAXIMUM		NUMBER
DISTCNT		NUMBER
LOWVAL		RAW(32)
HIVAL		RAW(32)
DENSITY		NUMBER
INTCOL#	NOT NULL	NUMBER
SPARE1		NUMBER
SPARE2		NUMBER

The **ICOL$** table contains information about all indexed columns in the database.

Listing A.31   Description of the data dictionary table ICOL$.

Name	Null?	Type
OBJ#	NOT NULL	NUMBER
BO#	NOT NULL	NUMBER
COL#	NOT NULL	NUMBER

```
POS#                              NOT NULL NUMBER
SEGCOL#                           NOT NULL NUMBER
SEGCOLLENGTH                      NOT NULL NUMBER
OFFSET                            NOT NULL NUMBER
INTCOL#                           NOT NULL NUMBER
SPARE1                                     NUMBER
SPARE2                                     NUMBER
SPARE3                                     NUMBER
SPARE4                                     VARCHAR2(1000)
SPARE5                                     VARCHAR2(1000)
SPARE6                                     DATE
```

The **IDL_CHAR$** table is used internally by Oracle.

Listing A.32 Description of the data dictionary table IDL_CHAR$.

Name	Null?	Type
OBJ#	NOT NULL	NUMBER
PART	NOT NULL	NUMBER
VERSION		NUMBER
PIECE#	NOT NULL	NUMBER
LENGTH	NOT NULL	NUMBER
PIECE	NOT NULL	LONG

IDL_SB4$ is used internally by Oracle.

Listing A.33 Description of the data dictionary table IDL_SB4$.

Name	Null?	Type
OBJ#	NOT NULL	NUMBER
PART	NOT NULL	NUMBER
VERSION		NUMBER
PIECE#	NOT NULL	NUMBER
LENGTH	NOT NULL	NUMBER
PIECE	NOT NULL	UNDEFINED

IDL_UB1$ is used internally by Oracle.

Listing A.34 Description of the data dictionary table IDL_UB1$.

Name	Null?	Type
OBJ#	NOT NULL	NUMBER
PART	NOT NULL	NUMBER
VERSION		NUMBER
PIECE#	NOT NULL	NUMBER
LENGTH	NOT NULL	NUMBER
PIECE	NOT NULL	LONG RAW

IDL_UB2$ is used internally by Oracle.

Listing A.35   Description of the data dictionary table IDL_UB2$.

Name	Null?	Type
OBJ#	NOT NULL	NUMBER
PART	NOT NULL	NUMBER
VERSION		NUMBER
PIECE#	NOT NULL	NUMBER
LENGTH	NOT NULL	NUMBER
PIECE	NOT NULL	UNDEFINED

ID_GENS$ is used internally by Oracle.

Listing A.36   Description of the data dictionary table ID_GENS$.

Name	Null?	Type
TOTAL	NOT NULL	NUMBER

The **INCEXP$** table keeps track of the objects that have been incrementally exported.

Listing A.37   Description of the data dictionary table INCEXP$.

Name	Null?	Type
OWNER#	NOT NULL	NUMBER
NAME	NOT NULL	VARCHAR2(30)
TYPE#	NOT NULL	NUMBER
CTIME		DATE
ITIME	NOT NULL	DATE
EXPID	NOT NULL	NUMBER(3)

The **INCFILE** table tracks incremental export file names.

Listing A.38   Description of the data dictionary table INCFILE.

Name	Null?	Type
EXPID	NOT NULL	NUMBER(3)
EXPTYPE	NOT NULL	VARCHAR2(1)
EXPFILE	NOT NULL	VARCHAR2(100)
EXPDATE	NOT NULL	DATE
EXPUSER	NOT NULL	VARCHAR2(30)

The **INCVID** table tracks export identification numbers for the current incremental exports.

Listing A.39 Description of the data dictionary table INCVID.

Name	Null?	Type
EXPID	NOT NULL	NUMBER(3)

The **IND$** table keeps track of all system indexes.

Listing A.40 Description of the data dictionary table IND$.

Name	Null?	Type
OBJ#	NOT NULL	NUMBER
DATAOBJ#		NUMBER
TS#	NOT NULL	NUMBER
FILE#	NOT NULL	NUMBER
BLOCK#	NOT NULL	NUMBER
BO#	NOT NULL	NUMBER
INDMETHOD#	NOT NULL	NUMBER
COLS	NOT NULL	NUMBER
PCTFREE$	NOT NULL	NUMBER
INITRANS	NOT NULL	NUMBER
MAXTRANS	NOT NULL	NUMBER
PCTTHRES$		NUMBER
TYPE#	NOT NULL	NUMBER
FLAGS	NOT NULL	NUMBER
PROPERTY	NOT NULL	NUMBER
BLEVEL		NUMBER
LEAFCNT		NUMBER
DISTKEY		NUMBER
LBLKKEY		NUMBER
DBLKKEY		NUMBER
CLUFAC		NUMBER
ANALYZETIME		DATE
SAMPLESIZE		NUMBER
ROWCNT		NUMBER
INTCOLS	NOT NULL	NUMBER
DEGREE		NUMBER
INSTANCES		NUMBER
TRUNCCNT		NUMBER
SPARE1		NUMBER
SPARE2		NUMBER
SPARE3		NUMBER
SPARE4		VARCHAR2(1000)
SPARE5		VARCHAR2(1000)
SPARE6		DATE

The **INDPART$** table tracks all partitioned indexes in the database.

Listing A.41 Description of the data dictionary table INDPART$.

Name	Null?	Type
OBJ#	NOT NULL	NUMBER
DATAOBJ#	NOT NULL	NUMBER
BO#	NOT NULL	NUMBER
PART#	NOT NULL	NUMBER
HIBOUNDLEN	NOT NULL	NUMBER
HIBOUNDVAL		LONG
FLAGS	NOT NULL	NUMBER
TS#	NOT NULL	NUMBER
FILE#	NOT NULL	NUMBER
BLOCK#	NOT NULL	NUMBER
PCTFREE$	NOT NULL	NUMBER
PCTTHRES$		NUMBER
INITRANS	NOT NULL	NUMBER
MAXTRANS	NOT NULL	NUMBER
ANALYZETIME		DATE
SAMPLESIZE		NUMBER
ROWCNT		NUMBER
BLEVEL		NUMBER
LEAFCNT		NUMBER
DISTKEY		NUMBER
LBLKKEY		NUMBER
DBLKKEY		NUMBER
CLUFAC		NUMBER
SPARE1		NUMBER
SPARE2		NUMBER
SPARE3		NUMBER
INCLCOL		NUMBER

The **JOB$** table tracks all defined jobs for the internal job queues.

Listing A.42 Description of the data dictionary table JOB$.

Name	Null?	Type
JOB	NOT NULL	NUMBER
LOWNER	NOT NULL	VARCHAR2(30)
POWNER	NOT NULL	VARCHAR2(30)
COWNER	NOT NULL	VARCHAR2(30)
LAST_DATE		DATE
THIS_DATE		DATE
NEXT_DATE	NOT NULL	DATE
TOTAL	NOT NULL	NUMBER
INTERVAL#	NOT NULL	VARCHAR2(200)
FAILURES		NUMBER

```
FLAG                            NOT NULL NUMBER
WHAT                                     VARCHAR2(4000)
NLSENV                                   VARCHAR2(4000)
ENV                                      RAW(32)
CUR_SES_LABEL                            RAW MLSLABEL
CLEARANCE_HI                             RAW MLSLABEL
CLEARANCE_LO                             RAW MLSLABEL
CHARENV                                  VARCHAR2(4000)
FIELD1                                   NUMBER
```

The **KOPM$** table is used internally by Oracle.

Listing A.43   Description of the data dictionary table KOPM$.
```
Name                            Null?    Type
------------------------------- -------- ----
NAME                            NOT NULL VARCHAR2(30)
LENGTH                          NOT NULL NUMBER
METADATA                                 RAW(255)
```

The **LAB$** table is used with Secure Oracle to track **MLSLABEL** values.

Listing A.44   Description of the data dictionary table LAB$.
```
Name                            Null?    Type
------------------------------- -------- ----
LAB#                            NOT NULL RAW MLSLABEL
OLAB                                     RAW(255)
ALIAS#                                   VARCHAR2(30)
```

The **LIBRARY$** table is used to track library objects. Library objects are references
to external locations where DLL libraries are stored. This is used for external procedure calls.

Listing A.45   Description of the data dictionary table LIBRARY$.
```
Name                            Null?    Type
------------------------------- -------- ----
OBJ#                            NOT NULL NUMBER
FILESPEC                                 VARCHAR2(2000)
PROPERTY                                 NUMBER
AUDIT$                          NOT NULL VARCHAR2(38)
```

The **LINK$** table tracks all database links defined for this database.

Listing A.46   Description of the data dictionary table LINK$.

Name	Null?	Type
OWNER#	NOT NULL	NUMBER
NAME	NOT NULL	VARCHAR2(128)
CTIME	NOT NULL	DATE
HOST		VARCHAR2(2000)
USERID		VARCHAR2(30)
PASSWORD		VARCHAR2(30)
FLAG		NUMBER
AUTHUSR		VARCHAR2(30)
AUTHPWD		VARCHAR2(30)

The **LOB$** table tracks all **LOB**s used in the database (**BLOB**, **CLOB**, **NCLOB**, **BFILE**).

Listing A.47   Description of the data dictionary table LOB$.

Name	Null?	Type
OBJ#	NOT NULL	NUMBER
COL#	NOT NULL	NUMBER
INTCOL#	NOT NULL	NUMBER
LOBJ#	NOT NULL	NUMBER
PART#	NOT NULL	NUMBER
IND#	NOT NULL	NUMBER
TS#	NOT NULL	NUMBER
FILE#	NOT NULL	NUMBER
BLOCK#	NOT NULL	NUMBER
CHUNK	NOT NULL	NUMBER
PCTVERSION$	NOT NULL	NUMBER
FLAGS	NOT NULL	NUMBER
PROPERTY	NOT NULL	NUMBER
SPARE1		NUMBER
SPARE2		NUMBER
SPARE3		VARCHAR2(255)

The **METHOD$** table tracks all methods for all **TYPES** used in the database.

Listing A.48   Description of the data dictionary table METHOD$.

Name	Null?	Type
TOID	NOT NULL	RAW(16)
VERSION#	NOT NULL	NUMBER
METHOD#	NOT NULL	NUMBER
NAME	NOT NULL	VARCHAR2(30)
PROPERTIES	NOT NULL	NUMBER

```
PARAMETERS#                          NOT NULL NUMBER
RESULTS                              NOT NULL NUMBER
SPARE1                                        NUMBER
SPARE2                                        NUMBER
SPARE3                                        NUMBER
```

The **MIGRATE$** table is an artifact from the conversion process between Oracle7 and Oracle8 and can be disregarded.

Listing A.49   Description of the data dictionary table MIGRATE$.
```
Name                             Null?     Type
-------------------------------- --------- ----
VERSION#                                   VARCHAR2(30)
MIGDATE                                    DATE
MIGRATED                         NOT NULL  NUMBER
```

The **MLOG$** table tracks the snapshot logs created in this database.

Listing A.50   Description of the data dictionary table MLOG$.
```
Name                             Null?     Type
-------------------------------- --------- ----
MOWNER                           NOT NULL  VARCHAR2(30)
MASTER                           NOT NULL  VARCHAR2(30)
OLDEST                                     DATE
OLDEST_PK                                  DATE
OSCN                                       NUMBER
YOUNGEST                                   DATE
YSCN                                       NUMBER
LOG                              NOT NULL  VARCHAR2(30)
TRIG                                       VARCHAR2(30)
FLAG                                       NUMBER
MTIME                            NOT NULL  DATE
```

The **MLOG_REFCOL$** table tracks the reference columns used by the snapshot logs for this database.

Listing A.51   Description of the data dictionary table MLOG_REFCOL$.
```
Name                             Null?     Type
-------------------------------- --------- ----
MOWNER                           NOT NULL  VARCHAR2(30)
MASTER                           NOT NULL  VARCHAR2(30)
COLNAME                          NOT NULL  VARCHAR2(30)
OLDEST                                     DATE
FLAG                                       NUMBER(38)
```

The **NOEXP$** table is used to flag objects that should not be exported from this database.

Listing A.52 Description of the data dictionary table NOEXP$.

```
Name                            Null?     Type
------------------------------- --------  ----
OWNER                           NOT NULL  VARCHAR2(30)
NAME                            NOT NULL  VARCHAR2(30)
OBJ_TYPE                        NOT NULL  NUMBER
```

The **NTAB$** table tracks nested tables used in this database.

Listing A.53 Description of the data dictionary table NTAB$.

```
Name                            Null?     Type
------------------------------- --------  ----
OBJ#                            NOT NULL  NUMBER
COL#                            NOT NULL  NUMBER
INTCOL#                         NOT NULL  NUMBER
NTAB#                           NOT NULL  NUMBER
NAME                            NOT NULL  VARCHAR2(4000)
```

The **OBJ$** table tracks all objects in the database (tables, views, triggers, procedures, packages, etc.).

Listing A.54 Description of the data dictionary table OBJ$.

```
Name                            Null?     Type
------------------------------- --------  ----
OBJ#                            NOT NULL  NUMBER
DATAOBJ#                                  NUMBER
OWNER#                          NOT NULL  NUMBER
NAME                            NOT NULL  VARCHAR2(30)
NAMESPACE                       NOT NULL  NUMBER
SUBNAME                                   VARCHAR2(30)
TYPE#                           NOT NULL  NUMBER
CTIME                           NOT NULL  DATE
MTIME                           NOT NULL  DATE
STIME                           NOT NULL  DATE
STATUS                          NOT NULL  NUMBER
REMOTEOWNER                               VARCHAR2(30)
LINKNAME                                  VARCHAR2(128)
FLAGS                                     NUMBER
OID$                                      RAW(16)
SPARE1                                    NUMBER
SPARE2                                    NUMBER
SPARE3                                    NUMBER
```

```
SPARE4                           VARCHAR2(1000)
SPARE5                           VARCHAR2(1000)
SPARE6                           DATE
```

The **OBJAUTH$** table tracks all object authorizations (grants) for the database.

Listing A.55   Description of the data dictionary table OBJAUTH$.
```
Name                        Null?     Type
--------------------------- --------  ----
OBJ#                        NOT NULL  NUMBER
GRANTOR#                    NOT NULL  NUMBER
GRANTEE#                    NOT NULL  NUMBER
PRIVILEGE#                  NOT NULL  NUMBER
SEQUENCE#                   NOT NULL  NUMBER
PARENT                                ROWID
OPTION$                               NUMBER
COL#                                  NUMBER
```

The **OBJPRIV$** table maps between the **OBJ$** and the privilege map table.

Listing A.56   Description of the data dictionary table OBJPRIV$.
```
Name                        Null?     Type
--------------------------- --------  ----
OBJ#                        NOT NULL  NUMBER
PRIVILEGE#                  NOT NULL  NUMBER
```

The **OID$** table tracks all object identifiers for the database.

Listing A.57   Description of the data dictionary table OID$.
```
Name                        Null?     Type
--------------------------- --------  ----
USER#                       NOT NULL  NUMBER
OID$                        NOT NULL  RAW(16)
OBJ#                        NOT NULL  NUMBER
```

The **PARAMETER$** table tracks method parameters used in type methods.

Listing A.58   Description of the data dictionary table PARAMETER$.
```
Name                        Null?     Type
--------------------------- --------  ----
TOID                        NOT NULL  RAW(16)
VERSION#                    NOT NULL  NUMBER
METHOD#                     NOT NULL  NUMBER
NAME                        NOT NULL  VARCHAR2(30)
PARAMETER#                  NOT NULL  NUMBER
PARAM_TOID                  NOT NULL  RAW(16)
```

```
PARAM_VERSION#                  NOT NULL NUMBER
PROPERTIES                      NOT NULL NUMBER
CHARSETID                                NUMBER
CHARSETFORM                              NUMBER
DEFAULT$                                 VARCHAR2(4000)
SPARE1                                   NUMBER
SPARE2                                   NUMBER
SPARE3                                   NUMBER
```

The **PARTCOL$** table tracks the partitioning columns for partitioned tables.

Listing A.59 Description of the data dictionary table PARTCOL$.

```
Name                            Null?    Type
------------------------------- -------- ----
OBJ#                            NOT NULL NUMBER
INTCOL#                         NOT NULL NUMBER
COL#                            NOT NULL NUMBER
POS#                            NOT NULL NUMBER
SPARE1                                   NUMBER
```

The **PARTOBJ$** table tracks all partitioned objects in the database.

Listing A.60 Description of the data dictionary table PARTOBJ$.

```
Name                            Null?    Type
------------------------------- -------- ----
OBJ#                            NOT NULL NUMBER
PARTTYPE                        NOT NULL NUMBER
PARTCNT                         NOT NULL NUMBER
PARTKEYCOLS                     NOT NULL NUMBER
FLAGS                                    NUMBER
DEFTS#                          NOT NULL NUMBER
DEFPCTFREE                      NOT NULL NUMBER
DEFPCTUSED                      NOT NULL NUMBER
DEFPCTTHRES                              NUMBER
DEFINITRANS                     NOT NULL NUMBER
DEFMAXTRANS                     NOT NULL NUMBER
DEFTINIEXTS                     NOT NULL NUMBER
DEFEXTSIZE                      NOT NULL NUMBER
DEFMINEXTS                      NOT NULL NUMBER
DEFMAXEXTS                      NOT NULL NUMBER
DEFEXTPCT                       NOT NULL NUMBER
DEFLISTS                        NOT NULL NUMBER
DEFGROUPS                       NOT NULL NUMBER
DEFLOGGING                      NOT NULL NUMBER
SPARE1                                   NUMBER
SPARE2                                   NUMBER
SPARE3                                   NUMBER
DEFINCLCOL                               NUMBER
```

The **PENDING_SESSIONS$** table is used for distributed transaction monitoring.

Listing A.61 Description of the data dictionary table PENDING_SESSIONS$.

Name	Null?	Type
LOCAL_TRAN_ID	NOT NULL	VARCHAR2(22)
SESSION_ID	NOT NULL	NUMBER(38)
BRANCH_ID	NOT NULL	RAW(64)
INTERFACE	NOT NULL	VARCHAR2(1)
TYPE#		NUMBER
PARENT_DBID		VARCHAR2(16)
PARENT_DB		VARCHAR2(128)
DB_USERID	NOT NULL	NUMBER(38)

The **PENDING_SUB_SESIONS$** table tracks distributed transactions.

Listing A.62 Description of the data dictionary table PENDING_SUB_ SESSIONS$.

Name	Null?	Type
LOCAL_TRAN_ID	NOT NULL	VARCHAR2(22)
SESSION_ID	NOT NULL	NUMBER(38)
SUB_SESSION_ID	NOT NULL	NUMBER(38)
INTERFACE	NOT NULL	VARCHAR2(1)
DBID	NOT NULL	VARCHAR2(16)
LINK_OWNER	NOT NULL	NUMBER(38)
DBLINK	NOT NULL	VARCHAR2(128)
BRANCH_ID		RAW(64)
SPARE		RAW(64)

The **PENDING_TRANS$** table tracks distributed transactions in the database.

Listing A.63 Description of the data dictionary table PENDING_TRANS$.

Name	Null?	Type
LOCAL_TRAN_ID	NOT NULL	VARCHAR2(22)
GLOBAL_TRAN_FMT	NOT NULL	NUMBER(38)
GLOBAL_ORACLE_ID		VARCHAR2(64)
GLOBAL_FOREIGN_ID		RAW(64)
TRAN_COMMENT		VARCHAR2(2000)
STATE	NOT NULL	VARCHAR2(16)
STATUS	NOT NULL	VARCHAR2(1)
HEURISTIC_DFLT		VARCHAR2(1)
SESSION_VECTOR	NOT NULL	RAW(4)
RECO_VECTOR	NOT NULL	RAW(4)
TYPE#		NUMBER

```
FAIL_TIME                        NOT NULL DATE
HEURISTIC_TIME                            DATE
RECO_TIME                        NOT NULL DATE
TOP_DB_USER                               VARCHAR2(30)
TOP_OS_USER                               VARCHAR2(2000)
TOP_OS_HOST                               VARCHAR2(2000)
TOP_OS_TERMINAL                           VARCHAR2(2000)
GLOBAL_COMMIT#                            VARCHAR2(16)
SPARE1                                    NUMBER
SPARE2                                    VARCHAR2(30)
SPARE3                                    NUMBER
SPARE4                                    VARCHAR2(30)
```

The **PROCEDURE$** table is used to track all stored procedures in the database.

Listing A.64   Description of the data dictionary table PROCEDURE$.

```
Name                             Null?    Type
-------------------------------  -------- ----
OBJ#                             NOT NULL NUMBER
AUDIT$                           NOT NULL VARCHAR2(38)
STORAGESIZE                               NUMBER
OPTIONS                                   NUMBER
```

The **PROFILE$** table tracks the resource limits for all profiles in the database.

Listing A.65   Description of the data dictionary table PROFILE$.

```
Name                             Null?    Type
-------------------------------  -------- ----
PROFILE#                         NOT NULL NUMBER
RESOURCE#                        NOT NULL NUMBER
TYPE#                            NOT NULL NUMBER
LIMIT#                           NOT NULL NUMBER
```

The **PROFNAME$** table is used to store the map between profile number and profile name for the database.

Listing A.66   Description of the data dictionary table PROFNAME$.

```
Name                             Null?    Type
-------------------------------  -------- ----
PROFILE#                         NOT NULL NUMBER
NAME                             NOT NULL VARCHAR2(30)
```

The **PROPS$** table is used to track National Language Support (NLS) values for the database.

Listing A.67 Description of the data dictionary table PROPS$.

Name	Null?	Type
NAME	NOT NULL	VARCHAR2(30)
VALUE$		VARCHAR2(4000)
COMMENT$		VARCHAR2(4000)

PSTUBTBL is used for Oracle Forms 3 client activity.

Listing A.68 Description of the data dictionary table PSTUBTBL.

Name	Null?	Type
USERNAME		VARCHAR2(30)
DBNAME		VARCHAR2(128)
LUN		VARCHAR2(30)
LUTYPE		VARCHAR2(3)
LINENO		NUMBER
LINE		VARCHAR2(1800)

The **REFCON$** table tracks the referential constraints in the database.

Listing A.69 Description of the data dictionary table REFCON$.

Name	Null?	Type
OBJ#	NOT NULL	NUMBER
COL#	NOT NULL	NUMBER
INTCOL#	NOT NULL	NUMBER
REFTYP	NOT NULL	NUMBER
STABID		RAW(16)

The **REG_SNAP$** table is used to track the registered snapshots for this database.

Listing A.70 Description of the data dictionary table REG_SNAP$.

Name	Null?	Type
SOWNER	NOT NULL	VARCHAR2(30)
SNAPNAME	NOT NULL	VARCHAR2(30)
SNAPSITE	NOT NULL	VARCHAR2(128)
SNAPSHOT_ID		NUMBER(38)
FLAG		NUMBER
REP_TYPE		NUMBER
COMMENT$		VARCHAR2(4000)
QUERY_TXT		LONG

The **RESOURCE_COST$** table is used to track the defined resource cost values for profiles used in this database.

Listing A.71 Description of the data dictionary table RESOURCE_COST$.

```
Name                                Null?     Type
------------------------------      --------  ----
RESOURCE#                           NOT NULL  NUMBER
COST                                NOT NULL  NUMBER
```

The **RESOURCE_MAP** table maps the reference number for a resource to its name for use with profiles in this database.

Listing A.72 Description of the data dictionary table RESOURCE_MAP.

```
Name                                Null?     Type
------------------------------      --------  ----
RESOURCE#                           NOT NULL  NUMBER
TYPE#                               NOT NULL  NUMBER
NAME                                NOT NULL  VARCHAR2(32)
```

The **RESULT$** table is used to track results returned by methods in user-defined types for this database.

Listing A.73 Description of the data dictionary table RESULT$.

```
Name                                Null?     Type
------------------------------      --------  ----
TOID                                NOT NULL  RAW(16)
VERSION#                            NOT NULL  NUMBER
METHOD#                             NOT NULL  NUMBER
RESULT#                             NOT NULL  NUMBER
RESULT_TOID                         NOT NULL  RAW(16)
RESULT_VERSION#                     NOT NULL  NUMBER
PROPERTIES                          NOT NULL  NUMBER
CHARSETID                                     NUMBER
CHARSETFORM                                   NUMBER
SPARE1                                        NUMBER
SPARE2                                        NUMBER
SPARE3                                        NUMBER
```

The **RGCHILD$** table is used by the refresh group process to determine which objects (snap_shots) should be refreshed with which refresh group.

Listing A.74 Description of the data dictionary table RGCHILD$.

```
Name                                Null?     Type
------------------------------      --------  ----
OWNER                               NOT NULL  VARCHAR2(30)
NAME                                NOT NULL  VARCHAR2(30)
TYPE#                                         VARCHAR2(30)
FIELD1                                        NUMBER
REFGROUP                                      NUMBER
```

The **RGROUP$** table is used to track refresh groups for snapshots used in this database.

Listing A.75   Description of the data dictionary table RGROUP$.

```
Name                                Null?     Type
---------------------------------   --------  ----
REFGROUP                                      NUMBER
OWNER                               NOT NULL  VARCHAR2(30)
NAME                               NOT NULL  VARCHAR2(30)
FLAG                                          NUMBER
ROLLBACK_SEG                                  VARCHAR2(30)
FIELD1                                        NUMBER
JOB                                NOT NULL  NUMBER
```

The **SEG$** table is used to track all segments in the database. Segments are maps to the physical disk areas for the objects contained in datafiles.

Listing A.76   Description of the data dictionary table SEG$.

```
Name                                Null?     Type
---------------------------------   --------  ----
FILE#                              NOT NULL  NUMBER
BLOCK#                             NOT NULL  NUMBER
TYPE#                              NOT NULL  NUMBER
TS#                                NOT NULL  NUMBER
BLOCKS                             NOT NULL  NUMBER
EXTENTS                            NOT NULL  NUMBER
INIEXTS                            NOT NULL  NUMBER
MINEXTS                            NOT NULL  NUMBER
MAXEXTS                            NOT NULL  NUMBER
EXTSIZE                            NOT NULL  NUMBER
EXTPCT                             NOT NULL  NUMBER
USER#                              NOT NULL  NUMBER
LISTS                                         NUMBER
GROUPS                                        NUMBER
BITMAPRANGES                       NOT NULL  NUMBER
CACHEHINT                          NOT NULL  NUMBER
SCANHINT                           NOT NULL  NUMBER
HWMINCR                            NOT NULL  NUMBER
SPARE1                                        NUMBER
SPARE2                                        NUMBER
```

The **SEQ$** table contains information on all sequences defined in the database.

Listing A.77 Description of the data dictionary table SEQ$.

Name	Null?	Type
OBJ#	NOT NULL	NUMBER
INCREMENT$	NOT NULL	NUMBER
MINVALUE		NUMBER
MAXVALUE		NUMBER
CYCLE#	NOT NULL	NUMBER
ORDER$	NOT NULL	NUMBER
CACHE	NOT NULL	NUMBER
HIGHWATER	NOT NULL	NUMBER
AUDIT$	NOT NULL	VARCHAR2(38)

The **SLOG$** table contains data on all snapshot logs in the database.

Listing A.78 Description of the data dictionary table SLOG$.

Name	Null?	Type
MOWNER	NOT NULL	VARCHAR2(30)
MASTER	NOT NULL	VARCHAR2(30)
SNAPSHOT		DATE
SNAPID		NUMBER(38)
SSCN		NUMBER
SNAPTIME	NOT NULL	DATE
TSCN		NUMBER
USER#		NUMBER

The **SNAP$** table contains information on all snapshots defined in the database.

Listing A.79 Description of the data dictionary table SNAP$.

Name	Null?	Type
SOWNER	NOT NULL	VARCHAR2(30)
VNAME	NOT NULL	VARCHAR2(30)
TNAME	NOT NULL	VARCHAR2(30)
MVIEW		VARCHAR2(30)
MOWNER		VARCHAR2(30)
MASTER		VARCHAR2(30)
MLINK		VARCHAR2(128)
CAN_USE_LOG		VARCHAR2(1)
SNAPSHOT		DATE
SNAPID		NUMBER(38)
SSCN		NUMBER
SNAPTIME		DATE
TSCN		NUMBER
ERROR#		NUMBER
AUTO_FAST		VARCHAR2(1)

```
AUTO_FUN                              VARCHAR2(200)
AUTO_DATE                             DATE
REFGROUP                              NUMBER
USTRG                                 VARCHAR2(30)
USLOG                                 VARCHAR2(30)
STATUS                                NUMBER(38)
MASTER_VERSION                        NUMBER(38)
TABLES                                NUMBER(38)
FIELD1                                NUMBER
FIELD2                                VARCHAR2(30)
FLAG                                  NUMBER
QUERY_TXT                             LONG
LOBMASKVEC                            RAW(255)
MTIME                        NOT NULL DATE
MAS_ROLL_SEG                          VARCHAR2(30)
```

The **SNAP_COLMAP$** table maps columns to snapshots for all snapshots in the database.

Listing A.80   Description of the data dictionary table SNAP_COLMAP$.

Name	Null?	Type
SOWNER	NOT NULL	VARCHAR2(30)
VNAME	NOT NULL	VARCHAR2(30)
SNACOL	NOT NULL	VARCHAR2(30)
TABNUM	NOT NULL	NUMBER(38)
MASCOL		VARCHAR2(30)
MASPOS		NUMBER(38)
COLROLE		NUMBER

The **SNAP_REFOP$** table contains information on all snapshot refresh operations in the current database.

Listing A.81   Description of the data dictionary table SNAP_REFOP$.

Name	Null?	Type
SOWNER	NOT NULL	VARCHAR2(30)
VNAME	NOT NULL	VARCHAR2(30)
TABNUM	NOT NULL	NUMBER(38)
OPERATION#	NOT NULL	NUMBER(38)
COLS		NUMBER
FCMASKVEC		RAW(255)
EJMASKVEC		RAW(255)
SQL_TXT		LONG

The **SNAP_REFTIME$** table contains information on all snapshot refresh times for the database.

Listing A.82 Description of the data dictionary table SNAP_REFTIME$.

Name	Null?	Type
SOWNER	NOT NULL	VARCHAR2(30)
VNAME	NOT NULL	VARCHAR2(30)
TABLENUM	NOT NULL	NUMBER(38)
SNAPTIME		DATE
MOWNER		VARCHAR2(30)
MASTER		VARCHAR2(30)

The **SOURCE$** table contains the source code for stored objects in this database.

Listing A.83 Description of the data dictionary table SOURCE$.

Name	Null?	Type
OBJ#	NOT NULL	NUMBER
LINE	NOT NULL	NUMBER
SOURCE		VARCHAR2(4000)

STMT_AUDIT_OPTION_MAP contains the map from **OPTION#** values used in other data dictionary tables to the actual name of the audit option.

Listing A.84 Description of the data dictionary table STMT_AUDIT_ OPTION_MAP.

Name	Null?	Type
OPTION#	NOT NULL	NUMBER
NAME	NOT NULL	VARCHAR2(40)

The **SYN$** table maps database **SYNONYM**s back to their source objects.

Listing A.85 Description of the data dictionary table SYN$.

Name	Null?	Type
OBJ#	NOT NULL	NUMBER
NODE		VARCHAR2(128)
OWNER		VARCHAR2(30)
NAME	NOT NULL	VARCHAR2(30)

The **SYSAUTH$** table contains information on system-level **GRANT**s.

Listing A.86 Description of the data dictionary table SYSAUTH$.

Name	Null?	Type
GRANTEE#	NOT NULL	NUMBER
PRIVILEGE#	NOT NULL	NUMBER
SEQUENCE#	NOT NULL	NUMBER
OPTION$		NUMBER

SYSTEM_PRIVILEGE_MAP contains mapping from the **PRIVILEGE** number value used in other data dictionary tables to the actual privilege name.

Listing A.87 Description of the data dictionary table SYSTEM_PRIVILEGE_MAP.

Name	Null?	Type
PRIVILEGE	NOT NULL	NUMBER
NAME	NOT NULL	VARCHAR2(40)

The **TAB$** table contains information about all **TABLE**s in the database.

Listing A.88 Description of the data dictionary table TAB$.

Name	Null?	Type
OBJ#	NOT NULL	NUMBER
DATAOBJ#		NUMBER
TS#	NOT NULL	NUMBER
FILE#	NOT NULL	NUMBER
BLOCK#	NOT NULL	NUMBER
BOBJ#		NUMBER
TAB#		NUMBER
COLS	NOT NULL	NUMBER
CLUCOLS		NUMBER
PCTFREE$	NOT NULL	NUMBER
PCTUSED$	NOT NULL	NUMBER
INITRANS	NOT NULL	NUMBER
MAXTRANS	NOT NULL	NUMBER
FLAGS	NOT NULL	NUMBER
AUDIT$	NOT NULL	VARCHAR2(38)
ROWCNT		NUMBER
BLKCNT		NUMBER
EMPCNT		NUMBER
AVGSPC		NUMBER
CHNCNT		NUMBER
AVGRLN		NUMBER
AVGSPC_FLB		NUMBER
FLBCNT		NUMBER

```
ANALYZETIME                              DATE
SAMPLESIZE                               NUMBER
DEGREE                                   NUMBER
INSTANCES                                NUMBER
INTCOLS                         NOT NULL NUMBER
KERNELCOLS                      NOT NULL NUMBER
PROPERTY                        NOT NULL NUMBER
TRIGFLAG                                 NUMBER
SPARE1                                   NUMBER
SPARE2                                   NUMBER
SPARE3                                   NUMBER
SPARE4                                   VARCHAR2(1000)
SPARE5                                   VARCHAR2(1000)
SPARE6                                   DATE
```

The **TABLE_PRIVILEGE_MAP** table maps the table privilege number back to the actual privilege name for table privileges used in other data dictionary tables.

Listing A.89   Description of the data dictionary table TABLE_ PRIVILEGE_MAP.

```
Name                            Null?    Type
------------------------------- -------- ----
PRIVILEGE                       NOT NULL NUMBER
NAME                            NOT NULL VARCHAR2(40)
```

The **TABPART$** table stores information concerning all partitioned table partitions in the database.

Listing A.90   Description of the data dictionary table TABPART$.

```
Name                            Null?    Type
------------------------------- -------- ----
OBJ#                            NOT NULL NUMBER
DATAOBJ#                        NOT NULL NUMBER
BO#                             NOT NULL NUMBER
PART#                           NOT NULL NUMBER
HIBOUNDLEN                      NOT NULL NUMBER
HIBOUNDVAL                               LONG
TS#                             NOT NULL NUMBER
FILE#                           NOT NULL NUMBER
BLOCK#                          NOT NULL NUMBER
PCTFREE$                        NOT NULL NUMBER
PCTUSED$                        NOT NULL NUMBER
INITRANS                        NOT NULL NUMBER
MAXTRANS                        NOT NULL NUMBER
FLAGS                           NOT NULL NUMBER
ANALYZETIME                              DATE
```

```
SAMPLESIZE                          NUMBER
ROWCNT                              NUMBER
BLKCNT                             NUMBER
EMPCNT                            NUMBER
AVGSPC                          NUMBER
CHNCNT                         NUMBER
AVGRLN                        NUMBER
SPARE1                       NUMBER
SPARE2                      NUMBER
SPARE3                      NUMBER
```

The **TRIGGER$** table contains information about all **TRIGGER**s built in this database.

Listing A.91   Description of the data dictionary table TRIGGER$.

```
Name                            Null?      Type
------------------------------- --------   ----

OBJ#                            NOT NULL NUMBER
TYPE#                           NOT NULL NUMBER
UPDATE$                         NOT NULL NUMBER
INSERT$                         NOT NULL NUMBER
DELETE$                         NOT NULL NUMBER
BASEOBJECT                      NOT NULL NUMBER
REFOLDNAME                               VARCHAR2(30)
REFNEWNAME                               VARCHAR2(30)
DEFINITION                               VARCHAR2(4000)
WHENCLAUSE                               VARCHAR2(4000)
ACTION#                                  LONG
ACTIONSIZE                               NUMBER
ENABLED                                  NUMBER
PROPERTY                        NOT NULL NUMBER
```

The **TRIGGERCOL$** table contains data on all columns that have triggers in the database. A join between **TRIGGER$** and **TRIGGERCOL$** is required to produce complete information about a trigger.

Listing A.92   Description of the data dictionary table TRIGGERCOL$.

```
Name                            Null?      Type
------------------------------- --------   ----

OBJ#                            NOT NULL NUMBER
COL#                            NOT NULL NUMBER
TYPE#                           NOT NULL NUMBER
POSITION#                                NUMBER
INTCOL#                         NOT NULL NUMBER
```

The **TRUSTED_LIST$** table is used in Secure Oracle to establish a list of trusted users.

Listing A.93 Description of the data dictionary table TRUSTED_LIST$.

```
Name                                  Null?    Type
------------------------------------  -------- ----
DBNAME                                NOT NULL VARCHAR2(128)
USERNAME                              NOT NULL VARCHAR2(4000)
```

The **TS$** table contains information about all tablespaces for this database.

Listing A.94 Description of the data dictionary table TS$.

```
Name                                  Null?    Type
------------------------------------  -------- ----
TS#                                   NOT NULL NUMBER
NAME                                  NOT NULL VARCHAR2(30)
OWNER#                                NOT NULL NUMBER
ONLINE$                               NOT NULL NUMBER
CONTENTS$                             NOT NULL NUMBER
UNDOFILE#                                      NUMBER
UNDOBLOCK#                                     NUMBER
BLOCKSIZE                             NOT NULL NUMBER
INC#                                  NOT NULL NUMBER
SCNWRP                                         NUMBER
SCNBAS                                         NUMBER
DFLMINEXT                             NOT NULL NUMBER
DFLMAXEXT                             NOT NULL NUMBER
DFLINIT                              NOT NULL NUMBER
DFLINCR                              NOT NULL NUMBER
DFLMINLEN                            NOT NULL NUMBER
DFLEXTPCT                            NOT NULL NUMBER
DFLOGGING                            NOT NULL NUMBER
AFFSTRENGTH                          NOT NULL NUMBER
BITMAPPED                            NOT NULL NUMBER
PLUGGED                              NOT NULL NUMBER
DIRECTALLOWED                        NOT NULL NUMBER
FLAGS                                NOT NULL NUMBER
PITRSCNWRP                                     NUMBER
PITRSCNBAS                                     NUMBER
OWNERINSTANCE                                  VARCHAR2(30)
BACKUPOWNER                                    VARCHAR2(30)
GROUPNAME                                      VARCHAR2(30)
SPARE1                                         NUMBER
SPARE2                                         NUMBER
SPARE3                                         VARCHAR2(1000)
SPARE4                                         DATE
```

The **TSQ$** table contains information on all quota grants made on tablespaces to users in this database.

Listing A.95   Description of the data dictionary table TSQ$.

Name	Null?	Type
TS#	NOT NULL	NUMBER
USER#	NOT NULL	NUMBER
GRANTOR#	NOT NULL	NUMBER
BLOCKS	NOT NULL	NUMBER
MAXBLOCKS		NUMBER
PRIV1	NOT NULL	NUMBER
PRIV2	NOT NULL	NUMBER
PRIV3	NOT NULL	NUMBER

The **TYPE$** table contains information on all user-defined **TYPE**s in the database.

Listing A.96   Description of the data dictionary table TYPE$.

Name	Null?	Type
TOID	NOT NULL	RAW(16)
VERSION#	NOT NULL	NUMBER
VERSION	NOT NULL	VARCHAR2(30)
TVOID	NOT NULL	RAW(16)
TYPECODE	NOT NULL	NUMBER
PROPERTIES	NOT NULL	NUMBER
ATTRIBUTES		NUMBER
METHODS		NUMBER
SUPERTYPES		NUMBER
SUBTYPES		NUMBER
SPARE1		NUMBER
SPARE2		NUMBER
SPARE3		NUMBER

The **TYPED_VIEW$** table contains information about object view generated pseudo-OIDs for this database.

Listing A.97   Description of the data dictionary table TYPED_VIEW$.

Name	Null?	Type
OBJ#	NOT NULL	NUMBER
TYPEOWNER		VARCHAR2(30)
TYPENAME		VARCHAR2(30)
TYPETEXTLENGTH		NUMBER
TYPETEXT		VARCHAR2(4000)
OIDTEXTLENGTH		NUMBER

```
OIDTEXT                         VARCHAR2(4000)
TRANSTEXTLENGTH                 NUMBER
TRANSTEXT                       LONG
```

The **TYPE_MISC$** is used to store type-miscellaneous information, such as the auditing information.

Listing A.98   Description of the data dictionary table TYPE_MISC$.

Name	Null?	Type
OBJ#	NOT NULL	NUMBER
AUDIT$	NOT NULL	VARCHAR2(38)
PROPERTIES	NOT NULL	NUMBER

The **UET$** table contains information on all of the used extents in the database. Its opposite is the **FET$** table, which contains information on the free extents in the database.

Listing A.99   Description of the data dictionary table UET$.

Name	Null?	Type
SEGFILE#	NOT NULL	NUMBER
SEGBLOCK#	NOT NULL	NUMBER
EXT#	NOT NULL	NUMBER
TS#	NOT NULL	NUMBER
FILE#	NOT NULL	NUMBER
BLOCK#	NOT NULL	NUMBER
LENGTH	NOT NULL	NUMBER

The **UGROUP$** table is used to group rollback segments (U=UNDO=ROLLBACK). This may be used for parallel server or maybe future enhancement to allow specification of rollback segment groups. For normal 8.0.3 databases, it doesn't seem to be used.

Listing A.100   Description of the data dictionary table UGROUP$.

Name	Null?	Type
UGRP#	NOT NULL	NUMBER
NAME	NOT NULL	VARCHAR2(30)
SEQ#		NUMBER
SPARE1		NUMBER
SPARE2		VARCHAR2(30)
SPARE3		NUMBER

The **UNDO$** table is used to store data about the **ROLLBACK SEGMENT**s (UNDO=ROLLBACK) for this database.

Listing A.101 Description of the data dictionary table UNDO$.

Name	Null?	Type
US#	NOT NULL	NUMBER
NAME	NOT NULL	VARCHAR2(30)
USER#	NOT NULL	NUMBER
FILE#	NOT NULL	NUMBER
BLOCK#	NOT NULL	NUMBER
SCNBAS		NUMBER
SCNWRP		NUMBER
XACTSQN		NUMBER
UNDOSQN		NUMBER
INST#		NUMBER
STATUS$	NOT NULL	NUMBER
TS#		NUMBER
UGRP#		NUMBER
KEEP		NUMBER
OPTIMAL		NUMBER
FLAGS		NUMBER
SPARE1		NUMBER
SPARE2		NUMBER
SPARE3		NUMBER
SPARE4		VARCHAR2(1000)
SPARE5		VARCHAR2(1000)
SPARE6		DATE

The **USER$** table stores information about all **USER**s for this database. The password for all users is stored in encrypted form, but it can still be used for DBA work by using the **VALUES** clause of the **ALTER** or **CREATE USER** commands. For example, if you want to use another account and are in a privileged account, save the value of the users' current encrypted password, reset the pasword to something you can remember, and use the account. Then, use the **ALTER USER x IDENTIFIED BY VALUES** "encrypted value"; command to reset the password back to the original encrypted value.

Listing A.102 Description of the data dictionary table USER$.

Name	Null?	Type
USER#	NOT NULL	NUMBER
NAME	NOT NULL	VARCHAR2(30)
TYPE#	NOT NULL	NUMBER
PASSWORD		VARCHAR2(30)

```
DATATS#                         NOT NULL NUMBER
TEMPTS#                         NOT NULL NUMBER
CTIME                           NOT NULL DATE
PTIME                                    DATE
EXPTIME                                  DATE
LTIME                                    DATE
RESOURCE$                       NOT NULL NUMBER
AUDIT$                                   VARCHAR2(38)
DEFROLE                         NOT NULL NUMBER
DEFGRP#                                  NUMBER
DEFGRP_SEQ#                              NUMBER
ASTATUS                         NOT NULL NUMBER
LCOUNT                          NOT NULL NUMBER
DEFSCHCLASS                              VARCHAR2(30)
EXT_USERNAME                             VARCHAR2(4000)
SPARE1                                   NUMBER
SPARE2                                   NUMBER
SPARE3                                   NUMBER
SPARE4                                   VARCHAR2(1000)
SPARE5                                   VARCHAR2(1000)
SPARE6                                   DATE
```

The **USER_ASTATUS_MAP** table stores the relationship betweeen a user's status numeric value and the actual status name value. The concept of user status is new with Oracle8 and is used only if you enable password checking via resources and profiles.

Listing A.103   Description of the data dictionary table USER_ASTATUS_MAP.

```
Name                              Null?    Type
--------------------------------  -------- ----
STATUS#                           NOT NULL NUMBER
STATUS                            NOT NULL VARCHAR2(32)
```

The **USER_HISTORY$** table stores information about a user's password history. This table is used only if password checking is enabled through resources and profiles.

Listing A.104   Description of the data dictionary table USER_HISTORY$.

```
Name                              Null?    Type
--------------------------------  -------- ----
USER#                             NOT NULL NUMBER
PASSWORD                                   VARCHAR2(30)
PASSWORD_DATE                              DATE
```

The **VIEW$** table tracks information about all **VIEW**s in the database. By selecting the maximum value of the text length variable, you can find out where to set your long value for view reports (**SET LONG** in SQL*Plus). A bad long setting will result in truncated output of the **TEXT** field.

Listing A.105 Description of the data dictionary table VIEW$.

```
Name                              Null?     Type
-------------------------------   --------  ----
OBJ#                              NOT NULL  NUMBER
AUDIT$                            NOT NULL  VARCHAR2(38)
COLS                             NOT NULL  NUMBER
INTCOLS                          NOT NULL  NUMBER
PROPERTY                         NOT NULL  NUMBER
FLAGS                            NOT NULL  NUMBER
TEXTLENGTH                                 NUMBER
TEXT                                       LONG
```

The "**_default_auditing_options_**" table stores the default auditing option designator for the database. To describe or **SELECT** from this table, you must enclose the name in double quotes because the underscore is not a normally allowed name character in Oracle.

Listing A.106 Description of the data dictionary table _default_auditing_ options_.

```
Name                              Null?     Type
-------------------------------   --------  ----
A                                          VARCHAR2(1)
```

The Dynamic Performance Tables (**GV$** Views Of The **GV_$** Fixed Views)

In the beginning, there were just the **V_$** dynamic performance tables (DPTs) and their views, the **V$** views. In Oracle8, the **V_$** DPTs were usurped from their top position by the **GV_$** DPTs. The major difference between the two is that the **GV_$** DPTs contain the instance number for situations where Oracle Parallel Server is in use. The **V_$** tables have been replaced by instance-specific views that extract the applicable entries for the current instance only. The **GV$** views are views made against the **GV_$** DPTs to allow the granting of permissions (permissions cannot be granted against the fixed views). The **V$** views are views based on the **V_$** views.

Based directly (in most cases) on the **K** and **X$** C language strucs that are the foundation for the Oracle data dictionary, the **GV$** views (actually views on the **GV_$** DPTs) are dynamic (they reflect the current state of these structures, not just a snapshot of historical data) in nature and are used for statistical monitoring of the database and process state.

The **V_$** and **V$** views are subsets of the **GV$** views stripped for one instance (the current) only. For single-instance databases, the data in both **GV$** and **V$** tables of the same name should be identical except that the **GV$** tables will have an extra instance number field. I will not show the definitions for **GV_$**, **V_$**, or **V$** views, because this data would be redundant.

The **GV$ACCESS** DPT reflects the currently used objects that have locks in the database.

Listing A.107 Description of the data dictionary dynamic performance table GV$ACCESS.

```
Name                             Null?     Type
-------------------------------- --------  ----
INST_ID                                    NUMBER
SID                                        NUMBER
OWNER                                      VARCHAR2(64)
OBJECT                                     VARCHAR2(1000)
TYPE                                       VARCHAR2(12)

GV$ACCESS            select distinct s.inst_id,s.ksusenum,o.kglnaown,o.kglnaobj,
                     decode(o.kglobtyp,
                       0, 'CURSOR', 1, 'INDEX', 2, 'TABLE', 3, 'CLUSTER',
                       4, 'VIEW', 5, 'SYNONYM', 6, 'SEQUENCE', 7, 'PROCEDURE',
                       8, 'FUNCTION', 9, 'PACKAGE', 10,'NON-EXISTENT', 11,'PACKAGE
BODY',
                     12,'TRIGGER', 13,'CLASS', 14,'SET', 15,'OBJECT', 16,'USER',
                     17,'DBLINK', 'INVALID TYPE') from x$ksuse
                     s,x$kglob o,x$kgldp d,x$kgllk l where l.kgllkuse=s.addr and
                     l.kgllkhdl=d.kglhdadr and l.kglnahsh=d.kglnahsh and
                     o.kglnahsh=d.kglrfhsh and o.kglhdadr=d.kglrfhdl
```

The **GV$ACTIVE_INSTANCES** table shows which instances for a parallel instance setup are currently active (not used for nonparallel server installations).

Listing A.108 Description of the dynamic performance table GV$ACTIVE_ INSTANCES.

```
Name                             Null?     Type
-------------------------------- --------  ----
INST_ID                                    NUMBER
INST_NUMBER                                NUMBER
INST_NAME                                  VARCHAR2(60)

GV$ACTIVE_INSTANCES   select inst_id, ksiminum, rpad(ksimstr,60) from x$ksimsi
```

The **GV$ARCHIVE** DPT shows the current status of the archive logs.

Listing A.109 **Description of the data dictionary dynamic performance table GV$ARCHIVE.**

Name	Null?	Type
INST_ID		NUMBER
GROUP#		NUMBER
THREAD#		NUMBER
SEQUENCE#		NUMBER
CURRENT		VARCHAR2(3)
FIRST_CHANGE#		NUMBER

```
GV$ARCHIVE        select le.inst_id,le.lenum,le.lethr,le.leseq,
                  decode(bitand(le.leflg,8),0,'NO','YES'),to_number(le.lelos)
                  from x$kccle le,x$kccdi di where bitand(di.diflg,1)!=0 and
                  le.ledup!=0 and bitand(le.leflg,1)=0 and
                  (to_number(le.lelos)<=to_number(di.difas) or
                  bitand(le.leflg,8)=0)
```

The **GV$ARCHIVED_LOG** DPT shows the current status of all archived redo logs.

Listing A.110 **Description of the data dictionary dynamic performance table GV$ARCHIVED_LOG.**

Name	Null?	Type
INST_ID		NUMBER
RECID		NUMBER
STAMP		NUMBER
NAME		VARCHAR2(513)
THREAD#		NUMBER
SEQUENCE#		NUMBER
RESETLOGS_CHANGE#		NUMBER
RESETLOGS_TIME		DATE
FIRST_CHANGE#		NUMBER
FIRST_TIME		DATE
NEXT_CHANGE#		NUMBER
NEXT_TIME		DATE
BLOCKS		NUMBER
BLOCK_SIZE		NUMBER
ARCHIVED		VARCHAR2(3)
DELETED		VARCHAR2(3)
COMPLETION_TIME		DATE

```
GV$ARCHIVED_LOG      select
                     inst_id,alrid,alstm,alnam,althp,alseq,to_number(alrls),
                     to_date(alrlc,'MM/DD/RR HH24:MI:SS'), to_number(allos),
```

```
to_date(allot,'MM/DD/RR HH24:MI:SS'), to_number(alnxs),
to_date(alnxt,'MM/DD/RR HH24:MI:SS'),albct,albsz,
decode(bitand(alflg, 2) ,0,'NO','YES'),
decode(bitand(alflg,1),0,'NO','YES'),
to_date(altsm,'MM/DD/RR HH24:MI:SS')from
x$kccal
```

The **GV$ARCHIVE_DEST** table shows the current location where archived logs are written.

Listing A.111   Description of the data dictionary dynamic performance table GV$ARCHIVE_DEST.

Name	Null?	Type
INST_ID		NUMBER
ARCMODE		VARCHAR2(12)
STATUS		VARCHAR2(8)
DESTINATION		VARCHAR2(256)

```
GV$ARCHIVE_DEST       select inst_id, decode(kcrrdmod,1,'MUST
                      SUCCEED',2,'BEST-EFFORT'),
                      decode(kcrrdsta,1,'NORMAL',2,'DISABLED'),kcrrdest from
                      x$kcrrdest
```

The **GV$BACKUP** DPT gives the current backup status for all files in the database instance identified by the specific instance number.

Listing A.112   Description of the data dictionary dynamic performance table GV$BACKUP.

Name	Null?	Type
INST_ID		NUMBER
FILE#		NUMBER
STATUS		VARCHAR2(18)
CHANGE#		NUMBER
TIME		DATE

```
GV$BACKUP             select inst_id,hxfil,
                      decode(hxerr, 0,decode(bitand(fhsta,1),
                      0,'NOT ACTIVE','ACTIVE'),
                      1,'FILE MISSING',
                      2,'OFFLINE NORMAL',
                      3,'NOT VERIFIED',
                      4,'FILE NOT FOUND',
                      5,'CANNOT OPEN FILE',
                      6,'CANNOT READ HEADER',
```

```
7,'CORRUPT HEADER',
8,'WRONG FILE TYPE',
9,'WRONG DATABASE',
10,'WRONG FILE NUMBER',
11,'WRONG FILE CREATE', 12,'WRONG FILE CREATE',
13,'WRONG FILE SIZE', 'UNKNOWN ERROR'), to_number(fhbsc),
to_date(fhbti,'MM/DD/RR HH24:MI:SS') from x$kcvfhonl
```

The **GV$BACKUP_CORRUPTION** DPT gives information on all pieces (for incremental backups) of backup data that show corruption problems.

Listing A.113 Description of the data dictionary dynamic performance table GV$BACKUP_CORRUPTION.

Name	Null?	Type
INST_ID		NUMBER
RECID		NUMBER
STAMP		NUMBER
SET_STAMP		NUMBER
SET_COUNT		NUMBER
PIECE#		NUMBER
FILE#		NUMBER
BLOCK#		NUMBER
BLOCKS		NUMBER
CORRUPTION_CHANGE#		NUMBER
MARKED_CORRUPT		VARCHAR2(3)

```
GV$BACKUP_CORRUPTION select
            inst_id,fcrid,fcstm,fcbss,fcbsc,fcpno,fcdfp,fcblk,fccnt,
            to_number(fcscn),decode(bitand(fcflg,1),1,'YES','NO') from
            x$kccfc
```

The **GV$BACKUP_DATAFILE** DPT shows the file map for the backup sets for the RMAN (recovery manager) backup sets.

Listing A.114 Description of the data dictionary dynamic performance table GV$BACKUP_DATAFILE.

Name	Null?	Type
INST_ID		NUMBER
RECID		NUMBER
STAMP		NUMBER
SET_STAMP		NUMBER
SET_COUNT		NUMBER
FILE#		NUMBER

```
CREATION_CHANGE#                    NUMBER
CREATION_TIME                       DATE
RESETLOGS_CHANGE#                   NUMBER
RESETLOGS_TIME                      DATE
INCREMENTAL_LEVEL                   NUMBER
INCREMENTAL_CHANGE#                 NUMBER
CHECKPOINT_CHANGE#                  NUMBER
CHECKPOINT_TIME                     DATE
ABSOLUTE_FUZZY_CHANGE#              NUMBER
MARKED_CORRUPT                      NUMBER
MEDIA_CORRUPT                       NUMBER
LOGICALLY_CORRUPT                   NUMBER
DATAFILE_BLOCKS                     NUMBER
BLOCKS                             NUMBER
BLOCK_SIZE                          NUMBER
OLDEST_OFFLINE_RANGE                NUMBER
```

```
GV$BACKUP_DATAFILE    select
                      inst_id,bfrid,bfstm,bfbss,bfbsc,bfdfp,to_number(bfcrs),
                      to_date(bfcrt,'MM/DD/RR HH24:MI:SS'), to_number(bfrls),
                      to_date(bfrlc,'MM/DD/RR HH24:MI:SS'),
                      decode(bitand(bfflg,1),1,bflvl,NULL),
                      to_number(bfics), to_number(bfcps),
                      to_date(bfcpt,'MM/DD/RR HH24:MI:SS'),to_number(bfafs),
                      bfncb,bfmcb,bflcb,bffsz,bfbct,
                      bfbsz,bflor,to_date(bftsm, 'MM/DD/RR HH24:MI:SS') from
                      x$kccbf
```

The **GV$BACKUP_DEVICE** DPT shows the backup devices available for use by the RMAN utility for the instance specified by the specific instance number.

Listing A.115   Description of the data dictionary dynamic performance table GV$BACKUP_DEVICE.

```
Name                            Null?    Type
------------------------------- -------- ----
INST_ID                                  NUMBER
DEVICE_TYPE                              VARCHAR2(17)
DEVICE_NAME                              VARCHAR2(513)
```

```
GV$BACKUP_DEVICE     select inst_id, devtype, devname from x$ksfhdvnt
```

The **GV$BACKUP_PIECE** DPT contains information about the pieces of backup sets backed up through the RMAN.

Listing A.116 Description of the data dictionary dynamic performance table GV$BACKUP_PIECE.

Name	Null?	Type
INST_ID		NUMBER
RECID		NUMBER
STAMP		NUMBER
SET_STAMP		NUMBER
SET_COUNT		NUMBER
PIECE#		NUMBER
DEVICE_TYPE		VARCHAR2(17)
HANDLE		VARCHAR2(513)
COMMENTS		VARCHAR2(81)
MEDIA		VARCHAR2(65)
CONCUR		VARCHAR2(3)
TAG		VARCHAR2(32)
DELETED		VARCHAR2(3)
START_TIME		DATE
COMPLETION_TIME		DATE
ELAPSED_SECONDS		NUMBER

```
GV$BACKUP_PIECE       select
                      inst_id,bprid,bpstm,bpbss,bpbsc,bpnum,bpdev,bphdl,bpcmt,bpmd
                      h,decode(bitand(bpflg,2),1,'YES','NO'),bptag,
                      decode(bitand(bpflg,1),1,'YES','NO'),
                      to_date(bptsm,'MM/DD/RR HH24:MI:SS'),
                      to_date(bptim,'MM/DD/RR HH24:MI:SS'),
                      (to_date(bptim,'MM/DD/RR HH24:MI:SS')-
                       to_date(bptsm,'MM/DD/RR HH24:MI:SS'))*86400
                      from x$kccbp
```

The **GV$BACKUP_REDOLOG** DPT shows the redo log backup status for the RMAN.

Listing A.117 Description of the data dictionary dynamic performance table GV$BACKUP_REDOLOG.

Name	Null?	Type
INST_ID		NUMBER
RECID		NUMBER
STAMP		NUMBER
SET_STAMP		NUMBER
SET_COUNT		NUMBER
THREAD#		NUMBER
SEQUENCE#		NUMBER
RESETLOGS_CHANGE#		NUMBER
RESETLOGS_TIME		DATE
FIRST_CHANGE#		NUMBER

```
FIRST_TIME                                      DATE
NEXT_CHANGE#                                     NUMBER
NEXT_TIME                                        DATE
BLOCKS                                           NUMBER
BLOCK_SIZE                                       NUMBER

GV$BACKUP_REDOLOG       select
                        inst_id,blrid,blstm,blbss,blbsc,blthp,blseq,to_number(blrls),
                        to_date(blrlc,'MM/DD/RR HH24:MI:SS'), to_number(bllos),
                        to_date(bllot,'MM/DD/RR HH24:MI:SS'), to_number(blnxs),
                        to_date(blnxt,'MM/DD/RR HH24:MI:SS'),blbct,blbsz from x$kccbl
```

The **GV$BACKUP_SET** DPT provides the mapping of backup set pieces to specific
backup sets for the RMAN.

**Listing A.118   Description of the data dictionary dynamic performance
table GV$BACKUP_SET.**

```
Name                            Null?    Type
------------------------------- -------- ----
INST_ID                                  NUMBER
RECID                                    NUMBER
STAMP                                    NUMBER
SET_STAMP                                NUMBER
SET_COUNT                                NUMBER
BACKUP_TYPE                              VARCHAR2(1)
CONTROLFILE_INCLUDED                     VARCHAR2(3)
INCREMENTAL_LEVEL                        NUMBER
PIECES                                   NUMBER
START_TIME                               DATE
COMPLETION_TIME                          DATE
ELAPSED_SECONDS                          NUMBER
BLOCK_SIZE                               NUMBER

GV$BACKUP_SET           select
                        inst_id,bsrid,bsstm,bsbss,bsbsc,decode(bitand(bstyp,11),1,'D',
                        2,'I',8,'L'),decode(bitand(bstyp,4),4,'YES','NO'),
                        decode(bitand(bstyp,16),16,bslvl,NULL),bspct,
                        to_date(bsbst,'MM/DD/RR HH24:MI:SS'),
                        to_date(bstsm,'MM/DD/RR HH24:MI:SS'),
                        (to_date(bstsm,'MM/DD/RR HH24:MI:SS')-
                         to_date(bsbst,'MM/DD/RR HH24:MI:SS'))*86400,bsbsz from
x$kccbs
```

The **GV$BGPROCESS** DPT gives the current status for all possible database back-
ground processes.

Listing A.119 Description of the data dictionary dynamic performance table GV$BGPROCESS.

```
Name                              Null?    Type
--------------------------------- -------- ----
INST_ID                                    NUMBER
PADDR                                      RAW(4)
NAME                                       VARCHAR2(5)
DESCRIPTION                                VARCHAR2(64)
ERROR                                      NUMBER


GV$BGPROCESS          select p.inst_id,
                      p.ksbdppro,p.ksbdpnam,d.ksbdddsc,p.ksbdperr  from x$ksbdp
                      p,x$ksbdd d where p.indx=d.indx
```

The **GV$BH** DPT is used in parallel server to track the SGA buffer pool. This useful DPT is built using the CATPARR.SQL script. It isn't automatically built for nonparallel server instances.

Listing A.120 Description of the dynamic performance table GV$BH.

```
Name                              Null?    Type
--------------------------------- -------- ----
INST_ID                                    NUMBER
FILE#                                      NUMBER
BLOCK#                                     NUMBER
CLASS#                                     NUMBER
STATUS                                     VARCHAR2(4)
XNC                                        NUMBER
FORCED_READS                               NUMBER
FORCED_WRITES                              NUMBER
LOCK_ELEMENT_ADDR                          RAW(4)
LOCK_ELEMENT_NAME                          NUMBER
LOCK_ELEMENT_CLASS                         NUMBER
DIRTY                                      VARCHAR2(1)
TEMP                                       VARCHAR2(1)
PING                                       VARCHAR2(1)
STALE                                      VARCHAR2(1)
DIRECT                                     VARCHAR2(1)
NEW                                        CHAR(1)
OBJD                                       NUMBER


GV$BH                 select bh.inst_id, file#, dbablk, class,
                      decode(state,0,'free',1,'xcur',2,'scur',3,'cr',4,'read',
                        5,'mrec',6,'irec'), x_to_null, forced_reads, forced_writes,
                      bh.le_addr, name,le_class,
                      decode(bitand(flag,1), 0, 'N', 'Y'),
                      decode(bitand(flag,16), 0, 'N', 'Y'),
```

```
decode(bitand(flag,1536), 0, 'N', 'Y'),
decode(bitand(flag,16384), 0, 'N', 'Y'),
decode(bitand(flag,65536), 0, 'N', 'Y'), 'N', obj from x$bh
bh, x$le le where bh.le_addr = le.le_addr
```

The **GV$BUFFER_POOL** DPT displays information about all buffer pools available for the database.

Listing A.121 Description of the dynamic performance table GV$BUFFER_POOL.

```
Name                                    Null?       Type
-------------------------------------- --------    ----
INST_ID                                            NUMBER
ID                                                 NUMBER
NAME                                               VARCHAR2(20)
LO_SETID                                           NUMBER
HI_SETID                                           NUMBER
SET_COUNT                                          NUMBER
BUFFERS                                            NUMBER
LO_BNUM                                            NUMBER
HI_BNUM                                            NUMBER

GV$BUFFER_POOL       select inst_id, bp_id, bp_name, bp_lo_sid, bp_hi_sid,
                     bp_set_ct, bp_size, bp_lo_bnum, bp_hi_bnum from x$kcbwbpd
```

The **V$CACHE** DPV (dynamic performance view) is a parallel server view and contains information from the headers of each SGA of the current instance as related to specific database objects. There is no corresponding **GV$** DPT.

Listing A.122 Description of the dynamic performance view V$CACHE.

```
Name                                    Null?       Type
-------------------------------------- --------    ----
FILE#                                              NUMBER
BLOCK#                                             NUMBER
CLASS#                                             NUMBER
STATUS                                             VARCHAR2(4)
XNC                                                NUMBER
FORCED_READS                                       NUMBER
FORCED_WRITES                                      NUMBER
NAME                                               VARCHAR2(30)
PARTITION_NAME                                     VARCHAR2(30)
KIND                                               VARCHAR2(15)
OWNER#                                             NUMBER
LOCK_ELEMENT_ADDR                                  RAW(4)
LOCK_ELEMENT_NAME                                  NUMBER
```

V$CACHE

```
select bh.file#,
bh.block#,
bh.class#,
bh.status,
bh.xnc,
bh.forced_reads,
bh.forced_writes,
ob.name,
ob.subname partition_name,
decode (ob.type#,  1, 'INDEX',
2, 'TABLE',
3, 'CLUSTER',
4, 'VIEW',
5, 'SYNONYM',
6, 'SEQUENCE',
7, 'PROCEDURE',
8,  'FUNCTION',
9, 'PACKAGE',
10, 'NON-EXISTENT',
11, 'PACKAGE BODY',
12, 'TRIGGER',
13, 'TYPE',
14, 'TYPE BODY',
19, 'TABLE PARTITION',
20, 'INDEX PARTITION',
21, 'LOB',
22, 'LIBRARY',
'UNKNOWN') kind,
ob.owner#,
lock_element_addr,
lock_element_name
from gv$bh bh, obj$ ob
where (bh.objd = ob.dataobj#)
union all
select bh.file#,
bh.block#,
bh.class#,
bh.status,
bh.xnc,
bh.forced_reads,
bh.forced_writes,
un.name,
NULL              partition_name,
'UNDO'            kind,
un.user#          owner#,
lock_element_addr,
lock_element_name
```

```
from v$bh bh, undo$ un
where (bh.class# >= 11) and
(un.us# = floor((bh.class# - 11) / 2))
```

The **V$CACHE_LOCK** DPV contains information similar to the **GV$CACHE** DPT, except the platform-specific lock manager identifiers are used. Using the **INDX** and **CLASS** values, additional queries to the **GV$BH** DPT are made to gain more information.

Listing A.123   Description of the dynamic performance view V$CACHE_LOCK.

Name	Null?	Type
FILE#		NUMBER
BLOCK#		NUMBER
STATUS		VARCHAR2(4)
XNC		NUMBER
FORCED_READS		NUMBER
FORCED_WRITES		NUMBER
NAME		VARCHAR2(30)
KIND		VARCHAR2(15)
OWNER#		NUMBER
LOCK_ELEMENT_ADDR		RAW(4)
LOCK_ELEMENT_NAME		NUMBER
INDX		NUMBER
CLASS		NUMBER

```
V$CACHE_LOCK          select file#, block#, status, xnc,
                      forced_reads, forced_writes,
                      name, kind, owner#, c.lock_element_addr,
                      c.lock_element_name,
                      indx, class
                      from v$cache c, v$lock_element l
                      where l.lock_element_addr = c.lock_element_addr
```

The **GV$CIRCUIT** DPT tracks the multithreaded server circuit status information for the specified instance.

Listing A.124   Description of the data dictionary dynamic performance table GV$CIRCUIT.

Name	Null?	Type
INST_ID		NUMBER
CIRCUIT		RAW(4)
DISPATCHER		RAW(4)
SERVER		RAW(4)

```
WAITER                          RAW(4)
SADDR                           RAW(4)
STATUS                          VARCHAR2(16)
QUEUE                           VARCHAR2(16)
MESSAGE0                        NUMBER
MESSAGE1                        NUMBER
MESSAGES                        NUMBER
BYTES                           NUMBER
BREAKS                          NUMBER

GV$CIRCUIT          select inst_id,addr,kmcvcdpc,
                    decode(kmcvcpro,kmcvcdpc,hextoraw('00'),kmcvcpro),
                    kmcvcwat,kmcvcses,kmcvcsta,kmcvcque,
                    kmcvcsz0,kmcvcsz1,kmcvcnmg,kmcvcnmb,kmcvcbrk from x$kmcvc
                    where bitand(ksspaflg,1)!=0
```

The **GV$CLASS_PING** table displays the number of blocks pinged per block class. A ping is an attempt to get a block that is already in use. Use this table to compare contentions for blocks of different classes.

Listing A.125 Description of the dynamic performance table GV$CLASS_PING.

```
Name                            Null?     Type
------------------------------- --------  ----
INST_ID                                   NUMBER
CLASS                                     VARCHAR2(18)
X_2_NULL                                  NUMBER
X_2_NULL_FORCED_WRITE                     NUMBER
X_2_NULL_FORCED_STALE                     NUMBER
X_2_S                                     NUMBER
X_2_S_FORCED_WRITE                        NUMBER
X_2_SSX                                   NUMBER
X_2_SSX_FORCED_WRITE                      NUMBER
S_2_NULL                                  NUMBER
S_2_NULL_FORCED_STALE                     NUMBER
SS_2_NULL                                 NUMBER
NULL_2_X                                  NUMBER
S_2_X                                     NUMBER
SSX_2_X                                   NUMBER
NULL_2_S                                  NUMBER
NULL_2_SS                                 NUMBER

GV$CLASS_PING select inst_id,  decode(indx,1,'data block',2,'sort block',
              3,'save undo block',
              4,'segment header',5,'save undo header',6,'free list',
              7,'extent map', 8,'bitmap block',
              9,'bitmap index block',10,'unused',11,'undo header',
```

```
                  12,'undo block'),
                  CLASS_X2NC,   CLASS_X2NFWC, CLASS_X2NFSC,   CLASS_X2SC,
CLASS_X2SFWC,

                  CLASS_X2SSXC, CLASS_X2SSXFWC, CLASS_S2NC,   CLASS_S2NFSC,
                  CLASS_SS2NC, CLASS_N2XC,
                  CLASS_S2XC, CLASS_SSX2XC,
                  CLASS_N2SC, CLASS_N2SSC
              from x$class_stat
```

The **GV$COMPATIBILITY** DPT lists compatibility (version of Oracle that the specific instance component is compatible with) levels for all Oracle8 components.

Listing A.126 Description of the data dictionary dynamic performance table GV$COMPATIBILITY.

```
Name                             Null?    Type
-------------------------------- -------- ----
INST_ID                                   NUMBER
TYPE_ID                                   VARCHAR2(8)
RELEASE                                   VARCHAR2(60)
DESCRIPTION                               VARCHAR2(64)

GV$COMPATIBILITY     select inst_id,kcktyid, kcktyrls, kcktydsc from x$kckty
```

The **GV$COMPATSEG** DPT stores information about the release level of the instance versus the set compatibility level.

Listing A.127 Description of the data dictionary dynamic performance table GV$COMPATSEG.

```
Name                             Null?    Type
-------------------------------- -------- ----
INST_ID                                   NUMBER
TYPE_ID                                   VARCHAR2(8)
RELEASE                                   VARCHAR2(60)
UPDATED                                   VARCHAR2(60)

GV$COMPATSEG         select inst_id,kckceid, kckcerl, kckcevsn from x$kckce
```

The **GV$CONTROLFILE** DPT lists locations and status for all controlfiles.

Listing A.128 Description of the data dictionary dynamic performance table GV$CONTROLFILE.

```
Name                             Null?    Type
-------------------------------- -------- ----
INST_ID                                   NUMBER
STATUS                                    VARCHAR2(7)
NAME                                      VARCHAR2(513)
```

```
GV$CONTROLFILE          select
                        inst_id,decode(bitand(cfflg,1),0,'',1,'INVALID'),cfnam from
                        x$kcccf
```

The **GV$CONTROLFILE_RECORD_SECTION** table lists the current contents of the various controlfile record areas (new with Oracle8 and used mostly with RMAN).

Listing A.129 Description of the data dictionary dynamic performance table GV$CONTROLFILE_RECORD_SECTION.

```
Name                                Null?     Type
----------------------------------  --------  ----
INST_ID                                       NUMBER
TYPE                                          VARCHAR2(17)
RECORD_SIZE                                   NUMBER
RECORDS_TOTAL                                 NUMBER
RECORDS_USED                                  NUMBER
FIRST_INDEX                                   NUMBER
LAST_INDEX                                    NUMBER
LAST_RECID                                    NUMBER


GV$CONTROLFILE_RECORD_SECTION select inst_id,
                        decode(indx,0,'DATABASE',1, 'CKPT PROGRESS',
                        2, 'REDO THREAD',3,'REDO LOG', 4,'DATAFILE',
5,'FILENAME',
                        6,'TABLESPACE', 7,'RESERVED1',
                        8,'RESERVED2',9,'LOG HISTORY',10,'OFFLINE RANGE',
                        11,'ARCHIVED LOG', 12,'BACKUP SET', 13,'BACKUP
PIECE',
                        14,'BACKUP DATAFILE', 15, 'BACKUP REDOLOG',
                        16,'DATAFILE COPY', 17,'BACKUP CORRUPTION',
                        18,'COPY CORRUPTION',19,'DELETED  OBJECT',
20,'RESERVED3',
                        21,'RESERVED4', 'UNKNOWN'),rsrsz,rsnum
                        ,rsnus,rsiol,rsilw,rsrlw from x$kccrs
```

The **GV$COPY_CORRUPTION** DPT is used by RMAN to track problems with backup sets.

Listing A.130 Description of the data dictionary dynamic performance table GV$COPY_CORRUPTION.

```
Name                                Null?     Type
----------------------------------  --------  ----
INST_ID                                       NUMBER
RECID                                         NUMBER
STAMP                                         NUMBER
COPY_RECID                                    NUMBER
```

```
COPY_STAMP                              NUMBER
FILE#                                   NUMBER
BLOCK#                                  NUMBER
BLOCKS                                  NUMBER
CORRUPTION_CHANGE#                      NUMBER
MARKED_CORRUPT                          VARCHAR2(3)
```

```
GV$COPY_CORRUPTION      select
                        inst_id,ccrid,ccstm,ccdcp,ccdcs,ccdfp,ccblk,cccnt,to_number(
                        ccscn),decode(bitand(ccflg,1),1,'YES','NO') from x$kcccc
```

The **GV$DATABASE** DPT tracks information about the specific database, such as database name, creation date, and log status.

Listing A.131 Description of the data dictionary dynamic performance table GV$DATABASE.

```
Name                                Null?     Type
---------------------------------   --------  ----
INST_ID                                       NUMBER
DBID                                          NUMBER
NAME                                          VARCHAR2(9)
CREATED                                       DATE
RESETLOGS_CHANGE#                             NUMBER
RESETLOGS_TIME                                DATE
LOG_MODE                                      VARCHAR2(12)
CHECKPOINT_CHANGE#                            NUMBER
ARCHIVE_CHANGE#                               NUMBER
CONTROLFILE_TYPE                              VARCHAR2(7)
CONTROLFILE_CREATED                           DATE
CONTROLFILE_SEQUENCE#                         NUMBER
CONTROLFILE_CHANGE#                           NUMBER
CONTROLFILE_TIME                              DATE
OPEN_RESETLOGS                                VARCHAR2(11)
```

```
GV$DATABASE             select inst_id,didbi,didbn,
                        to_date(dicts,'MM/DD/RR HH24:MI:SS'),to_number(dirls),
                        to_date(dirlc,'MM/DD/RR HH24:MI:SS'),to_number(diprs),
                        to_date(diprc,'MM/DD/RR HH24:MI:SS'),
                        decode(bitand(diflg,1),0,'NOARCHIVELOG','ARCHIVELOG'),
                        to_number(discn),to_number(difas),
                        decode(bitand(diflg
                        ,256),256,'CREATED',decode(bitand(diflg,1024),1024,'STANDBY'
                        ,decode(bitand(diflg,32768),32768,'CLONE',
                        decode(bitand(diflg,4096),
                         4096,'BACKUP','CURRENT')))),to_date(dicct, 'MM/DD/RR
                        HH24:MI:SS'),dicsq,to_number(dickp_scn),to_date(dickp_tim,
```

```
'MM/DD/RR HH24:MI:SS'),decode(bitand(diflg,4),4,'REQUIRED',
decode(diirs,
 0,'NOT ALLOWED','ALLOWED')),
to_date(divts, 'MM/DD/RR HH24:MI:SS') from x$kccdi
```

The **GV$DATAFILE** DPT tracks the current status of all datafiles.

Listing A.132   Description of the data dictionary dynamic performance table GV$DATAFILE.

Name	Null?	Type
INST_ID		NUMBER
FILE#		NUMBER
CREATION_CHANGE#		NUMBER
CREATION_TIME		DATE
TS#		NUMBER
RFILE#		NUMBER
STATUS		VARCHAR2(7)
ENABLED		VARCHAR2(10)
CHECKPOINT_CHANGE#		NUMBER
CHECKPOINT_TIME		DATE
UNRECOVERABLE_CHANGE#		NUMBER
UNRECOVERABLE_TIME		DATE
LAST_CHANGE#		NUMBER
LAST_TIME		DATE
OFFLINE_CHANGE#		NUMBER
ONLINE_CHANGE#		NUMBER
ONLINE_TIME		DATE
BYTES		NUMBER
BLOCKS		NUMBER
CREATE_BYTES		NUMBER
BLOCK_SIZE		NUMBER
NAME		VARCHAR2(513)

```
GV$DATAFILE        select fe.inst_id,fe.fenum,to_number(fe.fecrc_scn),
                   to_date(fe.fecrc_tim,'MM/DD/RR HH24:MI:SS'),fe.fetsn,fe.ferfn,
                 decode(fe.fetsn,0,decode(bitand(fe.festa,2),0,'SYSOFF','SYSTEM'),
                   decode(bitand(fe.festa,18),0,'OFFLINE',2,'ONLINE','RECOVER')),
                   decode(bitand(fe.festa, 12), 0,'DISABLED',4,'READ ONLY',
                   12,'READ WRITE','UNKNOWN'),
                   to_number(fe.fecps),to_date(fe.fecpt,'MM/DD/RR HH24:MI:SS'),
                   to_number(fe.feurs),to_date(fe.feurt,'MM/DD/RR HH24:MI:SS'),
                   to_number(fe.fests),
                   decode(fe.fests,NULL,to_date(NULL),
                   to_date(fe.festt,'MM/DD/RR HH24:MI:SS')),
                   to_number(fe.feofs),to_number(fe.feonc_scn),
                   to_date(fe.feonc_tim,'MM/DD/RR HH24:MI:SS'),
```

```
fh.fhfsz*fe.febsz,fh.fhfsz,fe.fecsz*fe.febsz,fe.febsz,fn.fnnam
from x$kccfe fe, x$kccfn fn, x$kcvfh fh where
fn.fnfno=fe.fenum and fn.fnfno=fh.hxfil and
fe.fefnh=fn.fnnum and fe.fedup!=0 and fn.fntyp=4 and
fn.fnnam is not null
```

The **GV$DATAFILE_COPY** DPT tracks backup information for the RMAN about datafile backups.

Listing A.133 Description of the data dictionary dynamic performance table GV$DATAFILE_COPY.

```
Name                             Null?     Type
-------------------------------- --------- ----
INST_ID                                    NUMBER
RECID                                      NUMBER
STAMP                                      NUMBER
NAME                                       VARCHAR2(513)
TAG                                        VARCHAR2(32)
FILE#                                      NUMBER
RFILE#                                     NUMBER
CREATION_CHANGE#                           NUMBER
CREATION_TIME                              DATE
RESETLOGS_CHANGE#                          NUMBER
RESETLOGS_TIME                             DATE
INCREMENTAL_LEVEL                          NUMBER
CHECKPOINT_CHANGE#                         NUMBER
CHECKPOINT_TIME                            DATE
ABSOLUTE_FUZZY_CHANGE#                     NUMBER
RECOVERY_FUZZY_CHANGE#                     NUMBER
RECOVERY_FUZZY_TIME                        DATE
ONLINE_FUZZY                               VARCHAR2(3)
BACKUP_FUZZY                               VARCHAR2(3)
MARKED_CORRUPT                             NUMBER
MEDIA_CORRUPT                              NUMBER
LOGICALLY_CORRUPT                          NUMBER
BLOCKS                                     NUMBER
BLOCK_SIZE                                 NUMBER
OLDEST_OFFLINE_RANGE                       NUMBER
DELETED                                    VARCHAR2(3)
COMPLETION_TIME                            DATE

GV$DATAFILE_COPY       select
                       inst_id,dcrid,dcstm,dcnam,dctag,dcdfp,dcrfn,to_number(dccrs)
                       ,to_date(dccrt,'MM/DD/RR HH24:MI:SS'),
                       to_number(dcrls),to_date(dcrlc,'MM/DD/RR HH24:MI:SS'),
                       decode(bitand(dcflg,8),8,0,NULL),to_number(dccps),
                       to_date(dccpt,'MM/DD/RR HH24:MI:SS'),
```

```
to_number(dcafs),to_number(dcrfs),
to_date(dcrft,'MM/DD/RR HH24:MI:SS'),decode(bitand(dcflg,
2),0,'NO','YES'),decode(bitand(dcflg,
4),0,'NO','YES'),dcncb,dcmcb,dclcb,dcbct,dcbsz,dclor,decode(
bitand(dcflg, 1),0,'NO','YES'),
to_date(dctsm,'MM/DD/RR HH24:MI:SS')from x$kccdc
```

The **GV$DATAFILE_HEADER** DPT tracks information about the datafile headers for the database.

Listing A.134   Description of the data dictionary dynamic performance table GV$DATAFILE_HEADER.

Name	Null?	Type
INST_ID		NUMBER
FILE#		NUMBER
STATUS		VARCHAR2(7)
ERROR		VARCHAR2(18)
RECOVER		VARCHAR2(3)
FUZZY		VARCHAR2(3)
CREATION_CHANGE#		NUMBER
CREATION_TIME		DATE
TABLESPACE_NAME		VARCHAR2(30)
TS#		NUMBER
RFILE#		NUMBER
RESETLOGS_CHANGE#		NUMBER
RESETLOGS_TIME		DATE
CHECKPOINT_CHANGE#		NUMBER
CHECKPOINT_TIME		DATE
CHECKPOINT_COUNT		NUMBER
BYTES		NUMBER
BLOCKS		NUMBER
NAME		VARCHAR2(513)

```
GV$DATAFILE_HEADER    select inst_id,hxfil,decode(hxons, 0, 'OFFLINE',
                      'ONLINE'),decode(hxerr, 0, NULL, 1,'FILE MISSING',
                      2,'OFFLINE NORMAL', 3,'NOT VERIFIED', 4,'FILE NOT FOUND',
                      5,'CANNOT OPEN FILE', 6,'CANNOT READ HEADER',
                      7,'CORRUPT HEADER',8,'WRONG FILE TYPE', 9,'WRONG DATABASE',
                      10,'WRONG FILE NUMBER',11,'WRONG FILE CREATE',
                      12,'WRONG FILE CREATE',13,'WRONG FILE SIZE',
                      14, 'WRONG RESETLOGS', 15,'OLD CONTROLFILE', 'UNKNOWN ERROR'),
                      hxver,decode(hxnrcv, 0,'NO',
                      1,'YES', NULL),decode(hxifz, 0,'NO', 1,'YES',
                      NULL),to_number(fhcrs),
                      to_date(fhcrt,'MM/DD/RR HH24:MI:SS'),
```

```
fhtnm,fhtsn,fhrfn,to_number(fhrls),to_date(fhrl
c,'MM/DD/RR HH24:MI:SS'),to_number(fhscn),
to_date(fhtim,'MM/DD/RR HH24:MI:SS'),
fhcpc,fhfsz*fhbsz,fhfsz,hxfnm from x$kcvfh
```

The **GV$DBFILE** DPT tracks the current file number and datafile locations for the database.

Listing A.135   Description of the data dictionary dynamic performance table GV$DBFILE.

Name	Null?	Type
INST_ID		NUMBER
FILE#		NUMBER
NAME		VARCHAR2(513)

```
GV$DBFILE          select inst_id,fnfno,fnnam from x$kccfn where fnnam is not
                   null and fntyp=4
```

The **GV$DBLINK** DPT provides data about database links for the database. The current status includes whether or not the link is currently in use.

Listing A.136   Description of the data dictionary dynamic performance table GV$DBLINK.

Name	Null?	Type
INST_ID		NUMBER
DB_LINK		VARCHAR2(128)
OWNER_ID		NUMBER
LOGGED_ON		VARCHAR2(3)
HETEROGENEOUS		VARCHAR2(3)
PROTOCOL		VARCHAR2(6)
OPEN_CURSORS		NUMBER
IN_TRANSACTION		VARCHAR2(3)
UPDATE_SENT		VARCHAR2(3)
COMMIT_POINT_STRENGTH		NUMBER

```
GV$DBLINK          select inst_id,nconam, ncouid, decode(bitand(hstflg, 32), 0,
                   'NO', 'YES'),   decode(bitand(hstflg, 8), 0, 'NO', 'YES'),
                   decode(hstpro, 1, 'V5', 2, 'V6', 3, 'V6_NLS', 4, 'V7',
                   'UNKN'),   ncouct, decode(bitand(ncoflg, 2), 0, 'NO', 'YES'),
                   decode(bitand(ncoflg, 8), 0, 'NO', 'YES'), nco2pstr   from
                   x$uganco where bitand(hstflg, 1) != 0
```

The **GV$DB_OBJECT_CACHE** DPT shows the current status of all object caches specified for the database. The cache is for internal database objects and not the client-side object cache.

Listing A.137 Description of the data dictionary dynamic performance table GV$DB_OBJECT_CACHE.

```
Name                             Null?    Type
-------------------------------- -------- ----
INST_ID                                   NUMBER
OWNER                                     VARCHAR2(64)
NAME                                      VARCHAR2(1000)
DB_LINK                                   VARCHAR2(64)
NAMESPACE                                 VARCHAR2(15)
TYPE                                      VARCHAR2(14)
SHARABLE_MEM                              NUMBER
LOADS                                     NUMBER
EXECUTIONS                                NUMBER
LOCKS                                     NUMBER
PINS                                      NUMBER
KEPT                                      VARCHAR2(3)


GV$DB_OBJECT_CACHE    select inst_id,kglnaown,kglnaobj,kglnadlk,
                 decode(kglhdnsp,1,'TABLE/PROCEDURE',2,'BODY',3,'TRIGGER',
                  4,'INDEX',5,'CLUSTER',6,'OBJECT'),
                 decode(bitand(kglobflg,3),0,'NOT LOADED',
                  2,'NON-EXISTENT',3,'INVALID STATUS',
                 decode(kglobtyp, 1,'INDEX',2,'TABLE',3,'CLUSTER',4,'VIEW',
              5,'SYNONYM',6,'SEQUENCE',7,'PROCEDURE',8,'FUNCTION',9,'PACKAGE',
                 10, 'NON-EXISTENT',11,'PACKAGE BODY',
                 12,'TRIGGER',13,'CLASS',14,'SET',
                 15,'OBJECT',16,'USER',17,'DBLINK','INVALID TYPE')),
              kglobhs0+kglobhs1+kglobhs2+kglobhs3+kglobhs4+kglobhs5+kglobhs6,
               kglhdldc,kglhdexc,kglhdlkc,kglobpc0,decode(kglhdkmk,0,'NO','
               YES') from x$kglob where kglhdnsp between 1 and 6
```

The **GV$DB_PIPES** DPT contains information on database pipes created with the **DBMS_PIPES** package.

Listing A.138 Description of the data dictionary dynamic performance table GV$DB_PIPES.

```
Name                             Null?    Type
-------------------------------- -------- ----
INST_ID                                   NUMBER
OWNERID                                   NUMBER
NAME                                      VARCHAR2(1000)
TYPE                                      VARCHAR2(7)
SIZE                                      NUMBER
```

```
GV$DB_PIPES          select inst_id,decode(kglobt00,1,kglobt17,null),kglnaobj,
                     decode(kglobt00,1,'PRIVATE','PUBLIC'),
                     kglobhs0+kglobhs1+kglobhs2+kglobhs3+kglobhs4+kglobhs5+kglobhs6
                     from x$kglob where kglhdnsp=7
```

The **GV$DELETED_OBJECT** DPT collects information on currently deleted objects, such as archive logs, datafile copies, or backup piece.

Listing A.139 Description of the data dictionary dynamic performance table GV$DELETED_OBJECT.

```
Name                              Null?     Type
-------------------------------- -------- ----
INST_ID                                    NUMBER
RECID                                      NUMBER
STAMP                                      NUMBER
TYPE                                       VARCHAR2(13)
OBJECT_RECID                               NUMBER
OBJECT_STAMP                               NUMBER
```

```
GV$DELETED_OBJECT    select inst_id,dlrid,dlstm,
                     decode(dltyp,11,'ARCHIVED LOG',13,'BACKUP PIECE',
                       16,'DATAFILE COPY','UNKNOWN'),dlobp,dlosm from x$kccdl
```

The **GV$DISPATCHER** DPT provides current information concerning the multithreaded server dispatcher processes.

Listing A.140 Description of the data dictionary dynamic performance table GV$DISPATCHER.

```
Name                              Null?     Type
-------------------------------- -------- ----
INST_ID                                    NUMBER
NAME                                       VARCHAR2(5)
NETWORK                                    VARCHAR2(128)
PADDR                                      RAW(4)
STATUS                                     VARCHAR2(16)
ACCEPT                                     VARCHAR2(3)
MESSAGES                                   NUMBER
BYTES                                      NUMBER
BREAKS                                     NUMBER
OWNED                                      NUMBER
CREATED                                    NUMBER
IDLE                                       NUMBER
BUSY                                       NUMBER
LISTENER                                   NUMBER
```

```
GV$DISPATCHER          select inst_id,kmmdinam,kmmdinet,kmmdipro,kmmdista,
                       decode(kmmdiacc,0,'NO','YES'),kmmdinmg,kmmdinmb,kmmdibrk,
                       kmmdinvo,kmmditnc,kmmdiidl,kmmdibsy,kmmdiler from x$kmmdi
                       where kmmdiflg!=0
```

The **GV$DISPATCHER_RATE** DPT provides rate statistics for the MTS dispatcher processes.

Listing A.141   Description of the data dictionary dynamic performance table GV$DISPATCHER_RATE.

Name	Null?	Type
INST_ID		NUMBER
NAME		VARCHAR2(5)
PADDR		RAW(4)
CUR_LOOP_RATE		NUMBER
CUR_EVENT_RATE		NUMBER
CUR_EVENTS_PER_LOOP		NUMBER
CUR_MSG_RATE		NUMBER
CUR_SVR_BUF_RATE		NUMBER
CUR_SVR_BYTE_RATE		NUMBER
CUR_SVR_BYTE_PER_BUF		NUMBER
CUR_CLT_BUF_RATE		NUMBER
CUR_CLT_BYTE_RATE		NUMBER
CUR_CLT_BYTE_PER_BUF		NUMBER
CUR_BUF_RATE		NUMBER
CUR_BYTE_RATE		NUMBER
CUR_BYTE_PER_BUF		NUMBER
CUR_IN_CONNECT_RATE		NUMBER
CUR_OUT_CONNECT_RATE		NUMBER
CUR_RECONNECT_RATE		NUMBER
MAX_LOOP_RATE		NUMBER
MAX_EVENT_RATE		NUMBER
MAX_EVENTS_PER_LOOP		NUMBER
MAX_MSG_RATE		NUMBER
MAX_SVR_BUF_RATE		NUMBER
MAX_SVR_BYTE_RATE		NUMBER
MAX_SVR_BYTE_PER_BUF		NUMBER
MAX_CLT_BUF_RATE		NUMBER
MAX_CLT_BYTE_RATE		NUMBER
MAX_CLT_BYTE_PER_BUF		NUMBER
MAX_BUF_RATE		NUMBER
MAX_BYTE_RATE		NUMBER
MAX_BYTE_PER_BUF		NUMBER
MAX_IN_CONNECT_RATE		NUMBER
MAX_OUT_CONNECT_RATE		NUMBER
MAX_RECONNECT_RATE		NUMBER

```
AVG_LOOP_RATE                    NUMBER
AVG_EVENT_RATE                   NUMBER
AVG_EVENTS_PER_LOOP              NUMBER
AVG_MSG_RATE                     NUMBER
AVG_SVR_BUF_RATE                 NUMBER
AVG_SVR_BYTE_RATE                NUMBER
AVG_SVR_BYTE_PER_BUF             NUMBER
AVG_CLT_BUF_RATE                 NUMBER
AVG_CLT_BYTE_RATE                NUMBER
AVG_CLT_BYTE_PER_BUF             NUMBER
AVG_BUF_RATE                     NUMBER
AVG_BYTE_RATE                    NUMBER
AVG_BYTE_PER_BUF                 NUMBER
AVG_IN_CONNECT_RATE              NUMBER
AVG_OUT_CONNECT_RATE             NUMBER
AVG_RECONNECT_RATE               NUMBER
NUM_LOOPS_TRACKED                NUMBER
NUM_MSG_TRACKED                  NUMBER
NUM_SVR_BUF_TRACKED              NUMBER
NUM_CLT_BUF_TRACKED              NUMBER
NUM_BUF_TRACKED                  NUMBER
NUM_IN_CONNECT_TRACKED           NUMBER
NUM_OUT_CONNECT_TRACKED          NUMBER
NUM_RECONNECT_TRACKED            NUMBER
SCALE_LOOPS                      NUMBER
SCALE_MSG                        NUMBER
SCALE_SVR_BUF                    NUMBER
SCALE_CLT_BUF                    NUMBER
SCALE_BUF                        NUMBER
SCALE_IN_CONNECT                 NUMBER
SCALE_OUT_CONNECT                NUMBER
SCALE_RECONNECT                  NUMBER
```

GV$DISPATCHER_RATE select

```
            inst_id,kmmdinam,kmmdipro,kmmdicrle,kmmdicre,kmmdicepl,kmmdicrm,
            kmmdicrus,kmmdicrys,kmmdicyus,kmmdicruc,kmmdicryc,kmmdicyuc,kmmdicru,
            kmmdicry,kmmdicyu,kmmdicic,kmmdicoc,kmmdicrr,kmmdimrle,kmmdimre,
            kmmdimepl,kmmdimrm,kmmdimrus,kmmdimrys,kmmdimyus,kmmdimruc,kmmdimryc,
            kmmdimyuc,kmmdimru,kmmdimry,kmmdimyu,kmmdimic,kmmdimoc,kmmdimrr,
            kmmdiarle,kmmdiare,kmmdiaepl,kmmdiarm,kmmdiarus,kmmdiarys,kmmdiayus,
            kmmdiaruc,kmmdiaryc,kmmdiayuc,kmmdiaru,kmmdiary,kmmdiayu,kmmdiaic,
            kmmdiaoc,kmmdiarr,kmmdinrle,kmmdinrm,kmmdinrus,kmmdinruc,kmmdinru,
            kmmdinic,kmmdinoc,kmmdinrr,kmmdisrle,kmmdisrm,kmmdisrus,kmmdisruc,
            kmmdisru,kmmdisic,kmmdisoc,kmmdisrr
            from x$kmmdi where kmmdiflg!=0
```

The **GV$DLM_CONVERT_LOCAL** DPT displays the elapsed time for local dynamic lock manager (DLM) lock conversion operations.

Listing A.142 Description of the dynamic performance table GV$DLM_CONVERT_LOCAL.

Name	Null?	Type
INST_ID		NUMBER
CONVERT_TYPE		VARCHAR2(64)
AVERAGE_CONVERT_TIME		NUMBER
CONVERT_COUNT		NUMBER

```
GV$DLM_CONVERT_LOCAL   select inst_id, kjicvtnam, kjicvtalt, kjicvtalc from
x$kjicvt
```

The **GV$DLM_CONVERT_REMOTE** DPT displays the elapsed time for a remote DLM lock conversion operation.

Listing A.143 Description of the dynamic performance table GV$DLM_CONVERT_REMOTE.

Name	Null?	Type
INST_ID		NUMBER
CONVERT_TYPE		VARCHAR2(64)
AVERAGE_CONVERT_TIME		NUMBER
CONVERT_COUNT		NUMBER

```
GV$DLM_CONVERT_REMOTE   select inst_id, kjicvtnam, kjicvtart, kjicvtarc from
x$kjicvt
```

The **GV$DLM_LATCH** DPT displays statistics about the DLM latch performance. The table reports total for each type of latch rather than for each latch.

Listing A.144 Description of the dynamic performance table GV$DLM_LATCH.

Name	Null?	Type
INST_ID		NUMBER
LATCH_TYPE		VARCHAR2(64)
IMM_GETS		NUMBER
TTL_GETS		NUMBER

```
GV$DLM_LATCH           select inst_id, kjilftdesc, kjilftimgt, kjilfttlgt from
x$kjilft
```

The **GV$DLM_MISC** DPT displays miscellaneous DLM statistics.

Listing A.145   Description of the dynamic performance table GV$DLM_MISC.

Name	Null?	Type
INST_ID		NUMBER
STATISTIC#		NUMBER
NAME		VARCHAR2(64)
VALUE		NUMBER

```
GV$DLM_MISC        select inst_id, indx, kjisftdesc, kjisftval from x$kjisft
```

The **GV$ENABLEDPRIVS** DPT shows the currently enabled privileges for the database.

Listing A.146   Description of the data dictionary dynamic performance table GV$ENABLEDPRIVS.

Name	Null?	Type
INST_ID		NUMBER
PRIV_NUMBER		NUMBER

```
GV$ENABLEDPRIVS        select inst_id,-indx from x$kzspr where x$kzspr.kzsprprv=1
```

The **GV$ENQUEUE_LOCK** DPT shows the current enqueue locks for the database.

Listing A.147   Description of the dynamic performance table GV$ENQUEUE_LOCK.

Name	Null?	Type
INST_ID		NUMBER
ADDR		RAW(4)
KADDR		RAW(4)
SID		NUMBER
TYPE		VARCHAR2(2)
ID1		NUMBER
ID2		NUMBER
LMODE		NUMBER
REQUEST		NUMBER
CTIME		NUMBER
BLOCK		NUMBER

```
GV$ENQUEUE_LOCK        select /*+ ordered use_nl(l), use_nl(s), use_nl(r) +*/
                       s.inst_id,l.addr,l.ksqlkadr,s.ksusenum,r.ksqrsidt,r.ksqrsid1
                       ,r.ksqrsid2, l.ksqlkmod, l.ksqlkreq,l.ksqlkctim,l.ksqlklblk
```

```
from x$ksqeq l,x$ksuse s,x$ksqrs r where l.ksqlkses=s.addr
and  bitand(l.kssobflg,1)!=0 and (l.ksqlkmod!=0 or
l.ksqlkreq!=0) and  l.ksqlkres=r.addr
```

The **GV$EVENT_NAME** DPT provides a list of all of the current event names for this release of Oracle. Also provided are any parameters that can be accessed for this event.

Listing A.148 Description of the data dictionary dynamic performance table GV$EVENT_NAME.

Name	Null?	Type
INST_ID		NUMBER
EVENT#		NUMBER
NAME		VARCHAR2(64)
PARAMETER1		VARCHAR2(64)
PARAMETER2		VARCHAR2(64)
PARAMETER3		VARCHAR2(64)

```
GV$EVENT_NAME       select inst_id, indx, kslednam, ksledp1, ksledp2, ksledp3
                    from x$ksled
```

The **GV$EXECUTION** DPT provides current data on any parallel query operations that are occurring.

Listing A.149 Description of the data dictionary dynamic performance table GV$EXECUTION.

Name	Null?	Type
INST_ID		NUMBER
PID		NUMBER
DEPTH		NUMBER
FUNCTION		VARCHAR2(10)
TYPE		VARCHAR2(7)
NVALS		NUMBER
VAL1		NUMBER
VAL2		NUMBER
SEQH		NUMBER
SEQL		NUMBER

```
GV$EXECUTION        select inst_id, pid, val0, func,
                    decode(id,1,'call',2,'return',3,'longjmp'), nvals,  val2,
                    val3, seqh, seql from x$kstex where op=10
```

The **V$FALSE_PING** DPV is a parallel server view that displays buffers that may be getting false pings. A false ping is defined as a buffer pinged more than 10 times that is protected by the same lock as another buffer that is pinged more than 10 times. If a buffer is getting false pings, it should be remapped in **GC_FILES_TO_LOCK** to reduce lock collisions.

Listing A.150   Description of the dynamic performance view V$FALSE_PING.

Name	Null?	Type
FILE#		NUMBER
BLOCK#		NUMBER
STATUS		VARCHAR2(4)
XNC		NUMBER
FORCED_READS		NUMBER
FORCED_WRITES		NUMBER
NAME		VARCHAR2(30)
PARTITION_NAME		VARCHAR2(30)
KIND		VARCHAR2(15)
OWNER#		NUMBER
LOCK_ELEMENT_ADDR		RAW(4)
LOCK_ELEMENT_NAME		NUMBER
LOCK_ELEMENT_CLASS		NUMBER

```
V$FALSE_PING   select file#,
                  block#,
                  status,
                  xnc,
                  p.forced_reads,
                  p.forced_writes,
                  name,
                  partition_name,
                  kind,
                  owner#,
                  p.lock_element_addr,
                  p.lock_element_name,
                  p.class#  lock_element_class
               from v$ping p, v$locks_with_collisions c
               where (p.forced_reads + p.forced_writes) > 5
                and  p.lock_element_addr = c.lock_element_addr
```

GV$FILE_PING is a shared server DPT that shows how often a specific file is pinged.

Listing A.151   Description of the dynamic performance table GV$FILE_PING.

Name	Null?	Type
INST_ID		NUMBER
FILE_NUMBER		NUMBER

```
FREQUENCY                           NUMBER
X_2_NULL                            NUMBER
X_2_NULL_FORCED_WRITE               NUMBER
X_2_NULL_FORCED_STALE               NUMBER
X_2_S                               NUMBER
X_2_S_FORCED_WRITE                  NUMBER
X_2_SSX                             NUMBER
X_2_SSX_FORCED_WRITE                NUMBER
S_2_NULL                            NUMBER
S_2_NULL_FORCED_STALE               NUMBER
SS_2_NULL                           NUMBER
WRB                                 NUMBER
WRB_FORCED_WRITE                    NUMBER
RBR                                 NUMBER
RBR_FORCED_WRITE                    NUMBER
RBR_FORCED_STALE                    NUMBER
CBR                                 NUMBER
CBR_FORCED_WRITE                    NUMBER
NULL_2_X                            NUMBER
S_2_X                               NUMBER
SSX_2_X                             NUMBER
NULL_2_S                            NUMBER
NULL_2_SS                           NUMBER


GV$FILE_PING        select inst_id, kcfiofno,KCFIOX2N,
                    KCFIOX2NC,KCFIOX2NFWC, KCFIOX2NFSC,  KCFIOX2SC,
                    KCFIOX2SFWC,  KCFIOX2SSXC, KCFIOX2SSXFWC,
                    KCFIOS2NC, KCFIOS2NFSC, KCFIOSS2NC,
                    KCFIOWRBC, KCFIOWRBFWC, KCFIORBRC,
                    KCFIORBRFWC, KCFIORBRFSC, KCFIOCBRC,KCFIOCBRFWC,
                    KCFION2XC, KCFIOS2XC, KCFIOSSX2XC, KCFION2SC, KCFION2SSC
                    from x$kcfio x
```

The **GV$FILESTAT** DPT gives current file statistics information for such operations as I/O against the database physical files.

Listing A.152   Description of the data dictionary dynamic performance table GV$FILESTAT.

Name	Null?	Type
INST_ID		NUMBER
FILE#		NUMBER
PHYRDS		NUMBER
PHYWRTS		NUMBER
PHYBLKRD		NUMBER
PHYBLKWRT		NUMBER
READTIM		NUMBER
WRITETIM		NUMBER

GV$FILESTAT   select k.inst_id,
                          k.kcfiofno,k.kcfiopyr,k.kcfiopyw,k.kcfiopbr,k.kcfiopbw,k.kcfioprt,
                          k.kcfiopwt from x$kcfio k,x$kccfe f
                          where f.fedup <> 0 and f.fenum=k.kcfiofno

The **GV$FIXED_TABLE** DPT provides current information on all fixed tables in the database. These are the **K** and **X$** tables.

Listing A.153   Description of the data dictionary dynamic performance table GV$FIXED_TABLE.

Name	Null?	Type
INST_ID		NUMBER
NAME		VARCHAR2(30)
OBJECT_ID		NUMBER
TYPE		VARCHAR2(5)
TABLE_NUM		NUMBER

```
GV$FIXED_TABLE         select inst_id,kqftanam, kqftaobj, 'TABLE', indx
                       from x$kqfta
                       union all
                       select inst_id,kqfvinam, kqfviobj, 'VIEW',
                       65537 from x$kqfvi
                       union all
                       select inst_id,kqfdtnam,
                       kqfdtobj, 'TABLE', 65537 from x$kqfdt
```

The **GV$FIXED_VIEW_DEFINITION** table provides descriptions and the physical definition of the **GV_$** DPT views.

Listing A. 154   Description of the data dictionary dynamic performance table GV$FIXED_VIEW_DEFINITION.

Name	Null?	Type
INST_ID		NUMBER
VIEW_NAME		VARCHAR2(30)
VIEW_DEFINITION		VARCHAR2(4000)

```
GV$FIXED_VIEW_DEFINITION select i.inst_id,kqfvinam,kqftpsel from x$kqfvi i, x$kqfvtt
                       where i.indx = t.indx
```

The **GV$GLOBAL_TRANSACTION** DPT provides information on current database global transaction operations.

Listing A.155 Description of the data dictionary dynamic performance table GV$GLOBAL_TRANSACTION.

Name	Null?	Type
INST_ID		NUMBER
FORMATID		NUMBER
GLOBALID		RAW(64)
BRANCHID		RAW(64)
BRANCHES		NUMBER
REFCOUNT		NUMBER
PREPARECOUNT		NUMBER
STATE		VARCHAR2(18)
FLAGS		NUMBER
COUPLING		VARCHAR2(15)

```
GV$GLOBAL_TRANSACTION select inst_id, K2GTIFMT, K2GTITID_EXT, K2GTIBID,
                      K2GTECNT, K2GTERCT, K2GTDPCT,
                      decode (K2GTDFLG,
                      0,'ACTIVE', 1, 'COLLECTING', 2, 'FINALIZED',
                      4,'FAILED', 8, 'RECOVERING', 16, 'UNASSOCIATED',
                      32,'FORGOTTEN', 64, 'READY FOR RECOVERY', 'COMBINATION'),
K2GTDFLG,
                      decode (K2GTETYP,
                      0, 'FREE',
                      1, 'LOOSELY COUPLED',
                      2, 'TIGHTLY COUPLED')  from
                      X$K2GTE2
```

The **GV$INDEXED_FIXED_COLUMN** DPT provides information on columns in the fixed table that are indexed tables (**X$**).

Listing A.156 Description of the data dictionary dynamic performance table GV$INDEXED_FIXED_COLUMN.

Name	Null?	Type
INST_ID		NUMBER
TABLE_NAME		VARCHAR2(30)
INDEX_NUMBER		NUMBER
COLUMN_NAME		VARCHAR2(30)
COLUMN_POSITION		NUMBER

```
GV$INDEXED_FIXED_COLUMN select c.inst_id,kqftanam, kqfcoidx, kqfconam, kqfcoipo
from
                      x$kqfco c, x$kqfta t where t.indx = c.kqfcotab and kqfcoidx
                      != 0
```

The **GV$INSTANCE** DPT gives information on current instance status.

Listing A.157 Description of the data dictionary dynamic performance table GV$INSTANCE.

Name	Null?	Type
INST_ID		NUMBER
INSTANCE_NUMBER		NUMBER
INSTANCE_NAME		VARCHAR2(16)
HOST_NAME		VARCHAR2(64)
VERSION		VARCHAR2(17)
STARTUP_TIME		DATE
STATUS		VARCHAR2(7)
PARALLEL		VARCHAR2(3)
THREAD#		NUMBER
ARCHIVER		VARCHAR2(7)
LOG_SWITCH_WAIT		VARCHAR2(11)
LOGINS		VARCHAR2(10)
SHUTDOWN_PENDING		VARCHAR2(3)

```
GV$INSTANCE          select
                     inst_id,ksuxsins,ksuxssid,ksuxshst,ksuxsver,ksuxstim,
                     decode(ksuxssts,0,'STARTED',1,'MOUNTED',2,'OPEN','UNKNOWN'),
                     decode(ksuxsshr,0,'NO',1,'YES',2,NULL),
                     ksuxsthr,
                     decode(ksuxsarc,0,'STOPPED',1,'STARTED','FAILED'),
                     decode(ksuxslsw,0,NULL,2,'ARCHIVE LOG',3,'CLEAR
LOG',4,'CHECKPOINT'),
                     decode(ksuxsdba,0,'ALLOWED','RESTRICTED '),
                     decode(ksuxsshp,0,'NO','YES') from x$ksuxsinst
```

The **GV$LATCH** table lists statistics for nonparent latches and summary statistics for parent latches. Parent-latch statistics contain roll-up data from all child latches of that parent.

Listing A.158 Description of the data dictionary dynamic performance table GV$LATCH.

Name	Null?	Type
INST_ID		NUMBER
ADDR		RAW(4)
LATCH#		NUMBER
LEVEL#		NUMBER
NAME		VARCHAR2(64)
GETS		NUMBER
MISSES		NUMBER
SLEEPS		NUMBER
IMMEDIATE_GETS		NUMBER
IMMEDIATE_MISSES		NUMBER
WAITERS_WOKEN		NUMBER

Name	Type
WAITS_HOLDING_LATCH	NUMBER
SPIN_GETS	NUMBER
SLEEP1	NUMBER
SLEEP2	NUMBER
SLEEP3	NUMBER
SLEEP4	NUMBER
SLEEP5	NUMBER
SLEEP6	NUMBER
SLEEP7	NUMBER
SLEEP8	NUMBER
SLEEP9	NUMBER
SLEEP10	NUMBER
SLEEP11	NUMBER

```
GV$LATCH          select
                  d.inst_id,d.kslldadr,la.latch#,d.kslldlvl,d.kslldnam,la.gets,
                  la.misses,
              la.sleeps,la.immediate_gets,la.immediate_misses,la.waiters_woken,
                  la.waits_holding_latch,la.spin_gets,la.sleep1,la.sleep2,
                  la.sleep3,la.sleep4,la.sleep5,la.sleep6,la.sleep7,la.sleep8,
                  la.sleep9,la.sleep10, la.sleep11 from x$kslld d,
                  (select kslltnum latch#, sum(kslltwgt)
                  gets,sum(kslltwff) misses,sum(kslltwsl) sleeps,
                  sum(kslltngt) immediate_gets,sum(kslltnfa) immediate_misses,
                  sum(kslltwkc) waiters_woken,sum(kslltwth)
                  waits_holding_latch,sum(ksllthst0)
                  spin_gets,sum(ksllthst1) sleep1,sum(ksllthst2) sleep2,
                  sum(ksllthst3) sleep3,sum(ksllthst4) sleep4,sum(ksllthst5)
                  sleep5, sum(ksllthst6) sleep6,sum(ksllthst7)
                  sleep7,sum(ksllthst8) sleep8, sum(ksllthst9)
                  sleep9,sum(ksllthst10) sleep10,sum(ksllthst11) sleep11
                  from x$ksllt group by kslltnum) la  where la.latch# = d.indx
```

The **GV$LATCHHOLDER** DPT contains information about the current latch holders for the database.

Listing A.159 Description of the data dictionary dynamic performance table GV$LATCHHOLDER.

Name	Null?	Type
INST_ID		NUMBER
PID		NUMBER
SID		NUMBER
LADDR		RAW(4)
NAME		VARCHAR2(64)

```
GV$LATCHHOLDER    select inst_id,ksuprpid,ksuprsid,ksuprlat,ksuprlnm from
                  x$ksuprlat
```

The **GV$LATCHNAME** DPT contains decoded latch name values for the latches shown in **GV$LATCH**. The two tables have a one-to-one correspondence.

Listing A.160   Description of the data dictionary dynamic performance table GV$LATCHNAME.

```
Name                                 Null?     Type
------------------------------       --------  ----
INST_ID                                        NUMBER
LATCH#                                         NUMBER
NAME                                           VARCHAR2(64)


GV$LATCHNAME               select inst_id,indx,kslldnam from x$kslld
```

The **GV$LATCH_CHILDREN** DPT contains information about the child latches in the database. If the latches have the same **LATCH#** value, they have the same parent.

Listing A.161   Description of the data dictionary dynamic performance table GV$LATCH_CHILDREN.

```
Name                                 Null?     Type
------------------------------       --------  ----
INST_ID                                        NUMBER
ADDR                                           RAW(4)
LATCH#                                         NUMBER
CHILD#                                         NUMBER
LEVEL#                                         NUMBER
NAME                                           VARCHAR2(64)
GETS                                           NUMBER
MISSES                                         NUMBER
SLEEPS                                         NUMBER
IMMEDIATE_GETS                                 NUMBER
IMMEDIATE_MISSES                               NUMBER
WAITERS_WOKEN                                  NUMBER
WAITS_HOLDING_LATCH                            NUMBER
SPIN_GETS                                      NUMBER
SLEEP1                                         NUMBER
SLEEP2                                         NUMBER
SLEEP3                                         NUMBER
SLEEP4                                         NUMBER
SLEEP5                                         NUMBER
SLEEP6                                         NUMBER
SLEEP7                                         NUMBER
SLEEP8                                         NUMBER
SLEEP9                                         NUMBER
SLEEP10                                        NUMBER
SLEEP11                                        NUMBER
```

```
GV$LATCH_CHILDREN        select
                         t.inst_id,t.addr,t.kslltnum,t.kslltcnm,n.kslldlvl,n.kslldnam,
                         t.kslltwgt,t.kslltwff,t.kslltwsl,t.ksllngt,t.ksllnfa,
                         t.kslltwkc,t.kslltwth,t.ksllthst0,t.ksllthst1,
                         t.ksllthst2,t.ksllthst3,t.ksllthst4,t.ksllthst5,
                         t.ksllthst6,t.ksllthst7,t.ksllthst8,
                         t.ksllthst9,t.ksllthst10, t.ksllthst11 from x$ksllt t,
                         x$kslld n  where t.kslltcnm > 0 and t.kslltnum = n.indx
```

The **GV$LATCH_MISSES** DPT contains information about missed attempts to acquire a latch.

Listing A.162 Description of the data dictionary dynamic performance table GV$LATCH_MISSES.

Name	Null?	Type
INST_ID		NUMBER
PARENT_NAME		VARCHAR2(50)
WHERE		VARCHAR2(64)
NWFAIL_COUNT		NUMBER
SLEEP_COUNT		NUMBER

```
GV$LATCH_MISSES          select t1.inst_id,t1.ksllasnam, t2.ksllwnam, t1.kslnowtf,
                         t1.kslsleep from  x$ksllw t2, x$kslwsc t1
                         where t2.indx = t1.indx
```

The **GV$LATCH_PARENT** DPT contains statistics about parent latches.

Listing A.163 Description of the data dictionary dynamic performance table GV$LATCH_PARENT.

Name	Null?	Type
INST_ID		NUMBER
ADDR		RAW(4)
LATCH#		NUMBER
LEVEL#		NUMBER
NAME		VARCHAR2(64)
GETS		NUMBER
MISSES		NUMBER
SLEEPS		NUMBER
IMMEDIATE_GETS		NUMBER
IMMEDIATE_MISSES		NUMBER
WAITERS_WOKEN		NUMBER
WAITS_HOLDING_LATCH		NUMBER
SPIN_GETS		NUMBER
SLEEP1		NUMBER

```
SLEEP2                                          NUMBER
SLEEP3                                          NUMBER
SLEEP4                                          NUMBER
SLEEP5                                          NUMBER
SLEEP6                                          NUMBER
SLEEP7                                          NUMBER
SLEEP8                                          NUMBER
SLEEP9                                          NUMBER
SLEEP10                                         NUMBER
SLEEP11                                         NUMBER
```

```
GV$LATCH_PARENT      select t.inst_id,t.addr,t.kslltnum,n.kslldlvl,n.kslldnam,
                     t.kslltwgt,t.kslltwff,t.kslltwsl,t.kslltngt,t.kslltnfa,
                     t.kslltwkc,t.kslltwth,t.ksllthst0,t.ksllthst1,
                     t.ksllthst2,t.ksllthst3,t.ksllthst4,t.ksllthst5,
                     t.ksllthst6,t.ksllthst7,t.ksllthst8,
                     t.ksllthst9,t.ksllthst10, t.ksllthst11 from x$ksllt t,
                     x$kslld n  where t.kslltcnm = 0 and t.kslltnum = n.indx
```

The **GV$LIBRARYCACHE** DPT contains current statistics about the library caches of the shared pool area of the SGA.

Listing A.164   Description of the data dictionary dynamic performance table GV$LIBRARYCACHE.

```
Name                              Null?     Type
--------------------------------  --------  ----
INST_ID                                     NUMBER
NAMESPACE                                   VARCHAR2(15)
GETS                                        NUMBER
GETHITS                                     NUMBER
GETHITRATIO                                 NUMBER
PINS                                        NUMBER
PINHITS                                     NUMBER
PINHITRATIO                                 NUMBER
RELOADS                                     NUMBER
INVALIDATIONS                               NUMBER
DLM_LOCK_REQUESTS                           NUMBER
DLM_PIN_REQUESTS                            NUMBER
DLM_PIN_RELEASES                            NUMBER
DLM_INVALIDATION_REQUESTS                   NUMBER
DLM_INVALIDATIONS                           NUMBER
```

```
GV$LIBRARYCACHE      select inst_id,
                     decode(indx,
                        0,'SQL AREA',
                        1,'TABLE/PROCEDURE',
                        2,'BODY',
```

```
              3,'TRIGGER',
              4,'INDEX',
              5,'CLUSTER',
              6,'OBJECT',
              7,'PIPE','?'),
        kglstget,kglstght,
        decode(kglstget,0,1,kglstght/kglstget),kglstpin,kglstpht,
        decode(kglstpin,0,1,kglstpht/kglstpin),kglstrld,kglstinv,
        kglstlrq,kglstprq,kglstprl,kglstirq,kglstmiv from x$kglst
        where indx<8
```

The **GV$LICENSE** DPT contains information about the current license limits, as specified by the initialization file parameters.

Listing A.165 Description of the data dictionary dynamic performance table GV$LICENSE.

Name	Null?	Type
INST_ID		NUMBER
SESSIONS_MAX		NUMBER
SESSIONS_WARNING		NUMBER
SESSIONS_CURRENT		NUMBER
SESSIONS_HIGHWATER		NUMBER
USERS_MAX		NUMBER

```
GV$LICENSE          select inst_id,ksullms,ksullws,ksullcs,ksullhs,ksullmu from
                    x$ksull
```

The **GV$LOADCSTAT** (cluster), **GV$LOADPSTAT** (partition), and **GV$LOADTSTAT** (table) DPTs contain SQL*Loader statistics compiled during the execution of a direct load and apply to the whole load. Any **SELECT** against these DPTs results in "no rows returned", because you cannot load data and do a query at the same time; hence, for users, these DPTs are useless.

Listing A.166 Description of the data dictionary dynamic performance table GV$LOADCSTAT.

Name	Null?	Type
INST_ID		NUMBER
READ		NUMBER
REJECTED		NUMBER
TDISCARD		NUMBER
NDISCARD		NUMBER

```
GV$LOADCSTAT                   select inst_id,kllcntnrd,kllcntnrj,kllcnttds,kllcntnds from
                               x$kllcnt
```

Listing A.167 Description of the data dictionary dynamic performance table GV$LOADPSTAT.

Name	Null?	Type
INST_ID		NUMBER
TABNAME		VARCHAR2(31)
PARTNAME		VARCHAR2(31)
LOADED		NUMBER

```
GV$LOADPSTAT                   select inst_id,klcpxtn,klcpxpn,klcpxrld from x$klpt
```

Listing A.168 Description of the data dictionary dynamic performance table GV$LOADTSTAT.

Name	Null?	Type
INST_ID		NUMBER
LOADED		NUMBER
REJECTED		NUMBER
FAILWHEN		NUMBER
ALLNULL		NUMBER
LEFT2SKIP		NUMBER
PTNLOADED		NUMBER

```
GV$LOADTSTAT                   select
                               inst_id,klltabnld,klltabnrj,klltabnfw,klltabnan,klltabnls,
                               klltabpld from x$klltab
```

The **GV$LOCK** DPT contains information about current locks and requested locks for the database.

Listing A.169 Description of the data dictionary dynamic performance table GV$LOCK.

Name	Null?	Type
INST_ID		NUMBER
ADDR		RAW(4)
KADDR		RAW(4)
SID		NUMBER
TYPE		VARCHAR2(2)
ID1		NUMBER
ID2		NUMBER

```
LMODE                                          NUMBER
REQUEST                                        NUMBER
CTIME                                          NUMBER
BLOCK                                          NUMBER

GV$LOCK              select /*+ ordered use_nl(l), use_nl(s), use_nl(r) +*/
                    s.inst_id,l.laddr,l.kaddr,s.ksusenum,r.ksqrsidt,r.ksqrsid1,
                    r.ksqrsid2,l.lmode, l.request,l.ctime,l.block
                    from v$_lock l,x$ksuse s,x$ksqrs r
                    where l.saddr=s.addr and
                    l.raddr=r.addr
```

The **GV$LOCKED_OBJECT** DPT contains information about currently locked objects and about all locks acquired by every transaction on the system.

Listing A.170 Description of the data dictionary dynamic performance table GV$LOCKED_OBJECT.

Name	Null?	Type
INST_ID		NUMBER
XIDUSN		NUMBER
XIDSLOT		NUMBER
XIDSQN		NUMBER
OBJECT_ID		NUMBER
SESSION_ID		NUMBER
ORACLE_USERNAME		VARCHAR2(30)
OS_USER_NAME		VARCHAR2(15)
PROCESS		VARCHAR2(9)
LOCKED_MODE		NUMBER

```
GV$LOCKED_OBJECT    select x.inst_id,x.kxidusn, x.kxidslt, x.kxidsqn,
                    l.ktadmtab,         s.indx, s.ksuudlna, s.ksuseunm,
                    s.ksusepid, l.ksqlkmod from x$ktcxb x, x$ktadm l, x$ksuse s
                    where x.ktcxbxba = l.kssobown and x.ktcxbses = s.addr
```

GV$LOCKS_WITH_COLLISIONS is a parallel server table showing locks that protect multiple buffers that have been force read or force written at least 10 times. This will probably correlate with high readings in the false pings DPT.

Listing A.171 Description of the dynamic performance table GV$LOCKS_WITH_COLLISIONS.

Name	Null?	Type
INST_ID		NUMBER
LOCK_ELEMENT_ADDR		RAW(4)

```
GV$LOCKS_WITH_COLLISIONS select inst_id, lock_element_addr
                        from gv$bh
                        where
                        (forced_writes + forced_reads) > 10
                        group by
                         lock_element_addr, inst_id
                        having
                         count(*) >= 2
```

GV$LOCK_ELEMENT is a parallel server table. It has one entry for each PCM lock used by the buffer cache.

Listing A.172 Description of the dynamic performance table GV$LOCK_ELEMENT.

```
Name                            Null?     Type
------------------------------- --------  ----
INST_ID                                   NUMBER
LOCK_ELEMENT_ADDR                         RAW(4)
INDX                                      NUMBER
CLASS                                     NUMBER
LOCK_ELEMENT_NAME                         NUMBER
MODE_HELD                                 NUMBER
BLOCK_COUNT                               NUMBER
RELEASING                                 NUMBER
ACQUIRING                                 NUMBER
INVALID                                   NUMBER
FLAGS                                     NUMBER

GV$LOCK_ELEMENT         select inst_id, addr, indx, le_class,
                        name, le_mode,
                        le_blks, le_rls,
                        le_acq, le_inv, le_flags
                        from x$le
```

The **GV$LOG** DPT contains information on the redo log files taken live from the control files.

Listing A.173 Description of the data dictionary dynamic performance table GV$LOG.

```
Name                            Null?     Type
------------------------------- --------  ----
INST_ID                                   NUMBER
GROUP#                                    NUMBER
THREAD#                                   NUMBER
SEQUENCE#                                 NUMBER
BYTES                                     NUMBER
```

```
MEMBERS                         NUMBER
ARCHIVED                        VARCHAR2(3)
STATUS                          VARCHAR2(16)
FIRST_CHANGE#                   NUMBER
FIRST_TIME                      DATE


GV$LOG              select
                   le.inst_id,le.lenum,le.lethr,le.leseq,le.lesiz*le.lebsz,ledup,
                   decode(bitand(le.leflg,1),0,'NO','YES'),
                   decode(bitand(le.leflg,24),
                    8,'CURRENT',
                    16,'CLEARING',
                    24,'CLEARING_CURRENT',
                    decode(sign(leseq),0,'UNUSED',
                   decode(sign((to_number(rt.rtckp_scn)-to_number(le.lenxs))*
                   bitand(rt.rtsta,2)),-1,'ACTIVE','INACTIVE'))),
                   to_number(le.lelos),
                   to_date(le.lelot,'MM/DD/RR HH24:MI:SS')
                   from x$kccle le, x$kccrt rt
                   where le.ledup!=0 and le.lethr=rt.rtnum and
                   le.inst_id = rt.inst_id
```

The **GV$LOGFILE** DPT contains information about the current status of all redo log files.

Listing A.174   Description of the data dictionary dynamic performance table GV$LOGFILE.

Name	Null?	Type
INST_ID		NUMBER
GROUP#		NUMBER
STATUS		VARCHAR2(7)
MEMBER		VARCHAR2(513)

```
GV$LOGFILE         select inst_id,fnfno,
                   decode(fnflg,0,'',1,'INVALID',2,'STALE',4,'DELETED','UNKNOWN'),
                   fnnam from x$kccfn where fnnam is not null and fntyp=3
```

The **GV$LOGHIST** DPT contains information about the redo log history for the redo log files from the controlfile. This is included only for backward consistency. All future references should be transferred to the **GV$LOG_HISTORY** DPT.

Listing A.175 Description of the data dictionary dynamic performance table GV$LOGHIST.

Name	Null?	Type
INST_ID		NUMBER
THREAD#		NUMBER
SEQUENCE#		NUMBER
FIRST_CHANGE#		NUMBER
FIRST_TIME		DATE
SWITCH_CHANGE#		NUMBER

```
GV$LOGHIST          select
                    inst_id,lhthp,lhseq,to_number(lhlos),
                    to_date(lhlot,'MM/DD/RR HH24:MI:SS'), to_number(lhnxs) from
x$kcclh
```

The **GV$LOG_HISTORY** DPT is the more current version of the **V$LOGHIST** DPT and should be used in its place.

Listing A.176 Description of the data dictionary dynamic performance table GV$LOG_HISTORY.

Name	Null?	Type
INST_ID		NUMBER
RECID		NUMBER
STAMP		NUMBER
THREAD#		NUMBER
SEQUENCE#		NUMBER
FIRST_CHANGE#		NUMBER
FIRST_TIME		DATE
NEXT_CHANGE#		NUMBER

```
GV$LOG_HISTORY      select
                    inst_id,lhrid,lhstm,lhthp,lhseq,to_number(lhlos),to_date(lhl
                    ot,'MM/DD/RR HH24:MI:SS'),to_number(lhnxs) from x$kcclh
```

The **GV$MLS_PARAMETERS** DPT gives the current value for all MLS parameters. This DPT is used only with the Secure Oracle option.

Listing A.177 Description of the data dictionary dynamic performance table GV$MLS_PARAMETERS.

Name	Null?	Type
INST_ID		NUMBER
NUM		NUMBER
NAME		VARCHAR2(64)
TYPE		NUMBER

```
VALUE                                     VARCHAR2(512)
ISDEFAULT                                 VARCHAR2(9)
ISSES_MODIFIABLE                          VARCHAR2(5)
ISSYS_MODIFIABLE                          VARCHAR2(9)
ISMODIFIED                                VARCHAR2(10)
ISADJUSTED                                VARCHAR2(5)
DESCRIPTION                               VARCHAR2(64)
```

The **GV$MTS** DPT gives the current status of the multithreaded server process.

Listing A.178   Description of the data dictionary dynamic performance table GV$MTS.

```
Name                            Null?     Type
------------------------------- --------  ----
INST_ID                                   NUMBER
MAXIMUM_CONNECTIONS                       NUMBER
SERVERS_STARTED                           NUMBER
SERVERS_TERMINATED                        NUMBER
SERVERS_HIGHWATER                         NUMBER

GV$MTS              select inst_id,kmmsgcmx,kmmsgsta+kmmsgutr,kmmsgtrm,kmmsgsmx
                    from x$kmmsg
```

The **GV$MYSTAT** DPT gives the current statistics for the current session. To translate the **STATISTIC#** column, join to the **GV$STATNAME** DPT.

Listing A.179   Description of the data dictionary dynamic performance table GV$MYSTAT.

```
Name                            Null?     Type
------------------------------- --------  ----
INST_ID                                   NUMBER
SID                                       NUMBER
STATISTIC#                                NUMBER
VALUE                                     NUMBER

GV$MYSTAT           select inst_id,ksusenum,ksusestn,ksusestv from x$ksumysta
                    where bitand(ksspaflg,1)!=0 and bitand(ksuseflg,1)!=0 and
                    ksusestn<(select count(*) from x$ksusd)
```

The **GV$NLS_PARAMETERS** DPT lists the current value for the National Language System (NLS) parameters.

Listing A.180 Description of the data dictionary dynamic performance table GV$NLS_PARAMETERS.

```
Name                                Null?     Type
-------------------------------     --------  ----
INST_ID                                       NUMBER
PARAMETER                                     VARCHAR2(64)
VALUE                                         VARCHAR2(64)
```

```
GV$NLS_PARAMETERS     select inst_id,parameter, value from x$nls_parameters where
                      parameter != 'NLS_SPECIAL_CHARS'
```

The **GV$NLS_VALID_VALUES** DPT lists all valid values for NLS parameters.

Listing A.181 Description of the data dictionary dynamic performance table GV$NLS_VALID_VALUES.

```
Name                                Null?     Type
-------------------------------     --------  ----
INST_ID                                       NUMBER
PARAMETER                                     VARCHAR2(64)
VALUE                                         VARCHAR2(64)
```

```
GV$NLS_VALID_VALUES   select inst_id,parameter, value from x$ksulv
```

The **GV$OBJECT_DEPENDENCY** DPT is used to determine the current dependency trees for objects in the database that are in the shared pool. Together with **GV$SESSION** and **GV$SQL**, it can be used to determine which tables are used in the SQL statement a user is currently executing.

Listing A.182 Description of the data dictionary dynamic performance table GV$OBJECT_DEPENDENCY.

```
Name                                Null?     Type
-------------------------------     --------  ----
INST_ID                                       NUMBER
FROM_ADDRESS                                  RAW(4)
FROM_HASH                                     NUMBER
TO_OWNER                                      VARCHAR2(64)
TO_NAME                                       VARCHAR2(1000)
TO_ADDRESS                                    RAW(4)
TO_HASH                                       NUMBER
TO_TYPE                                       NUMBER
```

```
GV$OBJECT_DEPENDENCY  select d.inst_id,d.kglhdpar, d.kglnahsh,           o.kglnaown,
                      o.kglnaobj, o.kglhdadr, o.kglnahsh, o.kglobtyp from x$kglob
                      o, x$kgldp d  where o.kglnahsh = d.kglrfhsh  and  o.kglhdadr
                      = d.kglrfhdl
```

The **GV$OFFLINE_RANGE** DPT gives information about datafiles that are currently offline. Records are created in this DPT when tablespaces or datafiles are altered offline **NORMAL** or **READ ONLY** only.

Listing A.183 Description of the data dictionary dynamic performance table GV$OFFLINE_RANGE.

```
Name                            Null?    Type
------------------------------- -------- ----
INST_ID                                  NUMBER
RECID                                    NUMBER
STAMP                                    NUMBER
FILE#                                    NUMBER
OFFLINE_CHANGE#                          NUMBER
ONLINE_CHANGE#                           NUMBER
ONLINE_TIME                              DATE


GV$OFFLINE_RANGE       select
                       inst_id,orrid,orstm,ordfp,to_number(orofs),to_number(orons),
                       to_date(oront,'MM/DD/RR HH24:MI:SS') from x$kccor
```

The **GV$OPEN_CURSOR** DPT provides information on currently opened and parsed cursors for each user.

Listing A.184 Description of the data dictionary dynamic performance table GV$OPEN_CURSOR.

```
Name                            Null?    Type
------------------------------- -------- ----
INST_ID                                  NUMBER
SADDR                                    RAW(4)
SID                                      NUMBER
USER_NAME                                VARCHAR2(30)
ADDRESS                                  RAW(4)
HASH_VALUE                               NUMBER
SQL_TEXT                                 VARCHAR2(60)


GV$OPEN_CURSOR         select inst_id,kgllkuse, kgllksnm, user_name, kglhdpar,
                       kglnahsh, kglnaobj from x$kgllk where kglhdnsp = 0 and
                       kglhdpar != kgllkhdl
```

The **GV$OPTION** DPT provides information on currently installed options for the database.

Listing A.185 Description of the data dictionary dynamic performance table GV$OPTION.

```
Name                              Null?    Type
---------------------------------- -------- ----
INST_ID                                    NUMBER
PARAMETER                                  VARCHAR2(64)
VALUE                                      VARCHAR2(64)

GV$OPTION              select inst_id,parameter, value from x$option
```

The **GV$PARAMETER** DPT provides information on all database initialization parameters.

Listing A.186 Description of the data dictionary dynamic performance table GV$PARAMETER.

```
Name                              Null?    Type
---------------------------------- -------- ----
INST_ID                                    NUMBER
NUM                                        NUMBER
NAME                                       VARCHAR2(64)
TYPE                                       NUMBER
VALUE                                      VARCHAR2(512)
ISDEFAULT                                  VARCHAR2(9)
ISSES_MODIFIABLE                           VARCHAR2(5)
ISSYS_MODIFIABLE                           VARCHAR2(9)
ISMODIFIED                                 VARCHAR2(10)
ISADJUSTED                                 VARCHAR2(5)
DESCRIPTION                                VARCHAR2(64)

GV$PARAMETER          select x.inst_id,x.indx+1,ksppinm,ksppity,ksppstvl,ksppstdf,
                      decode(bitand(ksppiflg/256,1),1,'TRUE','FALSE'),
                      decode(bitand(ksppiflg/65536,3),1,'IMMEDIATE',2,'DEFERRED',
                      3,'IMMEDIATE','FALSE'),
                      decode(bitand(ksppstvf,7),1,'MODIFIED',4,'SYSTEM_MOD','FALSE'),
                      decode(bitand(ksppstvf,2),2,'TRUE','FALSE'),   ksppdesc
                      from x$ksppi x, x$ksppcv y where x.indx = y.indx and
                      translate(ksppinm,'_','#') not like '#%'
```

The **GV$PQ_SESSTAT** DPT provides current session statistics on parallel query operations.

Listing A.187 Description of the data dictionary dynamic performance table GV$PQ_SESSTAT.

```
Name                                     Null?    Type
--------------------------------------   -------- ----
INST_ID                                           NUMBER
STATISTIC                                         VARCHAR2(30)
LAST_QUERY                                        NUMBER
SESSION_TOTAL                                     NUMBER

GV$PQ_SESSTAT           select inst_id, kxfpssnam, kxfpssval, kxfpsstot from
                        x$kxfpsst
```

The **GV$PQ_SLAVE** DPT provides current statistics for all parallel query slaves in the database.

Listing A.188 Description of the data dictionary dynamic performance table GV$PQ_SLAVE.

```
Name                                     Null?    Type
--------------------------------------   -------- ----
INST_ID                                           NUMBER
SLAVE_NAME                                        VARCHAR2(4)
STATUS                                            VARCHAR2(4)
SESSIONS                                          NUMBER
IDLE_TIME_CUR                                     NUMBER
BUSY_TIME_CUR                                     NUMBER
CPU_SECS_CUR                                      NUMBER
MSGS_SENT_CUR                                     NUMBER
MSGS_RCVD_CUR                                     NUMBER
IDLE_TIME_TOTAL                                   NUMBER
BUSY_TIME_TOTAL                                   NUMBER
CPU_SECS_TOTAL                                    NUMBER
MSGS_SENT_TOTAL                                   NUMBER
MSGS_RCVD_TOTAL                                   NUMBER

GV$PQ_SLAVE             select inst_id,kxfpdpnam, decode(bitand(kxfpdpflg, 16), 0,
                        'BUSY', 'IDLE'),  kxfpdpses, floor(kxfpdpcit / 6000),
                        floor(kxfpdpcbt / 6000),  floor(kxfpdpcct / 100),
                        kxfpdpclsnt + kxfpdpcrsnt,  kxfpdpclrcv + kxfpdpcrrcv,
                        floor((kxfpdptit + kxfpdpcit) / 6000),  floor((kxfpdptbt +
                        kxfpdpcbt) / 6000),  floor((kxfpdptct + kxfpdpcct) / 100),
                        kxfpdptlsnt + kxfpdpclsnt + kxfpdptrsnt + kxfpdpcrsnt,
                        kxfpdptlrcv + kxfpdpclrcv + kxfpdptrrcv + kxfpdpcrrcv  from
                        x$kxfpdp where bitand(kxfpdpflg, 8) != 0
```

The **GV$PQ_SYSSTAT** DPT provides current system-level statistics for parallel query operations for the database.

Listing A.189 Description of the data dictionary dynamic performance table GV$PQ_SYSSTAT.

```
Name                            Null?    Type
------------------------------- -------- ----
INST_ID                                  NUMBER
STATISTIC                                VARCHAR2(30)
VALUE                                    NUMBER


GV$PQ_SYSSTAT          select inst_id, rpad(kxfpysnam,30), kxfpysval from x$kxfpys
```

The **GV$PQ_TQSTAT** DPT provides statistics on the most currently run parallel query. It also provides information on the query tree regarding the number of rows processed for each branch of the parallel query operation.

Listing A.190 Description of the data dictionary dynamic performance table GV$PQ_TQSTAT.

```
Name                            Null?    Type
------------------------------- -------- ----
INST_ID                                  NUMBER
DFO_NUMBER                               NUMBER
TQ_ID                                    NUMBER
SERVER_TYPE                              VARCHAR2(10)
NUM_ROWS                                 NUMBER
BYTES                                    NUMBER
OPEN_TIME                                NUMBER
AVG_LATENCY                              NUMBER
WAITS                                    NUMBER
TIMEOUTS                                 NUMBER
PROCESS                                  VARCHAR2(10)
INSTANCE                                 NUMBER


GV$PQ_TQSTAT          select inst_id, kxfqsqn, kxfqsid, rpad(kxfqsty,10),
                      kxfqscnt, kxfqslen, kxfqset, kxfqsavl, kxfqsdw, kxfqsdt,
                      rpad(kxfqssid,10), kxfqsiid from x$kxfqsrow
```

The **GV$PROCESS** DPT provides information about the currently active processes.

Listing A.191 Description of the data dictionary dynamic performance table GV$PROCESS.

```
Name                            Null?    Type
------------------------------- -------- ----
INST_ID                                  NUMBER
ADDR                                     RAW(4)
PID                                      NUMBER
SPID                                     VARCHAR2(9)
USERNAME                                 VARCHAR2(15)
```

```
SERIAL#                              NUMBER
TERMINAL                             VARCHAR2(16)
PROGRAM                              VARCHAR2(64)
BACKGROUND                           VARCHAR2(1)
LATCHWAIT                            VARCHAR2(8)
LATCHSPIN                            VARCHAR2(8)

GV$PROCESS          select inst_id,
                    addr,indx,ksuprpid,ksuprunm,ksuprser,ksuprtid,ksuprpnm,
                    decode(bitand(ksuprflg,2),0,null,1),
                    decode(ksllawat,hextoraw('00'),null,ksllawat),
                    decode(ksllaspn,hextoraw('00'),null,ksllaspn) from x$ksupr
                    where bitand(ksspaflg,1)!=0
```

The **GV$PWFILE_USERS** DPT provides information on which users have been granted SYSDBA and SYSOPER privileges. It is derived from the external password file.

Listing A.192 Description of the data dictionary dynamic performance table GV$PWFILE_USERS.

Name	Null?	Type
INST_ID		NUMBER
USERNAME		VARCHAR2(30)
SYSDBA		VARCHAR2(5)
SYSOPER		VARCHAR2(5)

```
GV$PWFILE_USERS     select inst_id,username,decode(sysdba,1,'TRUE','FALSE'),
                    decode(sysoper,1,'TRUE','FALSE') from x$kzsrt where valid=1
```

The **GV$QUEUE** DPT provides information on the multithreaded server message queues.

Listing A.193 Description of the data dictionary dynamic performance table GV$QUEUE.

Name	Null?	Type
INST_ID		NUMBER
PADDR		RAW(4)
TYPE		VARCHAR2(10)
QUEUED		NUMBER
WAIT		NUMBER
TOTALQ		NUMBER

```
GV$QUEUE              select
                      inst_id,kmcqspro,
                      decode(indx,0,'COMMON',1,'OUTBOUND','DISPATCHER'),
                      kmcqsncq,kmcqswat,kmcqstnc from x$kmcqs where indx
                      in (0,1) or kmcqspro!=hextoraw('00')
```

These next three DPTs—**GV$RECOVERY_FILE_STATUS**, **GV$RECOVERY_LOG**, and **GV$RECOVERY_STATUS**—are visible only to the Recovery Manager, and hence, are not much use to anyone else.

Listing A.194 Description of the data dictionary dynamic performance table GV$RECOVERY_FILE_STATUS.

```
Name                             Null?     Type
-------------------------------- --------  ----
INST_ID                                    NUMBER
FILENUM                                    NUMBER
FILENAME                                   VARCHAR2(513)
STATUS                                     VARCHAR2(13)
```

```
GV$RECOVERY_FILE_STAUS select fn.inst_id, fn.fnfno, fn.fnnam,
                      decode(nvl(mf.cps,0),
                      0, 'NOT RECOVERED',
                      281474976710655, 'CURRENT',
                      'IN RECOVERY')
                      from x$kcrmx mx, x$kccfn fn, x$kccfe fe, x$kcrmf
                      mf where fn.fntyp = 4 and mf.fno(+) = fn.fnfno and
                      ((bitand(mx.flg,2) != 0 and fe.fedup != 0) or mf.fno =
                      fn.fnfno) and fe.fenum = fn.fnfno
```

Listing A.195 Description of the data dictionary dynamic performance table GV$RECOVERY_LOG.

```
Name                             Null?     Type
-------------------------------- --------  ----
INST_ID                                    NUMBER
THREAD#                                    NUMBER
SEQUENCE#                                  NUMBER
TIME                                       DATE
ARCHIVE_NAME                               VARCHAR2(513)
```

```
GV$RECOVERY_LOG       select
                      inst_id,lhthp,lhseq,to_date(lhlot,'MM/DD/RR HH24:MI:SS'),
                      lhnam from x$kcclh
                      where to_number(lhnxs) >
                      (select min(to_number(fhscn)) from x$kcvfhmrr where hxerr =
                      0) and lhseq not in (select leseq from x$kccle where lethr =
                      lhthp) and to_number(lhlos) < (select max(to_number(hxsts))
                      from x$kcvfhmrr where hxerr = 0)
```

Listing A.196 Description of the data dictionary dynamic performance table GV$RECOVERY_STATUS.

Name	Null?	Type
INST_ID		NUMBER
RECOVERY_CHECKPOINT		DATE
THREAD		NUMBER
SEQUENCE_NEEDED		NUMBER
SCN_NEEDED		VARCHAR2(16)
TIME_NEEDED		DATE
PREVIOUS_LOG_NAME		VARCHAR2(513)
PREVIOUS_LOG_STATUS		VARCHAR2(13)
REASON		VARCHAR2(13)

```
GV$RECOVERY_STATUS   select fx.inst_id, to_date(mx.ckptim,'MM/DD/RR HH24:MI:SS'),
                     mx.thr, mx.seq, mx.los, to_date(mx.tim,'MM/DD/RR
                     HH24:MI:SS'), nvl(mx.nam, 'NONE'),
                     decode(bitand(mx.mrs, 256 + 128 + 64 + 8),
                      8,'RELEASE',
                      64,'WRONG LOG',
                      128,'MISSING NAME',
                      256,'UNNEEDED NAME',
                      'NONE'),
                     decode(nvl(fx.err, 3),
                      1, 'NEED LOG',
                      3, 'END OF THREAD',
                      4, 'LOG REUSED',
                     'UNKNOWN')
                     from x$kcrmx mx, x$kcrfx fx where
                     fx.thr(+) = mx.thr
```

The **GV$RECOVER_FILE** DPT shows the current database files that need recovery.

Listing A.197 Description of the data dictionary dynamic performance table GV$RECOVER_FILE.

Name	Null?	Type
INST_ID		NUMBER
FILE#		NUMBER
ONLINE		VARCHAR2(7)
ERROR		VARCHAR2(18)
CHANGE#		NUMBER
TIME		DATE

```
GV$RECOVER_FILE         select inst_id,hxfil, decode(hxons, 0, 'OFFLINE', 'ONLINE'),
                        decode(hxerr,
                          0,'',
                          1,'FILE MISSING',
                          2,'OFFLINE NORMAL',
                          3,'NOT VERIFIED',
                          4,'FILE NOT FOUND',
                          5,'CANNOT OPEN FILE',
                          6,'CANNOT READ HEADER',
                          7,'CORRUPT HEADER',
                          8,'WRONG FILE TYPE',
                          9,'WRONG DATABASE',
                          10,'WRONG FILE NUMBER',
                          11,'WRONG FILE CREATE',
                          12,'WRONG FILE CREATE',
                          13,'WRONG FILE SIZE','UNKNOWN ERROR'), to_number(fhscn),
                        to_date(fhtim,'MM/DD/RR HH24:MI:SS') from x$kcvfhmrr
```

The **GV$REQDIST** DPT shows data for a histogram of the multithreaded server request times. There are 12 buckets that grow exponentially in time and size, based on bucket number.

Listing A.198   Description of the data dictionary dynamic performance table GV$REQDIST.

```
Name                             Null?     Type
-------------------------------- --------  ----
INST_ID                                    NUMBER
BUCKET                                     NUMBER
COUNT                                      NUMBER

GV$REQDIST              select inst_id,kmmrdbuc,sum(kmmrdcnt) from x$kmmrd where
                        kmmrdpro!=hextoraw('00') group by inst_id,kmmrdbuc
```

The **GV$RESOURCE** DPT contains system type resource-object names and addresses.

Listing A.199   Description of the data dictionary dynamic performance table GV$RESOURCE.

```
Name                             Null?     Type
-------------------------------- --------  ----
INST_ID                                    NUMBER
ADDR                                       RAW(4)
TYPE                                       VARCHAR2(2)
ID1                                        NUMBER
ID2                                        NUMBER

GV$RESOURCE            select inst_id,addr,ksqrsidt,ksqrsid1,ksqrsid2 from x$ksqrs
                       where bitand(ksqrsflg,2)!=0
```

The **GV$RESOURCE_LIMIT** DPT shows the current values for each global resource limit. These are not **PROFILE** resources, but the resources used by system operations.

Listing A.200   Description of the dynamic performance table GV$RESOURCE_LIMIT.

Name	Null?	Type
INST_ID		NUMBER
RESOURCE_NAME		VARCHAR2(30)
CURRENT_UTILIZATION		NUMBER
MAX_UTILIZATION		NUMBER
INITIAL_ALLOCATION		VARCHAR2(10)
LIMIT_VALUE		VARCHAR2(10)

```
GV$RESOURCE_LIMIT    select inst_id, ksurlmnm, ksurlmcv, ksurlmmv,
                     LPAD(decode(bitand(ksurlmfg, 1), 0, to_char(ksurlmia),
                     'UNLIMITED'),10),  LPAD(decode(bitand(ksurlmfg, 2), 0,
                     to_char(ksurlmlv), 'UNLIMITED'),10) from x$ksurlmt
```

The **GV$ROLLSTAT** DPT contains current rollback segment statistics.

Listing A.201   Description of the data dictionary dynamic performance table GV$ROLLSTAT.

Name	Null?	Type
INST_ID		NUMBER
USN		NUMBER
EXTENTS		NUMBER
RSSIZE		NUMBER
WRITES		NUMBER
XACTS		NUMBER
GETS		NUMBER
WAITS		NUMBER
OPTSIZE		NUMBER
HWMSIZE		NUMBER
SHRINKS		NUMBER
WRAPS		NUMBER
EXTENDS		NUMBER
AVESHRINK		NUMBER
AVEACTIVE		NUMBER
STATUS		VARCHAR2(15)
CUREXT		NUMBER
CURBLK		NUMBER

```
GV$ROLLSTAT          select
                     inst_id,kturdusn,kturdext,kturdsiz,kturdwrt,kturdnax,kturdge
                     t,kturdwat, decode(kturdopt, -1,to_number(null), kturdopt),
                     kturdhwm,kturdnsh,kturdnwp,kturdnex, kturdash,kturdaae,
                     decode(kturdflg, 0,'ONLINE', 2,'PENDING OFFLINE',
                     3,'OFFLINE',         4, 'FULL', 'UNKNOWN'), kturdcex,
                     kturdcbk from x$kturd where kturdsiz!=0 and kturdflg != 3
```

The **GV$ROWCACHE** DPT contains current statistics for the data dictionary row cache area.

Listing A.202   Description of the data dictionary dynamic performance table GV$ROWCACHE.

Name	Null?	Type
INST_ID		NUMBER
CACHE#		NUMBER
TYPE		VARCHAR2(11)
SUBORDINATE#		NUMBER
PARAMETER		VARCHAR2(32)
COUNT		NUMBER
USAGE		NUMBER
FIXED		NUMBER
GETS		NUMBER
GETMISSES		NUMBER
SCANS		NUMBER
SCANMISSES		NUMBER
SCANCOMPLETES		NUMBER
MODIFICATIONS		NUMBER
FLUSHES		NUMBER
DLM_REQUESTS		NUMBER
DLM_CONFLICTS		NUMBER
DLM_RELEASES		NUMBER

```
GV$ROWCACHE          select
                     inst_id,kqrstcid,decode(kqrsttyp,1,'PARENT','SUBORDINATE'),
                     decode(kqrsttyp,2,kqrstsno,null),kqrsttxt,kqrstcsz,kqrstusg,
                     kqrstfcs,
                     kqrstgrq,kqrstgmi,kqrstsrq,kqrstsmi,kqrstsco,kqrstmrq,kqrstm
                     fl, kqrstilr,kqrstifr,kqrstisr from x$kqrst
```

The **GV$SESSION** DPT provides current statistics for each current session.

Listing A.203 Description of the data dictionary dynamic performance table GV$SESSION.

Name	Null?	Type
INST_ID		NUMBER
SADDR		RAW(4)
SID		NUMBER
SERIAL#		NUMBER
AUDSID		NUMBER
PADDR		RAW(4)
USER#		NUMBER
USERNAME		VARCHAR2(30)
COMMAND		NUMBER
TADDR		VARCHAR2(8)
LOCKWAIT		VARCHAR2(8)
STATUS		VARCHAR2(8)
SERVER		VARCHAR2(9)
SCHEMA#		NUMBER
SCHEMANAME		VARCHAR2(30)
OSUSER		VARCHAR2(15)
PROCESS		VARCHAR2(9)
MACHINE		VARCHAR2(64)
TERMINAL		VARCHAR2(16)
PROGRAM		VARCHAR2(64)
TYPE		VARCHAR2(10)
SQL_ADDRESS		RAW(4)
SQL_HASH_VALUE		NUMBER
PREV_SQL_ADDR		RAW(4)
PREV_HASH_VALUE		NUMBER
MODULE		VARCHAR2(48)
MODULE_HASH		NUMBER
ACTION		VARCHAR2(32)
ACTION_HASH		NUMBER
CLIENT_INFO		VARCHAR2(64)
FIXED_TABLE_SEQUENCE		NUMBER
ROW_WAIT_OBJ#		NUMBER
ROW_WAIT_FILE#		NUMBER
ROW_WAIT_BLOCK#		NUMBER
ROW_WAIT_ROW#		NUMBER
LOGON_TIME		DATE
LAST_CALL_ET		NUMBER
PDML_ENABLED		VARCHAR2(3)
FAILOVER_TYPE		VARCHAR2(13)
FAILOVER_METHOD		VARCHAR2(10)
FAILED_OVER		VARCHAR2(3)

```
GV$SESSION              select
                        inst_id,addr,indx,ksuseser,ksuudses,ksusepro,ksuudlui,ksuudlna,
                        ksuudoct, ksusesow,
                        decode(ksusetrn,hextoraw('00'),null,ksusetrn),
                        decode(ksqpswat,hextoraw('00'),null,ksqpswat),
                        decode(bitand(ksuseidl,11),
                        1,'ACTIVE',
                        0, decode(bitand(ksuseflg,4096),
                          0,'INACTIVE','CACHED'),
                        2,'SNIPED',
                        3,'SNIPED',
                         'KILLED'),
                        decode(ksspatyp,1,'DEDICATED',2,'SHARED',3,'PSEUDO','NONE'),
                        ksuudsid,ksuudsna,ksuseunm,ksusepid,ksusemnm,ksusetid,ksusepnm,
                        decode(bitand(ksuseflg,19),
                         17,'BACKGROUND',
                         1,'USER',
                         2,'RECURSIVE','?'), ksusesql, ksusesqh, ksusepsq, ksusepha,
                        ksuseapp, ksuseaph,  ksuseact, ksuseach, ksusecli, ksusefix,
                        ksuseobj, ksusefil, ksuseblk, ksuseslt, ksuseltm, ksusectm,
                        decode(bitand(ksuseflg, 32768),0,'NO','YES'),
                        decode(ksuseft, 2,'SESSION',
                        4,'SELECT',8,'TRANSACTIONAL','NONE'),
                        decode(ksusefm,1,'BASIC',2,'PRECONNECT',4,'PREPARSE','NONE')
                        , decode(ksusefs, 1, 'YES', 'NO') from x$ksuse where
                        bitand(ksspaflg,1)!=0 and bitand(ksuseflg,1)!=0
```

The **GV$SESSION_CONNECT_INFO** DPT provides information about network connections for the current session.

Listing A.204 Description of the data dictionary dynamic performance table GV$SESSION_CONNECT_INFO.

```
Name                                Null?     Type
-----------------------------------  --------  ----
INST_ID                                        NUMBER
SID                                            NUMBER
AUTHENTICATION_TYPE                            VARCHAR2(15)
OSUSER                                         VARCHAR2(30)
NETWORK_SERVICE_BANNER                         VARCHAR2(4000)

GV$SESSION_CONNECT_INFO select distinct inst_id,trunc(indx/5, 0), decode(ksuseaty,
                        0, 'DATABASE', 1,  'PROTOCOL', 2, 'NETWORK SERVICE', '?'),
                        ksuseunm, ksuseban from x$ksusecon  where
                        bitand(ksuseflg,1)!=0 and bitand(ksuseflg,16)=0
```

The **GV$SESSION_CURSOR_CACHE** DPT provides information on the cursor cache usage for the current session.

Listing A.205 Description of the data dictionary dynamic performance table GV$SESSION_CURSOR_CACHE.

```
Name                            Null?    Type
-------------------------------- -------- ----
INST_ID                                  NUMBER
MAXIMUM                                  NUMBER
COUNT                                    NUMBER
OPENED_ONCE                              NUMBER
OPEN                                     NUMBER
OPENS                                    NUMBER
HITS                                     NUMBER
HIT_RATIO                                NUMBER

GV$SESSION_CURSOR_CACHE select
                inst_id,kgiccmax,kgicccnt,kgiccopd,kgiccope,kgiccopn,kgicchit,
                decode(kgiccopn,0,1,kgicchit/kgiccopn) from x$kgicc
```

The **GV$SESSION_EVENT** DPT provides information about waits that all sessions have logged. If your platform doesn't support a timing mechanism, all times will show zero. On platforms that support timing, set the **TIMED_STATISTICS** initialization parameter to **TRUE** to turn on gathering of time-based statistics and see values in the time fields.

Listing A.206 Description of the data dictionary dynamic performance table GV$SESSION_EVENT.

```
Name                            Null?    Type
-------------------------------- -------- ----
INST_ID                                  NUMBER
SID                                      NUMBER
EVENT                                    VARCHAR2(64)
TOTAL_WAITS                              NUMBER
TOTAL_TIMEOUTS                           NUMBER
TIME_WAITED                              NUMBER
AVERAGE_WAIT                             NUMBER

GV$SESSION_EVENT    select s.inst_id, s.kslessid, d.kslednam, s.ksleswts,
                    s.kslestmo, s.kslestim,  s.kslestim / s.ksleswts from
                    x$ksles s, x$ksled d where s.ksleswts != 0  and s.kslesenm =
                    d.indx
```

The **GV$SESSION_LONGOPS** DPT provides status of certain long-running jobs. The **SOFAR** and **TOTALWORK** columns provide progression reports on the following operations:

- Hash cluster creations

- Backup operations

- Recovery operations

Listing A.207 Description of the data dictionary dynamic performance table GV$SESSION_LONGOPS.

Name	Null?	Type
INST_ID		NUMBER
SID		NUMBER
SERIAL#		NUMBER
COMPNAM		VARCHAR2(30)
OBJID		NUMBER
CONTEXT		NUMBER
STEPID		NUMBER
MSG		VARCHAR2(512)
STEPSOFAR		NUMBER
STEPTOTAL		NUMBER
SOFAR		NUMBER
TOTALWORK		NUMBER

```
GV$SESSION_LONGOPS    select inst_id,ksulosno, ksulosrn, ksulosuc, ksulocna,
                      ksuloobj, ksuloctx, ksulostp, ksulomsg,
                      ksulossf, ksulosto, ksulosfr, ksulotot, ksuloap1,
                      ksuloap2, ksuloap3,
                      to_date(ksulostm,'MM/DD/RR HH24:MI:SS'),
                      to_date(ksulortm,'MM/DD/RR HH24:MI:SS'),
                      (to_date(ksulortm,'MM/DD/RR HH24:MI:SS')-
                      to_date(ksulostm,'MM/DD/RR HH24:MI:SS'))*86400
                      from  x$ksulop
```

The **GV$SESSION_OBJECT_CACHE** DPT provides statistics on object cache for the current user session. This is the server-side database object cache, not the client-side object cache.

Listing A.208 Description of the data dictionary dynamic performance table GV$SESSION_OBJECT_CACHE.

Name	Null?	Type
INST_ID		NUMBER
PINS		NUMBER
HITS		NUMBER
TRUE_HITS		NUMBER
HIT_RATIO		NUMBER
TRUE_HIT_RATIO		NUMBER
OBJECT_REFRESHES		NUMBER
CACHE_REFRESHES		NUMBER
OBJECT_FLUSHES		NUMBER
CACHE_FLUSHES		NUMBER
CACHE_SHRINKS		NUMBER
CACHED_OBJECTS		NUMBER
PINNED_OBJECTS		NUMBER
CACHE_SIZE		NUMBER
OPTIMAL_SIZE		NUMBER
MAXIMUM_SIZE		NUMBER

```
GV$SESSION_OBJECT_CACHE select
               inst_id,kocstpin,kocsthit,kocsttht,
               decode(kocstpin,0,1,kocsthit/kocstpin),
               decode(kocstpin,0,1,kocsttht/kocstpin),kocstorf,
               kocstrfs,kocstofs,kocstfls,kocstshr,kocstcnt,kocstpnd,kocs
               tsiz,kocstopt,kocstmax from x$kocst
```

The **GV$SESSION_WAIT** DPT provides information on resources or events for which active sessions are waiting.

Listing A.209 Description of the data dictionary dynamic performance table GV$SESSION_WAIT.

Name	Null?	Type
INST_ID		NUMBER
SID		NUMBER
SEQ#		NUMBER
EVENT		VARCHAR2(64)
P1TEXT		VARCHAR2(64)
P1		NUMBER
P1RAW		RAW(4)
P2TEXT		VARCHAR2(64)
P2		NUMBER
P2RAW		RAW(4)
P3TEXT		VARCHAR2(64)
P3		NUMBER

```
P3RAW                                   RAW(4)
WAIT_TIME                               NUMBER
SECONDS_IN_WAIT                         NUMBER
STATE                                   VARCHAR2(19)
```

```
GV$SESSION_WAIT        select
                       s.inst_id,s.indx,s.ksussseq,e.kslednam,e.ksledp1,s.ksussp1,
                       s.ksussp1r,e.ksledp2,
                       s.ksussp2,s.ksussp2r,e.ksledp3,s.ksussp3,s.ksussp3r,s.ksusstim,
                       s.ksusewtm,
                       decode(s.ksusstim,
                        0, 'WAITING',
                       -2, 'WAITED UNKNOWN TIME',
                       -1, 'WAITED SHORT TIME',
                       'WAITED KNOWN TIME')  from x$ksusecst s, x$ksled e where
                       bitand(s.ksspaflg,1)!=0 and bitand(s.ksuseflg,1)!=0 and
                       s.ksussseq!=0 and s.ksussopc=e.indx
```

The **GV$SESSTAT** DPT lists the user session statistics and must be joined to **GV$STATNAME** on the **STATISTIC#** column to get the statistic names.

Listing A.210 Description of the data dictionary dynamic performance table GV$SESSTAT.

Name	Null?	Type
INST_ID		NUMBER
SID		NUMBER
STATISTIC#		NUMBER
VALUE		NUMBER

```
GV$SESSTAT          select inst_id,indx,ksusestn,ksusestv from x$ksusesta where
                    bitand(ksspaflg,1)!=0 and bitand(ksuseflg,1)!=0 and
                    ksusestn<(select count(*) from x$ksusd)
```

The **GV$SESS_IO** DPT provides information on all I/O statistics for each user session.

Listing A.211 Description of the data dictionary dynamic performance table GV$SESS_IO.

Name	Null?	Type
INST_ID		NUMBER
SID		NUMBER
BLOCK_GETS		NUMBER
CONSISTENT_GETS		NUMBER

```
PHYSICAL_READS                          NUMBER
BLOCK_CHANGES                           NUMBER
CONSISTENT_CHANGES                      NUMBER

GV$SESS_IO          select inst_id,indx, ksusesbg, ksusescg, ksusespr, ksusesbc,
                    ksusescc from x$ksusio where bitand(ksspaflg,1)!=0 and
                    bitand(ksuseflg,1)!=0
```

The **GV$SGA** DPT contains summary information about all database shared global areas.

Listing A.212 Description of the data dictionary dynamic performance table GV$SGA.

```
Name                               Null?     Type
--------------------------------   --------  ----
INST_ID                                      NUMBER
NAME                                         VARCHAR2(20)
VALUE                                        NUMBER

GV$SGA              select inst_id,ksmsdnam,ksmsdval from x$ksmsd
```

The **GV$SGASTAT** DPT contains detailed information about the database shared global areas.

Listing A.213 Description of the data dictionary dynamic performance table GV$SGASTAT.

```
Name                               Null?     Type
--------------------------------   --------  ----
INST_ID                                      NUMBER
POOL                                         VARCHAR2(11)
NAME                                         VARCHAR2(26)
BYTES                                        NUMBER

GV$SGASTAT          select inst_id,'',ksmssnam,ksmsslen from x$ksmfs where
                    ksmsslen>1  union all select inst_id, 'shared
                    pool',ksmssnam,ksmsslen  from x$ksmss where ksmsslen>1 union
                    all select inst_id, 'large pool',  ksmssnam,ksmsslen from
                    x$ksmls where ksmsslen>1
```

The **GV$SHARED_POOL_RESERVED** DPT shows statistics useful for tuning the shared pool. The table is valid only if the **SHARED_POOL_RESERVED_SIZE** parameter is set in the initialization parameters for the database.

Listing A.214   Description of the data dictionary dynamic performance table GV$SHARED_POOL_RESERVED.

```
Name                                Null?    Type
----------------------------------- -------- ----
INST_ID                                      NUMBER
FREE_SPACE                                   NUMBER
AVG_FREE_SIZE                                NUMBER
FREE_COUNT                                   NUMBER
MAX_FREE_SIZE                                NUMBER
USED_SPACE                                   NUMBER
AVG_USED_SIZE                                NUMBER
USED_COUNT                                   NUMBER
MAX_USED_SIZE                                NUMBER
REQUESTS                                     NUMBER
REQUEST_MISSES                               NUMBER
LAST_MISS_SIZE                               NUMBER
MAX_MISS_SIZE                                NUMBER
REQUEST_FAILURES                             NUMBER
LAST_FAILURE_SIZE                            NUMBER
ABORTED_REQUEST_THRESHOLD                    NUMBER
ABORTED_REQUESTS                             NUMBER
LAST_ABORTED_SIZE                            NUMBER
```

```
GV$SHARED_POOL_RESERVED select
                    avg(x$ksmspr.inst_id),
                    sum(decode(ksmchcls,'R-free',ksmchsiz,0)),
                    avg(decode(ksmchcls,'R-free',ksmchsiz,0)),
                    sum(decode(ksmchcls,'R-free',1,0)),
                    max(decode(ksmchcls,'R-free',ksmchsiz,0)),
                    sum(decode(ksmchcls,'R-free',0,ksmchsiz)),
                    avg(decode(ksmchcls,'R-free',0,ksmchsiz)),
                    sum(decode(ksmchcls,'R-free',0,1)),
                    max(decode(ksmchcls,'R-free',0,ksmchsiz)), avg(kghlurcn),
                    avg(kghlurmi), avg(kghlurmz), avg(kghlurmx), avg(kghlunfu),
                    avg(kghlunfs), avg(kghlumxa), avg(kghlumer), avg(kghlumes)
                    from x$ksmspr, x$kghlu
                    where ksmchcom not like '%reserved sto%'
```

The **GV$SHARED_SERVER** DPT contains information about the shared server processes.

Listing A.215   Description of the data dictionary dynamic performance table GV$SHARED_SERVER.

```
Name                                Null?    Type
----------------------------------- -------- ----
INST_ID                                      NUMBER
NAME                                         VARCHAR2(5)
```

```
PADDR                                    RAW(4)
STATUS                                   VARCHAR2(16)
MESSAGES                                 NUMBER
BYTES                                    NUMBER
BREAKS                                   NUMBER
CIRCUIT                                  RAW(4)
IDLE                                     NUMBER
BUSY                                     NUMBER
REQUESTS                                 NUMBER
```

```
GV$SHARED_SERVER    select inst_id,kmmsinam,kmmsiprp,kmmsista,kmmsinmg,
                    kmmsinmb,kmmsibrk,kmmsivcp,kmmsiidl,kmmsibsy,kmmsitnc from
                    x$kmmsi where bitand(kmmsiflg,1)!=0
```

The **GV$SORT_SEGMENT** table contains information about every sort segment in a given database.

Listing A.216   Description of the data dictionary dynamic performance table GV$SORT_SEGMENT.

Name	Null?	Type
INST_ID		NUMBER
TABLESPACE_NAME		VARCHAR2(31)
SEGMENT_FILE		NUMBER
SEGMENT_BLOCK		NUMBER
EXTENT_SIZE		NUMBER
CURRENT_USERS		NUMBER
TOTAL_EXTENTS		NUMBER
TOTAL_BLOCKS		NUMBER
USED_EXTENTS		NUMBER
USED_BLOCKS		NUMBER
FREE_EXTENTS		NUMBER
FREE_BLOCKS		NUMBER
ADDED_EXTENTS		NUMBER
EXTENT_HITS		NUMBER
FREED_EXTENTS		NUMBER
FREE_REQUESTS		NUMBER
MAX_SIZE		NUMBER
MAX_BLOCKS		NUMBER
MAX_USED_SIZE		NUMBER
MAX_USED_BLOCKS		NUMBER
MAX_SORT_SIZE		NUMBER
MAX_SORT_BLOCKS		NUMBER
RELATIVE_FNO		NUMBER

```
GV$SORT_SEGMENT          select inst_id, tablespace_name, segment_file,
                         segment_block, extent_size, current_users, total_extents,
                         total_blocks, used_extents, used_blocks, free_extents,
                         free_blocks, added_extents, extent_hits, freed_extents,
                         free_requests, max_size, max_blocks, max_used_size,
                         max_used_blocks, max_sort_size, max_sort_blocks,
                         relative_fno from x$ktstssd
```

The **GV$SORT_USAGE** DPT describes sort usage in the database.

Listing A.217 Description of the data dictionary dynamic performance table GV$SORT_USAGE.

```
Name                              Null?    Type
--------------------------------  -------- ----
INST_ID                                    NUMBER
USER                                       VARCHAR2(30)
SESSION_ADDR                               RAW(4)
SESSION_NUM                                NUMBER
SQLADDR                                    RAW(4)
SQLHASH                                    NUMBER
TABLESPACE                                 VARCHAR2(31)
CONTENTS                                   VARCHAR2(9)
SEGFILE#                                   NUMBER
SEGBLK#                                    NUMBER
EXTENTS                                    NUMBER
BLOCKS                                     NUMBER
SEGRFNO#                                   NUMBER
```

```
GV$SORT_USAGE            select x$ktsso.inst_id, username, ktssoses, ktssosno,
                         prev_sql_addr, prev_hash_value, ktssotsn,
                         decode(ktssocnt,0,'PERMANENT',1,'TEMPORARY'),
                         ktssofno, ktssobno,
                         ktssoexts, ktssoblks, ktssorfno
                         from x$ktsso, v$session
                         where ktssoses = v$session.saddr
                         and ktssosno = v$session.serial#
```

The **GV$SQL** DPT shows the current statistics on the shared SQL area of the shared pool.

Listing A.218 Description of the data dictionary dynamic performance table GV$SQL.

```
Name                              Null?    Type
--------------------------------  -------- ----
INST_ID                                    NUMBER
SQL_TEXT                                   VARCHAR2(1000)
SHARABLE_MEM                               NUMBER
```

PERSISTENT_MEM	NUMBER
RUNTIME_MEM	NUMBER
SORTS	NUMBER
LOADED_VERSIONS	NUMBER
OPEN_VERSIONS	NUMBER
USERS_OPENING	NUMBER
EXECUTIONS	NUMBER
USERS_EXECUTING	NUMBER
LOADS	NUMBER
FIRST_LOAD_TIME	VARCHAR2(19)
INVALIDATIONS	NUMBER
PARSE_CALLS	NUMBER
DISK_READS	NUMBER
BUFFER_GETS	NUMBER
ROWS_PROCESSED	NUMBER
COMMAND_TYPE	NUMBER
OPTIMIZER_MODE	VARCHAR2(10)
OPTIMIZER_COST	NUMBER
PARSING_USER_ID	NUMBER
PARSING_SCHEMA_ID	NUMBER
KEPT_VERSIONS	NUMBER
ADDRESS	RAW(4)
TYPE_CHK_HEAP	RAW(4)
HASH_VALUE	NUMBER
CHILD_NUMBER	NUMBER
MODULE	VARCHAR2(64)
MODULE_HASH	NUMBER
ACTION	VARCHAR2(64)
ACTION_HASH	NUMBER
SERIALIZABLE_ABORTS	NUMBER

GV$SQL

```
            select inst_id,kglnaobj,
kglobhs0+kglobhs1+kglobhs2+kglobhs3+kglobhs4+kglobhs5+kglobhs6+kglobt16
        , kglobt08+kglobt11, kglobt10, kglobt01,
        decode(kglobhs6,0,0,1), decode(kglhdlmd,0,0,1), kglhdlkc,
        kglhdexc, kglobpc6, kglhdldc,
        substr(to_char(kglnatim,'YYYY-MM-DD/HH24:MI:SS'),1,19),
        kglhdivc, kglobt12, kglobt13, kglobt14, kglobt15, kglobt02,
        decode(kglobt32,
            0, 'NONE',
            1, 'ALL_ROWS',
            2, 'FIRST_ROWS',
            3, 'RULE',
            4, 'CHOOSE',
            'UNKNOWN'),
```

```
kglobtn0, kglobt17, kglobt18, kglhdkmk,
kglhdpar, kglobtp0, kglnahsh, kglobt09, kglobts0, kglobt19,
kglobts1, kglobt20, kglobt21
from x$kglcursor  where
kglhdadr != kglhdpar  and   kglobt02 != 0
```

The **GV$SQLAREA** DPT uses a **GROUP BY** clause to provide a summary of the **GV$SQL** area.

Listing A.219 Description of the data dictionary dynamic performance table GV$SQLAREA.

Name	Null?	Type
INST_ID		NUMBER
SQL_TEXT		VARCHAR2(1000)
SHARABLE_MEM		NUMBER
PERSISTENT_MEM		NUMBER
RUNTIME_MEM		NUMBER
SORTS		NUMBER
VERSION_COUNT		NUMBER
LOADED_VERSIONS		NUMBER
OPEN_VERSIONS		NUMBER
USERS_OPENING		NUMBER
EXECUTIONS		NUMBER
USERS_EXECUTING		NUMBER
LOADS		NUMBER
FIRST_LOAD_TIME		VARCHAR2(19)
INVALIDATIONS		NUMBER
PARSE_CALLS		NUMBER
DISK_READS		NUMBER
BUFFER_GETS		NUMBER
ROWS_PROCESSED		NUMBER
COMMAND_TYPE		NUMBER
OPTIMIZER_MODE		VARCHAR2(25)
PARSING_USER_ID		NUMBER
PARSING_SCHEMA_ID		NUMBER
KEPT_VERSIONS		NUMBER
ADDRESS		RAW(4)
HASH_VALUE		NUMBER
MODULE		VARCHAR2(64)
MODULE_HASH		NUMBER
ACTION		VARCHAR2(64)
ACTION_HASH		NUMBER
SERIALIZABLE_ABORTS		NUMBER

```
GV$SQLAREA          select inst_id,kglnaobj,
            sum(kglobhs0+kglobhs1+kglobhs2+kglobhs3+kglobhs4+kglobhs5+kglobhs6),
            sum(kglobt08+kglobt11), sum(kglobt10),
            sum(kglobt01), count(*)-1, sum(decode(kglobhs6,0,0,1)),
            decode(sum(decode(kglhdlmd,0,0,1)),0,0,sum(decode(kglhdlmd,0
            ,0,1))-1), sum(kglhdlkc)/2, sum(kglhdexc), sum(kglobpc6),
            sum(kglhdldc)-1,
            substr(to_char(kglnatim,'YYYY-MM-DD/HH24:MI:SS'),1,19),
            sum(kglhdivc), sum(kglobt12), sum(kglobt13), sum(kglobt14),
            sum(kglobt15), sum(decode(kglobt09,0,kglobt02,0)) ,
            decode(count(*)-1, 1,
             decode(sum(decode(kglobt09, 0, kglobt32, 0)),
             0, 'NONE',
             1, 'ALL_ROWS',
             2, 'FIRST_ROWS',
             3, 'RULE',
             4, 'CHOOSE',
             'UNKNOWN'),
             'MULTIPLE CHILDREN PRESENT'),
            sum(decode(kglobt09,0,kglobt17,0)),
            sum(decode(kglobt09,0,kglobt18,0)),
            decode(sum(decode(kglhdkmk,0,0,1)),0,0,
            sum(decode(kglhdkmk,0,0,1))-1),
            kglhdpar, kglnahsh, kglobts0, kglobt19, kglobts1,
            kglobt20, sum(kglobt21)
            from x$kglcursor group by
            inst_id,kglnaobj,kglhdpar,kglnahsh,kglnatim,
            kglobts0, kglobt19, kglobts1, kglobt20   having
            sum(decode(kglobt09,0,kglobt02,0)) != 0
```

The **GV$SQLTEXT** DPT provides information on the SQL text stored in the SGA shared pool. By linking on address or hash value and sorting by piece, the actual SQL in the SGA can be obtained for analysis.

Listing A.220 Description of the data dictionary dynamic performance table GV$SQLTEXT.

Name	Null?	Type
INST_ID		NUMBER
ADDRESS		RAW(4)
HASH_VALUE		NUMBER
COMMAND_TYPE		NUMBER
PIECE		NUMBER
SQL_TEXT		VARCHAR2(64)

```
GV$SQLTEXT          select inst_id,kglhdadr, kglnahsh, kgloboct, piece, name
                    from x$kglna where kgloboct != 0
```

The **GV$SQLTEXT_WITH_NEWLINES** DPT provides the same information as the **GV$SQL_TEXT** DPT, but adds new lines to the output to provide easier-to-read SQL.

Listing A.221   Description of the data dictionary dynamic performance table GV$SQLTEXT_WITH_NEWLINES.

Name	Null?	Type
INST_ID		NUMBER
ADDRESS		RAW(4)
HASH_VALUE		NUMBER
COMMAND_TYPE		NUMBER
PIECE		NUMBER
SQL_TEXT		VARCHAR2(64)

```
GV$SQLTEXT_WITH_NEWLINES select inst_id,kglhdadr, kglnahsh, kgloboct, piece, name
                        from x$kglna1 where kgloboct != 0
```

The **GV$SQL_BIND_DATA** DPT provides the actual bind data sent by the client for each distinct bind variable in each cursor owned by the session querying the view, if the data is still available on the server.

Listing A.222   Description of the data dictionary dynamic performance table GV$SQL_BIND_DATA.

Name	Null?	Type
INST_ID		NUMBER
CURSOR_NUM		NUMBER
POSITION		NUMBER
DATATYPE		NUMBER
SHARED_MAX_LEN		NUMBER
PRIVATE_MAX_LEN		NUMBER
ARRAY_SIZE		NUMBER
PRECISION		NUMBER
SCALE		NUMBER
SHARED_FLAG		NUMBER
SHARED_FLAG2		NUMBER
BUF_ADDRESS		RAW(4)
BUF_LENGTH		NUMBER
VAL_LENGTH		NUMBER
BUF_FLAG		NUMBER
INDICATOR		NUMBER
VALUE		VARCHAR2(4000)

```
GV$SQL_BIND_DATA    select inst_id,kxsbdcur, kxsbdbnd, kxsbddty, kxsbdmxl,
                    kxsbdpmx, kxsbdmal, kxsbdpre, kxsbdscl, kxsbdofl, kxsbdof2,
                    kxsbdbfp, kxsbdbln, kxsbdavl, kxsbdbfl, kxsbdind, kxsbdval
                    from x$kxsbd
```

The **GV$SQL_BIND_METADATA** displays the bind metadata provided by the client for each distinct bind variable in each cursor owned by the session querying the view.

Listing A.223 Description of the data dictionary dynamic performance table GV$SQL_BIND_METADATA.

```
Name                              Null?    Type
-------------------------------   -------- ----
INST_ID                                    NUMBER
ADDRESS                                    RAW(4)
POSITION                                   NUMBER
DATATYPE                                   NUMBER
MAX_LENGTH                                 NUMBER
ARRAY_LEN                                  NUMBER
BIND_NAME                                  VARCHAR2(30)

GV$SQL_BIND_METADATA select inst_id,kglhdadr, position, kkscbndt, kkscbndl,
               kkscbnda, kksbvnnam from x$kksbv
```

The **GV$SQL_CURSOR** DPT displays debugging data for each cursor associated with the session querying this view.

Listing A.224 Description of the data dictionary dynamic performance table GV$SQL_CURSOR.

```
Name                              Null?    Type
-------------------------------   -------- ----
INST_ID                                    NUMBER
CURNO                                      NUMBER
FLAG                                       NUMBER
STATUS                                     VARCHAR2(9)
PARENT_HANDLE                              RAW(4)
PARENT_LOCK                                RAW(4)
CHILD_LOCK                                 RAW(4)
CHILD_PIN                                  RAW(4)
PERS_HEAP_MEM                              NUMBER
WORK_HEAP_MEM                              NUMBER
BIND_VARS                                  NUMBER
DEFINE_VARS                               NUMBER
BIND_MEM_LOC                              VARCHAR2(64)
INST_FLAG                                  VARCHAR2(64)
INST_FLAG2                                 VARCHAR2(64)

GV$SQL_CURSOR          select inst_id,kxscccur, kxscccfl, decode(kxsccsta, 0,
                       'CURNULL', 1, 'CURSYNTAX', 2, 'CURPARSE', 3, 'CURBOUND', 4,
                       'CURFETCH', 5, 'CURROW', 'ERROR'), kxsccphd, kxsccplk,
                       kxsccclk, kxscccpn, kxscctbm, kxscctwm, kxscctbv, kxscctdv,
                       kxsccbdf, kxsccflg, kxsccfl2 from x$kxscc
```

The **GV$SQL_SHARED_MEMORY** DPT displays information about the cursor shared memory snapshot. Each SQL object stored in the shared pool has one or more child objects. Each child has a number of parts, one of which is the context heap that holds the query plan and other information.

Listing A.225 Description of the data dictionary dynamic performance table GV$SQL_SHARED_MEMORY.

```
Name                             Null?    Type
-------------------------------- -------- ----
INST_ID                                   NUMBER
SQL_TEXT                                  VARCHAR2(1000)
HASH_VALUE                                NUMBER
HEAP_DESC                                 RAW(4)
STRUCTURE                                 VARCHAR2(16)
FUNCTION                                  VARCHAR2(16)
COMMENT                                   VARCHAR2(16)
CHUNK_PTR                                 RAW(4)
CHUNK_SIZE                                NUMBER
ALLOC_CLASS                               VARCHAR2(8)
CHUNK_TYPE                                NUMBER
SUBHEAP_DESC                              RAW(4)

GV$SQL_SHARED_MEMORY select /*+use_nl(h,c)*/ c.inst_id,kglnaobj, kglnahsh,
                    kglobhd6,
                    rtrim(substr(ksmchcom, 1, instr(ksmchcom, ':', 1, 1) - 1)),
                    ltrim(substr(ksmchcom,-(length(ksmchcom)-
(instr(ksmchcom,':',1,1))),
                    (length(ksmchcom) -
                    (instr(ksmchcom, ':', 1, 1)) + 1))), ksmchcom, ksmchptr,
                    ksmchsiz, ksmchcls, ksmchtyp, ksmchpar from x$kglcursor c,
                    x$ksmhp h where ksmchds = kglobhd6 and kglhdadr != kglhdpar
```

The **GV$STATNAME** DPT Contains the map between **STATISTIC#** and the actual statistic name for all statistics in the various DPTs.

Listing A.226 Description of the data dictionary dynamic performance table GV$STATNAME.

```
Name                             Null?    Type
-------------------------------- -------- ----
INST_ID                                   NUMBER
STATISTIC#                                NUMBER
NAME                                      VARCHAR2(64)
CLASS                                     NUMBER

GV$STATNAME         select inst_id,indx,ksusdnam,ksusdcls from x$ksusd
```

The **GV$SUBCACHE** DPT contains data about the subordinate caches loaded into the library cache memory.

Listing A.227 Description of the data dictionary dynamic performance table GV$SUBCACHE.

```
Name                             Null?    Type
-------------------------------- -------- ----
INST_ID                                   NUMBER
OWNER_NAME                                VARCHAR2(64)
NAME                                      VARCHAR2(1000)
TYPE                                      NUMBER
HEAP_NUM                                  NUMBER
CACHE_ID                                  NUMBER
CACHE_CNT                                 NUMBER
HEAP_SZ                                   NUMBER
HEAP_ALOC                                 NUMBER
HEAP_USED                                 NUMBER

GV$SUBCACHE        select inst_id,kglnaown, kglnaobj, kglobtyp, kqlfshpn,
                   kqlfscid, kqlfsscc, kqlfsesp, kqlfsasp, kqlfsusp  from
                   x$kqlset
```

The **GV$SYSSTAT** DPT shows current system statistics. A join to **GV$STATNAME** on **STATISTIC#** is required to obtain the statistic name.

Listing A.228 Description of the data dictionary dynamic performance table GV$SYSSTAT.

```
Name                             Null?    Type
-------------------------------- -------- ----
INST_ID                                   NUMBER
STATISTIC#                                NUMBER
NAME                                      VARCHAR2(64)
CLASS                                     NUMBER
VALUE                                     NUMBER

GV$SYSSTAT         select inst_id,indx,ksusdnam,ksusdcls,ksusgstv from
                   x$ksusgsta
```

The **GV$SYSTEM_CURSOR_CACHE** DPT contains data nearly identical to **GV$SESSION_CURSOR_CACHE**, except the data is systemwide.

Listing A.229 Description of the data dictionary dynamic performance table GV$SYSTEM_CURSOR_CACHE.

```
Name                              Null?    Type
------------------------------    -------- ----
INST_ID                                    NUMBER
OPENS                                      NUMBER
HITS                                       NUMBER
HIT_RATIO                                  NUMBER

GV$SYSTEM_CURSOR_CACHE select
                      inst_id,kgicsopn,kgicshit,decode(kgicsopn,0,1,kgicshit/
kgicsopn)

                      from x$kgics
```

The **GV$SYSTEM_EVENT** DPT contains information on total waits for an event. As with other timed statistics, any time values will show only if your system is capable of timing events and if the **TIMED_STATISTICS** initialization parameter is set to **TRUE**.

Listing A.230 Description of the data dictionary dynamic performance table GV$SYSTEM_EVENT.

```
Name                              Null?    Type
------------------------------    -------- ----
INST_ID                                    NUMBER
EVENT                                      VARCHAR2(64)
TOTAL_WAITS                                NUMBER
TOTAL_TIMEOUTS                             NUMBER
TIME_WAITED                                NUMBER
AVERAGE_WAIT                               NUMBER

GV$SYSTEM_EVENT       select d.inst_id, d.kslednam, s.ksleswts, s.kslestmo,
                      s.kslestim,  s.kslestim / s.ksleswts from x$kslei s, x$ksled
                      d where s.ksleswts != 0 and  s.indx = d.indx
```

The **GV$SYSTEM_PARAMETER** DPT contains information on system parameters.

Listing A.231 Description of the data dictionary dynamic performance table GV$SYSTEM_PARAMETER.

```
Name                              Null?    Type
------------------------------    -------- ----
INST_ID                                    NUMBER
NUM                                        NUMBER
NAME                                       VARCHAR2(64)
TYPE                                       NUMBER
VALUE                                      VARCHAR2(512)
ISDEFAULT                                  VARCHAR2(9)
ISSES_MODIFIABLE                           VARCHAR2(5)
```

```
ISSYS_MODIFIABLE                        VARCHAR2(9)
ISMODIFIED                              VARCHAR2(8)
ISADJUSTED                             VARCHAR2(5)
DESCRIPTION                            VARCHAR2(64)

GV$SYSTEM_PARAMETER    select x.inst_id,x.indx+1,ksppinm,ksppity,ksppstvl,ksppstdf,
                       decode(bitand(ksppiflg/256,1),1,'TRUE','FALSE'),
                       decode(bitand(ksppiflg/65536,3),
                        1,'IMMEDIATE',
                        2,'DEFERRED',
                        'FALSE'),
                       decode(bitand(ksppstvf,7),1,'MODIFIED','FALSE'),
                       decode(bitand(ksppstvf,2),2,'TRUE','FALSE'),
                       ksppdesc
                       from
                       x$ksppi x, x$ksppsv y where x.indx = y.indx and
                       translate(ksppinm,'_','#') not like '#%'
```

The **GV$TABLESPACE** DPT contains information about the tablespaces gleaned
from the controlfiles.

Listing A.232 Description of the data dictionary dynamic performance table GV$TABLESPACE.

Name	Null?	Type
INST_ID		NUMBER
TS#		NUMBER
NAME		VARCHAR2(30)

```
GV$TABLESPACE          select inst_id,tstsn,tsnam from x$kccts where tstsn != -1
```

The **GV$THREAD** DPT contains information about redo log threads gleaned from
the controlfiles.

Listing A.233 Description of the data dictionary dynamic performance table GV$THREAD.

Name	Null?	Type
INST_ID		NUMBER
THREAD#		NUMBER
STATUS		VARCHAR2(6)
ENABLED		VARCHAR2(8)
GROUPS		NUMBER
INSTANCE		VARCHAR2(16)
OPEN_TIME		DATE
CURRENT_GROUP#		NUMBER

```
```

```
SEQUENCE#                                         NUMBER
CHECKPOINT_CHANGE#                                 NUMBER
CHECKPOINT_TIME                                    DATE
ENABLE_CHANGE#                                     NUMBER
ENABLE_TIME                                        DATE
DISABLE_CHANGE#                                    NUMBER
DISABLE_TIME                                       DATE

GV$THREAD               select
                        inst_id,rtnum,decode(bitand(rtsta,1),1,'OPEN','CLOSED'),
                        decode(bitand(rtsta,6),
                         0,'DISABLED',
                         2,'PRIVATE',
                         6,'PUBLIC','
                          UNKNOWN'),
                        rtnlf,rtsid,
                        to_date(rtots,'MM/DD/RR HH24:MI:SS'),rtcln,rtseq,
                        to_number(rtckp_scn),
                        to_date(rtckp_tim,'MM/DD/RR HH24:MI:SS'),
                        to_number(rtenb),
                        to_date(rtets,'MM/DD/RR HH24:MI:SS'),
                        to_number(rtdis),
                        to_date(rtdit,'MM/DD/RR HH24:MI:SS')
                        from x$kccrt where rtnlf!=0
```

The **GV$TIMER** DPT displays the elapsed time in hundredths of a second. The value wraps to 0 approximately every 497 days.

Listing A.234 Description of the data dictionary dynamic performance table GV$TIMER.

```
Name                              Null?     Type
-------------------------------   --------  ----
INST_ID                                     NUMBER
HSECS                                       NUMBER

GV$TIMER                select inst_id,ksutmtim from x$ksutm
```

The **GV$TRANSACTION** DPT contains information on all active transactions in the database.

Listing A.235 Description of the data dictionary dynamic performance table GV$TRANSACTION.

```
Name                              Null?     Type
-------------------------------   --------  ----
INST_ID                                     NUMBER
ADDR                                        RAW(4)
XIDUSN                                      NUMBER
```

```
XIDSLOT                         NUMBER
XIDSQN                          NUMBER
UBAFIL                          NUMBER
UBABLK                          NUMBER
UBASQN                          NUMBER
UBAREC                          NUMBER
STATUS                          VARCHAR2(16)
START_TIME                      VARCHAR2(20)
START_SCNB                      NUMBER
START_SCNW                      NUMBER
START_UEXT                      NUMBER
START_UBAFIL                    NUMBER
START_UBABLK                    NUMBER
START_UBASQN                    NUMBER
START_UBAREC                    NUMBER
SES_ADDR                        RAW(4)
FLAG                            NUMBER
SPACE                           VARCHAR2(3)
RECURSIVE                       VARCHAR2(3)
NOUNDO                          VARCHAR2(3)
PTX                             VARCHAR2(3)
PRV_XIDUSN                      NUMBER
PRV_XIDSLT                      NUMBER
PRV_XIDSQN                      NUMBER
PTX_XIDUSN                      NUMBER
PTX_XIDSLT                      NUMBER
PTX_XIDSQN                      NUMBER
DSCN-B                          NUMBER
DSCN-W                          NUMBER
USED_UBLK                       NUMBER
USED_UREC                       NUMBER
LOG_IO                          NUMBER
PHY_IO                          NUMBER
CR_GET                          NUMBER
CR_CHANGE                       NUMBER

GV$TRANSACTION       select
                     inst_id,ktcxbxba,kxidusn,kxidslt,kxidsqn,ktcxbkfn,kubablk,
                     kubaseq,kubarec,
                     decode(ktcxbsta,
                         0,'IDLE',
                         1,'COLLECTING',
                         2,'PREPARED',
                         3,'COMMITTED',
                         4,'HEURISTIC ABORT',
                         5,'HEURISTIC COMMIT',
                         6,'HEURISTIC DAMAGE',
```

```
                            7,'TIMEOUT',
                            9,'INACTIVE',
                            10,'ACTIVE',
                            11,'PTX PREPARED',
                            12,'PTX COMMITTED',
                            'UNKNOWN'), ktcxbstm,ktcxbssb,ktcxbssw,
                    ktcxbsen,ktcxbsfl,ktcxbsbk,ktcxbssq,ktcxbsrc,
                    ktcxbses,ktcxbflg, decode(bitand(ktcxbflg,16),0,'NO','YES'),
                    decode(bitand(ktcxbflg,32),0,'NO','YES'),
                    decode(bitand(ktcxbflg,64),0,'NO','YES'),
                    decode(bitand(ktcxbflg,8388608),0,'NO','YES'),
                    ktcxbpus,ktcxbpsl,ktcxbpsq, ktcxbpxu,ktcxbpxs,ktcxbpxq,
                    ktcxbdsb, ktcxbdsw,
                    ktcxbubk,ktcxburc,ktcxblio,ktcxbpio,ktcxbcrg,ktcxbcrc from
                    x$ktcxb where bitand(ksspaflg,1)!=0 and
                    bitand(ktcxbflg,2)!=0
```

The **GV$TRANSACTION_ENQUEUE** DPT contains information on the locks owned by transaction state objects.

Listing A.236 Description of the dynamic performance table GV$TRANSACTION_ENQUEUE.

```
Name                            Null?     Type
-----------------------------   --------  ----
INST_ID                                   NUMBER
ADDR                                      RAW(4)
KADDR                                     RAW(4)
SID                                       NUMBER
TYPE                                      VARCHAR2(2)
ID1                                       NUMBER
ID2                                       NUMBER
LMODE                                     NUMBER
REQUEST                                   NUMBER
CTIME                                     NUMBER
BLOCK                                     NUMBER
```

```
GV$TRANSACTION_ENQUEUE select /*+ ordered use_nl(l), use_nl(s), use_nl(r) +*/
                      s.inst_id,l.addr,l.ksqlkadr,s.ksusenum,r.ksqrsidt,r.ksqrsid1
                      ,r.ksqrsid2, l.ksqlkmod, l.ksqlkreq,l.ksqlkctim,l.ksqlklblk
                      from x$ktcxb l,x$ksuse s,x$ksqrs r where l.ksqlkses=s.addr
                      and  bitand(l.ksspaflg,1)!=0 and (l.ksqlkmod!=0 or
                      l.ksqlkreq!=0) and  l.ksqlkres=r.addr
```

The **GV$TYPE_SIZE** DPT lists the sizes of various database components for use in estimating data block capacity.

Listing A.237 Description of the data dictionary dynamic performance table GV$TYPE_SIZE.

```
Name                                Null?    Type
-------------------------------- --------  ----
INST_ID                                     NUMBER
COMPONENT                                   VARCHAR2(8)
TYPE                                        VARCHAR2(8)
DESCRIPTION                                 VARCHAR2(32)
SIZE                                        NUMBER

GV$TYPE_SIZE            select inst_id,kqfszcom,kqfsztyp,kqfszdsc,kqfszsiz from
                       x$kqfsz
```

The **GV$VERSION** DPT contains the version numbers of the core library components in the Oracle server, one row for each component.

Listing A.238 Description of the data dictionary dynamic performance table GV$VERSION.

```
Name                                Null?    Type
-------------------------------- --------  ----
INST_ID                                     NUMBER
BANNER                                      VARCHAR2(64)

GV$VERSION             select inst_id, banner from x$version
```

The **GV$WAITSTAT** DPT lists block contention statistics. This table is updated only when the **TIMED_STATISTIC** initialization parameter is set to **TRUE**.

Listing A.239 Description of the data dictionary dynamic performance table GV$WAITSTAT.

```
Name                                Null?    Type
-------------------------------- --------  ----
INST_ID                                     NUMBER
CLASS                                       VARCHAR2(18)
COUNT                                       NUMBER
TIME                                        NUMBER

GV$WAITSTAT            select inst_id,
                      decode(indx,
                        1,'data block',
                        2,'sort block',
                        3,'save undo block',
                        4,'segment header',
                        5,'save undo header',
                        6,'free list',
                        7,'extent map',
```

```
        8,'bitmap block',
        9,'bitmap index block',
        10,'unused',
        11,'system undo header',
        12,'system undo block',
        13,'undo header',14,'undo block'),
   count,time from x$kcbwait where indx!=0
```

The **GV$_LOCK** DPT stores database-wide lock statistics.

Listing A.240 Description of the data dictionary dynamic performance table GV$_LOCK.

```
Name                              Null?    Type
--------------------------------  -------- ----
INST_ID                                    NUMBER
LADDR                                      RAW(4)
KADDR                                      RAW(4)
SADDR                                      RAW(4)
RADDR                                      RAW(4)
LMODE                                      NUMBER
REQUEST                                    NUMBER
CTIME                                      NUMBER
BLOCK                                      NUMBER


GV$_LOCK              select
                     USERENV('Instance'),laddr,kaddr,saddr,raddr,lmode,request,ct
                     ime,  block from v$_lock1 union all select
                     inst_id,addr,ksqlkadr,ksqlkses,ksqlkres,ksqlkmod,ksqlkreq,
                     ksqlkctim,ksqlklblk from x$ktadm where bitand(kssobflg,1)!=0
                     and (ksqlkmod!=0 or ksqlkreq!=0)
                     union all
                     select
                     inst_id,addr,ksqlkadr,ksqlkses,ksqlkres,ksqlkmod,ksqlkreq,
                     ksqlkctim,ksqlklblk from x$ktcxb where bitand(ksspaflg,1)!=0
                     and (ksqlkmod!=0 or ksqlkreq!=0)
```

The **DBA_** Views

The **DBA_** views are based on the dollar tables and each other. The purpose of the **DBA_** views is to provide the information contained in the dollar tables in a more user-friendly format. The view definitions make extensive use of joins to map tables and decodes to translate unclear numeric codes to text values. The **DBA_** tables should be used to monitor most database hard objects, such as indexes, clusters, and tables, as well as datafile logs and other external database objects.

Because the **ALL_** and **USER_** views are usually just cuts of the data contained in the **DBA_** views, I will not define them here. The **ALL_** views show all objects in the category of the view that the user has grants or permissions against. The **USER_** views show all the objects of the view's domain that the user owns.

Descriptions Of The **DBA_** Views (The Base Views For **USER_** And **ALL_** Views)

The **DBA_2PC_NEIGHBORS** view is used to show incoming and outgoing connections for pending transactions (for distributed databases). 2PC stands for two-phase commit.

Listing A.241   Description of the DBA_ view DBA_2PC_NEIGHBORS.

```
Name                             Null?     Type
-------------------------------- --------  ----
LOCAL_TRAN_ID                              VARCHAR2(22)
IN_OUT                                     VARCHAR2(3)
DATABASE                                   VARCHAR2(128)
DBUSER_OWNER                               VARCHAR2(30)
INTERFACE                                  VARCHAR2(1)
DBID                                       VARCHAR2(16)
SESS#                                      NUMBER
BRANCH                                     VARCHAR2(128)


DBA_2PC_NEIGHBORS   select  local_tran_id,'in',parent_db,db_user,interface,
parent_dbid,
                    session_id, rawtohex(branch_id)
              from sys.ps1$
          union all
        select  local_tran_id, 'out', dblink, owner_name, interface, dbid,
               session_id, to_char(sub_session_id)
            from sys.pss1$
```

The **DBA_2PC_PENDING** view contains information about pending transactions that require recovery for distributed systems.

Listing A.242   Description of the DBA_ view DBA_2PC_PENDING.

```
Name                        Null?     Type
--------------------------- --------  ----
LOCAL_TRAN_ID               NOT NULL  VARCHAR2(22)
GLOBAL_TRAN_ID                        VARCHAR2(169)
STATE                       NOT NULL  VARCHAR2(16)
MIXED                                 VARCHAR2(3)
ADVICE                                VARCHAR2(1)
```

```
TRAN_COMMENT                           VARCHAR2(255)
FAIL_TIME               NOT NULL DATE
FORCE_TIME                       DATE
RETRY_TIME              NOT NULL DATE
OS_USER                          VARCHAR2(64)
OS_TERMINAL                      VARCHAR2(255)
HOST                             VARCHAR2(128)
DB_USER                          VARCHAR2(30)
COMMIT#                          VARCHAR2(16)


DBA_2PC_PENDING   select  local_tran_id,
                     nvl(global_oracle_id, global_tran_fmt||'.'||global_foreign_id),
                  state, decode(status,'D','yes','no'), heuristic_dflt, tran_comment,
                         fail_time, heuristic_time, reco_time,
                         top_os_user, top_os_terminal, top_os_host,
                         top_db_user, global_commit#
                  from  sys.pending_trans$
```

The **DBA_ALL_TABLES** view shows information of all tables in the database, including object and relational tables.

Listing A.243   Description of the DBA_ view DBA_ALL_TABLES.

```
Name                               Null?     Type
---------------------------------- --------- ----
OWNER                                        VARCHAR2(30)
TABLE_NAME                                   VARCHAR2(30)
TABLESPACE_NAME                              VARCHAR2(30)
CLUSTER_NAME                                 VARCHAR2(30)
IOT_NAME                                     VARCHAR2(30)
PCT_FREE                                     NUMBER
PCT_USED                                     NUMBER
INI_TRANS                                    NUMBER
MAX_TRANS                                    NUMBER
INITIAL_EXTENT                               NUMBER
NEXT_EXTENT                                  NUMBER
MIN_EXTENTS                                  NUMBER
MAX_EXTENTS                                  NUMBER
PCT_INCREASE                                 NUMBER
FREELISTS                                    NUMBER
FREELIST_GROUPS                              NUMBER
LOGGING                                      VARCHAR2(3)
BACKED_UP                                    VARCHAR2(1)
NUM_ROWS                                     NUMBER
BLOCKS                                       NUMBER
EMPTY_BLOCKS                                 NUMBER
AVG_SPACE                                    NUMBER
CHAIN_CNT                                    NUMBER
```

```
AVG_ROW_LEN                      NUMBER
AVG_SPACE_FREELIST_BLOCKS        NUMBER
NUM_FREELIST_BLOCKS              NUMBER
DEGREE                           VARCHAR2(10)
INSTANCES                        VARCHAR2(10)
CACHE                            VARCHAR2(5)
TABLE_LOCK                       VARCHAR2(8)
SAMPLE_SIZE                      NUMBER
LAST_ANALYZED                    DATE
PARTITIONED                      VARCHAR2(3)
IOT_TYPE                         VARCHAR2(12)
TABLE_TYPE_OWNER                 VARCHAR2(30)
TABLE_TYPE                       VARCHAR2(30)
TEMPORARY                        VARCHAR2(1)
NESTED                           VARCHAR2(3)
BUFFER_POOL                      VARCHAR2(7)


DBA_ALL_TABLES    select OWNER, TABLE_NAME, TABLESPACE_NAME, CLUSTER_NAME, IOT_NAME,
                         PCT_FREE, PCT_USED,
                         INI_TRANS, MAX_TRANS,
                         INITIAL_EXTENT, NEXT_EXTENT,
                         MIN_EXTENTS, MAX_EXTENTS, PCT_INCREASE,
                         FREELISTS, FREELIST_GROUPS, LOGGING,
                         BACKED_UP, NUM_ROWS, BLOCKS, EMPTY_BLOCKS,
                         AVG_SPACE, CHAIN_CNT, AVG_ROW_LEN,
                         AVG_SPACE_FREELIST_BLOCKS, NUM_FREELIST_BLOCKS,
                         DEGREE, INSTANCES, CACHE, TABLE_LOCK,
                         SAMPLE_SIZE, LAST_ANALYZED, PARTITIONED,
                         IOT_TYPE, NULL, NULL, TEMPORARY, NESTED,
                         BUFFER_POOL
                  from dba_tables
                  union all
                  select OWNER,TABLE_NAME,TABLESPACE_NAME,CLUSTER_NAME,IOT_NAME,
                         PCT_FREE,
                  PCT_USED,INI_TRANS,MAX_TRANS,INITIAL_EXTENT,NEXT_EXTENT,MIN_EXTENTS,
                         MAX_EXTENTS,PCT_INCREASE,FREELISTS,FREELIST_GROUPS,LOGGING,
                         BACKED_UP,
                         NUM_ROWS,BLOCKS,EMPTY_BLOCKS,AVG_SPACE,CHAIN_CNT,AVG_ROW_LEN,
                  AVG_SPACE_FREELIST_BLOCKS,NUM_FREELIST_BLOCKS,DEGREE,INSTANCES,CACHE,
                         TABLE_LOCK,SAMPLE_SIZE,LAST_ANALYZED,PARTITIONED,IOT_TYPE,
                         TABLE_TYPE_OWNER,TABLE_TYPE,TEMPORARY,NESTED,BUFFER_POOL
                  from dba_object_tables
```

The **DBA_ANALYZE_OBJECTS** view lists all objects that have been analyzed.

Listing A.244 Description of the DBA_ view DBA_ANALYZE_OBJECTS.

```
Name                             Null?     Type
-------------------------------- --------  ----
OWNER                            NOT NULL VARCHAR2(30)
OBJECT_NAME                      NOT NULL VARCHAR2(30)
OBJECT_TYPE                               VARCHAR2(7)


DBA_ANALYZE_OBJECTS select u.name, o.name, decode(o.type#, 2, 'TABLE', 3, 'CLUSTER')
                   from sys.user$ u, sys.obj$ o, sys.tab$ t
                   where o.owner# = u.user#
                   and   o.obj# = t.obj# (+)
                   and   t.bobj# is null
                   and   o.type# in (2,3)
                   and   o.linkname is null
```

The **DBA_AUDIT_EXISTS** view shows all audit trail entries generated by the **AUDIT NOT EXISTS** and **AUDIT EXISTS** commands.

Listing A.245 Description of the DBA_ view DBA_AUDIT_EXISTS.

```
Name                             Null?     Type
-------------------------------- --------  ----
OS_USERNAME                               VARCHAR2(255)
USERNAME                                  VARCHAR2(30)
USERHOST                                  VARCHAR2(128)
TERMINAL                                  VARCHAR2(255)
TIMESTAMP                        NOT NULL DATE
OWNER                                     VARCHAR2(30)
OBJ_NAME                                  VARCHAR2(128)
ACTION_NAME                               VARCHAR2(27)
NEW_OWNER                                 VARCHAR2(30)
NEW_NAME                                  VARCHAR2(128)
OBJ_PRIVILEGE                             VARCHAR2(16)
SYS_PRIVILEGE                             VARCHAR2(40)
GRANTEE                                   VARCHAR2(30)
SESSIONID                        NOT NULL NUMBER
ENTRYID                          NOT NULL NUMBER
STATEMENTID                      NOT NULL NUMBER
RETURNCODE                       NOT NULL NUMBER


DBA_AUDIT_EXISTS     select os_username, username, userhost, terminal, timestamp,
   owner, obj_name, action_name, new_owner, new_name,
   obj_privilege, sys_privilege, grantee,
   sessionid, entryid, statementid, returncode
                from dba_audit_trail
```

```
where returncode in
(942, 943, 959, 1418, 1432, 1434, 1435, 1534, 1917,
 1918, 1919, 2019, 2024, 2289, 4042, 4043, 4080, 1, 951,
 955, 957, 1430, 1433,
 1452, 1471, 1535, 1543,
 1758, 1920, 1921, 1922, 2239, 2264, 2266, 2273,
 2292, 2297, 2378, 2379, 2382, 4081, 12006, 12325)
```

The **DBA_AUDIT_OBJECT** view contains the audit trail records for all objects in the system.

Listing A.246   Description of the DBA_ view DBA_AUDIT_OBJECT.

```
Name                            Null?    Type
------------------------------- -------- ----
OS_USERNAME                              VARCHAR2(255)
USERNAME                                 VARCHAR2(30)
USERHOST                                 VARCHAR2(128)
TERMINAL                                 VARCHAR2(255)
TIMESTAMP                       NOT NULL DATE
OWNER                                    VARCHAR2(30)
OBJ_NAME                                 VARCHAR2(128)
ACTION_NAME                              VARCHAR2(27)
NEW_OWNER                                VARCHAR2(30)
NEW_NAME                                 VARCHAR2(128)
SES_ACTIONS                              VARCHAR2(19)
COMMENT_TEXT                             VARCHAR2(4000)
SESSIONID                       NOT NULL NUMBER
ENTRYID                         NOT NULL NUMBER
STATEMENTID                     NOT NULL NUMBER
RETURNCODE                      NOT NULL NUMBER
PRIV_USED                                VARCHAR2(40)
OBJECT_LABEL                             RAW MLSLABEL
SESSION_LABEL                            RAW MLSLABEL


DBA_AUDIT_OBJECT     select OS_USERNAME, USERNAME, USERHOST, TERMINAL, TIMESTAMP,
                            OWNER, OBJ_NAME, ACTION_NAME, NEW_OWNER, NEW_NAME,
                            SES_ACTIONS, COMMENT_TEXT, SESSIONID, ENTRYID,
                            STATEMENTID,
                            RETURNCODE, PRIV_USED, OBJECT_LABEL, SESSION_LABEL
                     from dba_audit_trail
                     where (action between 1 and 16)
                        or (action between 19 and 29)
                        or (action between 32 and 41)
                        or (action = 43)
                        or (action between 51 and 99)
                        or (action = 103)
                        or (action between 110 and 113)
```

```
            or (action between 116 and 121)
            or (action between 123 and 128)
```

The **DBA_AUDIT_SESSION** view shows all audit records for **CONNECT** and **DIS-CONNECT** audit actions.

Listing A.247   Description of the DBA_ view DBA_AUDIT_SESSION.

```
Name                              Null?    Type
--------------------------------- -------- ----
OS_USERNAME                                VARCHAR2(255)
USERNAME                                   VARCHAR2(30)
USERHOST                                   VARCHAR2(128)
TERMINAL                                   VARCHAR2(255)
TIMESTAMP                         NOT NULL DATE
ACTION_NAME                                VARCHAR2(27)
LOGOFF_TIME                                DATE
LOGOFF_LREAD                               NUMBER
LOGOFF_PREAD                               NUMBER
LOGOFF_LWRITE                              NUMBER
LOGOFF_DLOCK                               VARCHAR2(40)
SESSIONID                        NOT NULL NUMBER
RETURNCODE                       NOT NULL NUMBER
SESSION_LABEL                              RAW MLSLABEL

DBA_AUDIT_SESSION    select os_username, username, userhost, terminal,
                            timestamp,action_name,
                            logoff_time,logoff_lread,logoff_pread,
                            logoff_lwrite, logoff_dlock,
                            sessionid, returncode, session_label
                     from dba_audit_trail
                     where action between 100 and 102
```

The **DBA_AUDIT_STATEMENT** view contains all audit trail records for **GRANT**, **REVOKE**, **AUDIT**, **NOAUDIT**, and **ALTER SYSTEM** statements.

Listing A.248   Description of the DBA_ view DBA_AUDIT_STATEMENT.

```
Name                              Null?    Type
--------------------------------- -------- ----
OS_USERNAME                                VARCHAR2(255)
USERNAME                                   VARCHAR2(30)
USERHOST                                   VARCHAR2(128)
TERMINAL                                   VARCHAR2(255)
TIMESTAMP                         NOT NULL DATE
OWNER                                      VARCHAR2(30)
OBJ_NAME                                   VARCHAR2(128)
```

```
ACTION_NAME                         VARCHAR2(27)
NEW_NAME                            VARCHAR2(128)
OBJ_PRIVILEGE                       VARCHAR2(16)
SYS_PRIVILEGE                       VARCHAR2(40)
ADMIN_OPTION                        VARCHAR2(1)
GRANTEE                             VARCHAR2(30)
AUDIT_OPTION                        VARCHAR2(40)
SES_ACTIONS                         VARCHAR2(19)
COMMENT_TEXT                        VARCHAR2(4000)
SESSIONID           NOT NULL NUMBER
ENTRYID             NOT NULL NUMBER
STATEMENTID         NOT NULL NUMBER
RETURNCODE          NOT NULL NUMBER
PRIV_USED                           VARCHAR2(40)
SESSION_LABEL                       RAW MLSLABEL

DBA_AUDIT_STATEMENT select OS_USERNAME, USERNAME, USERHOST, TERMINAL, TIMESTAMP,
                   OWNER, OBJ_NAME, ACTION_NAME, NEW_NAME,
                   OBJ_PRIVILEGE, SYS_PRIVILEGE, ADMIN_OPTION,
                   GRANTEE, AUDIT_OPTION,
                   SES_ACTIONS, COMMENT_TEXT, SESSIONID, ENTRYID,
STATEMENTID,
                   RETURNCODE, PRIV_USED, SESSION_LABEL
            from dba_audit_trail
            where action in (  17 /* GRANT OBJECT   */,
                               18 /* REVOKE OBJECT */,
                               30 /* AUDIT OBJECT */,
                               31 /* NOAUDIT OBJECT */,
                               49 /* ALTER SYSTEM */,
                              104 /* SYSTEM AUDIT */,
                              105 /* SYSTEM NOAUDIT */,
                              106 /* AUDIT DEFAULT */,
                              107 /* NOAUDIT DEFAULT */,
                              108 /* SYSTEM GRANT */,
                              109 /* SYSTEM REVOKE */,
                              114 /* GRANT ROLE */,
                              115 /* REVOKE ROLE */ )
```

The **DBA_AUDIT_TRAIL** view contains audit records for all audit trail entries.

Listing A.249 Description of the DBA_ view DBA_AUDIT_TRAIL.

```
Name                              Null?      Type
-------------------------------   --------   ----
OS_USERNAME                                  VARCHAR2(255)
USERNAME                                     VARCHAR2(30)
USERHOST                                     VARCHAR2(128)
TERMINAL                                     VARCHAR2(255)
```

```
          TIMESTAMP                       NOT NULL DATE
          OWNER                                    VARCHAR2(30)
          OBJ_NAME                                 VARCHAR2(128)
          ACTION                          NOT NULL NUMBER
          ACTION_NAME                              VARCHAR2(27)
          NEW_OWNER                                VARCHAR2(30)
          NEW_NAME                                 VARCHAR2(128)
          OBJ_PRIVILEGE                            VARCHAR2(16)
          SYS_PRIVILEGE                            VARCHAR2(40)
          ADMIN_OPTION                             VARCHAR2(1)
          GRANTEE                                  VARCHAR2(30)
          AUDIT_OPTION                             VARCHAR2(40)
          SES_ACTIONS                              VARCHAR2(19)
          LOGOFF_TIME                              DATE
          LOGOFF_LREAD                             NUMBER
          LOGOFF_PREAD                             NUMBER
          LOGOFF_LWRITE                            NUMBER
          LOGOFF_DLOCK                             VARCHAR2(40)
          COMMENT_TEXT                             VARCHAR2(4000)
          SESSIONID                       NOT NULL NUMBER
          ENTRYID                         NOT NULL NUMBER
          STATEMENTID                     NOT NULL NUMBER
          RETURNCODE                      NOT NULL NUMBER
          PRIV_USED                                VARCHAR2(40)
          OBJECT_LABEL                             RAW MLSLABEL
          SESSION_LABEL                            RAW MLSLABEL

  DBA_AUDIT_TRAIL        select spare1    /* OS_USERNAME */,
                                userid    /* USERNAME */,
                                userhost  /* USERHOST */,
                                terminal  /* TERMINAL */,
                                timestamp#        /* TIMESTAMP */,
                                obj$creator  /* OWNER */,
                                obj$name  /* OBJECT_NAME */,
                                aud.action#  /* ACTION */,
                                act.name  /* ACTION_NAME */,
                                new$owner         /* NEW_OWNER */,
                                new$name  /* NEW_NAME */,
                                decode(aud.action#,
          108 /* grant  sys_priv */, null,
          109 /* revoke sys_priv */, null,
          114 /* grant  role */, null,
          115 /* revoke role */, null,
          auth$privileges)
          /* OBJ_PRIVILEGE */,
                                decode(aud.action#,
```

```
108 /* grant   sys_priv */, spm.name,
109 /* revoke sys_priv */, spm.name,
null)
/* SYS_PRIVILEGE */,
                decode(aud.action#,
108 /* grant   sys_priv */, substr(auth$privileges,1,1),
109 /* revoke sys_priv */, substr(auth$privileges,1,1),
114 /* grant   role */, substr(auth$privileges,1,1),
115 /* revoke role */, substr(auth$privileges,1,1),
null)
/* ADMIN_OPTION */,
                auth$grantee       /* GRANTEE */,
                decode(aud.action#,
104 /* audit    */, aom.name,
105 /* noaudit */, aom.name,
null)
/* AUDIT_OPTION  */,
                ses$actions  /* SES_ACTIONS   */,
                logoff$time  /* LOGOFF_TIME   */,
                logoff$lread /* LOGOFF_LREAD  */,
                logoff$pread /* LOGOFF_PREAD  */,
                logoff$lwrite/* LOGOFF_LWRITE */,
                decode(aud.action#,
104 /* audit    */, null,
                    105 /* noaudit */, null,
108 /* grant   sys_priv */, null,
109 /* revoke sys_priv */, null,
114 /* grant   role */, null,
115 /* revoke role */, null,
aud.logoff$dead)
/* LOGOFF_DLOCK */,
                comment$text       /* COMMENT_TEXT */,
                sessionid  /* SESSIONID */,
                entryid    /* ENTRYID */,
                statement  /* STATEMENTID */,
                returncode /* RETURNCODE */,
                spx.name           /* PRIVILEGE */,
                rawtolab(obj$label)        /* OBJECT_LABEL */,
                rawtolab(ses$label)        /* SESSION_LABEL */
from sys.aud$ aud, system_privilege_map spm, system_privilege_map spx,
        STMT_AUDIT_OPTION_MAP aom, audit_actions act
        where   aud.action#      = act.action     (+)
          and - aud.logoff$dead = spm.privilege (+)
          and   aud.logoff$dead = aom.option#    (+)
          and - aud.priv$used   = spx.privilege (+)
```

The **DBA_BLOCKERS** view, created by the CATBLOCK.SQL script, contains an entry for each session that is causing a block through a lock that is not being blocked by another session.

Listing A.250   Description of the DBA_ view DBA_BLOCKERS.

```
Name                            Null?    Type
------------------------------- -------- ----
HOLDING_SESSION                          NUMBER

DBA_BLOCKERS       select /*+ all_rows */ holding_session from dba_waiters
                   minus
                     select /*+ all_rows */ session_id from dba_locks w
                       where w.mode_requested != 'None'
```

The **DBA_CATALOG** view lists all tables, views, synonyms, and sequences for the database.

Listing A.251   Description of the DBA_ view DBA_CATALOG.

```
Name                            Null?    Type
------------------------------- -------- ----
OWNER                           NOT NULL VARCHAR2(30)
TABLE_NAME                      NOT NULL VARCHAR2(30)
TABLE_TYPE                               VARCHAR2(11)

DBA_CATALOG        select u.name, o.name,
                          decode(o.type#, 0, 'NEXT OBJECT', 1, 'INDEX',
                                          2, 'TABLE', 3, 'CLUSTER', 4, 'VIEW',
                                          5, 'SYNONYM', 6, 'SEQUENCE',
                                          'UNDEFINED')
                   from sys.user$ u, sys.obj$ o
                   where o.owner# = u.user#
                     and o.linkname is null
                     and ((o.type# in (4, 5, 6))
                         or
                         (o.type# = 2   /* tables,excluding iot-overflow,nested
                                                     tables */
                          and
                          not exists (select null
           from sys.tab$ t
         where t.obj# = o.obj#
           and (bitand(t.property, 512) = 512 or
               bitand(t.property, 8192) = 8192))))
```

The **DBA_CLUSTERS** view lists all clusters defined in the database.

Listing A.252 Description of the DBA_ view DBA_CLUSTERS.

Name	Null?	Type
OWNER	NOT NULL	VARCHAR2(30)
CLUSTER_NAME	NOT NULL	VARCHAR2(30)
TABLESPACE_NAME	NOT NULL	VARCHAR2(30)
PCT_FREE		NUMBER
PCT_USED	NOT NULL	NUMBER
KEY_SIZE		NUMBER
INI_TRANS	NOT NULL	NUMBER
MAX_TRANS	NOT NULL	NUMBER
INITIAL_EXTENT		NUMBER
NEXT_EXTENT		NUMBER
MIN_EXTENTS	NOT NULL	NUMBER
MAX_EXTENTS	NOT NULL	NUMBER
PCT_INCREASE	NOT NULL	NUMBER
FREELISTS		NUMBER
FREELIST_GROUPS		NUMBER
AVG_BLOCKS_PER_KEY		NUMBER
CLUSTER_TYPE		VARCHAR2(5)
FUNCTION		VARCHAR2(15)
HASHKEYS		NUMBER
DEGREE		VARCHAR2(10)
INSTANCES		VARCHAR2(10)
CACHE		VARCHAR2(5)
BUFFER_POOL		VARCHAR2(7)

```
DBA_CLUSTERS      select u.name, o.name, ts.name,
                    mod(c.pctfree$, 100), c.pctused$,
c.size$,c.initrans,c.maxtrans,
                    s.iniexts * ts.blocksize, s.extsize * ts.blocksize,
                    s.minexts, s.maxexts, s.extpct,
                    decode(s.lists, 0, 1, s.lists), decode(s.groups, 0, 1,
                    s.groups),
                    c.spare4, decode(c.hashkeys, 0, 'INDEX', 'HASH'),
                    decode(c.hashkeys, 0, NULL,
                        decode(c.func, 0, 'COLUMN', 1, 'DEFAULT',
                            2, 'HASH EXPRESSION', 3, 'DEFAULT2', NULL)),
                c.hashkeys,
            lpad(decode(c.degree, 32767, 'DEFAULT', nvl(c.degree,1)),10),
            lpad(decode(c.instances, 32767, 'DEFAULT', nvl(c.instances,1)),10),
                lpad(decode(bitand(c.flags, 8), 8, 'Y', 'N'), 5),
                decode(s.cachehint, 0, 'DEFAULT', 1, 'KEEP', 2, 'RECYCLE',
                NULL)
                from sys.user$ u, sys.ts$ ts, sys.seg$ s, sys.clu$ c, sys.obj$o
                where o.owner# = u.user#
```

```
and o.obj# = c.obj#
and c.ts# = ts.ts#
and c.ts# = s.ts#
and c.file# = s.file#
and c.block# = s.block#
```

The **DBA_CLUSTER_HASH_EXPRESSIONS** view shows the hash expressions for all hash clusters defined in the database.

Listing A.253   Description of the DBA_ view DBA_CLUSTER_ HASH_EXPRESSIONS.

```
Name                                  Null?     Type
------------------------------------- --------- ----
OWNER                                 NOT NULL  VARCHAR2(30)
CLUSTER_NAME                          NOT NULL  VARCHAR2(30)
HASH_EXPRESSION                                 LONG

DBA_CLUSTER_HASH_EXPRESSIONS          select us.name, o.name, c.condition
                                      from sys.cdef$ c, sys.user$ us, sys.obj$ o
                                      where c.type# = 8
                                        and c.obj#   = o.obj#
                                        and us.user# = o.owner#
```

The **DBA_CLU_COLUMNS** view shows all of the cluster columns defined in the database.

Listing A.254   Description of the DBA_ view DBA_CLU_COLUMNS.

```
Name                                  Null?     Type
------------------------------------- --------- ----
OWNER                                 NOT NULL  VARCHAR2(30)
CLUSTER_NAME                          NOT NULL  VARCHAR2(30)
CLU_COLUMN_NAME                       NOT NULL  VARCHAR2(30)
TABLE_NAME                            NOT NULL  VARCHAR2(30)
TAB_COLUMN_NAME                                 VARCHAR2(4000)

DBA_CLU_COLUMNS       select u.name, oc.name, cc.name, ot.name,
                             decode(bitand(tc.property, 1), 1, ac.name, tc.name)
                      from sys.user$ u, sys.obj$ oc, sys.col$ cc, sys.obj$ ot,
                           sys.col$ tc,
                           sys.tab$ t,  sys.attrcol$ ac
                      where oc.owner#  = u.user#
                        and oc.obj#    = cc.obj#
                        and t.bobj#    = oc.obj#
                        and t.obj#     = tc.obj#
                        and tc.segcol# = cc.segcol#
                        and t.obj#     = ot.obj#
```

```
                    and oc.type#  = 3
                    and tc.obj#   = ac.obj#(+)
                    and tc.intcol# = ac.intcol#(+)
```

The **DBA_COLL_TYPES** view contains information on all named collection types in
the database (**VARRAY**s, nested tables, object tables, etc.).

Listing A.255 Description of the DBA_ view DBA_COLL_TYPES.

```
Name                                  Null?      Type
------------------------------------  --------   ----
OWNER                                 NOT NULL   VARCHAR2(30)
TYPE_NAME                             NOT NULL   VARCHAR2(30)
COLL_TYPE                             NOT NULL   VARCHAR2(30)
UPPER_BOUND                                      NUMBER
ELEM_TYPE_MOD                                    VARCHAR2(7)
ELEM_TYPE_OWNER                                  VARCHAR2(30)
ELEM_TYPE_NAME                                   VARCHAR2(30)
LENGTH                                           NUMBER
PRECISION                                        NUMBER
SCALE                                            NUMBER
CHARACTER_SET_NAME                               VARCHAR2(44)

DBA_COLL_TYPES      select u.name, o.name, co.name, c.upper_bound,
                        decode(bitand(c.properties, 32768), 32768, 'REF',
                        decode(bitand(c.properties, 16384), 16384, 'POINTER')),
                        decode(bitand(et.properties, 64), 64, null, eu.name),
                        decode(et.typecode,
                            52, decode(c.charsetform, 2, 'NVARCHAR2', eo.name),
                            53, decode(c.charsetform, 2, 'NCHAR', eo.name),
                            54, decode(c.charsetform,2,'NCHAR VARYING',eo.name),
                            61, decode(c.charsetform, 2, 'NCLOB', eo.name),
                                         eo.name),
                             c.length, c.precision, c.scale,
                             decode(c.charsetform, 1, 'CHAR_CS',
                                    2, 'NCHAR_CS',
                                    3, NLS_CHARSET_NAME(c.charsetid),
                                    4, 'ARG:'||c.charsetid)
                    from sys.user$ u, sys.obj$ o, sys.collection$ c,
                        sys.obj$ co, sys.obj$ eo, sys.user$ eu,
                        sys.type$ et
                    where o.owner# = u.user#
                    and o.oid$ = c.toid
                    and o.type# <> 10 -- must not be invalid
                    and c.coll_toid = co.oid$
                    and c.elem_toid = eo.oid$
                    and eo.owner# = eu.user#
```

```
                              and c.elem_toid = et.toid
                              and c.elem_version# = et.version#
```

The **DBA_COL_COMMENTS** view lists all comments on all columns that have had comments entered in the database.

Listing A.256   Description of the DBA_ view DBA_COL_COMMENTS.

```
Name                              Null?    Type
-------------------------------   -------- ----
OWNER                             NOT NULL VARCHAR2(30)
TABLE_NAME                        NOT NULL VARCHAR2(30)
COLUMN_NAME                       NOT NULL VARCHAR2(30)
COMMENTS                                   VARCHAR2(4000)


DBA_COL_COMMENTS      select u.name, o.name, c.name, co.comment$
                      from sys.obj$ o, sys.col$ c, sys.user$ u, sys.com$ co
                      where o.owner# = u.user#
                        and o.type# in (2, 4)
                        and o.obj# = c.obj#
                        and c.obj# = co.obj#(+)
                        and c.col# = co.col#(+)
                        and bitand(c.property, 32) = 0 /* not hidden column */
```

The **DBA_COL_PRIVS** view shows all grants made on columns in the database.

Listing A.257   Description of the DBA_ view DBA_COL_PRIVS.

```
Name                              Null?    Type
-------------------------------   -------- ----
GRANTEE                           NOT NULL VARCHAR2(30)
OWNER                             NOT NULL VARCHAR2(30)
TABLE_NAME                        NOT NULL VARCHAR2(30)
COLUMN_NAME                       NOT NULL VARCHAR2(30)
GRANTOR                           NOT NULL VARCHAR2(30)
PRIVILEGE                         NOT NULL VARCHAR2(40)
GRANTABLE                                  VARCHAR2(3)


DBA_COL_PRIVS         select ue.name, u.name, o.name, c.name, ur.name, tpm.name,
                             decode(oa.option$, 1, 'YES', 'NO')
                      from sys.objauth$ oa, sys.obj$ o, sys.user$ u,
                             sys.user$ ur, sys.user$ ue, sys.col$ c,
table_privilege_map tpm
                      where oa.obj# = o.obj#
                        and oa.grantor# = ur.user#
                        and oa.grantee# = ue.user#
                        and oa.obj# = c.obj#
```

```
and oa.col# = c.col#
and bitand(c.property, 32) = 0 /* not hidden column */
and oa.col# is not null
and oa.privilege# = tpm.privilege
and u.user# = o.owner#
```

The **DBA_CONSTRAINTS** view shows all constraints on all tables in the database. Linking **DBA_CONSTRAINTS** with **DBA_CONS_COLUMNS** gives a complete picture of the constraints in the database.

Listing A.258   Description of the DBA_ view DBA_CONSTRAINTS.

Name	Null?	Type
OWNER	NOT NULL	VARCHAR2(30)
CONSTRAINT_NAME	NOT NULL	VARCHAR2(30)
CONSTRAINT_TYPE		VARCHAR2(1)
TABLE_NAME	NOT NULL	VARCHAR2(30)
SEARCH_CONDITION		LONG
R_OWNER		VARCHAR2(30)
R_CONSTRAINT_NAME		VARCHAR2(30)
DELETE_RULE		VARCHAR2(9)
STATUS		VARCHAR2(8)
DEFERRABLE		VARCHAR2(14)
DEFERRED		VARCHAR2(9)
VALIDATED		VARCHAR2(13)
GENERATED		VARCHAR2(14)
BAD		VARCHAR2(3)
LAST_CHANGE		DATE

```
DBA_CONSTRAINTS     select ou.name, oc.name,
                      decode(c.type#, 1, 'C', 2, 'P', 3, 'U',
                             4, 'R', 5, 'V', 6, 'O', 7,'C', '?'),
                      o.name, c.condition, ru.name, rc.name,
                      decode(c.type#, 4,
                      decode(c.refact, 1, 'CASCADE', 'NO ACTION'), NULL),
                      decode(c.type#, 5, 'ENABLED',
                      decode(c.enabled, NULL, 'DISABLED', 'ENABLED')),
                      decode(bitand(c.defer, 1), 1, 'DEFERRABLE', 'NOT
                      DEFERRABLE'),
                      decode(bitand(c.defer, 2), 2, 'DEFERRED', 'IMMEDIATE'),
                      decode(bitand(c.defer, 4), 4, 'VALIDATED', 'NOT VALIDATED'),
                      decode(bitand(c.defer, 8), 8, 'GENERATED NAME', 'USER NAME'),
                      decode(bitand(c.defer,16),16, 'BAD', null),
                      c.mtime
```

```
        from sys.con$ oc, sys.con$ rc, sys.user$ ou, sys.user$ ru,
             sys.obj$ o, sys.cdef$ c
        where oc.owner# = ou.user#
          and oc.con# = c.con#
          and c.obj# = o.obj#
          and c.type# != 8          /* don't include hash expressions */
          and c.rcon# = rc.con#(+)
          and rc.owner# = ru.user#(+)
```

The **DBA_CONS_COLUMNS** view lists all columns that have constraints assigned in the database.

Listing A.259   Description of the DBA_ view DBA_CONS_COLUMNS.

```
Name                                 Null?     Type
-------------------------------      --------  ----
OWNER                                NOT NULL  VARCHAR2(30)
CONSTRAINT_NAME                      NOT NULL  VARCHAR2(30)
TABLE_NAME                           NOT NULL  VARCHAR2(30)
COLUMN_NAME                                    VARCHAR2(4000)
POSITION                                       NUMBER
```

```
DBA_CONS_COLUMNS    select u.name, c.name, o.name,
                           decode(bitand(col.property, 1), 1, ac.name, col.name),
                    cc.pos#
                    from sys.user$ u, sys.con$ c, sys.col$ col,
                         sys.ccol$ cc, sys.cdef$ cd,
                         sys.obj$ o, sys.attrcol$ ac
                    where c.owner# = u.user#
                      and c.con# = cd.con#
                      and cd.con# = cc.con#
                      and cc.obj# = col.obj#
                      and cc.intcol# = col.intcol#
                      and cc.obj# = o.obj#
                      and col.obj# = ac.obj#(+)
                      and col.intcol# = ac.intcol#(+)
```

The **DBA_DATA_FILES** view provides information on all tablespace datafiles assigned to the database.

Listing A.260   Description of the DBA_ view DBA_DATA_FILES.

```
Name                                 Null?     Type
-------------------------------      --------  ----
FILE_NAME                                      VARCHAR2(513)
FILE_ID                              NOT NULL  NUMBER
TABLESPACE_NAME                      NOT NULL  VARCHAR2(30)
```

```
BYTES                                    NUMBER
BLOCKS                        NOT NULL   NUMBER
STATUS                                   VARCHAR2(9)
RELATIVE_FNO                             NUMBER
AUTOEXTENSIBLE                           VARCHAR2(3)
MAXBYTES                                 NUMBER
MAXBLOCKS                                NUMBER
INCREMENT_BY                             NUMBER

DBA_DATA_FILES    select v.name, f.file#, ts.name,
                         ts.blocksize * f.blocks, f.blocks,
                         decode(f.status$, 1, 'INVALID', 2, 'AVAILABLE',
                         'UNDEFINED'),
                         f.relfile#, decode(f.inc, 0, 'NO', 'YES'),
                         ts.blocksize * f.maxextend, f.maxextend, f.inc
                    from sys.file$ f, sys.ts$ ts, sys.v$dbfile v
                    where v.file# = f.file#
                      and f.ts# = ts.ts#
```

The **DBA_DB_LINKS** view provides information on all database links assigned to the database.

Listing A.261   Description of the DBA_ view DBA_DB_LINKS.

```
Name                                Null?      Type
----------------------------------  --------   ----
OWNER                               NOT NULL   VARCHAR2(30)
DB_LINK                             NOT NULL   VARCHAR2(128)
USERNAME                                       VARCHAR2(30)
HOST                                           VARCHAR2(2000)
CREATED                             NOT NULL   DATE

DBA_DB_LINKS      select u.name, l.name, l.userid, l.host, l.ctime
                    from sys.link$ l, sys.user$ u
                    where l.owner# = u.user#
```

The **DBA_DDL_LOCKS** view shows all Data Definition Language (DDL) locks currently held in the database. DDL locks are granted when objects are created, dropped, or altered. This view is created by the CATBLOCK.SQL script.

Listing A.262   Description of the DBA_ view DBA_DDL_LOCKS.

```
Name                                Null?      Type
----------------------------------  --------   ----
SESSION_ID                                     NUMBER
OWNER                                          VARCHAR2(30)
NAME                                           VARCHAR2(30)
```

```
TYPE                                       VARCHAR2(40)
MODE_HELD                                  VARCHAR2(9)
MODE_REQUESTED                             VARCHAR2(9)

DBA_DDL_LOCKS    select  s.sid session_id,
                    substr(ob.kglnaown,1,30) owner,
                    substr(ob.kglnaobj,1,30) name,
                    decode(ob.kglhdnsp, 0, 'Cursor', 1, 'Table/Procedure', 2, 'Body',
                                3, 'Trigger', 4, 'Index', 5, 'Cluster', 'Unknown')
                                type,
                    decode(lk.kgllkmod, 0, 'None', 1, 'Null', 2, 'Share', 3,
                            'Exclusive', 'Unknown') mode_held,
                    decode(lk.kgllkreq, 0,'None', 1, 'Null', 2, 'Share', 3,
                            'Exclusive', 'Unknown') mode_requested
                    from v$session s, x$kglob ob, x$kgllk lk
                    where lk.kgllkhdl = ob.kglhdadr
                    and   lk.kgllkuse = s.saddr
                    and   ob.kglhdnsp != 0
```

The **DBA_DEPENDENCIES** view lists all to and from dependencies between objects in the database.

Listing A.263   Description of the DBA_ view DBA_DEPENDENCIES.

```
Name                               Null?    Type
-------------------------------    -------- ----
OWNER                              NOT NULL VARCHAR2(30)
NAME                              NOT NULL VARCHAR2(30)
TYPE                                       VARCHAR2(12)
REFERENCED_OWNER                           VARCHAR2(30)
REFERENCED_NAME                            VARCHAR2(64)
REFERENCED_TYPE                            VARCHAR2(12)
REFERENCED_LINK_NAME                       VARCHAR2(128)
DEPENDENCY_TYPE                            VARCHAR2(4)

DBA_DEPENDENCIES    select u.name, o.name,
                        decode(o.type#, 0, 'NEXT OBJECT', 1, 'INDEX',
                                    2, 'TABLE', 3, 'CLUSTER',
                                    4, 'VIEW', 5, 'SYNONYM',
                                    6, 'SEQUENCE', 7, 'PROCEDURE',
                                    8, 'FUNCTION', 9, 'PACKAGE',
                                    10, 'NON-EXISTENT',
                                    11, 'PACKAGE BODY', 12, 'TRIGGER',
                                    13, 'TYPE', 14, 'TYPE BODY', 'UNDEFINED'),
                        decode(po.linkname, null, pu.name, po.remoteowner), po.name,
```

```
decode(po.type#, 0, 'NEXT OBJECT', 1, 'INDEX',
                 2, 'TABLE', 3, 'CLUSTER',
                 4, 'VIEW', 5, 'SYNONYM', 6, 'SEQUENCE',
                 7, 'PROCEDURE', 8, 'FUNCTION','9',PACKAGE,
                 10, 'NON-EXISTENT',
                 11, 'PACKAGE BODY', 12, 'TRIGGER',
                 13, 'TYPE', 14, 'TYPE BODY', 'UNDEFINED'),
       po.linkname,
       decode(d.property, 2, 'REF', 'HARD')
from sys.obj$ o, sys.disk_and_fixed_objects po,
     sys.dependency$ d, sys.user$ u,sys.user$ pu
where o.obj# = d.d_obj#
  and o.owner# = u.user#
  and po.obj# = d.p_obj#
  and po.owner# = pu.user#
```

The **DBA_DIRECTORIES** view provides information on all **DIRECTORY** specifications in the database. **DIRECTORY** assignments are used when dealing with **BFILE** datatypes.

Listing A.264   Description of the DBA_ view DBA_DIRECTORIES.

Name	Null?	Type
OWNER	NOT NULL	VARCHAR2(30)
DIRECTORY_NAME	NOT NULL	VARCHAR2(30)
DIRECTORY_PATH		VARCHAR2(4000)

```
DBA_DIRECTORIES    select u.name, o.name, d.os_path
                   from sys.user$ u, sys.obj$ o, sys.dir$ d
                   where u.user# = o.owner#
                     and o.obj# = d.obj#
```

The **DBA_DML_LOCKS** view shows all Data Manipulation Locks currently held in the database. DML locks are granted through **SELECT**, **INSERT**, **DELETE**, and **UPDATE** operations.

Listing A.265   Description of the DBA_ view DBA_DML_LOCKS.

Name	Null?	Type
SESSION_ID		NUMBER
OWNER	NOT NULL	VARCHAR2(30)
NAME	NOT NULL	VARCHAR2(30)
MODE_HELD		VARCHAR2(13)
MODE_REQUESTED		VARCHAR2(13)
LAST_CONVERT		NUMBER

```
       BLOCKING_OTHERS                          VARCHAR2(40)

DBA_DML_LOCKS        select
                           sid session_id,
                           u.name owner,
                           o.name,
                           decode(lmode,
                            0, 'None',              /* Mon Lock equivalent */
                            1, 'Null',             /* N */
                            2, 'Row-S (SS)',       /* L */
                            3, 'Row-X (SX)',       /* R */
                            4, 'Share',            /* S */
                            5, 'S/Row-X (SSX)',    /* C */
                            6, 'Exclusive',        /* X */
                             'Invalid') mode_held,
                           decode(request,
                            0, 'None',              /* Mon Lock equivalent */
                            1, 'Null',             /* N */
                            2, 'Row-S (SS)',       /* L */
                            3, 'Row-X (SX)',       /* R */
                            4, 'Share',            /* S */
                            5, 'S/Row-X (SSX)',    /* C */
                            6, 'Exclusive',        /* X */
                             'Invalid') mode_requested,
                           l.ctime last_convert,
                           decode(block,
                            0, 'Not Blocking',  /* Not blocking any other
                                                        processes */
                            1, 'Blocking',       /* This lock blocks other
                                                        processes */
                            2, 'Global',        /* This lock is global,so we can't
                                                        tell */
                           to_char(block)) blocking_others
                     from v$lock l, obj$ o, user$ u
                     where l.id1 = o.obj#
                     and   o.owner# = u.user#
                     and   l.type = 'TM'
```

The **DBA_ERRORS** view shows all current errors for the stored objects (procedures, functions, packages, etc.) in the database.

Listing A.266 Description of the DBA_ view DBA_ERRORS.

```
Name                               Null?    Type
---------------------------------- -------- ----
OWNER                              NOT NULL VARCHAR2(30)
NAME                              NOT NULL VARCHAR2(30)
TYPE                                       VARCHAR2(12)
SEQUENCE                          NOT NULL NUMBER
LINE                             NOT NULL NUMBER
POSITION                          NOT NULL NUMBER
TEXT                             NOT NULL VARCHAR2(4000)


DBA_ERRORS          select u.name, o.name,
                          decode(o.type#, 4, 'VIEW', 7, 'PROCEDURE',
                                          8, 'FUNCTION', 9, 'PACKAGE',
                                          11, 'PACKAGE BODY', 12, 'TRIGGER',
                                          13, 'TYPE', 14, 'TYPE BODY',
                                                'UNDEFINED'),
                          e.sequence#, e.line, e.position#, e.text
                    from sys.obj$ o, sys.error$ e, sys.user$ u
                    where o.obj# = e.obj#
                      and o.owner# = u.user#
                      and o.type# in (4, 7, 8, 9, 11, 12, 13, 14)
```

The **DBA_EXP_FILES** view contains a description of all current export files.

Listing A.267 Description of the DBA_ view DBA_EXP_FILES.

```
Name                               Null?    Type
---------------------------------- -------- ----
EXP_VERSION                       NOT NULL NUMBER(3)
EXP_TYPE                                   VARCHAR2(11)
FILE_NAME                         NOT NULL VARCHAR2(100)
USER_NAME                         NOT NULL VARCHAR2(30)
TIMESTAMP                         NOT NULL DATE


DBA_EXP_FILES       select o.expid,
                          decode(o.exptype, 'X', 'COMPLETE', 'C', 'CUMULATIVE',
                                            'I', 'INCREMENTAL', 'UNDEFINED'),
                          o.expfile, o.expuser, o.expdate
                    from sys.incfil o
```

The **DBA_EXP_OBJECTS** view lists all objects that have been incrementally exported.

Listing A.268 Description of the DBA_ view DBA_EXP_OBJECTS.

```
Name                             Null?    Type
------------------------------   -------- ----
OWNER                            NOT NULL VARCHAR2(30)
OBJECT_NAME                      NOT NULL VARCHAR2(30)
OBJECT_TYPE                               VARCHAR2(12)
CUMULATIVE                                DATE
INCREMENTAL                      NOT NULL DATE
EXPORT_VERSION                   NOT NULL NUMBER(3)


DBA_EXP_OBJECTS    select u.name, o.name,
                         decode(o.type#, 1, 'INDEX', 2, 'TABLE', 3, 'CLUSTER',
                                4, 'VIEW', 5, 'SYNONYM', 6, 'SEQUENCE','7',PROCEDURE,
                                8, 'FUNCTION', 9, 'PACKAGE', 11, 'PACKAGE BODY',
                                12, 'TRIGGER', 13, 'TYPE', 14, 'TYPE BODY',
                                22, 'LIBRARY', 'UNDEFINED'),
                          o.ctime, o.itime, o.expid
                   from sys.incexp o, sys.user$ u
                   where o.owner# = u.user#
```

The **DBA_EXP_VERSION** view contains the version number of the last export session.

Listing A.269 Description of the DBA_ view DBA_EXP_VERSION.

```
Name                             Null?    Type
------------------------------   -------- ----
EXP_VERSION                      NOT NULL NUMBER(3)


DBA_EXP_VERSION          select o.expid
                         from sys.incvid o
```

The **DBA_EXTENTS** view contains information on all segment extents in the database.

Listing A.270 Description of the DBA_ view DBA_EXTENTS.

```
Name                             Null?    Type
------------------------------   -------- ----
OWNER                                     VARCHAR2(30)
SEGMENT_NAME                              VARCHAR2(81)
PARTITION_NAME                            VARCHAR2(30)
SEGMENT_TYPE                              VARCHAR2(17)
TABLESPACE_NAME                           VARCHAR2(30)
EXTENT_ID                        NOT NULL NUMBER
FILE_ID                          NOT NULL NUMBER
BLOCK_ID                         NOT NULL NUMBER
```

```
BYTES                                   NUMBER
BLOCKS                         NOT NULL NUMBER
RELATIVE_FNO                   NOT NULL NUMBER


DBA_EXTENTS           select ds.owner, ds.segment_name, ds.partition_name,
                             ds.segment_type, ds.tablespace_name,e.ext#,
                             f.file#, e.block#, e.length * ds.blocksize, e.length,
                             e.file#
                      from sys.uet$ e, sys.sys_dba_segs ds, sys.file$ f
                      where e.segfile# = ds.relative_fno
                        and e.segblock# = ds.header_block
                        and e.ts# = ds.tablespace_id
                        and e.ts# = f.ts#
                        and e.file# = f.relfile#
```

The **DBA_FREE_SPACE** view lists the free extents available in the database.

Listing A.271   Description of the DBA_ view DBA_FREE_SPACE.

```
Name                              Null?     Type
-------------------------------- --------- ----
TABLESPACE_NAME                  NOT NULL VARCHAR2(30)
FILE_ID                          NOT NULL NUMBER
BLOCK_ID                         NOT NULL NUMBER
BYTES                                     NUMBER
BLOCKS                           NOT NULL NUMBER
RELATIVE_FNO                     NOT NULL NUMBER


DBA_FREE_SPACE        select ts.name, fi.file#, f.block#,
                             f.length * ts.blocksize, f.length, f.file#
                      from sys.fet$ f, sys.ts$ ts, sys.file$ fi
                      where f.ts# = ts.ts#
                        and f.ts# = fi.ts#
                        and f.file# = fi.relfile#
```

The **DBA_FREE_SPACE_COALESCED** view contains statistics about coalesced tablespaces in the database.

Listing A.272   Description of the DBA_ view DBA_FREE_SPACE_COALESCED.

```
Name                              Null?     Type
-------------------------------- --------- ----
TABLESPACE_NAME                  NOT NULL VARCHAR2(30)
TOTAL_EXTENTS                              NUMBER
EXTENTS_COALESCED                         NUMBER
PERCENT_EXTENTS_COALESCED                 NUMBER
TOTAL_BYTES                               NUMBER
```

```
BYTES_COALESCED                             NUMBER
TOTAL_BLOCKS                                NUMBER
BLOCKS_COALESCED                            NUMBER
PERCENT_BLOCKS_COALESCED                     NUMBER

DBA_FREE_SPACE_COALESCED        select
                                    name,total_extents, extents_coalesced,
                                    extents_coalesced/total_extents*100,
                                    total_blocks*c.blocksize,
                                    blocks_coalesced*c.blocksize,
                                    total_blocks,
                                    blocks_coalesced,
                                    blocks_coalesced/total_blocks*100
                                from DBA_FREE_SPACE_COALESCED_TMP1 a,
                                    DBA_FREE_SPACE_COALESCED_TMP2 b,
                                sys.ts$
                                where a.ts#=b.ts# and a.ts#=c.ts#
```

The **DBA_FREE_SPACE_COALESCED_TMP1** and **DBA_FREE_SPACE_COALESCED_TMP2** views are used to hold intermediate calculation results for the the **DBA_FREE_SPACE_COALESCED** view.

Listing A.273 Description of the DBA_ view DBA_FREE_SPACE_COALESCED_TMP1.

```
Name                                Null?    Type
--------------------------------    -------- ----
TS#                                 NOT NULL NUMBER
EXTENTS_COALESCED                            NUMBER
BLOCKS_COALESCED                             NUMBER

DBA_FREE_SPACE_COALESCED_TMP1       select ts#, count(*) extents_coalesced,
                                            sum(length) blocks_coalesced
                                    from sys.fet$ a
                                    where not exists (
                                                    select * from sys.fet$ b
                                                    where b.ts#=a.ts# and
                                                            b.file#=a.file#
                                            and
                                                    a.block#=b.block#+b.length)
                                    group by ts#
```

Listing A.274 Description of the DBA_ view DBA_FREE_SPACE_ COALESCED_TMP2.

```
Name                              Null?    Type
--------------------------------  -------- ----
TS#                               NOT NULL NUMBER
TOTAL_EXTENTS                              NUMBER
TOTAL_BLOCKS                               NUMBER


DBA_FREE_SPACE_COALESCED_TMP2          select ts#, count(*) total_extents,
                                              sum(length) total_blocks
                                       from sys.fet$
                                       group by ts#
```

The **DBA_INDEXES** view contains storage information and statistics on all of the indexes in the database. Note that the detailed statistics generated by the **ANALYZE** command are placed in the one-row view **INDEX_STATS** and must be viewed there before the next index is analyzed.

Listing A.275 Description of the DBA_ view DBA_INDEXES.

```
Name                              Null?    Type
--------------------------------  -------- ----
OWNER                             NOT NULL VARCHAR2(30)
INDEX_NAME                        NOT NULL VARCHAR2(30)
INDEX_TYPE                                 VARCHAR2(12)
TABLE_OWNER                       NOT NULL VARCHAR2(30)
TABLE_NAME                        NOT NULL VARCHAR2(30)
TABLE_TYPE                                 VARCHAR2(11)
UNIQUENESS                                 VARCHAR2(9)
TABLESPACE_NAME                            VARCHAR2(30)
INI_TRANS                                  NUMBER
MAX_TRANS                                  NUMBER
INITIAL_EXTENT                             NUMBER
NEXT_EXTENT                                NUMBER
MIN_EXTENTS                                NUMBER
MAX_EXTENTS                                NUMBER
PCT_INCREASE                               NUMBER
PCT_THRESHOLD                              NUMBER
INCLUDE_COLUMN                             NUMBER
FREELISTS                                  NUMBER
FREELIST_GROUPS                            NUMBER
PCT_FREE                                   NUMBER
LOGGING                                    VARCHAR2(3)
BLEVEL                                     NUMBER
LEAF_BLOCKS                                NUMBER
DISTINCT_KEYS                              NUMBER
AVG_LEAF_BLOCKS_PER_KEY                    NUMBER
```

```
       AVG_DATA_BLOCKS_PER_KEY                    NUMBER
       CLUSTERING_FACTOR                          NUMBER
       STATUS                                     VARCHAR2(8)
       NUM_ROWS                                   NUMBER
       SAMPLE_SIZE                                NUMBER
       LAST_ANALYZED                              DATE
       DEGREE                                     VARCHAR2(40)
       INSTANCES                                  VARCHAR2(40)
       PARTITIONED                                VARCHAR2(3)
       TEMPORARY                                  VARCHAR2(1)
       GENERATED                                  VARCHAR2(1)
       BUFFER_POOL                                VARCHAR2(7)

DBA_INDEXES              select u.name, o.name,
                             decode(i.type#, 1, 'NORMAL', 2, 'BITMAP',
                                             3, 'CLUSTER', 4, 'IOT - TOP',
                                             5, 'IOT - NESTED', 6, 'SECONDARY',
                                             7, 'ANSI', 8, 'LOB'),
                             iu.name, io.name,
                             decode(io.type#, 0, 'NEXT OBJECT', 1, 'INDEX',
                                              2, 'TABLE',
                                              3, 'CLUSTER', 4, 'VIEW', 5, 'SYNONYM',
                                              6, 'SEQUENCE', 'UNDEFINED'),
                             decode(bitand(i.property, 1), 0, 'NONUNIQUE',
                                              1, 'UNIQUE', 'UNDEFINED'),
                             decode(bitand(i.property, 2),0, ts.name, null),
                             decode(bitand(i.property, 2),0, i.initrans, null),
                             decode(bitand(i.property, 2),0, i.maxtrans, null),
                             s.iniexts * ts.blocksize, s.extsize * ts.blocksize,
                             s.minexts, s.maxexts, s.extpct, i.pctthres$,
                             i.trunccnt,
                             decode(s.lists, 0, 1, s.lists),
                             decode(s.groups, 0, 1, s.groups),
                             decode(bitand(i.property, 2),0,i.pctfree$,null),
                             decode(bitand(i.property, 2), 2, NULL,
                             decode(bitand(i.flags, 4), 0, 'YES', 'NO')),
                             i.blevel, i.leafcnt, i.distkey, i.lblkkey,
                             i.dblkkey, i.clufac,
                             decode(bitand(i.property, 2), 2, 'N/A',
                             decode(bitand(i.flags, 1), 1, 'UNUSABLE', 'VALID')),
                             rowcnt, samplesize, analyzetime,
                             decode(i.degree, 32767, 'DEFAULT', nvl(i.degree,1)),
                             decode(i.instances, 32767, 'DEFAULT',
                             nvl(i.instances,1)),
                             decode(bitand(i.property, 2), 2, 'YES', 'NO'),
                             decode(bitand(o.flags, 2), 0, 'N', 2, 'Y', 'N'),
                             decode(bitand(o.flags, 4), 0, 'N', 4, 'Y', 'N'),
                             decode(s.cachehint,0,'DEFAULT',1, 'KEEP', 2, 'RECYCLE',
                             NULL)
```

```
                        from sys.ts$ ts, sys.seg$ s,
                            sys.user$ iu, sys.obj$ io, sys.user$ u, sys.ind$ i,
    sys.obj$ o
                        where u.user# = o.owner#
                          and o.obj# = i.obj#
                          and i.bo# = io.obj#
                          and io.owner# = iu.user#
                          and i.ts# = ts.ts# (+)
                          and i.file# = s.file# (+)
                          and i.block# = s.block# (+)
                          and i.ts# = s.ts# (+)
```

The **DBA_IND_COLUMNS** view contains information about all indexed columns.
To get a complete picture of the indexes in the database, a join between
DBA_INDEXES and **DBA_IND_COLUMNS** is required.

Listing A.276   Description of the DBA_ view DBA_IND_COLUMNS.

```
Name                                   Null?     Type
------------------------------------   --------  ----
    INDEX_OWNER                        NOT NULL VARCHAR2(30)
    INDEX_NAME                         NOT NULL VARCHAR2(30)
    TABLE_OWNER                        NOT NULL VARCHAR2(30)
    TABLE_NAME                         NOT NULL VARCHAR2(30)
    COLUMN_NAME                                 VARCHAR2(4000)
    COLUMN_POSITION                    NOT NULL NUMBER
    COLUMN_LENGTH                      NOT NULL NUMBER


    DBA_IND_COLUMNS        select io.name, idx.name, bo.name, base.name,
                               decode(bitand(c.property,1),1,ac.name, c.name),
                               ic.pos#, c.length
                        from sys.col$ c, sys.obj$ idx, sys.obj$ base, sys.icol$ ic,
                            sys.user$ io, sys.user$ bo, sys.ind$ i, sys.attrcol$ ac
                        where base.obj# = c.obj#
                          and ic.intcol# = c.intcol#
                          and ic.bo# = base.obj#
                          and io.user# = idx.owner#
                          and bo.user# = base.owner#
                          and ic.obj# = idx.obj#
                          and idx.obj# = i.obj#
                          and i.type# in (1, 2, 3, 4, 6, 7)
                          and c.obj# = ac.obj#(+)
                          and c.intcol# = ac.intcol#(+)
```

The **DBA_IND_PARITIONS** view contains information on all partitioned indexes
in the database.

Listing A.277 Description of the DBA_ view DBA_IND_PARTITIONS.

Name	Null?	Type
INDEX_OWNER	NOT NULL	VARCHAR2(30)
INDEX_NAME	NOT NULL	VARCHAR2(30)
PARTITION_NAME		VARCHAR2(30)
HIGH_VALUE		LONG
HIGH_VALUE_LENGTH	NOT NULL	NUMBER
PARTITION_POSITION	NOT NULL	NUMBER
STATUS		VARCHAR2(8)
TABLESPACE_NAME	NOT NULL	VARCHAR2(30)
PCT_FREE	NOT NULL	NUMBER
INI_TRANS	NOT NULL	NUMBER
MAX_TRANS	NOT NULL	NUMBER
INITIAL_EXTENT		NUMBER
NEXT_EXTENT		NUMBER
MIN_EXTENT	NOT NULL	NUMBER
MAX_EXTENT	NOT NULL	NUMBER
PCT_INCREASE	NOT NULL	NUMBER
FREELISTS		NUMBER
LOGGING		VARCHAR2(3)
BLEVEL		NUMBER
LEAF_BLOCKS		NUMBER
DISTINCT_KEYS		NUMBER
AVG_LEAF_BLOCKS_PER_KEY		NUMBER
AVG_DATA_BLOCKS_PER_KEY		NUMBER
CLUSTERING_FACTOR		NUMBER
NUM_ROWS		NUMBER
SAMPLE_SIZE		NUMBER
LAST_ANALYZED		DATE
BUFFER_POOL		VARCHAR2(7)

```
DBA_IND_PARTITIONS    select u.name, o.name, o.subname,
                      ip.hiboundval, ip.hiboundlen, ip.part#,
                      decode(bitand(ip.flags, 1), 1, 'UNUSABLE', 'USABLE'),
                      ts.name, ip.pctfree$,ip.initrans, ip.maxtrans,
                      s.iniexts * ts.blocksize,
                      s.extsize * ts.blocksize, s.minexts, s.maxexts,
                      s.extpct,
                      decode(s.lists, 0, 1, s.lists),
                      decode(mod(trunc(ip.flags / 4), 2), 0, 'YES', 'NO'),
                      ip.blevel, ip.leafcnt, ip.distkey, ip.lblkkey,
                      ip.dblkkey,
                      ip.clufac, ip.rowcnt, ip.samplesize, ip.analyzetime,
                      decode(s.cachehint, 0, 'DEFAULT', 1, 'KEEP',
                                          2, 'RECYCLE', NULL)
```

```
                  from obj$ o, indpart$ ip, ts$ ts, sys.seg$ s, user$ u
             where o.obj# = ip.obj# and ts.ts# = ip.ts# and ip.file#=s.file#
                 and ip.block#=s.block# and ip.ts#=s.ts# and o.owner#=u.user#
```

The **DBA_JOBS** view contains information on all submitted jobs in the database.
The **DBMS_JOB** package is used to submit and control jobs in the Oracle job queues.

Listing A.278 Description of the DBA_ view DBA_JOBS.

Name	Null?	Type
JOB	NOT NULL	NUMBER
LOG_USER	NOT NULL	VARCHAR2(30)
PRIV_USER	NOT NULL	VARCHAR2(30)
SCHEMA_USER	NOT NULL	VARCHAR2(30)
LAST_DATE		DATE
LAST_SEC		VARCHAR2(8)
THIS_DATE		DATE
THIS_SEC		VARCHAR2(8)
NEXT_DATE	NOT NULL	DATE
NEXT_SEC		VARCHAR2(8)
TOTAL_TIME		NUMBER
BROKEN		VARCHAR2(1)
INTERVAL	NOT NULL	VARCHAR2(200)
FAILURES		NUMBER
WHAT		VARCHAR2(4000)
CURRENT_SESSION_LABEL		MLSLABEL
CLEARANCE_HI		MLSLABEL
CLEARANCE_LO		MLSLABEL
NLS_ENV		VARCHAR2(4000)
MISC_ENV		RAW(32)

```
DBA_JOBS           select JOB, lowner LOG_USER, powner PRIV_USER,
                     cowner SCHEMA_USER,LAST_DATE,
                     substr(to_char(last_date,'HH24:MI:SS'),1,8) LAST_SEC,
                     THIS_DATE,
                     substr(to_char(this_date,'HH24:MI:SS'),1,8) THIS_SEC,
                     NEXT_DATE,
                     substr(to_char(next_date,'HH24:MI:SS'),1,8) NEXT_SEC,
                     (total+(sysdate-nvl(this_date,sysdate)))*86400
                     TOTAL_TIME,
                     decode(mod(FLAG,2),1,'Y',0,'N','?') BROKEN,
                     INTERVAL# interval, FAILURES, WHAT,
                     cur_ses_label CURRENT_SESSION_LABEL,
                     CLEARANCE_HI, CLEARANCE_LO,
                     nlsenv NLS_ENV, env MISC_ENV
                   from sys.job$ j
```

The **DBA_JOBS_RUNNING** view displays information on any jobs from the Oracle job queues that are currently running.

Listing A.279 Description of the DBA_ view DBA_JOBS_RUNNING.

```
Name                             Null?     Type
------------------------------- --------   ----
SID                                        NUMBER
JOB                                        NUMBER
FAILURES                                   NUMBER
LAST_DATE                                  DATE
LAST_SEC                                   VARCHAR2(8)
THIS_DATE                                  DATE
THIS_SEC                                   VARCHAR2(8)

DBA_JOBS_RUNNING     select v.SID, v.id2 JOB, j.FAILURES,
                            LAST_DATE,
                            substr(to_char(last_date,'HH24:MI:SS'),1,8) LAST_SEC,
                            THIS_DATE,
                            substr(to_char(this_date,'HH24:MI:SS'),1,8) THIS_SEC
                     from sys.job$ j, v$lock v
                     where v.type = 'JQ' and j.job (+)= v.id2
```

The **DBA_KEEPSIZES** view is created by the DBMSPOOL.SQL and PRVTPOOL.PLB scripts and is used by the **DBMS_SHARED_POOL** package to help maintain the shared pool. The view holds information on shared SQL area items and their sizes.

Listing A.280 Description of the DBA_ view DBA_KEEPSIZES.

```
Name                             Null?     Type
------------------------------- --------   ----
TOTSIZE                                    NUMBER
OWNER                            NOT NULL  VARCHAR2(30)
NAME                             NOT NULL  VARCHAR2(30)

DBA_KEEPSIZES        select trunc((sum(parsed_size)+sum(code_size))/1000),
                            owner, name
                     from dba_object_size
                     where type in
                        ('PACKAGE','PROCEDURE','FUNCTION','PACKAGE BODY','TRIGGER')
                     group by owner, name
```

The **DBA_KGLLOCK** view contains information on global locks used internally by Oracle. This view is created by the CATBLOCK.SQL script.

Listing A.281 Description of the DBA_ view DBA_KGLLOCK.

```
Name                                  Null?    Type
-------------------------------- -------- ----
KGLLKUSE                                        RAW(4)
KGLLKHDL                                        RAW(4)
KGLLKMOD                                        NUMBER
KGLLKREQ                                        NUMBER
KGLLKTYPE                                       VARCHAR2(4)


DBA_KGLLOCK          select kgllkuse, kgllkhdl, kgllkmod,
                            kgllkreq, 'Lock' kgllktype
                     from x$kgllk
                     union all
                     select kglpnuse, kglpnhdl, kglpnmod, kglpnreq, 'Pin'  kgllktype
                     from x$kglpn
```

The **DBA_LIBRARIES** view contains information on all **LIBRARY** entries for the database. A **LIBRARY** entry is used to hold a pointer to an external DLL library for use by external procedure calls.

Listing A.282 Description of the DBA_ view DBA_LIBRARIES.

```
Name                                  Null?    Type
-------------------------------- -------- ----
OWNER                                 NOT NULL VARCHAR2(30)
LIBRARY_NAME                          NOT NULL VARCHAR2(30)
FILE_SPEC                                      VARCHAR2(2000)
DYNAMIC                                        VARCHAR2(1)
STATUS                                         VARCHAR2(7)


DBA_LIBRARIES        select u.name,
                            o.name,
                            l.filespec,
                            decode(bitand(l.property, 1), 0, 'Y', 1, 'N', NULL),
                            decode(o.status, 0, 'N/A', 1, 'VALID', 'INVALID')
                     from sys.obj$ o, sys.library$ l, sys.user$ u
                     where o.owner# = u.user#
                       and o.obj# = l.obj#
```

The **DBA_LOBS** view contains information about all defined **LOB** datatypes in use in the database (**BLOB**, **CLOB**, **NCLOB**, **BFILE**).

Listing A.283 Description of the DBA_ view DBA_LOBS.

```
Name                                  Null?    Type
-------------------------------- -------- ----
OWNER                                 NOT NULL VARCHAR2(30)
TABLE_NAME                            NOT NULL VARCHAR2(30)
COLUMN_NAME                                    VARCHAR2(4000)
```

```
         SEGMENT_NAME                    NOT NULL VARCHAR2(30)
         INDEX_NAME                      NOT NULL VARCHAR2(30)
         CHUNK                                    NUMBER
         PCTVERSION                      NOT NULL NUMBER
         CACHE                                    VARCHAR2(3)
         LOGGING                                  VARCHAR2(3)
         IN_ROW                                   VARCHAR2(3)


DBA_LOBS              select u.name, o.name,
                             decode(bitand(c.property, 1), 1, ac.name, c.name),
                             lo.name, io.name,
                             l.chunk * ts.blocksize, l.pctversion$,
                             decode(l.flags, 0, 'YES', 'NO'),
                             decode(bitand(l.flags, 2), 2, 'NO', 'YES'),
                             decode(l.property, 0, 'NO', 'YES')
                      from sys.obj$ o, sys.col$ c, sys.attrcol$ ac,
                           sys.lob$ l, sys.obj$ lo, sys.obj$ io, sys.user$ u,
                           sys.ts$ ts
                      where o.owner# = u.user#
                        and o.obj# = c.obj#
                        and c.obj# = l.obj#
                        and c.intcol# = l.intcol#
                        and l.lobj# = lo.obj#
                        and l.ind# = io.obj#
                        and l.ts# = ts.ts#
                        and c.obj# = ac.obj#(+)
                        and c.intcol# = ac.intcol#(+)
```

The **DBA_LOCK** view contains information on all locks currently active or requested in the database. This view is created by the CATBLOCK.SQL script.

Listing A.284   Description of the DBA_ view DBA_LOCK.

```
Name                             Null?    Type
-------------------------------- -------- ----
SESSION_ID                                NUMBER
LOCK_TYPE                                 VARCHAR2(26)
MODE_HELD                                 VARCHAR2(40)
MODE_REQUESTED                            VARCHAR2(40)
LOCK_ID1                                  VARCHAR2(40)
LOCK_ID2                                  VARCHAR2(40)
LAST_CONVERT                              NUMBER
BLOCKING_OTHERS                           VARCHAR2(40)
```

```
DBA_LOCK        select
                   sid session_id,
                   decode(type,
                    'MR', 'Media Recovery',
                    'RT', 'Redo Thread',
                    'UN', 'User Name',
                    'TX', 'Transaction',
                    'TM', 'DML',
                    'UL', 'PL/SQL User Lock',
                    'DX', 'Distributed Xaction',
                    'CF', 'Controlfile',
                    'IS', 'Instance State',
                    'FS', 'File Set',
                    'IR', 'Instance Recovery',
                    'ST', 'Disk Space Transaction',
                    'TS', 'Temp Segment',
                    'IV', 'Library Cache Invalidation',
                    'LS', 'Log Start or Switch',
                    'RW', 'Row Wait',
                    'SQ', 'Sequence Number',
                    'TE', 'Extend Table',
                    'TT', 'Temp Table',
                    type) lock_type,
                   decode(lmode,
                    0, 'None',              /* Mon Lock equivalent */
                    1, 'Null',              /* N */
                    2, 'Row-S (SS)',        /* L */
                    3, 'Row-X (SX)',        /* R */
                    4, 'Share',             /* S */
                    5, 'S/Row-X (SSX)',     /* C */
                    6, 'Exclusive',         /* X */
                    to_char(lmode)) mode_held,
                       decode(request,
                    0, 'None',              /* Mon Lock equivalent */
                    1, 'Null',              /* N */
                    2, 'Row-S (SS)',        /* L */
                    3, 'Row-X (SX)',        /* R */
                    4, 'Share',             /* S */
                    5, 'S/Row-X (SSX)',     /* C */
                    6, 'Exclusive',         /* X */
                    to_char(request)) mode_requested,
                       to_char(id1) lock_id1, to_char(id2) lock_id2,
                   ctime last_convert,
                   decode(block,
                       0, 'Not Blocking',  /* Not blocking any other
                                              processes */
```

```
                   1, 'Blocking',        /* This lock blocks other processes */
                   2, 'Global',     /* This lock is global, so we can't tell */
                   to_char(block)) blocking_others
            from v$lock        /* processes waiting on or holding enqueues */
```

The **DBA_LOCK_INTERNAL** view contains information about all internal locks held
or requested in the database. This view is created by the CATBLOCK.SQL script.

Listing A.285   Description of the DBA_ view DBA_LOCK_INTERNAL.
```
Name                             Null?    Type
-------------------------------- -------- ----
SESSION_ID                                NUMBER
LOCK_TYPE                                 VARCHAR2(56)
MODE_HELD                                 VARCHAR2(40)
MODE_REQUESTED                            VARCHAR2(40)
LOCK_ID1                                  VARCHAR2(1130)
LOCK_ID2                                  VARCHAR2(40)


DBA_LOCK_INTERNAL    select
                        sid session_id,
                        decode(type,
                             'MR', 'Media Recovery',
                             'RT', 'Redo Thread',
                             'UN', 'User Name',
                             'TX', 'Transaction',
                             'TM', 'DML',
                             'UL', 'PL/SQL User Lock',
                             'DX', 'Distributed Xaction',
                             'CF', 'Controlfile',
                             'IS', 'Instance State',
                             'FS', 'File Set',
                             'IR', 'Instance Recovery',
                             'ST', 'Disk Space Transaction',
                             'TS', 'Temp Segment',
                             'IV', 'Library Cache Invalidation',
                             'LS', 'Log Start or Switch',
                             'RW', 'Row Wait',
                             'SQ', 'Sequence Number',
                             'TE', 'Extend Table',
                             'TT', 'Temp Table',
                              type) lock_type,
                          decode(lmode,
                             0, 'None',              /* Mon Lock equivalent */
                             1, 'Null',              /* N */
                             2, 'Row-S (SS)',        /* L */
                             3, 'Row-X (SX)',        /* R */
                             4, 'Share',             /* S */
```

```
            5, 'S/Row-X (SSX)',      /* C */
            6, 'Exclusive',          /* X */
            to_char(lmode)) mode_held,
        decode(request,
            0, 'None',                    /* Mon Lock equivalent */
            1, 'Null',               /* N */
            2, 'Row-S (SS)',         /* L */
            3, 'Row-X (SX)',         /* R */
            4, 'Share',              /* S */
            5, 'S/Row-X (SSX)',      /* C */
            6, 'Exclusive',     /* X */
        to_char(request)) mode_requested,
        to_char(id1) lock_id1, to_char(id2) lock_id2
    from v$lock    /* processes waiting on or holding enqueues */
    union all                        /* procs holding latches */
select s.sid, 'LATCH', 'Exclusive', 'None', rawtohex(laddr), ' '
    from v$process p, v$session s, v$latchholder h
    where h.pid  = p.pid       /* 6 = exclusive, 0 = not held */
    and   p.addr = s.paddr
    union all                        /* procs waiting on latch */
  select sid, 'LATCH', 'None', 'Exclusive', latchwait,' '
    from v$session s, v$process p
    where latchwait is not null
    and   p.addr = s.paddr
    union all                        /* library cache locks */
  select  s.sid,
    decode(ob.kglhdnsp, 0, 'Cursor', 1, 'Table/Procedure', 2,
    'Body', 3, 'trigger', 4, 'Index', 5, 'Cluster',
        to_char(ob.kglhdnsp))
      || ' Definition ' || lk.kgllktype,
    decode(lk.kgllkmod, 0, 'None', 1, 'Null',
                  2, 'Share', 3, 'Exclusive',
                  to_char(lk.kgllkmod)),
    decode(lk.kgllkreq,  0, 'None', 1, 'Null',
                  2, 'Share', 3, 'Exclusive',
                  to_char(lk.kgllkreq)),
    decode(ob.kglnaown, null,'', ob.kglnaown || '.') ||
      ob.kglnaobj ||
    decode(ob.kglnadlk, null, '', '@' || ob.kglnadlk),
    rawtohex(lk.kgllkhdl)
  from v$session s, x$kglob ob, dba_kgllock lk
    where lk.kgllkhdl = ob.kglhdadr
    and   lk.kgllkuse = s.saddr
```

The **DBA_METHOD_PARAMS** view lists all method parameters for the methods on types defined in the database.

Listing A.286   Description of the DBA_ view DBA_METHOD_PARAMS.

```
Name                            Null?     Type
------------------------------- --------  ----
OWNER                           NOT NULL  VARCHAR2(30)
TYPE_NAME                       NOT NULL  VARCHAR2(30)
METHOD_NAME                     NOT NULL  VARCHAR2(30)
METHOD_NO                       NOT NULL  NUMBER
PARAM_NAME                      NOT NULL  VARCHAR2(30)
PARAM_NO                        NOT NULL  NUMBER
PARAM_MODE                                VARCHAR2(6)
PARAM_TYPE_MOD                            VARCHAR2(7)
PARAM_TYPE_OWNER                          VARCHAR2(30)
PARAM_TYPE_NAME                           VARCHAR2(30)
CHARACTER_SET_NAME                        VARCHAR2(44)


DBA_METHOD_PARAMS    select u.name, o.name, m.name, m.method#,
                            p.name, p.parameter#,
                            decode(bitand(p.properties, 768), 768, 'IN OUT',
                                    decode(bitand(p.properties, 256), 256, 'IN',
                                            decode(bitand(p.properties, 512), 512,
                                            'OUT'))),
                            decode(bitand(p.properties, 32768), 32768, 'REF',
                                    decode(bitand(p.properties, 16384), 16384,
                                    'POINTER')),
                            decode(bitand(pt.properties, 64), 64, null, pu.name),
                            decode(pt.typecode,
                                    52, decode(p.charsetform, 2, 'NVARCHAR2',
                                    po.name),
                                    53, decode(p.charsetform, 2, 'NCHAR', po.name),
                                    54, decode(p.charsetform, 2, 'NCHAR VARYING',
                                    po.name),
                                    61, decode(p.charsetform, 2, 'NCLOB', po.name),
                                    po.name),
                            decode(p.charsetform, 1, 'CHAR_CS',
                                                  2, 'NCHAR_CS',
                                                  3, NLS_CHARSET_NAME(p.charsetid),
                                                  4, 'ARG:'||p.charsetid)
                    from sys.user$ u, sys.obj$ o, sys.method$ m, sys.parameter$ p,
                         sys.obj$ po, sys.user$ pu, sys.type$ pt
                    where o.owner# = u.user#
                      and o.type# <> 10 -- must not be invalid
                      and o.oid$ = m.toid
```

```
and m.toid = p.toid
and m.version# = p.version#
and m.method# = p.method#
and p.param_toid = po.oid$
and po.owner# = pu.user#
and p.param_toid = pt.toid
and p.param_version# = pt.version#
```

The **DBA_METHOD_RESULTS** view contains descriptions of all method results in the database.

Listing A.287 Description of the DBA_ view DBA_METHOD_RESULTS.

```
Name                                  Null?     Type
------------------------------------- --------  ----
OWNER                                 NOT NULL  VARCHAR2(30)
TYPE_NAME                             NOT NULL  VARCHAR2(30)
METHOD_NAME                           NOT NULL  VARCHAR2(30)
METHOD_NO                             NOT NULL  NUMBER
RESULT_TYPE_MOD                                 VARCHAR2(7)
RESULT_TYPE_OWNER                               VARCHAR2(30)
RESULT_TYPE_NAME                                VARCHAR2(30)
CHARACTER_SET_NAME                              VARCHAR2(44)

DBA_METHOD_RESULTS   select u.name, o.name, m.name, m.method#,
                            decode(bitand(r.properties, 32768), 32768, 'REF',
                                   decode(bitand(r.properties, 16384), 16384,
                                   'POINTER')),
                            decode(bitand(rt.properties, 64), 64, null, ru.name),
                            decode(rt.typecode,
                                   52, decode(r.charsetform, 2, 'NVARCHAR2',
                                   ro.name),
                                   53, decode(r.charsetform, 2, 'NCHAR', ro.name),
                                   54, decode(r.charsetform, 2, 'NCHAR VARYING',
                                   ro.name),
                                   61, decode(r.charsetform, 2, 'NCLOB', ro.name),
                                   ro.name),
                            decode(r.charsetform, 1, 'CHAR_CS',
                                                  2, 'NCHAR_CS',
                                                  3, NLS_CHARSET_NAME(r.charsetid),
                                                  4, 'ARG:'||r.charsetid)
                     from sys.user$ u, sys.obj$ o, sys.method$ m, sys.result$ r,
                          sys.obj$ ro, sys.user$ ru, sys.type$ rt
                     where o.owner# = u.user#
                       and o.type# <> 10 -- must not be invalid
                       and o.oid$ = m.toid
```

```
                     and m.toid = r.toid
                     and m.version# = r.version#
                     and m.method# = r.method#
                     and r.result_toid = ro.oid$
                     and ro.owner# = ru.user#
                     and r.result_toid = rt.toid
                     and r.result_version# = rt.version#
```

The **DBA_NESTED_TABLES** view provides information on all nested tables in the database.

Listing A.288 Description of the DBA_ view DBA_NESTED_TABLES.

```
Name                             Null?     Type
-------------------------------- --------  ----
OWNER                                      VARCHAR2(30)
TABLE_NAME                                 VARCHAR2(30)
TABLE_TYPE_OWNER                           VARCHAR2(30)
TABLE_TYPE_NAME                            VARCHAR2(30)
PARENT_TABLE_NAME                          VARCHAR2(30)
PARENT_TABLE_COLUMN                        VARCHAR2(4000)

DBA_NESTED_TABLES    select u.name, o.name, ut.name, ot.name, op.name, ac.name
                     from sys.ntab$ n, sys.obj$ o, sys.obj$ op, sys.obj$ ot,
                       sys.col$ c, sys.coltype$ ct, sys.user$ u,
                       sys.user$ ut, sys.attrcol$ ac
                     where o.owner# = u.user#
                       and n.obj# = op.obj#
                       and n.ntab# = o.obj#
                       and c.obj# = op.obj#
                       and n.intcol# = c.intcol#
                       and c.obj# = ac.obj#
                       and c.intcol# = ac.intcol#
                       and op.obj# = ct.obj#
                       and ct.toid = ot.oid$
                       and ct.intcol#=n.intcol#
                       and ot.owner# = ut.user#
                       and bitand(ct.flags,4)=4
                     union all
                     select u.name, o.name, ut.name, ot.name, op.name, c.name
                     from sys.ntab$ n, sys.obj$ o, sys.obj$ op, sys.obj$ ot,
                       sys.col$ c, sys.coltype$ ct, sys.user$ u, sys.user$ ut
                     where o.owner# = u.user#
                       and n.obj# = op.obj#
                       and n.ntab# = o.obj#
                       and c.obj# = op.obj#
                       and n.intcol# = c.intcol#
```

```
                        and bitand(c.property,1)=0
                        and op.obj# = ct.obj#
                        and ct.toid = ot.oid$
                        and ct.intcol#=n.intcol#
                        and ot.owner# = ut.user#
                        and bitand(ct.flags,4)=4
```

The **DBA_OBJECTS** view contains information for all database objects. Objects are partitions (index or table), packages, package bodies, clusters, tables, indexes, sequences, synonyms, types, type bodies, views, directories, libraries, or triggers.

Listing A.289 Description of the DBA_ view DBA_OBJECTS.

```
Name                              Null?    Type
--------------------------------  -------- ----
OWNER                                      VARCHAR2(30)
OBJECT_NAME                                VARCHAR2(128)
SUBOBJECT_NAME                             VARCHAR2(30)
OBJECT_ID                                  NUMBER
DATA_OBJECT_ID                             NUMBER
OBJECT_TYPE                                VARCHAR2(15)
CREATED                                    DATE
LAST_DDL_TIME                              DATE
TIMESTAMP                                  VARCHAR2(19)
STATUS                                     VARCHAR2(7)
TEMPORARY                                  VARCHAR2(1)
GENERATED                                  VARCHAR2(1)


DBA_OBJECTS       select u.name, o.name, o.subname, o.obj#, o.dataobj#,
                      decode(o.type#,
                              0, 'NEXT OBJECT', 1, 'INDEX',
                              2, 'TABLE', 3, 'CLUSTER',
                              4, 'VIEW', 5, 'SYNONYM', 6, 'SEQUENCE',
                              7, 'PROCEDURE', 8, 'FUNCTION', 9, 'PACKAGE',
                              11, 'PACKAGE BODY', 12, 'TRIGGER',
                              13, 'TYPE', 14, 'TYPE BODY',
              19, 'TABLE PARTITION', 20, 'INDEX PARTITION',
              22, 'LIBRARY', 23, 'DIRECTORY', 'UNDEFINED'),
                      o.ctime, o.mtime,
                      to_char(o.stime, 'YYYY-MM-DD:HH24:MI:SS'),
                      decode(o.status, 0, 'N/A', 1, 'VALID', 'INVALID'),
                      decode(bitand(o.flags, 2), 0, 'N', 2, 'Y', 'N'),
                      decode(bitand(o.flags, 4), 0, 'N', 4, 'Y', 'N')
                  from sys.obj$ o, sys.user$ u
                  where o.owner# = u.user#
                    and o.linkname is null
```

```
                      and (o.type# not in (1   /* INDEX - handled below */,
        10 /* NON-EXISTENT */)
                      or
                      (o.type# = 1 and 1 = (select 1
        from sys.ind$ i
      where i.obj# = o.obj#
        and i.type# in (1, 2, 3, 4, 6, 7))))
                  and o.name != '_NEXT_OBJECT'
                  and o.name != '_default_auditing_options_'
              union all
              select u.name, l.name, NULL, to_number(null), to_number(null),
                      'DATABASE LINK',
                      l.ctime, to_date(null), NULL, 'VALID','N','N'
              from sys.link$ l, sys.user$ u
              where l.owner# = u.user#
```

The **DBA_OBJECT_SIZE** view lists the size in bytes of various database objects. Objects have to exhibit that they are at least partially filled in order to be displayed. To be honest, I don't see the usefulness of this view.

Listing A.290   Description of the DBA_ view DBA_OBJECT_SIZE.

```
Name                             Null?    Type
-------------------------------- -------- ----
OWNER                            NOT NULL VARCHAR2(30)
NAME                             NOT NULL VARCHAR2(30)
TYPE                                      VARCHAR2(12)
SOURCE_SIZE                               NUMBER
PARSED_SIZE                               NUMBER
CODE_SIZE                                 NUMBER
ERROR_SIZE                                NUMBER

DBA_OBJECT_SIZE    select u.name, o.name,
                     decode(o.type#, 2, 'TABLE', 4, 'VIEW', 5, 'SYNONYM', 6,
                            'SEQUENCE', 7,  'PROCEDURE', 8, 'FUNCTION', 9, 'PACKAGE',
                            11, 'PACKAGE BODY', 13, 'TYPE', 14, 'TYPE BODY',
                            'UNDEFINED'),
                     nvl(s.bytes,0), nvl(p.bytes,0), nvl(c.bytes,0),
                         nvl(e.bytes,0)
                     from sys.obj$ o, sys.user$ u,
                      sys.source_size s, sys.parsed_size p, sys.code_size c,
                      sys.error_size e
                     where o.type# in (2, 4, 5, 6, 7, 8, 9, 11, 13, 14)
                       and o.owner# = u.user#
                       and o.obj# = s.obj# (+)
```

```
                  and o.obj# = p.obj# (+)
                  and o.obj# = c.obj# (+)
                  and o.obj# = e.obj# (+)
             and nvl(s.bytes,0) + nvl(p.bytes,0) + nvl(c.bytes,0) +
                                nvl(e.bytes,0) > 0
```

The **DBA_OBJECT_TABLES** view contains the descriptions of all object tables in the database.

Listing A.291   Description of the DBA_ view DBA_OBJECT_TABLES.

Name	Null?	Type
OWNER	NOT NULL	VARCHAR2(30)
TABLE_NAME	NOT NULL	VARCHAR2(30)
TABLESPACE_NAME	NOT NULL	VARCHAR2(30)
CLUSTER_NAME		VARCHAR2(30)
IOT_NAME		VARCHAR2(30)
PCT_FREE		NUMBER
PCT_USED		NUMBER
INI_TRANS		NUMBER
MAX_TRANS		NUMBER
INITIAL_EXTENT		NUMBER
NEXT_EXTENT		NUMBER
MIN_EXTENTS		NUMBER
MAX_EXTENTS		NUMBER
PCT_INCREASE		NUMBER
FREELISTS		NUMBER
FREELIST_GROUPS		NUMBER
LOGGING		VARCHAR2(3)
BACKED_UP		VARCHAR2(1)
NUM_ROWS		NUMBER
BLOCKS		NUMBER
EMPTY_BLOCKS		NUMBER
AVG_SPACE		NUMBER
CHAIN_CNT		NUMBER
AVG_ROW_LEN		NUMBER
AVG_SPACE_FREELIST_BLOCKS		NUMBER
NUM_FREELIST_BLOCKS		NUMBER
DEGREE		VARCHAR2(10)
INSTANCES		VARCHAR2(10)
CACHE		VARCHAR2(5)
TABLE_LOCK		VARCHAR2(8)
SAMPLE_SIZE		NUMBER
LAST_ANALYZED		DATE
PARTITIONED		VARCHAR2(3)

```
IOT_TYPE                                          VARCHAR2(12)
TABLE_TYPE_OWNER                      NOT NULL VARCHAR2(30)
TABLE_TYPE                            NOT NULL VARCHAR2(30)
TEMPORARY                                         VARCHAR2(1)
NESTED                                            VARCHAR2(3)
BUFFER_POOL                                       VARCHAR2(7)
```

DBA_OBJECT_TABLES

```
select u.name, o.name, ts.name,
          decode(bitand(t.property, 1024), 0, null, co.name),
          decode(bitand(t.property, 512), 0, null, co.name),
          decode(bitand(t.property, 32), 0, mod(t.pctfree$, 100),
          null),
          decode(bitand(t.property, 32), 0, t.pctused$, null),
          decode(bitand(t.property, 32), 0, t.initrans, null),
          decode(bitand(t.property, 32), 0, t.maxtrans, null),
          s.iniexts * ts.blocksize, s.extsize * ts.blocksize,
          s.minexts, s.maxexts, s.extpct,
          decode(s.lists, 0, 1, s.lists),
          decode(s.groups, 0, 1, s.groups),
          decode(bitand(t.property, 32), 32, null,
        decode(bitand(t.flags, 32), 0, 'YES', 'NO')),
          decode(bitand(t.flags,1), 0, 'Y', 1, 'N', '?'),
          t.rowcnt, t.blkcnt, t.empcnt, t.avgspc, t.chncnt,
          t.avgrln,
          t.avgspc_flb, t.flbcnt,
       lpad(decode(t.degree, 32767,'DEFAULT', nvl(t.degree,1)),10),
       lpad(decode(t.instances, 32767,'DEFAULT',
                    nvl(t.instances,1)),10),
          lpad(decode(bitand(t.flags, 8), 8, 'Y', 'N'),5),
          decode(bitand(t.flags, 6), 0, 'ENABLED', 'DISABLED'),
          t.samplesize, t.analyzetime,
          decode(bitand(t.property, 32), 32, 'YES', 'NO'),
          decode(bitand(t.property, 64), 64, 'IOT',
          decode(bitand(t.property,512),512,'IOT_OVERFLOW',
          null)),
          tu.name, ty.name,
          decode(bitand(o.flags, 2), 0, 'N', 2, 'Y', 'N'),
          decode(bitand(t.property, 8192), 8192, 'YES', 'NO'),
          decode(s.cachehint,0,'DEFAULT',1, 'KEEP', 2, 'RECYCLE',
          NULL)
   from sys.user$ u, sys.ts$ ts, sys.seg$ s,
        sys.obj$ co, sys.tab$ t, sys.obj$ o,
        sys.coltype$ ac, sys.obj$ ty, sys.user$ tu, sys.col$ tc
  where o.owner# = u.user#
    and o.obj# = t.obj#
    and bitand(t.property, 1) = 1
```

```
and t.obj# = tc.obj#
and tc.name = 'SYS_NC_ROWINFO$'
and tc.obj# = ac.obj#
and tc.intcol# = ac.intcol#
and ac.toid = ty.oid$
and ty.owner# = tu.user#
and ty.type# <> 10
and t.bobj# = co.obj# (+)
and t.ts# = ts.ts#
and t.file# = s.file# (+)
and t.block# = s.block# (+)
and t.ts# = s.ts# (+)
```

The **DBA_OBJ_AUDIT_OPTS** view lists the auditing options for all tables and views in the database.

Listing A.292   Description of the DBA_ view DBA_OBJ_AUDIT_OPTS.

```
Name                              Null?    Type
-------------------------------   -------- ----
OWNER                                      VARCHAR2(30)
OBJECT_NAME                                VARCHAR2(30)
OBJECT_TYPE                                VARCHAR2(9)
ALT                                        VARCHAR2(3)
AUD                                        VARCHAR2(3)
COM                                        VARCHAR2(3)
DEL                                        VARCHAR2(3)
GRA                                        VARCHAR2(3)
IND                                        VARCHAR2(3)
INS                                        VARCHAR2(3)
LOC                                        VARCHAR2(3)
REN                                        VARCHAR2(3)
SEL                                        VARCHAR2(3)
UPD                                        VARCHAR2(3)
REF                                        VARCHAR2(3)
EXE                                        VARCHAR2(3)
CRE                                        VARCHAR2(3)
REA                                        VARCHAR2(3)
WRI                                        VARCHAR2(3)

DBA_OBJ_AUDIT_OPTS    select u.name, o.name, 'TABLE',
                substr(t.audit$, 1, 1) || '/' || substr(t.audit$, 2, 1),
                substr(t.audit$, 3, 1) || '/' || substr(t.audit$, 4, 1),
                substr(t.audit$, 5, 1) || '/' || substr(t.audit$, 6, 1),
                substr(t.audit$, 7, 1) || '/' || substr(t.audit$, 8, 1),
                substr(t.audit$, 9, 1) || '/' || substr(t.audit$, 10, 1),
                substr(t.audit$, 11, 1) || '/' || substr(t.audit$, 12, 1),
```

```
            substr(t.audit$, 13, 1) || '/' || substr(t.audit$, 14, 1),
            substr(t.audit$, 15, 1) || '/' || substr(t.audit$, 16, 1),
            substr(t.audit$, 17, 1) || '/' || substr(t.audit$, 18, 1),
            substr(t.audit$, 19, 1) || '/' || substr(t.audit$, 20, 1),
            substr(t.audit$, 21, 1) || '/' || substr(t.audit$, 22, 1),
            substr(t.audit$, 23, 1) || '/' || substr(t.audit$, 24, 1),
            substr(t.audit$, 25, 1) || '/' || substr(t.audit$, 26, 1),
            substr(t.audit$, 27, 1) || '/' || substr(t.audit$, 28, 1),
            substr(t.audit$, 29, 1) || '/' || substr(t.audit$, 30, 1),
            substr(t.audit$, 31, 1) || '/' || substr(t.audit$, 32, 1)
    from sys.obj$ o, sys.user$ u, sys.tab$ t
    where o.type# = 2
      and not (o.owner# = 0 and o.name =
'_default_auditing_options_')
        and o.owner# = u.user#
        and o.obj# = t.obj#
    union all
    select u.name, o.name, 'VIEW',
            substr(v.audit$, 1, 1) || '/' || substr(v.audit$, 2, 1),
            substr(v.audit$, 3, 1) || '/' || substr(v.audit$, 4, 1),
            substr(v.audit$, 5, 1) || '/' || substr(v.audit$, 6, 1),
            substr(v.audit$, 7, 1) || '/' || substr(v.audit$, 8, 1),
            substr(v.audit$, 9, 1) || '/' || substr(v.audit$, 10, 1),
            substr(v.audit$, 11, 1) || '/' || substr(v.audit$, 12, 1),
            substr(v.audit$, 13, 1) || '/' || substr(v.audit$, 14, 1),
            substr(v.audit$, 15, 1) || '/' || substr(v.audit$, 16, 1),
            substr(v.audit$, 17, 1) || '/' || substr(v.audit$, 18, 1),
            substr(v.audit$, 19, 1) || '/' || substr(v.audit$, 20, 1),
            substr(v.audit$, 21, 1) || '/' || substr(v.audit$, 22, 1),
            substr(v.audit$, 23, 1) || '/' || substr(v.audit$, 24, 1),
            substr(v.audit$, 25, 1) || '/' || substr(v.audit$, 26, 1),
            substr(v.audit$, 27, 1) || '/' || substr(v.audit$, 28, 1),
            substr(v.audit$, 29, 1) || '/' || substr(v.audit$, 30, 1),
            substr(v.audit$, 31, 1) || '/' || substr(v.audit$, 32, 1)
    from sys.obj$ o, sys.user$ u, sys.view$ v
    where o.type# = 4
      and o.owner# = u.user#
      and o.obj# = v.obj#
    union all
    select u.name, o.name, 'SEQUENCE',
            substr(s.audit$, 1, 1) || '/' || substr(s.audit$, 2, 1),
            substr(s.audit$, 3, 1) || '/' || substr(s.audit$, 4, 1),
            substr(s.audit$, 5, 1) || '/' || substr(s.audit$, 6, 1),
            substr(s.audit$, 7, 1) || '/' || substr(s.audit$, 8, 1),
            substr(s.audit$, 9, 1) || '/' || substr(s.audit$, 10, 1),
            substr(s.audit$, 11, 1) || '/' || substr(s.audit$, 12, 1),
            substr(s.audit$, 13, 1) || '/' || substr(s.audit$, 14, 1),
```

```
                    substr(s.audit$, 15, 1) || '/' || substr(s.audit$, 16, 1),
                    substr(s.audit$, 17, 1) || '/' || substr(s.audit$, 18, 1),
                    substr(s.audit$, 19, 1) || '/' || substr(s.audit$, 20, 1),
                    substr(s.audit$, 21, 1) || '/' || substr(s.audit$, 22, 1),
                    substr(s.audit$, 23, 1) || '/' || substr(s.audit$, 24, 1),
                    substr(s.audit$, 25, 1) || '/' || substr(s.audit$, 26, 1),
                    substr(s.audit$, 27, 1) || '/' || substr(s.audit$, 28, 1),
                    substr(s.audit$, 29, 1) || '/' || substr(s.audit$, 30, 1),
                    substr(s.audit$, 31, 1) || '/' || substr(s.audit$, 32, 1)
              from sys.obj$ o, sys.user$ u, sys.seq$ s
              where o.type# = 6
                and o.owner# = u.user#
                and o.obj# = s.obj#
              union all
              select u.name, o.name, 'PROCEDURE',
                    substr(p.audit$, 1, 1) || '/' || substr(p.audit$, 2, 1),
                    substr(p.audit$, 3, 1) || '/' || substr(p.audit$, 4, 1),
                    substr(p.audit$, 5, 1) || '/' || substr(p.audit$, 6, 1),
                    substr(p.audit$, 7, 1) || '/' || substr(p.audit$, 8, 1),
                    substr(p.audit$, 9, 1) || '/' || substr(p.audit$,
```

The **DBA_PART_COL_STATISTICS** view contains the statistics for all partitioned object partition columns in the database. This data is used in partition histograms.

Listing A.293   Description of the DBA_ view DBA_PART_COL_STATISTICS.

Name	Null?	Type
OWNER	NOT NULL	VARCHAR2(30)
TABLE_NAME	NOT NULL	VARCHAR2(30)
PARTITION_NAME		VARCHAR2(30)
COLUMN_NAME		VARCHAR2(30)
NUM_DISTINCT		NUMBER
LOW_VALUE		RAW(32)
HIGH_VALUE		RAW(32)
DENSITY		NUMBER
NUM_NULLS		NUMBER
NUM_BUCKETS		NUMBER
SAMPLE_SIZE		NUMBER
LAST_ANALYZED		DATE

```
DBA_PART_COL_STATISTICS select u.name, o.name, o.subname, tp.cname,
                               h.distcnt, h.lowval, h.hival,
                               h.density, h.null_cnt,
                               decode(h.row_cnt, 0, 1, 1, 1, h.row_cnt-1),
                               h.sample_size, h.timestamp#
```

```
             from sys.obj$ o, sys.hist_head$ h, tp$ tp, user$ u
            where o.obj# = tp.obj# and o.owner# = u.user#
             and tp.obj# = h.obj#(+) and tp.intcol# = h.intcol#(+)
             and o.type# = 19 /* TABLE PARTITION */
```

The **DBA_PART_HISTOGRAMS** view contains the histogram data (endpoints per histogram) for histograms on all table partitions.

Listing A.294 Description of the DBA_ view DBA_PART_HISTOGRAMS.

```
Name                                 Null?     Type
-------------------------------- --------  ----
OWNER                                      VARCHAR2(30)
TABLE_NAME                                 VARCHAR2(30)
PARTITION_NAME                             VARCHAR2(30)
COLUMN_NAME                                VARCHAR2(30)
BUCKET_NUMBER                              NUMBER
ENDPOINT_VALUE                             NUMBER

DBA_PART_HISTOGRAMS select u.name,
                      o.name, o.subname,
                      c.name,
                      h.bucket,
                      h.endpoint
                  from sys.col$ c, sys.obj$ o, sys.histgrm$ h, sys.user$ u,
                      tabpart$ tp
                  where o.obj# = tp.obj# and tp.bo# = c.obj#
                    and o.owner# = u.user#
                    and tp.obj# = h.obj# and c.intcol# = h.intcol#
                    and o.type# = 19 /* TABLE PARTITION */
                  union
                  select u.name,
                      o.name, o.subname,
                      c.name,
                      0,
                      h.minimum
                  from sys.col$ c, sys.obj$ o, sys.hist_head$ h,
                      sys.user$ u, tabpart$ tp
                   where o.obj# = tp.obj# and tp.bo# = c.obj#
                    and o.owner# = u.user#
                    and tp.obj# = h.obj# and c.intcol# = h.intcol#
                    and o.type# = 19 /* TABLE PARTITION */
                    and h.bucket_cnt = 1
                  union
                  select u.name,
                      o.name, o.subname,
                      c.name,
```

```
                 1,
                 h.maximum
       from sys.col$ c, sys.obj$ o, sys.hist_head$ h,
             sys.user$ u, tabpart$ tp
        where o.obj# = tp.obj# and tp.bo# = c.obj#
          and o.owner# = u.user#
          and tp.obj# = h.obj# and c.intcol# = h.intcol#
          and o.type# = 19 /* TABLE PARTITION */
          and h.bucket_cnt = 1
```

The **DBA_PART_INDEXES** lists the object-level partitioning information for all partitioned indexes.

Listing A.295 Description of the DBA_ view DBA_PART_INDEXES.

Name	Null?	Type
OWNER	NOT NULL	VARCHAR2(30)
INDEX_NAME	NOT NULL	VARCHAR2(30)
PARTITIONING_TYPE		VARCHAR2(7)
PARTITION_COUNT	NOT NULL	NUMBER
PARTITIONING_KEY_COUNT	NOT NULL	NUMBER
LOCALITY		VARCHAR2(6)
ALIGNMENT		VARCHAR2(12)
DEF_TABLESPACE_NAME		VARCHAR2(30)
DEF_PCT_FREE	NOT NULL	NUMBER
DEF_INI_TRANS	NOT NULL	NUMBER
DEF_MAX_TRANS	NOT NULL	NUMBER
DEF_INITIAL_EXTENT	NOT NULL	NUMBER
DEF_NEXT_EXTENT	NOT NULL	NUMBER
DEF_MIN_EXTENTS	NOT NULL	NUMBER
DEF_MAX_EXTENTS	NOT NULL	NUMBER
DEF_PCT_INCREASE	NOT NULL	NUMBER
DEF_FREELISTS	NOT NULL	NUMBER
DEF_LOGGING		VARCHAR2(7)
DEF_BUFFER_		

```
DBA_PART_INDEXES    select u.name, o.name, decode(po.parttype, 1, 'RANGE',
                          'UNKNOWN'),
                      po.partcnt, po.partkeycols,
                      decode(bitand(po.flags, 1), 1, 'LOCAL',    'GLOBAL'),
                      decode(bitand(po.flags, 2), 2, 'PREFIXED',
                      'NON_PREFIXED'),
                      ts.name, po.defpctfree, po.definitrans,
                      po.defmaxtrans, po.deftiniexts, po.defextsize,
                      po.defminexts,
                      po.defmaxexts, po.defextpct, po.deflists,
```

```
                    decode(po.deflogging, 0, 'NONE', 1, 'YES',
                                          2, 'NO', 'UNKNOWN'),
                    decode(po.spare1, 0, 'DEFAULT', 1, 'KEEP', 2, 'RECYCLE',
                    NULL)
        from    sys.obj$ o, sys.partobj$ po, sys.ts$ ts,
                sys.ind$ i, sys.user$ u
        where   o.obj# = po.obj# and po.defts# = ts.ts# (+) and
                i.obj# = o.obj# and u.user# = o.owner#
```

The **DBA_PART_KEY_COLUMNS** view describes the partitioning key columns for
all partitioned objects.

Listing A.296 Description of the DBA_ view DBA_PART_KEY_COLUMNS.

```
Name                                   Null?    Type
-------------------------------------- -------- ----
OWNER                                           VARCHAR2(30)
NAME                                            VARCHAR2(30)
COLUMN_NAME                                     VARCHAR2(30)
COLUMN_POSITION                                 NUMBER


DBA_PART_KEY_COLUMNS select u.name, o.name, c.name, pc.pos#
                       from partcol$ pc, obj$ o, col$ c, user$ u
                     where pc.obj# = o.obj#
                       and pc.obj# = c.obj# and c.intcol# = pc.intcol#
                       and u.user# = o.owner#
                     union
                     select u.name, o.name, c.name, pc.pos#
                     from partcol$ pc, obj$ o, col$ c, user$ u, ind$ i
                     where pc.obj# = i.obj# and i.obj# = o.obj# and i.bo# = c.obj#
                     and
                         c.intcol# = pc.intcol# and u.user# = o.owner#
```

The **DBA_PART_TABLES** view contains information on all partitioned tables in the
database.

Listing A.297 Description of the DBA_ view DBA_PART_TABLES.

```
Name                                   Null?    Type
-------------------------------------- -------- ----
OWNER                                  NOT NULL VARCHAR2(30)
TABLE_NAME                             NOT NULL VARCHAR2(30)
PARTITIONING_TYPE                               VARCHAR2(7)
PARTITION_COUNT                        NOT NULL NUMBER
PARTITIONING_KEY_COUNT                 NOT NULL NUMBER
DEF_TABLESPACE_NAME                    NOT NULL VARCHAR2(30)
DEF_PCT_FREE                           NOT NULL NUMBER
```

```
DEF_PCT_USED                        NOT NULL NUMBER
DEF_INI_TRANS                       NOT NULL NUMBER
DEF_MAX_TRANS                       NOT NULL NUMBER
DEF_INITIAL_EXTENT                  NOT NULL NUMBER
DEF_NEXT_EXTENT                     NOT NULL NUMBER
DEF_MIN_EXTENTS                     NOT NULL NUMBER
DEF_MAX_EXTENTS                     NOT NULL NUMBER
DEF_PCT_INCREASE                    NOT NULL NUMBER
DEF_FREELISTS                       NOT NULL NUMBER
DEF_FREELIST_GROUPS                 NOT NULL NUMBER
DEF_LOGGING                                  VARCHAR2(7)
DEF_BUFFER_POOL                              VARCHAR2(7)


DBA_PART_TABLES     select u.name, o.name,
                      decode(po.parttype, 1, 'RANGE', 'UNKNOWN'), po.partcnt,
                      po.partkeycols, ts.name, po.defpctfree, po.defpctused,
                      po.definitrans,
                      po.defmaxtrans, po.deftiniexts, po.defextsize, po.defminexts,
                      po.defmaxexts, po.defextpct, po.deflists, po.defgroups,
                      decode(po.deflogging, 0, 'NONE', 1, 'YES', 2, 'NO', 'UNKNOWN'),
                      decode(po.spare1, 0, 'DEFAULT', 1, 'KEEP', 2, 'RECYCLE', NULL)
                    from  sys.obj$ o, sys.partobj$ po, sys.ts$ ts, sys.tab$ t,
                    sys.user$ u
                      where  o.obj# = po.obj# and po.defts# = ts.ts# and t.obj# =
                        o.obj#
                        and
                      o.owner# = u.user#
```

The **DBA_PENDING_TRANSACTIONS** view contains information on pending distributed transactions. This is a shared server view.

Listing A.298   Description of the DBA_ view DBA_PENDING_ TRANSACTIONS.

Name	Null?	Type
FORMATID		NUMBER
GLOBALID		RAW(64)
BRANCHID		RAW(64)

```
DBA_PENDING_TRANSACTIONS (((select formatid, globalid, branchid
                          from   gv$global_transaction
                    where  refcount = preparecount)
                    minus
               (select global_tran_fmt, global_foreign_id, branch_id
                from   sys.pending_trans$ tran, sys.pending_sessions$ sess
```

```
       where  tran.local_tran_id = sess.local_tran_id
         and  tran.state != 'collecting'
         and  BITAND(TO_NUMBER(tran.session_vector),
              POWER(2, (sess.session_id - 1))) = sess.session_id))
      union
      (select global_tran_fmt, global_foreign_id, branch_id
       from   sys.pending_trans$ tran, sys.pending_sessions$ sess
       where  tran.local_tran_id = sess.local_tran_id
         and  tran.state != 'collecting'
         and  BITAND(TO_NUMBER(tran.session_vector),
          POWER(2, (sess.session_id - 1))) = sess.session_id))
```

The **DBA_PRIV_AUDIT_OPTS** view contains information on all audited system privileges across the system and by user.

Listing A.299   Description of the DBA_ view DBA_PRIV_AUDIT_OPTS.

```
Name                                 Null?     Type
-------------------------------      --------  ----
USER_NAME                                      VARCHAR2(30)
PRIVILEGE                            NOT NULL  VARCHAR2(40)
SUCCESS                                        VARCHAR2(10)
FAILURE                                        VARCHAR2(10)


DBA_PRIV_AUDIT_OPTS select decode(aud.user#, 1 /* System wide auditing*/, null,
                                  usr.name)
                                  /* USER_NAME */,
                           prv.name   /* PRIVILEGE */,
                           decode(aud.success, 1, 'BY SESSION',
                                             2, 'BY ACCESS', 'NOT SET')
                                  /* SUCCESS */,
                           decode(aud.failure, 1, 'BY SESSION',
                                             2, 'BY ACCESS', 'NOT SET')
                                  /* FAILURE */
                    from sys.user$ usr, system_privilege_map prv, sys.audit$ aud
                    where aud.option# = -prv.privilege
                      and aud.user# = usr.user#
```

The **DBA_PROFILES** view shows information on all defined **PROFILE**s in the database.

Listing A.300   Description of the DBA_ view DBA_PROFILES.

```
Name                                 Null?     Type
-------------------------------      --------  ----
PROFILE                              NOT NULL  VARCHAR2(30)
RESOURCE_NAME                        NOT NULL  VARCHAR2(32)
RESOURCE_TYPE                                  VARCHAR2(8)
LIMIT                                          VARCHAR2(40)
```

```
DBA_PROFILES          select n.name, m.name,
                             decode (u.type#, 0, 'KERNEL', 1, 'PASSWORD',
                             'INVALID'),
               decode (u.limit#, 0, 'DEFAULT', 2147483647, 'UNLIMITED',
                             decode(u.resource#, 4,
                             decode (u.type#, 1, o.name, u.limit#),
                             decode(u.type#, 0, u.limit#,
                             decode(u.resource#, 1, trunc(u.limit#/86400,
                             4), 2,
                          trunc(u.limit#/86400, 4), 5, trunc(u.limit#/
                             86400, 4),
                               6, trunc(u.limit#/86400, 4), u.limit#))))
               from sys.profile$ u, sys.profname$ n, sys.resource_map m,
                             sys.obj$ o
               where u.resource# = m.resource#
               and u.type#=m.type#
               and o.obj# (+) = u.limit#
               and n.profile# = u.profile#
```

The **DBA_QUEUES** view shows information for every queue in the database. This is an advanced queuing option view.

Listing A.301 Description of the DBA_ view DBA_QUEUES.

Name	Null?	Type
OWNER	NOT NULL	VARCHAR2(30)
NAME	NOT NULL	VARCHAR2(30)
QUEUE_TABLE	NOT NULL	VARCHAR2(30)
QID	NOT NULL	NUMBER
QUEUE_TYPE		VARCHAR2(15)
MAX_RETRIES		NUMBER
RETRY_DELAY		NUMBER
ENQUEUE_ENABLED		VARCHAR2(7)
DEQUEUE_ENABLED		VARCHAR2(7)
RETENTION		VARCHAR2(40)
USER_COMMENT		VARCHAR2(50)

```
DBA_QUEUES            select u.name OWNER, q.name NAME, t.name QUEUE_TABLE, q.eventid
                      QID,
                           decode(q.usage, 1, 'EXCEPTION_QUEUE', 'NORMAL_QUEUE')
                           QUEUE_TYPE,
                               q.max_retries MAX_RETRIES, q.retry_delay RETRY_DELAY,
                      decode(bitand(q.enable_flag, 1),1,' YES', 'NO')ENQUEUE_ENABLED,
                      decode(bitand(q.enable_flag,2), 2 , ' YES ', ' NO
                           ')DEQUEUE_ENABLED,
                           decode(q.ret_time, -1, ' FOREVER', q.ret_time)
                           RETENTION,
```

```
                    substr(q.queue_comment, 1, 50) USER_COMMENT
        from system.aq$_queues q, system.aq$_queue_tables t,
        sys.user$u
        where u.name  = t.schema
        and   q.table_objno = t.objno
```

The **DBA_QUEUE_TABLES** view shows information on all advanced queuing queue
tables.

Listing A.302   Description of the DBA_ view DBA_QUEUE_TABLES.

```
Name                             Null?    Type
-------------------------------- -------- ----
OWNER                                     VARCHAR2(30)
QUEUE_TABLE                               VARCHAR2(30)
TYPE                                      VARCHAR2(7)
OBJECT_TYPE                               VARCHAR2(61)
SORT_ORDER                                VARCHAR2(22)
RECIPIENTS                                VARCHAR2(8)
MESSAGE_GROUPING                          VARCHAR2(13)
USER_COMMENT                              VARCHAR2(50)


DBA_QUEUE_TABLES    select t.schema OWNER, t.name QUEUE_TABLE,
                        decode(t.udata_type, 1 , 'OBJECT', 2, 'VARIANT', 3, 'RAW')
                        TYPE,
                        u.name || '.' || o.name OBJECT_TYPE,
                        decode(t.sort_cols, 0, 'NONE', 1, 'PRIORITY', 2,
                        'ENQUEUE_TIME',
              3, 'PRIORITY, ENQUEUE_TIME',
              7, 'ENQUEUE_TIME, PRIORITY') SORT_ORDER,
                   decode(bitand(t.flags, 1), 1, 'MULTIPLE', 0, 'SINGLE')
                           RECIPIENTS,
                   decode(bitand(t.flags,2),2,'TRANSACTIONAL',
                                          0, 'NONE')MESSAGE_GROUPING,
                   substr(t.table_comment, 1, 50) USER_COMMENT
                from system.aq$_queue_tables t,sys.col$ c, sys.coltype$ ct,
                     sys.obj$ o,
                sys.user$ u
                where c.col# = ct.col#
                and c.obj# = ct.obj#
                and c.name = 'USER_DATA'
                and t.objno = c.obj#
                and o.oid$ = ct.toid
                and o.owner# = u.user#
                union
                select t.schema OWNER, t.name QUEUE_TABLE,
                    decode(t.udata_type, 1 , 'OBJECT', 2, 'VARIANT', 3, 'RAW')
                    TYPE,
```

```
                   null OBJECT_TYPE,
                   decode(t.sort_cols, 0, 'NONE', 1, 'PRIORITY', 2,
                   'ENQUEUE_TIME',
          3, 'PRIORITY, ENQUEUE_TIME',
          7, 'ENQUEUE_TIME, PRIORITY') SORT_ORDER,
               decode(bitand(t.flags, 1), 1, 'MULTIPLE', 0, 'SINGLE')
                  RECIPIENTS,
        decode(bitand(t.flags,2),2,'TRANSACTIONAL',0,'NONE')MESSAGE_GROUPING,
              substr(t.table_comment, 1, 50) USER_COMMENT
           from system.aq$_queue_tables t
           where (t.udata_type = 2
           or t.udata_type = 3)
```

The **DBA_RCHILD** view contains information on all children in any refresh group.

Listing A.303   Description of the DBA_ view DBA_RCHILD.

```
Name                             Null?     Type
------------------------------   --------  ----
REFGROUP                                   NUMBER
OWNER                            NOT NULL  VARCHAR2(30)
NAME                                       VARCHAR2(30)
TYPE#                                      VARCHAR2(30)


DBA_RCHILD              select REFGROUP, OWNER, NAME, TYPE# from rgchild$
```

The **DBA_REFRESH** view contains information on all refresh groups defined in the database.

Listing A.304   Description of the DBA_ view DBA_REFRESH.

```
Name                             Null?     Type
------------------------------   --------  ----
ROWNER                           NOT NULL  VARCHAR2(30)
RNAME                            NOT NULL  VARCHAR2(30)
REFGROUP                                   NUMBER
IMPLICIT_DESTROY                           VARCHAR2(1)
PUSH_DEFERRED_RPC                          VARCHAR2(1)
REFRESH_AFTER_ERRORS                       VARCHAR2(1)
ROLLBACK_SEG                               VARCHAR2(30)
JOB                                        NUMBER
NEXT_DATE                                  DATE
INTERVAL                                   VARCHAR2(200)
BROKEN                                     VARCHAR2(1)
PURGE_OPTION                               NUMBER(38)
PARALLELISM                                NUMBER(38)
HEAP_SIZE                                  NUMBER(38)
```

```
DBA_REFRESH          select r.owner ROWNER, r.name RNAME, r.REFGROUP,
                            decode(bitand(r.flag,1),1,'Y',0,'N','?')
                            IMPLICIT_DESTROY,
                            decode(bitand(r.flag,2),2,'Y',0,'N','?')
                            PUSH_DEFERRED_RPC,
                            decode(bitand(r.flag,4),4,'Y',0,'N','?')
REFRESH_AFTER_ERRORS,
                            r.rollback_seg ROLLBACK_SEG,
                            j.JOB, j.NEXT_DATE, j.INTERVAL# interval,
                            decode(bitand(j.flag,1),1,'Y',0,'N','?') BROKEN,
                            r.purge_opt#    PURGE_OPTION,
                            r.parallelism# PARALLELISM,
                            r.heap_size#   HEAP_SIZE
                     from rgroup$ r, job$ j
                     where r.job = j.job(+)
```

The **DBA_REFRESH_CHILDREN** view lists all of the objects in all refresh groups.

Listing A.305 Description of the DBA_ view DBA_REFRESH_CHILDREN.

Name	Null?	Type
OWNER	NOT NULL	VARCHAR2(30)
NAME		VARCHAR2(30)
TYPE		VARCHAR2(30)
ROWNER	NOT NULL	VARCHAR2(30)
RNAME	NOT NULL	VARCHAR2(30)
REFGROUP		NUMBER
IMPLICIT_DESTROY		VARCHAR2(1)
PUSH_DEFERRED_RPC		VARCHAR2(1)
REFRESH_AFTER_ERRORS		VARCHAR2(1)
ROLLBACK_SEG		VARCHAR2(30)
JOB		NUMBER
NEXT_DATE		DATE
INTERVAL		VARCHAR2(200)
BROKEN		VARCHAR2(1)
PURGE_OPTION		NUMBER(38)
PARALLELISM		NUMBER(38)
HEAP_SIZE		NUMBER(38)

```
DBA_REFRESH_CHILDREN select rc.owner OWNER, rc.name NAME, rc.TYPE# TYPE,
                            r.owner ROWNER, r.name RNAME, r.REFGROUP,
                            decode(bitand(r.flag,1),1,'Y',0,'N','?')
                            IMPLICIT_DESTROY,
                            decode(bitand(r.flag,2),2,'Y',0,'N','?')
                            PUSH_DEFERRED_RPC,
                            decode(bitand(r.flag,4),4,'Y',0,'N','?')
                            REFRESH_AFTER_ERRORS,
```

```
                    r.rollback_seg ROLLBACK_SEG,
                    j.job, j.NEXT_DATE, j.INTERVAL# interval,
                    decode(bitand(j.flag,1),1,'Y',0,'N','?') BROKEN,
                    r.purge_opt#   PURGE_OPTION,
                    r.parallelism# PARALLELISM,
                    r.heap_size#   HEAP_SIZE
             from rgroup$ r, rgchild$ rc, job$ j
             where r.refgroup = rc.refgroup
                and r.job = j.job (+)
```

The **DBA_REFS** view contains information on all defined **REF** values in the database, including all **REF** columns and **REF** attributes.

Listing A.306 Description of the DBA_ view DBA_REFS.

Name	Null?	Type
OWNER	NOT NULL	VARCHAR2(30)
TABLE_NAME	NOT NULL	VARCHAR2(30)
COLUMN_NAME		VARCHAR2(4000)
WITH_ROWID		VARCHAR2(3)
IS_SCOPED		VARCHAR2(3)
SCOPE_TABLE_OWNER		VARCHAR2(30)
SCOPE_TABLE_NAME		VARCHAR2(30)

```
DBA_REFS          select u.name, o.name,
                         decode(bitand(c.property, 1), 1, ac.name, c.name),
                         decode(bitand(rc.reftyp, 2), 2, 'YES', 'NO'),
                         decode(bitand(rc.reftyp, 1), 1, 'YES', 'NO'),
                         su.name, so.name
                  from sys.obj$ o, sys.col$ c, sys.user$ u, sys.refcon$ rc,
                    sys.obj$ so,
                  sys.user$ su, sys.attrcol$ ac
                  where o.owner# = u.user#
                    and o.obj# = c.obj#
                    and c.obj# = rc.obj#
                    and c.col# = rc.col#
                    and c.intcol# = rc.intcol#
                    and rc.stabid = so.oid$(+)
                    and so.owner# = su.user#(+)
                    and c.obj# = ac.obj#(+)
                    and c.intcol# = ac.intcol#(+)
```

The **DBA_REGISTERED_SNAPSHOTS** view contains information on all remote snapshots for objects in this database.

Listing A.307 Description of the DBA_ view DBA_REGISTERED_SNAPSHOTS.

```
Name                            Null?    Type
------------------------------- -------- ----
OWNER                           NOT NULL VARCHAR2(30)
NAME                            NOT NULL VARCHAR2(30)
SNAPSHOT_SITE                   NOT NULL VARCHAR2(128)
CAN_USE_LOG                              VARCHAR2(3)
UPDATABLE                                VARCHAR2(3)
REFRESH_METHOD                           VARCHAR2(11)
SNAPSHOT_ID                              NUMBER(38)
VERSION                                  VARCHAR2(17)
QUERY_TXT                                LONG


DBA_REGISTERED_SNAPHOTS select sowner, snapname, snapsite,
                       decode(bitand(flag,1), 0 , 'NO', 'YES'),
                       decode(bitand(flag,2), 0 , 'NO', 'YES'),
                       decode(bitand(flag,32), 0 , 'ROWID', 'PRIMARY KEY'),
                       snapshot_id,
                       decode(rep_type, 1, 'ORACLE 7 SNAPSHOT',
                                        2, 'ORACLE 8 SNAPSHOT',
                                        3, 'REPAPI SNAPSHOT',
                                           'UNKNOWN'),
                        query_txt
                       from sys.reg_snap$
```

The **DBA_RGROUP** view contains information about all refresh groups in the database.

Listing A.308 Description of the DBA_ view DBA_RGROUP.

```
Name                            Null?    Type
------------------------------- -------- ----
REFGROUP                                 NUMBER
OWNER                           NOT NULL VARCHAR2(30)
NAME                            NOT NULL VARCHAR2(30)
IMPLICIT_DESTROY                         VARCHAR2(1)
PUSH_DEFERRED_RPC                        VARCHAR2(1)
REFRESH_AFTER_ERRORS                     VARCHAR2(1)
ROLLBACK_SEG                             VARCHAR2(30)
JOB                             NOT NULL NUMBER
PURGE_OPTION                             NUMBER(38)
PARALLELISM                              NUMBER(38)
HEAP_SIZE                                NUMBER(38)


DBA_RGROUP             select REFGROUP, OWNER, NAME,
                          decode(bitand(flag,1),1,'Y',0,'N','?')
                          IMPLICIT_DESTROY,
```

```
                              decode(bitand(flag,2),2,'Y',0,'N','?')
                              PUSH_DEFERRED_RPC,
                              decode(bitand(flag,4),4,'Y',0,'N','?')
                              REFRESH_AFTER_ERRORS,
                               ROLLBACK_SEG,
                               JOB,
                               purge_opt#   PURGE_OPTION,
                               parallelism# PARALLELISM,
                               heap_size#   HEAP_SIZE
                     from rgroup$
```

The **DBA_ROLES** view contains information about all defined roles in the database. To get a complete picture of a role's assigned privileges, you must join to the **DBA_ROLE_PRIVS**, **DBA_TAB_PRIVS**, **DBA_COL_PRIVS**, and **DBA_SYS_PRIVS** views.

Listing A.309   Description of the DBA_ view DBA_ROLES.

```
Name                                   Null?    Type
------------------------------------   -------- ----
ROLE                                   NOT NULL VARCHAR2(30)
PASSWORD_REQUIRED                               VARCHAR2(8)


DBA_ROLES          select name, decode(password, null, 'NO', 'EXTERNAL', 'EXTERNAL',
                       'YES')
                   from  user$
                   where type# = 0 and name not in ('PUBLIC', '_NEXT_USER')
```

The **DBA_ROLE_PRIVS** view provides information on roles assigned to users and roles in the database.

Listing A.310   Description of the DBA_ view DBA_ROLE_PRIVS.

```
Name                                   Null?    Type
------------------------------------   -------- ----
GRANTEE                                         VARCHAR2(30)
GRANTED_ROLE                           NOT NULL VARCHAR2(30)
ADMIN_OPTION                                    VARCHAR2(3)
DEFAULT_ROLE                                    VARCHAR2(3)


DBA_ROLE_PRIVS     select decode(sa.grantee#, 1, 'PUBLIC', u1.name), u2.name,
                       decode(min(option$), 1, 'YES', 'NO'),
                       decode(min(u1.defrole), 0, 'NO', 1, 'YES',
                           2, decode(min(ud.role#),null,'NO','YES'),
                           3, decode(min(ud.role#),null,'YES','NO'), 'NO')
                   from sysauth$ sa,defrole$ ud, user$ u1, user$ u2
                   where sa.grantee#=ud.user#(+)
                     and sa.privilege#=ud.role#(+) and u1.user#=sa.grantee#
```

```
                        and u2.user#=sa.privilege#
                    group by decode(sa.grantee#,1,'PUBLIC',u1.name),u2.name
```

The **DBA_ROLLBACK_SEGS** view contains information about rollback segments for this database.

Listing A.311   Description of the DBA_ view DBA_ROLLBACK_SEGS.

```
Name                              Null?      Type
--------------------------------  --------   ----
SEGMENT_NAME                      NOT NULL   VARCHAR2(30)
OWNER                                        VARCHAR2(6)
TABLESPACE_NAME                   NOT NULL   VARCHAR2(30)
SEGMENT_ID                        NOT NULL   NUMBER
FILE_ID                           NOT NULL   NUMBER
BLOCK_ID                          NOT NULL   NUMBER
INITIAL_EXTENT                               NUMBER
NEXT_EXTENT                                  NUMBER
MIN_EXTENTS                       NOT NULL   NUMBER
MAX_EXTENTS                       NOT NULL   NUMBER
PCT_INCREASE                      NOT NULL   NUMBER
STATUS                                       VARCHAR2(16)
INSTANCE_NUM                                 VARCHAR2(40)
RELATIVE_FNO                      NOT NULL   NUMBER


DBA_ROLLBACK_SEGS      select un.name, decode(un.user#,1,'PUBLIC','SYS'),
                              ts.name, un.us#, f.file#, un.block#,
                              s.iniexts * ts.blocksize, s.extsize * ts.blocksize,
                              s.minexts, s.maxexts, s.extpct,
                              decode(un.status$, 2, 'OFFLINE', 3, 'ONLINE',
                                                 4, 'UNDEFINED', 5, 'NEEDS RECOVERY',
                                                 6, 'PARTLY AVAILABLE', 'UNDEFINED'),
                              decode(un.inst#, 0, NULL, un.inst#), un.file#
                        from sys.undo$ un, sys.seg$ s, sys.ts$ ts, sys.file$ f
                       where un.status$ != 1
                         and un.ts# = s.ts#
                         and un.file# = s.file#
                         and un.block# = s.block#
                         and s.type# = 1
                         and s.ts# = ts.ts#
                         and un.ts# = f.ts#
                         and un.file# = f.relfile#
```

The **DBA_SEGMENTS** view contains information on all storage allocations for segments in the database. Segments correspond to any database object that has assigned or default storage clauses.

Listing A.312 Description of the DBA_ view DBA_SEGMENTS.

Name	Null?	Type
OWNER		VARCHAR2(30)
SEGMENT_NAME		VARCHAR2(81)
PARTITION_NAME		VARCHAR2(30)
SEGMENT_TYPE		VARCHAR2(17)
TABLESPACE_NAME		VARCHAR2(30)
HEADER_FILE		NUMBER
HEADER_BLOCK		NUMBER
BYTES		NUMBER
BLOCKS		NUMBER
EXTENTS		NUMBER
INITIAL_EXTENT		NUMBER
NEXT_EXTENT		NUMBER
MIN_EXTENTS		NUMBER
MAX_EXTENTS		NUMBER
PCT_INCREASE		NUMBER
FREELISTS		NUMBER
FREELIST_GROUPS		NUMBER
RELATIVE_FNO		NUMBER
BUFFER_POOL		VARCHAR2(7)

```
DBA_SEGMENTS        select owner, segment_name, partition_name,
                       segment_type, tablespace_name,
                       header_file, header_block, bytes, blocks, extents,
                       initial_extent,
                       next_extent, min_extents, max_extents, pct_increase,
                       freelists,
                       freelist_groups, relative_fno, buffer_pool
                    from sys_dba_segs
```

The **DBA_SEQUENCES** view contains information on all sequences in the database.

Listing A.313 Description of the DBA_ view DBA_SEQUENCES.

Name	Null?	Type
SEQUENCE_OWNER	NOT NULL	VARCHAR2(30)
SEQUENCE_NAME	NOT NULL	VARCHAR2(30)
MIN_VALUE		NUMBER
MAX_VALUE		NUMBER
INCREMENT_BY	NOT NULL	NUMBER
CYCLE_FLAG		VARCHAR2(1)
ORDER_FLAG		VARCHAR2(1)

```
CACHE_SIZE                       NOT NULL NUMBER
LAST_NUMBER                      NOT NULL NUMBER

DBA_SEQUENCES        select u.name, o.name,
                            s.minvalue, s.maxvalue, s.increment$,
                            decode (s.cycle#, 0, 'N', 1, 'Y'),
                            decode (s.order$, 0, 'N', 1, 'Y'),
                            s.cache, s.highwater
                     from sys.seq$ s, sys.obj$ o, sys.user$ u
                     where u.user# = o.owner#
                       and o.obj# = s.obj#
```

The **DBA_SNAPSHOTS** view contains information on all local snapshots for this database.

Listing A.314   Description of the DBA_ view DBA_SNAPSHOTS.

Name	Null?	Type
OWNER	NOT NULL	VARCHAR2(30)
NAME	NOT NULL	VARCHAR2(30)
TABLE_NAME	NOT NULL	VARCHAR2(30)
MASTER_VIEW		VARCHAR2(30)
MASTER_OWNER		VARCHAR2(30)
MASTER		VARCHAR2(30)
MASTER_LINK		VARCHAR2(128)
CAN_USE_LOG		VARCHAR2(3)
UPDATABLE		VARCHAR2(3)
REFRESH_METHOD		VARCHAR2(11)
LAST_REFRESH		DATE
ERROR		NUMBER
FR_OPERATIONS		VARCHAR2(10)
CR_OPERATIONS		VARCHAR2(10)
TYPE		VARCHAR2(8)
NEXT		VARCHAR2(200)
START_WITH		DATE
REFRESH_GROUP		NUMBER
UPDATE_TRIG		VARCHAR2(30)
UPDATE_LOG		VARCHAR2(30)
QUERY		LONG
MASTER_ROLLBACK_SEG		VARCHAR2(30)

```
DBA_SNAPSHOTS        select s.sowner, s.vname, tname, mview, t.mowner, t.master,
                     mlink,
                            decode(bitand(flag,1),  0, 'NO', 'YES'),
                            decode(bitand(flag,2),  0, 'NO', 'YES'),
                            decode(bitand(flag,16), 16, 'ROWID',
                            (decode(bitand(flag,32), 32, 'PRIMARY KEY',
```

```
               (decode(bitand(flag,256), 256, 'COMPLEX',
               'UNKNOWN')))))),
          s.snaptime, error#,
          decode(bitand(status,1), 0, 'REGENERATE', 'VALID'),
          decode(bitand(status,2), 0, 'REGENERATE', 'VALID'),
          decode(auto_fast,
                 'C', 'COMPLETE',
                 'F', 'FAST',
                 '?', 'FORCE',
                 null, 'FORCE', 'ERROR'),
          s.auto_fun, s.auto_date, r.refgroup, s.ustrg, s.uslog,
          s.query_txt, s.mas_roll_seg
     from sys.snap$ s, sys.rgchild$ r, sys.snap_reftime$ t
     where t.sowner = s.sowner
     and t.vname = s.vname
     and t.tablenum = 0
     and t.sowner  = r.owner (+)
     and t.vname = r.name (+)
     and r.type# (+) = 'SNAPSHOT'
```

The **DBA_SNAPSHOT_LOGS** view contains information on all snapshot logs for this database.

Listing A.315   Description of the DBA_ view DBA_SNAPSHOT_LOGS.

```
Name                              Null?    Type
-------------------------------- -------- ----
LOG_OWNER                         NOT NULL VARCHAR2(30)
MASTER                            NOT NULL VARCHAR2(30)
LOG_TABLE                         NOT NULL VARCHAR2(30)
LOG_TRIGGER                                VARCHAR2(30)
ROWIDS                                     VARCHAR2(3)
PRIMARY_KEY                                VARCHAR2(3)
FILTER_COLUMNS                             VARCHAR2(3)
CURRENT_SNAPSHOTS                          DATE
SNAPSHOT_ID                                NUMBER(38)

DBA_SNAPSHOT_LOGS    select m.mowner, m.master, m.log, m.trig,
                            decode(bitand(m.flag,1), 0, 'NO', 'YES'),
                            decode(bitand(m.flag,2), 0, 'NO', 'YES'),
                            decode(bitand(m.flag,4), 0, 'NO', 'YES'),
                            s.snaptime, s.snapid
                     from sys.mlog$ m, sys.slog$ s
                     where s.mowner (+) = m.mowner
                       and s.master (+) = m.master
```

The **DBA_SNAPSHOT_LOG_FILTER_COLS** view contains information on all defined snapshot log filter columns. Filter columns are used to restrict the scope of a snapshot.

Listing A.316 Description of the DBA_ view DBA_SNAPSHOT_ LOG_FILTER_COLS.

```
Name                              Null?    Type
--------------------------------  -------- ----
OWNER                             NOT NULL VARCHAR2(30)
NAME                              NOT NULL VARCHAR2(30)
COLUMN_NAME                       NOT NULL VARCHAR2(30)

DBA_SNAPSHOT_LOG_FILTER_COLS select mowner, master, colname from sys.mlog_refcol$
```

The **DBA_SNAPSHOT_REFRESH_TIMES** view provides information on all local snapshot refresh times.

Listing A.317 Description of the DBA_ view DBA_SNAPSHOT_ REFRESH_TIMES.

```
Name                              Null?    Type
--------------------------------  -------- ----
OWNER                             NOT NULL VARCHAR2(30)
NAME                              NOT NULL VARCHAR2(30)
MASTER_OWNER                               VARCHAR2(30)
MASTER                                     VARCHAR2(30)
LAST_REFRESH                               DATE

DBA_SNAPSHOT_REFRESH_TIMES select sowner, vname, mowner, master, snaptime
                           from sys.snap_reftime$
```

The **DBA_SOURCE** view contains the source code for all stored objects (procedures, packages, package bodies, functions, types, type bodies).

Listing A.318 Description of the DBA_ view DBA_SOURCE.

```
Name                              Null?    Type
--------------------------------  -------- ----
OWNER                             NOT NULL VARCHAR2(30)
NAME                             NOT NULL VARCHAR2(30)
TYPE                                      VARCHAR2(12)
LINE                             NOT NULL NUMBER
TEXT                                      VARCHAR2(4000)

DBA_SOURCE         select u.name, o.name,
                   decode(o.type#, 7, 'PROCEDURE', 8, 'FUNCTION', 9, 'PACKAGE',
                   11, 'PACKAGE BODY', 13, 'TYPE', 14, 'TYPE BODY', 'UNDEFINED'),
                   s.line, s.source
```

```
from sys.obj$ o, sys.source$ s, sys.user$ u
where o.obj# = s.obj#
  and o.owner# = u.user#
  and o.type# in (7, 8, 9, 11, 13, 14)
```

The **DBA_STMT_AUDIT_OPTS** view contains information on all statement audit options for the database, such as **WHENEVER SUCCESSFUL** or **WHENEVER NOT SUCCESSFUL** auditing actions.

Listing A.319   Description of the DBA_ view DBA_STMT_AUDIT_OPTS.

```
Name                            Null?    Type
------------------------------- -------- ----
USER_NAME                                VARCHAR2(30)
AUDIT_OPTION                    NOT NULL VARCHAR2(40)
SUCCESS                                  VARCHAR2(10)
FAILURE                                  VARCHAR2(10)


DBA_STMT_AUDIT_OPTS select decode(aud.user#,
                   1 /*System wide auditing*/,null,usr.name) /* USER_NAME */,
                   aom.name                          /* AUDIT_OPTION */,
                   decode(aud.success, 1, 'BY SESSION',
                   2, 'BY ACCESS', 'NOT SET')     /* SUCCESS */,
                   decode(aud.failure, 1, 'BY SESSION',
                   2, 'BY ACCESS', 'NOT SET')     /* FAILURE */
                 from sys.user$ usr, STMT_AUDIT_OPTION_MAP aom, sys.audit$ aud
                 where aud.option# = aom.option#
                   and aud.user# = usr.user#
```

The **DBA_SYNONYMS** view contains information about all **SYNONYM**s defined in the database.

Listing A.320   Description of the DBA_ view DBA_SYNONYMS.

```
Name                            Null?    Type
------------------------------- -------- ----
OWNER                           NOT NULL VARCHAR2(30)
SYNONYM_NAME                    NOT NULL VARCHAR2(30)
TABLE_OWNER                              VARCHAR2(30)
TABLE_NAME                      NOT NULL VARCHAR2(30)
DB_LINK                                  VARCHAR2(128)


DBA_SYNONYMS          select u.name, o.name, s.owner, s.name, s.node
                    from sys.user$ u, sys.syn$ s, sys.obj$ o
                    where o.obj# = s.obj#
                      and o.type# = 5
                      and o.owner# = u.user#
```

The **DBA_SYS_PRIVS** view lists all system privileges granted to users and roles in the database.

Listing A.321   Description of the DBA_ view DBA_SYS_PRIVS.

```
Name                              Null?     Type
-------------------------------   --------  ----
GRANTEE                           NOT NULL  VARCHAR2(30)
PRIVILEGE                         NOT NULL  VARCHAR2(40)
ADMIN_OPTION                                VARCHAR2(3)

DBA_SYS_PRIVS      select u.name,spm.name,decode(min(option$),1,'YES','NO')
                   from  sys.system_privilege_map spm, sys.sysauth$ sa, user$ u
                   where sa.grantee#=u.user# and sa.privilege#=spm.privilege
                   group by u.name,spm.name
```

The **DBA_TABLES** view contains information on all relational tables in the database.

Listing A.322   Description of the DBA_ view DBA_TABLES.

```
Name                              Null?     Type
-------------------------------   --------  ----
OWNER                             NOT NULL  VARCHAR2(30)
TABLE_NAME                        NOT NULL  VARCHAR2(30)
TABLESPACE_NAME                             VARCHAR2(30)
CLUSTER_NAME                                VARCHAR2(30)
IOT_NAME                                    VARCHAR2(30)
PCT_FREE                                    NUMBER
PCT_USED                                    NUMBER
INI_TRANS                                   NUMBER
MAX_TRANS                                   NUMBER
INITIAL_EXTENT                             NUMBER
NEXT_EXTENT                                 NUMBER
MIN_EXTENTS                                 NUMBER
MAX_EXTENTS                                 NUMBER
PCT_INCREASE                               NUMBER
FREELISTS                                   NUMBER
FREELIST_GROUPS                            NUMBER
LOGGING                                     VARCHAR2(3)
BACKED_UP                                   VARCHAR2(1)
NUM_ROWS                                    NUMBER
BLOCKS                                      NUMBER
EMPTY_BLOCKS                               NUMBER
AVG_SPACE                                   NUMBER
CHAIN_CNT                                   NUMBER
AVG_ROW_LEN                                 NUMBER
AVG_SPACE_FREELIST_BLOCKS                   NUMBER
```

```
NUM_FREELIST_BLOCKS                  NUMBER
DEGREE                               VARCHAR2(10)
INSTANCES                            VARCHAR2(10)
CACHE                                VARCHAR2(5)
TABLE_LOCK                           VARCHAR2(8)
SAMPLE_SIZE                          NUMBER
LAST_ANALYZED                        DATE
PARTITIONED                          VARCHAR2(3)
IOT_TYPE                             VARCHAR2(12)
TEMPORARY                            VARCHAR2(1)
NESTED                               VARCHAR2(3)
BUFFER_POOL                          VARCHAR2(7)
```

DBA_TABLES

```
select u.name, o.name, decode(bitand(t.property, 32), 32, null,
        decode(bitand(t.property, 64), 64, null, ts.name)),
        decode(bitand(t.property, 1024), 0, null, co.name),
        decode(bitand(t.property, 512), 0, null, co.name),
        decode(bitand(t.property, 32), 0, mod(t.pctfree$, 100),
        null),
        decode(bitand(t.property, 32), 0, t.pctused$, null),
        decode(bitand(t.property, 32), 0, t.initrans, null),
        decode(bitand(t.property, 32), 0, t.maxtrans, null),
        s.iniexts * ts.blocksize, s.extsize * ts.blocksize,
        s.minexts, s.maxexts, s.extpct,
    decode(s.lists, 0, 1, s.lists), decode(s.groups, 0, 1,
        s.groups),
        decode(bitand(t.property, 32), 32, null,
  decode(bitand(t.flags, 32), 0, 'YES', 'NO')),
        decode(bitand(t.flags,1), 0, 'Y', 1, 'N', '?'),
        t.rowcnt, t.blkcnt, t.empcnt, t.avgspc, t.chncnt,
        t.avgrln,
        t.avgspc_flb, t.flbcnt,
        lpad(decode(t.degree, 32767, 'DEFAULT',
                nvl(t.degree,1)),10),
    lpad(decode(t.instances, 32767, 'DEFAULT',
                nvl(t.instances,1)),10),
        lpad(decode(bitand(t.flags, 8), 8, 'Y', 'N'),5),
        decode(bitand(t.flags, 6), 0, 'ENABLED', 'DISABLED'),
        t.samplesize, t.analyzetime,
        decode(bitand(t.property, 32), 32, 'YES', 'NO'),
        decode(bitand(t.property, 64), 64, 'IOT',
          decode(bitand(t.property, 512), 512, 'IOT_OVERFLOW',
          null)),
        decode(bitand(o.flags, 2), 0, 'N', 2, 'Y', 'N'),
        decode(bitand(t.property, 8192), 8192, 'YES',
  decode(bitand(t.property, 1), 0, 'NO', 'YES')),
        decode(s.cachehint, 0, 'DEFAULT', 1, 'KEEP', 2, 'RECYCLE',
        NULL)
```

```
            from sys.user$ u, sys.ts$ ts, sys.seg$ s, sys.obj$ co,
                sys.tab$ t, sys.obj$ o
            where o.owner# = u.user#
              and o.obj# = t.obj#
              and bitand(t.property, 1) = 0
              and t.bobj# = co.obj# (+)
              and t.ts# = ts.ts#
              and t.file# = s.file# (+)
              and t.block# = s.block# (+)
              and t.ts# = s.ts# (+)
```

The **DBA_TABLESPACES** view provides information on all tablespaces defined in the database.

Listing A.323   Description of the DBA_ view DBA_TABLESPACES.

```
Name                              Null?     Type
--------------------------------  --------  ----
TABLESPACE_NAME                   NOT NULL  VARCHAR2(30)
INITIAL_EXTENT                              NUMBER
NEXT_EXTENT                                 NUMBER
MIN_EXTENTS                       NOT NULL  NUMBER
MAX_EXTENTS                       NOT NULL  NUMBER
PCT_INCREASE                      NOT NULL  NUMBER
MIN_EXTLEN                                  NUMBER
STATUS                                      VARCHAR2(9)
CONTENTS                                    VARCHAR2(9)
LOGGING                                     VARCHAR2(9)


DBA_TABLESPACES     select ts.name, ts.blocksize * ts.dflinit,
                           ts.blocksize * ts.dflincr, ts.dflminext,
                           ts.dflmaxext, ts.dflextpct,
                           ts.blocksize * ts.dflminlen,
                           decode(ts.online$, 1, 'ONLINE', 2, 'OFFLINE',
                                  4, 'READ ONLY', 'UNDEFINED'),
                           decode(ts.contents$, 0, 'PERMANENT', 1, 'TEMPORARY'),
                           decode(ts.dflogging, 0, 'NOLOGGING', 1, 'LOGGING')
                    from sys.ts$ ts
                    where ts.online$ != 3
```

The **DBA_TAB_COLUMNS** view describes all table columns defined in the database. To see a full table definition, you must join this view to the **DBA_TABLES** view.

Listing A.324   Description of the DBA_ view DBA_TAB_COLUMNS.

Name	Null?	Type
OWNER	NOT NULL	VARCHAR2(30)
TABLE_NAME	NOT NULL	VARCHAR2(30)
COLUMN_NAME	NOT NULL	VARCHAR2(30)
DATA_TYPE		VARCHAR2(30)
DATA_TYPE_MOD		VARCHAR2(3)
DATA_TYPE_OWNER		VARCHAR2(30)
DATA_LENGTH	NOT NULL	NUMBER
DATA_PRECISION		NUMBER
DATA_SCALE		NUMBER
NULLABLE		VARCHAR2(1)
COLUMN_ID	NOT NULL	NUMBER
DEFAULT_LENGTH		NUMBER
DATA_DEFAULT		LONG
NUM_DISTINCT		NUMBER
LOW_VALUE		RAW(32)
HIGH_VALUE		RAW(32)
DENSITY		NUMBER
NUM_NULLS		NUMBER
NUM_BUCKETS		NUMBER
LAST_ANALYZED		DATE
SAMPLE_SIZE		NUMBER
CHARACTER_SET_NAME		VARCHAR2(44)

```
DBA_TAB_COLUMNS     select u.name, o.name,
                     c.name,
                    decode(c.type#, 1, decode(c.charsetform, 2, 'NVARCHAR2',
                            'VARCHAR2'),
                                        2, decode(c.scale, null,
                                        decode(c.precision#, null, 'NUMBER',
                                        'FLOAT'),
                                                'NUMBER'),
                                        8, 'LONG',
                            9, decode(c.charsetform, 2, 'NCHAR VARYING',
                                    'VARCHAR'),
                                        12, 'DATE', 23, 'RAW', 24, 'LONG RAW',
                                        69, 'ROWID',
                                        96, decode(c.charsetform, 2, 'NCHAR',
                                         'CHAR'),
                                        105, 'MLSLABEL',
                                        106, 'MLSLABEL',
                                        111, ot.name,
                                        112, decode(c.charsetform, 2, 'NCLOB',
                                         'CLOB'),
```

```
                              113, 'BLOB', 114, 'BFILE', 115, 'CFILE',
                              121, ot.name,
                              122, ot.name,
                              123, ot.name,
                              'UNDEFINED'),
                decode(c.type#, 111, 'REF'), ut.name,
                c.length, c.precision#, c.scale,
                decode(sign(c.null$),-1,'D', 0, 'Y', 'N'), c.col#,
                    c.deflength,
                c.default$, h.distcnt, h.lowval, h.hival, h.density,
                h.null_cnt,
        decode(h.row_cnt, 0, 1, 1, 1, h.row_cnt-1), h.timestamp#,
                h.sample_size,
                decode(c.charsetform, 1, 'CHAR_CS',
                                      2, 'NCHAR_CS',
                                      3, NLS_CHARSET_NAME(c.charsetid),
                                      4, 'ARG:'||c.charsetid)
        from sys.col$ c, sys.obj$ o, sys.hist_head$ h, sys.user$ u,
                sys.coltype$ ac, sys.obj$ ot, sys.user$ ut
        where o.obj# = c.obj#
          and o.owner# = u.user#
          and c.obj# = h.obj#(+) and c.intcol# = h.intcol#(+)
          and bitand(c.property, 32) = 0 /* not hidden column */
          and c.obj# = ac.obj#(+) and c.col# = ac.col#(+)
          and ac.toid = ot.oid$(+)
          and ot.owner# = ut.user#(+)
          and (o.type# in (3, 4)        /* cluster, view */
             or
               (o.type# = 2 /* tables,excluding iot-overflow, nested
                              tables */
                  and
                  not exists (select null
     from sys.tab$ t
    where t.obj# = o.obj#
      and (bitand(t.property, 512) = 512 or
           bitand(t.property, 8192) = 8192))))
```

The **DBA_TAB_COL_STATISTICS** view contains column statistics and histogram information. This view is a companion view and subset of the **DBA_TAB_COLUMNS** view.

Listing A.325   Description of the DBA_ view DBA_TAB_COL_STATISTICS.

```
Name                                Null?     Type
----------------------------------- --------- ----
TABLE_NAME                          NOT NULL VARCHAR2(30)
COLUMN_NAME                         NOT NULL VARCHAR2(30)
NUM_DISTINCT                                 NUMBER
```

```
LOW_VALUE                               RAW(32)
HIGH_VALUE                              RAW(32)
DENSITY                                 NUMBER
NUM_NULLS                               NUMBER
NUM_BUCKETS                             NUMBER
LAST_ANALYZED                           DATE
SAMPLE_SIZE                             NUMBER

DBA_TAB_COL_STATISTICS select table_name, column_name, num_distinct,
                         low_value, high_value,
                         density, num_nulls, num_buckets, last_analyzed,
sample_size
                    from dba_tab_columns
                    where last_analyzed is not null
```

The **DBA_TAB_COMMENTS** view contains all the comments defined on tables in the database. I highly suggest using **DBA_TAB_COMMENTS** and **DBA_TAB_COL_STATISTICS** to provide internal documentation for your tables and views in the database.

Listing A.326   Description of the DBA_ view DBA_TAB_COMMENTS.

```
Name                                    Null?    Type
-----------------------------------     -------- ----
OWNER                                   NOT NULL VARCHAR2(30)
TABLE_NAME                              NOT NULL VARCHAR2(30)
TABLE_TYPE                                       VARCHAR2(11)
COMMENTS                                          VARCHAR2(4000)

DBA_TAB_COMMENTS      select u.name, o.name,
                        decode(o.type#, 0, 'NEXT OBJECT', 1, 'INDEX',
                                        2, 'TABLE', 3, 'CLUSTER',
                                        4, 'VIEW', 5, 'SYNONYM', 'UNDEFINED'),
                        c.comment$
                    from sys.obj$ o, sys.user$ u, sys.com$ c
                    where o.owner# = u.user#
                      and (o.type# in (4) /* view */
                          or
                          (o.type# = 2 /*tables,excluding iot-overflow nested
                                      tables */
                          and
                          not exists (select null
            from sys.tab$ t
          where t.obj# = o.obj#
            and (bitand(t.property, 512) = 512 or
                                      bitand(t.property, 8192) = 8192))))
                    and o.obj# = c.obj#(+)
                    and c.col#(+) is null
```

The **DBA_TAB_HISTOGRAMS** lists the histogram information for all histogram columns of all tables.

Listing A.327   Description of the DBA_ view DBA_TAB_HISTOGRAMS.

```
Name                             Null?    Type
-------------------------------- -------- ----
OWNER                                     VARCHAR2(30)
TABLE_NAME                                VARCHAR2(30)
COLUMN_NAME                               VARCHAR2(4000)
ENDPOINT_NUMBER                           NUMBER
ENDPOINT_VALUE                            NUMBER


DBA_TAB_HISTOGRAMS   select u.name,
                            o.name,
                            decode(bitand(c.property, 1), 1, a.name, c.name),
                            h.bucket,
                            h.endpoint
                     from sys.col$ c, sys.obj$ o, sys.histgrm$ h,
                        sys.user$ u, sys.attrcol$ a
                      where o.obj# = c.obj#
                        and o.owner# = u.user#
                        and c.obj# = h.obj# and c.intcol# = h.intcol#
                        and (o.type# in (3, 4)       /* cluster, view */
                            or
                            (o.type# = 2 /* tables, excluding iot-overflow,nested
                                           tables*/
                             and
                             not exists (select null
                             from sys.tab$ t
                             where t.obj# = o.obj#
                               and (bitand(t.property, 512) = 512 or
                                              bitand(t.property, 8192) = 8192))))
                                     and c.obj# = a.obj#(+)
                                     and c.intcol# = a.intcol#(+)
                     union all
                     select u.name,
                            o.name,
                            decode(bitand(c.property, 1), 1, a.name, c.name),
                            0,
                            h.minimum
                     from sys.col$ c, sys.obj$ o, sys.hist_head$ h,
                        sys.user$ u, sys.attrcol$ a
                         where o.obj# = c.obj#
                         and o.owner# = u.user#
                         and c.obj# = h.obj# and c.intcol# = h.intcol#
                         and (o.type# in (3, 4)            /* cluster, view */
                          or
```

```
                    (o.type# = 2 /* tables, excluding iot-overflow,nested
                                 tables */
           and  not exists (select null
                  from sys.tab$ t
                 where t.obj# = o.obj#
                   and (bitand(t.property, 512) = 512 or
                                         bitand(t.property, 8192) = 8192))))
           and h.bucket_cnt = 1
           and c.obj# = a.obj#(+)
           and c.intcol# = a.intcol#(+)
      union all
      select u.name,
             o.name,
             decode(bitand(c.property, 1), 1, a.name, c.name),
             1,
             h.maximum
       from sys.col$ c, sys.obj$ o, sys.hist_head$ h,
        sys.user$ u, sys.attrcol$ a
       where o.obj# = c.obj#
         and o.owner# = u.user#
         and c.obj# = h.obj# and c.intcol# = h.intcol#
         and (o.type# in (3, 4)          /* cluster, view */
             or
    (o.type# = 2  /* tables,excluding iot - overflow nested tables */
         and
         not exists (select null
               from sys.tab$ t
              where t.obj# = o.obj#
                and (bitand(t.property, 512) = 512 or
                                         bitand(t.property, 8192) = 8192))))
         and h.bucket_cnt = 1
         and c.obj# = a.obj#(+)
         and c.intcol# = a.intcol#(+)
```

The **DBA_TAB_PARTITIONS** describes the partition-level partitioning information, storage information, and various partition statistics for all table partitions in the database.

Listing A.328   Description of the DBA_ view DBA_TAB_PARTITIONS.

Name	Null?	Type
TABLE_OWNER	NOT NULL	VARCHAR2(30)
TABLE_NAME	NOT NULL	VARCHAR2(30)
PARTITION_NAME		VARCHAR2(30)
HIGH_VALUE		LONG
HIGH_VALUE_LENGTH	NOT NULL	NUMBER

```
PARTITION_POSITION              NOT NULL NUMBER
TABLESPACE_NAME                 NOT NULL VARCHAR2(30)
PCT_FREE                        NOT NULL NUMBER
PCT_USED                        NOT NULL NUMBER
INI_TRANS                       NOT NULL NUMBER
MAX_TRANS                       NOT NULL NUMBER
INITIAL_EXTENT                           NUMBER
NEXT_EXTENT                              NUMBER
MIN_EXTENT                      NOT NULL NUMBER
MAX_EXTENT                      NOT NULL NUMBER
PCT_INCREASE                    NOT NULL NUMBER
FREELISTS                                NUMBER
FREELIST_GROUPS                          NUMBER
LOGGING                                  VARCHAR2(3)
NUM_ROWS                                 NUMBER
BLOCKS                                   NUMBER
EMPTY_BLOCKS                             NUMBER
AVG_SPACE                                NUMBER
CHAIN_CNT                                NUMBER
AVG_ROW_LEN                              NUMBER
SAMPLE_SIZE                              NUMBER
LAST_ANALYZED                            DATE
BUFFER_POOL                              VARCHAR2(7)


DBA_TAB_PARTITIONS   select u.name, o.name, o.subname, tp.hiboundval, tp.hiboundlen,
                            Tp.part#, ts.name,
                            tp.pctfree$, tp.pctused$, initrans, maxtrans,
                            s.iniexts * ts.blocksize,
                            s.extsize * ts.blocksize, s.minexts, s.maxexts,
                            s.extpct,
                         decode(s.lists, 0, 1, s.lists), decode(s.groups, 0, 1,
                            s.groups),
                            decode(mod(trunc(tp.flags / 4), 2), 0, 'YES', 'NO'),
                            tp.rowcnt, tp.blkcnt, tp.empcnt, tp.avgspc, tp.chncnt,
                            tp.avgrln,tp.samplesize, tp.analyzetime,
                          decode(s.cachehint, 0, 'DEFAULT', 1, 'KEEP', 2, 'RECYCLE',
                            NULL)
                     from   obj$ o, tabpart$ tp, ts$ ts, sys.seg$ s, user$ u
                     where  o.obj# = tp.obj# and ts.ts# = tp.ts#
                            and u.user# = o.owner# and
                            tp.file#=s.file# and tp.block#=s.block# and tp.ts#=s.ts#
```

The **DBA_TAB_PRIVS** view provides information on all grants made at the table
level to all users or roles in the database.

Listing A.329 Description of the DBA_ view DBA_TAB_PRIVS.

```
Name                                Null?    Type
----------------------------------- -------- ----
GRANTEE                             NOT NULL VARCHAR2(30)
OWNER                              NOT NULL VARCHAR2(30)
TABLE_NAME                         NOT NULL VARCHAR2(30)
GRANTOR                            NOT NULL VARCHAR2(30)
PRIVILEGE                          NOT NULL VARCHAR2(40)
GRANTABLE                                   VARCHAR2(3)

DBA_TAB_PRIVS         select ue.name, u.name, o.name, ur.name, tpm.name,
                             decode(oa.option$, 1, 'YES', 'NO')
                      from sys.objauth$ oa, sys.obj$ o, sys.user$ u, sys.user$ ur,
                           sys.user$ ue,
                           table_privilege_map tpm
                      where oa.obj# = o.obj#
                        and oa.grantor# = ur.user#
                        and oa.grantee# = ue.user#
                        and oa.col# is null
                        and oa.privilege# = tpm.privilege
                        and u.user# = o.owner#
```

The **DBA_TRIGGERS** view contains information on all database triggers.

Listing A.330 Description of the DBA_ view DBA_TRIGGERS.

```
Name                                Null?    Type
----------------------------------- -------- ----
OWNER                              NOT NULL VARCHAR2(30)
TRIGGER_NAME                       NOT NULL VARCHAR2(30)
TRIGGER_TYPE                                VARCHAR2(16)
TRIGGERING_EVENT                            VARCHAR2(26)
TABLE_OWNER                        NOT NULL VARCHAR2(30)
TABLE_NAME                         NOT NULL VARCHAR2(30)
REFERENCING_NAMES                          VARCHAR2(87)
WHEN_CLAUSE                                 VARCHAR2(4000)
STATUS                                     VARCHAR2(8)
DESCRIPTION                                VARCHAR2(4000)
TRIGGER_BODY                               LONG

DBA_TRIGGERS          select trigusr.name, trigobj.name,
                      decode(t.type#, 0, 'BEFORE STATEMENT',
                                      1, 'BEFORE EACH ROW',
                                      2, 'AFTER STATEMENT',
                                      3, 'AFTER EACH ROW',
                                      4, 'INSTEAD OF',
                                      'UNDEFINED'),
```

```
decode(t.insert$*100 + t.update$*10 + t.delete$,
                  100, 'INSERT',
                  010, 'UPDATE',
                  001, 'DELETE',
                  110, 'INSERT OR UPDATE',
                  101, 'INSERT OR DELETE',
                  011, 'UPDATE OR DELETE',
                  111, 'INSERT OR UPDATE OR DELETE', 'ERROR'),
tabusr.name, tabobj.name,
'REFERENCING NEW AS '||t.refnewname||' OLD AS '||t.refoldname,
t.whenclause,decode(t.enabled, 0, 'DISABLED', 1, 'ENABLED',
                  'ERROR'),
t.definition,t.action#
from sys.obj$ trigobj, sys.obj$ tabobj, sys.trigger$ t,
      sys.user$ tabusr, sys.user$ trigusr
where trigobj.obj#   = t.obj#
  and tabobj.obj#    = t.baseobject
  and tabobj.owner#  = tabusr.user#
  and trigobj.owner# = trigusr.user#
```

The **DBA_TRIGGER_COLS** view contains information on all table columns that have triggers defined for them.

Listing A.331 Description of the DBA_ view DBA_TRIGGER_COLS.

```
Name                              Null?     Type
--------------------------------  --------  ----
TRIGGER_OWNER                     NOT NULL  VARCHAR2(30)
TRIGGER_NAME                      NOT NULL  VARCHAR2(30)
TABLE_OWNER                       NOT NULL  VARCHAR2(30)
TABLE_NAME                        NOT NULL  VARCHAR2(30)
COLUMN_NAME                                 VARCHAR2(4000)
COLUMN_LIST                                 VARCHAR2(3)
COLUMN_USAGE                                VARCHAR2(17)


DBA_TRIGGER_COLS select /*+ ORDERED NOCOST */ u.name, o.name, u2.name, o2.name,
                decode(bitand(c.property, 1), 1, ac.name, c.name),
                max(decode(tc.type#,0,'YES','NO')) COLUMN_LIST,
                decode(sum(decode(tc.type#, 5,  1, -- one instance of new in
                                           6,  2, -- one instance of old in
                                           9,  4, -- one instance of new out
                                          10,  8, -- one instance of old out
                                                  -- (impossible)
                                         13,  5, -- one instance of new in out
                                         14, 10, -- one instance of old in out
                                                  -- (imp.)         null)
```

```
                    ), -- result in thesecombinations across occurrences
                    1, 'NEW IN', 2, 'OLD IN',
                    3, 'NEW IN OLD IN',
                    4, 'NEW OUT',
                    5, 'NEW IN OUT',
                    6, 'NEW OUT OLD IN',
                    7, 'NEW IN OUT OLD IN',
                    'NONE')
          from sys.trigger$ t, sys.obj$ o, sys.user$ u, sys.user$ u2,
               sys.col$ c, sys.obj$ o2, sys.triggercol$ tc,
               sys.attrcol$ ac
          where t.obj# = tc.obj#   -- find corresponding trigger
                                   -- definition
            and o.obj# = t.obj#   --    and corresponding trigger name
            and c.obj# = t.baseobject  -- and corresponding row in COL$ of
            and c.intcol# = tc.intcol# --   the referenced column
            and o2.obj# = t.baseobject -- and name of the table containing
                                       -- the trigger
            and u2.user# = o2.owner# -- and name of the user who owns the
                                     -- table and u.user# = o.owner#
                                     -- and name of user who owns the trigger
          and c.intcol# = ac.intcol#(+)
        group by u.name, o.name, u2.name, o2.name,
                 decode(bitand(c.property, 1), 1, ac.name, c.name)
```

The **DBA_TS_QUOTAS** view provides information on all tablespace quotas granted to users in the database on database tablespaces.

Listing A.332 Description of the DBA_ view DBA_TS_QUOTAS.

Name	Null?	Type
TABLESPACE_NAME	NOT NULL	VARCHAR2(30)
USERNAME	NOT NULL	VARCHAR2(30)
BYTES		NUMBER
MAX_BYTES		NUMBER
BLOCKS	NOT NULL	NUMBER
MAX_BLOCKS		NUMBER

```
DBA_TS_QUOTAS        select ts.name, u.name,
                            q.blocks * ts.blocksize,
                            decode(q.maxblocks, -1, -1, q.maxblocks * ts.blocksize),
                            q.blocks, q.maxblocks
                     from sys.tsq$ q, sys.ts$ ts, sys.user$ u
                     where q.ts# = ts.ts#
                       and q.user# = u.user#
                       and q.maxblocks != 0
```

The **DBA_TYPES** view contains information on all user-defined types in the database.

Listing A.333   Description of the DBA_ view DBA_TYPES.

```
Name                               Null?     Type
-------------------------------    --------  ----
OWNER                                        VARCHAR2(30)
TYPE_NAME                          NOT NULL  VARCHAR2(30)
TYPE_OID                           NOT NULL  RAW(16)
TYPECODE                                     VARCHAR2(30)
ATTRIBUTES                                   NUMBER
METHODS                                      NUMBER
PREDEFINED                                   VARCHAR2(3)
INCOMPLETE                                   VARCHAR2(3)

DBA_TYPES          select decode(bitand(t.properties, 64), 64, null, u.name),
                          o.name,
                            t.toid,decode(t.typecode, 108, 'OBJECT',
                                                      122, 'COLLECTION',
                                          o.name),
                        t.attributes, t.methods,
                        decode(bitand(t.properties, 16), 16, 'YES', 0, 'NO'),
                        decode(bitand(t.properties, 256), 256, 'YES', 0, 'NO')
                   from sys.user$ u, sys.type$ t, sys.obj$ o
                   where o.owner# = u.user#
                     and o.oid$ = t.toid
                     and o.type# <> 10 -- must not be invalid
                     and bitand(t.properties, 2048) = 0 -- not system-generated
```

The **DBA_TYPE_ATTRS** view contains information on all attributes used in user-defined types in the database.

Listing A.334   Description of the DBA_ view DBA_TYPE_ATTRS.

```
Name                               Null?     Type
-------------------------------    --------  ----
OWNER                                        VARCHAR2(30)
TYPE_NAME                          NOT NULL  VARCHAR2(30)
ATTR_NAME                          NOT NULL  VARCHAR2(30)
ATTR_TYPE_MOD                                VARCHAR2(7)
ATTR_TYPE_OWNER                              VARCHAR2(30)
ATTR_TYPE_NAME                               VARCHAR2(30)
LENGTH                                       NUMBER
PRECISION                                    NUMBER
SCALE                                        NUMBER
CHARACTER_SET_NAME                           VARCHAR2(44)
```

```
DBA_TYPE_ATTRS          select decode(bitand(t.properties, 64), 64, null, u.name),
                               o.name,
                               a.name,
                                     decode(bitand(a.properties, 32768), 32768, 'REF',
                                         decode(bitand(a.properties, 16384), 16384,
                                         'POINTER')),
                               decode(bitand(at.properties, 64), 64, null, au.name),
                               decode(at.typecode,
                                     52, decode(a.charsetform, 2, 'NVARCHAR2',
                                         ao.name),
                                     53, decode(a.charsetform, 2, 'NCHAR', ao.name),
                                     54, decode(a.charsetform, 2, 'NCHAR VARYING',
                                         ao.name),
                                     61, decode(a.charsetform, 2, 'NCLOB', ao.name),
                                         ao.name),
                               a.length, a.precision#, a.scale,
                               decode(a.charsetform, 1, 'CHAR_CS',
                                                     2, 'NCHAR_CS',
                                                     3, NLS_CHARSET_NAME(a.charsetid),
                                                     4, 'ARG:'||a.charsetid)
                        from sys.user$ u, sys.obj$ o, sys.type$ t, sys.attribute$ a,
                             sys.obj$ ao, sys.user$ au, sys.type$ at
                        where o.owner# = u.user#
                          and o.oid$ = t.toid
                          and o.type# <> 10 -- must not be invalid
                          and bitand(t.properties, 2048) = 0 -- not system-generated
                          and t.toid = a.toid
                          and t.version# = a.version#
                          and a.attr_toid = ao.oid$
                          and ao.owner# = au.user#
                          and a.attr_toid = at.toid
                          and a.attr_version# = at.version#
```

The **DBA_TYPE_METHODS** view contains information on all user-defined type methods defined in the database.

Listing A.335   Description of the DBA_ view DBA_TYPE_METHODS.

```
Name                              Null?    Type
-------------------------------   -------- ----
OWNER                             NOT NULL VARCHAR2(30)
TYPE_NAME                         NOT NULL VARCHAR2(30)
METHOD_NAME                       NOT NULL VARCHAR2(30)
METHOD_NO                         NOT NULL NUMBER
METHOD_TYPE                                VARCHAR2(6)
PARAMETERS                        NOT NULL NUMBER
RESULTS                           NOT NULL NUMBER
```

```
DBA_TYPE_METHODS        select u.name, o.name, m.name, m.method#,
                              decode(bitand(m.properties, 512), 512, 'MAP',
                                     decode(bitand(m.properties, 2048), 2048, 'ORDER',
                                        'PUBLIC')), m.parameters#, m.results
                        from sys.user$ u, sys.obj$ o, sys.method$ m
                        where o.owner# = u.user#
                          and o.type# <> 10 -- must not be invalid
                          and o.oid$ = m.toid
```

The **DBA_UPDATABLE_COLUMNS** view contains information on all columns involved in a join view that can be updated by the database administrator.

Listing A.336   Description of the DBA_ view DBA_UPDATABLE_COLUMNS.

```
Name                            Null?    Type
------------------------------- -------- ----
OWNER                           NOT NULL VARCHAR2(30)
TABLE_NAME                      NOT NULL VARCHAR2(30)
COLUMN_NAME                     NOT NULL VARCHAR2(30)
UPDATABLE                                VARCHAR2(3)
INSERTABLE                               VARCHAR2(3)
DELETABLE                                VARCHAR2(3)


DBA_UPDATABLE_COLUMNS select u.name, o.name, c.name,
                            decode(bitand(c.fixedstorage,2),
                                  2, decode(bitand(v.flags,8192), 8192, 'YES',
                                     'NO'),
                                  'YES'),
                            decode(bitand(c.fixedstorage,2),
                                  2, decode(bitand(v.flags,4096), 4096, 'YES',
                                     'NO'),
                                  'YES'),
                            decode(bitand(c.fixedstorage,2),
                                  2, decode(bitand(v.flags,16384), 16384, 'YES',
                                     'NO'),
                                  'YES')
                      from sys.obj$ o, sys.user$ u, sys.col$ c, sys.view$ v
                      where u.user# = o.owner#
                        and c.obj# = o.obj#
                        and c.obj# = v.obj#(+)
                        and bitand(c.property, 32) = 0 /* not hidden column */
```

The **DBA_USERS** view contains information on all users defined for the database.

Listing A.337 Description of the DBA_ view DBA_USERS.

```
Name                              Null?     Type
------------------------------    --------  ----
USERNAME                          NOT NULL  VARCHAR2(30)
USER_ID                           NOT NULL  NUMBER
PASSWORD                                    VARCHAR2(30)
ACCOUNT_STATUS                    NOT NULL  VARCHAR2(32)
LOCK_DATE                                   DATE
EXPIRY_DATE                                 DATE
DEFAULT_TABLESPACE                NOT NULL  VARCHAR2(30)
TEMPORARY_TABLESPACE              NOT NULL  VARCHAR2(30)
CREATED                           NOT NULL  DATE
PROFILE                           NOT NULL  VARCHAR2(30)
EXTERNAL_NAME                               VARCHAR2(4000)


DBA_USERS            select u.name, u.user#, u.password,
                        m.status,
                        decode(u.astatus, 4, u.ltime,
                                          5, u.ltime,
                                          6, u.ltime,
                                          12, u.ltime,NULL),
                        decode(u.astatus, 1, u.exptime,
                               2, u.exptime,
                               6, u.exptime,
                               10, u.exptime,
                               14, u.exptime,
                               5, u.exptime,
                               9, u.exptime,
                               13, u.exptime,
                               decode(u.ptime, '', NULL,
                                 decode(pr.limit#, 2147483647, NULL,
                                   decode(pr.limit#, 0,
                                   decode(dp.limit#, 2147483647, NULL, u.ptime +
                                       dp.limit#/86400),
                                     u.ptime + pr.limit#/86400)))),
                        dts.name, tts.name, u.ctime, p.name, u.ext_username
                        from sys.user$ u, sys.ts$ dts, sys.ts$ tts,
      sys.profname$ p,
                           sys.user_astatus_map m, sys.profile$ pr,
      sys.profile$ dp
                        where u.datats# = dts.ts#
                        and u.resource$ = p.profile#
                        and u.tempts# = tts.ts#
                        and u.astatus = m.status#
                        and u.type# = 1
                        and u.resource$ = pr.profile#
                        and dp.profile# = 0
```

```
                      and dp.type#=1
                      and dp.resource#=1
                      and pr.type# = 1
                      and pr.resource# = 1
```

The **DBA_VIEWS** view contains information for all defined views in the database.

Listing A.338   Description of the DBA_ view DBA_VIEWS.

```
Name                             Null?     Type
-------------------------------  --------  ----
OWNER                            NOT NULL  VARCHAR2(30)
VIEW_NAME                        NOT NULL  VARCHAR2(30)
TEXT_LENGTH                                NUMBER
TEXT                                       LONG
TYPE_TEXT_LENGTH                           NUMBER
TYPE_TEXT                                  VARCHAR2(4000)
OID_TEXT_LENGTH                            NUMBER
OID_TEXT                                   VARCHAR2(4000)
VIEW_TYPE_OWNER                            VARCHAR2(30)
VIEW_TYPE                                  VARCHAR2(30)


DBA_VIEWS            select u.name, o.name, v.textlength, v.text, t.typetextlength,
                           t.typetext, t.oidtextlength, t.oidtext, t.typeowner,
                           t.typename
                    from sys.obj$ o, sys.view$ v, sys.user$ u, sys.typed_view$ t
                    where o.obj# = v.obj#
                      and o.obj# = t.obj#(+)
                      and o.owner# = u.user#
```

The **DBA_WAITERS** view contains information on all sessions waiting on a lock to clear. This view is created using the CATBLOCK.SQL script.

Listing A.339   Description of the DBA_ view DBA_WAITERS.

```
Name                             Null?     Type
-------------------------------  --------  ----
WAITING_SESSION                            NUMBER
HOLDING_SESSION                            NUMBER
LOCK_TYPE                                  VARCHAR2(26)
MODE_HELD                                  VARCHAR2(40)
MODE_REQUESTED                             VARCHAR2(40)
LOCK_ID1                                   VARCHAR2(40)
LOCK_ID2                                   VARCHAR2(40)
```

```
DBA_WAITERS          select /*+ all_rows */ w.session_id   waiting_session,
   h.session_id   holding_session,
   w.lock_type,
   h.mode_held,
   w.mode_requested,
   w.lock_id1,
   w.lock_id2
                     from dba_locks w, dba_locks h
                    where h.blocking_others = 'Blocking'
                     and   h.mode_held   !=  'None'
                     and   h.mode_held   !=  'Null'
                     and   w.mode_requested !=  'None'
                     and   w.lock_type    =  h.lock_type
                     and   w.lock_id1  =   h.lock_id1
                     and   w.lock_id2        =   h.lock_id2
```

Using the information in this appendix, developers and DBAs can obtain any piece of informatioin about virtually any database object. If you need more detailed information, I suggest you consult the *Oracle8 Server Reference*, Release 8.0, Part No. A54645-01, June 1997, Oracle Corporation.

Index

Symbols

D

The Ultimate Technical Cheat Sheets

Out of every advanced technology comes a body of "black art." The Black Book Series captures that black art into the ultimate high-tech "cheat sheet." This is where the unknown network configuration magic, or blistering server performance expertise, resides. Where other titles may present advanced projects, Black Book presents advanced knowledge.

Encyclopedic and organized by topic, with superb indexes, Black Books allow readers to access information quickly and easily.

The Black Book Series

1-57610-114-2	1-57610-149-5	1-57610-174-6	1-57610-162-2	1-57610-189-4	1-57610-185-1	1-57610-187-8	1-57610-188-6
$39.99/$55.99	$39.99/$55.99	$59.99/$83.99	$39.99/$55.99	$49.99/$69.99	$49.99/$69.99	$49.99/$69.99	$49.99/$69.99
(US/CAN)	(US/CAN)	(US/CAN)	(US/CAN)	(US/CAN)	(US/CAN)	(US/CAN)	(US/CAN)
Available Now	*Available Now*	*Available Now*	*Available Now*	*January '98*	*January '98*	*January '98*	*February '98*

COMING SOON:
Oracle8 & Windows NT Black Book
1-57610-248-3
$49.99/$69.99 (US/CAN)

AFC Black Book
1-57610-235-1
$49.99/$69.99 (US/CAN)

 **CORIOLIS GROUP BOOKS**
An International Thomson Publishing Company ITP

(800) 410-0192 • International Callers (602) 483-0192 • Fax (602) 483-0193 • www.coriolis.com